1295

An outline of
The Law of Contract

CW00321586

An outline of
The Law of Contract

Fourth edition

G H Treitel QC, DCL, FBA
Honorary Bencher of Gray's Inn,
Fellow of All Souls College,
Vinerian Professor of English Law

Butterworths
London
1989

United Kingdom	Butterworth & Co (Publishers) Ltd, 88 Kingsway, LONDON WC2B 6AB and 4 Hill Street, EDINBURGH EH2 3JZ
Australia	Butterworths Pty Ltd, SYDNEY, MELBOURNE, BRISBANE, ADELAIDE, PERTH, CANBERRA and HOBART
Canada	Butterworths Canada Ltd, TORONTO and VANCOUVER
Ireland	Butterworth (Ireland) Ltd, DUBLIN
Malaysia	Malayan Law Journal Sdn Bhd, KUALA LUMPUR
New Zealand	Butterworths of New Zealand Ltd, WELLINGTON and AUCKLAND
Singapore	Butterworth & Co (Asia) Pte Ltd, SINGAPORE
USA	Butterworths Legal Publishers, ST PAUL, Minnesota, SEATTLE, Washington, BOSTON, Massachusetts, AUSTIN, Texas, and D & S Publishers, CLEARWATER, Florida

A CIP Catalogue record for this book is available from the British Library.

ISBN 0 406 66849 3

Set in Singapore by Colset Pte Ltd
Printed and bound in Great Britain by Billing & Sons Ltd, Worcester

Preface

The aims of this book remain as they were in previous editions. They are to state the general principles of the subject in such a way as to make them intelligible to the non-specialist; to give such a reader an insight into the policies which have shaped the subject; and to make him or her aware of the difficulties (and of some of the defects) of the subject, while avoiding technical detail as much as possible.

Five years is a long time in the law of contract, so that the text has again been extensively revised. The most important changes are as follows. In chapter 2 the discussion of offer and acceptance has been recast in the light (particularly) of recent arbitration cases; in chapter 7 account is taken of many recent decisions on the effects of exemption clauses, both between the contracting parties and with regard to third parties; in chapter 10 important changes in the law of undue influence, as well as the decline of the doctrine of inequality of bargaining power, are noted; in chapter 11 new developments in the law relating to restraint of trade and illegality generally are considered; in chapter 12 the section on minors has been rewritten in the light of the Minors' Contracts Act 1987, and that on the Crown and other public authorities been deleted (that subject being more generally studied in administrative law than in contract courses); in chapter 13 the relation between liability in negligence to third parties and the doctrine of privity of contract now receives fuller discussion; and chapters 16, 17 and 18 have been extensively revised to take account of important new decisions in the areas of performance, breach, frustration and remedies. Many less extensive changes have been made in every chapter, and on almost every page, of the book. The new text takes account of such provisions of the Financial Services Act 1986, the Insolvency Act 1986 and the Consumer Protection Act 1987 as are relevant to the law of contract. The result of all these changes is that about a quarter of the text is new.

This edition was completed in the late summer of 1988 but developments up to the end of that year have been incorporated in proof. I am particularly grateful to the publishers for making this possible in spite of my absence abroad at the relevant time; their help and forbearance in many other respects is also gratefully acknowledged.

15 January 1989   G.H.T.

Contents

Preface   v
Table of Statutes   xi
List of Cases   xvii

CHAPTER 1   **Introduction**   1
1   Definition of contract   1
2   Contract and contracts   1
3   Agreement   2
4   Freedom of contract   3
5   Reasons for enforcing contracts   4
6   Common law and equity   6

CHAPTER 2   **Agreement**   7
1   Offer and invitation to treat   7
2   Acceptance and counter-offer   10
3   Communication of acceptance   11
4   Postal acceptance   12
5   Method of acceptance prescribed by offer   15
6   Silence as acceptance   15
7   Acceptance requires knowledge of offer   16
8   Unilateral contracts   16
9   Termination of offer   18
10   Cases in which there is no identifiable offer and
       acceptance   21
11   Vague or incomplete agreements   21
12   Conditional agreements   24

CHAPTER 3   **Consideration**   25
1   Definition   25
2   Gratuitous and onerous promises   26
3   Benefit and detriment   27
4   Irrelevance of adequacy of consideration; nominal
       consideration   28
5   Past consideration is insufficient   30
6   Consideration must move from the promisee   31

7   Mutual promises as consideration 31
8   Compromises and forbearances 34
9   Existing duties as consideration 35
10 Promissory estoppel 41
11 Estoppel by convention 43
12 Part payment of a debt 44
13 Proprietary estoppel 47
14 Irrevocable offers 49

CHAPTER 4   **Contractual intention** 51
1   Express provisions 51
2   Vague agreements 52
3   Discretionary agreements 53
4   Social and domestic agreements 53
5   Other illustrations 54

CHAPTER 5   **Form** 56
1   Nature and purpose of formal requirements 56
2   Form generally not required 57
3   Types of formal requirements 57
4   Effects of failure to use the required form 59
5   Rescission and variation of written contracts 61

CHAPTER 6   **The contents of a contract** 62
1   Ascertainment of express terms 62
2   Implied terms 63
3   The parol evidence rule 66

CHAPTER 7   **Standard terms and exemption clauses** 72
1   Incorporation of exemption clauses 73
2   The scope of exemption clauses 75
3   The effectiveness of exemption clauses at common law 85
4   The Unfair Contract Terms Act 1977 88
5   Other legislative techniques 96

CHAPTER 8   **Mistake** 98
1   Introduction 98
2   Mistakes which may nullify consent 99
3   Mistakes which may negative consent 107
4   Documents signed under a mistake 116
5   Mistakes in recording agreements 118

CHAPTER 9   **Misrepresentation** 122
1   General requirements 122
2   Effects of misrepresentation 127
3   Non-disclosure 141

CHAPTER 10   **Improper pressure**   147
1   Duress   147
2   Undue influence   148
3   Protection of particular groups of persons   149

CHAPTER 11   **Illegality**   152
1   Contracts contrary to law   152
2   Contracts contrary to public policy   156
3   Contracts in restraint of trade   164
4   The effects of illegality   175

CHAPTER 12   **Contractual capacity**   188
1   Minors   188
2   Mental patients   198
3   Drunken persons   198
4   Corporations   198

CHAPTER 13   **The parties to a contract**   203
1   Promises by more than one person   203
2   Promises to more than one person   206
3   Promises in favour of a third party   208
4   Promises purporting to bind a third party   219

CHAPTER 14   **Transfer of contractual rights**   223
1   Law and equity   223
2   Effects of the Judicature Act 1873   225
3   Assignment distinguished from authority to pay   228
4   Formalities   229
5   Notice to the debtor   230
6   Consideration   230
7   The assignee's title   234
8   Negotiability distinguished from assignment   235
9   Limits on assignability   236
10   Involuntary assignment   240
11   Assignment distinguished from transfer of liabilities   241

CHAPTER 15   **Agency**   245
1   Introduction   245
2   Creation of agency   246
3   Effects of agency   255
4   Termination of agency   263

CHAPTER 16   **Performance and breach**   265
1   The duty to perform   265
2   Method of performance   270

3   Rescission for failure in performance   271
4   Anticipatory breach   294

CHAPTER 17   **Frustration**   298
1   Operation of the doctrine   299
2   Limitations on the doctrine   307
3   Legal consequences of frustration   311

CHAPTER 18   **Remedies for breach of contract**   315
1   Classification   315
2   Damages   316
3   Action for an agreed sum   349
4   Specific enforcement   351
5   Restitutionary remedies   359

Index   365

Table of Statutes

References in this Table to Statutes are to Halsbury's Statutes of England (Fourth Edition) showing the volume and page at which the annotated text of the Act will be found.

PAGE

Administration of Justice Act 1982
(11 *Statutes* 886)
s 15 342
Sch 1 342
Apportionment Act 1870 (23 *Statutes* 38) 278
s 2, 5, 7 291
Arbitration Act 1950 (2 *Statutes* 535)
s 4 (1) 161
Arbitration Act 1975 (2 *Statutes* 603)
s 1 (1) 161
Arbitration Act 1979 (2 *Statutes* 608)
s 1 (2) 161
2 161
3 (6), (7) 161
Auctions (Bidding Agreements) Act 1927 (4 *Statutes* 5) . . . 175
Auctions (Bidding Agreements) Act 1969 (4 *Statutes* 10) . . . 175
Bills of Exchange Act 1882 (5 *Statutes* 346)
s 27 (1) 236
(b) 30
(2) 236
29 236
30 236
53 (1) 229
62 39
73 234
Bills of Lading Act 1855 (39 *Statutes* 422)
s 1 . . . . . . 230, 243
2 243

PAGE

Carriage by Air Act 1961 (4 *Statutes* 19)
Sch 1
art 25A 87
Carriage of Goods by Road Act 1965
Schedule 96
Carriage of Goods by Sea Act 1924
Sch 3
art 3 58
Carriage of Goods by Sea Act 1971
(39 *Statutes* 831)
Schedule 96
art IVbis 87
Chancery Amendment Act 1858
s 2 358
Child Benefit Act 1975
s 12 240
Civil Code (West Germany)
s 518 26
Civil Liability (Contribution) Act 1978 (13 *Statutes* 533)
s 3 . . . . 205, 261
Companies Act 1985 (8 *Statutes* 107)
s 4 199
35 . . . . . 201, 250, 254
(1) 21
36 (4) 254, 260
182 (1) 230
282 253
378 199
395, 396 229
Competition Act 1980 (47 Statutes 463) 171
s 2, 3, 5 172
Consumer Arbitration Agreements Act 1988 161

PAGE

Consumer Credit Act 1974 (11 *Statutes* 15)

s 8, 55 56
56 (3) (a) 246
57 (3) 246
60 56
61 . . . . 56, 57
62–64 57
65 59
67, 68 151
69 151
(6) 246
70–73 151
88 277
99 269
100 (1), (3) 347
102 246
127 59
137 151
138 151
(1) 151
139 151
(2) 151
Sch 4
para 35 267
Consumer Protection Act 1987 . 91, 245
s 7 . . . . 90, 91
10 91
41 (1) 91
(3) 177
(4) 91
Criminal Justice Act 1988
s 104 . . . . . 136, 315
105 136
Criminal Law Act 1967 (12 *Statutes* 742)
s 5 (1) 162
13 224
14 . . . . . . 152, 224
Defective Premises Act 1972 (31 *Statutes* 195)
s 1 (1) 90
6 (3) 90
Domestic Proceedings and Magistrates' Courts Act 1978 (27 *Statutes* 791)
s 6 160
Domestic Violence and Matrimonial Proceedings Act 1976 (27 *Statutes* 788)
s 2 (1) 158
Employment Act 1980 (16 *Statutes* 639)
s 4 (1), (2) 171

PAGE

Employment of Children Act 1973 (6 *Statutes* 332) 191
Employment Protection (Consolidation) Act 1978 (16 *Statutes* 381)
s 1, 3 58
69–71 354
74 (4) 339
Enduring Powers of Attorney Act 1985
s 1 (1)(a)–(c) 264
2, 6 264
7 (1) (a) 264
8 (3) 264
9 264
Estate Agents Act 1979 (1 *Statutes* 69)
s 13 (1) (a) 246
15 246
18 58
European Communities Act 1972
s 9 (1) 201
Fair Trading Act 1973 (47 *Statutes* 125) 172
s 2 96
3 151
13 (1) 151
(a), (b) 97
14 . . . . . . 96, 151
17 (2) (c) 151
(d) 97, 151
22, 23 . . . . 97, 151, 177
26 97
35, 37 . . . . . 97, 151
Family Law Reform Act 1969 (6 *Statutes* 213)
s 1 188
Finance Act 1988
s 69 330
Financial Services Act 1986 (30 *Statutes* 254)
s 5 . . . . . . 177, 182
47 136
56 . . . . 151, 177, 182
57 . . . . . 177, 182
61 136
86 90
131 . . . . . 177, 182
132 . . . 155, 177, 178, 182
146 145
150 146
163 145
166 146

PAGE

Fires Prevention (Metropolis) Act
1774 (22 *Statutes* 9)
  s 83 218
Honours (Prevention of Abuses) Act
1925 (33 *Statutes* 279) 163
Housing Act 1961
  s 33 (6), (7) 96
Income and Corporation Taxes Act
1988
  s 148 330
    188 (4) 330
Inheritance (Provision for Family
and Dependants) Act 1975 (17
Statutes 344)
  s 10, 11 29
Insolvency Act 1986 (4 *Statutes* 717)
  s 44 (1) 260
    178 243
    238 29
    283 (1) (a) 261
    306 261
    310 (2) 261
    311 (4) 240
    315 243
    339 29
    344 229
    345 (4) 207
    403 261
    423 29
Insurance Companies Act 1982 (22
Statutes 153)
  s 76 151
International Transport Conven-
tions Act 1983 (36 *Statutes* 560)
  s 1 96
Landlord and Tenant Act 1927 (23
Statutes 55)
  s 18 (1) 325
Landlord and Tenant Act 1985 (23
Statutes 322)
  s 4 58
    11, 12 96
    17 356
Law of Property Act 1925 (37 *Stat-
utes* 72)
  s 40 (1) 58, 60
    41 285
    47 218
    49 (2) 347
    52 . . . . 57, 59
    53 (1) 229, 232
    56 (1) 218, 219
    73 26
    81 207

PAGE

Law of Property Act 1925 — *contd*
  s 84 174
    136 (1) . . . 226, 228, 229
    137 (3) 230
    146 277
    174 150
    205 (1) 218
Law of Property Act 1969 (37 *Statutes* 391)
  s 28 174
Law Reform (Contributory Negligence) Act 1945 (31 *Statutes* 185) . 340,
                          341
Law Reform (Enforcement of Contracts) Act 1954 58
Law Reform (Frustrated Contracts)
Act 1943 (11 *Statutes* 209) . 362, 363
  s 1 (2) 311
    (3) 312
      (b) 313
    2 (3) (a) 313
    (4), (5) 313
Law Reform Miscellaneous Provisions Act 1970 (27 *Statutes* 543)
  s 1 160
    2 (1) 160
Life Assurance Act 1774 (22 *Statutes* 7)
  s 1 153
Limitation Act 1980 (24 *Statutes*
629)
  s 29 (5), (7) 30
    30 (1) 30
Marine Insurance Act 1906 (22 *Statutes* 15)
  s 4 (1) 153
    20 (2) 125
    22 61
    50 230
    84 (1), 3(a) 138
    86 255
Married Women's Property Act
1882 (27 *Statutes* 566)
  s 11 217
Matrimonial and Family Proceedings Act 1984 (27 *Statutes* 852)
  s 10 160
Matrimonial Causes Act 1973 (27
Statutes 700)
  s 7 160
    34 161
Mercantile Law Amendment Act
1856 (11 *Statutes* 207)
  s 3 58

PAGE

Merchant Shipping Act 1979 (39
    Statutes 904)
    s 14 96
    Sch 3 96
Minors' Contracts Act 1987
    s 1 193
    2 204
    3 (1) . . . 194, 195, 196, 197
        (2) 195
    4 (2) 193
Misrepresentation Act 1967 (29
    Statutes 724) 122, 289
    s 1 (a) 137, 282, 288
    2 146
        (1) . . . 129, 130, 133, 134,
                            146, 343
        (2) . . . 132, 133, 137, 138,
                            146, 282, 288
    3 93
Mobile Homes Act 1983 (32 *Statutes*
    514)
    s 1 58
Occupiers' Liability Act 1984 (31
    Statutes 213)
    s 2 89
Partnership Act 1890 (32 *Statutes*
    636)
    s 9 205
    29, 30 317
Police Act 1964 (33 *Statutes* 597)
    s 15 36
Police and Criminal Evidence Act
    1984 (12 *Statutes* 941)
    s 24 (1) 162
Policies of Assurance Act 1867 (22
    Statutes 11) 230
Powers of Attorney Act 1971 (1 *Stat-
    utes* 62)
    s 4 264
    5 (1) 262
        (2) 264
Powers of Criminal Courts Act 1973
    (12 *Statutes* 597)
    s 35 . . . . . . 136, 315
    38 136
Protection from Eviction Act 1977
    (23 *Statutes* 293)
    s 1 315
Public Passenger Vehicles Act 1981
    s 29 90
Race Relations Act 1976 (6 *Statutes*
    765) 4
Real Property Act 1845
    s 5 218

PAGE

Rent Act 1977 (23 *Statutes* 405)
    s 57, 94, 125 182
Resale Prices Act 1976 (44 *Statutes*
    386) 175
    s 9 221
    11 4
    14, 26 221
Restrictive Trade Practices Act 1976
    (47 *Statutes* 321) 171
    s 5, 34 174
Road Traffic Act 1972
    s 62 (1), (2) 177
    148 (3) 74
        (4) 217
    149, 150 217
Sale of Goods Act 1979 (39 *Statutes*
    106) 331
    s 3 . . . . . 190, 198, 363
    6 105
    7 313
    8 (2) 22, 363
    9 (1) 23
    10 (1) 285
    11 (2), (4) 287
    12 (2) 281
    13 280
    14 64
        (3) 67
    28 273
    30 (1) 278
    35 288
    49 (1), (2) 349
    50 (3) 328, 329
    51 (3) 327, 331
    53 (1) (a) 326
        (3) 326
    57 (2) 9
Sale of Reversions Act 1867 . . . 150
Sex Discrimination Act 1975 (6 *Stat-
    utes* 696) 171
    s 13 4
Sex Discrimination Act 1986 . . . 171
Social Security Act 1975
    s 87 240
Solicitors Act 1974 (41 *Statutes* 12) . 217
Statute of Frauds (1677) (11 *Statutes*
    205)
    s 4 58
    9 232
Suicide Act 1961 (12 *Statutes* 341) . 155
Supply of Goods and Services Act
    1982 (39 *Statutes* 161)
    s 4, 9 267
    13 . . . . 64, 267

PAGE

Supply of Goods and Services Act
1982 — *contd*
s 15 363
    (1) 22
    16(2)(a) 267
    17(2) 91
    (3) 92
Supply of Goods (Implied Terms)
Act 1973 (11 *Statutes* 8)
s 9—11 267
Supreme Court Act 1981 (11 *Statutes* 756)
s 35A 342
    49 358
    (1) 205
    50 358
Supreme Court of Judicature Act
1873 . . . . . . 223, 226
s 25 (I) 285
    (II) 205
Theft Act 1968 (12 *Statutes* 514)
s 15 136
    (4) 136
    16 136
Theft Act 1978 (12 *Statutes* 780)
s 1, 5 136
Third Parties (Rights against
Insurers) Act 1930 (4 *Statutes*
688)
s 1 217
Torts (Interference with Goods)
Act 1977 (45 *Statutes* 658)
s 6 252
    12, 13 . . . . . . 251, 252
    Sch 1 . . . . . . 251, 252
Trade Descriptions Act 1968 (39
Statutes 41)
s 1(1)(a) 136, 315
Trade Union and Labour Relations
Act 1974 (16 *Statutes* 248)
s 2(5) 171
    16 354
    18(1), (2), (4) 52
Trading with the Enemy Act 1939
(48 *Statutes* 808) 163
Transport Act 1962 (36 *Statutes*
245)
s 43(7) 90

PAGE

Unfair Contract Terms Act 1977
(11 *Statutes* 214) 72, 77, 78,
                85, 88, 289, 345
s 1 (1) 95
    (2) 96
    (3) 89, 91, 95
2 89
    (1) 90, 93
    (2) 91, 93
3(1) 92
    (2)(a), (b) 92, 277
4 93
5 . . . . 89, 90
6 . . . . 89, 90
    (1) 91
    (2) 64, 91
    (3) 64, 92, 94
    (4) 91, 92, 95
7 . . . . 89, 90
    (2) 91
    (3) 92
    (3A) 91
    (4) 92
8 93
9(1), (2) 94
10 95
11(1), (2), (4) 93
    (5) 91
12(1)(a), (b) 89
13(1), (2) 89
14 89
26(1) 64, 96
27(1) 96
    (2) 95
29 96
Sch 1
    para 1 96
Sch 2 93
Uniform Commercial Code (USA)
s 2-328(3) 9
    2-715(1) 325
Uniform Laws on International
Sales Act 1967 (39 *Statutes* 17)
Sch 2 14
    art 5(4) 14
    6(1) 14
    9(2) 15
    12(1) 14
Wages Act 1986 278

List of Cases

PAGE

A

AG Securities v Vaughan
(1988) 67

Aberfoyle Plantations Ltd v
Cheng (1960) 286

Adamastos Shipping Co Ltd v
Anglo-Saxon Petroleum Co
Ltd (1959) 62

Adams v Lindsell (1818) . . . 13

Adamson v Jarvis (1827) . . . 155

Addis v Gramophone Co Ltd
(1909) 319

Adelfa, The (1988) 308

Adler v Dickson (1955) . . . 86

Affréteurs Réunis SA v Leopold
Walford (London) Ltd
(1919) 215

Afovos Shipping Co SA v
Pagnan and Lli, The Afovos
(1983) 277, 295

Agip SpA v Navigazione Alta
Italia SpA, The Nai Genova
and Nai Superba (1984) . . 119

Agrabele, The. See Gebr Van
Weelde Scheepvaartkantor BV
v Cia Naviera Sea Orient SA,
The Agrabele

Ahlstrom Osakeyhtio v EC
Commission: 89, 104, 114, 116,
117, 125-129/85 (1988) . . 174

Ailion v Spiekermann (1976) . 154

Ailsa Craig Fishing Co Ltd v
Malvern Fishing Co Ltd and
Securicor (Scotland) Ltd
(1983) 76, 81

Ajayi (trading under the name
and style of Colony Carrier
Co) v R T Briscoe (Nigeria)
Ltd (1964) 46

Akerhielm v De Mare (1959) . 125

Aktion Maritime Corpn of
Liberia v S Kasmas & Bros
Ltd, The Aktion (1987) . . 332

PAGE

Al-Kandari v J R Brown & Co
(1988) 212

Alaskan Trader, The. See Clea
Shipping Corpn v Bulk Oil
International Ltd, The Alaskan
Trader

Alder v Moore (1961) . . . 346

Alexander v Railway Executive
(1951) 81

Alexander v Rayson (1936) . . 162

Aliakmon, The. See Leigh and
Sillivan Ltd v Aliakmon
Shipping Co Ltd, The
Aliakmon

Allan (J M) (Merchandising) Ltd
v Cloke (1963) 176

Allcard v Skinner (1887) . . . 149

Allcard v Walker (1896) . . . 103

Allen v Pink (1838) 69

Allen v Waters & Co (1935) . . 211

Alliance Bank Ltd v Broom
(1864) 34

Allied Marine Transport Ltd v
Vale do Rio Doce Navegacao
SA, The Leonidas D (1985) . 2, 7,
16, 41

Alpenstow Ltd v Regalian
Properties plc (1985) . . . 23

Amalgamated Investment and
Property Co Ltd v John
Walker & Sons Ltd (1976) . 101,
103, 304, 306

Amalgamated Investment and
Property Co Ltd (in
liquidation) v Texas
Commerce International Bank
Ltd (1982) 43

Amalgamated Society of Railway
Servants v Osborne (1910) . 163

xvii

PAGE

American Accord, The. See
United City Merchants
(Investments) Ltd and Glass
Fibres and Equipments Ltd v
Royal Bank of Canada,
Vitrorefuerzos SA and Banco
Continental SA, The American
Accord
Amoco Australia Pty Ltd v
Rocca Bros Motor Engineering
Co Pty Ltd (1975) 181
Anderson v Martindale (1801) . 206
Anderson (W B) & Sons Ltd v
Rhodes (Liverpool) Ltd
(1967) 129
Andre & Cie SA v Ets Michel
Blanc & Fils (1977) . . . 134
André et Cie v Cook Industries
Inc (1987) 270
Andre et Cie SA v Marine
Transocean Ltd, The Splendid
Sun (1981) 7
Andrews Bros (Bournemouth)
Ltd v Singer & Co Ltd
(1934) 79
Angelia, The. See Trade and
Transport Incorporated v Iino
Kaiun Kaisha, The Angelia
Angelic Star, The (1988) . . 345
Angell v Duke (1875) . . . 70
Anglia Television Ltd v Reed
(1972) 321
Anglo-Russian Merchant Traders
and John Batt & Co (London),
Re (1917) 24, 268
Antares (No 2), The. See Kenya
Railways v Antares Co Pte
Ltd, The Antares (No 2)
Antclizo, The. See Food Corpn of
India v Antclizo Shipping
Corpn, The Antclizo
Appleby v Myers (1867) . . . 299
Archbolds (Freightage) Ltd v S
Spanglett Ltd (Randall, Third
Party) (1961) 176
Archdale (James) & Co Ltd v
Comservices Ltd (1954) . . 77
Archer v Brown (1985) . . 135, 336
Arcos Ltd v EA Ronaasen & Son
(1933) 269, 280
Argy Trading Development Co
Ltd v Lapid Developments Ltd
(1977) 26, 42

PAGE

Armagas Ltd v Mundogas SA,
The Ocean Frost (1986) . 248, 249
Armstrong v Jackson (1917) . . 139
Armstrong v Stokes (1872) . . 258
Aron (J) & Co Inc v Comptoir
Wegimont (1921) 289
Arrale v Costain Civil
Engineering Ltd (1976) . 29, 44,
150
Ashbury Railway Carriage and
Iron Co Ltd v Riche (1875) . 254
Ashmore Benson Pease & Co Ltd
v A V Dawson Ltd (1973) . 176
Ashton v Corrigan (1871) . . 353
Aspinalls to Powell and
Scholefield (1889) . . . 106, 274
Associated Japanese Bank
(International) Ltd v Credit du
Nord SA (1988) . . 99, 100, 103,
105
Astley v Reynolds (1731) . . 148
Astley Industrial Trust Ltd v
Grimley (1963) 283
Astro Exito Navegacion SA v
Southland Enterprise Co Ltd,
The Messiniaki Tolmi (1983) . 352
Aswan Engineering
Establishment Co v Lupdine
Ltd (Thurgar Bolle, Third
Party) (1987) 213
Athos, The. See Telfair Shipping
Corpn v Athos Shipping Co
SA, Solidor Shipping Co Ltd,
Horizon Finance Corpn and
AN Cominos, The Athos
Atkinson v Cotesworth (1825) . 260
Atkinson v Denby (1862) . . 183
Atlantic Baron, The. See North
Ocean Shipping Co Ltd v
Hyundai Construction Co Ltd,
The Atlantic Baron
Atlantic Lines and Navigation
Co Inc v Didymi Corpn and
Leon Corpn, The Didymi and
Leon (1984) 302
Atlantic Lines and Navigation
Co Inc v Hallam Ltd, The
Lucy (1983) 127, 133
Attica Sea Carriers Corpn v
Ferrostaal Poseidon Bulk
Reederei GmbH, The Puerto
Buitrago (1976) 351
A-G v Guardian Newspapers Ltd
(No 2) (1988) 165, 317

PAGE

A-G for Ceylon v Silva (1953) . 248
A-G of Hong Kong v
  Humphreys Estate (Queen's
  Gardens) Ltd (1987) . . . 48
Attwood v Lamont (1920) . 168, 180
August Leonhardt, The. See
  Lokumal (K) & Sons (London)
  Ltd v Lotte Shipping Co Pte
  Ltd, The August Leonhardt
Autry v Republic Productions
  Inc (1947) 309
Avery v Bowden (1855); affd
  (1856) 297
Awilco A/S v Fulvia SpA di
  Navigazione, The Chikuma
  (1981) 277

B

B & S Contracts and Design Ltd
  v Victor Green Publications
  Ltd (1984) 40, 147
BICC plc v Burndy Corpn
  (1985) 277
BP Exploration Co (Libya) Ltd v
  Hunt (No 2) (1982); affd
  (1983) 312, 313
BTP Tioxide Ltd v Pioneer
  Shipping Ltd and Armada
  Marine SA, The Nema
  (1982) 161, 305
Badagry, The. See Terkol
  Rederierne v Petroleo
  Brasileiro SA and Frota
  Nacional De Petroleiros, The
  Badagry
Badische Co etc, Re (1921) . . 305
Bagot v Stevens, Scanlan & Co
  Ltd (1966) 267
Bain v Fothergill (1874) . . . 342
Bainbridge v Firmstone (1838) . 27
Balfour v Balfour (1919) . . . 54
Ballett v Mingay (1943) . . . 194
Balsamo v Medici (1984) . . . 213
Banco de Portugal v Waterlow &
  Sons Ltd (1932) 339
Bank Line Ltd v Arthur Capel &
  Co (1919) . . 300, 305, 309, 311
Bank of Baroda v Panessar
  (1987) 270
Bank of New Zealand v Simpson
  (1900) 68

PAGE

Bank of Nova Scotia v Hellenic
  Mutual War Risks Association
  (Bermuda) Ltd, The Good
  Luck (1988) 145, 341
Bannerman v White (1861) . 131, 279
Banque Financière de la Cité SA
  v Westgate Insurance Co Ltd
  (1988) 144, 146
Barnes & Co v Toye (1884) . . 190
Barrow, Lane and Ballard Ltd v
  Phillip Phillips & Co Ltd
  (1929) 105
Bartlett v Wells (1862) . . . 196
Basham, Re (1987) . . . 48
Baskcomb v Beckwith (1869) . 115
Bass Holdings Ltd v Morton
  Music Ltd (1987) 284
Batard v Hawes (1853) . . . 205
Beach v Reed Corrugated Cases
  Ltd (1956) 330
Beale v Kyte (1907) 119
Beauchamp Bros, Re, ex p
  Beauchamp (1894) 204
Beauforte (Jon) (London) Ltd,
  Re, Applications of Grainger
  Smith & Co (Builders) Ltd,
  John Wright & Son (Veneers)
  Ltd and Lowell Baldwin Ltd
  (1953) 200
Beaumont v Humberts (1988) . 126
Bedford Insurance Co Ltd v
  Instituto de Resseguros do
  Brasil (1985) 177, 255
Behn v Burness (1863) . . 130, 280
Behnke v Bede Shipping Co Ltd
  (1927) 353
Bell v Lever Bros Ltd (1932) . 100,
                101, 103, 106
Bell Houses Ltd v City Wall
  Properties Ltd (1966) . . . 202
Belvoir Finance Co Ltd v
  Stapleton (1971) 186
Bennett v Bennett (1952) . 179, 181
Bentall, Horsley and Baldry v
  Vicary (1931) 17
Bentley (Dick) Productions Ltd v
  Harold Smith (Motors) Ltd
  (1965) 131
Bentsen v Taylor Sons & Co (No
  2) (1893) 287
Beresford v Royal Insurance Co
  Ltd (1938) 155
Berg v Sadler and Moore
  (1937) 138

PAGE

Berger & Co Inc v Gill & Duffus
SA (1984) . . 271, 273, 293, 333
Bergerco USA v Vegoil Ltd
(1984) 279
Bernard v Williams (1928) . . 286
Bernstein v Pamson Motors
(Golders Green) Ltd (1987) . 320
Berry v Berry (1929) . . . 61
Beswick v Beswick (1966); affd
(1968) . . 209, 210, 214, 218, 352
Betterbee v Davis (1811) . . . 270
Bettini v Gye (1876) 275
Bickerton v Burrell (1816) . . 259
Bigos v Bousted (1951) . . 154, 183,
184
Bisset v Wilkinson (1927) . . 123
Black v Smallwood (1966) . . 260
Blackburn Bobbin Co v TW
Allen & Sons (1918) . . . 301
Blackburn Building Society v
Cunliffe Brooks & Co (1882);
affd sub nom Cunliffe Brooks
& Co v Blackburn and District
Benefit Building Society
(1884) 201
Blades v Free (1829) . . . 247, 263
Blankenstein, The. See Damon
Cia Naviera SA v
Hapag-Lloyd International SA
Blay v Pollard and Morris
(1930) 119
Bliss v South East Thames
Regional Health Authority
(1987) 319
Blyth v Fladgate (1891) . . . 205
Bolton Partners v Lambert
(1889) 255
Bone v Ekless (1860) 186
Borag, The. See Compania
Financiera Soleada SA,
Netherlands Antilles Ships
Management Corpn Ltd and
Dammers and Van der Heide's
Shipping and Trading Co Ltd
v Hamoor Tanker Corpn Inc,
The Borag
Boston Deep Sea Fishing and Ice
Co v Ansell (1888) 278
Boulton v Jones (1857) . . . 112
Bowes v Shand (1877) . . . 280
Bowmakers Ltd v Barnet
Instruments Ltd (1945) . . 185
Boyd v Hind (1857) 45

PAGE

Bradburn v Great Western Rly
Co (1874) 340
Brandts (William) Sons & Co v
Dunlop Rubber Co Ltd
(1905) 229
Branwhite v Worcester Works
Finance Ltd (1969) . . . 362
Bremer Handelsgesellschaft mbH
v Continental Grain Co
(1983) 310
Bremer Handelsgesellschaft mbH
v Mackprang Jr (1979) . . 310
Bremer Handelsgesellschaft mbH
v Vanden Avenne-Izegem
PVBA (1978) 282, 331
Bremer Vulkan Schiffbau und
Maschinenfabrik v South India
Shipping Corpn Ltd (1981) . 290
Brewer v Westminster Bank Ltd
(1952) 208
Brice v Bannister (1878) . . . 230
Bridge v Deacons (a firm)
(1984) 166, 168, 169
Bridges and Salmon Ltd v The
Swan (Owner), The Swan
(1968) 259
Brikom Investments Ltd v Carr
(1979) 38, 45, 70
Brimnes, The. See Tenax SS Co
Ltd v Reinante Transoceania
Navegacion SA, The Brimnes
Brinkibon Ltd v Stahag Stahl
und
Stahlwarenhandelsgesellschaft
mbH (1983) . . . 11, 13, 14
British and Beningtons Ltd v
North Western Cachar Tea Co
Ltd (1923) . . 61, 269, 273, 296
British and Commonwealth
Group plc v Quadrex Holdings
Inc (1988) 286
British Crane Hire Corpn Ltd v
Ipswich Plant Hire Ltd
(1975) 66, 75
British Motor Trade Association
v Salvadori (1949) . . . 221, 222
British Road Services Ltd v
Arthur V Crutchley & Co Ltd
(Factory Guards Ltd, Third
Parties) (1967); on appeal
(1968) 11
British Steel Corpn v Cleveland
Bridge and Engineering Co
Ltd (1984) 22, 23, 363

PAGE

British Transport Commission v
Gourley (1956) 330
British Waggon Co v Lea
(1880) 243
British Westinghouse Electric and
Manufacturing Co Ltd v
Underground Electric Rlys Co
of London Ltd (1912) . . . 339
Brodie v Brodie (1917) . . . 159
Brogden v Metropolitan Rly Co
(1877) 11
Brook v Hook (1871) 255
Brown v Brine (1875) . . . 36
Brown v Byrne (1854) . . . 69
Brown, Jenkinson & Co Ltd v
Percy Dalton (London) Ltd
(1957) 156
Browning v Provincial Insurance
Co of Canada (1873) . . . 256
Brownton Ltd v Edward Moore
Inbucon Ltd (1985) . . . 239
Bruce v Warwick (1815) . . . 193
Bruner v Moore (1904) . . . 13
Buckland v Farmer and Moody
(a firm) (1978) 293
Bunge Corpn v Tradax SA
(1981) . . . 271, 280, 282, 285
Burnard v Haggis (1863) . . 194
Burrell v Jones (1819) . . . 259
Burrows v Rhodes (1899) . . 178
Bute (Marquis) v Thompson
(1844) 104
Butler Machine Tool Co Ltd v
Ex-Cell-O Corpn (England)
Ltd (1979) 11
Butterworth v Kingsway Motors
Ltd (1954) 361
Butwick v Grant (1924) . . . 247
Byrne v Schiller (1871) . . . 313
Byrne & Co v Leon Van
Tienhoven & Co (1880) . 13, 18

C

C and P Haulage (a firm) v
Middleton (1983) 323
CCC Films (London) Ltd v
Impact Quadrant Films Ltd
(1985) 323
CN Marine Inc v Stena Line A/B
and Regie Voor Maritiem
Transport, The Stena Nautica
(No 2) (1982) 220, 353

PAGE

Calabar Properties Ltd v Stitcher
(1984) . . . 270, 319, 325, 356
Callisher v Bischoffsheim (1870) . 35
Campbell Discount Co Ltd v
Bridge (1961); revsd sub nom
Bridge v Campbell Discount
Co Ltd (1962) 346
Canada SS Lines Ltd v R
(1952) 76
Cannon v Hartley (1949) . . 355
Caparo Industries plc v Dickman
(1988) 129
Car and Universal Finance Co
Ltd v Caldwell (1965) . . . 137
Caribonum Co Ltd v Le Couch
(1913) 165
Carlill v Carbolic Smoke Ball Co
(1893) 8, 16
Carney v Herbert (1985) . . 181, 182
Carrington v Roots (1837) . . 60
Casey's Patents, Re, Stewart v
Casey (1892) 30
Cassell & Co Ltd v Broome
(1972) 319
Castle v Wilkinson (1870) . . 356
Catlin v Cyprus Finance Corpn
(London) Ltd (1983) . . . 208
Cehave NV v Bremer
Handelsgesellschaft mbH, The
Hansa Nord (1976) . . 276, 281,
283
Cellulose Acetate Silk Co Ltd v
Widnes Foundry (1925) Ltd
(1933) 345
Central London Property Trust
Ltd v High Trees House Ltd
(1947) 45
Centrovincial Estates plc v
Merchant Investors Assurance
Co Ltd (1983) . . . 34, 113
Cerealmangimi SpA v Toepfer,
The Eurometal (1981) . . . 270
Chande v East African Airways
Corpn (1964) 319
Chanter v Hopkins (1838) . 79, 288
Chapelton v Barry UDC (1940) . 73
Chaplin v Hicks (1911) . . . 329
Chaplin v Leslie Frewin
(Publishers) Ltd (1966) . 191, 194
Chappell v Times Newspapers
Ltd (1975) 357
Chappell & Co Ltd v Nestlé Co
Ltd (1960) 28
Chapple v Cooper (1844) . . 189

PAGE

Chaproniere v Lambert (1917) . 60
Charge Card Services Ltd, Re
  (1987); on appeal (1988) . 31, 271
Charnock v Liverpol Corpn
  (1968) 208
Charter v Sullivan (1957) . . 328
Charterhouse Credit Co Ltd v
  Tolly (1963) 326, 361
Chaudhry v Prabhakar (1988) . 27,
                                 129
Cheall v Association of
  Professional, Executive,
  Clerical and Computer Staff
  (1983) 157, 171, 291
Chelini v Nieri (1948) . . . 319
Chess (Oscar) Ltd v Williams
  (1957) 130, 131, 133
Chief Constable of Leicestershire
  v M (1988) 186
Chikuma, The. See Awilco A/S v
  Fulvia SpA di Navigazione,
  The Chikuma
Chilean Nitrate Sales Corpn v
  Marine Transportation Co Ltd
  and Pansuiza Compania de
  Navegacion SA (1978 C No
  2915), The Hermosa (1982) . 275,
                                 295
Chillingworth v Esche (1924) . 23
China National Foreign Trade
  Transportation Corpn v
  Evlogia Shipping Co SA of
  Panama, The Mihalios Xilas
  (1979) 287
China-Pacific SA v Food Corpn
  of India, The Winson (1982) . 252
Christopher (E) & Co v Essig
  (1948) 17
Christy v Row (1808) . . . 290
Churchward v R (1865) . . . 266
Circle Freight International Ltd
  v Mideast Gulf Exports Ltd
  (1988) 75
City and Westminster Properties
  (1934) Ltd v Mudd (1959) . 70
Clapham v Draper (1885) . . 291
Clark v Kirby-Smith (1964) . . 267
Clark v Lindsay (1903) . . . 307
Clarke v Chadburn (1985) . . 152
Clarke v Dickson (1858) . . . 139
Clarke v Earl of Dunraven and
  Mount-Earl, The Satanita. See
  Satanita, The

PAGE

Clarkson, Booker Ltd v Andjel
  (1964) 261
Clay v Yates (1856) 153
Clayton (Herbert) and Jack
  Waller Ltd v Oliver (1930) . 266
Clea Shipping Corpn v Bulk Oil
  International Ltd, The Alaskan
  Trader (1983) 351
Cleaver v Mutual Reserve Fund
  Life Association (1892) . . 210
Clements v London and North
  Western Rly Co (1894) . . 191
Clifford (Lord) v Watts (1870) . 104
Clifford (Frank W) Ltd v Garth
  (1956) 182
Clydebank Engineering and
  Shipbuilding Co Ltd v Don
  Jose Ramos Yzquierdo y
  Castaneda (1905) 343
Cochrane v Moore (1890) . . 232
Coggs v Bernard (1703) . . . 27
Cohen v Roche (1927) . . . 352
Coldunell Ltd v Gallon (1986) . 151
Colebrook's Conveyances, Re,
  Taylor v Taylor (1973) . . 120
Collen v Wright (1857) . . . 262
Collin v Duke of Westminster
  (1985) 39
Collins v Associated Greyhound
  Racecourses Ltd (1930) . . 256
Collins v Blantern (1767) . . 162
Combe v Combe (1951) . . . 42
Commercial Plastics Ltd v
  Vincent (1965) 165
Compania Financiera Soleada SA
  v Hamoor Tanker Corpn Inc,
  The Borag (1981) . . . 338
Condor v Barron Knights Ltd
  (1966) 300
Congimex Companhia Geral de
  Comercio Importadora e
  Exportadora SARL v Tradax
  Export SA (1983) 304
Connolly Shaw Ltd v
  Nordenfjeldske SS Co (1934) . 82
Constantine (Joseph) SS Line Ltd
  v Imperial Smelting Corpn
  Ltd, The Kingswood (1942) . 310
Container Transport
  International Inc and Reliance
  Group Inc v Oceanus Mutual
  Underwriting Association
  (Bermuda) Ltd (1984) . . . 144
Cook v S (1967) 320

PAGE

Cook v Wright (1861) . . . 35
Cooke (Isaac) & Sons v Eshelby
(1887) 257
Coombes v Smith (1986) . . . 48
Cooper v Micklefield Coal and
Lime Co Ltd (1912) . . . 237
Cooper v National Provincial
Bank Ltd (1946) 144
Cooper v Parker (1855) . . . 44
Cooper v Phibbs (1867) . 99, 103, 106
Coral Leisure Group Ltd v
Barnett (1981) 158, 176
Corby v Morrison (1980) . 163, 176
Corpe v Overton (1833) . . . 193
Cory v Patton (1872) 142
Cotman v Brougham (1918) . . 200
Couchman v Hill (1947) . . 67, 85
Coulls v Bagot's Executor and
Trustee Co Ltd (1967) . . 207, 210,
211
Coulthart v Clementson (1879) . 20
County Hotel and Wine Co v
London and North Western
Rly Co (1918) 239
County Personnel (Employment
Agency) Ltd v Alan R Pulver
& Co (1987) 326
Court Line Ltd v Aktiebolaget
Gøtaverken, The Halcyon the
Great (1984) 227
Courtney and Fairbairn Ltd v
Tolaini Bros (Hotels) Ltd
(1975) 22
Couturier v Hastie (1856) . . 105
Coventry v Great Eastern Rly
Co (1883) 141
Cowern v Nield (1912) . . 191, 197
Crabb v Arun District Council
(1976) 48, 49
Crane v Hegeman-Harris Co Inc
(1939) 121
Craven-Ellis v Canons Ltd
(1936) 363
Cresswell v Potter (1978) . . . 150
Cricklewood Property and
Investment Trust Ltd v
Leighton's Investment Trust
Ltd (1945) 306
Cullinane v British Rema
Manufacturing Co Ltd
(1954) 324
Cundy v Lindsay (1878) . . 109, 116,
127, 137, 194
Cunningham v Harrison (1973) . 211

PAGE

Curlewis v Birkbeck (1863) . . 257
Currie v Misa (1875) 25
Curtis v Chemical Cleaning and
Dyeing Co Ltd (1951) . . . 85
Czarnikow v Roth, Schmidt &
Co (1922) 161

D

D v National Society for the
Prevention of Cruelty to
Children (1978) 157
D & C Builders Ltd v Rees
(1966) 46, 150
D & F Estates Ltd v Church
Comrs for England (1988) . 213, 214,
244
Dakin v Oxley (1864) . . 276, 278
Damon Cia Naviera SA v
Hapag-Lloyd International SA,
The Blankenstein (1985) . 293, 348
Daniel, Re, Daniel v Vassall
(1917) 342
Daniels and Daniels v R White
& Sons Ltd and Tarbard
(1938) 267
Danube and Black Sea Railway
and Kustenjie Harbour Co Ltd
v Xenos (1863) 296
Darbishire v Warran (1963) . . 326
Daulia Ltd v Four Millbank
Nominees Ltd (1978) . . . 17
Davenport v R (1877) . . . 291
Davies v Beynon-Harris (1931) . 192
Davies v Collins (1945) . . 80, 244
Davies v Parry (1988) . . . 90
Davies v Presbyterian Church of
Wales (1986) 55
Davis v Johnson (1979) . . . 158
Davis Contractors Ltd v Fareham
UDC (1956) 303
Davis (Clifford) Management
Ltd v WEA Records Ltd
(1975) 168
Davison v Donaldson (1882) . . 261
Dawood (Ebrahim) Ltd v Heath
(Est 1927) Ltd (1961) . . . 360
Day v Singleton (1899) . . . 342
Dean v Ainley (1987) . . . 326
Dearle v Hall (1828) 230
Debenham v Mellon (1880) . . 247
Debenham v Sawbridge (1901) . 103
Debenham's, Ltd v Perkins
(1925) 261

PAGE

Decro-Wall International SA v
Practitioners in Marketing Ltd
(1971) 274
De Francesco v Barnum (1889) . 191
Defries v Milne (1913) . . . 238
De Lassalle v Guildford (1901) . 132
De Meza and Stuart v Apple,
Van Straten, Shena and Stone
(1974); affd (1975) . . . 340, 341
Denman v Brise (1949) . . . 306
Denmark Productions Ltd v
Boscobel Productions Ltd
(1969) 263, 310, 350
Dennis & Co Ltd v Munn
(1949) 154, 177
Denny Mott and Dickson Ltd v
James B Fraser & Co Ltd
(1944) 305
Denton v Great Northern Rly Co
(1856) 9
Derry v Peek (1889) 128
Dewar v Mintoft (1912) . . . 348
De Wutz v Hendricks (1824) . 163
Diana Prosperity, The. See
Reardon Smith Line Ltd v
Yngvar Hansen-Tangen and
Sanko SS Co Ltd, The Diana
Prosperity
Dibbins v Dibbins (1896) . . 254
Dickinson v Dodds (1876) . 18, 19,
49
Didymi and Leon, The. See
Atlantic Lines and Navigation
Co Inc v Didymi Corpn and
Leon Corpn, The Didymi and
Leon
Didymi Corpn v Atlantic Lines
and Navigation Co Inc
(1988) 23
Dies v British and International
Mining and Finance Corpn
Ltd (1939) 347
Diesen v Samson (1971) . . . 319
Dietman v Brent London
Borough Council (1987); affd
(1988) 291
Dillwyn v Llewelyn (1862) . 47, 48
Dimmock v Hallett (1866) . . 123
Dixon v Clark (1848) . . . 270
Dodsworth v Dodsworth (1973) . 48
Domb v Isoz (1980) . . . 23, 332

PAGE

Dominion Coal Co Ltd v
Dominion Iron and Steel Co
Ltd and National Trust Co Ltd
(1909) 355
Donnelly v Joyce (1974) . . . 211
Doyle v Olby (Ironmongers) Ltd
(1969) 135
Doyle v White City Stadium
(1935) 191
Drake v Beckham (1849) . . . 241
Drane v Evangelou (1978) . . 319
Drew v Nunn (1879) 263
Dunkirk Colliery Co v Lever
(1878) 327
Dunlop v Higgins (1848) . . . 13
Dunlop Pneumatic Tyre Co Ltd
v New Garage and Motor Co
Ltd (1915) 343
Dunlop Pneumatic Tyre Co Ltd
v Selfridge & Co Ltd (1915) . 208,
221
Dunn v Macdonald (1897) . . 262
Durham Bros v Robertson
(1898) 227
Dyster v Randall & Sons
(1926) 256

E

Eagle, The. See Hollingworth v
Southern Ferries Ltd, The
Eagle
Earle v Peale (1712) 190
East Ham Borough Council (or
Corpn) v Bernard Sunley &
Sons Ltd (1966) 331
Eastham v Newcastle United
Football Club Ltd (1964) . . 170
Easton v Pratchett (1835) . . 236
Eastwood v Kenyon (1840) . . 30
Ecclesiastical Comrs for
England's Conveyance, Re, Re
Law of Property Act 1925
(1936) 219
Edgington v Fitzmaurice (1885) . 123
Edler v Auerbach (1950) . . . 184
Edwards v Carter (1893) . . . 192
Edwards v Newland & Co (E
Burchett Ltd, Third Party)
(1950) 244
Edwards v Skyways Ltd (1964) . 51
Edwards v Society of Graphical
and Allied Trades (1971) . . 339
Ehrman v Bartholomew (1898) . 357

PAGE

Elena d'Amico, The. See Koch
Marine Inc v d'Amica Societa
di Navigazione arL, The Elena
d'Amico
Elias v George Sahely & Co
(Barbados) Ltd (1983) . . . 58
Elliott v Richardson (1870) . . 162
Ellis v Torrington (1920) . . 239
Emanuel (Lewis) & Son Ltd v
Sammut (1959) 267
Embiricos v Sydney Reid & Co
(1914) 305
Empire Meat Co Ltd v Patrick
(1939) 167
Empresa Exportadora de Azucar
v Industria Azucarera
Nacional SA, The Playa Larga
and The Marble Islands
(1983) 303
Empresa Lineas Maritimas
Argentinas v Oceanus Mutual
Underwriting Association
(Bermuda) Ltd (1984) . . . 43
Enderby Town Football Club
Ltd v Football Association Ltd
(1971) 156
England v Davidson (1840) . . 36
Entores Ltd v Miles Far East
Corpn (1955) 11, 13
Erlanger v New Sombrero
Phosphate Co (1878) . . . 139
Errington v Errington and
Woods (1952) 17
Ertel Bieber & Co v Rio Tinto
Co (1918) 308
Esso Petroleum Co Ltd v
Harper's Garage (Stourport)
Ltd (1968) . . . 172, 173, 174
Esso Petroleum Co Ltd v
Kingswood Motors
(Addlestone) Ltd (1974) . . 174
Esso Petroleum Co Ltd v Mardon
(1976) . . . 123, 128, 129, 132,
135, 341
Esso Petroleum Ltd v Customs
and Excise Comrs (1976) . . 8, 55
Etablissement Biret & Cie SA v
Yukiteru Kaiun KK and
Nissui Shipping Corpn, The
Sun Happiness (1984) . . . 259
Eugenia, The. See Ocean Tramp
Tankers Corpn v V/O
Sovfracht, The Eugenia

PAGE

Euro-Diam Ltd v Bathurst
(1988) 187
Eurometal, The. See
Cerealmangimi SpA v Toepfer,
The Eurometal
Eurymedon, The. See New
Zealand Shipping Co Ltd v A
M Satterthwaite & Co. Ltd
Evans v Llewellin (1787) . . . 150
Evans (J) & Son (Portsmouth)
Ltd v Andrea Merzario Ltd
(1976) 53
Evans Marshall & Co v Bertola
SA (1973) 352
Evening Standard Co Ltd v
Henderson (1987) . 169, 291, 357
Eves v Eves (1975) . . 47, 54, 158
Evia (No 2), The. See Kodros
Shipping Corpn of Monrovia v
Empresa Cubana de Fletes,
The Evia (No 2)
Excomm Ltd v Guan Guan
Shipping (Pte) Ltd, The
Golden Bear (1987) . . . 2, 16
Eximenco Handels AG v
Partrederiet Oro Chief and
Levantes Maritime Corpn, The
Oro Chief (1983) 353
Export Credits Guarantee
Department v Universal Oil
Products Co (1983) 346
Eyre v Johnson (1946) . . . 306
Eyre v Measday (1986) . . 62, 267

F

F & B Entertainments Ltd v
Leisure Enterprises Ltd
(1976) 134
Faccenda Chicken Ltd v Fowler
(1986) 165, 169
Fairline Shipping Corpn v
Adamson (1975) 15
Falcke v Gray (1859) . . . 354
Falcke v Scottish Imperial
Insurance Co (1886) . . . 252
Faraday v Tamworth Union
(1916) 119
Farnworth Finance Facilities Ltd
v Attryde (1970) 80
Fawcett v Smethurst (1914) . . 194

PAGE

Federal Commerce and
  Navigation Co Ltd v Molena
  Alpha Inc, The Nanfri
  (1979) 281, 282, 284
Feise v Parkinson (1812) . . . 138
Fellowes v Lord Gwydyr (1829) . 259
Fellows v Fisher (1976) . . . 168
Felthouse v Bindley (1862); affd
  (1863) 15
Fender v St John-Mildmay
  (1938) 160
Fenwick v Macdonald Fraser &
  Co (1904) 9
Fercometal SARL v MSC
  Mediterranean Shipping Co
  SA, The Simona (1988) . 273, 297,
  333
Fibrosa Spolka Akcyjna v
  Fairbairn Lawson Combe
  Barbour Ltd (1943) . . 305, 314,
  360
Financings Ltd v Baldock
  (1963) 292
Financings Ltd v Stimson
  (1962) 20
Finkielkraut v Monohan (1949) . 286
Firbank's Executors v
  Humphreys (1886) 201
First National Securities Ltd v
  Jones (1978) 26
Fisher & Co v Apollinaris Co
  (1875) 162
Fishmongers' Co v Robertson
  (1843) 33
Fitch v Dewes (1921) 168
Fitzroy v Cave (1905) . . . 224
Flavell, Re, Murray v Flavell
  (1883) 216
Fletcher v Tayleur (1855) . . 342
Flight v Bolland (1828) . . . 193
Flight v Booth (1834) . . . 274
Flint v Brandon (1803) . . . 355
Foakes v Beer (1884) . . . 41
Foley v Classique Coaches Ltd
  (1934) 23
Food Corpn of India v Antclizo
  Shipping Corpn, The Antclizo
  (1987); on appeal (1988) . 7, 113,
  290
Ford Motor Co Ltd v
  Amalgamated Union of
  Engineering and Foundry
  Workers (1969) 52

PAGE

Forman & Co Pty Ltd v The
  Liddesdale (1900) 253
Forsikringsaktieselskapet Vesta v
  Butcher (1988) 340, 341
Foster v Driscoll (1929) . . . 163
Foster v London, Chatham and
  Dover Rly Co (1895) . . . 200
Foster v Mackinnon (1869) . . 116
Freeman and Lockyer (a firm) v
  Buckhurst Park Properties
  (Mangal) Ltd (1964) . . 249, 250
Freeth v Burr (1874) 283
Frost v Aylesbury Dairy Co
  (1905) 267
Furness Bridge, The. See
  Seabridge Shipping Ltd v
  Antco Shipping Co Ltd, The
  Furness Bridge

G

Gadd v Thompson (1911) . . 191
Gage v King (1961) 53
Galbraith v Mitchenall Estates
  Ltd (1965) 348
Gallagher Ltd v British Road
  Services Ltd and Containerway
  and Roadferry Ltd (1974) . . 85
Galloway v Galloway (1914) . 99
Gardner v Coutts & Co (1967) . 63
Gardner v Moore (1984) . . 156, 217
Garforth v Fearon (1787) . . 163
Garnac Grain Co Inc v H M F
  Faure and Fairclough Ltd and
  Bunge Corpn (1968) . . . 246
Garrard v Frankel (1862) . . 119
Gator Shipping Corpn v
  Trans-Asiatic Oil Ltd SA and
  Occidental Shipping
  Establishment, The Odenfeld
  (1978) 351
Gebr Van Weelde
  Scheepvaartkantor BV v Cia
  Naviera Sea Orient SA, The
  Agrabele (1987) 7
Geier (formerly Braun) v
  Kujawa Weston and Warne
  Bros (Transport) Ltd (1970) . 74
Geismar v Sun Alliance and
  London Insurance Ltd (1978) . 187
General Accident Fire and Life
  Assurance Corpn v Tanter,
  The Zephyr (1985) . . 26, 212
George v Clagett (1797) . . . 257

PAGE

German v Yates (1915) . . . 233

Gewa Chartering BV v Remco
Shipping Lines Ltd, The
Remco (1984) 259

Gibson v Manchester City
Council (1979) . . . 8, 19, 21

Gilbert & Partners (a firm) v
Knight (1968) 362

Gillespie Bros & Co v Cheney,
Eggar & Co (1896) . . . 69

Gillespie Bros & Co Ltd v Roy
Bowles Transport Ltd (1973) . 76

Glafki Shipping Co SA v Pinios
Shipping Co No 1, The Maira
(No 2) (1985); affd (1986) . 308

Glaholm v Hays (1841) . . . 280

Glasbrook Bros Ltd v Glamorgan
County Council (1925) . . 36

Glegg v Bromley (1912) . . . 231

Gluckstein v Barnes (1900) . . 86

Glynn v Margetson & Co
(1893) 82

Gold v Haringey Health
Authority (1987) 267

Golden Bear, The. See Excomm
Ltd v Guan Guan Shipping
(Pte) Ltd, The Golden Bear

Golden Leader, The. See
Mineralimportexport v Eastern
Mediterranean Maritime, The
Golden Leader

Goldsoll v Goldman (1915) . 167, 180

Goldsworthy v Brickell (1987) . 149

Good Luck, The. See Bank of
Nova Scotia v Hellenic Mutual
War Risks Association
(Bermuda) Ltd, The Good
Luck

Gordon and Teixeira v Selico
and Select Management Ltd
(1986) 126, 142

Gore v Gibson (1845) . . . 198

Gore v Van der Lann (1967) . 32

Goring, The (1988) . . . 251

Gosling v Anderson (1972) . . 130

Goss v Lord Nugent (1833) . . 61

Gould v Gould (1970) . . . 54

Grant v Edwards (1986) . . . 54

Gray v Barr (1971) . . . 156

Gray v Southouse (1949) . . . 183

Great Northern Rly Co v
Swaffield (1874) 252

PAGE

Greater Nottingham
Co-operative Society Ltd v
Cementation Piling and
Foundations Ltd (1988) . . 212

Green (R W) Ltd v Cade Bros
Farms (1978) 94

Greenwood v Bennett (1973) . 252

Greenwood v Greenwood
(1863) 144

Greenwood v Martins Bank Ltd
(1933) 250

Gregory v Wilson (1852) . . . 355

Greig v Insole (1978) 170

Griffith v Brymer (1903) . . . 101

Grist v Bailey (1967) . . 101, 106

Griswold v Haven (1862) . . 141

Grover and Grover Ltd v
Mathews (1910) 255

Gunton v
Richmond-upon-Thames
London Borough Council
(1981) 291

Gurtner v Circuit (1968) . . . 217

H

Hadley v Baxendale (1854) . 333, 334

Hagedorn v Bazett (1813) . . 207

Hain SS Co Ltd v Tate and Lyle
Ltd (1936) 79

Halbot v Lens (1901) 262

Halcyon the Great, The. See
Court Line Ltd v Aktiebolaget
Gøtaverken, The Halcyon the
Great

Hall (R & H) Ltd and W H
Pim, Jr & Co's Arbitration, Re
(1928) 328

Hamilton, Re, FitzGeorge v
FitzGeorge (1921) 229

Hamilton v Forrester (1825) . . 247

Hands v Slaney (1800) . . . 189

Hannah Blumenthal, The. See
Wilson (Paal) & Co A/S v
Partenreederei Hannah
Blumenthal, The Hannah
Blumenthal

Hannan's Empress Gold Mining
and Development Co, Re,
Carmichael's Case (1896) . . 264

Hansa Nord, The. See Cehave
NV v Bremer
Handelsgesellschaft mbH, The
Hansa Nord

PAGE

Harbutt's Plasticine Ltd v Wayne
Tank and Pump Co Ltd
(1970) 318
Harding v Harding (1886) . . 233
Hardwick v Johnson (1978) . . 54
Hare v Nicoll (1966) . . . 284
Harling v Eddy (1951) . . 67, 85
Harlow and Jones Ltd v Panex
(International) Ltd (1967) . . 331
Harris v Nickerson (1873) . . . 9
Harris v Pepperell (1867) . . 119
Harris v Sheffield United
Football Club Ltd (1988) . . 36
Harris v Wyre Forest District
Council (1988) 87, 90
Harrison v Harrison (1910) . . 159
Harrison and Jones Ltd v Bunten
and Lancaster Ltd (1953) . . 100
Harse v Pearl Life Assurance Co
(1904) 153, 184
Hart v A R Marshall & Sons
(Bulwell) Ltd (1978) . . . 300
Hart v O'Connor (1985) . . . 198
Hartley v Hymans (1920) . . 285
Hartog v Colin and Shields
(1939) 111, 114
Harvela Investments Ltd v Royal
Trust Co of Canada (CI) Ltd
(1986) 9, 17, 54
Haryanto v E D & F Man
(Sugar) Ltd (1986) . . . 51
Hasham v Zenab (1960) . . . 358
Hayes v Dodds (1988) . . . 319
Head v Tattersall (1871) . . . 139
Heald v Kenworthy (1855) . . 258
Heard v Pilley (1869) . . . 247
Hector v Lyons (1988) . . . 108
Hedley Byrne & Co Ltd v Heller
& Partners Ltd (1964) . . 90, 128
Heilbut, Symons & Co v
Buckleton (1913) 70
Helstan Securities Ltd v
Hertfordshire County Council
(1978) 237
Henderson v Arthur (1907) . . 70
Henrik Sif, The. See Pacol Ltd v
Trade Lines Ltd
Henthorn v Fraser (1892) . . 13
Hermann v Charlesworth
(1905) 159, 187

PAGE

Hermosa, The. See Chilean
Nitrate Sales Corpn v Marine
Transportation Co Ltd and
Pansuiza Compania de
Navegacion SA (1978 C No
2915), The Hermosa
Herne Bay Steam Boat Co v
Hutton (1903) 304
Heron II, The. See Koufos v C
Czarnikow Ltd, The Heron II
Hershey Farms v State (1952) . 275, 287
Heskell v Continental Express
Ltd (1950) 337
Heyman v Darwins Ltd (1942) . 291
Heywood v Wellers (1976) . . 320
Hill v C A Parsons & Co Ltd
(1972) 354
Hill v Hill (1947) 58
Hill Steam Shipping Co v Hugo
Stinnes Ltd (1941) 259
Hillas & Co Ltd v Arcos Ltd
(1932) 22
Hirachand Punamchand v
Temple (1911) . . . 45, 212, 243
Hispanica de Petroleos SA v
Vencedora Oceanica
Navegacion SA, The Kapetan
Markos NL (No 2) (1987) . . 88
Hitchman v Stewart (1855) . . 203
Hobbs v Marlowe (1978) . . 238
Hochster v De La Tour (1853) . 296
Hoenig v Isaacs (1952) . . 279, 326
Hollier v Rambler Motors
(AMC) Ltd (1972) . . . 75, 77
Hollingworth v Southern Ferries
Ltd, The Eagle (1977) . . . 9, 74
Hollins v J Davy Ltd (1963) . . 81
Holman v Johnson (1775) . . 176
Holt v Heatherfield Trust Ltd
(1942) 230, 233
Holt v Ward Clarencieux
(1732) 33
Holwell Securities Ltd v Hughes
(1974) 13, 14
Home Insurance Co and St Paul
Fire and Marine Insurance Co
v Administratia Asigurarilor
de Stat (1983) 51
Hong Kong Fir Shipping Co Ltd
v Kawasaki Kisen Kaisha Ltd
(1962) . . . 275, 276, 281, 283, 296, 336
Hopper v Burness (1876) . . . 290

PAGE

Horrocks v Forray (1976) . 54, 158
Horsley & Weight Ltd, Re
(1982) 200
Horwood v Millar's Timber and
Trading Co Ltd (1917) . . 164
Houghton v Trafalgar Insurance
Co Ltd (1954) 76
Household Fire and Carriage
Accident Insurance Co v Grant
(1879) 13
Howard Marine and Dredging
Co Ltd v A Ogden & Sons
(Excavations) Ltd (1978) . . 129
Howe v Smith (1884) . . . 347
Howell v Coupland (1876) . . 301
Hudson v Temple (1860) . . 286
Hughes v Liverpool Victoria
Legal Friendly Society (1916) . 183
Hughes v Metropolitan Rly Co
(1877) 41
Hughes v Pump House Hotel Co
(1902) 232
Hummingbird Motors Ltd v
Hobbs (1986) . . . 130, 131
Hurley v Dyke (1979) . . . 143
Hussey v Horne-Payne (1879) . 10
Hussey v Palmer (1972) . . . 47
Hutchinson v Harris (1978) . . 320
Hutton v Warren (1836) . . . 68
Hutton v Watling (1948) . 69, 70
Huxford v Stoy Hayward & Co
(1989) 128
Hyams v Coombes (1912) . . 35
Hyde v Wrench (1840) . . . 19
Hyland v J H Barker (North
West) Ltd (1985) 163
Hyman v Hyman (1929) . . . 161
Hyundai Heavy Industries Co
Ltd v Papadopolous (1980) . 292,
347, 348
Hyundai Shipbuilding and
Heavy Industries Co Ltd v
Pournaras (1978) . 292, 347, 348

I

Imperial Loan Co v Stone
(1892) 198
Independent Broadcasting
Authority v EMI Electronics
Ltd and BICC Construction
Ltd (1980) 267

PAGE

Industrial Properties (Barton
Hill) Ltd v Associated
Electrical Industries Ltd
(1977) 125
Ingram v Little (1961) . . . 111
Interfoto Picture Library Ltd v
Stiletto Visual Programmes
Ltd (1988) 74, 85
International Minerals and
Chemical Corpn v Karl O
Helm AG (1986) 342
International Sales and Agencies
Ltd v Marcus (1982) . . . 201
International Sea Tankers Inc v
Hemisphere Shipping Co Ltd,
The Wenjiang (No 2) (1983) . 300,
305
Intertradex SA v
Lesieur-Tourteaux SARL
(1978) 267, 310
Introductions Ltd, Re,
Introductions Ltd v National
Provincial Bank Ltd (1970) . 199
Inwards v Baker (1965) . . 47, 48
Ion, The. See Nippon Yusen
Kaisha v Pacifica Navegacion
SA, The Ion
Irani v Southampton and South
West Hampshire Health
Authority (1985) 354
Irvine & Co v Watson & Sons
(1880) 258

J

JEB Fasteners Ltd v Marks,
Bloom & Co (a firm) (1983) . 127
Jackson v Horizon Holidays Ltd
(1975) 210, 211
Jackson v Union Marine
Insurance Co Ltd (1874) . 300, 308
Jacob and Youngs v Kent
(1921) 326
Jacobs v Batavia and General
Plantations Trust Ltd (1924) . 62,
66
Jacobs v Morris (1902) . . . 249
James v Heim Gallery (London)
Ltd (1980) 42
James Miller & Partners Ltd v
Whitworth Street Estates
(Manchester) Ltd (1970) . . 68
Jarvis v Swans Tours Ltd
(1973) 319

PAGE

Jefferys v Jefferys (1841) . .   29, 355
Jendwine v Slade (1797) . . .   123
Jenkin v Pharmaceutical Society
  of Great Britain (1921) . .   199
Jenkins v Jenkins (1928) . . .   204
Jervis v Howle and Talke
  Colliery Co Ltd (1937) . .   120
Jeune v Queens Cross Properties
  Ltd (1974)   356
Jewsbury v Newbold (1857) . .   247
Jobson v Johnson (1988) . . .   343
Johnson v Agnew (1980) . .   293, 294,
                       332, 348, 359
Johnson v Bragge (1901) . . .   120
Johnson v Moreton (1980) . .   157
Johnson v Raylton Dixon & Co
  (1881)   244
Johnson v Shrewsbury and
  Birmingham Rly Co (1853) .   354
Johnson Matthey Bankers Ltd v
  State Trading Corpn of India
  Ltd (1984)   308
Jones v Padavatton (1969) .   37, 54
Jones v Rimmer (1880) . . .   105
Joscelyne v Nissen (1970) . .   120
Joseph v National Magazine Co
  (1959)   355
Junior Books Ltd v Veitchi Co
  Ltd (1983) 87, 212, 321

K

Kapetan Markos NL, The (No
  2). See Hispanica de Petroleos
  SA v Vencedora Oceanica
  Navegacion SA, The Kapetan
  Markos NL (No 2)
Kaufman v Gerson (1904) . .   149
Kaye Steam Navigation Co Ltd
  v W & R Barnett Ltd (1932) .   330
Kearley v Thomson (1890) . .   184
Keighley, Maxsted & Co v
  Durant (1901)   253
Keir v Leeman (1846) . . .   162
Kelner v Baxter (1866) . . .   254
Kemp v Baerselman (1906) . .   238
Kendall v Hamilton (1879) . .   205
Kennedy v Panama New
  Zealand and Australian Royal
  Mail Co Ltd (1867) . . .   100
Kenya Railways v Antares Co
  Pte Ltd, The Antares (No 2)
  (1987) 78, 84

PAGE

Kenyon Son and Craven Ltd v
  Baxter Hoare & Co Ltd
  (1971)   81
Kerr v Morris (1987) . . .   166, 169
King v Michael Faraday &
  Partners Ltd (1939) . . .   164
King v Victoria Insurance Co
  Ltd (1896)   238
King's Norton Metal Co Ltd v
  Edridge, Merrett & Co Ltd
  (1897)   110
Kingswood Estate Co Ltd v
  Anderson (1963) . . .   51, 60
Kingswood, The. See Constantine
  (Joseph) SS Ltd v Imperial
  Smelting Corpn Ltd, The
  Kingswood
Kiriri Cotton Co Ltd v Dewani
  (1960)   183
Kirklees Metropolitan Borough
  Council v Yorkshire Woollen
  District Transport Co Ltd
  (1978)   303
Kish v Taylor (1912)   80
Kleinwort Benson Ltd v
  Malaysia Mining Corpn Bhd
  (1988)   51
Koch Marine Inc v d'Amica
  Societa di Navigazione arL,
  The Elena d'Amico (1980) .   338
Kodros Shipping Corpn of
  Monrovia v Empresa Cubana
  de Fletes, The Evia (No 2)
  (1983)   300
Kores Manufacturing Co Ltd v
  Kolok Manufacturing Co Ltd
  (1959)   170
Koufos v C Czarnikow Ltd, The
  Heron II (1969) . . .   335, 336
Krell v Henry (1903) . .   305, 308
Kydon Compania Naviera SA v
  National Westminster Bank
  Ltd, The Lena (1981) . . .   270
Kyprianou (Phoebus D) Co v
  Wm H Pim Jnr & Co (1977) .   331

L

Lacey (William) (Hounslow) Ltd
  v Davis (1957)   9
Laconia, The. See Mardorf Peach
  & Co Ltd v Attica Sea
  Carriers Corpn of Liberia, The
  Laconia

PAGE

Lake v Bayliss (1974) . . . 317
Lake v Simmons (1927) . . 110
Lamare v Dixon (1873) . . 353
Landom Trust Ltd v Hurrell
(1955) 344
Langston v Amalgamated Union
of Engineering Workers
(1974) 266
Langston v Amalgamated Union
of Engineering Workers (No
2) (1974) 266
Langton v Waite (1868) . . 256
La Pintada Cia Navegacion SA v
President of India, The La
Pintada (1985) 342
Larissa, The. See Showa Oil
Tanker Co Ltd of Japan v
Maravan SA of Caracas, The
Larissa
Latter v Braddell (1880); on
appeal (1881) 147
Laurence v Lexcourt Holdings
Ltd (1978) 102
Lavarack v Woods of Colchester
Ltd (1967) 339
Laws v London Chronicle
(Indicator Newspapers) Ltd
(1959) 283
Layton v Martin (1986) . . 48
Lazenby Garages Ltd v Wright
(1976) 329
Leaf v International Galleries
(1950) 140
Lee v Showmen's Guild of Great
Britain (1952) . . . 86, 161
Lee (Paula) Ltd v Robert Zehil
& Co Ltd (1983) . . 63, 330
Leeman v Stocks (1951) . . 246
Leigh and Sillivan Ltd v
Aliakmon Shipping Co Ltd,
The Aliakmon (1986) . . 87, 213
Lemenda Trading Co Ltd v
African Middle East Petroleum
Co Ltd (1988) 163
Lena, The. See Kydon Compania
Naviera SA v National
Westminster Bank Ltd, The
Lena
Leonidas D, The. See Allied
Marine Transport Ltd v Vale
do Rio Doce Navegacao SA,
The Leonidas D
Leslie (R) Ltd v Sheill (or Shiell)
(1914) 196, 197

PAGE

L'Estrange v F Graucob Ltd
(1934) 73
Levison v Patent Steam Carpet
Cleaning Co Ltd (1978) . 84, 85, 150
Lewis v Averay (1972) . . 111, 137
Lexmead (Basingstoke) Ltd v
Lewis (1982) . . . 52, 341
Licenses Insurance Corpn and
Guarantee Fund Ltd v Lawson
(1896) 55
Linck, Moeller & Co v Jameson
& Co (1885) 257
Lind (Peter) & Co Ltd v Mersey
Docks and Harbour Board
(1972) 363
Lips, The. See President of India
v Lips Maritime Corpn, The
Lips
Lister v Romford Ice and Cold
Storage Co Ltd (1957) . . . 63
Liverpool City Council v Irwin
(1977) 63, 65
Liverpool Corpn v Wright
(1859) 240
Livesey (formerly Jenkins) v
Jenkins (1985) 143
Lloyd's v Harper (1880) . . 17
Lloyds Bank Ltd v Bundy
(1975) 149, 150
Lobb (Alec) (Garages) Ltd v
Total Oil GB Ltd (1985) . 168, 173, 181
Lock v Bell (1931) . . . 286
Lokumal (K) & Sons (London)
Ltd v Lotte Shipping Co Pte
Ltd, The August Leonhardt
(1985) 43
Lombard North Central plc v
Butterworth (1987) . . . 293
Lombard Tricity Finance Ltd v
Paton (1988) 40
London and Northern Estates Co
v Schlesinger (1916) . . . 306
London and South of England
Building Society v Stone
(1983) 338
London, Chatham and Dover
Rly Co v South Eastern Rly
Co (1893) 342
London Congregational Union
Inc v Harriss and Harriss
(1988) 213

PAGE

London County Commercial
  Reinsurance Office Ltd, Re
  (1922) 153
Long v Lloyd (1958) 140
Lord Strathcona SS Co v
  Dominion Coal Co (1926) . . 222
Lound v Grimwade (1888) . . 181
Lovell and Christmas v
  Beauchamp (1894) 192
Lowe v Hope (1970) 348
Lowe v Peers (1768) 159
Lucas (T) & Co Ltd v Mitchell
  (1972) 168
Lucy, The. See Atlantic Lines
  and Navigation Co Inc v
  Hallam Ltd, The Lucy
Lumley v Wagner (1852) . . 357
Luna, The (1920) 73
Luxor (Eastbourne) Ltd v
  Cooper (1941) 17, 63
Lyus v Prowsa Developments Ltd
  (1982) 216

M

M and S Drapers (a firm) v
  Reynolds (1956) 168
Macara (James) Ltd v Barclay
  (1944); affd (1945) 347
McArdle, Re, (1951) 234
McCall v Abelesz (1976) . . . 315
McCann (John) & Co (a firm) v
  Pow (1974) 17, 244
McCutcheon v David MacBrayne
  Ltd (1964) 75
McDonald v Dennys Lascelles
  Ltd (1933) 348
Macdonald v Longbottom
  (1859) 68
McEllistrim v Ballymacelligott
  Co-operative Agricultural and
  Dairy Society Ltd (1919) . . 170
McEvoy v Belfast Banking Co
  Ltd (1935) 207
McFarlane v Daniell (1938) . . 182
McGregor v McGregor (1888) . 162
Mackay v Dick (1881) . . . 24
Mackenzie v Coulson (1869) . . 120
MacLeod v Kerr (1965) . . . 137
McRae v Commonwealth
  Disposals Commission (1950) . 105,
                          322, 329

PAGE

MacRobertson Miller Airline
  Services v Comr of State
  Taxation of State of Western
  Australia (1975) 9
Maddison v Alderson (1883) . . 60
Magee v Pennine Insurance Co
  Ltd (1969) 101, 106
Maharaj v Chand (1986) . . . 42
Mahmoud and Ispahani, Re
  (1921) 155, 177
Mahony v East Holyford Mining
  Co (1875) 249
Maira (No 2), The. See Glafki
  Shipping Co SA v Pinios
  Shipping Co No 1, The Maira
  (No 2)
Maira, The. See National Bank
  of Greece SA v Pinios
  Shipping Co No 1, The Maira
Malas (Hamzeh) & Sons v
  British Imex Industries Ltd
  (1958) 50
Malhotra v Choudhury (1980) . 342
Malins v Freeman (1836) . 114, 198
Malloch v Aberdeen Corpn
  (1971) 355
Malpass, Re, Lloyds Bank plc v
  Malpass (1985) 23
Manches v Trimborn (1946) . . 198
Manchester Diocesan Council for
  Education v Commercial and
  General Investments Ltd
  (1970) 15
Mangles v Dixon (1852) . . . 234
Mann v Nunn (1874) . . . 70
Manubens v Leon (1919) . . 329
Maple Flock Co Ltd v Universal
  Furniture Products (Wembley)
  Ltd (1934) 275
Mardorf Peach & Co Ltd v
  Attica Sea Carriers Corpn of
  Liberia, The Laconia (1977) . 277
Maredelanto Cia Naviera SA v
  Bergbau-Handel GmbH, The
  Mihalis Angelos (1971) . 277, 295,
                                  333
Maritime National Fish Ltd v
  Ocean Trawlers Ltd (1935) . 309
Marley v Forward Trust Group
  Ltd (1986) 52
Marley Tile Co Ltd v Johnson
  (1982) 168
Marlow v Pitfeild (1719) . . . 190
Marrison v Bell (1939) . . . 269

PAGE

Marshall v Harland and Wolff
Ltd (1972) 269, 300
Martin v Pycroft (1852) . . 67, 354
Martin-Baker Aircraft Co Ltd v
Canadian Flight Equipment
Ltd (1955) 263
Marvin v Marvin (1976) . . . 158
Mason v Burningham (1949) . 361
Mason v Provident Clothing and
Supply Co Ltd (1913) . . . 168
Massalia, The. See Société Franco
Tunisienne d'Armement v
Sidermar SpA, The Massalia
Matthews v Baxter (1873) . . 198
Matthey v Curling (1922) . . 306
May and Butcher Ltd v R
(1934) 23
Mears v Safecar Security Ltd
(1983) 65, 269
Mendelssohn v Normand Ltd
(1970) 75
Meng Leong Development Pte
Ltd v Jip Hong Trading Co
Pte Ltd (1985) 332
Mercantile Credit Co Ltd v
Hamblin (1965) . . . 245
Mercantile Union Guarantee
Corpn Ltd v Ball (1937) . . 191
Mersey Steel and Iron Co v
Naylor Benzon & Co (1884) . 284
Messiniaki Tolmi, The. See Astro
Exito Navegacion SA v
Southland Enterprise Co Ltd,
The Messiniaki Tolmi
Methodist Conference (President)
v Parfitt (1984) 55
Metropolitan Electric Supply Co
Ltd v Ginder (1901) . . . 358
Metropolitan Water Board v
Dick Kerr & Co (1918) . . 307
Michael v Hart & Co (1902) . 294
Michael (John) Design plc v
Cooke (1987) 166
Midland Bank Trust Co Ltd v
Green (1981) . . . 25, 28
Midland Bank Trust Co Ltd v
Hett, Stubbs and Kemp (a
firm) (1979) 341
Midland Bank plc v Shephard
(1988) 149

PAGE

Mihalios Xilas, The. See China
National Foreign Trade
Transportation Corpn v
Evlogia Shipping Co SA of
Panama, The Mihalios Xilas
Mihalis Angelos, The. See
Maredelanto Cia Naviera SA v
Bergbau-Handel GmbH, The
Mihalis Angelos
Mildred, Goyeneche & Co v
Maspons Y Hermano (1883) . 257
Miles v New Zealand Alford
Estate Co (1886) . . . 34, 35
Miles v Wakefield Metropolitan
District Council (1987) . 273, 278,
290, 291, 293, 364
Miliangos v George Frank
(Textiles) Ltd (1976) . . . 352
Millar's Machinery Co Ltd v
Way & Son (1935) . . . 293, 323
Miller v Karlinski (1945) . . 163
Millichamp v Jones (1983) . . 348
Mills v Fox (1887) 121
Milner (JH) & Son v Percy
Bilton Ltd (1966) 52
Milroy v Lord (1862) . . 231, 232
Mineralimportexport v Eastern
Mediterranean Maritime, The
Golden Leader (1980) . . . 76
Mirams, Re (1891) 240
Mitchell v Ealing London
Borough Council (1979) . . 27
Mitchell (George) (Chesterhall)
Ltd v Finney Lock Seeds Ltd
(1983); affd (1983) . 77, 78, 79, 81,
82, 94, 95
Mitchill v Lath (1928) . . . 70
Mitsubishi Corpn v Alafouzos
(1988) 162
Monarch SS Co Ltd v A/B
Karlshamns Oljefabriker
(1949) 337
Morgan v Palmer (1824) . . 36, 157
Moriarty v Regent's Garage Co
(1921) 291
Morris v Baron & Co (1918) . 61, 68
Morris v CW Martin & Sons Ltd
(1966) 88
Morris v MacCullock (1763) . 163, 187
Morris (Herbert) Ltd v Saxelby
(1916) 166
Mortimore v Wright (1840) . . 248

PAGE

Moschi v LEP Air Services Ltd
(1973)   292
Mountford v Scott (1975) . .   353
Muirhead v Industrial Tank
Specialities Ltd (1986) . .   87, 214
Multitank Holsatia, The. See
Tankrederei Ahrenkeil GmbH
v Frahuil SA, The Multitank
Holsatia
Munro v Willmott (1949) . .   252
Mussen v Van Diemen's Land Co
(1938)   348
Mutual Life and Citizens'
Assurance Co Ltd v Evatt
(1971)   128
Myers (G H) & Co v Brent Cross
Service Co (1934)   268

N

Nagle v Feilden (1966) . .   4, 171
Nai Genova and Nai Superba,
The. See Agip SpA v
Navigazione Alta Italia SpA,
The Nai Genova and Nai
Superba
Nanfri, The. See Federal
Commerce and Navigation Co
Ltd v Molena Alpha Inc, The
Nanfri
Nash v Dix (1898)   256
Nash v Halifax Building Society
(1979)   183
Nash v Inman (1908)   190
National Bank of Greece SA v
Pinios Shipping Co No 1, The
Maira (1988)   63
National Carriers Ltd v
Panalpina (Northern) Ltd
(1981)   306
National Coal Board v National
Union of Mineworkers
(1986)   52
National Westminster Bank plc v
Morgan (1985) 149, 151
Neilson v London and North
Western Rly Co (1922) . .   80
Nema, The. See BTP Tioxide
Ltd v Pioneer Shipping Ltd
and Armada Marine SA, The
Nema
Nevill v Snelling (1880) . . .   150
Neville v Dominion of Canada
News Co Ltd (1915) . . .   157

PAGE

New Hart Builders Ltd v
Brindley (1975)   60
New York Star, The. See Port
Jackson Stevedoring Pty Ltd v
Salmond & Spraggon
(Australia) Pty Ltd, The New
York Star
New Zealand Shipping Co Ltd v
A M Satterthwaite & Co Ltd,
sub nom The Eurymedon
(1975) 21, 37, 87
New Zealand Shipping Co Ltd v
Société des Ateliers et
Chantiers de France (1919) .   291
Newborne v Sensolid (GB) Ltd
(1954)   260
Newell v Radford (1867) . .   68
Newfoundland Government v
Newfoundland Rly Co (1888) .   235
Nicholson v Revill (1836) . .   204
Nicholson and Venn v Smith
Marriott (1947)   101
Nickoll and Knight v Ashton
Edridge & Co (1901) . . .   301
Nile Co for the Export of
Agricultural Crops v H & J M
Bennett (Commodities) Ltd
(1986) 23, 309
Nippon Yusen Kaisha v Pacifica
Navegacion SA, The Ion
(1980)   42
Nittan (UK) Ltd v Solent Steel
Fabrication Ltd trading as
Sargrove Automation and
Cornhill Insurance Co Ltd
(1981)   120
Nokes v Doncaster Amalgamated
Collieries Ltd (1940) . . .   237
Nordenfelt v Maxim Nordenfelt
Guns and Ammunition Co
(1894) 167, 168
North Central (or General)
Wagon and Finance Co Ltd v
Graham (1950)   185
North Ocean Shipping Co Ltd v
Hyundai Construction Co Ltd,
The Atlantic Baron (1979) .   40,
147
North Western Rly Co v
M'Michael (1850)   192
Northern Construction Co Ltd v
Gloge Heating and Plumbing
(1984)   49

PAGE

Northgran Finance Ltd v Ashley
(1963) 246
Norwegian American Cruises A/S
(formerly Norwegian
American Lines A/S) v Paul
Mundy Ltd, The Vistafjord
(1988) 43
Norwich City Council v Paul
Clarke Harvey (1987) . . . 87
Notara v Henderson (1872) . . 251
Notcutt v Universal Equipment
Co (London) Ltd (1986) . . 301
Nottingham Patent Brick and
Tile Co v Butler (1886) . . 142
Nottingham Permanent Benefit
Building Society v Thurstan
(1903) 193

O

Occidental Worldwide
Investment Corpn v Skibs A/S
Avanti, Skibs A/S Glarona,
Skibs A/S Navalis, The Siboen
and The Sibotre (1976) . 125, 147,
317
Ocean Frost, The. See Armagas
Ltd v Mundogas SA, The
Ocean Frost
Ocean Tramp Tankers Corpn v
V/O Sovfracht, The Eugenia
(1964) . . . 302, 309, 363
Odenfeld, The. See Gator
Shipping Corpn v
Trans-Asiatic Oil Ltd SA and
Occidental Shipping
Establishment, The Odenfeld
Offord v Davies (1862) . . . 17
Ogilvy v Hope-Davies (1976) . 42
Olearia Tirrena SpA v
Algemeene Oliehandel NV,
The Osterbek (1973) . . . 285
Olley v Marlborough Court Ltd
(1949) 73
Olsson v Dyson (1969) . . . 233
Olympia Sauna Shipping Co SA
v Shinwa Kaiun Kaisha Ltd,
The Ypatia Halcoussi (1985) . 119
Oom v Bruce (1810) 184
Oro Chief, The. See Eximenco
Handels AG v Partrederiet
Oro Chief and Levantes
Maritime Corpn, The Oro
Chief

PAGE

Osman v J Ralph Moss Ltd
(1970) 156
Osterbek, The. See Olearia
Tirrena SpA v Algemeene
Oliehandel NV, The Osterbek
O'Sullivan v Management
Agency & Music Ltd (1985) . 149,
173
O'Sullivan v Thomas (1895) . . 186

P

Pacific Associates Inc v Baxter
(1988) 213
Pacol Ltd v Trade Lines Ltd and
R/I Sif IV, The Henrik Sif
(1982) 42
Page One Records Ltd v Britton
(trading as The Troggs)
(1968) 357
Paget v Marshall (1884) . . . 119
Pagnan SpA v Feed Products Ltd
(1987) 21, 23
Pagnan SpA v Tradax Ocean
Transportation SA (1987) . . 24
Paine v Meller (1801) . . . 306
Palgrave, Brown & Son Ltd v SS
Turid (1922) 69
Palmco Shipping Inc v
Continental Ore Corpn
(1970) 302
Pancommerce SA v Veecheema
BV (1983) 75
Pao On v Lau Yiu Long (1980) . 30,
37, 47, 68, 147, 148,
150
Parker v Clark (1960) . . . 54
Parker v South Eastern Rly Co
(1877) 73
Parker v Winlow (or Winlo)
(1857) 259
Parker (Harry) Ltd v Mason
(1940) 184
Parkin v Thorold (1852) . . . 285
Parkinson v College of
Ambulance Ltd and Harrison
(1925) 163
Parsons v BNM Laboratories Ltd
(1964) 330
Parsons (H) (Livestock) Ltd v
Uttley Ingham & Co Ltd
(1978) 336
Partridge v Crittenden (1968) . . 8
Pascoe v Turner (1979) . . 47, 48

PAGE

Patel v Ali (1984)   353
Pateman v Pay (1974) . . .   52
Paul v Constance (1977) . .   158
Payzu Ltd v Saunders (1919) .   338
Pearce v Brooks (1866) . .   158, 175
Pearson (S) & Son Ltd v Dublin
   Corpn (1907) 85, 126
Peco Arts Inc v Hazlitt Gallery
   Ltd (1983) 101, 104
Peevyhouse v Garland Coal
   Mining Co (1962)   325
Pegase, The. See Satef-Huttenes
   Albertus SpA v Paloma
   Tercera Shipping Co SA, The
   Pegase
Penarth Dock Engineering Co
   Ltd v Pounds (1963) . . .   317
Percival Ltd v LCC Asylums and
   Mental Deficiency Committee
   (1918)   9
Perera v Vandiyar (1953) . .   319
Perry v Sidney Phillips & Son (a
   firm) (1982) . .   318, 319, 325
Perry (Howard E) & Co Ltd v
   British Railways Board
   (1980)   353
Perrylease Ltd v Imecar AG
   (1987)   68
Peters v Fleming (1840) . . .   189
Peters v General Accident Fire
   and Life Assurance Corpn Ltd
   (1937)   237
Peyman v Lanjani (1985) . . .   287
Pharmaceutical Society of Great
   Britain v Boots Cash Chemists
   (Southern) Ltd (1953) . . .   8
Philips v Ward (1956) . . .   318
Phillips v Brooks Ltd (1919) . .   110
Phillips Products Ltd v Hyland
   (1987)   93
Phoenix General Insurance Co of
   Greece SA v Administratia
   Asigurarilo de Stat (1986) .   155, 178
Phonogram Ltd v Lane (1982) .   260
Phonographic Equipment (1958)
   Ltd v Muslu (1961) . . .   344
Photo Production Ltd v Securicor
   Transport Ltd (1980) .   78, 81, 83,
                  271, 274, 291, 293,
                  318
Pickersgill (William) & Sons Ltd
   v London and Provincial
   Marine and General Insurance
   Co Ltd (1912)   234

PAGE

Pilmore v Hood (1838) . . .   126
Pinnel's Case (1602)   44
Pioneer Shipping Ltd v BTP
   Tioxide Ltd. See BTP Tioxide
   Ltd v Pioneer Shipping Ltd
   and Armada Marine SA, The
   Nema
Pirie v Richardson (1927) . .   204
Planché v Colburn (1831) .   289, 364
Playa Larga, The. See Empresa
   Exportadora de Azucar v
   Industria Azucarera Nacional
   SA, The Playa Larga and The
   Marble Islands
Plowman (G W) & Son Ltd v
   Ash (1964)   168
Plumpton v Burkinshaw (1908) .   253
Polhill v Walter (1832) . . .   128
Port Jackson Stevedoring Pty Ltd
   v Salmond & Spraggon
   (Australia) Pty Ltd, The New
   York Star (1980)   87
Port Line Ltd v Ben Line
   Steamers Ltd (1958) . . .   222
Portavon Cinema Co Ltd v Price
   and Century Insurance Co Ltd
   (1939)   218
Portuguese Consolidated Copper
   Mines Ltd, Re, ex p Badman,
   ex p Bosanquet (1890) . .   254
Posner v Scott-Lewis (1987) . .   355
Post Chaser, The. See Société
   Italo-Belge pour le Commerce
   et l'Industrie SA v Palm and
   Vegetable Oils (Malaysia) Sdn
   Bhd, The Post Chaser
Potter v Sanders (1846) . . .   14
Poussard v Spiers and Pond
   (1876) 275, 301
Powell v Brent London Borough
   Council (1988)   354
Powell v Brodhurst (1901) . .   207
Powell Duffryn Steam Coal Co v
   Taff Vale Rly Co (1874) . .   355
Preece v Lewis (1963) . . .   70
Prehn v Royal Bank of Liverpool
   (1870)   342
Prenn v Simmonds (1971) . .   68
President of India v Lips
   Maritime Corpn, The Lips
   (1987)   342
Price v Barker (1855) . . .   204
Price v Jenkins (1877) . . .   32
Price v Strange (1978) .   356, 358

PAGE

Printers and Finishers Ltd v
Holloway (1964) . . . 165
Production Technology
Consultants Ltd v Bartlett
(1988) 133
Proodos C, The. See Syros
Shipping Co SA v Elaghill
Trading Co, The Proodos C
Protector Endowment Loan and
Annuity Co v Grice (1880) . 345
Public Works Comr v Hills
(1906) 347
Puerto Buitrago, The. See Attica
Sea Carriers Corpn v
Ferrostaal Poseidon Bulk
Reederei GmbH, The Puerto
Buitrago
Pusey v Pusey (1684) . . . 352
Pye v British Automobile
Commercial Syndicate Ltd
(1906) 347
Pym v Campbell (1856) . . 24, 67
Pyrene Co Ltd v Scindia Steam
Navigation Co Ltd (1954) . . 88

Q

Quadrangle Development and
Construction Co Ltd v Jenner
(1974) 286

R

R v Civil Service Appeal Board,
ex p Bruce (1988) 55
R v Lambie (1982) 31
R and B Customs Brokers Co Ltd
v United Dominions Trust Ltd
(Saunders Abbott (1980) Ltd,
third party) (1988) 89
Rabin v Gerson Berger
Association Ltd (1986) . . 66, 69
Radford v De Froberville
(1978) 210, 326, 332
Raffles v Wichelhaus (1864) . 108, 112
Rainbow v Howkins (1904) . . 262
Raineri v Miles (1981) . . . 285
Ramsgate Victoria Hotel Co v
Montefiore (1866) 20
Rashdall v Ford (1866) . . 202, 262
Rasnoimport V/O v Guthrie &
Co Ltd (1966) 262

PAGE

Reardon Smith Line Ltd v
— Yngvar Hansen-Tangen and
Sanko SS Co Ltd, The Diana
Prosperity (1976) 281
Redgrave v Hurd (1881) . . . 126
Redland Bricks Ltd v Morris
(1970) 353
Reed v Kilburn Co-operative
Society (1875) 271
Regal (Hastings) Ltd v Gulliver
(1942) 317
Remco, The. See Gewa
Chartering BV v Remco
Shipping Lines Ltd, The
Remco
Richards (Michael) Properties
Ltd v Corpn of Wardens of St
Saviour's Parish, Southwark
(1975) 154, 347
Richardson v Mellish (1824) . . 156
Richmond Gate Property Co Ltd,
Re (1964) 53
Rickards (Charles) Ltd v
Oppenhaim (or Oppenheim)
(1950) 38
Ridgway v Hungerford Market
Co (1835) 269
Rigby v Ferodo Ltd (1987) . . 291
Rignall Developments Ltd v
Halil (1988) 145
Rijn, The. See Santa Martha
Baay Scheepvaart and
Handelsmaatschappij NV v
Scanbulk A/S, The Rijn
Rio Claro, The. See Transworld
Oil Ltd v North Bay Shipping
Corpn, The Rio Claro
Ritchie v Atkinson (1808) . . 278
Riverlate Properties Ltd v Paul
(1975) 115, 119
Roberts v Elwells Engineers Ltd
(1972) 350
Roberts v Gray (1913) . . . 190
Roberts v Hayward (1828) . . 16
Robinson v Davison (1871) . . 300
Robinson v Geisel (1894) . . 205
Robinson v Harman (1848) . 320, 359
Robinson v Mollett (1875) . 65, 247
Robson v Drummond (1831) . 244
Rolled Steel Products (Holdings)
Ltd v British Steel Corpn
(1986) 200
Romer and Haslam, Re (1893) . 270
Rookes v Barnard (1964) . . 214

PAGE

Roper v Johnson (1873) . . . 332
Roscorla v Thomas (1842) . . 30
Rose and Frank Co v JR
  Crompton & Bros Ltd (1925) . 51
Rose (Frederick E) (London) Ltd
  v William H Pim Jnr & Co
  Ltd (1953) 120
Ross v Caunters (1980) . . . 212
Rossiter v Miller (1878) . . . 23
Roth (L) & Co Ltd v Taysen,
  Townsend & Co and Grant
  and Grahame (1895) . . . 332
Rover International Ltd v
  Cannon Films Sales Ltd (No 2)
  (1987); revsd (1988) . . 254, 360,
                                363
Rowland v Divall (1923) . . 360
Rowlands (Mark) Ltd v Berni
  Inns Ltd (1986) 218, 340
Royal British Bank v Turquand
  (1856) 250
Rozanes v Bowen (1928) . . . 144
Ruben v Great Fingall
  Consolidated (1906) . . . 250
Rust v Abbey Life Assurance Co
  Ltd (1978); affd (1979) . . 16
Rutter v Palmer (1922) . . . 77
Ryan v Mutual Tontine
  Westminster Chambers
  Association (1893) 355
Ryan v Pilkington (1959) . . 246
Ryder v Wombwell (1868) . . 189

S

Sadler v Imperial Life Assurance
  Co of Canada Ltd (1988) . . 169
Said v Butt (1920) 256
St Enoch Shipping Co Ltd v
  Phosphate Mining Co (1916) . 278
St John Shipping Corpn v Joseph
  Rank Ltd (1957) . . . 154, 176
Sajan Singh v Sardara Ali
  (1960) 186
Samick Lines Co Ltd v Antonis P
  Lemos (Owners) (1985) . . 212
Samuel (P) & Co Ltd v Dumas
  (1924) 207
Sanko SS Co Ltd v Eacom
  Timber Sales Ltd, The Sanko
  Iris and Sanko Venus (1987) . 295

PAGE

Santa Carina, The. See
  Vlassopulos (N & J) Ltd v Ney
  Shipping Ltd, The Santa
  Carina
Santa Martha Baay Scheepvaart
  and Handelsmaatschappij NV
  v Scanbulk A/S, The Rijn
  (1981) 330
Satanita, The (1895); affd sub
  nom Clarke v Earl of
  Dunraven and Mount-Earl,
  The Satanita (1897) . . . 21
Satef-Huttenes Albertus SpA v
  Paloma Tercera Shipping Co
  SA, The Pegase (1981) . . 336
Saunders (Executrix of Will of
  Gallie) v Anglia Building
  Society (1971) 117, 118
Saunders v Edwards (1987) . . 178
Sayers v Harlow UDC (1958) . 340
Scammell (G) and Nephew Ltd v
  Ouston (1941) 22
Scandinavian Trading Tanker
  Co AB v Flota Petrolera
  Ecuatoriana, The Scaptrade
  (1983) 41, 277, 347
Scaptrade, The. See
  Scandinavian Trading Tanker
  Co AB v Flota Petrolera
  Ecuatoriana, The Scaptrade
Scarf v Jardine (1882) . . . 261
Scarfe v Adams (1981) . . . 68
Schebsman, Re, ex p Official
  Receiver, Trustee v Cargo
  Superintendents (London) Ltd
  and Schebsman (1944) . . . 216
Schindler v Pigault (1975) . . 347
Schmaltz (or Schmalz) v Avery
  (1851) 259
Schneider v Norris (1814) . . 58
Schroeder Music Publishing Co
  Ltd v Macaulay (1974) . 165, 166,
                              168, 169, 173
Schuler (L) AG v Wickman
  Machine Tool Sales Ltd
  (1974) 279
Schwabacher, Re, Stern v
  Schwabacher, Koritschoner's
  Claim (1907) 352
Scott v Avery (1856) 161
Scott v Brown, Doering, McNab
  & Co (1892) 152, 182
Scott v Coulson (1903) . . . 102

PAGE

Scott v Frank F Scott (London)
Ltd (1940) 121

Scriven Bros v Hindley & Co
(1913) 114

Scruttons Ltd v Midland
Silicones Ltd (1962) . . . 86

Seabridge Shipping Ltd v Antco
Shipping Co Ltd, The Furness
Bridge (1977) 302

Segap Garages Ltd v Gulf Oil
(Great Britain) Ltd (1988) . 273,
293

Sethia (K C) (1944) Ltd v
Partabmull Rameshwar
(1950); affd sub nom
Partabmuli Rameshwar v K C
Sethia (1944) Ltd (1951) . . 63

Shadwell v Shadwell (1860) . 27, 37

Shamia v Joory (1958) . . . 224

Shanklin Pier Ltd v Detel
Products Ltd (1951) . . . 53

Sharneyford Supplies Ltd v Edge
(Barrington Black Austin &
Co, Third Party) (1987) . 342, 343

Sharpe (C) & Co v Nosawa &
Co (1917) 331

Shaw v Groom (1970) . . 59, 154

Sheffield Gas Consumers' Co v
Harrison (1853) 355

Sheikh Bros v Ochsner (1957) . 100

Shell UK Ltd v Lostock Garage
Ltd (1976) 64, 354

Shelley v Paddock (1980) . . 178

Shepherd (F C) & Co Ltd v
Jerrom (1987) . . . 310, 311

Sherdley v Sherdley (1988) . . 189

Shine, Re, ex p Shine (1892) . 241

Shipping Corpn of India v
Naviera Letasa SA (1976) . . 331

Shipton Anderson & Co and
Harrison Bros & Co, Re
(1915) 300

Shirlaw v Southern Foundries
(1926) Ltd (1939); affd sub
nom Southern Foundries
(1926) Ltd v Shirlaw (1940) . 63

Shove v Downs Surgical plc
(1984) 319, 330

Showa Oil Tanker Co Ltd of
Japan v Maravan SA of
Caracas, The Larissa (1983) . 131

Shuey v US (1875) 19

PAGE

Siboen, The and The Sibotre. See
Occidental Worldwide
Investment Corpn v Skibs A/S
Avanti, Skibs A/S Glarona,
Skibs A/S Navalis, The Siboen
and The Sibotre

Silver Coast Shipping Co Ltd v
Union Nationale des
Co-operatives Agricoles des
Cereales, The Silver Sky
(1981) 337

Sim v Rotherham Metropolitan
Borough Council (1987) . . 293

Simaan General Contracting Co
v Pilkington Glass Ltd (No 2)
(1988) 87, 213

Simona, The. See Fercometal
SARL v MSC Mediterranean
Shipping Co SA, The Simona

Simpson v John Reynolds & Co
(Insurances) Ltd (1975) . . 30

Sims v Bond (1833) 259

Sinclair v Brougham (1914) . . 201

Sinclair's Life Policy, Re (1938) . 209,
216

Singer Co (UK) v Tees and
Hartlepool Port Authority
(1988) 88, 93

Skeate v Beale (1840) 148

Sky Petroleum Ltd v VIP
Petroleum Ltd (1974) . . . 353

Smart v Sandars (1848) . . . 264

Smeaton Hanscomb & Co Ltd v
Sassoon I Setty, Son & Co
(1953) 79

Smith v Eric S Bush (1987) . 77, 94

Smith v Green (1875) . . . 324

Smith v Harrison (1857) . . . 104

Smith v Hughes (1871) . 108, 111,
114

Smith v Kay (1859) 125

Smith v Land and House
Property Corpn (1884) . . 123

Smith v South Wales Switchgear
Ltd (1978) 74, 76

Smith v Wilson (1832) . . . 69

Smith (WH) & Son v Clinton
and Harris (1908) 156

Smyth (or Smith) v Anderson
(1849) 258

Snelling v John G Snelling Ltd
(1973) 45, 87

PAGE

Société des Industries
M'tallurgiques SA v Bronx
Engineering Co Ltd (1975) · 353
Société Franco Tunisienne
d'Armement v Sidermar SpA,
The Massalia (1961) · · · 363
Société Italo-Belge pour le
Commerce et l'Industrie SA v
Palm and Vegetable Oils
(Malaysia) Sdn Bhd, The Post
Chaser (1981) · · · · 42, 282
Sole v W J Hallt Ltd (1973) · · 340
Solholt, The. See Sotiros
Shipping Inc and Aeco
Maritime SA v Sameiet
Solholt, The Solholt
Solle v Butcher (1950) · · 101, 106,
116
Sorrell v Finch (1977) · · · 246
Sorsbie v Park (1843) · · · 206
Sotiros Shipping Inc and Aeco
Maritime SA v Sameiet
Solholt, The Solholt (1983) · 292,
338
South of England Natural Gas
and Petroleum Co Ltd, Re
(1911) · · · · · · · 146
Southern Water Authority v
Carey (1985) · · · · 87
Spector v Ageda (1973) · · 187
Spence v Crawford (1939) · · 140
Spencer v Harding (1870) · · · 9
Spencer v Macmillan's Trustees
(1958) · · · · · · 330
Spencer v Marchington (1988) · 167,
168
Spiers v Hunt (1908) · · · · 160
Spiro v Lintern (1973) · 15, 246, 250
Splendid Sun, The. See Andre et
Cie SA v Marine Transocean
Ltd, The Splendid Sun
Sport International Bussum BV v
Inter-Footwear Ltd (1984) · 277
Spriggs v Sotheby Parke Bernet
& Co Ltd (1986) · · · · 76
Spring v National Amalgamated
Stevedores and Dockers Society
(1956) · · · · · · · 63
Spurling (J) Ltd v Bradshaw
(1956) · · · · · · · 75
Staffordshire Area Health
Authority v South
Staffordshire Waterworks Co
(1978) · · · · · · 303

PAGE

Stapleton-Bretherton, Re,
Weld-Blundell v
Stapleton-Bretherton (1941) · 212
Starside Properties Ltd v
Mustapha (1974) · · · · 348
Steadman v Steadman (1976) · 60
Steeds v Steeds (1889) · · 206, 207
Stein, Forbes & Co v County
Tailoring Co (1916) · · · 349
Steinberg v Scala (Leeds) Ltd
(1923) · · · · · · · 192
Stena Nautica (No 2), The. See
CN Marine Inc v Stena Line
A/B and Regie Voor Maritiem
Transport, The Stena Nautica
(No 2)
Stenhouse Australia Ltd v
Phillips (1974) · · · · · 169
Stephens v Venables (1862) · · 235
Stevenson, Jaques & Co v
McLean (1880) · · · · · 19
Stewart v Oriental Fire and
Marine Insurance Co Ltd
(1985) · · · · · · · 178
Stewart v Reavell's Garage
(1952) · · · · · · · 244
Stewart (Robert) & Sons Ltd v
Carapanayoti & Co Ltd
(1962) · · · · · · · 325
Stickney v Keeble (1915) · · 285
Stilk v Myrick (1809) · · 39, 157
Stockloser v Johnson (1954) · · 348
Stocks v Wilson (1913) · · 194, 196
Stoddart v Union Trust Ltd
(1912) · · · · · · · 235
Stokes v Whicher (1920) · · · 58
Strongman (1945) Ltd v Sincock
(1955) · · · · · · · 179
Strover v Harrington (1988) · · 126
Strutt v Whitnell (1975) · · · 338
Sturcke v S W Edwards Ltd
(1971) · · · · · · · 306
Sudbrook Trading Estate Ltd v
Eggleton (1983) · · · · 23
Suisse Atlantique Société
d'Armement Maritime SA v
Rotterdamsche Kolen Centrale
NV (1967) · · · 78, 80, 82, 283
Summers v Solomon (1857) · · 248
Sumnal v Statt (1984) · · · 310
Sumpter v Hedges (1898) · 278, 287,
289

PAGE

Sun Happiness, The. See
Etablissement Biret & Cie SA
v Yukiteru Kaiun KK and
Nissui Shipping Corpn, The
Sun Happiness
Sutton v Sutton (1984) . 1, 160, 161, 356
Swain v Law Society (1983) . 214, 215, 217
Swan v Bank of Scotland (1836) 204
Swan, The. See Bridges and
Salmon Ltd v The Swan
(Owner), Marine Diesel
Service (Grimsby) Ltd v The
Swan (Owner), The Swan
Swiss Bank Corpn v Lloyds Bank
Ltd (1979); revsd (1982); affd
(1982) 220, 222, 353
Sybron Corpn v Rochem Ltd (1984) 100, 145
Synge v Synge (1894) . . . 296
Syros Shipping Co SA v Elaghill
Trading Co, The Proodos C (1980) 35
Sze Hai Tong Bank Ltd v
Rambler Cycle Co Ltd (1959) 82

T

TC Industrial Plant Pty Ltd v
Roberts Quensland Pty Ltd (1964) 324
TCB Ltd v Gray (1986); affd (1988) 26
TFL Prosperity, The. See Tor
Line AB v Alltrans Group of
Canada Ltd, The TFL
Prosperity
Tai Hing Cotton Mill Ltd v
Kamsing Knitting Factory (1979) 332
Tai Hing Cotton Mill Ltd v Liu
Chong Hing Bank Ltd (1986) . 65
Tamplin v James (1879) . . . 115
Tamplin (F A) SS Co v
Anglo-Mexican Petroleum
Products Co (1916) 300
Tancred v Delagoa Bay and East
Africa Rly Co (1889) . . . 227
Tankrederei Ahrenkeil GmbH v
Frahuil SA, The Multitank
Holsatia (1988) 7, 16, 21

PAGE

Tanner v Tanner (1975) . . 54, 158
Tate v Williamson (1866) . . 149
Tate and Lyle Industries Ltd v
Greater London Council (1983) 213
Tatem Ltd v Gamboa (1939) . 309
Taylor v Bowers (1876) . . . 184
Taylor v Brewer (1813) . . . 53
Taylor v Caldwell (1863) . 299, 310
Taylor v Chester (1869) . . . 185
Taylor v Webb (1937) . . . 273
Taylor (C R) (Wholesale) Ltd v
Hepworths Ltd (1977) . . . 326
Telfair Shipping Corpn v Athos
Shipping Co SA, Solidor
Shipping Co Ltd, Horizon
Finance Corpn and AN
Cominos, The Athos (1981);
affd (1983) 287
Tenant Radiant Heat Ltd v
Warrington Development
Corpn (1987) 341
Tenax SS Co Ltd v Reinante
Transoceania Navegacion SA,
The Brimnes (1975) . . . 18
Terkol Rederierne v Petroleo
Brasileiro SA and Frota
Nacional De Petroleiros, The
Badagry (1985) 302
Tetley v Shand (1871) . . . 271
Thackwell v Barclays Bank plc (1986) 186
Thake v Maurice (1986) . . 62, 267
Thavorn v Bank of Credit and
Commerce International SA (1985) 208
Thomas, Re, Jaquess v Thomas (1894) 152
Thomas v Brown (1876) . . . 60
Thomas v Thomas (1842) . . 31
Thompson v ASDA-MFI Group
plc (1988) 291
Thompson v London, Midland
and Scottish Rly Co (1930) . 74
Thompson v T Lohan (Plant
Hire) Ltd (1987) 93
Thompson (W L) Ltd v
Robinson (Gunmakers) Ltd (1955) 328
Thomson v Davenport (1829) . 261
Thomson v Eastwood (1877) . . 149
Thorley (Joseph) Ltd v Orchis
SS Co Ltd (1907) 79

PAGE

Thornton v Shoe Lane Parking
  Ltd (1971) 8, 9, 74, 85
Thorpe v Fasey (1949) . . . 287
Thorpe v Jackson (1837) . . . 205
Tiedemann and Ledermann
  Frѐres, Re (1899) 253
Tinline v White Cross Insurance
  Association Ltd (1921) . . . 155
Tinn v Hoffmann & Co (1873) . 10,
                                16
Tito v Waddell (No 2) (1977) . 242,
                           326, 353
Toepfer v Lenersan-Poortman
  NV (1980) 282
Tolhurst v Associated Portland
  Cement Manufacturers (1900)
  Ltd (1903) 238
Tool Metal Manufacturing Co
  Ltd v Tungsten Electric Co
  Ltd (1955) 41
Tooth v Hallett (1869) . . . 234
Toprak Mahsulleri Ofisi v
  Finagrain Cie Commerciale
  Agricole et Financière SA
  (1979) 331, 332
Tor Line AB v Alltrans Group of
  Canada Ltd, The TFL
  Prosperity (1984) 84
Torkington v Magee (1902);
  revsd (1903) 228
Torrance v Bolton (1872) . 108, 115
Tradax Export SA v André &
  Cie SA (1976) 303
Tradax Export SA v European
  Grain and Shipping Ltd
  (1983) 282
Tradax Internacional SA v
  Goldschmidt SA (1977) . . 282
Trade and Transport
  Incorporated v Iino Kaiun
  Kaisha, The Angelia (1973) . 269
Trade Indemnity Co Ltd v
  Workington Harbour and
  Dock Board (1937) 145
Traill v Baring (1864) . . 125, 143
Trans Trust SPRL v Danubian
  Trading Co Ltd (1952) . . 342
Transworld Oil Ltd v North Bay
  Shipping Corpn, The Rio
  Claro (1987) 335
Travers (Joseph) & Sons Ltd v
  Cooper (1915) 76
Trego v Hunt (1896) 164

PAGE

Trendtex Trading Corpn v
  Crédit Suisse (1982) . . . 152, 239
Trollope and Colls Ltd v North
  West Metropolitan Regional
  Hospital Board (1973) . . . 63
Tsakiroglou & Co Ltd v Noblee
  Thorl GmbH (1962) . . 302, 303
Turner v Sawdon & Co (1901) . 266
Tweddell v Henderson (1975) . 52,
                                58
Tweddle v Atkinson (1861) . . 208
Tyers v Rosedale and Ferryhill
  Iron Co (1875) 61
Tyrie v Fletcher (1777) . . . 313

U

UCB Leasing Ltd v Holtom (t/a
  David Holtom & Co) (1987) . 292,
                                320
Unique Mariner, The (1978) . 113
United Bank of Kuwait v
  Hammoud (1988) 248
United City Merchants
  (Investments) Ltd and Glass
  Fibres and Equipments Ltd v
  Royal Bank of Canada,
  Vitrorefuerzos SA and Banco
  Continental SA, The American
  Accord (1983) 50, 187
United Dominions Trust Ltd v
  Western (1976) 118
United Fresh Meat Co Ltd v
  Charterhouse Cold Storage Ltd
  (1974) 80
United Scientific Holdings Ltd v
  Burnley Borough Council
  (1978) 285
Universal Cargo Carriers Corpn
  v Citati (1957) 295
Universal Corpn v Five Ways
  Properties Ltd (1979) . . 266, 347
Universal Steam Navigation Co
  Ltd v James McKelvie & Co
  (1923) 259
Universe Sentinel, The. See
  Universe Tankships Inc of
  Monrovia v International
  Transport Workers Federation,
  The Universe Sentinel

PAGE

Universe Tankships Inc of
    Monrovia v International
    Transport Workers Federation,
    The Universe Sentinel (1982) .   40,
                                    147, 148
Uxbridge Permanent Benefit
    Building Society v Pickard
    (1939)   250

V

Vanbergen v St Edmunds
    Properties Ltd (1933) . . .   38
Victoria Laundry (Windsor) Ltd
    v Newman Industries Ltd
    (1949)   334
Victoria Seats Agency v Paget
    (1902)   307
Vincent v Premo Enterprises
    (Voucher Sales) Ltd (1969) .   26
Vistafjord, The. See Norwegian
    American Cruises A/S
    (formerly Norwegian
    American Lines A/S) v Paul
    Mundy Ltd, The Vistafjord
Vlassopulos (N & J) Ltd v Ney
    Shipping Ltd, The Santa
    Carina (1977)   259
Voest Alpine Intertrading GmbH
    v Chevron International Oil
    Co Ltd (1987)   23

W

Wade v Waldon (1909) . . .   274
Wadsworth v Lydall (1981) . .   342
Wake v Harrop (1861); affd
    (1862)   67
Wakeham v Mackenzie (1968) .   60
Wakeham v Wood (1982) . .   357
Wales v Wadham (1977) . . .   143
Walker, Re (1905)   198
Walker v Boyle (1982) . 85, 90, 274,
                                    289
Walker v Bradford Old Bank Ltd
    (1884)   231
Wall v Rederiaktiebolaget
    Luggude (1915)   346
Wallersteiner v Moir (No 2)
    (1975)   152
Wallis v Smith (1882) . . .   342
Wallis Chlorine Syndicate Ltd v
    American Alkali Co Ltd
    (1901)   342
Walsh v Lonsdale (1882) . . .   59

PAGE

Walter v James (1871) . . .   255
Walter and Sullivan Ltd v J
    Murphy & Sons Ltd (1955) .   228
Walton v Mascall (1844) . . .   270
Ward v Byham (1956) . . 36, 158
Warlow v Harrison (1859) . . .   9
Warman v Southern Counties
    Car Finance Corpn Ltd, WJ
    Ameris Car Sales (Third
    Party) (1949)   362
Warmington v Miller (1973) .   356
Warner Bros Pictures Inc v
    Nelson (1937)   357
Warner Bros Records Inc v
    Rollgreen Ltd (1976) . . .   230
Watford Borough Council v
    Watford Rural District
    Council (1987)   303
Watkins v Watkins (1896) . .   239
Watson v Davies (1931) . . .   255
Watteau v Fenwick (1893) . .   251
Watts v Spence (1976) . . 343, 356
Waugh v Morris (1873) . . .   176
Webster v Bosanquet (1912) . .   344
Webster v Higgin (1948) . . .   75
Weddell v J A Pearce & Major
    (1988) 225, 239
Weld-Blundell v Stephens
    (1920)   335
Wenjiang, The (No 2). See
    International Sea Tankers Inc
    v Hemisphere Shipping Co
    Ltd, The Wenjiang (No 2)
Wessex Dairies Ltd v Smith
    (1935)   165
West v Houghton (1879) . . .   216
West Country Cleaners
    (Falmouth) Ltd v Saly (1966) .   284
Westlake v Adams (1858) . .   28
Westminster (Duke) v Guild
    (1985)   63
Wettern Electric Ltd v Welsh
    Development Agency (1983) .   15
White v Bijou Mansions Ltd
    (1937); affd (1938)   219
White v Bluett (1853) . . .   29
White v John Warrick & Co Ltd
    (1953)   76
White v London Transport
    Executive (1971)   217
White and Carter (Councils) Ltd
    v McGregor (1962) . . .   350
Whittaker v Campbell (1984) . 111,
                                    113

PAGE

Whittingham v Murdy (1889) . 192
Whittington v Seale-Hayne
(1900) 135
Whitwood Chemical Co v
Hardman (1891) . . . 357
Wigan v English and Scottish
Law Life Assurance
Association (1909) . . . 35
Wilkie v London Passenger
Transport Board (1947) . . 9
Wilkinson v Byers (1834) . . 44
Wilkinson v Coverdale (1793) . 27
Williams v Atlantic Assurance
Co Ltd (1933) 227
Williams v Moor (1843) . . 193
Williams v Reynolds (1865) . 327
Williams v Stern (1879) . . 42
Williams Bros v E T Agius Ltd
(1914) 327
Willson v Love (1896) . . . 344
Wilson v Kearse (1800) . . . 193
Wilson v Wilson (1848) . . . 159
Wilson (Paal) & Co A/S v
Partenreederei Hannah
Blumenthal, The Hannah
Blumenthal (1983) . 2, 7, 290, 309
Wilson & Sons v Pike (1949) . 246
Wilson Sons & Co v Balcarres
Brook SS Co (1893) . . . 205
Windhill Local Board of Health
v Vint (1890) 162
Winson, The. See China-Pacific
SA v Food Corpn of India,
The Winson
With v O'Flanagan (1936) . . 143
Withers v Bircham (1824) . . 206
Wolverhampton Corpn v
Emmons (1901) . . . 356
Woodar Investment Development
Ltd v Wimpey Construction
UK Ltd (1980) . . 210, 214, 284
Woodstead Finance Ltd v Petrou
(1986) 149
Woolf v Collis Removal Service
(1948) 80

PAGE

Woolfe v Horne (1877) . . . 285
Worboys v Carter (1987) . . 250
Workman, Clark & Co Ltd v
Lloyd Brazileno (1908) . . 349
Wright v Carter (1903) . . . 149
Wright v Wright (1750) . . . 224
Wroth v Tyler (1974) . . 332, 359
Wrotham Park Estate Co v
Parkside Homes Ltd (1974) . 317
Wyatt v Kreglinger and Fernau
(1933) 33, 169
Wyatt v Marquis of Hertford
(1802) 258
Wyvern Developments Ltd, Re
(1974) 42

X

Xenos v Wickham (1866) . . 26

Y

Yasin, The (1979) 340
Yeoman Credit Ltd v Apps
(1962) 80, 361
Yeoman Credit Ltd v
Waragowski (1961) . . . 293
Yetton v Eastwoods Froy Ltd
(1966) 338
Yianni v Edwin Evans & Sons
(1982) 126, 128, 212
Yonge v Toynbee (1910) . . 262, 263
Yorkshire Railway Wagon Co v
Maclure (1882) 204
Young v Kitchin (1878) . . . 242
Young and Marten Ltd v
McManus Childs Ltd (1969) . 268
Ypatia Halcoussi, The. See
Olympia Sauna Shipping Co
SA v Shinwa Kaiun Kaisha
Ltd, The Ypatia Halcoussi

Z

Zephyr, The. See General
Accident Fire and Life
Assurance Corpn v Tanter,
The Zephyr

Chapter 1

Introduction

1 DEFINITION OF CONTRACT

A contract may be defined as an agreement which is either enforced by law or recognised by law as affecting the legal rights or duties of the parties. The law of contract is, therefore, primarily concerned with three questions: is there an agreement? is it one which should be legally recognised or enforced? and just how is the agreement enforced, or, in other words, what remedies are available to the injured party when a contract has been broken?

A detailed discussion of these questions forms the subject-matter of the remaining chapters of this book. The present chapter is devoted to a number of general points arising mainly, though not exclusively, out of the three questions just put.

2 CONTRACT AND CONTRACTS

The subject-matter of this book is 'the law of contract'. It was formerly the fashion, which in some parts of the common law world still persists, to refer to the law of contracts (in the plural). The point of modern references to a law of contract (in the singular) is to indicate that the law has a general or unified theory of contract, that is, one which applies to all contracts irrespective of their content or subject-matter. A contract may relate to any one or more of a large number of transactions, such as sale of goods, land or shares, employment, carriage, hire, lease, mortgage and so forth. A general theory of contract asserts that there is at least a substantial body of rules which applies to all contracts in common; and that these rules constitute 'the law of contract'. This is the theory of modern English law. On the other hand it has been said that Roman law had 'not a theory of contract, but a theory of contracts'.[1] What is meant is, that the rules which governed the formation and effects of a contract depended either on its content (eg whether it was sale or loan) or on its form (eg whether it was expressed orally or in writing). Neither theory can be accepted without qualification. In most modern systems of law there is, indeed, a body of

---

[1] Buckland and McNair *Roman Law and Common Law* (2nd edn) p 195.

rules which applies to contracts generally. These rules may, however, apply to particular transactions such as sale, employment or carriage, subject to certain modifications; and such transactions may also be governed by special rules peculiar to them, in the sense that they have no close analogy at all with general rules which apply to other transactions. In this book our concern will be with the general rules, and to some extent with the modified form in which they apply to particular transactions. Rules peculiar to particular transactions will not in general be discussed, nor will any attempt be made to give any systematic account of the rules governing any one or more particular or special contracts. At the same time, it is necessary to warn the reader that the general 'law of contract' is something of an abstraction, since most contracts obviously concern some particular class of transaction; and since there is always some degree of danger in assuming that a 'general' rule applies (at least without modification) to a contract of the particular type under consideration.

3 AGREEMENT

In the normal case, a contract results from an agreement between the parties to it; and much of the law of contract is concerned with the process of reaching agreement, and with the contents of the agreement when reached. Nevertheless, the description of a contract as an agreement is subject to a number of important qualifications.

The first of these is that the law generally speaking applies an objective test of agreement. If one party, A, so conducts himself as to induce the other, B, reasonably to believe that A is assenting to certain terms proposed by B, then A will generally be held so to have assented, whatever his actual state of mind may have been.[2] The law adopts this objective test because a person who reasonably believed that a contractual proposal had been made to him might be seriously prejudiced if he could not take it at its face value. The principle is, however, one of convenience only, so that it will not be applied where, on balance, the inconvenience to A of applying the objective test, exceeds the inconvenience to B of allowing A to rely on his actual intention: for example, where B knows that A's actual state of mind was not in accordance with the objective appearance created by A's conduct.[3]

The second qualification is that, even where agreement determines the existence of a contract, it does not necessarily determine all the contents or scope of a contract. These matters are often determined by so-called 'implied terms'. These may be divided into terms implied *in*

---

[2]   *The Hannah Blumenthal* [1983] 1 A C 854, as intepreted in *The Leonidas D* [1985] 2 All E R 796; see p 7, post.

[3]   See *The Golden Bear* [1987] 1 Lloyd's Rep 330, 341; and see p 113, post.

fact and terms implied *in law* : this distinction will be explained in Chapter 6. Only terms implied in fact are truly based on the intention of the parties. Terms implied in law are duties prima facie imposed by law; and with respect to them, the intention of the parties is relevant only insofar as it may be open to the parties to exclude the implied terms by express contrary agreement.

Thirdly, there are cases, commonly discussed under the general heading of contract, in which the obligation does not truly arise out of an agreement between two parties, but rather out of a promise made by one of them. This would be the position where a person made a gratuitous promise in such a form that it was legally binding: for example, in a deed under seal. In such a case, the promisee would at most 'agree' by accepting the gift or by indicating his willingness to accept it. But even this is not necessary: a promise of this kind can bind even before it is communicated to the promisee.

Fourthly, the idea that contract depends on agreement must be qualified in cases in which one party is in a very much stronger bargaining position than the other, so that the former can in a sense impose his terms on the latter. This possibility is illustrated by the standard form contracts which are used by many commercial suppliers of goods or services. Under such contracts the customer may be bound by terms of which he is not aware because he has taken his chance of whatever terms were contained in the form, or he may have agreed reluctantly, or he may not in truth have 'agreed' at all.

4 FREEDOM OF CONTRACT

In its most obvious sense, the expression 'freedom of contract' is used to refer to the general principle that the law does not restrict the terms on which parties may contract: it will not give relief merely because the terms of the contract are harsh or unfair to one party. Many of the basic principles of the modern law of contract were settled in the last century, when, in the light of the prevailing *laissez faire* philosophy, it was thought wrong to interfere with private agreements on such grounds. The present trend is rather to stress abuses to which the principle of 'freedom of contract' can give rise; so that the principle has been considerably restricted, both by legislation and by judicial decision. Very substantial legislative inroads on the principle have, for example, been made in the law of landlord and tenant, and in the law of consumer sales and consumer credit; while restrictions on the effectiveness of exemption clauses in standard form contracts are due partly to judicial decisions and partly to legislation.[4] Such developments now give a good deal of protection to the person who is assumed to be the

---

[4] See ch 7, post.

weaker party to a contractual relationship. But in most transactions between businessmen, bargaining at arm's length, the principle of 'freedom of contract' remains an important one.

'Freedom of contract' is also used in another sense, to refer to the principle that, in general, a person is not by law compelled to enter into a contract. Here again the law has from time to time made exceptions to the general rule on grounds of public interest. The earliest exceptions applied to persons who engaged in the so-called 'common callings', by holding themselves out as ready to provide services of a certain kind to the public in general. The best known examples were common carriers and innkeepers. Such persons could not refuse their services as they pleased: they could only do so on certain grounds specified by law. In modern times a similar principle has been extended over a wider area so that, for example, a supply of goods may not be refused to a retailer on the ground of price-cutting;[5] nor, in certain circumstances, may employment or accommodation or certain other facilities be refused to a person on grounds of race or sex.[6] And it seems that arbitrary exclusion of a person from an association (eg on religious or political grounds), depriving that person of the opportunity to exercise a particular profession, may in certain circumstances be actionable as a matter of general common law.[7]

It is obvious that, the more the law interferes with the relationship of the parties, the less important the factor of agreement becomes. In some situations the degree of interference is so large that it becomes improper to describe the relationship between the parties as a contract. One obvious illustration of such a relationship is that of marriage. Here, the parties can only decide whether or not to enter into the relationship. Once they have done so, its essential incidents are determined by law: for example, an agreement that a marriage should last for a trial period of three years would not have any legal effect. In other cases, one of the parties may not have any choice at all: for example where a person's property is compulsorily acquired against his will under statutory powers. These cases differ from those discussed in the preceding paragraph. In those cases, the relationship is contractual because the parties have a considerable degree of legal freedom to decide upon the terms of their relationship, even though they may enter it under some degree of legal compulsion.

5 REASONS FOR ENFORCING CONTRACTS

The legal enforceability of contractual agreements is so well esta-

---

[5] Resale Prices Act 1976, s 11.
[6] Race Relations Act 1976, Pts II and III; Sex Discrimination Act 1975, Pts II and III.
[7] See *Nagle v Feilden* [1966] 2 Q B 633 (a case of sex discrimination, now unlawful under Sex Discrimination Act 1975, s 13).

blished, in all western systems of law, that a discussion of the reasons for it may seem to be superfluous. Yet such a discussion is important in relation to the topic of remedies for breach of contract, since the principles on which enforcement is based will determine the often difficult question of the extent to which enforcement is to be carried. Three reasons for the enforcement of contracts are commonly given,[8] and they may be illustrated by some simple hypothetical cases. First, A has agreed to buy something from B and paid for it in advance but B has not delivered it. If B could nevertheless keep the advance payment, he would be unjustly enriched; and it is therefore generally agreed that he should at the very least pay back the money to A. This process is sometimes referred to as protecting A's 'restitution interest'. Secondly, A has agreed to render some service to B at a distant place. He incurs travelling expenses in getting to that place but on his arrival there B repudiates the agreement. Here A's expenditure has not enriched B, but it is nevertheless generally held that A should have a remedy against B, in respect of the wasted expenditure which he has incurred in reliance on the contract. This process is sometimes called the protection of A's 'reliance interest'. But the law of contract goes beyond protecting the restitution and reliance interests, as a third illustration will show. A offers to buy a picture from B for £20,000 and B accepts the offer. The same day, before A has paid B or incurred any expense in reliance on the contract, B repudiates it by refusing to deliver the picture. There is no doubt that A can enforce the contract; and the reason given is, that A's expectations arising out of the contract have been disappointed. It is said that the law here protects A's *expectation interest*. The protection of such expectations is the characteristic feature of the law of contract. Of course, other expectations are protected by other branches of the law: for example, under the law of torts a person who has been injured by another's negligence may recover damages for loss of his expected earnings. But this expectation exists independently of the negligence giving rise to the legal liability to compensate for its loss. The law of contract, on the other hand, protects expectations which owe their existence solely to the very agreement for breach of which the action is brought. The common explanation of this state of the law is that such protection is necessary in the interests of commercial convenience: that 'business could not go on' unless contractual expectations were protected by law. This is probably too extreme a view. In practice, a good deal of business does go on without the sanction of legal enforceability of expectations. One may instance the very considerable credit betting industry; or business arrangements which are so vague as not to amount to binding contracts, or which are expressed to

---

[8] See further pp 320–322, post.

be 'gentlemen's agreements'. On the other hand, one could point to the practice of 'gazumping' to show that the failure of the law to enforce certain types of agreement may lead, if not to a commercially intolerable situation, at least to serious inconvenience. The protection of contractual expectations does mitigate such inconvenience and so tends to promote stability; it also provides the legal framework for the operation of share, commodity and similar markets. This is the best explanation for the general principle that the law will protect these expectations, even where there has been no receipt of benefit under the contract and no loss suffered by action in reliance on it.

6 COMMON LAW AND EQUITY

English law recognises a distinction between common law and equity; and hence between legal and equitable rights, remedies and defences. Originally, the distinction was based on the fact that common law and equity were distinct systems of law, administered in separate courts. This separate administration of the two systems was abolished over a hundred years ago, so that both are now administered in the same courts. Even so, the distinction remains of considerable importance to an understanding of the law of contract. Although generalisations on the point are hazardous, it is broadly speaking true that equity often takes a less rigid or literal approach than the common law to contract problems; that it pays greater regard to substance than to form; and that it often provides more satisfactory remedies than those available at common law. Differences between the common law and equitable approaches to contract problems will therefore have to be discussed at many points in the following chapters.

Chapter 2

Agreement

This chapter is concerned with the process by which the parties to a contract reach agreement. Generally, that process can be analysed into the acceptance by one party of an offer made by another. Thus, in the simplest case, A may offer to sell B 20 tons of coal for £500. When B says 'I accept' (or uses words to that effect) a contract is concluded. In practice, the course of contractual negotiations is often very much more complex than this. When parties begin to negotiate there may be considerable differences between them as to price, quantity, quality, delivery dates, terms of credit and so forth. Gradually, by a series of concessions, they move towards agreement, and it is often very difficult to say just when an offer has been accepted. For the purpose of answering this question, the law distinguishes between various steps or stages in negotiations.

1 OFFER AND INVITATION TO TREAT

An offer is a statement to the effect that the person making it is willing to contract on the terms stated, as soon as these are accepted by the person to whom the statement is addressed. The person making the statement is called the *offeror* ; the person to whom it is made is called the *offeree* or (if he accepts the offer) the *acceptor* . The offer may be made to an individual, or to a group of persons, or to the public at large; it may be made expressly or by conduct. Under the objective test,[1] conduct by A can constitute an offer, in spite of the fact that A did not actually intend to make one, if it induces B reasonably to believe that A had such an intention. Even failure by A to act may occasionally suffice: for example, the fact that he has allowed an arbitration claim to remain dormant for a long period may amount to an offer to abandon the arbitration, at least when combined with other circumstances indicative of the necessary intention.[2] But by itself such inactivity will only very rarely have this effect since it is usually too equivocal to give B reasonable grounds for thinking that A is making an offer to him.[3]

---

[1] Ante, p 2.

[2] *The Splendid Sun* [1981] QB 694; *The Multitank Holsatia* [1988] 2 Lloyd's Rep 486.

[3] *The Hannah Blumenthal* [1983] 1 AC 854; *The Leonidas D* [1985] 2 All ER 796; *The Agrabele* [1987] 2 Lloyd's Rep 223; *The Antclizo* [1988] 2 All ER 513.

The essential feature of an offer is that the person making it must (actually or objectively) intend to be bound without further negotiation, by a simple acceptance of his terms. Thus there is no offer where the owner of a house, in response to an enquiry from a person who wishes to buy it, states the price at which he might be prepared to sell;[4] nor even where the owner wishes to sell and invites offers at or about a specified price. In the latter case he is said to make an 'invitation to treat', and he is not bound to accept the highest or any other offer. In border-line cases it is obviously hard to determine with what intention the statement was made; but the difficulty is mitigated in two ways. First, it is enough to show that the statement was reasonably understood by the person to whom it was addressed as indicating an intention to be bound; and secondly, the character of certain frequently-recurring types of statements is settled by rules of law, at any rate in the absence of clear evidence of contrary intention.

Thus it is generally accepted in England that a display of price-marked goods in a shop-window, or on the shelves of a self-service shop, is merely an invitation to treat.[5] The offer in such a case comes from the customer. An indication of the price at which petrol is to be sold at a filling station is, similarly, only an invitation to treat.[6] Likewise, advertisements in newspapers or in tradesmen's circulars are commonly held not to amount to offers.[7] These rules may apply even though the person making the statement calls it an offer: a shop's 'special offer' may well be nothing more than an invitation to treat. But it should not be supposed that all displays and advertisements are only invitations to treat. For example, it has been said that a notice displayed at the entrance to an automatic car-park was an offer, presumably because no further act of acceptance on the part of the proprietor was contemplated after the customer drove in.[8] For the same reason, advertisements of rewards for the return of (for example) lost property are commonly held to be offers. Similarly, in *Carlill v Carbolic Smoke Ball Co*[9] the manufacturers of carbolic smoke balls promised to pay £100 to any person who caught influenza after using the appliance as directed; and they added that they had deposited £1000 with a named bank 'shewing our sincerity in the matter'. It was held that the advertisement was an offer.

It is a common commercial practice to ask for 'tenders' for the purchase or sale of goods, or for the supply of services. In this situation, the person asking for tenders normally makes an invitation to treat; the offer comes from the person making the tender. Where the tender

---

4 *Gibson v Manchester City Council* [1979] 1 All ER 972.
5 *Pharmaceutical Society of Great Britain v Boots Cash Chemists* [1953] 1 QB 401.
6 *Esso Petroleum Ltd v Customs and Excise Comrs* [1976] 1 WLR 1 at 5, 6, 11.
7 *Partridge v Crittenden* [1968] 2 All ER 421.
8 *Thornton v Shoe Lane Parking Ltd* [1971] 2 QB 163 at 169.
9 [1893] 1 QB 256.

is for an indefinite amount (eg for 'so much coal, not exceeding 1,000 tons, as you may order') it constitutes a standing offer which may be accepted from time to time as specific quantities are ordered.[10] A person to whom a tender is made can normally accept or reject it as he pleases. He is not bound to accept the best tender unless he has clearly indicated in his invitation that he would do so.[11] In that event, the invitation will be an offer even though it calls for the submission of 'offers'; and an 'offer' that complies with its terms will be an acceptance.[12]

In the case of auction sales, no offer for sale is made by the advertisement of the auction;[13] nor by putting the goods up for bidding. The offer is made by the bidder and accepted by the auctioneer in the customary manner, ie usually by the 'fall of the hammer'.[14] Even where the auction is expressly said to be 'without reserve' there is no contract *of sale* if the auctioneer refuses to knock the goods down to the highest bidder; though it has been held that the auctioneer was liable for breach of a separate undertaking that the auction would be without reserve.[15] This reasoning seems to be unduly refined: if the bidder's interests are worth protecting in such a case, it would be better to hold that the auctioneer had made an offer and that this was accepted by the highest bidder, so that a contract of sale had been concluded between the latter and the seller.[16]

In contracts for the carriage of passengers, many views have been expressed on the question when and by whom the offer is made. At the one extreme, a railway time-table has been held to be an offer;[17] and it has been suggested that the act of running a bus constitutes an offer to intending passengers.[18] Another view is that the carrier does not make the offer until he issues the ticket, and that the contract is made when the passenger keeps the ticket without objection,[19] or when he claims his seat.[20] Where a booking is made in advance, the offer may come from the passenger, for it has been said that the contract is made as soon as the carrier 'accepts' the booking.[1] There is no single rule which determines the time when the contract of carriage is made: the

10 *Percival v L C C Asylum Committee* (1918) 87 L J K B 677.
11 See *Spencer v Harding* (1870) L R 5 C P 561; *William Lacey (Hounslow) Ltd v Davis* [1957] 1 W L R 932 at 939.
12 *Harvela Investments Ltd v Royal Trust Co of Canada (CI) Ltd* [1986] A C 207.
13 *Harris v Nickerson* (1873) L R 8 Q B 286.
14 Sale of Goods Act 1979, s 57(2)
15 *Warlow v Harrison* (1859) 1 E & E 309, contrast, in Scotland, *Fenwick v Macdonald Fraser & Co Ltd* (1904) 6 F 850.
16 *Cf* American Uniform Commercial Code, s 2–328(3).
17 *Denton v Great Northern Rly Co* (1856) 5 E & B 860.
18 *Wilkie v London Passenger Transport Board* [1947] 1 All E R 258 at 259.
19 *Thornton v Shoe Lane Parking Co Ltd* [1971] 2 Q B 163 at 169.
20 *MacRobertson Miller Airline Services v Com of State Taxation of State of Western Australia* (1975) 8 A L R 131.
1 *The Eagle* [1977] 2 Lloyd's Rep 70.

question depends in each case on the wording of the relevant document and on the circumstances in which it was issued.

2 ACCEPTANCE AND COUNTER-OFFER

Assuming that an offer has been made, a contract comes into existence when the offer is accepted. To accept an offer, the offeree must indicate his assent to the terms of the offer. He may do this either expressly (by words of acceptance) or by conduct. In most cases, the acceptance, no less than the offer, contains a promise. The contract is then said to be a *bilateral* one, that is, one under which each party undertakes obligations: for example one party agrees to deliver goods and the other to accept and to pay for them. There may also be a *unilateral* contract, under which only one party comes under an obligation. The stock examples are a promise by A to pay £100 to B, if B walks from London to York; or one to pay B £100 if he refrains from smoking until he is 21. Here, only A undertakes an obligation: B does not promise to do, or to refrain from doing, anything.

The most important rule with regard to an acceptance is that it must correspond with the offer. If it seeks to qualify or to vary the offer, it is ineffective as an acceptance: for example, an offer to sell 1,200 tons of iron is not accepted by a reply stating that the offeree will take 800 tons.[2] Trivial variations between the terms of the offer and acceptance may be disregarded; and the same is true of variations which merely make express a term which the law would in any event imply. Subject to these qualifications, a purported acceptance which introduces different terms is not in law an acceptance but a counter-offer. As such it may have two legal consequences. First, it rejects the original offer, so that the original offeree cannot subsequently accept it: eg in the above example he cannot send a second letter accepting the offer to sell 1,200 tons. Secondly, it amounts to a fresh offer, which the original offeror (who has now become the offeree under the counter-offer) may accept. A counter-offer may be followed by a further communication of the same character; and complicated negotiations may take the form of a long series of counter-offers, alleged to have culminated in a concluded agreement when one of the counter-offers is finally accepted without, or with only trivial, variations. In such a situation, the court must look at the whole course of negotiations[3] to determine whether, and, if so, exactly when the parties have reached agreement.

The rules relating to counter-offers are particularly important in the increasingly common situation, commonly known as the 'battle of

[2] *Tinn v Hoffman & Co* (1873) 29 L T 271.
[3] *Hussey v Horne-Payne* (1879) 4 App Cas 311.

forms', in which each party sends the other a previously prepared form containing the terms on which he is prepared to contract. For example, a buyer offers to buy goods on the terms of his 'purchase form' and the seller purports to accept the offer on the terms of his 'sales form'. If, as is probable, the terms of the forms differ (since the one is drafted in the buyer's, and the other in the seller's, interest) there is at this stage no contract. All that has happened is that the seller has made a counter-offer. This counter-offer may be accepted by conduct when the buyer takes delivery of the goods. In that event, there will be a contract on the terms of the seller's form.[4] On the other hand, the contract would be on the buyer's terms if the original offer had come from the seller, and had been followed by a buyer's counter-offer which had in turn been accepted by the conduct of the seller. Thus victory in the 'battle of forms' normally goes to the party who fires the last shot, ie to the party by whom the last form in the series is despatched. But this is not invariably true; for if that party has, in his own last communication, indicated his acceptance of the terms stated in the other party's form, the contract will be made on those terms.[5]

3 COMMUNICATION OF ACCEPTANCE

As a general rule, an acceptance has no effect unless and until it is communicated to the offeror.[6] This means that the fact of acceptance must be brought to the notice of the offeror. If the words of acceptance are 'drowned by an aircraft flying overhead,' or spoken into a telephone which has gone dead, there is no contract.[7] The reason for this rule is that it might be unjust to the offeror to hold him bound if he did not know that his offer had been accepted. On the other hand, no injustice is normally caused to the offeree by holding that there is no contract. In the cases put, he knows at once that there has been a failure of communication, so that he can take steps to retrieve the situation by making a second attempt to communicate the acceptance. For the purpose of the present rule, the acceptance need not be communicated to the offeror personally. It is sufficient to communicate it to an agent authorised to receive it, such as a company's senior official. Obviously, leaving a message with a porter would not suffice.

There are three exceptions to the general rule that an acceptance must actually be communicated. The first, for which there is as yet

---

4 See *British Road Services v A V Crutchley Ltd* [1967] 2 All E R 785 at 787 and [1968] 1 All E R 811 at 817.

5 *Butler Machine Tool Co Ltd* v *Ex-Cell-O Corpn (England) Ltd* [1979] 1 All E R 965.

6 *Brogden v Metropolitan Rly* (1877) 2 App Cas 666; *Brinkibon Ltd v Stahag Stahl und Stahlwarenhandelsgesellschaft mbH* [1983] 2 A C 34.

7 *Entores Ltd v Miles Far East Corpn* [1955] 2 Q B 327 at 333.

little authority, is that there may be a contract when the failure in communication is in some sense due to the fault, or at any rate to the act or omission, of the offeror himself.[8] This would be the position if the offeror did not hear words of acceptance spoken into a telephone simply because, at the crucial point, he had put the telephone down without telling the offeree that he was doing this. The second exception arises where the terms of the offer expressly, or by implication, dispense with communication of acceptance. For example, in *Carlill v Carbolic Smoke Ball Co* [9] the plaintiff accepted the defendants' offer by simply using the smoke ball: she did not at this stage need to tell them that she had done so. Where goods are ordered from a supplier, it may be that the offer to buy can similarly be accepted by simply despatching the goods. The third exception relates to acceptances sent through the post. This is a complex subject calling for separate treatment.

4 POSTAL ACCEPTANCE

There are many possible answers to the question when an acceptance sent by post should become operative. At the one extreme, it is possible to take the view that such an acceptance should only take effect when it is actually brought to the notice of the offeror; at the other extreme, there is the view that such an acceptance should take effect as soon as it is posted. Intermediate possibilities are that the acceptance should take effect when it is delivered to the offeror's address, or when it should have arrived there in the ordinary course of post. Any view is bound to give rise to the possibility of some hardship to one or other of the parties, especially where the acceptance is lost or delayed in the post. If the contract is complete on posting, the offeror may be bound before he knows of the acceptance; and this result may be justified by saying that he takes the risk of being placed in such a position by initiating negotiations through the medium of the post. But when it is recalled that a contract may result from a lengthy sequence of counter-offers leading in the end to an acceptance, it will be obvious that the final offeror is not necessarily the person who has initiated the negotiations. If, on the other hand, the contract is not complete till the acceptance reaches the offeror, then the offeree will find it hard to know exactly when he can rely on having secured a firm contract. There is no way of reconciling the conflicting interests of the parties. The choice between the various solutions is an arbitrary one and can only be justified on grounds of convenience. Even this justification inevitably takes the point of view of one or other party. English law looks primarily to the convenience of

[8] Ibid.
[9] See p 8, ante.

the offeree, and this is best served by holding that the acceptance takes effect as soon as it is posted.[10] The rule does not apply where 'instantaneous' methods of long-distance communication are used, such as telex or the telephone. In such cases, actual communication of acceptance is generally necessary;[11] and this rule need cause no hardship to the offeree, because he will usually know of any failure in communication in time to retrieve the situation. Where a letter of acceptance goes astray, on the other hand, the offeree will usually not know this until it is too late to make a further communication.

The rule with respect to posted acceptances is subject to a number of commonsense limitations. In the first place, it must be reasonable in all the circumstances to use the post.[12] Obviously it would not be reasonable to reply by second class mail to a telexed offer, or to send an acceptance by post on the eve of a postal strike. Secondly, the general rule presupposes that the letter of acceptance is properly addressed and stamped. If this is not the case, any loss due to resulting delay should fall on the party who is responsible for the defect in the communication. This will normally be the offeree; but it may be the offeror: for example, where he sends out an offer in which he fails to give his own correct or complete address. Finally, the general rule can be excluded by the terms of the offer, which may require the acceptance to be actually communicated to the offeror, or at least to be delivered at his address.[13]

Where the general rule does apply, it leads to a number of practical consequences. The first, and by far the most important, is to curtail the offeror's power to withdraw his offer. The posting of an acceptance concludes the contract even though, after the acceptance has been posted but before it has reached the offeror, he communicates a withdrawal of the offer to the offeree; and even though, before the acceptance was posted, the offeror had posted a withdrawal which had not yet reached the offeree when the latter posted the acceptance.[14] The second consequence of the rule is to put the risk of accidents in the post on the offeror: thus there is a good contract although the acceptance is delayed in the post;[15] and the same is true even if it is lost in the post, so that it never reaches the offeror at all.[16] This is perhaps the case in which the 'posted acceptance' rule can cause the greatest hardship to the offeror; but to hold that there was no contract could cause equal

---

[10] *Adams v Lindsell* (1818) 1 B & Ald 681; *Henthorn v Fraser* [1892] 2 Ch 27 at 33; *Bruner v Moore* [1904] 1 Ch 305 (telegram, now replaced for inland purposes by telemessage).

[11] *Entores Ltd v Miles Far East Corpn* [1955] 2 QB 327; *Brinkibon Ltd v Stahag Stahl und Stahlwarenhandelsgesellschaft mbH* [1983] 2 AC 34; for exceptions, see pp 11–12, ante.

[12] *Henthorn v Fraser* [1892] 2 Ch 27.

[13] *Holwell Securities Ltd v Hughes* [1974] 1 All ER 161.

[14] *Byrne & Co v Leon Van Tienhoven* (1880) 5 CPD 344.

[15] *Dunlop v Higgins* (1848) 1 HL Cas 381.

[16] *Household Insurance v Grant* (1879) 4 ExD 216.

hardship to the offeree, if he had acted in reliance on his posted acceptance. Thirdly, the contract is taken to have been made at the time of posting:[17] this may be important in order to determine the priority of two or more competing claimants each of whom has made a contract affecting the same subject-matter.

It should not be supposed that the 'posted acceptance' rule necessarily applies in all situations to which it could logically be applied. The rule will not be applied where it would lead to 'manifest inconvenience and absurdity':[18] in each new situation the question must be asked whether the rule produces, on balance, a convenient result.[19] This is the test which should be applied to the difficult question whether a posted acceptance can be revoked by the offeree, if he manages actually to communicate the revocation to the offeror before the latter has received the acceptance. One view is that the offeree should be allowed to do this, since the offeror cannot have acted in reliance on an acceptance of which he is as yet unaware. Another view is that, just as the posting of the acceptance curtails the offeror's power to withdraw the offer, so it should curtail the offeree's power to revoke his acceptance. For, if it did not have this effect, an offeree could, on a fluctuating market, post an acceptance and rely on it if the market moved in his favour; while he could revoke it later on the same day, if the market moved against him. Although the rule of convenience exists to protect the offeree, it does not seem that he should be allowed to exploit it in this way.

Certain contracts for the international sale of goods may, if the parties so choose, be governed by an international convention known as the Uniform Law on the Formation of Contracts for the International Sale of Goods (or ULFIS).[20] Under this Uniform Law an acceptance does not take effect on posting, but only when it is 'communicated' to the offeror, that is, when it is delivered at his address.[1] One important effect of the English posting rule is, however, preserved in the Uniform Law: a revocation of an offer is only effective if communicated to the offeree before the latter has despatched his acceptance.[2] Thus, if the acceptance is posted before the revocation has been communicated, there will be a contract, though the contract will be formed when the acceptance is communicated—not when it is posted. If the acceptance is lost in the post, there will be no contract under the Uniform Law. If the acceptance is 'communicated late' (eg because it

17 *Potter v Sanders* (1846) 6 Hare 1.
18 *Holwell Securities Ltd v Hughes* [1974] 1 All ER 161 at 166.
19 *Brinkibon Ltd v Stahag Stahl und Stahlwarenhandelsgesellschaft mbH* [1983] 2 AC 34 at 41.
20 Uniform Laws on International Sales Act 1967, Sch 2.
1 Ibid arts 6(1), 12(1).
2 Ibid art 5(4).

is delayed in the post) there will be a contract unless the offeror promptly repudiates.[3]

5 METHOD OF ACCEPTANCE PRESCRIBED BY OFFER

An offeror may in his offer expressly require the acceptance to be made in a certain way, eg by letter or telex. *Prima facie*, the offeree can then accept only in that way, as the offeror has made the requirement for his own protection; an attempt to accept it in some other way amounts at most to a counter-offer.[4] To this rule there are, however, two exceptions. First, an acceptance made in a different manner may be effective, if the manner actually adopted is no less efficacious from the offeror's point of view: ie if it is in every way as quick and reliable as the prescribed method. Secondly, allowance must be made for the fact that an offer is often made on a form supplied by the offeree: for example where land is to be sold by tender and the seller requires tenders (ie offers) to be made on printed forms issued by him. Here the stipulation as to the manner of acceptance exists for the benefit of the *offeree*, so that the stipulation can be waived by him, at least so long as this does not prejudice the offeror.[5]

6 SILENCE AS ACCEPTANCE

An offer may stipulate that it can be accepted by silence. If the offeree makes no response to such an offer, the general rule is that he is not bound. For example, A may write to B offering to buy B's car, and adding: 'If I hear no more about it, I shall consider it mine.' There is no contract if B simply ignores the letter.[6] It would obviously be undesirable to enable A to force a contract on B by ultimatum, or to oblige B to take active steps to avoid liability. It is by no means equally obvious that, in the above situation, A should not be bound if B has acted in reliance on the offer: for example, if B has turned away another offer to buy the car, thinking that he had a contract with A. If A stood by, knowing that B was about to act in this way in reliance on the offer, he might be estopped from denying that there was a contract.[7]

The rule that there can be no acceptance by 'silence' does not mean

---

3 Ibid art 9(2).
4 *Wettern Electric Ltd v Welsh Development Agency* [1983] QB 796.
5 *Manchester Diocesan Council for Education v Commercial and General Investments Ltd* [1970] 1 WLR 241.
6 *Felthouse v Bindley* (1862) 11 CBNS 869, (1863) 1 New Rep 401.
7 *Spiro v Lintern* [1973] 1 WLR 1002 at 1011; but see *Fairline Shipping Corpn v Adamson* [1975] QB 180 at 189; for estoppel cf p 141, post.

that it is always necessary to communicate *words* of acceptance to the offeror. An acceptance may be inferred from the conduct of the offeree, and communication of acceptance may be dispensed with. Where this is the case, the acceptance is said to be by conduct rather than by silence.[8] 'Conduct' here refers to some action on the part of the offeree, so that mere inaction is not normally sufficient. It can only amount to an acceptance 'in the most exceptional circumstances;'[9] eg where the offeree began the negotiations by soliciting the offer and then failed to reply to it in circumstances leading the offeror reasonably to believe that the offer had been accepted.[10]

7 ACCEPTANCE REQUIRES KNOWLEDGE OF OFFER

A person may do an act which appears to amount to acceptance of an offer but be unaware of the offer: for example, he may give information for which a reward has been advertised without knowing of the advertisement. In such a case there is no agreement, and hence no contract. On the other hand, if the person doing the act does know of the offer, it is probably immaterial that he did the act with some motive other than that of claiming the reward. Thus, in *Carlill v Carbolic Smoke Ball Co*,[11] the plaintiff recovered the £100, although she presumably did not use the smoke ball with this aim in view, but rather to stave off the various diseases against which the appliance was meant to give protection.

One application of the rule, that a person can only accept an offer of which he knows, is to be found in cases of so-called identical cross-offers. If A writes to B offering to buy B's car for £5000 and by the same post B writes to A offering to sell the car for £5000 there is, it is said, no contract.[12] Yet it could be argued that A and B were in agreement; and the probable reason for the rule is that parties to such a correspondence would be left in some degree of uncertainty. This is best resolved by some further communication between them.

8 UNILATERAL CONTRACTS

In the case of a bilateral contract, acceptance of the offer normally takes the form of a counter-promise (though this may be inferred from conduct), and the moment of acceptance is, as a general rule, that of

---

[8] *Roberts v Hayward* (1828) 3 C & P 432.

[9] *The Leonidas D* [1985] 2 All E R 796 at 805; so far as contra, *The Golden Bear* [1987] 1 Lloyd's Rep 330 is open to doubt. Cf *The Multitank Holsatia* [1988] 2 Lloyd's Rep 486 (not a case of *mere* inaction).

[10] *Rust v Abbey Life Assurance Co* [1979] 2 Lloyd's Rep 334 at 340; affg [1978] 2 Lloyd's Rep 386 at 393.

[11] [1893] 1 Q B 256.

[12] *Tinn v Hoffman & Co* (1873) 29 L T 271 at 278.

the communication of the counter-promise. Where the contract is unilateral, however, there is no counter-promise. The person to whom £100 is promised if he walks to York, or forbears from smoking until he is 21, does not promise to do these things. He can, without breach of contract, give up walking or start smoking at any time after he has begun to engage in the required course of conduct. Hence it was sometimes thought that the person who promised the £100 should likewise have the power to withdraw until the walk had been completed or the abstinence fully accomplished; and in support of this view it was said that there had been no acceptance until the terms of the promise had been fully performed. In some cases such a solution may indeed be in accordance with the intention of the parties and a perfectly fair one. It is, for example, sometimes possible to regard a contract between a prospective seller of a house and an estate agent as a unilateral one, by which the agent is to receive his commission if he effects a sale, without promising to do anything to that end.[13] In such a case it might be perfectly reasonable to allow the owner to revoke without liability, even if the agent had taken steps in performance, such as advertising the property. But the ground for this view would be that such a result was in accordance with the intention of the parties, and not that the contract was unilateral: the position would be exactly the same where the agent *had* made some promise (eg to use his best endeavours to effect a sale, or to advertise the property at his own expense[14]), so that the contract would be bilateral. More generally, in the case of a unilateral contract, the parties' intention would not be to allow the promisor to revoke without liability after part performance by the promisee (eg walking as far as Doncaster); and the prevailing modern view is that the offer of a unilateral contract cannot be revoked after part performance by the promisee.[15] This view, however, presupposes that the contract is simply to pay a lump sum for the performance of the act. It may amount to a promise to make a number of payments in response to each of a series of acts; and in that case the promise is revocable, in the sense that the promisor can escape liability in respect of acts done after (but not before) revocation. An application of these principles is to be found in cases of so-called continuing guarantees.[16] These are cases in which A promises B to guarantee liabilities which C may incur to B. The contract between A and B is unilateral since B does not promise A to give credit to C. If the guarantee is in respect of a single

---

13 See *Luxor (Eastbourne) Ltd v Cooper* [1941] A C 108 at 124.
14 *Christopher v Essig* [1948] W N 461; *John McCann & Co v Pow* [1974] 1 W L R 1643 at 1647; cf *Bentall, Horsley and Baldry v Vicary* [1931] 1 K B 253.
15 See *Errington v Errington and Woods* [1952] 1 K B 290 at 295; *Daulia Ltd v Four Millbank Nominees Ltd* [1978] Ch 231 at 238; *Harvela Investments Ltd v Royal Trust Co of Canada (CI) Ltd* [1986] A C 207 at 224; and the enforceability of bankers' irrevocable credits, p 49, post.
16 See *Offord v Davies* (1862) 12 C B N S 748; *Lloyds v Harper* (1880) 16 Ch D 290.

transaction between B and C it is 'indivisible' and A cannot withdraw after B has begun to give credit to C. But the position is different if the guarantee is given in respect of a series of loans each of which is a separate transaction. In such a case the guarantee is 'divisible' and A can revoke it with respect to loans made by B after notice of revocation.

9 TERMINATION OF OFFER

Events may occur after an offer has been made which bring it to an end so that it can no longer be accepted. This happens when the offer is withdrawn by the offeror, or rejected by the offeree; and it may happen by lapse of time, by the occurrence of a condition, or by the death or supervening incapacity of one of the parties.

a Withdrawal

An offeror may withdraw his offer at any time before the offeree has accepted it.[17] This is so even though the offer expressly states that it will be left open for a fixed time. Generally such a statement is (as we shall see in the next chapter) a promise without consideration and therefore does not bind the offeror.[18]

The law does, however, limit the offeror's power to withdraw his offer, by insisting that the withdrawal must be communicated to the offeree. Thus if A has offered to sell his car to B, he cannot withdraw the offer simply by changing his mind or by selling the car to C: B must have notice of the withdrawal. Of course, B may not actually be able to get the car (which may in the meanwhile have been delivered to C). But if he accepts A's offer before its withdrawal has been communicated to him, B is entitled to damages for breach of contract against A. For the purpose of the present rule the notice of withdrawal must, as a general rule, actually reach the offeree's address. Once this happens, the withdrawal takes effect, even though the offeree does not actually read it, at least if it arrives during business hours.[19] But a mere posting of the withdrawal is not enough. Thus, if A posts a withdrawal, and B then posts an acceptance before the withdrawal has reached him, there is a contract between A and B.[20] This is so, even though there may never have been any agreement between them. The rule is an important one: if it did not exist, no offeree could safely act in reliance on his acceptance of an offer; for the possibility that a withdrawal was in the post could never be ruled out. So long as the withdrawal is commmunicated *to the offeree* , it need not, however, be communicated *by the offeror* .

17 *Offord v Davies,* supra.
18 *Dickinson v Dodds* (1876) 2 Ch D 463; for criticism, see p 49, post.
19 Cf *The Brimnes* [1975] Q B 929.
20 *Byrne & Co v Leon Van Tienhoven* (1880) 5 C P D 344.

It suffices if the offeree gets to know from a reliable source that the offeror no longer intends to deal with him on the terms of the offer.[1]

In some exceptional cases, a withdrawal may be effective even though it is neither actually communicated to the offeree, nor delivered to his address. For example, a withdrawal delivered to the offeree's last known address would probably be effective if he had moved without notifying the offeror. And where an offer is made by public advertisement, a withdrawal is probably sufficient if it is published in such a way that it is reasonably likely to come to the attention of those who saw the original advertisement.[2]

b Rejection

If an offeree rejects an offer, he cannot subsequently change his mind and accept it. Rejection is considered to put an end to the offer. In this connection, it is important to recall that a counter-offer amounts to a rejection. Hence an offeree who makes a counter-offer thereby loses the power of accepting the original offer.[3] But an offer is not rejected by a mere enquiry whether the offeror would be prepared to depart from its terms. A distinction is drawn between a rejection (including a counter-offer) and a request for information.[4] For example, an offer to sell at a stated price would not be rejected by an enquiry whether the seller was prepared to give credit, or even whether he was prepared to reduce the price, so long as the enquiry was 'merely exploratory'.[5] The distinction between such a request or enquiry and a rejection depends on the intention of the offeree, as reasonably understood by the offeror.

Although there is no authority on the point, it seems that a rejection does not take effect on posting, but only when it reaches the offeror. Until this happens, the offeree can still accept, provided he does so by a communication which overtakes the posted rejection, eg by telephone. The offeror is not prejudiced by this rule, since a rejection gives him no rights and since he cannot act in reliance on it until he actually receives it.

c Lapse

An offer may come to an end by lapse of time. If a time limit for acceptance is expressly stated in the offer, it clearly cannot be accepted after that time. If no time is stated, the offer lapses at the end of a reasonable time. What is a reasonable time is a question of fact, depending on such

---

[1] *Dickinson v Dodds* (1876) 2 Ch D 463.
[2] Cf *Shuey v US* 92 US 73 (1875).
[3] *Hyde v Wrench* (1840) 3 Beav 334.
[4] *Stevenson, Jaques & Co v McLean* (1880) 5 QBD 346.
[5] *Gibson v Manchester City Council* [1979] 1 All ER 972 at 978.

circumstances as the nature of the subject-matter and the general market conditions in which the offer is made.[6]

d Occurrence of condition

An offer may be so expressed as to come to an end on the occurrence of a condition: for example, where a tender to sell goods from time to time is made subject to the seller's being himself able to obtain adequate supplies. Where an offer is made to buy goods, there is an implied term to the effect that it cannot be accepted after the goods have been seriously damaged.[7]

e Death and incapacity

One possible view is that an offer cannot be accepted after the death of either party, since the fact of death makes it impossible for them to reach agreement. But the strict application of such a rule might cause hardship. Suppose that A makes a continuing offer to B, to guarantee loans to be made by B to C. If A dies and B in ignorance of this fact makes a further loan to C, he might well be prejudiced by a rule that A's death automatically terminated the offer, and it seems that in such a situation B is entitled to sue A's estate on the guarantee.[8] It is always open to A's personal representatives to terminate the offer by giving notice of withdrawal in the ordinary way. Similarly, there seems to be no *a priori* reason why an offer should be determined by the death of the offeree, since acceptance by the personal representatives of the offeree would not normally prejudice the offeror. Of course there are certain contracts which are 'personal' in the sense that they would be terminated by the death of either party: for example, contracts of personal service.[9] It is obvious that offers to enter into such contracts must be terminated by the death of either party.

Supervening incapacity may be involuntary, as where one of the parties becomes mentally ill. The question whether an acceptance made after this had happened bound either party, would depend on the general rules governing contracts with mental patients.[10] Supervening incapacity may also be voluntary, as where a company changes its objects so that the contract to which the offer relates is no longer within the powers of the company.[11] There is no hardship in holding that a company which voluntarily acts in this way loses the power to accept the offer. But it is submitted that the company cannot in this way

---

6 *Ramsgate Victoria Hotel Co Ltd v Montefiore* (1866) LR 1 Exch 109.
7 *Financings Ltd v Stimson* [1962] 3 All ER 386.
8 See *Coulthart v Clementson* (1879) 5 QBD 42 at 46.
9 See p 300, post.
10 See p 198, post.
11 See p 199, post.

deprive a person, to whom it had made an offer, of the power of accepting it.[12] The point is only important where the company has effectively bound itself not to withdraw the offer (eg by granting an option)[13]: if this is not the position the company is free to withdraw its offer by notice in the ordinary way.

10 CASES IN WHICH THERE IS NO IDENTIFIABLE OFFER AND ACCEPTANCE

In certain exceptional situations, there is undoubtedly a contract, but the process of reaching agreement cannot readily be analysed into the normal stages of offer and acceptance.[14] For example, the parties may negotiate through the same broker who eventually obtains their consent to the same terms. Here it is very hard to say which of them has made the offer and which the acceptance.[15] Again, it has been held that the competitors in a regatta enter into a contract, not only with the club which organises the race, but also with each other, to the effect that each will abide by the regatta rules.[16] In this situation, too, it is far from clear exactly when each competitor makes his offer to the others and when that offer is accepted.

11 VAGUE OR INCOMPLETE AGREEMENTS

So far, we have been concerned with what may be called the mechanics of agreement. Even where the rules relating to offer and acceptance are complied with, the agreement may still suffer from defects, making it impossible or very difficult for the courts to determine on exactly what terms the parties were agreed. The task of the courts in this area is a delicate one. They do not, on the one hand, want to impose on the parties terms to which they never agreed, or, as it is put, to 'make a contract for the parties'. On the other hand, they will often do their best to uphold loosely worded agreements. They recognise that businessmen often do not have the time to work out the terms of their agreements in meticulous detail; and that it may be desirable to avoid too much precision and rigidity in commercial agreements, if these are to stand up to the stresses of changing economic circumstances.

It is common to find in commercial contracts references to 'fair

---

[12] This will sometimes follow from s 35 of the Companies Act 1985; see p 201, post.

[13] See p 49, post.

[14] *New Zealand Shipping Co Ltd v A M Satterthwaite & Co Ltd* [1975] A C 154 at 167; *Gibson v Manchester City Council* [1979] 1 W L R 294 at 297; *The Multitank Holsatia* [1988] 2 Lloyd's Rep 486 at 491.

[15] *Pagnan SpA v Feed Products Ltd* [1987] 2 Lloyd's Rep 601 at 616.

[16] *The Satanita* [1895] P 248; affd sub nom *Clarke v Dunraven* [1897] A C 59.

quality' or to terms which are 'usual' in the course of business at a particular place. Such vague terms do not necessarily vitiate the contract: their want of precision may be made good by reference to any relevant local custom or to the standard of reasonableness.[17] This standard can be applied even to fill gaps on which the contract is completely silent. For example an agreement for the sale or for the supply of goods may amount to a contract even though no price is agreed: in that event, a reasonable price must be paid.[18] On the other hand, failure to agree on such an important point as the amount to be paid may indicate that there was no concluded contract.[19] Even where this is the case, a party doing work under the agreement may be entitled to a reasonable recompense;[20] but, as there is no contract, he would not be liable in damages, eg for delay in doing the work.[1]

Where a contract contains vague or meaningless provisions on matters which are not considered to be of vital importance, those provisions can be ignored and the rest of the contract enforced. But if the vague provisions relate to a vital matter and cannot be resolved in any of the ways described above, there is no contract. This was, for example, held to be the position in a case in 1941 in which an agreement was made to supply a van 'on hire-purchase terms'.[2] Even at the present time, when hire-purchase is a far more common and standardised transaction, an agreement in these words would still not be a contract if such vital matters as the amount of the deposit and the number of instalments were left unspecified.

Even greater difficulty arises where the parties are unable or unwilling to reach agreement on certain vital points and provide that these are to be settled by future agreement. When long-term contracts are made in times of fluctuating markets, it is natural to find the parties reluctant to bind themselves to fixed prices. But an agreement for the sale of goods 'at a price to be agreed' is in a sense more difficult to enforce than one which simply says nothing about the price. In the latter case, the courts can claim merely to be supplementing the agreement of the parties by determining the amount of the reasonable price which the buyer has to pay. In the former case they may be overriding the agreement, if they substitute their own notion of what was reasonable for a figure which the parties might have reached after further bargaining. The agreement of the parties in such a case can be regarded as a mere agreement to negotiate, or as a 'contract to make a contract'; and in law such an agreement is 'too uncertain to have any

17 *Hillas & Co Ltd v Arcos Ltd* (1932) 147 LT 503.
18 Sale of Goods Act 1979, s 8(2); Supply of Goods and Services Act 1982, s 15 (1).
19 *Courtney and Fairbairn Ltd v Tolaini Bros (Hotels) Ltd* [1975] 1 All ER 716.
20 Post p 363.
 1 *British Steel Corpn v Cleveland Bridge & Engineering Co Ltd* [1984] 1 All ER 504.
 2 *G Scammell & Nephew Ltd v Ouston* [1941] AC 251.

binding force'.³ Accordingly, there are cases in which agreements containing such 'open price' terms have been held not to constitute binding contracts.⁴ However, where it is clear that the parties intended to be bound the court will give effect to such an agreement⁵ and may do so even if so important a matter as the price is left to be decided by subsequent agreement.⁶ In the law of insurance, agreements made 'at a premium to be arranged' are commonly regarded as binding.

Parties who cannot agree on all vital points at once may provide some machinery or standard for resolving such matters: eg they may say that prices or rents are to be fixed by reference to market values, or by arbitration, or by the decision of a designated third party. Such agreements are binding, though they may be avoided if the agreed machinery breaks down: eg if the third party fails to make the valuation.⁷ However, if the agreed machinery is merely 'subsidiary and incidental'⁸ its failure to operate is not fatal to the formation of a contract. In one such case, a party tried to defeat the agreed machinery by refusing to appoint a valuer. The House of Lords upheld the agreement, construing it as one to sell for a reasonable price which could be determined by the court itself.⁹

In the cases just considered, vital matters such as the price are left over for further agreement. There is a further group of cases in which the parties may have reached agreement on all vital terms, but stipulate for the execution of some formal agreement. Such a stipulation may have a number of different purposes. First, it may be evidence of the intention of the parties not to be bound till the formal agreement is drawn up and duly executed.¹⁰ This is the purpose of the stipulation commonly found in agreements for the sale of land that the agreement is 'subject to contract'. The normal¹¹ effect of this phrase is that neither party is bound until formal contracts are 'exchanged',¹² a process that may be completed by telephone.¹³ Secondly, the purpose of the stipulation may simply be to provide written evidence of the conclusion of the contract and of its terms. In such a case, there is a good contract even though the formal contract has not been executed.¹⁴ A

3 *Nile Co for the Export of Agricultural Crops v H & J M Bennett (Commodities) Ltd* [1986] 1 Lloyd's Rep 555 at 587.
4 Eg *May and Butcher v R* [1934] 2 KB 17n.
5 *Pagnan SpA v Feed Products Ltd* [1987] 2 Lloyd's Rep 601.
6 *Foley v Classique Coaches* [1934] 2 KB 1; *Voest Alpine Intertrading GmbH v Chevron International Oil Co Ltd* [1987] 2 Lloyd's Rep 547; *Didymi Corpn v Atlantic Lines and Navigation Co Inc* [1988] 2 Lloyd's Rep 108 (price *adjustment* to be agreed).
7 Sale of Goods Act 1979, s 9(1)
8 *Re Malpass* [1985] Ch 42 at 50.
9 *Sudbrook Trading Estate Ltd v Eggleton* [1983] 1 AC 444.
10 Eg *British Steel Corpn v Cleveland Bridge and Engineering Co Ltd* [1984] 1 All ER 504.
11 Ie unless the contrary intention is made extremely clear, as in *Alpenstow Ltd v Regalian Properties plc* [1985] 2 All ER 545.
12 *Chillingworth v Esche* [1924] 1 Ch 97.
13 *Domb v Isoz* [1980] Ch 548.
14 *Rossiter v Miller* (1878) 3 App Cas 1124.

third possible purpose of the stipulation is that the parties, having agreed on essentials, look to the formal document for the solution of points of detail which may be quite important, such as the delivery dates, precise technical specifications and terms of payment. At a time of increasing complexity in contractual relations, it is this third purpose which gives rise to the greatest difficulties and as to which the authorities, as yet, provide the least guidance. Probably there are two factors on which the existence of a contract in these cases primarily depends, namely, the degree of importance of the terms left to be settled by the formal agreement, and the extent to which the parties have acted on the informal agreement.

12 CONDITIONAL AGREEMENTS

The expression 'condition' is used in the law of contract in a confusing variety of senses, some of which are discussed later in this book.[15] At this point, we are concerned with a condition in the sense of an event on which the operation of the contract depends, but which neither party is bound to bring about. For example, a person may agree to buy a machine on condition that it proves, on trial, to have a stated capacity; or to buy a house on condition that he can raise a mortgage of a stated amount. In these cases the agreement is said to be subject to a *condition precedent*. The effect of such a condition depends on its construction. It may mean that, until the event occurs, neither party is bound at all, so that each party is free to withdraw from the transaction without legal liability.[16] A second, more common, interpretation would be that until the event occurred neither party was bound by the main agreement, but in the meantime he must not do anything to prevent the occurrence of the event: for example in the first case put above, neither must impede the trial of the machine.[17] It may even be that one party is bound to do his best to bring about the event without absolutely undertaking to do so: for example where goods are sold 'subject to export licence'. In such a case one of the parties (usually the exporter) will have to make reasonable efforts to obtain the licence; but if, in spite of his having done so, no licence is obtained, neither he nor the other party will be under any liability.[18] He will only be liable if the terms of the contract, on their true construction, amount to an absolute undertaking that a licence will be obtained.[19]

A contract may be subject to a *condition subsequent* , that is, it may come to an end when a future event occurs: for example, where a father contracts to pay his daughter an allowance 'until you marry'.

[15] See pp 273, 279, post.
[16] *Pym v Campbell* (1856) 6 E & B 370.
[17] *Mackay v Dick* (1881) 6 App Cas 251.
[18] *Re Anglo-Russian Merchant Traders* [1917] 2 K B 679.
[19] As in *Pagnan Sp A v Tradax Ocean Transportation SA* [1987] 3 All E R 565.

Chapter 3

Consideration

1 DEFINITION

Legal systems do not regard all agreements whatsoever as contracts. They use various devices for limiting the area of enforceable agreements: they may insist on the use of some formality, or on part performance, or on compliance with some other requirement. In English law, an agreement (even if made with the requisite contractual intention)[1], is not a contract unless it is *either* made under seal *or* supported by some 'consideration'.

The basic notion of consideration is that of *reciprocity* : that a promisee should not be able to enforce the promise, unless he has given (or promised to give), or unless the promisor has obtained (or been promised), something in exchange for it. This idea underlies the often repeated judicial definition that consideration is a benefit to the promisor, or a detriment to the promisee.[2] Only one limb of the definition needs to be satisfied: if there is a detriment to the promisee there is a contract, even though there is no benefit to the promisor; and conversely. In the great majority of cases the detriment to the promisee (eg parting with goods under a contract of sale) will also be the benefit to the promisor (ie receipt of the same goods).

Where the contract is bilateral, each party will both make and receive a promise. In such a case, it is the consideration *for each promise* that is under discussion: it is confusing and wrong to think of the consideration *for the contract.* Thus in the case of a contract for the sale of goods, the consideration for the buyer's promise to pay is the seller's promise to deliver the goods, or their actual delivery. This is a detriment to the seller, in that he will part with the goods; and for the purpose of the requirement of consideration, it is quite irrelevant whether he has sold the goods for more, or for less, than they are worth. The question whether he has suffered a detriment is, in other words, determined simply by looking at his performance, without regard to what he will receive in exchange when the buyer performs his promise to pay. Conversely, the consideration for the seller's promise

---

[1] See ch 4, post.
[2] Eg *Currie v Misa* (1875) LR 10 Exch 153, 162; *Midland Bank Trust Co Ltd v Green* [1981] AC 513 at 531.

to deliver is the buyer's promise to pay, or the payment of, the price. The detriment to the buyer is that he will part with his money: again, this is looked at in isolation, irrespective of the exchange which he receives for it.

2 GRATUITOUS AND ONEROUS PROMISES

The idea behind the doctrine of consideration being that of reciprocity, it follows that a gratuitous promise, such as a promise to make a gift to a charity for no return, is not supported by consideration. This does not mean that such a promise cannot be made legally enforceable. To produce this result, it is only necessary to make the promise under seal, a practice which is often adopted in any case, for tax reasons. Compliance with this requirement is now a simple matter, requiring the signature[3] of a document bearing the word 'seal' or some similar indication that it is intended to take effect as a deed under seal.[4] The 'delivery' of a deed to which reference is made in the phrase 'signed, sealed and delivered' merely means conduct indicating that the signer intends to be bound by the deed.[5] Thus it is only *informal* gratuitous promises which are not binding in English law, as a result of the doctrine of consideration. This fact should be stressed when comparing English law with other systems of law in which there is no doctrine of consideration, but in which gratuitous promises are nevertheless enforceable only if they are made in some special form, eg by a notarised writing.[6] The purpose of such requirements is to provide some safeguard against rash promises to make gifts.

The central idea of a gratuitous promise is easy enough to understand: it is a promise to make a gift, ie one to give or do something of value, for no return. To take the most obvious case, a promise by A to make a present of a car to B is a gratuitous promise; and so is a promise by A to lend B his car for one day without charge, or to give B a free lift from London to Edinburgh. If A goes back on any of these promises, B has in English law no right to damages for breach of contract. The position would be the same if A agreed to undertake the safe-keeping of B's car without reward, or agreed (again without reward) to arrange to insure B's car.[7] If in the first of these cases A withdrew his promise before the car had come into his possession, or if in the second he simply forgot to insure the car, he would not be under any liability to B for breach of contract.[8] But if, instead of simply

3 Law of Property Act 1925, s 73.
4 *First National Securities v Jones* [1978] Ch 109; contrast *TCB Ltd v Gray* [1986] Ch 621; affd on other grounds [1988] 1 All E R 108.
5 *Xenos v Wickham* (1866) L R 2 H L 296; *Vincent v Premo Enterprise Ltd* [1969] 2 Q B 609.
6 See, for example, s 518 of the German Civil Code.
7 *Argy Trading Development Co Ltd v Lapid Developments Ltd* [1977] 3 All E R 785.
8 *The Zephyr* [1985] 2 Lloyd's Rep 529 at 538.

doing nothing to fulfill the gratuitous promise, A starts to perform it and in the course of so doing negligently causes loss to B, he may be liable to B under the law of tort. This would, for example, be the position where A promised to look after B's car, actually received it and then negligently damaged it;[9] or where he caused loss to his friend B in the course of gratuitously rendering him some other service.[10] In one case A was even held liable for carelessly giving free advice to B in connection with the purchase of a second-hand car which turned out to be seriously defective.[11]

In all the above examples, it is assumed that B makes no counter-promise. If he does make such a counter-promise there is usually no difficulty in finding consideration for both promises. Thus if A promised to lend B his car for a week, without charge, and in return B promised to wash the car, there would be a good contract binding both parties.[12] That is, A would be contractually liable if he did not lend the car and B would similarly be liable if he did not wash it. One situation which gives rise to particular difficulty is that in which B's counter-promise is simply one not to complain of defects in A's performance: this is discussed below.[13]

3 BENEFIT AND DETRIMENT

The doctrine of consideration, however, does not prevent the enforcement of all informal promises which, on a commonsense view, are gratuitous; while, on the other hand, it has prevented the enforcement of many transactions which do not in any very obvious sense amount to gratuitous promises. The doctrine has from time to time served many different purposes, so that it is almost possible to regard it as a collection of separate doctrines. The courts have used it as a substitute for other, imperfectly developed, doctrines; they were able to do this because of the essential vagueness of the twin notions of 'benefit' and 'detriment'. They have sometimes taken the view that any 'benefit' or 'detriment' *which could be detected by the court* was sufficient consideration, even though the person suffering the alleged 'detriment' may not have regarded it as such, but rather as a benefit. In one case, for example, a young man was held to have provided consideration for his uncle's promise to pay him an allowance, by suffering the 'detriment' of marrying his fiancée.[14] This approach often makes it

9 *Coggs v Bernard* (1703) 2 Ld Raym 909; *Mitchell v Ealing London Borough* [1979] QB 1.
10 *Wilkinson v Coverdale* (1793) 1 Esp 74.
11 *Chaudhry v Prabhakar* [1988] 3 All ER 718.
12 Cf *Bainbridge v Firmstone* (1838) 8 Ad & El 743.
13 See p 32, post.
14 *Shadwell v Shadwell* (1860) 9 CBNS 159.

possible for the courts to 'find' or invent a consideration for a promise which would strike a layman as gratuitous. On the other hand, the courts have sometimes held that acts or promises, which are in fact benefits or detriments, should not be regarded as such in law, simply because the thing done or promised *was already legally due*. For example, the general rule (to be further discussed below) is that part payment of a debt is no consideration for a promise by the creditor to forgo the balance. These different shades in the meaning of 'benefit' and 'detriment' make a comprehensive definition of 'consideration' impossible. The precise meaning, or meanings, of the term can be gathered only from a survey of the many varying situations in which it has been applied.

Promises which are not supported by consideration do not give rise to full contractual liability but may nevertheless have certain limited legal effects. The point has already been illustrated in our discussion of liability for gratuitous services;[15] and in other cases to be discussed later in this chapter the law provides remedies against a person who goes back on a promise, even though it was not supported by consideration.[16] But such promises are not *binding as contracts*; so that the remedies for their breach are generally less advantageous to the promisee than those available in respect of promises which are supported by consideration.[17]

4 IRRELEVANCE OF ADEQUACY OF CONSIDERATION; NOMINAL CONSIDERATION

Although there must be some consideration for a promise, it is well settled that 'the law will not enter into an enquiry as to the adequacy of the consideration'.[18] The doctrine of consideration is not concerned with the question whether the bargain which the parties have made is particularly favourable to one of them, and consequently unfavourable to the other. One striking result of this rule is the device of nominal consideration. An agreement by which A promises to pay B £1,000 in exchange for a peppercorn, or to convey a house in exchange for £1, does not suffer from want of consideration. This device provides a second way (in addition to the promise under seal) in which a gratuitous promise can be made legally binding. It makes no difference that the thing received by way of nominal consideration is of no actual use to the recipient. In one case,[19] chocolate manufacturers sold

---

15 See pp 26–27, ante.
16 See pp 41–43, 47–49, post.
17 See pp 43, 49, post.
18 *Westlake v Adams* (1858) 5 C B N S 248 at 265; *Midland Bank Trust Co Ltd v Green* [1981] A C 513.
19 *Chappell & Co Ltd v Nestlé Co Ltd* [1960] A C 87.

gramophone records for a sum of money, plus three wrappers of their bars of chocolate. It was held that the wrappers formed part of the consideration (and there seems to be no doubt that, in legal theory, they could have formed the whole consideration) even though they were simply thrown away. However, if it is clear that one party's performance cannot have any value at all, there would be no consideration: for example, if A agreed to pay B £100 for the contents of B's cellar, which was known by both to be empty. The position would be different if there was a chance, however slight, of the cellar containing something.

These general rules are well established, but it is obvious that courts cannot be insensitive to the problems raised by unequal bargains; so that the general rules are subject to a number of exceptions, to be discussed later in this book.[20] In none of these exceptional cases, however, is a promise held to be invalid *merely* because inadequate value has been given for it: some other factor must be established, such as a relationship enabling one party to take unfair advantage of the other.

Conversely, the courts sometimes feel that promises which are truly gratuitous do not deserve the same degree of enforcement as those for which substantial value has been given. For this reason, equity refuses to aid a 'volunteer,' ie a person who has given no *substantial* consideration for a promise; this rule applies even though the promise is under seal or supported by nominal consideration and so binding at common law.[1] The fact that adequate value is not given for a promise may also operate to the prejudice of third parties such as the creditors of the promisor or his dependants. The interests of such persons are protected by special statutory rules.[2]

Although a nominal consideration will suffice at law, there are cases in which the act or forbearance, promised or performed, is of such a trifling character that it becomes doubtful whether it can be regarded as consideration at all. It has, for example, been held that a son did not provide consideration for his father's promise not to enforce a debt, by promising not to bore his father with complaints.[3] It is, moreover, 'no consideration to refrain from a course of action which it was never intended to pursue':[4] eg where a promise to pay £100 is made to a confirmed teetotaller if he will abstain from alcohol for a week. The reason for this rule is, however, not to be found in the trifling value of the consideration, but in the requirement that it must be given in exchange for the promise.

---

[20] See pp 144–151, 168, 353.
[1] *Jefferys v Jefferys* (1841) Cr & Ph 138.
[2] Eg Inheritance (Provision for Family and Dependants) Act 1975 ss 10, 11; Insolvency Act 1986 ss 238, 339, 423.
[3] *White v Bluett* (1853) 23 LJ Ex 36.
[4] *Arrale v Costain Civil Engineering Ltd* [1976] 1 Lloyd's Rep 98 at 106.

5 PAST CONSIDERATION IS INSUFFICIENT

This last requirement also explains the general rule that 'past consideration' is no consideration. This means that an act done *before* the promise was made cannot normally be the consideration for it.[5] Consideration is, for example, past where, after an employee has retired, his employer promises to pay him a sum of money in recognition of his past services.[6] The same is true where goods are sold and at some later time the seller gives a guarantee as to their quality.[7] But there is obviously some elasticity in the notion of past consideration. If the promise and the previous act are substantially one transaction, the consideration is not past merely because there is a (relatively short) interval of time between them. There is quite commonly such an interval in the ordinary case, in which a buyer of goods claims the benefit of a manufacturer's guarantee. Although some days may elapse between the original purchase and the giving of the guarantee, it is not thought that the consideration for such a guarantee would be regarded as past.

An act may be done for which no recompense is fixed beforehand, or at the time when it was done. A subsequent promise to pay for the act is binding if the act was done at the request of the promisor, if the understanding of the parties was that the act was to be paid for, and if a promise to pay for it would, had it been made in advance, have been legally enforceable.[8] The rule covers the common case in which services are rendered on a commercial basis, but the rate of remuneration is only agreed after they have been rendered. On the same principle, a past *promise* made at the request of one party can constitute consideration for a counter-promise later made by that party.[9]

By way of exception to the rule that consideration must not be past, an 'antecedent debt or liability' is good consideration for a bill of exchange;[10] and a promise by an adult to perform an obligation contracted by him during minority is enforceable.[11] Moreover, a debtor who makes a written acknowledgement of a debt may thereby extend the period of limitation during which the debt can be sued for,[12] provided that, when the acknowledgement was made, that period had not already expired.[13]

---

[5] *Eastwood v Kenyon* (1840) 11 Ad & El 438.
[6] Cf *Simpson v John Reynolds* [1975] 2 All ER 88.
[7] *Roscorla v Thomas* (1842) 3 QB 234.
[8] *Re Casey's Patents* [1892] 1 Ch 104 at 115–116.
[9] *Pao On v Lau Yiu Long* [1980] AC 614.
[10] Bills of Exchange Act 1882, s 27(1)(b).
[11] Post, p 193.
[12] Limitation Act 1980, ss 29(5), 30(1).
[13] Ibid s 29(7).

6 CONSIDERATION MUST MOVE FROM THE PROMISEE

The rule that consideration must 'move from the promisee'[14] means that a person cannot enforce a promise (though made to him) if the consideration for it moved wholly from some other person. If, for example, A promised B to pay £1000 to B if C did the same, B could not enforce A's promise, since the only possible consideration for it moved from C. But it is not necessary for B to provide the whole consideration, and it should also be stressed that B may provide consideration by procuring C to do an act in favour of A. Thus, a promise by A to B to pay B a commission of 5 per cent on any loan which B might persuade C to make to A, would not suffer from lack of consideration.

Although consideration must move from the promisee, it is equally well settled that it need not move to the promisor. The 'benefit' of which the consideration consists may equally well be conferred on a third party. A common example is provided by the case of goods bought from a shop and paid for by use of a cheque-card or credit-card. In such a case the issuer of the card makes a promise to the shopkeeper that the cheque will be honoured or that the shopkeeper will be paid; and the shopkeeper provides consideration for this promise by delivering the goods to the customer.[15]

7 MUTUAL PROMISES AS CONSIDERATION

There is no doubt that mutual promises can be, and generally are, consideration for each other: eg where A and B agree today on a sale of goods, to be delivered and paid for tomorrow. Writers have had considerable difficulty in explaining this rule. Obviously, it will not do to say that each party suffers a detriment because he is bound by his own promise, for this presupposes the conclusion which it is sought to prove, viz the binding force of each promise. Probably the explanation is a simpler one: the making of a promise in fact (and quite apart from legal enforceability) generates a commercial pressure for its performance; and similarly, its receipt generates a commercial expectation that performance will be rendered. This pressure and this expectation are the detriment and benefit by virtue of which one promise can be said to be consideration for another. It is, however, not the case that all mutual promises are consideration for each other. Three qualifications must be made.

First, a promise is only consideration if the thing promised would, if

14 *Thomas v Thomas* (1842) 2 QB 851 at 859.
15 See *R v Lambie* [1982] AC 449; *Re Charge Card Services Ltd* [1987] Ch 150; affd [1988] 3 All ER 702.

performed, itself amount to consideration. For example, a debtor's promise to pay part of a debt already due would not be consideration for a promise by the creditor to release the balance, since (as we shall see)[16] the actual part payment would not be consideration for such a promise.

Secondly, a promise to accept a gift is not consideration for a promise to make it. Just as the receipt of £100 cannot be regarded as a detriment, so the promise to accept the money cannot be so regarded. Of course, the position is different if burdens are attached to the subject-matter of the gift and the donee promises to discharge them. Thus, a promise to accept a gift of a leasehold house and to perform the donor's obligations (eg to pay rent and to do repairs) is good consideration for the promise to make the gift.[17] A further complication arises if a person to whom a gift is promised makes a counter-promise not to complain, or sue, in respect of defects in the gift. Here again, it seems at first sight obvious that the counter-promise is no consideration: it is ridiculous to suppose that a promise to give someone a horse could be made binding by a counter-promise not to look the horse in the mouth. But, if performance of the promise has begun, and brought the parties into a relationship in which defective performance would normally give rise to legal liability to the 'donee', a promise by him not to enforce that liability could perfectly well amount to consideration. This would be the position where A promised to give B a free ride and B promised not to sue A for negligence in the performance of A's promise. There could be a contract, at least once A had begun to perform his promise.[18]

Thirdly, a promise is no consideration for a counter-promise if the former promise is freely revocable at the will of the person making it. This would be the position where a person promised to do something if he felt like it, or unless he cancelled the promise.[19] Such obviously illusory promises are not in practice bargained for, nor do they give rise to any legal difficulty; but more subtle variants do occur and give rise to problems. For example, A may promise to buy from B 'all the coal I require for my works'. Here, if A requires nothing, he is not bound to buy anything, but it is generally held that his promise is nevertheless a real one and so provides consideration for B's promise to supply any coal ordered. As A has promised to buy *all* his requirements from B, he is not at liberty to buy from anyone else and this restriction is a sufficient detriment.

---

[16] See p 41, post.
[17] *Price v Jenkins* (1877) 5 Ch D 619.
[18] *Gore v Van der Lann* [1967] 2 QB 31; and see next note.
[19] See p 92, post, for possible limitations on the effectiveness of certain provisions of this kind.

A further difficulty, which arises where mutual promises are alleged to constitute consideration for each other, is that one of them may not be binding under some rule of law: for example because it was procured by fraud, or because the party giving it lacked contractual capacity, or because the promise was illegal. At first sight it might seem logical to say that a promise which was not binding on a party for such a reason therefore could not be consideration for the counter-promise. Some cases adopt this reasoning. Thus if A promises B a pension in return for B's promise not to compete with him, A can escape liability by showing that B's promise is illegal under the rules relating to restraint of trade.[20] Here B's promise is invalid in the public interest; but where it is invalid in the interest of B or of a class to which he belongs, it is generally held that this invalidity does not prevent it from constituting good consideration for A's counter-promise. Thus, if B is not bound because he is under age and so lacks contractual capacity, A is nevertheless bound, ie B's promise, though it does not bind B, is good consideration for A's promise.[1] A further possibility arises where B has the legal option of declaring his promise binding or not: for example, where A, by fraud, induces B to enter into a contract with him. Here, if B elects to treat his promise as not binding, the whole contract is at an end.[2] But if B wishes to enforce A's promise, he is entitled to do so: by affirming the contract, he makes his own promise binding and so supplies consideration for A's promise. The same result will often follow where the party who is not bound actually performs his promise.[3] But this last rule does not apply where the contract is illegal. Thus, in the restraint of trade case put above,[4] the actual performance by B of his promise not to compete does not (any more than the giving of the promise) enable B to enforce A's promise to pay him a pension; for the law must not give the party making the illegal promise any incentive to perform it. The rules stated in this paragraph cannot be logically deduced from the doctrine of consideration. They are based rather on the different policy grounds which, in each of the situations discussed, invalidate one of a pair of mutual promises.

Although mutual promises are sufficient to constitute consideration, they are not necessary. Thus, in the case of a unilateral contract, performance of the requested act, or forbearance, can constitute consideration even though nothing was promised. Probably this is so even where the required performance has only been begun but not completed: this would seem to be a sufficient 'detriment' to satisfy the requirement of consideration.

---

20 *Wyatt v Kreglinger and Fernau* [1933] 1 K B 793; p 169, post.

1 *Holt v Ward Clarencieux* (1732) 2 Stra 937.

2 See p 136 et seq, post.

3 *Fishmonger's Co v Robertson* (1843) 5 Man & G 131.

4 See note 20 above.

8 COMPROMISES AND FORBEARANCES

If a person who has a legal claim against another promises not to
enforce it, there is in general no difficulty in seeing that he thereby
provides consideration for a counter-promise by the other party. For
example, if A is owed £100 by B payable to-day, A's promise not to
enforce the debt would be good consideration for B's promise to give
security for it. Similarly, if A had been injured in a motor accident by
B's negligence, A's promise not to sue B would be good consideration
for B's promise to pay £5,000 by way of compensation. In these cases,
A suffers a detriment by giving up a legal right and B gains a corresponding benefit.[5] But two further cases of this kind give rise to more
difficulty.

a Cases in which there is no promise to forbear

The person who forbears may not make any promise at all, but simply
forbear in fact. The question whether such actual forbearance amounts
to consideration appears to depend, in the first place, on the nature of
the claim forborne. In one case[6] a bank was owed £22,000 by one of its
customers and pressed him to give security. He promised to do so and
it was held that the bank had provided consideration for the promise by
forbearing to enforce the claim, even though it had not made any
promise to forbear. Here the claim was such that the bank would
almost certainly have taken steps to enforce it if the customer had not
made his promise. It was therefore quite obvious that the bank's forbearance was induced by that promise. In another case,[7] a seller of land
promised to pay certain sums of money to his dissatisfied buyer, who
later argued that he had provided consideration for the seller's promise
by forbearing to take proceedings to rescind the sale. The argument
was rejected because it was not shown that the buyer ever intended to
take such proceedings; and it was said that there was nothing (ie no
promise by the buyer) to bind him not to do so. The claim to rescind
was not such that the buyer would clearly have pursued it; nor was it
clear that his forbearance to do so was induced by the seller's promise.
In other words, the stronger the claim, the more likely it is that actual
forbearance (without a promise to forbear) will be consideration for a
promise made by the person liable to the claim.

The need to establish a causal connection between the forbearance
and the promise also accounts for the further rule, that the forbear-

[5] Cf *Centrovincial Estates plc v Merchant Investors Assurance Co Ltd* [1983] Com LR 158.
[6] *Alliance Bank v Broom* (1864) 2 Drew & Sm 289.
[7] *Miles v New Zealand Alford Estate Co* (1886) 32 Ch D 266.

ance must occur at the express or implied request of the promisor. Hence the mere fact that B owes a debt to A which A might have, but has not, enforced, is not sufficient to provide consideration for a promise made by B to A.[8] In technical language, the antecedent debt is past consideration, unless A's forbearance to enforce it was induced by B's promise.

b Doubtful and invalid claims

The claim which A gives up in exchange for B's promise may not, in fact or in law, be a good one. If A sued, he would therefore lose his action and have to pay costs, so that it can be argued that he suffers no detriment, but on the contrary gains a benefit, by his forbearance. Nevertheless the forbearance can be good consideration not only where A's claim is good, but also where it is doubtful in law and even where it is clearly bad in law.[9] For this rule to apply, there must be reasonable grounds for the claim; A must honestly believe that it has a fair chance of success; he must seriously intend to prosecute the claim; and he must not conceal from B any facts which would exonerate B.[10] The definition of the precise detriment to A, or of the benefit to B, in cases in which A's claim is clearly bad in law is a matter of very great theoretical difficulty. But the actual rule is well established and its existence is no doubt due to the desire of the courts to encourage reasonable compromises. It does not apply where A's claim is known to be bad. If A alone knows this, he is guilty of a kind of dishonesty which the law would obviously not want to encourage. But the position is sometimes the same even if A's knowledge is shared by B: thus, a 'compromise' of a gambling debt would not be enforced.[11]

9 EXISTING DUTIES AS CONSIDERATION

One of the most troublesome problems in the law of contract is whether a person can provide consideration by performing, or promising to perform, a pre-existing legal duty. In one sense, such a person suffers no detriment as he is already bound to render the performance in question; but he may find it economically expedient to break the duty and pay damages unless he has the benefit of some additional promise. Correspondingly, the person making that additional promise may benefit from the performance of the original duty; for the damages legally recoverable for its breach will not always compensate him fully

[8] *Wigan v English and Scottish Law Life Assurance Association* [1909] 1 Ch 291.
[9] *Callisher v Bischoffsheim* (1870) LR 5 QB 449.
[10] *Cook v Wright* (1861) 1 B & S 559 at 569; *Miles v New Zealand Alford Estate Co* (1886) 32 Ch D 266 at 284; *The Proodos C* [1980] 2 Lloyd's Rep 390 at 392.
[11] *Hyams v Coombs* (1912) 28 TLR 413.

for the loss which the breach would actually cause.[12] On the other hand, it may sometimes be undesirable to enforce promises made to secure the performance of a pre-existing legal duty. Such a state of the law might encourage the person under the duty to refuse to perform it unless some added inducement were held out to him, and so lead to results that were contrary to public policy.

a Public duty

This last argument is particularly strong where the pre-existing duty is one imposed by the general law. It is obvious that a person should not be held to provide consideration by merely forbearing to commit a breach of the criminal law;[13] and that a public officer should not be able to enforce a promise to pay him money for doing nothing more than his public duty.[14] On the other hand, if such an officer is induced by the promise to do more than his public duty he can enforce the promise. Thus, if a person promises to pay the police for affording to him or to his property a greater degree of protection than they reasonably think necessary, the promise is not invalid for lack of consideration.[15] By statute, a person is liable to pay for 'special police services' provided at his 'request'.[16] Such a request may be implied where a person organises an event which cannot safely take place without such special services: for this reason a football club has been held liable for the cost of policing matches held on its ground.[17]

Even a promise to do no more than the public duty may be enforceable. Thus in a number of cases, police officers have recovered rewards advertised for information leading to the capture of criminals, even though they were legally bound to transmit or act upon such information once they acquired it.[18] The tendency of such promises was to promote the administration of justice by encouraging extra effort, rather than to lead to the corruption of public officers. Although some of the older authorities can be cited in favour of the view that the performance of, or promise to perform, a duty imposed by law is no consideration for a counter-promise, the modern view is that the counter-promise is enforceable, unless there are grounds of public policy against its enforcement.[19]

---

[12] See p 333 et seq, post.
[13] *Brown v Brine* (1875) 1 Ex D 5.
[14] *Morgan v Palmer* (1824) 2 B & C 729 at 736.
[15] *Glasbrook Bros Ltd v Glamorgan County Council* [1925] A C 270.
[16] Police Act 1964 s 15.
[17] *Harris v Sheffield United Football Club Ltd* [1988] Q B 77.
[18] *Eg England v Davidson* (1840) 11 Ad & El 856.
[19] *Ward v Byham* [1956] 2 All ER 318.

b Duty imposed by contract with a third party

Where the pre-existing duty is imposed, not by law, but by an earlier contract, a distinction is drawn between two situations. In the first, the duty is imposed on the promisee by an earlier contract between him and the promisor; in the second that duty is imposed by an earlier contract between the promisee and a third party. As the law relating to the latter situation is relatively the more certain, it will be convenient to begin the discussion with cases of this kind.

Most authorities support the view that the performance of a contractual duty owed by A to B can be good consideration for a promise made by C to A.[20] Thus, in one case,[1] A (a stevedore) had contracted with B (a shipowner) to unload goods from B's ship. Some of the goods belonged to C who promised A not to make any claim against him if he damaged the goods while unloading them. It was held that A had provided consideration for this promise by unloading the goods even though this was something that he was already bound to do under his contract with B. Similarly, B may contract to do building work for C, and C may promise A (one of B's workmen) that he will pay him a bonus on completion of the work. This promise would be binding, even though A was already bound by his contract with B to work on the site. Again, A may be indebted to B, a company in which C is a substantial shareholder. If C made a promise to A in consideration of A's paying off the debt to B, C's promise to A would again be binding, in spite of the fact that A was only performing his contractual duty to B. In all these cases it might be argued that A suffered no detriment, as he did no more than he was already bound to do under his contract with B; but the performance of the duty is in fact a benefit to C, and this is sufficient to make C's promise binding. Where performance of the duty owed to the third party would be consideration, the promise to perform it has the same effect. Thus, in the last example, A's promise to perform his contract with the company (B), no less than its actual performance, would constitute consideration for C's promise to A.[2]

In all the above cases, A's performance of the duty imposed on him by his contract with B (or his promise to perform it) does constitute a real benefit to C. It is, however, necessary to guard against the danger that A may bring undue pressure to bear on C: for example, where the workman A tells the site-owner C that he will refuse to perform his contract with B unless C pays him a bonus. Such conduct may fall within the now expanding concept of duress.[3] If so, C's promise can

20 See *Shadwell v Shadwell* (1860) 9 CBNS 159, criticised on other grounds in *Jones v Padavatton* [1969] 1 WLR 328 at 333.
1 *The Eurymedon* [1975] A C 154.
2 *Pao On v Lau Yiu Long* [1980] A C 614.
3 See pp 147–148, post.

be avoided on that ground; but if there is in fact no duress the doctrine of consideration, which was formerly used to protect C against such forms of pressure, no longer presents any bar to the enforceability of the promise.

c Rescission or modification of contract between original parties

It commonly happens that parties who have entered into a contract subsequently agree to alter the terms of the contract, or even to abandon it altogether. In many cases such subsequent agreements give rise to no problems of consideration. Suppose that A on 1 May agrees to sell a car to B for £5,000, delivery and payment to take place on 1 June. If subsequently the parties agree to postpone delivery and payment until 1 July, there is no difficulty in finding consideration for the new promises. A suffers a detriment, in that he gets the money later, but gets a benefit in that he keeps the car for the extra time; and B gets a corresponding benefit and suffers a corresponding detriment. Moreover, as the law takes no account of adequacy of consideration, exactly the same arguments would apply if payment were postponed until 2 June and delivery until 1 July. It is assumed in the above cases that the variation is in fact made to secure some benefit (however small) for each party. If, though capable of benefiting both, it is in fact made for the benefit of one, it has been held that there is no consideration for the variation.[4] This would be the position where the place at which a loan is to be repaid was altered at the request, and for the sole convenience, of the debtor. Similarly, there is no consideration for a buyer's promise to accept late delivery of goods (even though the price is only payable on delivery), if the promise was made solely to accommodate the seller.[5]

Even where there is no consideration of the kind so far discussed, the variation can sometimes be enforced as a separate contract, collateral to the main transaction. Thus in one case[6] the owners of a block of flats had agreed to sell long leases of the flats to tenants. These leases required the tenants to contribute to the cost of roof repairs, but during the negotiations the owners had promised to repair certain existing defects in the roof 'at our own cost'. This promise was held binding as a collateral contract for which the tenants had provided consideration by executing the formal documents in which the leases were embodied.

Where contracting parties agree wholly to abandon the original contract, or, in technical language, to 'rescind' it, each of them suffers a detriment in not getting what he bargained for, and gains a benefit in not having to perform what he promised. This reasoning would apply

---

4 *Vanbergen v St Edmund's Properties Ltd* [1933] 2 K B 223.
5 *Charles Rickards Ltd v Oppenhaim* [1950] 1 K B 616.
6 *Brikom Investments Ltd v Carr* [1979] Q B 467.

even though the contract had been partly performed, so long as each party was still under some obligation and promised to give up rights under the contract:[7] each of them can then be said to give up and to obtain something, by way of consideration for the promise to release him.

Difficulties begin to arise where a 'rescission' occurs after one party has completely performed (so that only the other is released). Suppose that after a seller has delivered, but before the buyer has paid, the parties agree that nothing more is to be done under the contract. This looks like a promise to make a gift of the price to the buyer, and such a promise to renounce an accrued debt is not binding. To this rule there is an exception: if the holder of a bill of exchange or promissory note, after its maturity, unconditionally and in writing renounces his rights against any person liable on it, such person is discharged.[8] Thus in the case put, the seller could take a bill of exchange or promissory note in payment, and renounce it: in this way it is possible to evade the rule that a release without consideration is of no effect.

Further problems arise where the variation affects the obligation of only one of the parties: eg where a contract to sell a car is varied by an agreement to raise the price to £6,000 or to lower it to £4,000. In such cases, it is hard to find any consideration either for the buyer's promise to pay more or for the seller's promise to accept less, since the variation is capable of benefiting one party only (ie the seller in the first and the buyer in the second case). This difficulty about consideration is in principle the same whether the effect of such a one-sided variation is to increase or to reduce the obligation of one party (the buyer) while that of the other (the seller) remains constant. But for technical reasons the two situations require separate discussion.

d Variations increasing one party's obligation

Where the effect of the variation is simply to increase the obligation of one party, the orthodox view is that there is no consideration for the variation. This position was first established in a case[9] in which sailors, who had signed on for a voyage at a fixed rate of pay, were then promised extra pay for completing it. In a sense they suffered no detriment, as they merely did what they were legally bound to do; and the captain who made the promise got no benefit, since he was already legally entitled to their services. In fact, however, it is arguable that the captain did benefit, since he got the sailors' actual services, which were almost certainly worth more than the legal right to obtain them. It should be stressed that the orthodox view only strikes down the

---

[7] *Collin v Duke of Westminster* [1985] QB 581 at 598.
[8] Bills of Exchange Act 1882, s 62.
[9] *Stilk v Myrick* (1809) 2 Camp 317, 6 Esp 129.

variation where it is solely for the benefit of one party. If the party prin-
cipally benefited (ie, in the above case, the sailors) undertakes any
additional obligation, the requirement of consideration is satisfied.[10]
This is so, however small the additional obligation may be, for the law
will not investigate the adequacy of consideration.

A promise to pay increased wages to an employee will not suffer
from want of consideration in cases of short-term employment. In such
cases the employee is only obliged to work for the period of notice
required to determine the contract, and so he provides consideration
for the employer's promise by staying at work thereafter. Even a long-
term contract may be expressly or by implication made at the 'going
rate' of pay, whatever it may be from time to time;[10a] and in such a case
a promise to increase the rate of pay for part of the period would not
suffer from lack of consideration.

The principles stated above are not confined to contracts of
employment: they may equally apply where a building contractor
refuses to complete the agreed work unless he is promised extra pay, or
where a seller refuses to deliver unless he is promised a higher price. In
all cases of this kind, there is some danger that the variation may have
been obtained by improper pressure;[11] though it could equally well be a
perfectly reasonable arrangement, made to take account of changes in
the positions of the parties or of economic circumstances. The danger
of improper pressure may, moreover, exist even where the person to
whom the new promise is made has undertaken some small additional
obligation and so satisfied the technical requirement of consideration.
The importance of the doctrine of consideration in cases of this kind is
much reduced now that protection against improper pressure is more
satisfactorily provided by the expanding law of duress.[12]

e Variations reducing one party's obligation

A variation may simply reduce the obligation of one party: for
example, where a landlord promises to relieve his tenant from obligations to repair imposed by the lease; where a buyer, purely for the convenience of the seller, promises to accept delivery at a time later than
that agreed; or (in practice the most important case) where a creditor
agrees to accept part payment of a debt in full settlement. In all these
cases, the starting principle is that there is no consideration for the
variation, unless the party whose obligation is reduced also does, or
promises, something which he was not by the original contract bound
to do. Suppose, for example, that A is owed £100 by B and promises

10 *The Atlantic Baron* [1979] QB 705.
10a Cf *Lombard Tricity Finance Ltd v Paton* (1988) Times, 31 October (increase in
    interest rates made by lender).
11 Cf *B & S Contracts and Design Ltd v Victor Green Publications Ltd* [1984] ICR 419.
12 See *The Universe Sentinel* [1982] ICR 262 and p 147, post.

to accept £75 in full settlement. B duly pays the £75, but according to the decision of the House of Lords in *Foakes v Beer*,[13] A is nevertheless entitled to recover the remaining £25 from B. There is no consideration for A's promise to accept the £75 in full settlement since (it is said) B is already bound to pay A £100. Hence B suffers no detriment by paying less; and, since A is already entitled to £100 from B, he gains no benefit by receiving less. But such reasoning often ignores commercial realities. Part payment from a debtor who is in difficulties is in fact a benefit to the creditor; and the law has recognised this by imposing considerable limitations on the principle that a variation which simply reduces the obligation of one party is not legally binding. Many of these limitations apply specifically to promises to accept part payment of a debt in full settlement but one of them is of a more general character. We shall first consider this general limitation, which is commonly (if not very accurately) referred to as the doctrine of 'promissory estoppel', and then revert to the special rules relating to part payment of a debt.

10 PROMISSORY ESTOPPEL

This doctrine applies where one party to a contract by words or conduct makes a clear and unequivocal[14] promise or representation which leads the other party 'to suppose that the strict rights arising under the contract will not be enforced, or will be kept in suspense or held in abeyance'.[15] Its effect is that 'the person who otherwise might have enforced those rights will not be allowed to enforce them where it would be inequitable having regard to the dealings which have thus taken place between the parties'.[16] Under the doctrine of promissory estoppel, certain limited effects are given to promises without consideration. But there are several crucial differences between the legal effects of such a promise under that doctrine and the effects of a variation which is contractually binding because it is supported by consideration.

The first is that a variation alters the relations of the parties once for all; but, in general, promissory estoppel only *suspends*[17] the obligations of one of the parties. For example, a landlord who has promised not to enforce his tenant's obligation to repair cannot then turn round and peremptorily forfeit the lease because the tenant has not repaired; but

---

13 (1884) 9 App Cas 605.
14 See *The Scaptrade* [1983] 1 All E R 301; affd without reference to this point [1983] 2 A C 694; mere inactivity will not suffice, being at most equivocal: *The Leonidas D* [1985] 2 All E R 796 at 805.
15 *Hughes v Metropolitan Rly Co* (1877) 2 App Cas 439 at 448.
16 Ibid.
17 *Tool Metal Manufacturing Co Ltd v Tungsten Electric Co Ltd* [1955] 2 All E R 657.

he can reinstate the former contractual position by calling on the tenant to repair within a reasonable time, unless subsequent events make it impossible (or highly inequitable) to compel the tenant, as it were, to catch up on his original obligation.[18]

Secondly, the principle of promissory estoppel only applies when it would be 'inequitable' for the promisor to go back on his promise without due notice. The notion of what is 'inequitable' cannot be defined with anything approaching precision; but the basic idea is that the promisee must have acted in reliance on the promise so that he cannot be returned to the position in which he was before he acted in this way.[19] For example, he must have continued his attempts to perform the contract (as in the case of the seller who continues to make efforts to perform, in reliance on the buyer's promise that late delivery will be accepted); or he must have refrained from taking steps to safeguard his position (as in the case of the tenant neglecting to repair, in reliance on his landlord's promise that performance of the obligation to repair would not be enforced). Even where there has been such reliance, outside events may justify the promisor in going back on his promise; for example, retraction of a creditor's promise not to insist on punctual payment of a debt, may be justified by the fact that a third party is about to levy execution on the property which formed the security for the debt.[20] Nor will it be inequitable for the promisor to go back on his promise if he does so promptly, so that it remains possible to restore the promisee to the position in which he was before the promise was made.[1]

In English law the effect of the doctrine of promissory estoppel is also limited in another way. The doctrine prevents a party from asserting rights which he has under an existing contract; but the general view is that it does not operate so as to create entirely new rights.[2] Suppose, for example, that A promises B to pay any expenses which B may incur on a trip to Paris and B then incurs such expenses. B has no rights against A under the doctrine of promissory estoppel; and he will not be able to enforce A's promise, unless he can show that he provided consideration for it by going to Paris. Reliance on the doctrine of promissory estoppel in this situation would lead, not to the suspension of any right which A has against B, but to the creation of an entirely new right against A; and the doctrine of promissory estoppel does not

---

18 See *Ogilvy v Hope-Davies* [1976] 1 All E R 683 at 696; *The Ion* [1980] 2 Lloyd's Rep 245 at 251.

19 *Maharaj v Chand* [1986] A C 898.

20 *Williams v Stern* (1879) 5 Q B D 409.

1 *The Post Chaser* [1981] 2 Lloyd's Rep 695.

2 *Combe v Combe* [1951] 2 K B 215; *Argy Trading Development Co Ltd v Lapid Developments Ltd* [1977] 1 W L R 444 at 456; *James v Heim Gallery (London) Ltd* (1980) 256 Estates Gazette 819 at 821; contrast dicta in *Re Wyvern Development Ltd* [1974] 1 W L R 1097 at 1104-5; *The Henrik Sif* [1982] 1 Lloyd's Rep 456 at 466.

have this effect. For this reason the doctrine does not apply where the sole effect of the variation of a contract is to increase the obligations of one of the parties, eg where a contractor is promised extra pay for work which he had previously undertaken to do. He would, if he claimed the extra pay, be seeking to enforce a new right rather than to rely on his client's promise as a defence to an action on a pre-existing obligation.

None of these limitations on the scope of the doctrine of promissory estoppel applies where the subsequent promise is supported by consideration and so takes effect as a contractually binding variation. In that case, the promisee can enforce the variation without showing that it would be 'inequitable' for the promisor to go back on it; the effect of the variation will be to alter rights of the promisor permanently and not merely to suspend them; and the variation can create entirely new rights. The doctrine of promissory estoppel may have reduced, but it has not eliminated, the practical importance of consideration for the modification of contracts.

11 ESTOPPEL BY CONVENTION

Promissory estoppel must be distinguished from so called estoppel by convention. This arises where the parties to a transaction act on an assumed state of facts, the assumption being either shared by them both or made by one and acquiesced in by the other.[3] Its effect is to preclude the parties from denying the assumed facts if it would be unjust to allow them (or one of them) to go back on the assumption.[3a] For example, in one case[4] the parties to a guarantee assumed that it covered loans made not only by the company to which the guarantee was given, but also by one of its subsidiaries. As the parties had acted on this assumption, it was held that the guarantor could not deny its truth. Estoppel by convention may thus prevent a party from denying that a promise *has been made*, while promissory estoppel is concerned with the *legal effects* of a promise, the existence of which is not in doubt, but which is not supported by consideration. In our guarantee case the promise described above was clearly supported by consideration[5] and thus binding: the only issue was whether it could be taken to have been made. Where the assumed promise would, if made, have been *unsupported* by consideration, both types of estoppel may operate in the same case; estoppel by convention to prevent a party from denying that he has made the promise, and promissory estoppel to determine its legal effects.

3 *Empresa Lineas Maritimas Argentinas v Oceanus Mutual Underwriting Association (Bermuda) Ltd* [1984] 2 Lloyd's Rep 517; *The August Leonhardt* [1985] 2 Lloyd's Rep 28.
3a *The Vistafjord* [1988] 2 Lloyd's Rep 343.
4 *Amalgamated Investment and Property Co Ltd v Texas Commerce International Bank* [1982] QB 84.
5 See p 31, ante.

12 PART PAYMENT OF A DEBT

The rule that a variation of a contract is not *prima facie* supported by consideration, if it simply reduces the obligations of one party, has caused most trouble in cases arising out of promises by a creditor to accept part payment of a debt in full settlement. Under the rule in *Foakes v Beer*,[6] a creditor who has made such a promise can nevertheless sue for the balance, but the courts have created many qualifications and exceptions to this rule, so as to bring the law more or less into harmony with commercial needs.

In the first place the rule only applies to 'liquidated' claims,[7] ie to claims for a fixed sum, such as the agreed price for goods or services. It does not apply to unliquidated claims such as claims for damages, or to claims for a reasonable price, where none is fixed by the contract or subsequently agreed. In such cases the claim is of uncertain value; and, even though the overwhelming probability may be that it is worth *more* than the agreed settlement figure, the bare possibility of its being worth *less* is sufficient to provide consideration. This is so, because the law does not generally concern itself with the adequacy of consideration. There is an intermediate possibility where the creditor has both a liquidated and an unliquidated claim: for example, a dismissed employee may have a liquidated claim for arrears of wages and an unliquidated claim for damages for wrongful dismissal. Here a promise by him to accept the accrued wages in full settlement of both his claims would not be supported by consideration since the employer would, in paying the wages, only be doing what he was already legally bound to do; and the payment could not be worth more than the wages plus damages.[8] Secondly, the rule does not apply if the claim is in good faith disputed:[9] again, this makes its value uncertain, so that any settlement of it by the parties will be upheld. Thirdly, the rule does not apply if the method of performance is varied so as to benefit the creditor in some way:[10] eg if he agrees to accept part payment in full settlement even a single day before the full sum is due. Fourthly, the debtor might provide consideration for the creditor's promise in some other way. He might, in addition to paying the smaller sum, transfer to the creditor some benefit in kind, such as 'a hawk, horse or robe':[11] this is sufficient since the thing given *may* be worth more than the balance of the debt. Alternatively, the debtor might give up some cross-claim against the creditor: thus a seller's promise to accept part

---

6 See p 41, ante.
7 *Wilkinson v Byers* (1834) 1 Ad & El 106.
8 Cf *Arrale v Costain Civil Engineering Ltd* [1976] 1 Lloyd's Rep 98.
9 *Cooper v Parker* (1855) 15 C B 822.
10 *Pinnel's Case* (1602) 5 Co Rep 117a.
11 Ibid.

of the price in full settlement would be binding if the buyer gave up a claim for damages in respect of defects in the subject-matter.[12] Fifthly, a promise to accept part payment in full settlement may amount to a binding collateral contract reducing the debtor's liability under the principal transaction.[13] Finally, such a promise is binding if it is made under seal, or if it is supported by a nominal consideration (other than one in money): eg if it is expressed to be made in consideration of the debtor's delivering a peppercorn.

The above exceptions to the general rule can fairly easily be reconciled with the traditional reasoning of the doctrine of consideration. Two further exceptions are well established but harder to reconcile with the orthodox doctrine. First, a creditor who has accepted part payment *from a third party* in full settlement cannot then sue the debtor for the balance.[14] Secondly, a debtor may enter into a composition agreement with several creditors, by which each of these creditors agrees with the others and with the debtor to accept part payment in full settlement. A creditor who accepts such part payment cannot later sue the debtor for the balance of the debt.[15] The simplest explanation for these rules may be that a creditor who sues for the balance attempts to break his contract with the third party, or with the other creditors participating in the composition agreement. The court will not assist him in such an attempt and may indeed be able to restrain it: eg by allowing the third party to intervene so as to obtain a stay of the creditor's action against the debtor for the balance.[16]

A final exception to the general rule in *Foakes v Beer* is more controversial. It arises under the doctrine of promissory estoppel. That doctrine stretches back well into the 19th century, and promises to accept part payment of a debt in full settlement were literally within the formulation of the doctrine. Yet no one had thought of applying that doctrine to such promises; on the contrary, the rule that such promises were not binding was settled by the House of Lords *after* the doctrine was first laid down in the terms quoted above.[17] But in the *High Trees* case[18] in 1947 a landlord had promised his tenant to accept half the agreed rent in full settlement, so long as war-time difficulties of subletting continued; and it was said that the landlord was bound by the promise under the doctrine of promissory estoppel. The application of the doctrine to cases of this kind was new law; and if it is good law, such promises have some legal effect even though they are not supported by

---

[12] Cf *Brikom Investments Ltd v Carr* [1979] QB 467.
[13] Ibid, see p 38, ante.
[14] *Hirachand Punamchand v Temple* [1911] 2 KB 330.
[15] *Boyd v Hind* (1857) 1 H & N 938.
[16] Cf *Snelling v John G Snelling Ltd* [1973] QB 87.
[17] See p 41, ante.
[18] *Central London Property Trust Ltd v High Trees House Ltd* [1947] KB 130.

consideration. The problem is, how to reconcile this view with the rule in *Foakes v Beer*, that a promise to accept part payment in full settlement is not binding.

Probably the best reconciliation is to say that a promise which gives rise to a promissory estoppel is not binding *as a variation* of the contract, but has a more limited effect. In the first place, it may only suspend the creditor's right and not extinguish it. Sometimes, indeed, suspension may be all that is intended: eg where a debt is payable in instalments and the creditor agrees to reduce the amount of those instalments to tide the debtor over temporary financial difficulties, without intending to reduce the total amount due.[19] But where the intention is permanently to extinguish part of the debt, that intention would clearly be defeated by allowing the creditor to claim the full amount after reasonable notice. In some cases, such a result could perhaps be avoided by relying on the principle that promissory estoppel can operate extinctively in those exceptional cases where events after the promise make it highly inequitable to allow the promisor, even after reasonable notice, to reassert his original rights.[20] This principle could apply to the part payment of a debt cases: eg where the debtor had, in reliance on the creditor's promise, entered into fresh and irrevocable financial commitments. On the other hand, the creditor would not be acting inequitably in going back on his promise after reasonable notice merely because the debtor had relied on the promise by making the part payment. If, for example, there were a sudden improvement in the debtor's financial position, it might be perfectly reasonable, and in accordance with commercial morality, for the creditor to claim the balance.

The creditor may also be justified in going back on his promise by reason of the debtor's conduct in obtaining it. No doubt a creditor is normally thought of as the stronger party to a contractual relationship; but it is equally possible for that position to be occupied by the debtor and for him to use undue pressure to extort from the creditor a promise to accept part payment in full settlement. This was for example said to be the position in the *D & C Builders*[1] case, in which a houseowner owed a sum of money for work done to a small firm of builders, who were in desperate need of money. He induced them to promise to accept part of that sum in full settlement by threatening that, if they did not give such a promise, he would pay them nothing. It was held that the builders could go back on their promise and sue for the balance.

The purpose of the rule in *Foakes v Beer* was precisely to protect the creditor from this kind of pressure. But unfortunately the rule was

19 Eg *Ajayi v RT Briscoe (Nigeria) Ltd* [1964] 3 All ER 556.
20 Ante pp 41–42.
1 [1966] 2 QB 617.

explained on the ground that there was no consideration for the creditor's promise; and this reasoning applied even where that promise formed part of a perfectly reasonable variation, perhaps reflecting a change in circumstances after the making of the original contract. The protective function of the rule is now more satisfactorily performed by the expanding concept of duress;[2] and the rule should be replaced by one which struck only at variations extorted by duress. Meanwhile, the doctrine of promissory estoppel should not prevent a creditor from going back on a promise obtained in this way. Where, however, the debtor's conduct falls short of duress, the doctrine of promissory estoppel should not be excluded merely because the court views the debtor's conduct with some disapproval: such a vague category of 'improper conduct' is not only unnecessary but also 'unhelpful because it would make the law uncertain'.[3]

13 PROPRIETARY ESTOPPEL

The doctrine of proprietary estoppel applies to many situations, with only one of which we are here concerned. This arises where an owner of property (usually land) makes a representation or promise to another person that the latter has, or will be granted, legal rights in or over the property, and the latter acts to his detriment in reliance on that representation or promise. The landowner may then be prevented from denying the existence of those rights, or even be compelled to grant them; and, because the rights in question concern property, the estoppel has come to be known as 'proprietary'. Under this doctrine, some legal effect may be given to a promise even though it is not binding as a contract: eg because it is not intended to have contractual effect, or because it is not supported by consideration.

Typical illustrations of proprietary estoppel are provided by family arrangements between father and son, to the effect that, if the son will build himself a house on land belonging to the father, then the father will give the land to the son,[4] or allow him to stay there for life.[5] Such promises cannot be revoked after the son has built the house. Similarly, a promise by A to allow B to live in his house may induce B to believe that B has a legal right to stay there; such a promise cannot be revoked after B has, in reliance on it, made improvements to the house.[6] In these cases, the landowner would be unjustly enriched if he could freely revoke the promise, for he would then have the land

[2] See pp 147–148, post.
[3] *Pao On v Lau Yiu Long* [1980] AC 614 at 634.
[4] *Dillwyn v Llewelyn* (1862) 4 De GF & J 517.
[5] *Inwards v Baker* [1965] 2 QB 29.
[6] *Hussey v Palmer* [1972] 3 All ER 744; *Eves v Eves* [1975] 3 All ER 768; *Pascoe v Turner* [1979] 1 WLR 431.

together with the improvements made by the promisee. But action in reliance by the promisee can give rise to a proprietary estoppel even though it does not result in any improvement of the promisor's land. In one case [7] a local authority represented to a landowner that he had a right of way across its land to the public highway. It was held that the authority could not go back on that promise after the landowner had sold part of his land and so left himself with no access to the highway except over the authority's land. On the other hand, the doctrine will not apply merely because one party has acted in reliance on a promise affecting property. The promise must relate to identifiable property: it is not enough for the promisee to render services to another in the expectation (induced by the promise) of receiving some indeterminate benefit under the latter's will.[8] It is, moreover, necessary for the promisee to believe that the promise gives rise to a *legal* right to the property,[9] and for that belief to be induced by the words or conduct of the other party.[10]

The exact effects of proprietary estoppel vary widely from case to case. Sometimes, the promisor is actually compelled to convey the land to the promisee;[11] sometimes he is bound to allow him to stay there for life;[12] sometimes he is simply bound to compensate the promisee for his expenditure.[13] The court has a wide discretion as to the remedy to be granted to the promisee. It takes into account not only the terms of the promise but also the conduct of the promisor. Thus in one case the court made an order for the conveyance of a house on which only £230 had been spent in reliance on the promise, and did so in part because of the promisor's 'ruthlessness'[14] in seeking to evict the promisee.

Proprietary estoppel resembles promissory estoppel in that the promise remains revocable until the promisee has acted on it[15] or even thereafter if the promisee can still be restored to the position in which he was before he acted on the promise. On the other hand there are also important differences between them. The first is that promissory estoppel is not, while proprietary estoppel is, restricted to promises affecting property. And secondly, promissory estoppel cannot create

---

[7] *Crabb v Arun District Council* [1976] Ch 179.

[8] *Layton v Martin* [1986] 2 F L R 227; contrast *Re Basham* [1987] 1 All E R 405, where the property was more clearly defined.

[9] *Coombes v Smith* [1986] 1 W L R 808.

[10] *A-G of Hong Kong v Humphreys Estate (Queen's Gardens) Ltd* [1987] A C 114.

[11] *Dillwyn v Llewelyn* (1862) 4 De GF & J 517; *Pascoe v Turner* [1979] 1 W L R 431.

[12] *Inwards v Baker* [1965] 2 Q B 29.

[13] *Dodsworth v Dodsworth* 228 Estates Gazette 1115.

[14] *Pascoe v Turner* [1979] 1 W L R 431 at 439; cf *Crabb v Arun District Council* [1976] Ch 179 at 199.

[15] *Pascoe v Turner* [1979] 1 W L R 431 at 439; before action in reliance, promisee was said to have only a licence at will.

new rights,[16] while proprietary estoppel clearly can do so:[17] for example, it can give the promisee the right to have land conveyed to him.

A promise which gives rise to a proprietary estoppel is nevertheless less advantageous to the promisee than one which is binding contractually. In cases of proprietary estoppel, the promise may be revocable; the remedy for its breach is not available as of right but only at the discretion of the court; and in exercising that discretion the court may take into account the conduct of the promisor after the making of the promise. The enforceability of promises which have contractual force is not subject to any of these restrictions.

14 IRREVOCABLE OFFERS

In English law, an offer can be withdrawn at any time before it has been accepted. This is so even though the offeror has expressly or by implication promised to hold his offer open for a stated period. Such a promise is not binding unless it is under seal or unless consideration has been given for it:[18] for example, by the offeree's making some counter-promise, or by his buying an option or by doing some other act at the request of the promisor (such as making efforts to raise the money that will enable the offeree to accept the offer). In some contexts this rule is well understood by businessmen, who would not, for example, expect to be able to enforce wholly gratuitous share options. But in other contexts businessmen do, reasonably, rely on promises to hold offers open. For example, a builder may base his own offer to a client on offers for the supply of materials which he himself has received and which are expressed to remain 'firm' for a fixed period. Under the present law, those offers can be withdrawn within that period, even after the builder has bound himself contractually to a client in reliance on them. Here the rule causes hardship[19] to the builder and proposals for reform have from time to time been made.[20] These proposals have not so far been implemented; but exceptions to the rule have been created in the interests of commercial convenience. For example, in the case of certain international sales, the rule has been abolished by legislation.[1] A further important exception to it appears to be established where a contract for the sale of goods provides for payment by a banker's irrevocable credit. Under such a contract, the buyer will

---

[16] See p 42, ante.

[17] *Crabb v Arun District Council* [1976] Ch 179 at 187.

[18] *Dickinson v Dodds* (1876) 2 Ch D 463; see p 18, ante.

[19] Which Canadian courts have managed to avoid: see *Northern Construction Co Ltd v Gloge Heating & Plumbing* (1984) 6 D L R (4th) 450.

[20] See Law Commission, Working Paper No 60 (1975).

[1] See ULFIS (ante, p 14) Art 5 (2) and (3).

instruct his bank to notify the seller of the irrevocable credit; and the notification takes the shape of an irrevocable promise by the bank to pay the seller, usually on tender of specified shipping documents relating to the goods. The commercial understanding is that the bank is bound as soon as it notifies the seller of the credit and before the seller has done anything which can be said to amount to acceptance of the bank's offer, or to provide consideration for it. If, as seems likely, the courts accept this commercial view they can be said to enforce a promise not to revoke an offer, even though there is no consideration for it in the traditional sense.[2] The existence of these exceptions provides a final illustration of a point often made in this Chapter: that the doctrine of consideration requires considerable modification to enable the law of contract to remain in touch with modern business needs.

[2] See *Hamzeh Malas & Sons v British Imex Industries Ltd* [1958] 2 Q B 127; *The American Accord* [1983] 1 A C 168 at 183.

Chapter 4

Contractual intention

Even though the parties have reached agreement, and even though that agreement is supported by consideration, there may still be no contract because the agreement was made without any intention to affect legal relations. In the great majority of commercial transactions there is, however, no need, affirmatively, to prove that the parties had such an intention. On the contrary, it is up to the party denying the existence of a contract to disprove the intention and the onus of proof which he has to discharge is a heavy one.[1] Moreover, in deciding the issue of contractual intention, the courts apply an objective test, so that a party to an ordinary commercial arrangement cannot escape liability merely by showing that he did not, in his own mind, intend the agreement to affect legal relations.[2] The requirement of such intention is therefore chiefly important in a number of somewhat exceptional situations.

1 EXPRESS PROVISIONS

Contractual intention may be negatived by the terms of the agreement. This was, for example, held to be the effect of an 'honour clause' which provided that the agreement was not to be a 'legal agreement'.[3] But where a reinsurance contract provided that it was to be 'interpreted . . . as an honourable engagement rather than as a legal obligation', these words were held to affect only the *interpretation* of the agreement and not its binding character.[4] One rule which is well settled is that, in an agreement for the sale of land, contractual intention is normally negatived by the words 'subject to contract'.[5] But where these words are omitted from such an agreement it will amount to a binding contract even though one party subjectively believed that he was not to be bound until the usual 'exchange of

---

[1] *Edwards v Skyways Ltd* [1964] 1 W L R 349 at 355; *Haryanto v E D & F Man (Sugar) Ltd* [1986] 2 Lloyd's Rep 44; *Kleinwort Benson Ltd v Malaysia Mining Corpn Bhd* [1988] 1 All E R 714.

[2] *Kingswood Estate Co Ltd v Anderson* [1963] 2 Q B 169.

[3] *Rose & Frank Co v J R Crompton & Bros Ltd* [1925] A C 445.

[4] *Home Insurance Co and St Paul Fire and Marine Insurance Co v Administratia Asigurariltor de Stat* [1983] 2 Lloyd's Rep 674 at 677.

[5] See p 23, ante.

contracts' had taken place. The objective test would prevent that party from relying on the belief,[6] unless it was known to the other party.[7]

One important class of agreements which at common law were prima facie held to be binding in honour only, were collective agreements between trade unions and employers or associations of employers.[8] Under the Trade Union and Labour Relations Act 1974 such an agreement is 'conclusively presumed not to have been intended by the parties to be a legally enforceable contract' unless it is in writing and expressly provides that it is intended to be legally enforceable.[9] Whether or not the agreement is legally enforceable between the parties to it (ie the unions and the employers) some of its terms[10] may be incorporated, by reference, into individual contracts of employment and may then, if so intended, become binding between employers and employees.[11]

2 VAGUE AGREEMENTS

Contractual intention may be negatived by the inherent vagueness of the terms of the agreement. This principle is often applied in order to determine whether a particular statement forms part of an admitted contract. For this purpose the courts have distinguished between simple 'sales talk' which gives rise to no liability, 'mere representations' which have some legal effects without being contractually binding, and statements which are contractual terms.[12] Only statements which (on the objective test) are *intended* to be contractually binding will fall into the last of these classes. The same requirement may also determine the very existence of a contract. Thus in one case[13] it was held that no contract arose from claims made by a manufacturer in promotional literature that his product was 'foolproof' and that it 'required no maintenance'. In another case,[14] a property developer reached an 'understanding' with a firm of solicitors to employ them for legal work in connection with a proposed development; but the deliberately vague language used was held to negative contractual intention. Two factors which influence the courts in cases of this kind are, on the one

---

6 *Tweddell v Henderson* [1975] 2 All ER 1096.

7 *Pateman v Pay* (1974) 232 Estates Gazette 457.

8 *Ford Motor Co Ltd v Amalgamated Union of Engineering and Foundry Workers* [1969] 2 QB 303.

9 S 18 (1) and (2).

10 See s 18 (4) for special restrictions on incorporation of 'no strike' clauses.

11 *Marley v Forward Trust Group Ltd* [1986] ICR 891; *National Coal Board v National Union of Mineworkers* [1986] ICR 736.

12 See pp 121–124, 130–132, post.

13 *Lexmead (Basingstoke) Ltd v Lewis* [1982] AC 225, affd on other grounds ibid, at 271.

14 *JH Milner & Son v Percy Bilton Ltd* [1966] 2 All ER 894.

hand, the importance of the statement to the person to whom it is addressed[15] and, on the other, the degree of precision with which it is expressed. If A says to B 'You will come to no harm if you buy X's paint to paint your house', A's statement is unlikely to have contractual force. But the position is different if A says to B: 'If you buy X's paint to paint your house, I guarantee that it will last for seven years.'[16] In the second case the specific terms of A's 'guarantee' will make it highly probable that he intended to be legally bound, or at least that B reasonably received that impression.

3 DISCRETIONARY AGREEMENTS

Contractual intention may also be negatived because the terms of an agreement confer a wide discretion on one of the parties. In an old case, a promise to pay for services 'such remuneration as may be deemed right' was held to be 'merely an engagement of honour'[17] and thus not legally enforceable. Nowadays the courts are reluctant to interpret agreements in this way, especially after work has actually been done under them. But where the intention to negative contractual intention is clear, the courts will refuse to enforce the agreement.[18]

4 SOCIAL AND DOMESTIC AGREEMENTS

Many everyday social arrangements are not contractually binding, because this is obviously not the intention of the parties. No one would suppose that acceptance of an invitation to dinner created a contract; nor does a 'car-pool' arrangement between neighbours normally amount to a contract, even though it involves reciprocal services and even though it may provide for some sharing of expense. Similarly, most arrangements within the family which relate to the ordinary day-to-day running of the household are not contracts. A husband does not contract to pay his wife a housekeeping allowance, any more than a wife contracts to manage the household; nor is an arrangement under which husband and wife draw on a joint bank account normally a con-tract.[19] This position usually holds good even though the parties are temporarily living apart, eg because the husband's work has taken him

[15] *J Evans & Son (Portsmouth) Ltd v Andrea Merzario Ltd* [1976] 2 All E R 930.
[16] Cf *Shanklin Pier Ltd v Detel Products Ltd* [1951] 2 K B 854.
[17] *Taylor v Brewer* (1813) 1 M & S 290 at 291.
[18] *Re Richmond Gate Property Co Ltd* [1964] 3 All E R 936.
[19] *Gage v King* [1961] 1 Q B 188.

abroad.[20] Of course, when the parties live apart because of the break-up of their marriage, any agreement between them regulating the terms of separation is likely to be contractual in nature. Even in such a case, contractual intention may be negatived by the vague or discretionary terms of the arrangement: this was held to be the position where a husband, on leaving his wife, promised to pay her £15 per week 'so long as I can manage it.'[1] Somewhat similar principles apply between parent and child: for example, a parent's informal promise to pay the child an allowance during study would not normally be a binding contract. But where the promise was made in order to induce the child to give up one occupation and to qualify for another, the promise would prima facie be binding, though this inference could in turn be rebutted by the vagueness of the arrangement.[2] The fact that the promisee has taken some important step in reliance on the promise can also outweigh the significance normally attached to a 'family' relationship in negativing contractual intention. Thus it has been held that there was a contract where a young couple left their home and went to live with elderly relations on the faith of the latters' promise to provide for them by will.[3] Similar reasoning has been applied to house-sharing agreements between persons who lived together as husband and wife without being married.[4] The fact that one of the parties has helped to improve the property is also sometimes relied upon to give such an agreement contractual force.[5]

5 OTHER ILLUSTRATIONS

It is common to divide the cases in which there is no contractual intention into categories such as those which have been discussed in this Chapter. But these categories are not exhaustive and there are many other factors which may negative contractual intention. Thus, it has been held that an agreement which was intended merely to give effect to rights believed already to exist was not a contract, as the parties had no intention to enter into a new contract;[6] that the relationship between a minister of religion and the church which had appointed him was not a contract as it was not intended to be enforceable in the

---

20 *Balfour v Balfour* [1919] 2 K B 571.
1 *Gould v Gould* [1970] 1 Q B 275.
2 *Jones v Padavatton* [1969] 2 All E R 616; cf *Hardwick v Johnson* [1978] 2 All E R 935.
3 *Parker v Clark* [1960] 1 All E R 93.
4 *Tanner v Tanner* [1975] 3 All E R 776, contrast *Horrocks v Forray* [1976] 1 All E R 737.
5 *Eves v Eves* [1975] 1 W L R 1338 at 1345; cf *Grant v Edwards* [1986] Ch 638 (liability based on 'constructive trust').
6 *Harvela Investments Ltd v Royal Trust Co of Canada (CI) Ltd* [1986] A C 207.

courts;[7] that the same was true of the relationship between the Crown and one of its civil servants because the Crown did not have the requisite contractual intention;[8] and that contractual intention may be negatived where a promise is made in jest or anger, at least if this fact is apparent to the person to whom the promise is made.[9] On the other hand, special circumstances may establish contractual intention in a case within a category from which it is normally assumed to be absent, eg in the case of a domestic or social agreement. Occasionally, conflicting factors will lead to differences of judicial opinion on the issue of contractual intention. This was, for example, the position in a case[10] arising out of an advertising campaign by Esso in which so-called 'World Cup coins' were to be given away 'free' to motorists with every four gallons of petrol bought by them. Three members of the House of Lords regarded this arrangement as sufficiently precise to give rise to a contract between the motorists and garages with regard to the coins; while the other two thought that contractual intention was negatived by the fact that the coins were said to be 'going free' and by their minimal value. Whichever view may be preferred, the case shows that the categories discussed above are only useful in providing general guidance. They are not decisive since, in the last resort, the question of contractual intention is one of fact in each case.

[7] *President of the Methodist Conference v Parfitt* [1984] Q B 368; *Davies v Presbyterian Church of Wales* [1986] 1 All E R 705.
[8] *R v Civil Service Appeal Board, ex p Bruce* [1988] 3 All ER 686.
[9] *Licenses Insurance Corpn v Lawson* (1896) 12 T L R 501.
[10] *Esso Petroleum Ltd v Customs and Excise Comrs* [1976] 1 All E R 117.

Chapter 5

Form

1 NATURE AND PURPOSE OF FORMAL REQUIREMENTS

To say that a contract must be in a certain form means that its concl-usion must be marked or recorded in a prescribed manner. In modern systems of law, formal requirements invariably call for some kind of written instrument. Normally, such requirements must be satisfied in addition to the ordinary requirements of agreement, consideration and contractual intention, though occasionally form may replace one or more of these requirements. For example, a promise under seal to make a gift is binding, even in the absence of consideration and of agree-ment. In this chapter, however, we shall consider cases in which form is an *additional* (and not those in which it is a *substitute*) requirement.

There are several reasons why the law may impose formal require-ments. First, the use of a prescribed form leads to greater certainty, making it easier to tell when a contract has been made, what its terms are, and what type of contract it is (eg whether it is sale or hire-pur-chase). Secondly, a requirement of form acts as a warning against rashly entering into a contract. This was one of the functions of the instrument under seal in the days when an impression on wax was still necessary for its execution; and a modern equivalent can be seen in the formalities required by law for the execution of regulated consumer credit agreements (including hire-purchase agreements) under which the amount of credit does not exceed £15,000.[1] Here the debtor and creditor must sign a document drawn up in accordance with govern-ment regulations. The debtor must sign inside a 'signature box' warning him that he is signing a hire-purchase agreement; and the document must specify certain information which has to be given to the debtor. Such requirements also illustrate a third (increasingly important) function of form, which is to protect the weaker party to the transaction by giving him a written statement of its terms. Similar legislation exists to protect, for example, certain tenants and employees, who may have to be given written particulars of the terms on which they have contracted.[2]

---

[1] Consumer Credit Act 1974, ss 8, 55, 60, 61; SI 1983/1878.
[2] See p 58, post.

2 FORM GENERALLY NOT REQUIRED

Although there are thus many and good reasons for imposing formal requirements in certain cases, the general rule is that contracts can be made quite informally. In spite of a popular belief to the contrary, it is not even necessary for a contract to be in writing. Contracts for the sale of goods or shares worth millions of pounds can be made quite inform- ally, by word of mouth. In practice, such contracts are often made in writing, even when there is no such legal requirement; and this practice gives rise to problems which will be discussed in chapter 6.

The main reason for the general rule is that formal requirements are thought to be commercially inconvenient. The execution of a formal agreement takes time, when speed may be essential; and formal requirements are subject to pitfalls, so that a slip in the execution may enable a party to escape from a transaction on some technical ground. These factors justify the general principle, but there are many excep- tions to it. These now all depend on legislation dealing with particular types of contracts. Our concern is with the general principles of the law of contract and it would be quite impossible in a book of this kind to deal with the rules governing formal requirements in relation to each particular type of contract to which they apply. But there are two general problems to which formal requirements give rise. The first concerns the exact nature or type of formal requirements imposed by law, and the second, the effects of failing to comply with these require- ments. Since the answers to these two problems may apply to contracts generally, or at least to more than one type of contract, some discussion of them is appropriate here.

3 TYPES OF FORMAL REQUIREMENTS

Although all formal requirements involve writing of some kind, the exact nature of the writing required varies widely from case to case.

At the one extreme, the law may require the contract to be made *under seal*: this is, for example, the position with regard to a lease for more than three years.[3]

A second group of contracts must be *in writing*, but the writing does not have to be executed under seal: it simply has to be signed by one or both of the parties. Contracts in this group include bills of exchange and promissory notes. Similarly, a regulated consumer credit agree- ment is 'not properly executed' unless a document in the required form, containing the express terms of the agreement, is signed by both parties.[4]

---

[3] Law of Property Act 1925, s 52.
[4] Consumer Credit Act 1974, s 61. See also ss 62, 63, 64 for requirements as to delivery of copies and notice of 'cooling-off' period.

A third type of requirement is that there must be a *note or memorandum in writing* of the contract. This requirement exists in relation to contracts of guarantee[5] and to contracts for the sale or disposition of an interest in land.[6] Contracts within this group differ from those in the second group, in that the requirement is satisfied even though the document comes into existence after the time of contracting, so long as it recognises the existence of the contract[7] and comes into existence before an action is brought. For this reason it is sometimes said that contracts within this third group do not have to be *in writing*, but only *evidenced in writing*. The memorandum must identify the parties and the subject-matter of the contract and state its terms (though a memorandum of a guarantee need not state the consideration for the agreement).[8] It must also be 'signed' by the party to be charged; but this requirement has been very loosely interpreted, so that initials or a printed signature will do. The signature need not be at the foot of the document, so long as it authenticates the whole document.[9] A memorandum may even be put together from two or more documents, if the document signed by the party to be charged expressly, or by implication, refers to the other or others; or if, by placing the two side by side, their connection becomes obvious and does not have to be established by oral evidence.[10] These lax rules indicate the courts' dislike of the present requirement, which was often used to set up unmeritorious defences based on technical slips.

There is, finally, a fourth group of contracts which do not have to be in, or to be evidenced in, writing, but which are subject to the requirement that one party must (either spontaneously or on request) *supply certain written particulars* to the other: for example, under some tenancies, a landlord is bound to give his tenant a rent-book setting out certain particulars; an employer is often bound to give his employee a written document setting out the principal terms of the contract; estate agents are required by law to give certain information (relating to their right to commission) to their clients; and a carrier by sea may be obliged on demand of the shipper to issue a written bill of lading setting out certain specified particulars.[11]

---

5 Statute of Frauds 1677, s 4, repealed in relation to certain other contracts by Law Reform (Enforcement of Contracts) Act 1954.
6 Law of Property Act 1925, s 40(1).
7 *Tweddell v Henderson* [1975] 2 All E R 1096.
8 Mercantile Law Amendment Act 1856, s 3.
9 *Hill v Hill* [1947] Ch 231 at 240; *Schneider v Norris* (1814) 2 M & S 286.
10 *Stokes v Whicher* [1920] 1 Ch 411; *Elias v George Sahely & Co (Barbados) Ltd* [1983] 1 A C 646.
11 Landlord and Tenant Act 1985, s 4; Employment Protection (Consolidation) Act 1978, ss 1, 3; Estate Agents Act 1979, s 18; Carriage of Goods by Sea Act 1971, Sch 3, art 3; cf Mobile Homes Act 1983, s 1.

4 EFFECTS OF FAILURE TO USE THE REQUIRED FORM

The effect of failure to comply with a formal requirement imposed by law is hardly ever to make the contract a complete nullity. It varies according to the nature of the formal requirement.

The first possibility is that the failure may not affect the validity of the contract at all: this is, for example, the position where a landlord fails to give his tenant a rent book in accordance with the relevant legislation. In such a case the landlord commits a criminal offence, but he can nevertheless sue the tenant for rent;[12] and of course the tenant can enforce the lease against the landlord.

A second possibility is that the contract may still be binding as such, but that it does not produce all the legal effects which it would have produced, if it had been in the required form. This would, for example, be the position if a lease for over three years were simply in writing but not under seal. The document would be 'void for the purpose of creating a legal estate'[13] but it would be a perfectly valid agreement for a lease which could be enforced by the tenant.[14] The main difference between such an agreement and a duly executed lease is that the former might not, whereas the latter would, prevail against a third person to whom the landlord had sold the land.

A third possibility is that restrictions may be placed on the right of *one* of the parties to enforce the agreement. For example, a regulated hire-purchase or other consumer credit agreement cannot be enforced against the hirer or debtor if it has not been signed by him; and if it suffers from one or more of a number of other formal defects, it can only be enforced against the hirer or debtor on an order of the court.[15] In deciding whether to make such an order, the court can take into account factors such as the amount of prejudice caused to the debtor by the formal defect and the degree of culpability of the creditor. The court can also take various intermediate courses between allowing and refusing enforcement: for example it can enforce the contract as if it did not contain a term which should have been, but was not, included in the document signed by the hirer. The result of this judicial discretion will be to prevent a debtor from relying on unmeritorious defences based on technical formal slips. For the purpose of these rules, enforcement includes the retaking of any goods to which the agreement relates. Failure to comply with the statutory formalities has no effect on the right of the hirer or debtor to enforce the contract.

---

12 *Shaw v Groom* [1970] 2 QB 504.
13 Law of Property Act 1925, s 52.
14 *Walsh v Lonsdale* (1882) 21 Ch D 9.
15 Consumer Credit Act 1974, ss 65, 127.

A fourth possibility is that the contract can be enforced only against a party who has signed it or a note or memorandum of it. This is, for example, the position with regard to a contract for the disposition of an interest in land. If such a contract, or a note or memorandum of it, is 'signed' by only one party, but not by the other, it can be enforced against the former but not against the latter; if it is signed by neither party it cannot be enforced at all. But the rule simply is that 'no action may be brought'[16] upon the contract, which may be good for other purposes. For example, a deposit paid by the purchaser under it cannot be claimed back, so long as the vendor is willing to perform;[17] and a person who enters the land in reliance on the contract could set it up by way of defence, if he were sued for trespassing on the land.[18] Even with these limitations, however, the rule that an oral contract could not be enforced might cause considerable hardship to a party who had acted in reliance on it. To meet this hardship, Equity invented the so-called doctrine of part performance, under which a party, who had wholly or in part performed his side of the contract, could enforce it even though there was no note or memorandum in writing. At one time, it was thought that this doctrine was restricted to cases in which the acts of part performance could be referred *only* to a contract such as that alleged.[19] It remains true that the acts must not be purely equivocal: for example, it is not enough for a vendor to show that the purchaser helped him with a planning application, since this is commonly done even without a binding contract.[20] But the modern view is that the doctrine will apply if the most obvious explanation is that the acts were done under the alleged contract, even though some other explanation for them is also possible or even plausible.[1] A common act of part performance is for a purchaser or tenant to go into possession of the land in question.[2] On the other hand, payment of rent or of part of the purchase price in advance is not of itself sufficient part performance, either because it is an equivocal act, or because a defendant who has received money and then refuses to perform can be ordered to restore it, so that he will not be unjustly enriched by relying on the lack of writing.[3] But if the defendant cannot be made to pay the money back (eg because he is insolvent) and in certain other cases (eg where the land is of special value to the purchaser) the payment of money may be sufficient part performance.[4] The doctrine of part performance is, finally, restricted to contracts for the disposition of an

---

16 Law of Property Act 1925, s 40 (1).
17 *Thomas v Brown* (1876) 1 QBD 714.
18 See *Carrington v Roots* (1837) 2 M & W 248 at 255.
19 *Maddison v Alderson* (1883) 8 App Cas 467.
20 *New Hart Builders Ltd v Brindley* [1975] Ch 342 at 353.
1 *Wakeham v Mackenzie* [1968] 2 All ER 783 at 787; *Sutton v Sutton* [1984] Ch 184 at 188.
2 *Kingswood Estate Co Ltd v Anderson* [1963] 2 QB 169.
3 *Chapronière v Lambert* [1917] 2 Ch 356.
4 *Steadman v Steadman* [1976] AC 536.

interest in land. It does not apply to other contracts which are subject to formal requirements.

A fifth possibility is that a contract is not admissible in evidence at all unless it is embodied in a written document containing certain particulars. Such a rule is laid down by statute for policies of marine insurance.[5]

5 RESCISSION AND VARIATION OF WRITTEN CONTRACTS

So far, we have been concerned with the part that writing plays in the making, proof, or enforcement of a contract. It may also play a part where a contract which is required to be, or which in fact is, in writing is subsequently rescinded or varied by mutual consent[6].

A contract which is subject to a formal requirement can nevertheless be *rescinded* informally: for example, a contract for the disposition of an interest in land can be rescinded orally.[7] If an attempt is made to *vary* such a contract orally, two possibilities exist. First, the variation may be regarded as a rescission of the old contract, followed by the substitution of a new one on different terms. In that case the rescission will be effective, but the new contract will not satisfy the formal requirement and so there will be no legally enforceable contract on the new terms.[8] Secondly, the variation may be an attempt to add a term to the original contract, or to strike out one of its terms. In that case, the variation is ineffective and each party can sue (and can sue only) on the original contract.[9] For example, suppose that a contract for the sale of land is orally varied by a reduction of the area to be sold. In such a case the purchaser is not bound to pay the price, unless conveyance of the whole original area is tendered; and conversely, he could bring an action on the original agreement, disregarding the oral variation. At most, the variation might have a limited effect under the doctrine of a 'waiver', which is substantially similar to the doctrine of promissory estoppel discussed in chapter 3.[10]

If the contract is not subject to any formal requirement, but happens to have been made in writing or under seal, it may be rescinded or varied without the use of the same formality. For example, where a separation agreement was made by deed (though there was no legal requirement that it should be so made), it was held that it could be subsequently varied by a writing not under seal.[11]

[5] Marine Insurance Act 1906, s 22.
[6] For formalities required in cases of rescission by one party for the other's breach, without the latter's consent, see post, p 277.
[7] See *Morris v Baron & Co* [1918] A C 1.
[8] *Morris v Baron & Co,* supra.
[9] *Goss v Nugent* (1833) 5 B & Ad 58; *Tyers v Rosedale and Ferryhill Iron Co Ltd* (1875) L R 10 Exch 195.
[10] Pp 41–43, ante; *British and Beningtons Ltd v North Western Cachar Tea Co Ltd* [1923] A C 48.
[11] *Berry v Berry* [1929] 2 K B 316.

Chapter 6

The contents of a contract

A contract may contain both express and implied terms. Express terms depend on the words used by the parties in reaching or recording their agreement. Implied terms are included, for various reasons to be discussed in this chapter, even though they have not been expressly stated in words.

1 ASCERTAINMENT OF EXPRESS TERMS

The ascertainment of express terms raises two questions: what words did the parties use and what was the legal effect of those words? The first question is simply one of fact, but the second raises issues of law. In answering it, the court applies the objective test: a party cannot enforce the contract in the sense that he gave to the words, if that sense is not one in which a reasonable person would have understood them.[1]

Where the contract is in writing, there is normally no dispute as to the words contained in the document. But some difficulty may arise where a contract is set out in one document, which incorporates another document by express reference: eg where a contract is made subject to the rules of a trade association, or subject to the regulations in a time-table. Often, the document thus referred to is one of great length and complexity, running into many pages and sometimes into literally hundreds of clauses. In that case, the parties will often not be fully aware of the terms of the second document and they may include, in the first, provisions which are inconsistent with those contained in the second. The court then has to resolve the inconsistency as best it can; and, where possible, it will give primacy to the terms actually drawn up by the parties, as these are likely to represent their predominant intention.[2]

A contract may be contained in two documents, even though the principal one does not *expressly* refer to the other, if in the court's view it was the intention of the parties to incorporate the second document. For example in one case[3] a contract for the sale of certain securities was held to incorporate a term in a prospectus, even though that term was not set out in the contract of sale, while all the other terms in the prospectus were so set out.

1 *Eyre v Measday* [1986] 1 All ER 488; *Thake v Maurice* [1986] QB 644.
2 See *Adamastos Shipping Co Ltd v Anglo-Saxon Petroleum Co Ltd* [1959] AC 133.
3 *Jacobs v Batavia & General Plantations Trust Ltd* [1924] 1 Ch 287.

Where the contract is in writing, the so-called parol evidence rule may prevent a party from relying on other evidence as to its express terms. This rule will be considered after a discussion of implied terms.

2 IMPLIED TERMS

Implied terms may be divided into (a) terms implied in fact; (b) terms implied in law; and (c) terms implied by custom or usage.

a Terms implied in fact

A term implied in fact is one which was not expressly stated, but which (in the court's view) the parties must have intended to include, because it was 'so obvious that it goes without saying'; so that, if while the parties were making their bargain, an officious bystander were to suggest some express provision for it in the agreement, they would testily suppress him with a common 'Oh, of course!'[4] For example, in one case[5] land was sold and the vendor undertook that, if he later decided to *sell* certain adjoining land, the purchaser should have the 'first refusal' of it. It was held that a term must be implied, that the vendor would not defeat the purchaser's expectation by conveying the adjoining land to a third party by way of *gift*.

But there are relatively few cases in which the courts have been prepared to imply a term in fact under the 'officious bystander' test. They have, in the first place, insisted that the implication must be obvious to *both* parties, so that if one of them is ignorant of the matter to be implied, or has no view on it, the implication will fail.[6] Similarly, it is not sufficient to show that the parties would have made *some* provision for the matter, if it is not obvious that they would both have agreed to the *same* one.[7] In the second place, the court will not imply a term in fact unless this is 'necessary to give the transaction such business efficacy as the parties must have intended'.[8] It is not enough to show that the contract might have been a more reasonable one with the added term; for although the test of reasonableness may be used in *interpreting* express terms, [9] the court will not normally undertake the task of improving the contract by implying new terms into it.[10] This is

---

[4] *Shirlaw v Southern Foundries (1926) Ltd* [1939] 2 K B 206 at 227 (affd [1940] A C 701).
[5] *Gardner v Coutts & Co* [1967] 3 All E R 1064.
[6] *Spring v National Amalgamated Stevedores and Dockers Society* [1956] 2 All E R 221; *K C Sethia (1944) Ltd v Partabmull Rameshwar* [1950] 1 All E R 51; affd [1951] 2 All E R 352n.
[7] *Lister v Romford Ice and Cold Storage Co Ltd* [1957] A C 555.
[8] *Luxor (Eastbourne) Ltd v Cooper* [1941] A C 108 at 137; *Trollope & Colls Ltd v North West Metropolitan Hospital Board* [1973] 2 All E R 260.
[9] *Paula Lee Ltd v Robert Zehil & Co Ltd* [1983] 2 All E R 390; cf ante p 22.
[10] *Liverpool City Council v Irwin* [1977] A C 239; *Duke of Westminster v Guild* [1985] Q B 688 at 700; *The Maira (No 3)* [1988] 2 Lloyd's Rep 126.

particularly true 'where the parties have entered into a carefully drafted written contract containing detailed terms agreed between them'.[11] The judicial attitude is well illustrated by a case[12] arising out of a contract by which an oil company undertook to supply petrol and oil to a garage while the garage promised to buy such goods only from the company. During a price-war the company reduced the price of petrol to neighbouring retailers, so that the garage could only trade at a loss. The court (by a majority) refused to imply a term that the company should not 'abnormally discriminate' against the garage since it was not clear that the company would have agreed to it, and since it was too vague. Again, where an estate agent was to receive a commission 'on completion of sale', the court refused to imply a term to the effect that the owner should not sell the property privately, without using the agent's services.[13] An agent who wishes to rule out such a possibility must do so by express words, eg by stipulating for the 'sole and exclusive right to sell'.

b Terms implied in law

In many contractual relationships, certain obligations resting on one or other of the parties are said to be based on 'implied terms'. For example, a seller of goods may impliedly undertake that the goods are merchantable, or fit for the particular purpose for which the buyer requires them;[14] a person who contracts to supply services in the course of a business undertakes that he will carry them out with reasonable care and skill;[15] and an employer impliedly undertakes that he will not require his employee to do any unlawful act. Many of these implications have been developed in relation to various specific contracts, and detailed discussion of them will be found in works on sale of goods, contracts of employment, and so forth. Some of them are based on judicial decisions (though a number of these have been codified by statute); others owe their origin to statute. At common law, such terms can be excluded by express contrary provision; but the power to exclude them is now severely restricted by legislation. For example a term purporting to exclude liability for the terms as to quality implied by the Sale of Goods Act 1979 is invalid in a consumer sale, valid to the extent that it satisfies the test of reasonableness in a domestic non-consumer sale, but valid irrespective of reasonableness in an international sale.[16]

Obviously, an implied term which cannot be excluded has nothing

11 *Shell (UK) Ltd v Lostock Garages Ltd* [1976] 1 WLR 1187 at 1200.
12 *Shell (UK) Ltd v Lostock Garages Ltd,* supra.
13 *Luxor (Eastbourne) Ltd v Cooper,* supra.
14 Sale of Goods Act 1979, s 14.
15 Supply of Goods and Services Act 1982, s 13.
16 Unfair Contract Terms Act 1977, ss 6(2), 6(3) and 26(1); see pp 91–92, 96, post.

to do with the intention of the parties and is therefore very different in its legal nature from a term implied in fact. Where the implied term can be excluded, the intention of the parties is relevant, in that it may negative the term. But many terms (including those listed in the preceding paragraph) can be, and often are, implied even though it is plain that the 'officious bystander' test is not satisfied. Some of these terms are so complex that it is quite unrealistic to suppose that the parties had any positive common intention with respect to them; they have been described as 'legal incidents of [particular] kinds of contractual relationships'.[17] It has, indeed, been said that the implication rests on 'necessity';[18] but in determining what amounts to necessity the courts do not, in the present context,[19] look for evidence of common intention. They determine the existence, scope and content of terms implied in law rather by the citation of authorities and by reference to general considerations of policy. The distinction between the two processes of implication is illustrated by a case in which it was held to be an implied term of a lease of maisonette in a council block that the landlord should take reasonable care to keep the 'common parts' of the block in a reasonable state of repair.[20] The implication arose (in spite of the fact that the 'officious bystander' test was not satisfied) because it was thought desirable to impose some obligation on the landlord as to the maintenance of the common parts of the premises. In such cases the courts are really laying down, as a matter of law, how the parties to a contract ought to behave; and the parties will be bound by such standards of conduct unless they have effectively excluded or varied them by the terms of the contract.

c Terms implied by custom or usage

Where persons deal in a particular market, a custom of that market may be incorporated into their contract, so long as the custom is not inconsistent with the express terms of the contract, or with terms necessarily implied in the contract otherwise than by custom. In cases of such inconsistency, the custom is said to be 'unreasonable'. For example, in one case[1] a custom of the tallow market was proved, under which an agent, who had been engaged to buy goods for his principal, was allowed to sell goods of his own to the principal. It was held that the custom was inconsistent with the fundamental nature of the agency relationship and therefore unreasonable; for an agent engaged to buy must buy as cheaply as he can, while one who sold his own goods would seek to obtain the highest possible price. Although these rules are most

[17] *Mears v Safecar Securities Ltd* [1983] QB 54 at 78.
[18] *Tai Hing Cotton Mill Ltd v Liu Chong Hing Bank Ltd* [1986] AC 80 at 104–105.
[19] Contrast ante p 63 at n 8.
[20] *Liverpool City Council v Irwin* [1977] AC 239.
[1] *Robinson v Mollett* (1875) LR 7 HL 802.

easily illustrated by reference to a custom of a market, they apply equally to customs or usages of a particular locality or trade. For example, where persons engaged in the business of hiring out machinery regularly deal with each other on terms drawn up by a trade association, those terms may be implied in a particular transaction even though no express reference to them was made when that transaction was concluded.[2]

Where the custom is 'reasonable' the parties are bound by it whether they know of it or not. The suggestion that the incorporation of customary terms is based on the presumed common intention of the parties is therefore a somewhat artificial one. It becomes even less plausible in view of the fact that the question, whether a custom is reasonable, is one of law which the parties can scarcely be expected to resolve. Customary terms are best regarded as incorporated on grounds of convenience, irrespective of the intention of the parties.

3   THE PAROL EVIDENCE RULE

Where a contract is reduced to writing, the general rule is that neither party can rely on extrinsic evidence to add to, vary or contradict the written instrument.[3] The rule applies to any contract which is in fact in writing, whether or not it is required by law to be in writing. And although it is commonly called the parol evidence rule, it applies not only to oral evidence, but also to any other forms of evidence extrinsic to the document, such as evidence of another document, unless, of course, that document forms one of the contractual documents under the rules as to incorporation, discussed earlier in this chapter. The purpose of the rule is to promote certainty, and this can most clearly be seen where the parties have put the terms of their agreement into a formal, detailed written document. In such a case, it may often be reasonable to say that the parties intended their relations to be governed by that document and.by it alone. On the other hand, a less detailed contractual document may fail fully to express the intention of the parties, and, where this is the case, a strict application of the parol evidence rule would obviously cause injustice. For this reason the law has limited the scope of the rule and created exceptions to it, so that in the following situations it does not apply.

(1) The rule only relates to evidence as to the *contents* of a contract. It does not apply where evidence is introduced to show that the contract is not legally binding, eg for lack of consideration, or for mistake or misrepresentation. Nor does the rule prevent a party from relying on

---

2   *British Crane Hire Corpn Ltd v Ipswich Plant Hire Ltd* [1975] Q B 303.
3   *Jacobs v Batavia and General Plantations Trust Ltd* [1924] 1 Ch 287 at 295; *Rabin v Gerson Berger Association* Ltd [1986] 1 All E R 374 at 378, 382.

evidence to show that the contract is subject to a condition precedent, which is not stated in the written contract. For example, in one case[4] a written agreement was made for the sale of a patent, and the buyer was allowed to rely on oral evidence to show that the agreement was not to take effect until the patent had been approved by a third party.

(2) The written contract may be fully effective at law, but oral evidence may be relied on for the purpose of *establishing an equitable defence*. Thus a plaintiff's failure to perform an oral promise made before or at the time of the execution of the written contract may be a defence to a claim for specific performance, even though the defendant might not be able to rely on evidence of the oral promise in an action for damages.[5] Similarly an agent who, on behalf of his principal, signs a written contract by the terms of which he (the agent) is made personally liable, may be able to rely by way of equitable defence on the other party's oral promise to hold only the principal liable on the contract.[6]

(3) In general, the rule prevents a buyer from relying on evidence of so-called 'oral warranties'—ie of express undertaking as to the quality of the subject-matter. For example, a buyer of paint under a written contract containing no warranty could not rely on an oral promise by the seller that the paint would last for seven years. But such 'oral warranties' can be relied on for two purposes. First, an oral statement *of fact* (eg one that the paint contained no lead) may, if untrue, amount to a misrepresentation inducing the written contract[7] and so go to the *validity* of the contract and not as to its *contents*. Secondly, extrinsic evidence may be relied on by one party so as to deprive the other of the benefit of an exemption clause set out in the written contract. An oral statement made at an auction sale of cattle has, for example, been admitted so as to prevent the seller from relying on an exemption clause in the written particulars of sale.[8]

(4) The parol evidence rule only prevents a party from relying on extrinsic evidence as to the express terms of a written contract. Such evidence is admissible *to show that a term ought to be implied*. For example, a buyer of paint might have told the seller that he wanted to use the paint on the outside of his house. He could rely on such evidence to raise an implication that the paint was fit for that particular purpose.[9]

(5) The parol evidence rule only applies to evidence of statements

---

4   *Pym v Campbell* (1856) 6 E & B 370; cf *AG Securities v Vaughan* [1988] 3 All ER 1058 at 1072 (evidence that term in a document was a sham designed to evade the Rent Act).
5   *Martin v Pycroft* (1852) 2 DeGM&G 785.
6   *Wake v Harrop* (1861) 6 H & N 768; 1 H & C 202.
7   See p 122, post.
8   *Couchman v Hill* [1947] K B 554; *Harling v Eddy* [1951] 2 K B 739.
9   Under Sale of Goods Act 1979, s 14(3).

made before or at the time of the execution of the written contract. Extrinsic evidence can be used to show that the written contract has been *subsequently varied or rescinded*,[10] or to give rise to an estoppel.[11]

(6) The parol evidence rule applies to evidence as to what the express terms of a contract are. But extrinsic evidence can often be used to show *what the terms of a written document mean*. Such evidence can thus be used to explain ambiguous or vague expressions and technical terms.[12] On the same principle, extrinsic evidence can be used to identify the subject-matter of the contract (eg the area of land sold[13]), or the capacity in which the parties contract. In one case,[14] a contract was made to buy 'your wool' and evidence was admitted to show that this meant the wool produced not only on the seller's but also on a neighbour's farm. In another case,[15] a written contract for the sale of flour failed to make it clear which party was buyer and which was seller, and evidence was admitted to show that one of them was a baker and the other a flour-dealer. But evidence cannot be used for this purpose of *negotiations before* the document was executed (since the document is taken to supersede them)[16] or of the *conduct* of the parties *thereafter* (since this would change the meaning of the contract in the course of its operation).[17]

(7) Evidence of *custom* can be used for several of the purposes mentioned above: for example, evidence of custom can be used to imply a term, to show whether a person contracting as agent was personally liable on the contract, and as an aid to construction. Such evidence may be used 'to annex incidents to written contracts in matters with respect to which they are silent'.[18] The general rule is that custom may add to, but may not contradict, the written contract. Obviously, in borderline cases it is hard to distinguish between addition and contradiction. A practical test is to suppose that the custom was actually written out in the contract and then to ask whether the resulting document contains internal contradictions. In one case, a contract provided that the expenses of unloading goods from a ship should be borne by *one* party (the charterer) 'as customary', and evidence of a custom that those expenses should be borne by the *other* party (the

---

10 *Morris v Baron & Co* [1918] A C 1. For the *validity* of such variations, see p 61, ante.
11 *James Miller & Partners Ltd v Whitworth Street Estates (Manchester) Ltd* [1970] A C 583 at 611, 615.
12 *Bank of New Zealand v Simpson* [1900] A C 182; cf *Pao On v Lau Yiu Long* [1980] A C 614 at 631.
13 *Scarfe v Adams* [1981] 1 All E R 843; cf *Perry lease Ltd v Imecar AG* [1987] 2 All E R 373.
14 *Macdonald v Longbottom* (1859) 1 E & E 977.
15 *Newell v Radford* (1867) L R 3 C P 52.
16 *Prenn v Simmonds* [1971] 3 All E R 237.
17 *James Miller & Partners Ltd v Whitworth Street Estates (Manchester) Ltd* [1970] A C 583.
18 *Hutton v Warren* (1836) 1 M & W 466 at 475.

The parol evidence ruleThe parol evidence rule 69

shipowner) was rejected.[19] In another case,[20] a contract provided for payments at a certain rate and it was held that evidence of a customary discount did not contradict the contract, since the discount was calculated on the contract rate.

Evidence of custom can be used for the purpose of interpreting the contract, even though it does contradict the natural meaning of the words used in the contract. Thus evidence has been admitted to prove a local custom by which '1000 rabbits' meant '1200 rabbits'.[1]

(8) A document may fail fully or accurately to record a previous oral agreement, and, where this is due to a mistake in recording a previous oral agreement,[2] the document can be *rectified* ie brought into line with the oral agreement[3]. Rectification is necessarily based on extrinsic evidence; but the remedy is not available where the parties know that the document is at variance with the terms actually agreed.

(9) The mere existence of some document relating to a contract does not necessarily lead to the conclusion that all the terms of the contract are contained in that document. A distinction is drawn between, on the one hand, documents which are only *informal memoranda*, and, on the other, those which were intended as *complete contractual documents*, ie exhaustive records of the terms finally agreed. In one case[4] the seller of a horse gave the buyer a note simply recording the fact of sale and the price; and it was held that evidence of an oral warranty relating to the horse was admissible. In another case,[5] however, a document set out detailed provisions as to the terms on which a business had been sold, and it was held not to be a mere memorandum, so that extrinsic evidence of other terms was rejected. It has been suggested that this group of cases turns the parol evidence rule into 'no more than a circular statement',[6] which only prevents a party from relying on evidence of extrinsic terms if they were *not* intended to be part of the contract, so that the evidence would have no effect even if it were admitted. But the rule is in practice most likely to be important where one party (A) intended the extrinsic term to be part of the contract while the other (B) relies on the document as an exclusive record. In such a case, B can rely on a presumption [7] that a document which to a reasonable person *looks* like a complete contractual document was indeed intended to be an exclusive record,

[19] *Palgrave, Brown & Son Ltd v SS Turid (Owners)* [1922] 1 AC 397.
[20] *Brown v Byrne* (1854) 3 E & B 703.
[1] *Smith v Wilson* (1832) 3 B & Ad 728.
[2] Cf *Rabin v Gerson Berger Association Ltd* [1986] 1 All ER 374 at 380.
[3] Post, pp 118–121.
[4] *Allen v Pink* (1838) 4 M & W 140.
[5] *Hutton v Watling* [1948] Ch 398.
[6] Law Commission Paper 154 para 2.7.
[7] *Gillespie Bros & Co v Cheney, Eggar & Co* [1896] 2 QB 59 at 62.

so that extrinsic evidence of other terms is excluded.[8] The effect of this presumption is that B's view may prevail even though he does not show that he believed the document to contain all the terms of the contract. It is up to A to show that B had no such belief; and, in view of the importance attached (especially by non-lawyers) to writing in a contractual context, this will be no easy task. Where A fails to perform his task, he will be unable to rely on the extrinsic term even though he intended it to form part of the contract and even though B knew this: B will succeed simply because the term was not recorded in the document. In such cases, the parol evidence rule is more than a 'circular statement'; and, while the rule no doubt promotes certainty, the justice of its operation in such cases is open to question.[9]

(10) Although all the terms of a contract are contained in a written document, it may be possible to show that the parties made another, wholly separate contract relating to the same subject-matter; in which case this *collateral contract* can be proved by evidence extrinsic to the main written contract. In one case, for example, a written agreement for a lease did not refer to an oral agreement, made before the written one was executed, that the landlord would do certain specified repairs. It was held that the oral agreement could be enforced as an 'independent agreement.'[10] According to the older authorities,[11] a party could not rely on evidence of a collateral contract which actually *contradicted* the main contract. But a more recent case[12] rejects this restriction on the scope of the device, holding that a tenant could rely (by way of collateral contract) on an oral assurance that he could reside in the premises which had been let to him, even though the lease expressly provided that they were to be used for business purposes only. The scope of the collateral contract device is, however, restricted in two ways. First, the oral promise must have been intended to operate as a *separate* contract.[13] It could not, therefore, be relied on if it contained a term which one would expect to find in the main contract or which went to the essence of that contract; for in such cases the promise would have been intended as a term of the main contract.[14] Secondly, to take effect as a collateral contract, the promise must be supported by separate consideration: this follows from its nature as a

---

8 *Hutton v Watling* [1948] Ch 398 at 406.
9 Contrast Law Commission Working Paper 70 (recommending abolition of the rule) with Law Commission Paper 154 para 2.7.
10 *Mann v Nunn* (1874) 30 L T 526 at 527.
11 *Angell v Duke* (1875) 32 L T 320; *Henderson v Arthur* [1907] 1 K B 10.
12 *City and Westminster Properties (1934) Ltd v Mudd* [1959] Ch 129; cf *Brikom Investment Ltd v Carr* [1979] Q B 467 (where no point as to the admissibility of evidence was taken).
13 Cf *Heilbut, Symons & Co v Buckleton* [1913] A C 30.
14 Eg *Mitchill v Lath* 160 N E 646 (1928); cf *Preece v Lewis* (1963) 186 Estates Gazettes 113.

separate contract. These restrictions are necessary to preserve a formal consistency between the parol evidence rule and the collateral contract device; for if extrinsic evidence were always admissible to prove a collateral contract, the parol evidence rule would, in effect, cease to exist. But it must be admitted that the scope of the first restriction is hard to define, so that the courts are left with a large measure of discretion in deciding whether to admit, or to reject, evidence extrinsic to a written contract.

Chapter 7

Standard terms and
exemption clauses

Contracts are often made on standard terms prepared by one party and presented by him to the other. Usually such terms are set out in a printed form, which is either the contractual document or one to which reference is made at the time of contracting. Such terms are meant to govern a whole class of contracts, only the individual details being completed in each case. The practice has obvious advantages. It saves time; and, by creating a standard pattern of dealing, it enables the parties to know, in general terms, what sort of risks they will probably have to bear, and to cover by insurance. On the other hand, the practice was also open to abuse, particularly in contracts between commercial suppliers of goods or services and private consumers. The supplier might put into the printed form a clause limiting or altogether excluding a liability to which he would otherwise be subject, either by virtue of a term implied in law, or even irrespective of contract. The customer would often be in a weak position to resist the imposition of such exemption clauses. For one thing, he would generally not read the printed form: indeed, if he did so, its main purpose (of saving time) would be defeated. For another, he would often not be able to obtain the goods or services except on the standard terms, so that his only choice might be to secure them on these terms or to do without them altogether.

To some extent the courts were able to redress the balance in favour of the party prejudiced by such exemption clauses. To this end they developed stringent requirements for the incorporation of exemption clauses, and limited the scope and effectiveness of such clauses in various ways. At the same time Parliament has limited the effectiveness of exemption clauses in a number of statutes. The most important of these is the Unfair Contract Terms Act 1977, under which some exemption clauses are simply ineffective, while others are subject to a test of reasonableness. But many standard form contracts and exemption clauses remain outside the scope of the Act and are subject only to the judge-made limitations mentioned above. These therefore still require discussion, though many of the actual cases on which they are based would now be governed by the 1977 Act.

1 INCORPORATION OF EXEMPTION CLAUSES

A party who wishes to rely on an exemption clause, must first of all show that it has become part of the contract. He can do this in one of three ways.

a Signature

The first is to get the other party to sign the contractual document in which the clause is set out. The party signing is then *prima facie* bound,[1] even if he could not read or understand the document, eg because it was in a language which he did not know.[2]

b Notice

Many contracts are made without being signed by either party. In such cases, standard terms, including an exemption clause, may be contained in a notice posted up on the premises where the contract is made. Alternatively, they may be printed in a document which is simply handed or sent by one party to the other; or in one to which reference is made in the document, which is handed over: for example where a ticket refers to conditions set out in a time-table. In these situations the exemption clause will form part of the contract if, at or before the time of contracting, the party relying on the clause took reasonable steps to bring it to the other party's attention.[3] The question whether such reasonable steps have been taken is essentially one of fact; but some useful guidelines may be derived from the cases.

In the first place, a distinction is drawn between contractual documents and mere vouchers or receipts. A document is contractual if it is known to contain contractual terms, or if it is of a kind that could normally, in the ordinary course of business, be expected to contain such terms. Thus railway tickets or left luggage receipts are commonly regarded as contractual documents; while on the other hand a receipt given to a person to show that he had paid for the hire of a deck-chair at a seaside resort has been held to be a mere voucher.[4]

Secondly, the steps to notify the other party of the terms must be taken at or before the time of contracting. For example, where a contract between a hotel-keeper and a guest was made when the guest booked in at the reception desk, it was held that a printed notice which came to the guest's attention *later*, when he got to his room, did not form part of the contract.[5] Similarly, where a contract for the carriage

---

[1] *L'Estrange v F Graucob Ltd* [1934] 2 K B 394.
[2] *The Luna* [1920] P 22.
[3] *Parker v South Eastern Rly* (1877) 2 C P D 416.
[4] *Chapelton v Barry U D C* [1940] 1 K B 532.
[5] *Olley v Marlborough Court Ltd* [1949] 1 K B 532.

of a passenger was made when his booking was accepted through a travel agent,[6] it was held that conditions contained in the ticket later sent to the passenger were not incorporated in the contract.[7]

Thirdly, the steps must in all the circumstances be reasonably sufficient to bring home to the other party the existence of the exemption clause. This depends both on the manner in which the clause is displayed or set out, and on the nature of the clause. It is advisable to draw attention to the clause by clear words on the face of any document handed over at the time of contracting, especially if the clause is not contained in that document, but in another, which the first document incorporates by reference. Words such as 'For conditions see . . .' or 'subject to our conditions of contract, obtainable on request'[8] are commonly used. The amount of notice required increases in proportion to the unusualness of the clause. For example, a person who contracts to leave his car in a car-park might expect the proprietors to exclude liability for loss of or damage to the car; but a clause excluding liability for personal injury[9] would be more unusual, so that a higher degree of notice of such a clause would have to be given.[10] This could be done by printing or displaying such a clause in some particularly conspicuous manner: eg in block capitals or in red letters.

If reasonable steps have been taken, the clause becomes part of the contract, even though it does not *actually* come to the attention of the party adversely affected. In one case, for example, the clause took effect even though that party could not read it because she was illiterate.[11] However, the position may be different if the party relying on the clause *knows* that the other cannot read it. This would be the position if the clause was in English and the party relying on it was aware of the fact that the other party knew hardly any English.[12]

c Course of dealing

So far it has been assumed that the contract in question is an isolated transaction. But the parties may have entered into a series of contracts over a period of time; and they may regularly have used a form incorporating the same standard terms. Two problems may arise out of such a course of dealing.

---

6 See p 9, ante.
7 *The Eagle* [1977] 2 Lloyd's Rep 70.
8 *Smith v South Wales Switchgear Ltd* [1978] 1 All E R 18.
9 To the extent that it purported to exclude or restrict liability for personal injury *caused by negligence*, such a clause would now be ineffective; see p 90, post.
10 *Thornton v Shoe Lane Parking Ltd* [1971] 2 Q B 163; cf *Interfoto Picture Library Ltd v Stiletto Visual Programmes Ltd* [1988] 1 All E R 348 (where the clause *imposed* liability on the customer).
11 *Thompson v London Midland and Scottish Rly* [1930] 1 K B 41.
12 *Geier v Kujawa* [1970] 1 Lloyd's Rep 364; the clause in that case would now be invalid under the Road Traffic Act 1972, s 148 (3).

First, the steps normally taken to incorporate the clause may, by some oversight, be omitted on the crucial occasion when something goes wrong: eg a warehouseman may fail to hand over the usual warehouse receipt in relation to a particular consignment of goods, which is then stolen. The position is that the usual terms are nevertheless incorporated in that transaction by course of dealing, even though the customer had never actually read them, so long as reasonable notice of them has been given in the series of transactions as a whole.[13] To bring this rule into operation, there must be an established and regular course of dealing (and not, for example, just half a dozen transactions in the course of five years);[14] and it must be *consistent* (ie the same terms must have been used in all the transactions constituting the course of dealing).[15]

Secondly, the party normally handing over the document may wish to alter its terms in his own favour. In this situation, the person so altering the terms would have to take special steps to bring the alteration to the other party's notice, since prima facie the latter would be entitled to assume that a consistent course of dealing was continuing without alteration.[16]

In the cases so far considered, the course of dealing is one between the parties to the contract. A term may also be incorporated in a contract because of a general course of dealing amounting to a trade custom or usage.[17] It seems that an exemption clause can be incorporated in this way even between parties who have not previously dealt with each other.[18]

2 THE SCOPE OF EXEMPTION CLAUSES

a Construction in general

Assuming that an exemption clause has been duly incorporated, the party relying on it must next show that the breach and the loss complained of fall within its scope. Here the primary rule is that exemption clauses are construed strictly against the persons seeking to rely on them. For example, in one case[19] a hire-purchase agreement provided that 'no warranty, condition or description or representation *is* given';

[13] *J Spurling Ltd v Bradshaw* [1956] 2 All ER 121.
[14] *Hollier v Rambler Motors Ltd* [1972] 2 QB 71; *Circle Freight International Ltd v Mideast Gulf Exports Ltd* [1988] 2 Lloyd's Rep 427.
[15] See *McCutcheon v David MacBrayne Ltd* [1964] 1 All ER 430; *Mendelssohn v Normand* [1970] 1 QB 177.
[16] See *Pancommerce SA v Veecheema BV* [1983] 2 Lloyd's Rep 304 at 305 ('in bold type').
[17] See p 65, ante.
[18] See *British Crane Hire Corpn Ltd v Ipswich Plant Hire Ltd* [1975] QB 303 (indemnity clause; the same principle applies to exemption clauses).
[19] *Webster v Higgin* [1948] 2 All ER 127.

and it was held that this provision did not exclude liability for an under-taking which had been *previously* given. In another case,[20] a motor insurance policy provided that the insurer was not to be liable 'whilst the car is carrying any *load* in excess of that for which it was con-structed'; and it was held that this provision did not exclude liability where the car was carrying an excessive number of *passengers*. Although the present rule applies to all exemption clauses, it is less rigorously applied to those which merely limit liability than to those which attempt altogether to exclude it.[1]

b Liability for negligence

Liability for breach of contract is in many cases strict, ie it arises quite irrespective of negligence; while in other cases a contracting party is liable only for negligence.[2] By statute, clauses purporting to exempt a party from liability for negligence are often ineffective or subject to the test of reasonableness. But even where these statutory provisions do not apply the courts insist that 'clear words'[3] must be used to exclude liability for negligence. This requirement is most obviously satisfied if the clause refers expressly to 'negligence';[4] but it may also be satisfied by general words[5] of the kind to be discussed below. The effectiveness of such general words depends on the distinction between cases of strict liability and liability for negligence.

Where there is a realistic possibility[6] that a party can be made liable irrespective of negligence, an exemption clause in general terms (eg one simply excluding liability 'for loss or damage') will normally be construed to refer only to his strict liability.[7] If he is in fact negligent, he will therefore not be protected by such a clause. But the rule is one of construction only and will not be applied if the intention to exclude liability even for negligence is made clear.[8] This was, for example, held to be the position where an exemption clause excluded liability for loss or damage 'however caused which can be covered by insurance.'[9] Even in the present group of cases, moreover, general words which merely *limit* liability are more likely to be construed to cover

---

20 *Houghton v Trafalgar Insurance Co* [1954] 1 QB 247.
1 *Ailsa Craig Fishing Co Ltd v Malvern Fishing Co Ltd* [1983] 1 All ER 101.
2 See pp 266–268, post.
3 *Gillespie Bros & Co Ltd v Roy Bowles Transport Ltd* [1973] QB 400 at 419.
4 Eg, *Spriggs v Sotheby Parke Bernet & Co Ltd* [1986] 1 Lloyd's Rep 487.
5 *Canada SS Lines Ltd v R* [1952] AC 192 at 208; *Smith v South Wales Switchgear Ltd* [1978] 1 All ER 18 at 22, 26.
6 Ibid, p 27.
7 *Canada SS Lines Ltd v R* [1952] AC 192 at 208; *White v John Warrick Ltd* [1953] 2 All ER 1021.
8 *The Golden Leader* [1980] 2 Lloyd's Rep 573.
9 *Joseph Travers & Sons Ltd v Cooper* [1915] 1 KB 73.

negligence than similar words in a clause which purports altogether to *exclude* liability.[10]

Where the contract is one under which the party relying on the clause is *only* liable for negligence, the rule that general words do not normally exclude liability for negligence does not apply. Such words *may* therefore exempt the party in breach from liability for negligence.[11] But it by no means follows that they *will* have this effect: they may be construed simply as a warning to one party that the other is not in law liable except for negligence. Which of these constructions is adopted depends on the court's view as to the more obvious meaning of the clause to the injured party. Thus, in one case[12] a customer left a car with a garage on the terms that 'customers' cars are driven by our staff at customer's sole risk'. It was held that this clause protected the garage proprietor from liability for loss caused by the negligence of one of his staff, since he was only liable where such loss was due to negligence, and the obvious meaning of the clause was to exclude this liability. But in another similar case,[13] a provision that the garage was 'not responsible for damage caused by fire to customers' cars' was held to be only a warning that the garage was not legally liable in the *absence* of negligence. Accordingly it did not protect the garage for liability for damage to a customer's car caused by a fire due to the negligence of the garage.

c Seriousness of breach

Traditionally, the courts were not concerned with the fairness of contracts. But they nevertheless resisted attempts by contracting parties to exclude liability for particularly serious breaches; and to this end they developed the so-called doctrine of fundamental breach. According to one view, this doctrine made it impossible as a matter of substantive law to exclude liability for such breaches. This *substantive doctrine* was at one time a useful device for protecting consumers against unfair exemption clauses; but it is no longer needed for this purpose now that such clauses can be dealt with under the Unfair Contract Terms Act 1977. Moreover, the substantive doctrine was not restricted to cases involving private consumers; and when it was applied to commercial transactions negotiated between businessmen bargaining on equal terms it could create uncertainty and upset perfectly fair arrangements for allocating risks and the burden of insuring against them. For these reasons the House of Lords has rejected the substantive doctrine and has held that the doctrine of fundamental breach is a rule of

---

10 *George Mitchell (Chesterhall) Ltd v Finney Lock Seeds Ltd* [1983] 2 A C 803 at 814.
11 *J Archdale Ltd v Comservices Ltd* [1954] 1 All E R 210; *Smith v Eric S Bush* [1987] 3 All E R 179 (as to which see also p 94, post).
12 *Rutter v Palmer* [1922] 2 K B 87.
13 *Hollier v Rambler Motors Ltd* [1972] 2 Q B 71.

construction only.[14] In reaching this conclusion, the House of Lords overruled a small number of cases which were consistent only with the substantive doctrine; but it did not cast doubt on many other decisions which had previously determined the scope and effects of the rule of construction. That rule amounts to a presumption that general words in an exemption clause will not normally cover certain very serious breaches; but the presumption can be overcome if the words of the clause are sufficiently clear. Viewed in this way, the doctrine of fundamental breach can be regarded simply as an aspect of the principle that exemption clauses are to be construed strictly against parties who rely on them.[15] In applying that principle, the seriousness of the breach will remain an important (even though it is no longer a decisive) factor. Hence the old cases on fundamental breach (many of which were decided before the development of the substantive doctrine) will continue to provide some guidance on the *scope* of the rule of construction. It is also necessary to consider its exact legal *effects*. The practical importance of the subject is now largely restricted to clauses which are outside the scope of the Unfair Contract Terms Act 1977. A party obviously cannot rely on a clause (however clearly expressed) if it is simply ineffective under that Act; and where a clause is subject to the statutory reasonableness test, his right to rely on it is more likely to depend on the application of that test than on the construction of the clause at common law.[16]

i Scope of the rule

The scope of the rule of construction depends on three factors: the nature of the term broken, the effects of the breach and the manner in which the breach is committed.

So far as the first factor is concerned, we shall see in Chapter 16 that, as a general rule, relatively slight breaches give rise only to a right to damages, while more serious breaches give rise to a right to rescind the contract and also to a right to damages. But for the purpose of determining whether a breach gives rise to a right to rescind, the law further distinguishes between conditions, warranties and intermediate terms. Breach of a warranty or of an intermediate term does not, of itself, give the injured party the right to rescind the contract, and breaches of such terms are plainly not within the rule of construction here under discussion. Nor does that rule apply merely because the term broken is a condition, even though such a breach does give

---

[14] *Suisse Atlantique Société d'Armement Maritime SA v Rotterdamsche Kolen Centrale NV* [1967] 1 A C 361; *Photo Production Ltd v Securicor Transport Ltd* [1980] A C 827; *George Mitchell (Chesterhall) Ltd v Finney Lock Seeds Ltd* [1983] 2 A C 803; *The Antares (No 2)* [1987] 1 Lloyd's Rep 424 at 428.

[15] See p 75, ante. *George Mitchell (Chesterhall) Ltd v Finney Lock Seeds Ltd*, supra.

[16] Eg *George Mitchell (Chesterhall) Ltd v Finney Lock Seeds Ltd* [1983] 2 A C 803.

the injured party the right to rescind. But the rule does apply to the breach of what is known as a fundamental term: this is 'narrower than a condition'[17] and is so central to the purpose of the contract that the performance rendered is (as a result of the breach) essentially different from that promised. The stock example of a breach of such a term is provided by the case of a seller who contracts to deliver peas but instead delivers beans:[18] exemption clauses have been construed so as not to cover breaches of such terms.[19] By contrast, in *George Mitchell (Chesterhall) Ltd v Finney Lock Seeds Ltd*[20] a farmer bought seed for a crop of cabbage which totally failed because the seed was seriously defective. It was said that this was 'not a "peas and beans" case at all'[1] so that a clause limiting the seller's liability did, as a matter of construction, cover the breach.[2] The contract was evidently regarded as one for the sale of 'seed', and seed (though seriously defective seed) had indeed been delivered.

Whether the performance rendered is so fundamentally different from that promised, as to bring the case into the 'peas and beans' category, depends on two factors: the nature of the performance promised, and the extent to which the performance actually rendered differs from that promised. If, for example, the subject-matter of a sale is a car which turns out to be defective, one cannot classify the term broken simply by looking at the seriousness of the defects. One has to ask what the seller promised (expressly or by implication) at the time of sale. If he was a dealer who undertook that the car was in good running order, the defects necessary to constitute breach of a fundamental term will be relatively less serious than if the seller was a private person with no technical knowledge. Indeed, if the car was sold to an enthusiast as a pile of scrap metal, which might or might not be coaxed into running order, there would be no breach at all.

In contracts for the carriage of goods by sea it is well established that the term as to the route is fundamental. Hence the carrier loses the protection of an exemption clause if he deviates, that is, if without justification he departs from the agreed or customary route.[3] It makes no difference that the goods are ultimately carried to their destination, that the deviation was only slight, that the loss or damage was not caused by the deviation or by the extra length of the voyage, or indeed

---

[17] *Smeaton Hanscomb & Co Ltd v Sassoon I Setty & Co* [1953] 1 WLR 1468 at 1470.

[18] *Chanter v Hopkins* (1838) 4 M & W 399 at 404.

[19] Eg *Andrews Bros (Bournemouth) Ltd v Singer & Co Ltd* [1934] 1 KB 17.

[20] [1983] 2 AC 803.

[1] Ibid at 813.

[2] But the clause did not protect the seller as it failed to satisfy the statutory reasonableness test: see p 94 post.

[3] *Joseph Thorley Ltd v Orchis Ltd* [1907] 1 KB 660; *Hain SS Co v Tate & Lyle Ltd* (1936) 41 Com Cas 350; for the continued existence of the rule, see p 83, post.

that the deviation was 'for practical purposes irrelevant':[4] in other words, the *actual effects* of the deviation are not taken into account. The rule is based on the probable, or hypothetical, effects of the deviation: the owner of the goods may lose his effective insurance cover if the goods are carried by a different route from that covered by the policy, and therefore it is thought necessary to give him a remedy against the carrier in spite of the exemption clause.[5] The situation may be contrasted with that in which the goods are damaged because the ship is unseaworthy: the mere fact that the carrier has in some way broken his obligation in relation to seaworthiness does not deprive him of the protection of an exemption clause.[6] The principle of the deviation cases has been extended to land carriage,[7] and to cases which have nothing to do with carriage at all. For example, it has been applied to the case of a warehouseman who agrees to store goods in one particular warehouse and stores them in another;[8] and to a person who undertakes to do certain work (eg of cleaning or repairing) personally and then lets the work out to a sub-contractor.[9]

In a second group of cases it is the *effect of the breach* (rather than the *term broken*) which is the crucial point. For example, failure to perform at the agreed time is always a breach of the same term, but a clause which covers a slight delay may not cover one that is serious and prolonged. Again, a person who supplies a defective car under a contract of sale or hire-purchase will often be in breach of an implied condition as to quality. This is not a fundamental term;[10] but in a number of cases it has been held that the supplier was not protected by exemption clauses where the defects were so serious as to make the vehicles for practical purposes useless to the customer.[11] What is stressed in these cases is the *effect* of the breach. This must either be such as to make the performance rendered 'totally different from that which the contract contemplates'[12] or (as in the car cases just mentioned) merely cause *serious* prejudice to the injured party, without turning the performance rendered into something *totally* different from that promised. The exact degree of 'seriousness' required for this purpose cannot be precisely

---

[4] *Suisse Atlantique* case [1967] 1 AC 361 at 423.

[5] *Hain SS Co v Tate & Lyle Ltd*, supra, at 354.

[6] *Kish v Taylor* [1912] AC 604.

[7] *London and North Western Rly Co v Neilson* [1922] 2 AC 263.

[8] *Woolf v Collis Removal Services* [1948] 1 KB 11 at 15; cf *United Fresh Meat Co Ltd v Charterhouse Cold Storage Ltd* [1974] 2 Lloyd's Rep 286 (chilled instead of frozen store).

[9] *Davies v Collins* [1945] 1 All ER 247.

[10] See p 78, ante.

[11] *Yeoman Credit Ltd v Apps* [1962] 2 QB 508; *Farnsworth Finance Facilities Ltd v Attryde* [1970] 2 All ER 774.

[12] *Suisse Atlantique* case [1967] 1 AC 361, 393.

defined: all that can be said with certainty is that the difficulty of convincing the court that the clause covers a particular breach will increase with the gravity of that breach.

In a third group of cases the question whether an exemption clause applies turns on the *manner* (rather than on the *effect*) of the breach. Suppose that goods are entrusted to a person for safe-keeping or for carriage, and that person, in breach of contract, delivers them to someone who is not entitled to them, so that they are lost to the owner. Here a distinction is drawn: if the misdelivery is deliberate, an exemption clause is unlikely to protect the party in breach, because the probability is that 'the parties never contemplated that such a breach should be excused or limited';[13] but this reasoning does not apply where the misdelivery is merely negligent.[14] Nor would it apply where the goods were lost or damaged by a fire caused by negligence:[15] such a breach would only deprive the party in breach of the protection of the clause if he had been guilty of some particularly serious deficiency in his precautions against fire. In all these cases the *effect* of the breach is the same, viz wholly to deprive the owner of his goods; and the question whether an exemption clause should be construed so as to cover the breach was sometimes held to depend on whether it had been committed deliberately. But the mere fact that it was so committed is no longer regarded as decisive. Thus a person will not be deprived of the benefit of an exemption clause merely because he is guilty of a deliberate delay of one day in loading a ship under a charterparty;[16] for the prejudicial effect of such a delay is assumed to be slight. In the present group of cases, in other words, the breach must be deliberate *and* its effects must be serious.

ii Legal effects of the rule

Where the breach is a serious one in the sense of the preceding discussion, the effect of the rule of construction is that an exemption clause will only be construed so as to cover that breach if it is 'most clearly and unambiguously expressed'.[17] At one time, the courts were inclined, in applying this rule, to give a 'strained and artificial meaning'[18] to exemption clauses so as to exclude from their scope the serious breaches which had occurred. This approach no longer prevails[19]; but the court may still hold that general words which might seem to be

---

13 Ibid at 435; *Alexander v Railway Executive* [1951] 2 K B 882.
14 *Hollins v J Davy Ltd* [1963] 1 QB 844.
15 Cf *Kenyon & Craven Ltd v Baxter Hoare Ltd* [1971] 2 All E R 708.
16 *Suisse Atlantique* case, supra, at 435.
17 *Ailsa Craig Fishing Co Ltd v Malvern Fishing Co Ltd* [1983] 1 W L R 964 at 966.
18 *George Mitchell (Chesterhall) Ltd v Finney Lock Seeds Ltd* [1983] 2 A C 803 at 810.
19 Ibid at 814; *Ailsa Craig* case, supra, at 966; *Photo Production Ltd v Securicor Transport Ltd* [1980] A C 827 at 851.

capable of covering the breach should not be construed in this sense 'because this would lead to an absurdity or because it would defeat the main object of the contract . . .'[20] Thus in one case[1] a contract for the carriage of goods by sea provided that the carrier's responsibility was to cease after the goods had been discharged. It was held that he was not protected when he delivered the goods to someone who (as the carrier knew) was not entitled to them. Even where clauses do apply to breaches of fundamental terms, they are nevertheless strictly construed. This point is particularly well illustrated by cases in which contracts for the carriage of goods by sea contained clauses permitting deviation. Prima facie such clauses were construed so as to permit deviation only so long as the ship proceeded in the general direction contemplated by the contract.[2] And even if they expressly permitted for deviation 'in a contrary direction' they would not be taken absolutely literally: such a clause in a contract for the carriage of goods from London to Hamburg might justify a deviation to Newcastle, but not one to New York.[3]

It follows, however, from the status of the rule as one of construction that a clause can apply, notwithstanding the gravity of the breach, if it is clear from the words used that the parties intended the clause to have that effect. The courts are here, as elsewhere[4], more ready to hold that a clause protects the party in breach if it merely limits, than if it totally excludes, liability.[5] In the *Suisse Atlantique* case,[6] charterers under a long-term charterparty broke their part of the contract by causing the ship to be detained in port for very considerable periods; and the delays were so great as to amount to a 'fundamental breach'.[7] The contract provided that the charterers should pay $1,000 for each day of delay; and the House of Lords held that the shipowners could not recover more by way of damages, even though their actual loss far exceeded the stipulated amount. The clause effectively limited the charterers' liability because on its true construction it applied even to the very serious delays which had occurred. Similarly, in *George Mitchell (Chesterhall) Ltd v Finney Lock Seeds Ltd*[8] the seller's breach in supplying defective seed had the most serious consequence, in that the buyer's crop wholly failed. But the House of Lords nevertheless held that a clause limiting the seller's liability did, on its true construc-

---

20 *Suisse Atlantique* case [1967] 1 A C 361 at 396.
1 *Sze Hai Tong Bank Ltd v Rambler Cycle Co Ltd* [1959] A C 576.
2 *Glynn v Margetson* [1893] A C 351.
3 Cf *Connolly Shaw Ltd v Nordenfjeldske SS Co* (1934) 49 Ll L Rep 183.
4 See pp 76–77, ante.
5 *George Mitchell (Chesterhall) Ltd v Finney Lock Seeds Ltd* [1983] 2 A C 803.
6 [1967] 1 A C 361.
7 Ibid at 396.
8 [1983] 2 A C 803.

tion, cover the breach.[9] The character of the rule as one of construction is therefore firmly established; but three problems call for further consideration.

The first of these arises from the fact that a serious breach of the kind here under discussion normally gives the injured party two rights: a right to damages and a right to rescind the contract.[10] An exemption clause may be so drawn as to affect only one of these rights. Thus in the *Suisse Atlantique* case the clause only limited the shipowner's right to damages but said nothing about his right to rescind. Conversely, a contract may contain a non-rejection or non-cancellation clause which excludes the right to rescind, but says nothing about the injured party's right to damages. Such a clause may take away the right to rescind even for a breach of a most serious kind; but this would not prevent the injured party from claiming damages for that breach. The right to rescind may also be lost in other ways, in particular if the injured party affirms the contract. Such affirmation does not affect the operation of a clause which only excludes or limits the right to damages: in other words, that right continues, even after affirmation, to depend on the construction of the clause[11]. The position was at one time thought to be different where the injured party did not affirm, but rescinded on account of the breach. It used to be thought that such rescission brought the whole contract (including any clause restricting the right to damages) to an end, so that the injured party's right to damages was no longer affected by the clause. But this view amounted to a virtual reintroduction of the substantive doctrine of fundamental breach and it was rejected in *Photo Production Ltd v Securicor Transport Ltd.*[12] In that case a security firm had been engaged to protect a factory and one of its employees started a fire which got out of control, so that the factory was destroyed. The contract excluded the security firm's liability in damages; and the factory owners argued that they could get rid of the exemption clause by rescinding the contract for fundamental breach. But the House of Lords rejected the argument, holding that the clause, on its true construction, covered the breach, and that rescission only affected *future* performance: hence it did not retrospectively deprive the security firm of the benefit of the clause with respect to loss suffered before rescission. This rule seems, however, not to apply where a carrier of goods by sea deviates; for in such cases the carrier loses the benefit of exemption clauses in respect of losses which had occurred *before* rescission by the cargo-owner. Such cases can be regarded as a special exception to the general rule that rescission does not

---

[9] But the seller was held fully liable because the clause did not satisfy the statutory test of reasonableness: see p 94, post.

[10] See p 78, ante, p 283, post.

[11] As in the *Suisse Atlantique* case, *supra*.

[12] [1980] AC 827.

retrospectively affect exemption clauses;[13] or they can be explained on the ground that this result follows as a matter of construction from the special commercial considerations which justify the treatment of deviation as a breach of a fundamental term.[14]

The second problem arises from the fact that the law distinguishes between very *serious* breaches and those which make the performance rendered *totally* different from that bargained for.[15] In theory, the seller in the *George Mitchell* case might have drafted a clause that would have protected him even if, instead of delivering seeds, he had delivered grass clippings; but in practice he would find it hard to persuade the court that a clause in a contract for the sale of seeds was intended to lead to such a surprising result. The point is illustrated by *The TFL Prosperity*[16] where a clause in a charterparty exempting the shipowners from liability for 'damage' was held not to protect them when the charterer suffered economic loss because the ship was simply not of the size stipulated in the contract. To hold that the clause applied to this kind of breach would give the shipowners so much discretion in the performance of the charterparty as to turn it into 'no more than a statement of intent by the owners',[17] thus destroying its essential character as a contract. Since this did not accord with 'the true common intention of the parties',[18] the House of Lords cut down the scope of the exemption clause so as to make it consistent at the very least with the purpose of the contract as a whole.

The third problem relates to the burden of proof where a clause is held, as a matter of construction, not to extend to certain serious breaches and it is alleged that such a breach has occurred. Suppose, for example, that a bailee, such as a cleaner or carrier, loses goods that have been entrusted to him. In such a case it is not up to the owner of the goods to show that the loss is due to a breach so serious as not to be covered by the clause. The burden is on the bailee to show that the loss was *not* due to such a breach.[19] The law takes this view because, in the case put the question whether the breach is sufficiently serious depends on the manner[20] in which it was committed, and the bailee should be in a better position than the owner to prove just how the goods were lost. On the other hand, where the breach consists of delay and is serious because of its *effects*[1] (as in the *Suisse Atlantique* case) the burden is probably on the injured party, since he will be in a better

13 Ibid at 845.
14 See p 80, ante; cf *The Antares (No 2)* [1987] 1 Lloyd's Rep 424 at 430.
15 See p 80, ante.
16 [1984] 1 W L R 48.
17 Ibid at 58–59.
18 Ibid at 59.
19 *Levison v Patent Steam Carpet Cleaning Co Ltd* [1978] Q B 69.
20 See p 81, ante.
 1 See p 80, ante.

position than the party in breach to show that the prejudice resulting from the delay was indeed of the required degree of seriousness.

3 THE EFFECTIVENESS OF EXEMPTION CLAUSES AT COMMON LAW

Common law limitations on the effectiveness of exemption clauses remain important in cases not covered by the legislation to be discussed below;[2] and, even in cases which are so covered, common law rules may provide additional safeguards. One suggestion is that the courts will only hold a party bound by a contractual term when it would be fair and reasonable to do so.[3] But if this were true as a general rule many of the provisions of the Unfair Contract Terms Act 1977[4] would scarcely be necessary. As a matter of common law, the English courts have not, as yet, established any general rule that exemption clauses must be fair or reasonable. Rather, they have laid down a number of specific limitations on the effectiveness of such clauses.

The first of these is that a party cannot rely on an exemption clause if he has misrepresented the effect of the clause to the other party. This was held to be the position where a clause in a contract for the cleaning of a dress exempted the cleaner from liability for 'any damage, however arising' and the customer signed the contractual document after she had been told that the contract only excluded liability for damage to beads and sequins, and certain other specified risks.[5]

Secondly, the party in breach may, at the time of contracting, make an oral promise inconsistent with an exemption clause in a contractual document. That oral promise will then prevail: for example, where at an auction the auctioneer gives an oral assurance inconsistent with the printed conditions of sale.[6] A somewhat similar rule applies where a series of contracts is made under a 'master agreement'. An obligation imposed by that agreement may prevail over an exemption clause contained in one of the particular contracts made under it.[7]

Thirdly, the courts have held that there are certain kinds of conduct for which liability cannot be excluded. A party cannot, for example, exclude liability for his own fraud.[8] Clauses excluding liability for

---

[2] See pp 88–97, post.

[3] *Thornton v Shoe Lane Parking Ltd* [1971] 2 Q B 163 at 170; *Levison v Patent Steam Carpet Cleaning Co Ltd* [1978] Q B 69 at 79; *Interfoto Picture Library Ltd v Stiletto Visual Programmes Ltd* [1988] 1 All E R 348 at 357.

[4] Ie those imposing the requirement of reasonableness: post, pp 91–93.

[5] *Curtis v Chemical Cleaning and Dyeing Co Ltd* [1951] 1 K B 805.

[6] *Couchman v Hill* [1947] K B 554; *Harling v Eddy* [1951] 2 K B 739.

[7] *Gallagher v British Road Services Ltd* [1974] 2 Lloyd's Rep 440.

[8] *Pearson & Son Ltd v Dublin Corpn* [1907] A C 351 at 353, 362; *Walker v Boyle* [1982] 1 All E R 634.

fraud or other misrepresentation *inducing* a contract are discussed later in this chapter.[9] Here we are concerned with clauses excluding liability for fraud in the *performance* of the contract. For example, a carrier would not be protected by a clause protecting him from liability for short delivery if he had himself stolen the missing goods. A party similarly cannot exempt himself from liability for his own breach of fiduciary duty. The latter rule is particularly important in relation to the duty which the promoter of a company owes to the company, not to make a profit out of the promotion.[10] There is also some authority to support the view that a contract setting up a 'domestic tribunal' such as a private disciplinary body cannot effectively exclude the so-called rules of 'natural justice'.[11] These are rules of law designed to ensure that such a body exercises its powers fairly; in particular, by requiring the tribunal to give each party a fair hearing, and by disqualifying members of the tribunal who have a pecuniary interest in the dispute, or any other interest which is likely to bias them.

A fourth judicial limitation is to restrict the operation of exemption clauses to the parties to the contract, so that third parties may not be protected. In the leading *Midland Silicones*[12] case, for example, a contract for the carriage of a drum of chemicals from New York to London contained a clause by which the liability of the carriers was limited. While the drum was being unloaded it was damaged as a result of the negligence of a firm of stevedores, who had been employed by the carriers to unload the ship. It was held that the stevedores were not protected by the limitation of liability contained in the contract between the carriers and the owners of the drum. The rule is an inconvenient one, for it means that the injured party can very often get round an exemption clause, by simply suing the servant or agent of the protected party, who will then as a matter of business practice, or of good labour relations, have to 'stand behind' the actual defendant and to pay the damages. This may sometimes have been a useful device for protecting a private consumer against a more powerful contracting party[13] but it is no longer necessary for this purpose now that undesirable exemption clauses are directly controlled under the Unfair Contract Terms Act 1977.[14] Between businessmen, the rule gives rise to undesirable uncertainty, and it tends to falsify the assumptions on which each party to the contract bases certain important decisions: in particular decisions as to the risks against which each of them should insure. Hence in some cases the rule has been modified by legislation

9 See p 93, post.
10 *Gluckstein v Barnes* [1900] AC 240.
11 *Lee v Showmen's Guild of Great Britain* [1952] 2 QB 329 at 342.
12 *Scruttons Ltd v Midland Silicones Ltd* [1962] AC 446.
13 Eg *Adler v Dickson* [1955] 1 QB 158.
14 See p 88 et seq, post.

extending the benefit of exemption clauses to the servants or agents of the protected party.[15] Where such legislation does not apply, contracts now commonly provide that the benefit of the exemption clause is to be available to certain specified third parties. In spite of some theoretical difficulties which arise under the English doctrine of privity of contract,[16] the courts have upheld such provisions. A third party can, therefore, take advantage of them[17] if, while carrying out work under the contract on behalf of one of the contracting parties, he causes loss or injury to the other. The third party may also be protected on another ground, which can be illustrated by supposing that A has undertaken to build a house for B and has arranged for part of the work to be done by a subcontractor C. If B suffers loss as a result of defects in C's work, C may be liable in tort to B if he has been negligent, ie for breach of a duty of care; and it has been suggested that an exemption clause in the contract between A and B might 'limit the duty of care'[18] and so provide C with a defence. Although the suggestion has been doubted[19] it seems to be a reasonable one where B has assented to the clause and to A's employment of a subcontractor.

So far we have considered the question whether an exemption clause can *benefit* a third party. A further problem is whether such a clause can *bind* a third party. Here again, the starting principle is that it does not have this effect. The point may be illustrated by varying the example of the building contract just discussed and supposing that the exemption clause is contained, not in the main contract between A and B, but in the subcontract between A and C. Such a clause would not bind B,[20] and this seems to be a desirable result as B will not have assented to the clause. The example is based on the assumption that C has committed a *breach* of the subcontract. If he has *performed* that contract to the letter (eg by fitting the very components specified in it) he cannot be held liable merely because that performance turns out to be inadequate for B's purposes.[1] He can, in other words, rely on the

15 Eg Carriage by Air Act 1961, Sch 1 Art 25A; Carriage of Goods by Sea Act 1971, Sch Art IVbis.
16 See p 208, et seq, post.
17 *The Eurymedon* [1975] A C 154; *The New York Star* [1980] 3 All E R 257; cf *Snelling v John G Snelling Ltd* [1973] Q B 87.
18 *Junior Books Ltd v Veitchi Co Ltd* [1983] 1 A C 520 at 524; *Southern Water Authority v Carey* [1985] 2 All E R 1077 at 1086; *Norwich City Council v Harvey* (1987) 39 BLR 75; cf *Harris v Wyre Forest District Council* [1988] 1 All E R 691.
19 *The Aliakmon* [1986] A C 785 at 817; cf *Muirhead v Industrial Tank Specialities Ltd* [1986] Q B 507 at 525.
20 Cf *The Aliakmon* [1986] A C 785.
1 See *Junior Books Ltd v Veitchi Co Ltd* [1983] 1 A C 520, 534; *Simaan Contracting Co v Pilkington Glass Ltd (No 2)* [1988] 1 All E R 791 at 804.

subcontract as defining *what he has to do*, but not as excluding or limiting legal liability for *failing to do it*.

The general rule that an exemption clause cannot bind a third party is subject to exceptions which have been developed in the interests of commercial convenience. One such exception exists where goods are handed over, eg to a cleaner or repairer, under a contract of bailment which allows the work to be subcontracted. Here the owner of the goods may be bound by an exemption clause in the subcontract on the ground that he 'consented to the bailee making a sub-bailment containing those conditions'.[2] A second, more controversial, exception is based on a case[3] in which A bought goods from B and contracted with C to have the goods shipped abroad. It was held that B was bound by a limitation clause in the contract between A and C. The case may be reconciled with the doctrine of privity of contract either on the ground that A acted as B's agent in making the contract of carriage so far as it affected B;[4] or on the ground that, when B presented the goods to C for carriage, and C accepted them, an implied contract, incorporating the clause, sprang up between these parties.[5] The practical justification for the decision is that C is likely to make his insurance arrangements on the assumption that his liability will be limited by the terms of the contract, while B can be expected to cover his interest in the goods by insurance so long as they remain at his risk. In such a commercial context, there seems to be no good reason of policy for refusing to give effect to the contractual limitation of liability, even against a third party.

4 THE UNFAIR CONTRACT TERMS ACT 1977

This Act now contains the most important limitations on the effectiveness of exemption clauses. Under it some exemption clauses are simply ineffective, while others are made subject to a requirement of reasonableness.

a Terminology

Before discussing the operation of the Act it is necessary to say something about its terminology. Generally, the Act only applies to terms seeking to exclude or restrict 'business liability', that is liability arising from things done or to be done in the course of a business, or from the

---

2 *Morris v C W Martin & Sons Ltd* [1966] 1 QB 716 at 729; *Singer Co (UK) Ltd v Tees and Hartlepool Port Authority* [1988] 2 Lloyd's Rep 164.
3 *Pyrene Co Ltd v Scindia Navigation Co Ltd* [1954] 2 QB 402.
4 Ibid at 423–425.
5 *The Kapetan Markos NL (No 2)* [1987] 2 Lloyd's Rep 321 at 331.

occupation of business premises[6]. A person acting in the course of a business will in the following discussion be called B.

The Act gives special protection to a person who 'deals as consumer'. A person so deals if he does not make (or hold himself out as making) the contract in the course of a business, *and* the other party does make the contract in the course of a business.[7] If the contract is for the supply of goods, there is the additional requirement that they must be of a type ordinarily supplied for private use or consumption.[8] A person dealing as consumer will in the following discussion be called C.

Where neither party acts in the course of a business there can be no 'dealing as consumer' since it is an essential element of that concept that the other party must act in the course of a business. For example, if a car is sold to a 'private' buyer by a 'private' seller neither party deals as consumer.

The Act strikes at terms which 'exclude or restrict' liability. These words are not defined; but to the extent that the Act prevents exclusion or restriction of liability it also prevents a party from doing analogous things: for example, from imposing short time-limits on claims; or from excluding one remedy (eg rejection) without affecting another (eg damages).[9] A written arbitration agreement is not to be treated as excluding or restricting liability.[10]

While the Act prevents the parties from excluding or restricting *liabilities*, it generally leaves them free to define in their contract what *duties* each is undertaking. For example, if a seller promised to deliver goods by a certain date but made his promise 'subject to strikes', this qualification would not be within the Act. In certain cases, however, the Act specifically prevents a party from excluding or restricting duties. This is the position where a term purports to exclude the duty of care giving rise to liability in negligence,[11] or the duties arising out of terms implied by law in contracts for the supply of goods.[12] Even in these cases, however, there may be a distinction between terms which exclude or restrict a duty and those which prevent one from ever arising. Once all the circumstances giving rise to the duty are shown

---

[6] Unfair Contract Terms Act 1977, s 1(3). 'Business' includes a profession and activities of government departments and local or public authorities: s 14. Occupiers, Liability Act 1984, s 2 makes certain exceptions relating to access to premises for recreational or educational purposes.

[7] S 12(1)(a) and (b). A contract is only made in the course of a business if it is part of the *regular* course of dealing of that business: *R and B Customs Brokers Co Ltd v United Dominions Trust Ltd* [1988] 1 All E R 847.

[8] S 12(1)(c).

[9] S 13(1).

[10] S 13(2).

[11] See the reference to ss 2 and 5 in s 13(1).

[12] See the reference to ss 6 and 7 in s 13(1).

to exist, the Act applies to a term which attempts to exclude or restrict the duty: this would be the position where goods were sold in circumstances giving rise to the implied condition that the goods were of merchantable quality,[13] and the contract simply provided that the seller's liability for breach of that condition should be limited or excluded. The position may, however, be different where the exemption clause is one of the circumstances relevant to the question whether a duty exists: thus the Act has been held not to apply to a term by which A, when supplying information to B, expressly stated that he took no responsibility for its accuracy.[14] But in borderline cases the distinction between the two types of provisions is hard to draw; and the courts might refuse to regard terms as preventing duties from arising if they had obviously been drafted in this way to evade the Act.[15]

b Ineffective terms

In the first place, the Act makes ineffective any contract term or notice by which B seeks to exclude or restrict liability for death or personal injury resulting from negligence.[16] Terms or notices excluding or restricting *strict* liability[17] are not affected by this provision of the Act, but may be ineffective under some of its other provisions,[18] or under other legislation.[19]

Secondly, the Act strikes at exemption clauses in so-called manufacturers' guarantees of goods ordinarily supplied for private use as consumption. It provides[20] that in such guarantees B cannot exclude or restrict liability for loss or damage arising from defects in the goods while in 'consumer use', and resulting from the negligence of any person concerned in the manufacture or distribution of the goods. 'Consumer use' means use other than exclusively in the course of a business; thus it covers the case where a car is bought in the course of a business but also used partly for private purposes. A 'guarantee' is a written promise or assurance that defects will be made good. The present provision does not apply between the immediate parties to the contract for the supply of goods: exemption clauses in contracts between them are governed by the provisions to be discussed below.

Thirdly, a term is sometimes ineffective if it attemps to exclude or

---

13 Under Sale of Goods Act 1979, s 14(1).
14 *Harris v Wyre Forest District Council* [1988] 1 All ER 691; this was also the position in *Hedley Byrne & Co Ltd v Heller & Partners Ltd* [1964] AC 465, post, p 128.
15 See *Davies v Parry* [1988] 1 EGLR 147; cf *Walker v Boyle* [1982] 1 All ER 634.
16 S 2(1).
17 Cf pp 266–267, post.
18 Eg ss 6 and 7.
19 Eg Defective Premises Act 1972 ss 1(1) and 6(3); other legislation while not referring to negligence in practice deals with negligence liability: eg Public Passenger Vehicles Act 1981, s 29; Transport Act 1962 s 43(7); Financial Services Act 1986, s 86.
20 S 5. See also Consumer Protection Act 1987, s 7.

restrict liability for breach of undertakings implied by law[1] in contracts for the supply of goods. One group of such undertakings relates to the correspondence of the goods with description or sample, and (when the supplier acts in the course of a business) to their quality or fitness for a particular purpose. A term excluding or restricting the liability of B to C for breach of any of these implied undertakings is ineffective.[2] Another group of such terms relates to the supplier's title to the goods and to his right to give possession. In contracts of sale or hire-purchase, an attempt to exclude or restrict liability for breach of these undertakings is invalid whether or not the supplier acted in the course of a business.[3] Attempts to exclude or restrict such liability are also invalid in certain other contracts for the transfer of goods (such as contracts of exchange), but only if the supplier acts in the course of a business.[4]

Fourthly, certain exemption clauses are made ineffective by the Consumer Protection Act 1987. Part I of that Act makes producers liable if their products are 'defective' in the sense of being unsafe, and if the defect causes death, personal injury or certain kinds of harm to property. Such liability arises without proof of negligence and cannot be excluded by contract.[5] Part II of the Act makes it an offence to supply goods which do not comply with legislative safety standards. The Act gives a civil remedy to persons affected by contravention of these standards, and that liabilty cannot be excluded by contract.[6]

c The requirement of reasonableness

The Unfair Contract Terms Act makes a number of terms ineffective except in so far as they satisfy the requirement of reasonableness. The burden of showing that the requirement is satisfied lies on the party so claiming.[7]

i Cases to which the requirement applies

In the first place, the requirement of reasonableness applies where B by a contract term or notice seeks to exclude or restrict his liability for negligence giving rise to loss or damage *other than* death or personal injury.[8]

Secondly, the requirement applies in certain cases to terms purporting to exclude or restrict liability for breach of the undertakings implied by law in contracts for the supply of goods. We have seen that

---

[1] See p 64, ante.
[2] Ss 6(2), 7(2).
[3] Ss 6(1) and (4).
[4] Ss 1(3) and 7(3A), as inserted by the Supply of Goods and Services Act 1982, s 17(2).
[5] Consumer Protection Act 1987 s 7.
[6] Ibid ss 10, 41(1) and (4).
[7] Unfair Contract Terms Act 1977, s 11(5).
[8] S 2(2).

sometimes such terms are simply ineffective; but even where this is not the case they are often subject to the requirement of reasonableness. This is the position where B tries to exclude or restrict his liability to a person other than C for breach of the implied undertakings as to the correspondence of the goods with description or sample or as to their quality or fitness for a particular purpose;[9] where a person, even though not dealing in the course of a business, tries to exclude liability for breach of the implied undertakings as to correspondence of the goods with description or sample in a contract of sale or hire-purchase;[10] and where B tries to exclude the implied undertakings as to his right to transfer possession under certain contracts for the supply of goods (such as contracts of hire) by which the property in the goods is not transferred or to be transferred.[11]

Thirdly, the requirement of reasonableness applies to a term by which B seeks to exclude or restrict his liability for breach of any contract (regardless of its content) if the contract is made (a) between B and C or (b) on B's 'written standard terms of contract';[12] in the second of these cases the other party need not deal as consumer. This provision of the Act even extends the requirement of reasonableness to cases in which there may be no breach at all: it applies also to a term purporting to entitle B (i) to render a performance substantially different from that which was reasonably expected of him, or (ii) to render no performance at all.[13] The first situation would be illustrated by a provision in a tour operator's contract purporting to allow him to change itineraries and accommodations at will; the second by a clause purporting to give a contracting party a free discretion whether to perform. However, contract terms entitling a party to refuse to perform in the event of the other party's failure to perform his part,[14] and terms restricting the duty to perform (eg by making it 'subject to strikes')[15] would not seem to be within the present provision of the Act.

Fourthly, the requirement of reasonableness applies to certain 'indemnity clauses'. These are clauses by which one contracting party undertakes to indemnify the other for any liability incurred by the latter in the performance of a contract: for example, where equipment is hired out with a driver, and the contract provides that the hirer is to indemnify the owner for any liability incurred by the owner as a result of the driver's negligence. If the driver negligently injures, or causes damage to, a third party, and the hirer dealt as consumer,

9 Ss 6(3), 7(3).
10 Ss 6(3) and (4).
11 S 7(4), as amended by Supply of Goods and Services Act 1982, s 17(3); for similar clauses in contracts of sale, hire purchase and in certain other contracts for the transfer of goods, see p 91, ante.
12 Ss 3(1) and (2)(a).
13 S 3(2)(b).
14 See pp 273, 277–279, post.
15 Cf p 89, ante.

the owner's right to enforce the clause is subject to the requirement of reasonableness.[16] If the injury or damage was caused *to the hirer himself*, the clause will be invalid or subject to the requirement of reasonableness under the provisions of the Act (already discussed)[17] even if the hirer did *not* act as consumer. Between these parties the 'indemnity' is in substance an exemption clause:[18] there is no difference of substance between saying 'I am not liable to you' and 'you must indemnify me against any damages that I may have to pay to you'.

The requirement of reasonableness applies finally to any term purporting to exclude or restrict liability for misrepresentation inducing the making of a contract.[19] For this purpose the requirement applies to contracts of all types and whether or not one party acts in the course of a business or the other deals as consumer.

ii Rules relating to reasonableness

The requirement of reasonableness makes it hard to foretell just when an exemption clause will be upheld. The Act contains a number of provisions which to some extent reduce this uncertainty. First, it provides that the issue of reasonableness is to be determined by reference to the time when the contract was made.[20] If at that time the term was a reasonable one to be included, it will not become invalid as a result of later events. Secondly, the Act lays down certain guidelines for determining reasonableness. Where the clause places a monetary limit on a person's liability, regard is to be had to his resources; and to the extent to which it was open to him to cover himself by insurance.[1] Where the contract is one for the supply of goods, the Act lays down further guidelines:[2] these include the relative bargaining positions of the parties and the customer's knowledge, or means of knowledge, of the existence and extent of the term. These guidelines are not decisive: for example, a warehouseman may be able to rely on an exemption clause even though he *could* have insured against loss of goods stored with him; for he may know so little about their value that it is not reasonable to expect him to insure them[2a]. It follows that the guidelines do not eliminate the uncertainty arising from the requirement of reasonableness, but they do give some help, both to the courts in deciding

---

[16] S 4; if the hirer did not act as consumer the indemnity is not subject to the requirement of reasonableness: see *Thompson v T Lohan (Plant Hire) Ltd* [1987] 2 All E R 631.

[17] Ie s 2(1) and (2); ante pp 90, 91.

[18] *Phillips Products Ltd v Hyland* [1987] 2 All E R 620.

[19] Misrepresentation Act 1967, s 3, as amended by Unfair Contract Terms Act 1977, s 8.

[20] S 11(1).

[1] S 11(4).

[2] S 11(2) and Sch 2; applicable by analogy also to other contracts: *Singer Co (UK) Ltd v Tees and Hartlepool Port Authority* [1988] 2 Lloyd's Rep 164.

[2a] Ibid.

issues of reasonableness, and to those who draft exemption clauses in predicting the likely course of such decisions. The operation of the test of reasonableness is illustrated by further reference to the *George Mitchell* case,[3] where the seller's breach in supplying defective seed led to total crop failure, causing the buyer a loss of over £60,000, and a clause limiting the seller's liability to the return of the price (some £200) was held not to satisfy the test of reasonableness. The main reason for this conclusion was that it was the seller's practice not to rely on the clause but to negotiate reasonable claims.[4] This point would no longer be decisive now that reasonableness is judged by reference to the time of contracting and not (as under an earlier reasonableness test applicable in the *George Mitchell* case) at the time of reliance on the clause.

The case remains important, however, in showing that the common law rules of construction and the statutory reasonableness test remain separate requirements of the effectiveness of exemption clauses. The clause satisfied the common law rules[5] but failed to pass the statutory test; and this possibility exists also under the statutory reasonableness test that is now in force.[6] Of course, where the clause does not cover the breach under the common law rules, the stage of applying the statutory test will never be reached.

Where the test of reasonableness applies, a term which satisfies the test remains effective even though the contract has been terminated.[7] On the other hand, a term which does not satisfy the test remains ineffective even though the contract has been affirmed.[8]

d Partly effective terms

Under the Act, a term may be effective in part. For example, a seller of goods may seek to limit liability for 'any breach'. This would be ineffective to limit liability for defects of title but could protect the seller from liability for defects of quality if the buyer did not deal as consumer and the limitation was reasonable.[9] Moreover, a single clause might contain two terms: eg it might impose a reasonable time limit and an unreasonable financial limit on a claim. In such a case, the former limit can be upheld and the latter rejected.[10] But the court

---

3 [1983] 2 AC 803.
4 Ibid at 817.
5 Ante, pp 79, 82–83.
6 *Smith v Eric S Bush* [1987] 3 All ER 179.
7 S 9(1).
8 S 9(2).
9 Cf *George Mitchell (Chesterhall) Ltd v Finney Lock Seeds Ltd* [1983] QB 284 at 303, 309; affd [1983] 2 AC 803.
10 *R W Green Ltd v Cade Bros Farms* [1978] 1 Lloyd's Rep 602 (decided under an enactment now superseded by s 6(3) of the 1977 Act).

could not vary a term by, for example, substituting a reasonable limitation of liability for an unreasonable exclusion.[11] The question is whether '*the term* shall have been a fair and reasonable one to be included':[12] not whether some *other* term might reasonably have been included.

e Restrictions on evasion

The Act strikes at two possible devices for evading its provisions.

First, a term excluding or restricting liability may be contained not in the contract giving rise to the liability, but in a separate contract. The Act makes such a secondary contract ineffective so far as the rights which it tries to take away are rights to enforce a liability which under the Act cannot be excluded or restricted.[13] This provision in the Act gives rise to many difficulties of interpretation. It seems not to apply to a genuine renegotiation of a contract, which may result in a reasonable reduction of a previously agreed (and equally reasonable) limitation of liability. Nor would it seem to apply to a perfectly genuine out-of-court settlement of a claim for damages for breach of contract.

Secondly, an attempt may be made to evade the Act by means of a 'choice of law' clause, subjecting the contract to the law of another country under which the effectiveness of exemption clauses is not similarly restricted. The Act applies even though the contract contains such a clause if it was imposed wholly or mainly to evade the Act; and also where one of the parties was habitually resident in the United Kingdom and dealt as consumer, and the essential steps to the making of the contract were taken there.[14]

f Cases not covered by the Act

Some contract terms are not covered by the Act because they simply do not fall within its scope. Thus generally terms excluding or restricting the liability of a person not acting in the course of a business are not affected by the Act.[15] Even terms excluding or restricting the liability of a person who does so act may be outside the scope of the Act. Suppose, for example, that B1 sold goods to B2 and the contract was not made on B1's written standard terms of business. The Act would not apply to a clause by which B1 excluded or limited his liability for late delivery.

In other cases, exemption clauses would be within the Act if the

11 *George Mitchell (Chesterhall) Ltd v Finney Lock Seeds Ltd* [1983] 2 AC 803 at 816.
12 Unfair Contract Terms Act 1977, s 1 1(1).
13 S 10.
14 S 27(2).
15 S 1(3); an exception is made by s 6(4), see p 91, n 3 and p 92, n 10, ante.

contracts in which they are contained were not to some extent specifically excepted from its scope. These exceptions are extremely complex; but some illustrations of them may be given. The Act does not apply to contracts of insurance, or to any contract so far as it relates to the transfer of an interest in land.[16] The ordinary contract for the sale of a house is thus excepted. Nor does the Act apply to contracts for the international supply of goods.[17] Certain contracts, particularly those relating to the international carriage of goods and persons, are governed by international conventions to which the United Kingdom is a party, and which have been given the force of law.[18] These conventions often limit the liability of one party but make void any attempt further to reduce liability by contract. The 1977 Act preserves this position.[19] Finally, it often happens that international commercial contracts which have no substantial connection with England are governed by English law simply because they contain an express provision to this effect. Most of the provisions of the Act were not intended to apply, and do not apply, to such contracts.[20]

5 OTHER LEGISLATIVE TECHNIQUES

Other legislation illustrates two further techniques for dealing with the problem of exemption clauses.

The first is that of *supervised bargaining*: a court, or some other body, has to approve the clause to ensure that no undue advantage is taken of the weaker party. For example, the landlord's covenants to repair which are implied by statute in certain leases can only be excluded by a court order made with the consent of both parties.[1]

The second technique is to use *administrative action* to control exemption clauses. Under the Fair Trading Act 1973, it is the duty of the Director General of Fair Trading to keep under review commercial activities relating to the supply of goods and services to consumers.[2] The Act also sets up a Consumer Protection Advisory Committee, to which the Director or the appropriate Government Minister can refer 'consumer trade practices'.[3] These include the terms and conditions

---

[16] S 1(2) and Sch 1 para 1(a) and (b).
[17] S 26(1).
[18] Eg Carriage of Goods by Road Act 1965, Sch; Carriage of Goods by Sea Act 1971, Sch; Merchant Shipping Act 1979, s 14 and Sch 3; International Transport Conventions Act 1983, s 1.
[19] Unfair Contract Terms Act 1977, s 29.
[20] S 27(1).
[1] Landlord and Tenant Act 1985, ss 11 and 12.
[2] Fair Trading Act 1973, s 2.
[3] Ibid s 14.

on which goods or services are to be supplied to consumers, and the manner in which those terms and conditions are communicated to consumers.[4] If the terms in question are 'so adverse to [consumers] as to be inequitable', [5] the Director General can induce the Minister to legislate by Statutory Instrument against the practice;[6] and to make it an offence to continue the practice.[7] Under these powers some such practices have been made criminal: for example,[8] the use in a consumer sale of an exemption clause made void by legislation discussed earlier in this chapter.[9] If such a practice is nevertheless continued, the Restrictive Practices Court may order it to cease,[10] in which case its further continuation would amount to contempt of court. This method of administrative control recognises that private litigation is often an unsatisfactory way of controlling exemption clauses. The private consumer may well lack the means or the energy to contest even a plainly invalid provision. Serious abuses of such clauses therefore require the intervention of public authorities and, in the last resort, the sanction of a fine or even imprisonment.

[4] Ibid s 13(1)(a) and (b).
[5] Ibid s 17(2)(d).
[6] Ibid s 22. Such legislation is, however, not to invalidate contracts: s 26; nor is it envisaged that it will invalidate particular terms in contracts, such as exemption clauses.
[7] Ibid s 23.
[8] Consumer Transactions (Restrictions on Statements) Order 1976 (No 1813); Consumer Transactions (Restrictions on Statements) (Amendment) Order 1978 (No 127).
[9] See pp 90–91, ante.
[10] Fair Trading Act 1973, ss 35, 37.

Chapter 8

Mistake

1 INTRODUCTION

The cases in which the validity of a contract may be affected by mistake fall into two main types. In the first, both parties make the same mistake: for example both believe that the thing about which they are contracting is in existence when it has in fact ceased to exist. In the second type of case, the parties make different mistakes, so that they misunderstand each other: for example, one party thinks that they are contracting about one thing and the other about a different one. In the first type of case, the parties reach agreement, but the effect of the mistake may be to deprive that agreement of its normal contractual effect: here the mistake *nullifies* consent. In the second type of case, the effect of the mistake is to put the parties at cross purposes, and the reason why there is no contract is that they never reach agreement at all: here the mistake *negatives* consent.

At first sight there might appear to be little similarity between situations in which mistake prevents the parties from reaching agreement, and those in which it deprives an agreement of the effect of a binding contract. There is, however, an important feature which is common to both situations and which justifies the treatment of them under one heading. This is the requirement that the mistake must be *fundamental*. The concept of fundamental mistake will be further elaborated below; but the basic idea is that the mistake must relate to some crucially important element in the contract. A person who has made a bad bargain, can almost always say that he has made a 'mistake' of some kind; and it is obviously undesirable to allow him, merely on this ground, to escape from the contract. But the more important his 'mistake' becomes, the greater will be the hardship of holding him to the contract; and the law attempts to strike a balance between this hardship and the uncertainty which may be caused by holding contracts invalid on the ground of mistake.

The striking of this balance is in itself an extremely delicate task; and the difficulty of stating the present law is further increased by the different approaches to the subject at common law and in equity. The first main difference between the two approaches is that the common law, stressing the need for commercial certainty, only gives relief at all for a very narrowly defined range of mistakes. Equity, on the other hand, places greater emphasis on the factor of hardship to the mistaken party and so gives relief for many mistakes which are disregarded at common law. Secondly, the common law holds that, if a mistake has any effect at all, it makes the contract wholly void. In equity, mistake may have the more limited effect of giving rise to a right to have the contract rescinded, or to one of the other types of relief which will be discussed below.

2 MISTAKES WHICH MAY NULLIFY CONSENT

A contract may be void at common law, or to some lesser degree defective in equity, if both parties at the time of entering into the contract (or purported contract) make the same mistake about the subject-matter. Two topics arise for discussion: the types of mistake which may thus affect a contract, and the legal effects of the mistake.

a Types of mistake

At common law, a mistake only nullifies consent if it is a fundamental mistake of fact, but equity gives relief for certain other kinds of mistake.

i Fundamental mistake at common law

A mistake is most obviously fundamental where it relates to the existence of the subject-matter: for example, where a charter-party is made concerning a ship which (unknown to either party) had been previously sunk; where a contract is made to paint a portrait of a person believed to be alive but in fact deceased; or where a separation agreement is made between two persons who erroneously believed that they were married to each other.[1] A mistake of this kind may also affect an accessory contract, such as a guarantee. This was held to be the position where A promised B to guarantee C's liability under a lease of machinery which, unknown to A and B, did not exist.[2] Further examples of mistake which is fundamental are provided by cases in which the parties believe that it is possible to perform the contract when this is not the case. Thus, if a person agrees to buy property from another, and neither of them knows that it already belongs to the buyer, there is a fundamental mistake, since a person cannot in law buy his own property.[3] Similarly, a contract for the sale of ten tons of potatoes to be grown on a particular field would be affected by a fundamental mistake if, unknown to either party, the field could not,

[1] *Galloway v Galloway* (1914) 30 T L R 531.
[2] *Associated Japanese Bank (International) Ltd v Crédit du Nord SA* [1988] 3 All E R 902.
[3] *Cooper v Phibbs* (1867) L R 2 H L 149.

even in the most favourable circumstances, produce more than two tons.[4] A mistake would also be fundamental where it related to the identity of the subject-matter, eg where at an auction sale *both* parties believed that one lot was 'under the hammer' when in fact it was another. This is a rare situation: confusion of this kind generally exists in the mind of one party only and thus *negatives* consent, if it has any effect at all.

The above cases are relatively straightforward, but much greater difficulty arises where the mistake relates to some important quality of the subject-matter. Of course, if one of the parties *undertakes* that it has that quality, he is normally liable if the subject-matter in fact lacks the quality; and the other is in that event normally not bound to perform.[5] The difficult cases are those in which both parties simply *assume* that the thing has a certain quality which in fact is lacking. Many mistakes of this kind are obviously not fundamental: for example, if both buyer and seller of a horse believe it is sound, when it is not, there is no fundamental mistake. The position was held to be the same where kapok was sold under a brand name and both buyer and seller believed that kapok of that brand was pure when it in fact contained an admixture of other materials.[6] In these cases it can be said either that the mistake is not important enough to affect the validity of the contract, or that it related to a matter in respect of which the party prejudiced by the mistake could have been expected to protect himself, by expressly stipulating that the quality must exist: ie by providing in the contract that the horse must be sound or that the kapok must be pure.

To be 'fundamental' in the narrow common law sense, the mistake must, it has been said, be one 'as to the substance of the whole consideration [ie of the subject-matter] going, as it were, to the whole root of the matter.'[7] This requirement was very strictly interpreted in the leading case of *Bell v Lever Bros*.[8] In that case, Lever Bros wanted to terminate the service contracts of the chairman and vice-chairman of one of their subsidiary companies, and entered into an agreement to pay them £50,000 by way of compensation for loss of office. It was later discovered that the service contracts could legally have been terminated without paying any compensation at all, as the gentlemen in question had long ago committed breaches of duty which would have justified their summary dismissal. But these had been forgotten by them,[9] so that none of the parties to the compensation agreement

---

[4] Cf *Sheikh Bros Ltd v Ochsner* [1957] AC 136.
[5] *Associated Japanese Bank (International) Ltd v Crédit du Nord SA* [1988] 3 All E R 902.
[6] *Harrison and Jones Ltd v Bunten and LancasterLtd* [1953] 1 QB 646.
[7] *Kennedy v Panama Royal Mail Co* (1867) LR 2 QB 580 at 588.
[8] [1932] AC 161; contrast *Sybron Corpn v Rochem Ltd* [1984] Ch 112.
[9] They were under no duty to disclose the breaches: see post, p 142.

was (when that agreement was made) aware of the possibility of terminating the service contracts without compensation. In the lower courts it was held that this mistake was fundamental; but the House of Lords reversed their decision. Lever Bros, it was said, had got exactly what they bargained for. Their only mistake was as to a quality of the subject-matter of the compensation agreement, viz as to the legal enforceability of the underlying service agreements. Similarly, a mistaken belief that premises are suitable in the normal way for redevelopment, or free from rent control, or subject to a protected tenancy, is not fundamental in the common law sense; and the same conclusion has been reached where a claim on an insurance policy was settled in the belief that the policy was valid, when in fact it was voidable for misrepresentation.[10] Perhaps the most extreme illustration of the narrowness of the common law concept is to be found in an example given by Lord Atkin in *Bell v Lever Bros:* 'A buys a picture from B; both A and B believe it to be the work of an old master and a high price is paid. It turns out to be a modern copy. A has no remedy in the absence of representation or warranty.'[11]

The actual and hypothetical cases mentioned in the last paragraph so much restrict the concept of fundamental mistake that it has been doubted whether any mistake as to quality can ever be fundamental at common law. But some other decisions do provide illustrations of this possibility. In one case[12] a contract for the hire of a room for the purpose of viewing Edward VII's coronation procession was made in ignorance of the fact that the procession had been cancelled; and it was held that the mistake was fundamental. In another case,[13] table napkins were put up for auction and described in the catalogue as 'with the crest of Charles I and the authentic property of that monarch.' They were in fact Georgian and worth much less than the buyer had paid for them; and it was said that the buyer could have treated the contract as void for mistake. One possible view of the case is that the contract was for the sale of 'table linen', in which case a mistake as to its age would not be fundamental. But it is equally possible to say that the contract was for the sale of 'a personal relic of Charles I'; and on this view the mistake would be fundamental.

This last case provides a clue to the common law concept of a fundamental mistake. A thing which is the subject-matter of a contract will have many qualities such as age, colour, size and so on. Usually the contracting parties will have one or more (but not all) of these qualities

---

10 *Amalgamated Investment and Property Co Ltd v Walker & Sons Ltd* [1976] 3 All E R 509; *Solle v Butcher* [1950] 1 K B 671; *Grist v Bailey* [1967] Ch 532; *Magee v Pennine Insurance Co Ltd* [1969] 2 Q B 507.

11 [1932] A C at 224; contrast *Peco Arts Inc v Hazlitt Gallery Ltd* [1983] 3 All E R 193.

12 *Griffith v Brymer* (1903) 19 T L R 434.

13 *Nicholson and Venn v Smith Marriott* (1947) 177 L T 189.

in mind when they deal with the subject-matter. If the quality about which they are mistaken is *the* one by reference to which they have actually *identified* the subject-matter, then the mistake is fundamental at common law. A test for determining whether the mistake is as to an identifying quality is to imagine that one can ask the parties, immediately after the making of the contract, just what the subject-matter was. If, in the case of the napkins, their answer were to be 'antique table linen' the mistake would not be fundamental; but it would be fundamental if their answer were 'a Carolean relic.' Similarly, in *Bell v Lever Bros* the parties would have said that they were contracting about 'service contracts' and the possibility of terminating those contracts without compensation would not have entered their thoughts as part of the process of identifying the subject-matter.

Although this test of *the identifying quality* appears to state the gist of the common law concept of fundamental mistake, it does not by any means avoid all difficulties. Some of the older authorities take a rather wider view of mistakes which are fundamental: for example, in one case an insurance policy on the life of a person called Death was sold in the belief that he was alive when he was in fact dead. This mistake (which of course affected the value of the policy) was regarded by one of the judges as fundamental.[14] Yet the parties no doubt identified the subject-matter simply as 'the benefit of an insurance policy', which it was. On the other hand, a person who had just paid ten million pounds for what was believed to be an old master would surely say that he had bought (for example) 'a Rembrandt'. It would be simply facetious for him to say that he had just bought 'a picture'; and the better view (though not one that is generally accepted) is that the mistake should be regarded as fundamental.

ii Mistakes for which equity gives relief

Equity gives relief for certain mistakes which do not affect the validity of a contract at common law.

The first, and by far the most important, point here is that equity does not adopt the very narrow definition of fundamental mistake which has been discussed above. For example, a lease granted under the mistaken belief that the premises are free from rent control is valid at law, but may be set aside in equity. The same is true of a compromise of an insurance claim, made under the mistaken belief that the policy was valid (when it was actually voidable); and of the sale of a house at a low price under the mistaken belief that it was subject to a protected tenancy.[15] It is sometimes said that, in equity, too, the mistake must be

14 *Scott v Coulson* [1903] 2 Ch 249 at 252.
15 See the last three cases cited in n 10 supra; and cf *Laurence v Lexcourt Holdings Ltd* [1978] 2 All E R 810.

'fundamental', but all that this means is that some slight mistake will not be a ground for relief.[16] The mistake must go beyond the sort of 'mistake' of which anyone can complain when he has made a bad bargain. It must, moreover, relate to circumstances in existence at the time of contracting, and not merely to 'the expectation of the parties'.[17] For example, in one case[18] a contract was made for the sale of a London warehouse which the buyer intended to redevelop. Shortly afterwards it was listed as a building of special architectural or historic interest; this made it much less likely that permission to redevelop would be given, and substantially reduced the value of the property. It was held that the buyer's mistaken belief that the property was 'suitable for and capable of being redeveloped'[19] was not a sufficient ground for equitable intervention.

In the second place, a distinction must be drawn between mistakes of fact and mistakes of law. This is a troublesome distinction but in some cases at least it is clear. Thus, a belief that a ship is afloat when she has been sunk is obviously a mistake of fact; while a belief that a person of 14 has full contractual capacity is a mistake of law. Common law only takes account of mistakes of fact; but there is some (though rather dubious) authority to support the view that equity may give relief even for pure mistakes of law.[20] There is an intermediate category of so-called mistakes of private right. Such a mistake may, for example, arise out of the misconstruction of a will, as a result of which A is believed to be owner of something which legally belongs to B; or out of a belief that a contract is valid when it is voidable. In principle, both common law and equity can give relief against such mistakes of private right. But, except where such a mistake leads to an attempt by a person to buy his own property,[1] it is unlikely to be regarded as fundamental at common law.

b Effects of the mistake

i Contract void at common law

The general rule of common law is that a fundamental mistake makes a contract void.[2] Neither party therefore ever comes under any obligation to perform; and any performance rendered (or its value)

16 *Debenham v Sawbridge* [1901] 2 Ch 98.
17 *Amalgamated Investment and Property Co Ltd v Walker & Sons Ltd* [1976] 3 All E R 509 at 516.
18 *Amalgamated Investment and Property* case, supra.
19 Ibid, p 515.
20 *Allcard v Walker* [1896] 2 Ch 369.
1 See *Cooper v Phibbs* (1867) L R 2 H L 149 as explained in *Bell v Lever Bros Ltd* [1932] A C 161 at 218.
2 *Associated Japanese Bank (International) Ltd v Crédit du Nord SA* [1988] 3 All E R 902 at 909, 912.

must be returned: for example, money paid under such a contract must be paid back. The common law (subject to a possible exception mentioned below)[3] knows no half-way house between such complete voidness and complete validity. If the mistake is not fundamental, the contract is treated as completely valid, however much hardship this may cause to one of the parties.

ii *Risk of mistake taken by one party*

One of the contracting parties may consciously take the risk of having made even a fundamental mistake. In that case the contract is not void, and the party taking the risk may be liable in damages. Suppose, for example, that the seller of a picture believes that it is genuine and guarantees that it is so, but it turns out to be a copy.[4] In a sense, both he and the buyer are under a mistake; but, even if a mistake as to the authenticity of a picture could be regarded as fundamental at common law, the seller would clearly have taken the risk of being mistaken, and so be liable in damages. It is equally possible for the risk of mistake to be taken by both parties: for example, where a speculative picture is bought from a junk-shop for £50. If it turns out either that the picture is an old master of great value, or that it is in fact *completely* worthless, each party will be regarded as having impliedly taken the risk that the picture is worth more, or less, than the price, the implication being based on the circumstances in which the contract was made.

In some cases, contracts expressly allocate risks of this kind. This was, for example, the position where a seller of land sold 'my title, *if any*' to the land, and it was said that such a contract could be binding even if the seller had no title, unless the seller knew this.[5] Similarly, marine insurance policies may contain 'lost or not lost' clauses, the effect of which is that both parties are bound even though the subject-matter is already lost at the time the policy was made: that is, the insurer is liable for the loss if it was covered by the policy; and the insured is liable for the premium, even though the loss which occurred was not covered by the policy. Again, a mistake as to the productive capacity of a quarry or mine may relieve the tenant from liability for failing to extract the agreed minimum quantity;[6] but if he promises to pay a fixed rent or royalty *in any event*, he will be liable in full, even though the capacity of the mine falls short of the stipulated quantity.[7] In some of these cases of conscious risk-taking it is, indeed, scarcely appropriate to talk of mistake: they are hardly cases in which both

---

[3] See p 105, post.
[4] As in *Peco Arts Inc v Hazlitt Gallery Ltd* [1983] 3 All E R 193.
[5] *Smith v Harrison* (1857) 26 L J Ch 412.
[6] *Clifford v Watts* (1870) L R 5 C P 577.
[7] *Bute v Thompson* (1844) 13 M & W 487.

parties positively believed in one state of facts when a different one existed.

Even outside this area of conscious risk-taking the courts may impose the risk of a fundamental mistake on one of the parties and so hold him liable on the contract. In an Australian case[8] the Commonwealth Disposals Commission purported to sell the wreck of an oil tanker lying on a certain named reef. No such tanker had ever existed, but the Commission was held liable in damages to the buyer, on the ground that it had impliedly undertaken that a tanker such as that described did exist. A person may similarly be liable if he has no reasonable grounds for his mistaken belief.[9] Conversely, it is theoretically possible for the risk to be thrown on the buyer, so that he may have to pay the price even though the goods do not exist. In two English cases, however, such claims for the price were dismissed.[10] In one of these it was said that where specific goods were sold which did not exist, the case would not 'be treated as one in which the seller warrants the existence of these specific goods, but as one in which there has been failure of consideration and mistake'.[11] This view is reinforced by a provision in the Sale of Goods Act 1979 under which a contract for the sale of specific goods is void if, at the time when the contract was made, the goods had perished without the knowledge of either party.[12] It therefore seems that the courts would only throw the risk of a mistake as to the existence of the subject-matter on one of the parties in exceptional circumstances: for example, where he is somehow at fault in inducing the mistake in the other party's mind. This would be the position where the former party ought to have known that the subject-matter did not, or probably did not, exist and nevertheless entered into the contract without qualification. In this situation the party at fault would not be able to rely on the mistake, though the other party would probably be able to do so.

iii Bar to specific performance

Where a contract is void for mistake at common law, the equitable remedy of specific performance[13] is obviously not available. But equity may refuse specific performance on the ground of mistake even though at common law the contract is valid because the mistake is not fundamental.[14] This presents no acute conflict with the common law

---

[8] *McRae v Commonwealth Disposals Commission* (1950) 84 C L R 377.

[9] *Associated Japanese Bank (International) Ltd v Crédit du Nord SA* [1988] 3 All E R 902 at 913.

[10] *Couturier v Hastie* (1856) 5 H L Cas 673; *Barrow Lane & Ballard Ltd v Phillips & Co Ltd* [1929] 1 K B 574.

[11] *Barrow Lane & Ballard Ltd v Phillips & Co Ltd* supra at 582.

[12] Sale of Goods Act 1979, s 6.

[13] See ch 18, post.

[14] *Jones v Rimmer* (1880) 14 Ch D 588.

rules, since a claim for damages for breach of the contract remains available. Even mistakes which are not serious enough to justify rescission (which is discussed below) may lead to a refusal of specific performance. Moreover, we have here the first illustration of the greater flexibility of equitable relief: instead of simply refusing specific performance, the court may grant it *on terms*, those terms usually being designed to remove the prejudice which the mistake causes to one of the parties. For example where land sold is, because of some misdescription, supposed to be larger in area than it actually is, equity can grant specific performance on the terms that the price is reduced.[15]

iv Rescission on terms

A contract which is *void* at common law does not normally need to be rescinded by an order of the court. It can simply be disregarded by either party. A court order may, however, be necessary to secure a return to the status quo: for example, a person who has agreed to 'buy' his own property from another who had previously improved it may be ordered to pay for the improvements.[16] Such liability does not arise from the supposed contract but is imposed simply to prevent the unjust enrichment that would result if the 'buyer' could keep the improvements for nothing.

Equity can, however, rescind a contract which is *valid* at law, as it will be if the mistake is not fundamental in the common law sense. For example in the case, already mentioned,[17] of a compromise of a claim under an insurance policy which was believed to be valid when it was voidable, it was held that the compromise could be rescinded even though it was valid at common law. Here again the equitable remedy is a flexible one, in that the court can rescind the contract *on terms*. Thus where a flat was let in the mistaken belief that it was free from rent control, the court rescinded the lease, but gave the tenant the option of staying there on terms of his paying the extra rent which the landlord could have charged in respect of alterations, if he had known the true position in time.[18] Similarly, where a house was sold in the mistaken belief that it was subject to a protected tenancy, the contract was set aside on the terms that the purchaser should be given the opportunity of buying for 'a proper vacant possession price'.[19]

This equitable jurisdiction is very difficult to reconcile with the common law rules established in *Bell v Lever Bros.*[20] There is, it may be

---

15 *Aspinalls to Powell and Scholefield* (1889) 60 L T 595.
16 As in *Cooper v Phibbs* (1867) LR 2 HL 149.
17 *Magee v Pennine Insurance Co Ltd* [1969] 2 QB 507; see pp 101, 102 ante.
18 *Solle v Butcher* [1950] 1 KB 671.
19 *Grist v Bailey* [1967] Ch 532 at 543.
20 [1932] AC 161; see p 100, ante.

thought, little point in asserting that the contract is valid under these rules, if the court can then proceed to set it aside in equity. One view is that the two sets of rules cannot be reconciled at all and that the cases giving effect to the equitable jurisdiction were wrongly decided. There is much logical force in this view, but the courts in fact continue to exercise the equitable jurisdiction to rescind, and there seems to be no doubt that it is part of the present law. But it is not at all clear just when, or on what principles, the jurisdiction will be exercised. Perhaps the courts take into account the conduct of the parties: eg the fault of one in inducing the mistake, or in taking unconscionable advantage of it after becoming aware of the truth. In the present state of the authorities it is impossible to define the limits of the equitable jurisdiction with any degree of certainty.

Even where the right to rescind in principle exists, it may be lost on one of three grounds.[1] First, it is lost if the party seeking to rescind fails to do so within a reasonable time of the making of the contract. Secondly, a contract cannot be rescinded if the effect of rescission would be to deprive a third party of an interest in the subject-matter. Thirdly, a party can only rescind if the other party can be restored to substantially the position in which he was before the contract. Thus, he cannot rescind if he has consumed or disposed of the subject-matter of the contract. The position is the same if the other party (against whom rescission is sought) has acted in reliance on the contract in some way that makes rescission unfair to him. For example, where a tenant has farmed land and the lease was executed under a mistake prejudicial to the landlord, then the landlord cannot rescind unless he can make restitution to the tenant.

Equitable relief, whether by way of refusal of specific performance or by way of rescission, is available where the contract is valid at law *because the mistake is not 'fundamental'* in the narrow common law sense. There is (as we have seen) another reason why a mistake may not make a contract void, and this is that one party has, or is deemed to have, *taken the risk of the mistake.* It seems clear that equity would not give relief to a party who is held to a contract at law under this principle: eg because he had bought or sold a speculative picture.

3 MISTAKES WHICH MAY NEGATIVE CONSENT

Mistake is said to negative consent when it puts the parties so seriously at cross-purposes that they cannot be said to have agreed at all. We shall first discuss the types of mistake which are sufficiently serious to negative consent and then consider the legal effects of such mistakes.

[1] For details, cf pp 139–141, post.

It cannot be too strongly emphasised that in this type of case a mistake, though serious enough to negative consent, will not normally affect the validity of the contract at all. For reasons to be discussed later in this chapter,[2] the mistake will only impair the validity of the contract in a number of somewhat exceptional situations.

a Types of mistake

The cases provide illustrations of three types of mistake which may negative consent: mistakes as to the subject-matter, as to the person, and as to the terms of the contract.

i Mistake as to the subject-matter

Mistake will negative consent if one party intends to deal with one thing and the other with a different one. This principle is generally thought to explain the case of *Raffles v Wichelhaus*[3] where a contract was made for the sale of '125 bales of Surat Cotton . . . to arrive ex *Peerless* from Bombay.' Two ships of the name had left Bombay, one in October and the other in December. It was held that the buyer was not bound to accept the December shipment, as he had intended to buy the October shipment. On the assumption that the seller intended to sell the December shipment, consent would be negatived. If, on the other hand, the parties had both intended to deal with the December shipment, consent would not have been negatived merely because either party was mistaken as to the quality of the goods. Such a mistake would not be 'fundamental' and it would not create a misunderstanding sufficiently serious to negative consent.[4] The concept of a 'fundamental' mistake here is the same as that already discussed in relation to mistakes which nullify consent. A mistake of one party as to a quality of the subject-matter will only negative consent if it is a mistake as to *the* quality by which that party identified the subject-matter. It is again possible for equity to give relief in respect of a mistake which is not fundamental in the narrow common law sense.[5]

ii Mistake as to the person

This kind of mistake was not discussed above, in connection with mistakes which nullify consent. The reason for this is that the possibility of both parties making the *same* mistake about the identity or attributes of one of them is so remote as to be of no practical importance.[5a] But one party (A) may well make such a mistake about the other (B) and this most commonly happens where B makes

2 See p 113, post.
3 (1864) 2 H & C 906.
4 *Smith v Hughes* (1871) L R 6 Q B 597, see p 111, post.
5 Eg *Torrance v Bolton* (1872) 8 Ch App 118.
5a Cf *Hector v Lyons* (1988) Times, 19 December.

some pretence about himself in order to induce A to contract with him, or to give him credit. Usually (though not always), B is an impecunious rogue who pretends to be a person of means, and the question once again is whether A's mistake about B is sufficiently fundamental to negative consent. If the mistake is of this kind, its effect will usually be to make the contract void at common law.

As between the two parties to the alleged contract (A and B) the question whether the mistake is sufficiently fundamental to make the contract void is of small practical importance. B's pretence will almost always amount to fraud, so that the contract (if any) between them will be voidable on account of that fraud, in accordance with the principles to be discussed in Chapter 9. But the question of mistake is of crucial importance where (as often happens) B obtains goods under the contract without paying for them and then sells them to X who buys them in good faith. If the contract between A and B is void for mistake, no title in the goods will pass to B who will thus be unable to confer any title on X. Hence A can recover the goods (or their value) from X. If, on the other hand, the contract between A and B is only voidable for fraud, B will get a voidable title to the goods, which A will be unable to avoid, once X has in good faith acquired the goods. It follows that X will, as against A, be entitled to retain the goods. The likely effect of holding a contract is void for mistake is therefore to prejudice innocent third parties. This state of the law has been criticised by the Law Reform Committee,[6] who have recommended that the innocent third party (X) should be entitled to retain the goods even where the contract between A and B is void for mistake. But that recommendation has not been implemented; and the courts can only protect X by adopting a narrow definition of the kinds of mistake as to the person which will negative consent. For this purpose, a distinction has been drawn between mistakes as to identity and mistakes as to attributes. The former do, while the latter do not, negative consent.

In the leading case of *Cundy v Lindsay*,[7] Lindsay received an order for handkerchiefs from a rogue called Blenkarn, who signed his name so as to make it look like that of Blenkiron & Co, a respectable firm whom Lindsay knew by repute. Lindsay sent the handkerchiefs to the address given by Blenkarn, who did not pay for them and resold them to Cundy. It was held that the contract between Lindsay and Blenkarn was void, as Lindsay had made a mistake as to the identity of the other contracting party: they had dealt with Blenkarn when they thought they were dealing with Blenkiron & Co. Hence the handkerchiefs remained Lindsay's property throughout, so that Lindsay recovered their value from Cundy.

[6] 12th Report ((1966) Cmnd 2958) para 15.
[7] (1878) 3 App Cas 459.

110   *Mistake*

In *Cundy v Lindsay* the crucial fact was that A (Lindsay) believed that
he was dealing with B (Blenkiron & Co) when in fact he was dealing
with C (Blenkarn). The position would be different if A's only mistake
was about some attribute of B, but for the existence of which A would
not have been willing to deal with B. Thus, in a later case,[8] a rogue
called Wallis obtained goods on credit by using an impressive letter-
head purporting to come from a firm called 'Hallam & Co' which was
said to operate a large factory and various depots. There was in fact no
such entity as 'Hallam & Co', which was simply an alias for Wallis. It
was held that the sellers had not made a mistake as to the identity of the
other contracting party, but only as to one of his attributes, namely his
credit-worthiness. Accordingly, they were not entitled to recover the
goods from an innocent third party to whom Wallis had resold them.
As the sellers had sent goods on credit to a completely unknown
customer, without taking any steps to find out whether he was a good
credit risk, the decision is an eminently reasonable one.

It is obviously sensible for the law to take the view that a mistake as
to the particular attribute of credit-worthiness should not suffice to
negative consent. Any decision which one party makes as to the credit-
worthiness of the other involves the deliberate taking of a commercial
risk, and a person who takes such a risk should not be entitled to relief
against an innocent third party. But the cases leave open the possibility
that mistake as to some other attribute may negative consent. Here, an
analysis similar to that used in defining a fundamental mistake as to the
subject-matter may be adopted. A person has many attributes, and for
the purpose of a particular contract he may be identified by any one or
more of these. If the other party is mistaken about such an *identifying
attribute*, consent may be negatived. For example, a company may
identify persons with whom it wishes to deal simply as 'shareholders';
or a jeweller may identify the person with whom he wants to deal as 'the
wife of Z'.[9] If the persons dealt with lack those identifying attributes,
then it is suggested that a mistake as to identity has been made.

Of course, it may be very difficult to determine whether the mistake
which has been made in fact relates to an identifying attribute. To
some extent the law avoids the difficulty, by making certain provisional
assumptions about the way in which one contracting party identifies
the other. One very strong assumption is that parties who actually meet
face to face have identified each other by the normal process of sight
and hearing. This assumption is so strong that even a belief by the
mistaken party that he is dealing (face to face) with a totally different
person will not normally negative consent. In one case,[10] a jeweller sold

[8] *King's Norton Metal Co Ltd v Edridge, Merrett & Co Ltd* (1897) 14 TLR 98.
[9] See *Lake v Simmons* [1927] AC 487.
[10] *Phillips v Brooks Ltd* [1919] 2 KB 243.

a ring and delivered it on credit to a customer who had come into his shop and had falsely claimed to be Sir George Bullough, a wealthy man known by name to the jeweller. It was held that the contract was not void for mistake. In another case,[11] a dishonest person called on the owner of a car which had been advertised for sale, and in the negotiations leading up to the sale, falsely claimed to be the actor Richard Greene. As a result, he was allowed to take the car away in exchange for a cheque which was dishonoured; and it was again held that the contract was not void for mistake. In an earlier case,[12] two ladies in similar circumstances sold their car, and delivered it against a worthless cheque, to a person who had claimed to be 'PGM Hutchinson of Stanstead House, Stanstead Road, Caterham'. They only did so after one of them had checked in a telephone directory that there was such a person living at that address. It was held that the contract was void. The case has been doubted, but it can perhaps be justified on the ground that the very special circumstances rebutted the normal assumption as to the process of identification between persons who are actually in each others' presence. That assumption could also be rebutted where the dishonest person adopted an actual physical disguise. Even in this type of case, however, a distinction must be drawn. If A is induced to contract with B, by a disguise which simply leads him to believe that B *is not B*, the contract is not void for mistake, though it is voidable for fraud. To make the contract void, the disguise must induce A to believe that B *is C*, and C must be a distinct person either known to A or at least believed by A to exist. So long as A believes that there is a separately identifiable person called C, it seems to be immaterial that there is in fact no such person in existence: for example where, unknown to A, C had died before the transaction in question.

iii Mistake as to terms

Sometimes a mistake as to the terms of a transaction will negative consent. For example, in *Hartog v Colin and Shields*[13] a seller of skins intended to sell them at a fixed price per *piece* and the buyer to buy them at the same price per *pound*. There were about three pieces to the pound, and the contract was held void. It is obvious that in this case the parties were seriously at cross-purposes, but greater difficulty arises from the troublesome case of *Smith v Hughes*.[14] Oats were sold by a farmer to a trainer of racehorses, who was only interested in buying *old* oats and who refused to accept the oats which the farmer delivered, on

---

[11] *Lewis v Averay* [1972] 1 QB 198; cf *Whittaker v Campbell* [1984] QB 318 at 329.
[12] *Ingram v Little* [1961] 1 QB 31.
[13] [1939] 3 All E R 566.
[14] (1871) L R 6 QB 597.

the ground that they were in fact *new*. It was not an express term of the contract that the oats were old; and the buyer's mistaken belief that the oats *were old* would not have invalidated the contract, as this mistake as to quality would not be a fundamental one, within the principles already discussed. But it was said that a mistaken belief that the oats were *warranted to be old* would have negatived consent. It is not at all easy to see why a mistake of the latter kind should be so much more serious (than a simple mistake as to the age of the oats) as to negative consent; and another possible explanation of the decision will be put forward below.[15]

iv Mistake must induce the contract

A mistake will not negative consent merely because it is fundamental. It must, in addition, be as to a point of some commercial significance to the mistaken party, and it must induce him to enter into the contract. Suppose, for example, that a person orders goods from a shop with which he has long had dealings, but does so in ignorance of the fact that the shop has just been taken over by a new owner. His mistake is certainly fundamental: he thinks he is dealing with the old owner when in fact he is dealing with the new one. But in the great majority of cases this mistake will not matter in the least to the customer, so long as he in fact gets goods which satisfy his needs. To negative consent, further facts must be shown. For example, in one case[16] the buyer was owed money by the old owner of the shop and he intended to set off this debt against the price of the goods which he had ordered, so as not to have to pay cash. In these circumstances, it was held that there was no contract between him and the new owner.

The present requirement is additional to the requirement that the mistake must be fundamental. As was pointed out above, a mistake may be fundamental without operating as an inducement; and the converse is equally true. Nothing can amount to a stronger induce-ment than a mistake as to a person's creditworthiness, but such a mistake alone will not negative consent. To produce this effect, the mistake must be fundamental *and* induce the contract, as (for example) in *Cundy v Lindsay*. The present requirement is most commonly discussed in relation to cases of mistaken identity but it can also apply in relation to mistakes as to the subject-matter. Suppose that, in *Raffles v Wichelhaus,*[17] both *Peerlesses* had sailed (and arrived) on the same day. Probably, the validity of the contract would not have been affected by the fact that the buyer intended to buy goods arriving in the one ship and the seller to sell those arriving in the other.

[15] See p 114, post.
[16] *Boulton v Jones* (1857) 2 H & N 564.
[17] (1864) 2 H & C 906; see p 108, ante.

b Effects of the mistake

i *Contract generally valid at common law*

The fact that a mistake has been made which negatives consent does not generally invalidate a contract at common law. This is so because, generally, the mistaken party (A) will have conducted himself in such a way as to induce the other party (B) reasonably to believe that he, A, is in fact agreeing to the terms proposed by B. Hence the objective test of agreement[18] is satisfied (even though there is no agreement in fact) and there is a good contract. Suppose, for example, that at an auction sale a person thinks he is bidding for one lot when he is actually bidding for another, which is knocked down to him. He will normally be bound by the contract of sale even though his mistake was fundamental and induced the contract. Similarly, a landlord may, as a result of a clerical error, offer to grant a tenancy at an annual rent of £1,000, when he intended to charge £2,000. Once the tenant has accepted the offer, the landlord cannot treat the contract as void merely because he was under a mistake as to its terms.[19] Whenever the objective principle applies the contract is valid in spite of the fact that a mistake has been made. In such cases, it is therefore unnecessary to discuss the difficult question whether the mistake is 'fundamental' in the common law sense.[20]

ii *Contract exceptionally void at common law*

A mistake which negatives consent only affects the validity of a contract in three exceptional cases. It is only in these cases that the mistake is *operative*, and its effect then is to make the contract void.

First, the circumstances of the case may create such *perfect ambiguity* that the objective test provides no solution. This was the position in *Raffles v Wichelhaus*.[1] A reasonable person would have had no ground for believing that the buyer had agreed to buy the cotton on the December, rather than that on the October, *Peerless*.

Secondly, the mistake of one party will make the contract void if that mistake is *known to the other party*. The objective test exists to protect a person against the prejudice which he may suffer by relying on an appearance of agreement, and he can hardly complain if he actually knows that that appearance is false. Thus in *Cundy v Lindsay* the mistake made by Lindsay was operative because Blenkarn knew that Lindsay intended to deal with Blenkiron & Co. The contract may also be void if

18 Ante, p 2.
19 *Centrovincial Estates plc v Merchant Investors Assurance Co Ltd* [1983] Com LR 158, approved in *Whittaker v Campbell* [1984] QB 318 at 327 and in *The Antclizo* [1987] 2 Lloyd's Rep 130 at 146 (affd [1988] 2 All ER 513).
20 Eg *The Unique Mariner* [1978] 1 Lloyd's Rep 438 at 451–452.
1 See p 108 ante.

the mistake, though not actually known to the other party, is so obvious that it ought to have been known to him. This was the position in *Hartog v Colin and Shields*[2] where it was held that the buyer must, in the light of market prices and conditions, have known that the seller could not have intended the quoted price to apply to pounds but only to pieces. It is important to stress that, where a mistake is, or ought to be, known to the other party, it must still be fundamental if it is to make the contract void. If, for example, A mistakenly believes that B is rich, B's knowledge of A's mistake will not make the contract void, since it is a mistake as to an attribute only. Similarly, in *Smith v Hughes*,[3] a mistaken belief on the part of the buyer (A) that the oats *were old* would not have made the contract void, even if it had been known to the seller (B), since such a mistake would be as to a non-fundamental quality. To make the contract void, two elements would, in the court's view, have to be combined: (i) a mistaken belief on A's part that the oats were *warranted old*; and (ii) knowledge on B's part of *this* mistake.

It is (as suggested above) not altogether easy to see why a mistaken belief that oats were *warranted old* negatives consent, when a mistaken belief that they *were old* does not have this effect; and there may be an alternative explanation of *Smith v Hughes*. This is that a seller who knows of the buyer's belief that he is giving a warranty must be treated, on the objective principle, as if he had actually given the warranty. Hence he would be in breach of contract if he delivered new oats, and the buyer would be justified in rejecting the goods.[4]

Thirdly, the mistake of one party may make the contract void if it was *negligently induced by the other*. This rule was applied where auction particulars were so obscure as to lead a bidder to make a mistake as to what he was bidding for; and the contract was accordingly held void.[5]

iii Bar to specific performance

Equity may refuse specific performance even though the contract is not void at common law because the mistake is not fundamental. This principle has been discussed in relation to mistakes which nullify consent, and nothing more need be said about it here.

The contract may also be valid at common law, even though the mistake *is* fundamental, because the objective principle prevents the mistake from being operative. Here, too, specific performance is sometimes refused in equity. In one case[6] a buyer at an auction bid for

---

[2] [1939] 3 All ER 566; see p 111, ante.
[3] (1871) LR 6 QB 597; see pp 111–112, ante.
[4] 'Warranty' at that time was often used to refer to what would now be called a 'condition': see p 279, post for this distinction.
[5] *Scriven Bros v Hindley & Co* [1913] 3 KB 564.
[6] *Malins v Freeman* (1836) 2 Keen 25.

one lot in the mistaken belief that he was bidding for another, and specific performance was refused to the seller. But in another case of this kind, specific performance was granted to the seller where the buyer's only mistake was as to the extent of the land for which he was bidding. It was said that specific performance would only be refused (assuming that the contract was valid at common law) 'where a hardship amounting to injustice would have been inflicted upon [the mistaken party] by holding him to his bargain, and it was unreasonable to hold him to it.'[7] It follows from this statement that the *buyer* could have obtained specific performance, if he had been content with the smaller purchase. The court may also adopt the middle course of granting specific performance on terms. Thus, in one case,[8] a purchaser of a plot on an estate believed that the vendor had covenanted not to build a public house on the estate, when in fact such covenants had only been given by the purchasers of the other plots. It was held that the vendor could only obtain specific performance on the terms that he entered into a similar covenant.

iv Rescission on terms

The equitable remedy of rescission is generally discussed in relation to mistakes which nullify consent; and its most common (if controversial) application is to cases where the mistake is not fundamental in the common law sense. Equity may also rescind a contract where the parties are at cross-purposes and the mistake is not fundamental: for example, where only one of them makes a mistake about some quality which seriously affects the value of the subject-matter, but which is not *the* quality by which the parties identify the subject-matter.[9] If the court can rescind the contract, it can do so absolutely or on terms, and subject to the restrictions which have already been discussed.[10]

A contract may be valid at common law because the mistake, though *fundamental*, is, under the objective principle, not *operative*. To refuse specific performance in such a case leaves it open to the non-mistaken party to seek his remedy in damages. But to rescind the contract would (subject to the possible imposition of terms) deprive that party of all remedies and would thus seriously undermine the objective principle. The most recent authority therefore supports the view that rescission is not available when the mistake is not operative at common law.[11]

---

[7] *Tamplin v James* (1879) 15 Ch D 215 to 221.
[8] *Baskcomb v Beckwith* (1869) LR 8 Eq 100.
[9] Eg *Torrance v Bolton* (1872) 8 Ch App 118.
[10] See p 107, ante.
[11] *Riverlate Properties Ltd v Paul* [1975] Ch 133. In *Torrance v Bolton*, supra, the objective principle would not have applied as the one party's mistake was in part induced by misleading auction particulars issued on behalf of the other party: cf ante p 114.

It is sometimes said[12] that the power to order rescission exists even in relation to contracts which have been held *void* at common law: for example in such cases as *Cundy v Lindsay*.[13] The attraction of this view is that it would enable the law to protect innocent third parties, for the right to rescind would be lost once such third parties had acquired an interest in the subject-matter of the contract.[14] But as the law now stands, it is hard to see what there is for equity to rescind when the common law says that there is no contract at all. The better view (however regrettable it may be) is that the power to order rescission exists only in relation to contracts which are *valid* at common law.

4 DOCUMENTS SIGNED UNDER A MISTAKE

a The doctrine of non est factum

In general, a person who signs a contractual document is bound by its terms whether he has read the document or not: he may, for example, be bound by an exemption clause of which he is quite unaware.[15] But at the end of the 16th century, English law developed a special defence to protect illiterate persons who had executed deeds which had been incorrectly read over to them. This was the defence of non est factum, by which the signer pleaded that the instrument was 'not my deed'. In the 19th century, these cases were rationalised by saying that the alleged contract was void because 'the mind of the signer did not accompany the signature'.[16] But the mere fact that this is so does not, as we have seen, suffice to make a contract void for mistake. Under the objective principle, the contract will, on the contrary, generally be upheld. It will only be void in the exceptional cases discussed above;[17] and the only one of these that is likely to be relevant in the present context is the case in which the mistake of one party is known to the other. Usually, the signature of the mistaken party is procured by some kind of fraud; and if the document purports to be a contract between the mistaken and the fraudulent party, the contract may be held void without infringing the objective principle. More commonly, however, the document purports to be a contract between the mistaken party and some third party. This happens where A is induced by the fraud of B to sign a document addressed to C: for example B may wish to raise a loan from C and induce A to sign a guarantee in favour of C by representing that the document is an insurance proposal; or B may induce A to sign

---

12 *Solle v Butcher* [1950] 1 K B 671 at 692.
13 (1878) 3 App Cas 459.
14 See p 109, ante.
15 See p 73, ante.
16 *Foster v Mackinnon* (1869) L R 4 CP 704 at 711.
17 See pp 113–114 ante.

a promissory note in favour of C by representing that the signature is required for the purpose of witnessing a private document. In these cases, C may reasonably assume that A had agreed to the terms of the document; and to allow A to rely on the plea of non est factum would conflict with the objective principle and become a source of danger to innocent third parties. It is to minimise this danger that the law has developed a number of restrictions on the scope of the plea, which are designed to keep it within narrow limits.

b Restrictions on the doctrine

There are three such restrictions. They relate to the persons who can rely on the doctrine, the nature of the mistake necessary to bring it into operation, and the effect of carelessness on the part of the signer.

i Persons who can rely on the doctrine

The doctrine was originally devised to protect illiterate persons; and it might be thought that it should not apply at all to persons who could read the document but failed to do so. But in *Saunders v Anglia Building Society Ltd* the House of Lords rejected this perhaps somewhat Draconian view, and held that the doctrine could apply in favour of a person who has 'no real understanding' of the document 'whether . . . from defective education, illness or innate incapacity'.[18] Adult persons of normal attainments and capacity will only rarely be able to establish the plea.

ii Nature of the mistake

The doctrine is, secondly, restricted by a requirement which resembles that of fundamental mistake, discussed earlier in this chapter. In *Saunders v Anglia Building Society Ltd* the House of Lords held that the plea was only available where the difference between the document actually signed, and the document as it was believed to be, was a 'radical' or 'essential' or 'fundamental' or 'substantial' one. No attempt was made to define these terms, the question being treated as one of degree. In the actual case a widow of seventy-eight wanted to help her nephew to raise money for the purposes of his business, and to do so on the security of her house. A document was presented to her which she did not read because her glasses were broken. She thought that it was a deed making a gift of the house to her nephew, but in fact it purported to be a sale of the house to an intermediary called Lee, through whom the nephew had arranged to raise the money. Lee then mortgaged the house to a building society, but did not pay the purchase price to the widow, nor did he pay over any money to the nephew in

[18] [1971] AC 1004 at 1016.

accordance with the arrangement between them. It was assumed that the widow was the sort of person who could rely on the doctrine of non est factum, but it was held that her mistake was not serious enough to bring the doctrine into operation. Her purpose in executing the document was to help her nephew to raise money on the security of her house, and the document was in fact intended to serve that purpose, though by a different route from that envisaged by her. It is worth noting that the effect of the decision was to protect an innocent third party (the building society) which had advanced money on the faith of the document.

iii *Carelessness*

A further ground for the decision in *Saunders v Anglia Building Society Ltd* was that the plea of non est factum could only succeed if the person raising it showed that he or she was not careless in signing the document. The standard of care here seems to be a subjective one, depending on the actual capacities of the signer; but even an elderly widow of moderate educational attainments should not sign a document transferring her house, without at least making sure that the transfer is in favour of the right person. Similarly, a person cannot rely on the doctrine if he signs a document containing blanks which are later filled in otherwise than in accordance with his directions.[19]

Although the question of carelessness is one of fact in each case, it seems that there will be few cases in which a person will now be able to show that he was not careless in signing the document. The burden of disproving carelessness lies on the signer and is a heavy one. It could perhaps be discharged if he were told that he was witnessing a confidential document and had no reason to doubt this assertion, or by showing that a person of the signer's limited capicities could not have discovered the truth, even by reading the document.[20]

5 MISTAKES IN RECORDING AGREEMENTS

a Rectification of documents

So far, we have been concerned with mistakes which affect consent and hence invalidate contracts. There is a further group of cases in which mistakes only affect the process of *recording* agreements; and such mistakes may be corrected by means of the equitable remedy of rectification. This remedy is available where the parties fail to put into the document terms which were agreed, or put into it terms which were not agreed, or which differ from those which were agreed. In such

[19] *United Dominions Trust Ltd v Western* [1976] QB 513.
[20] *Saunders v Anglia Building Society Ltd* [1971] AC 1004 at 1023.

cases, the court may rectify the document so as to make it conform to the agreement. For example, if an oral agreement were made for the sale of peas and the written document recorded a sale of beans, the written document could be rectified by the substitution of 'peas' for 'beans'. Similarly, rectification is available where a lease states a rent other than that agreed, and where a conveyance is for a greater area of land than that covered by the preceding agreement.[1]

b Types of mistake

In general, the mistake on which a claim for rectification is based must be that of *both* parties. Hence the remedy is not available if the written document accurately expresses the intention of one party but not that of the other. Suppose that a lease stipulated for a rent of £1,000 per annum and that this accurately expressed the intention of the tenant. It would be obviously wrong to allow the landlord to obtain rectification merely because he (and he alone) intended the rent to be £2,000;[2] for this would impose on the tenant a liability to which he had never agreed. In such a case the landlord could only obtain rectification if he could show both that the lease did not record his true intention and that the tenant was guilty of fraud or knew of the landlord's mistake and tried to take advantage of it.[3] Even in the absence of such facts, it used to be thought that the landlord could force the tenant to choose between *either* having the lease rectified by the substitution of '£2,000' for '£1,000' *or* having it cancelled altogether.[4] But this view is inconsistent with the objective principle;[5] and it has accordingly been held that neither rectification nor rescission is available in such circumstances.[6] This is clearly the better view, for mistakes of this kind can arise simply because one party has wrongly added up a column of figures which the other party has never seen. It seems unreasonable to give relief to the mistaken party, unless the mistake was known to the other, or so obvious that he should have known of it.

A person who claims rectification only needs to show that the written document fails accurately to record the prior agreement. He does not have to establish that the prior agreement amounted to a *binding contract*. Thus if the prior agreement suffered from a formal defect, or was not intended to be legally binding until the written document was

---

[1] *Eg Beale v Kyte* [1907] 1 Ch 564.
[2] *Faraday v Tamworth Union* (1916) 86 L J Ch 436; cf *The Ypatia Halcoussi* [1985] 2 Lloyd's Rep 364.
[3] *Blay v Pollard & Morris* [1930] 1 K B 628 at 633; *Garrard v Frankel* (1862) 30 Beav 445 at 451.
[4] *Harris v Pepperell* (1867) L R 5 Eq 1; *Paget v Marshall* (1884) 28 Ch D 255.
[5] See p 113 ante.
[6] *Riverlate Properties Ltd v Paul* [1975] Ch 133; cf *The Nai Genova* [1984] 1 Lloyd's Rep 353.

executed, the written document may still be rectified. All that it is necessary to show is that the parties continued to entertain a common intention, evidenced by 'some outward expression of accord',[7] up to the time of the execution of the document, and that the document failed to record that intention.

On the other hand, if the written document does accurately record the prior agreement, it cannot be rectified on the ground that the prior agreement was itself made under some mistake; for equity does not rectify *contracts* but only *documents*.[8] If, for example, parties orally agreed on the sale of 'your picture of Salisbury Cathedral' and then reduced the contract to writing in these terms, the document could not be rectified on the ground that both parties believed the picture to be by John Constable, when in fact it was a copy. This would be so whether or not the mistake affected the validity of the contract.[9] Rectification is available for many mistakes which do not make the contract void at law and for some which are not even a ground for refusal of specific performance, or for rescission in equity: for example, in some cases for a mistake as to the legal effect of an agreement.[10] But the mistake must in all cases simply be one in *recording* the agreement. If the remedy were not limited in this way, it would indirectly subvert the principles which limit the kinds of mistake that affect the validity of contracts.

c Restrictions

The remedy of rectification is subject to restrictions, some of which resemble those already stated in relation to rescission. Thus, the remedy may be barred if it is not claimed within a reasonable time of the making of the contract; or by the intervention of third party rights (for example, where a third party in good faith acquires land which the seller had agreed to sell, but which was by mistake omitted from the conveyance). On the other hand, rectification differs from rescission, in that it is intended to give effect to the agreement of the parties, and not to restore them to the position in which they were before the contract was made. Hence the requirement that such restoration must be possible (which limits rescission) is quite inappropriate in relation to rectification.[11]

Mistakes in certain kinds of documents cannot be rectified, because the law provides other machinery for correcting such mistakes. For

---

[7] *Joscelyne v Nissen* [1970] 2 QB 86 at 98.

[8] *Mackenzie v Coulson* (1869) LR 8 Eq 368 at 375.

[9] Cf *Frederick E Rose (London) Ltd v William H Pim Jnr & Co Ltd* [1953] 2 QB 450.

[10] *Jervis v Howle & Talke Colliery Co Ltd* [1937] Ch 67. Cf *Re Colebrook's Conveyances* [1973] 1 All ER 132; contrast *Nittan (UK) Ltd v Solent Steel Fabrication Ltd* [1981] 1 Lloyd's Rep 633 (legal effect fully explained to party alleging mistake).

[11] Eg *Johnson v Bragge* [1901] 1 Ch 28.

example, a settlement of property which is binding by virtue of a court order cannot be rectified: if a mistake has been made in drawing up such a settlement, it can be corrected by applying to the court which ordered the settlement to be made, rather than by applying to another court to rectify it.[12] Similarly, articles of association of a company cannot be rectified even if they contain an obvious mistake.[13] Once such a document is registered in accordance with the Companies Act, it can only be altered in the manner provided for by that Act.

A claim to rectification may be, and often is, preceded by a dispute as to the construction of a document. That is, a party may claim, first, that a document bears a certain meaning, and secondly, that, if it does not bear that meaning, it should nevertheless be rectified on the ground that the meaning alleged by him represented the common intention of the parties, as expressed in a prior agreement. A party who wants to take this line should put forward *both* claims in the alternative in the same proceedings; for, if judgment is given against him on the point of construction, in proceedings in which he might have claimed rectification (but failed to do so), then his right to claim rectification will be barred. The purpose of this rule is to discourage multiple proceedings on substantially similar issues.[14]

---

12 *Mills v Fox* (1887) 37 Ch D 153.
13 *Scott v Frank F Scott (London) Ltd* [1940] Ch 794.
14 *Crane v Hegeman-Harris Co Inc* [1939] 4 All ER 68.

Chapter 9

Misrepresentation

In this chapter, the term misrepresentation refers to certain kinds of misleading statements by which persons may be induced to enter into contracts. The law relating to misrepresentation is complex because it is the product of three separate stages of development. First, the common law gave relief by way of damages or rescission for a misrepresentation, if it was either fraudulent or if it had been incorporated in the contract as one of its terms; more recently, the common law right to damages was extended to certain cases of negligent misrepresentation. Secondly, equity gave relief for wholly innocent misrepresentation but only by way of rescission and not by way of damages. Thirdly, the Misrepresentation Act 1967 has, in its first two sections, extended the scope of rescission and damages for misrepresentation. These sections give rise to many difficulties: in particular, the relationship between the new statutory remedies and those which continue to exist at common law and in equity is not made at all clear. It is, however, probably safe to say that the general trend of the law has been to increase the scope of the remedy of damages at the expense of rescission, so that damages will become the primary remedy for misrepresentation.

We shall begin by stating certain general conditions of liability before examining in detail the various remedies available for misrepresentation. Finally, we shall consider cases in which there is no active misrepresentation, but only a failure to disclose material facts known to one party but not to the other.

1 GENERAL REQUIREMENTS

a A representation of fact

As a general rule, relief for a misrepresentation, as such, will only be given in respect of statements of *existing fact*. These must be contrasted with statements of opinion or belief, statements as to the future, and statements of law.

i Statements of opinion or belief

These are sometimes so vague as to have no legal effect at all. Thus in one case,[1] a description of land as 'fertile and improveable' was held to give rise to no liability. Even statements which are more precise may fall into this category: in another case,[2] it was held that a seller of land was not liable for stating that it could support 2,000 sheep, as he had no personal knowledge of the facts and as the buyer knew this, so that it was understood that the seller could only state his belief. The statement is, however, likely to be treated as one of fact if the person making it had, or professed to have, some special knowledge or skill with regard to the matter stated.[3] Moreover, a statement of opinion or belief will generally, by implication, contain a representation that the person making the statement actually holds the opinion or belief, and it may contain a further implied statement that he holds the opinion or belief on reasonable grounds. Thus, if a person says that he believes a picture to be an original when he actually believes it to be a copy, he misrepresents a fact, namely the state of his belief.[4] The same is true if a person on selling a house says that it is 'let to a most desirable tenant', when the tenant has for a long time been in arrears with the rent.[5] In such a case it would not matter that the seller did not actually know this, since such a fact is one of which the buyer could reasonably have expected him to be aware.

ii Statements as to the future

A person who promises to do something in the future and then breaks that promise is, of course, liable for breach of contract if the promise amounted to a binding contract. But if the promise did not have contractual force he will not be subject to the remedies for misrepresentation, as he has not misrepresented an existing fact. For example, a person who obtains a loan of money by 'representing' that he *will* use it for one purpose is not liable for misrepresentation if he then changes his mind and uses the money for a different purpose. But he would be so liable if, when he made the representation, he had no intention of using the money for the stated purpose. In such a case, he would be misrepresenting his present intention and not his future conduct. In the words of Bowen LJ: 'There must be a misstatement of existing fact; but the state of a man's mind is as much a fact as the state of his digestion . . . A misrepresentation as to the state of a man's mind is, therefore, a misstatement of fact.'[6] A person would also be liable for

---

1 *Dimmock v Hallett* (1866) 2 Ch App 21.
2 *Bisset v Wilkinson* [1927] AC 177.
3 Eg *Esso Petroleum Co Ltd v Mardon* [1976] QB 801.
4 *Jendwine v Slade* (1797) 2 Esp 572 at 573.
5 *Smith v Land and House Property Corpn* (1884) 28 Ch D 7 at 15.
6 *Edgington v Fitzmaurice* (1885) 29 Ch D 459 at 482.

misrepresentation if he coupled a statement as to the future with one of existing fact: for example, if he untruthfully said that he *had* sold certain goods and *would* pay over the proceeds.

iii Statements of law

The distinction between statements of law and statements of fact is important, because damages are not awarded for misrepresentation of law. Rescission may be available for a deliberate misrepresentation of law, but probably not for one that is wholly innocent. The difficulties which arise in distinguishing between representations of fact and of law are similar to those already considered in relation to mistakes of fact and of law.[7] Thus, a misrepresentation as to the content and meaning of an Act of Parliament would be a misrepresentation of law. On the other hand, in the case of a misrepresentation as to the effects of a private document, a distinction would have to be drawn. If the misrepresentation related to the *content* of the document it would be one of fact, but if it related to the meaning of a document of known content it would be one of law, since the construction of a document is a question of law. However, a misrepresentation as to 'private right' would probably be treated as one of fact, even though it involved a misrepresentation as to the construction of a document. In some cases, it is quite impossible to tell from the statement itself whether it is a statement of law or of fact. For example, a statement that a will made by A is valid may involve a representation that A is 18 years old (the age at which persons acquire capacity to make a will) when in fact he is only 16, or a representation that A, though only 16, had fully testamentary capacity. If a contract is induced by such a statement, the question whether the representee is entitled to relief probably depends on which of these two representations in fact induced him to contract.

The distinction between representations of law and of fact is based on the theory that knowledge of the law is equally accessible to both parties: the representee ought not to rely on what the representor says about matters of law, but should rather take his own advice on such matters. In fact this is a wholly unrealistic theory; and the various refinements mentioned above show that the courts have tried, wherever possible, to soften its rigour. The result has been to blur the distinction to such an extent that it has become very hard to formulate, and almost impossible to justify, in practical terms. No harm would be done if the distinction were abolished and if the normal remedies were to become available for misrepresentation of law. If the representee did in fact take his own legal advice, these remedies would still be excluded on the principles to be discussed below.

[7] See p 103, ante.

b Other conditions of liability

Three further conditions must be satisfied before a misrepresentation (other than one having contractual force) will give rise to the remedies discussed later in this chapter.

i *Representation must be unambiguous*

A representation may be capable of bearing two meanings, one of which is true and the other false. If the representor (A) honestly intended it to bear the true meaning, he is not guilty of fraud merely because the representee (B) rightly understood it in the sense which was false.[8] But if A intended the representation to bear a meaning which he knew to be false, and B reasonably so understood it, A is guilty of fraud. He cannot escape liability for fraud by showing that the statement was also capable of bearing another meaning, which was true; or even that, as a matter of construction, it did bear such a meaning.[9]

ii *Representation must be material*

In the law of misrepresentation there is not (as in the law of mistake) any requirement that the misrepresentation must relate to a 'fundamental' matter. But often relief for misrepresentation which relates to a matter of only minor importance will not be available because of the requirement that the misrepresentation must be material.[10] This means that the misrepresentation must be one which would influence a reasonable person in deciding whether, or on what terms, or after what further enquiries, to enter into the contract. There are, however, two exceptions to this rule. First, it does not apply where the misrepresentation was made fraudulently.[11] And secondly, a contract may provide that every representation (however unimportant) is to be material. Contracts of insurance commonly provide that all statements in the proposal form are to be regarded as material. Indeed, they generally go further and provide that such statements are warranted to be true, or that they shall be the basis of the contract.

iii *Reliance on the representation*

Even if a reasonable person would have relied on the representation, there will be no liability if the representee did not rely on it in fact. This will obviously be the case if the representation never came to his

---

[8] *Akerhielm v De Mare* [1959] A C 789.
[9] *The Siboen and The Sibotre* [1976] 1 Lloyd's Rep 293 at 318.
[10] *Traill v Baring* (1864) 4 De GJ & Sm 318 at 326; *Industrial Properties Ltd v Associated Electrical Industries Ltd* [1977] QB 580; Marine Insurance Act 1906, s 20(2).
[11] *Smith v Kay* (1859) 7 H L Cas 750.

attention; but it may come to his attention even though it was not made directly to him: eg if it was made to a third person with the intention that it should be repeated to the claimant, and if it was so repeated.[12] The position is the same where the representor could reasonably have anticipated that the representation would be so repeated.[13]

Reliance is also negatived if the true facts were actually known to the representee, or to his agent acting within the scope of his authority.[14] More difficulty arises where the representee did not actually know the truth but took, or could have taken, steps to discover it. If he actually took such steps, but failed to discover the truth, it could be said that he did not rely on the misrepresentation but rather on his own judgment. Accordingly, he should not be entitled to relief, and this view certainly applies where the misrepresentation is innocent. But to deny relief where the misrepresentation is fraudulent would put a premium on skilful deception, so that in such cases relief is not barred simply because of an unsuccessful attempt by the representee to discover the truth.[15] Where the representee had, but simply did not take, an opportunity to discover the truth, he is similarly entitled to relief where the representation is fraudulent. According to the older authorities, this rule also applied where the representation was 'innocent'.[16] But at the time when these cases were decided the law did not recognise any separate category of negligent misrepresentation, so that 'innocent' misrepresentations included all those which could not be proved to be fraudulent. If the representor is indeed wholly innocent, while the representee is careless in not testing the accuracy of the representation, then the representee should be refused relief on the ground that it was, in all the circumstances, unreasonable for him to rely on the misrepresentation. This would, in particular, be the case where a private person made an innocent misrepresentation to a dealer who had a much better chance than the representor of discovering the truth.

If the representee relied on the misrepresentation, he may be entitled to relief even though there were also other factors which induced him to enter into the contract. Indeed this is the position in the great majority of cases. Relief for the misrepresentation will only be denied if the other inducements were so powerful as to show that the representee did not really rely on the misrepresentation at all: eg, if the

12 *Pilmore v Hood* (1838) 5 Bing N C 97.
13 Cf *Yianni v Edwin Evans & Sons* [1982] Q B 438; Contrast *Beaumont v Humberts* [1988] 29 E G 104.
14 *Strover v Harrington* [1988] 1 All E R 769.
15 See *S Pearson & Son Ltd v Dublin Corpn* [1907] A C 351; *Gordon v Selico Co Ltd* (1986) 278 Estates Gazette 53 at 61.
16 *Redgrave v Hurd* (1881) 20 Ch D 1.

evidence shows that he would have entered into the contract on the same terms even if he had known the truth.[17]

2 EFFECTS OF MISREPRESENTATION

Misrepresentation may give rise to certain claims for damages, to rescission, and to certain consequences under the doctrine of estoppel. Before these matters are discussed in detail, something must be said of the relationship between misrepresentation and mistake.

a Misrepresentation and mistake

The relationship between these subjects can best be understood by distinguishing between three possible situations.

First, a fundamental mistake may arise spontaneously, without any misrepresentation. In that case the remedies for misrepresentation do not apply. It is true that the cases sometimes refer to 'rescission' of a contract for mistake; but where the effect of mistake is to make a contract void there is no need to 'rescind', in the sense in which that word is used in the law of misrepresentation. Secondly, a misrepresentation may (and often will) induce a mistake which is not fundamental. In such a case the mistake will not make the contract void and the only remedies will be those for misrepresentation. Thirdly, there is an area of overlap in which a fundamental mistake is induced by a misrepresentation. Here both sets of remedies are available to the representee, who is entitled to choose that which is most favourable to him. This would, for example, be the position in the case of *Cundy v Lindsay*[18] which was discussed in chapter 8.

b Damages

There are no fewer than five separate legal grounds on which damages can be claimed for misrepresentation. We shall first consider these rights individually, then discuss the relationship between them, and finally refer, in the context of misrepresentation, to the power of a criminal court to make compensation orders.

i Damages for fraud

A person who suffers loss by relying on a fraudulent statement can recover damages in an action of deceit. This is an action in tort, available quite irrespective of the existence of any contract; but one possible application of it is to the situation in which a person has been induced by fraud to enter into a contract. Actions of deceit are not

17 *JEB Fasteners Ltd v Marks Bloom & Co* [1983] 1 All E R 583; *The Lucy* [1983] 1 Lloyd's Rep 188.
18 (1878) 3 App Cas 459; see p 109, ante.

commonly brought, as fraud is a serious charge which must be strictly substantiated. It must be shown that the person making the false statement *either* knew that it was false *or* had no belief in its truth *or* made it recklessly, not caring whether it was true or false.[19] Mere negligence in making a false statement does not amount to fraud, though it may entail liability in damages under two of the headings to be discussed below. Fraud requires some degree of conscious deception. But it is not necessary to show bad motive or intention to cause loss. A person may say that a certain state of facts exists when he knows it does not exist; and such a person is guilty of fraud even though he in good faith believes that the facts asserted will come true and that the present and temporary falsity of his statement will not prejudice the representee.[20]

ii Damages for negligence at common law

A claim for damages for negligent misrepresentation is again a claim in tort, available irrespective of contract. Before 1963, the common law did not allow such claims save in a number of highly exceptional situations. But it is now recognised that there may be liability where a statement is made carelessly and in breach of a duty to take reasonable care that it is accurate. The question whether the statement has been made carelessly depends on the circumstances of each case. The major problem is to determine whether any duty of care exists at all. Obviously, a duty of care may arise out of a contract, for example between a professional adviser such as an architect, or a solicitor, and his client. If such a duty is broken an action may be brought both for breach of contract, and in tort for negligence at common law.[1] The difficult cases are those in which there is *no* contract between the representor and representee; and here it is said that a duty of care arises if there is a 'special' relationship between them, by virtue of which the representor assumes responsibility for the accuracy of the statement.[2] Such a relationship may arise where a person in the exercise of his profession gives information or advice to a person *other* than his own client, knowing that that person is likely to rely on it. Thus, in one case a valuer employed by a building society negligently overvalued a house and was held liable to the purchaser to whom (as he could have anticipated) his report was shown and who had relied on it in buying the house.[3] According to one view, such liability only arises where the person making the statement is in the business or profession of giving information or advice.[4] But the more generally held view is

[19] *Derry v Peek* (1889) 14 App Cas 337.
[20] *Polhill v Walter* (1832) 3 B & Ad 114.
[1] See *Esso Petroleum Co Ltd v Mardon* [1976] QB 801 at 819; cf p 340, post.
[2] *Hedley Byrne & Co Ltd v Heller & Partners Ltd* [1964] AC 465.
[3] *Yianni v Edwin Evans & Sons* [1982] QB 438; cf *Caparo Industries plc v Dickman* [1988]NLJR 289; contrast *Huxford v Stoy Hayward & Co* (1989) Times, 11 January.
[4] *Mutual Life and Citizens Assurance Co Ltd v Evatt* [1971] AC 793.

that liability is not restricted to cases of this kind. For example, in *Esso Petroleum Co Ltd v Mardon*[5] the defendant was induced to take a lease of a filling station from an oil company by a statement, made by one of the company's salesmen, as to the potential turnover of the premises. It was held that the company owed a duty of care to the defendant as he had reasonably relied on the salesman's superior knowledge and experience. For the purposes of this chapter, however, it is generally unnecessary to show that such a duty exists. Our concern is with cases in which the misrepresentation induces a contract between misrepresentor and misrepresentee, and in such cases there is now a statutory liability in damages even in the absence of a 'special relationship'. Such liability is discussed in the immediately following section of this chapter. The question whether there is liability for negligent misrepresentation at common law only becomes acute where the misrepresentation does *not* lead to a contract between the representor and the representee. This was the position in the case of the valuer, mentioned above, where the contract which the representee made was with a third party, viz with the owner of the house.

iii Damages under Misrepresentation Act 1967, section 2(1)
This subsection creates a statutory liability in damages which arises 'where a person has entered into a contract after a misrepresentation has been made to him by another party thereto'. This cause of action is, from the representee's point of view, more favourable than common law liability for negligence. In the first place, he need only show that he entered into a contract with the representor after the misrepresentation had been made: he need *not* establish a 'special relationship' giving rise to a duty of care.[6] Section 2(1) would, for example, apply between buyer and seller, even though no 'special relationship' existed between them. Secondly, at common law the representee must prove negligence, but under section 2(1) the representor is liable 'unless *he proves* that he had reasonable ground to believe and did believe up to the time that the contract was made that the facts represented were true'. The cases show that the burden of proof which is thus placed on the representor is a difficult one to discharge. For example, where, during negotiations for the hire of barges, the owner's agent misstated their deadweight capacity in reliance on a wrong statement in Lloyd's Register, it was held that the burden had not been discharged, since documents in the owner's possession disclosed the true situation.[7] The representor's best hope

---

[5] [1976] QB 801; cf *Anderson & Sons Ltd v Rhodes (Liverpool) Ltd* [1967] 2 All ER 850. In *Chaudhry v Prabhakar* [1988] 3 All ER 718 (ante, p 27) a duty was admitted.
[6] *Howard Marine and Dredging Co Ltd v A Ogden & Sons (Excavations) Ltd* [1978] QB 574 at 596.
[7] *Howard Marine case*, supra.

will be to show that he had himself been previously induced to acquire the subject-matter by the same misrepresentation, and that he innocently repeated it before the contract now in question was concluded.[8]

Section 2(1) imposes a new statutory liability for misrepresentation, but it does so in a curious way, by a fiction of fraud. That is, it provides that, if the representor would be liable in damages if he were guilty of fraud, he shall be so liable even though he was not guilty of fraud. The point of the fiction may simply have been to make it clear that some liability in damages should exist, though for this purpose the fiction seems to be quite unnecessary. Another possible effect of the fiction is to make the statutory liability subject to rules which have been evolved in cases of actual fraud: eg the rule that a fraudulent representation need not be material.[9] But the courts are unlikely to take this view;[10] for many such rules would be quite inappropriate where the representor had acted in good faith and was liable simply because he could not disprove fault.

iv Damages for breach of contract

A statement made before the conclusion of a contract may be a 'mere' representation inducing the contract. Alternatively, it may actually have the force of contract: in other words, the person making the statement may undertake or promise that it is true. The distinction was of crucial importance before the law recognised liability for negligent misrepresentation. At that time, damages for misrepresentation could only be obtained either by proving fraud, or by showing that the misrepresentation had contractual force. As fraud was hard to prove, the latter alternative was in practice the more important one. Now that damages can be awarded for negligent, and sometimes even for wholly innocent, misrepresentation, the distinction has lost much of its former importance. But even today the distinction retains some significance, as the right to damages for breach of contract differs in several ways from the other rights to damages for misrepresentation.

Where the statement actually appears in the written contract, the question whether the maker undertakes that it is true is one of construction. Such a statement will generally be a term,[11] but the representor's intention to guarantee its truth may be excluded by express contrary provision, or by other circumstances. The statement may be a term even though the other party had not read the document and so could not have relied on the statement in entering into the contract.

---

[8] As in *Oscar Chess Ltd v Williams* [1957] 1 All ER 325 and in *Hummingbird Motors Ltd v Hobbs* [1986] RTR 276.

[9] Ante p 125; and see p 126.

[10] See *Gosling v Anderson* (1972) 223 Estates Gazette 1743.

[11] *Behn v Burness* (1863) 3 B & S 751.

Where the statement is not actually incorporated in the written contract, the question whether it has contractual force depends on the
intention (objectively ascertained) with which it was made.[12] This is a
question of fact, so that no 'rules' can be laid down on the point; but the
cases do provide illustrations of factors which are taken into account in
determining whether the requisite intention exists. Of the many factors
relevant to this issue, three are of particular significance.

The first, and most obvious, factor is the *wording of the statement*. An
express guarantee that it was true would clearly give it contractual
force.[13] This situation may be contrasted with a case in which the seller
of a car said that to the best of his knowledge and belief the odometer
reading was correct. It was held that this statement had no contractual
force, so that the seller was not liable merely because the odometer had
(unknown to him) been tampered with before he had acquired the
car.[14]

The second relevant factor is the *importance* which is attached by the
representee to the statement. For example, a statement as to the quality
of goods would be a term of the contract if, before the sale, the buyer
had made it clear to the seller that he would not be interested at all in
goods which did not have that quality.[15] On the other hand if the
statement merely affected the price which the buyer was willing to pay
it will not necessarily be incorporated in the contract. Thus a
representation as to the age of a car is (as will be seen below) not
necessarily a term of the ensuing sale.

Thirdly, the courts stress the *relative abilities of the parties to determine the
truth* of the statement. Two cases may be contrasted here. In *Oscar Chess
Ltd v Williams*[16] a private seller sold a car to a dealer in part exchange,
representing in good faith that it was 1948 model. It had been
previously sold to him as such, with a forged log-book, but it was in fact
a 1939 model. It was held that the seller had not warranted the car to be
a 1948 model, and the main reason for the decision was that the buyer,
as a dealer, was in at least as good a position as the seller to check the
truth of the statement. But in *Dick Bentley Productions Ltd v Harold Smith
(Motors) Ltd*[17] a dealer sold a Bentley car to a customer, representing
that it had done only 20,000 miles since having a replacement engine
fitted, when in fact it had covered 100,000 miles since then. Here the
dealer was in a better position than the customer to check the truth of
the statement, and it was held that the statement as to mileage was a
term of the contract.

12 *Howard Marine* case, supra n 6, at 595.
13 *The Larissa* [1983] 2 Lloyd's Rep 325, 330.
14 *Hummingbird Motors v Hobbs* [1986] RTR 276.
15 *Bannerman v White* (1861) 10 CBNS 844.
16 [1957] 1 All ER 325.
17 [1965] 2 All ER 65.

So far, it has been assumed that, if the statement is to have contractual force, it must be incorporated as a term in the contract which it has induced. It may be impossible for the statement to take effect in this way because it is oral and the contract is either in writing (so that extrinsic evidence cannot be used to add to it or to vary it[18]) or subject to some formal requirement. In such cases it is nevertheless possible for the statement to take effect as a *collateral contract*. For example, the statement made on behalf of the oil company in *Esso Petroleum Co Ltd v Mardon*[19] as to the potential turnover of the filling station was held to be a collateral contract. For such a contract to arise, the representor must intend the statement to be binding as a *separate* contract (and not just as a term of the main contract), and the representee must provide separate consideration for it. Some of the older cases do not seem to have insisted very strictly on these requirements, perhaps because the courts were anxious to use the collateral contract device to get round the former rule that there was no liability in damages for innocent or negligent misrepresentation. Now that the law recognises such liability, there is less need to extend the scope of the collateral contract device in this part of the law.

v *Damages in lieu of rescission*
Before 1967, the primary remedy for a 'mere' misrepresentation (not incorporated in the contract) was rescission, damages being only available in cases of fraud and, since 1963, in certain cases of negligence. This was an unsatisfactory state of the law; for it meant that the only remedy available to the victim of a wholly innocent misrepresentation was completely to set aside the contract, even though the misrepresentation related to some relatively minor defect. The victim might prefer to keep the subject-matter of the contract with some monetary adjustment; while the representor might prefer to pay a sum of money instead of having the subject-matter of the contract thrown back on his hands. It was therefore provided by s 2(2) of the Misrepresentation Act 1967 that the court should have a discretion to uphold the contract and award damages in lieu of rescission 'where a person has entered into a contract after a misrepresentation has been made to him otherwise than fraudulently, and he would be entitled, by reason of the misrepresentation, to rescind the contract . . . .'.

Under this subsection, the court can award damages even though the misrepresentation was wholly innocent (ie not even negligent) and even though no contractual undertaking as to its accuracy was given. This is a remarkable extension of the power to award damages, but the power is, or may be, limited in a number of ways. First, the subsection

---

[18] Because of the parol evidence rule: ante, p 66.
[19] [1976] QB 801, see p 129, ante; cf *De Lassalle v Guildford* [1901] 2 KB 215.

gives no *right* to damages: it only gives the court a discretion to make such an award. Secondly, the damages are awarded in lieu of rescission. Thus the victim of a wholly innocent misrepresentation cannot rescind *and* claim damages; by contrast both these possibilities are open to the victim of a fraudulent or negligent misrepresentation, and may be open to the victim of a misrepresentation which has contractual force. If the victim of a wholly innocent misrepresentation wants to get rid of the subject-matter of the contract, he can sometimes, as part of the process of rescission, get what is called an indemnity.[20] In this way he can rescind *and* get a sum of money, but the sum is (as we shall see) assessed on more restricted principles than damages. A third limitation on the court's discretion under section 2(2) is more controversial. The right to rescind the contract is in certain cases lost[1] eg if the representee has disposed of the subject-matter so that he can no longer restore it to the representor. There is no very good reason why the court's discretion to award damages should be lost at the same time; but the wording of section 2(2) does suggest that the court must have a real choice between rescission and damages, and that damages therefore cannot be claimed after the right to rescind has been lost.[2]

vi *Relationship between the various rights to damages*

The relationship between the above rights to damages gives rise to two questions: what facts must be shown to establish, or to defeat, any particular claim? and how much can the plaintiff recover under the various headings which have been discussed?

In discussing the first of these questions it will be helpful to take an example based on *Oscar Chess Ltd v Williams*,[3] and to suppose that a 1985 car is sold after a representation has been made that it is a 1988 model. If the buyer claims damages for fraud, he will have to show that the seller knew that his statement as to the age of the car was false, or at least that he was reckless in this respect. In practice the buyer will find it very hard to substantiate such a charge. To succeed in an action for negligence at common law, the buyer will have to show that there was a 'special relationship' giving rise to a duty of care at common law; and that the seller failed to take reasonable care to ensure that his statement as to the age of the car was accurate. If the buyer claims damages under s 2(1) of the Misrepresentation Act, his position is much more favourable: he only has to show that the false statement was made, and it is then up to the seller to show that he believed on reasonable grounds that the statement was correct. In practice this is therefore the claim which the buyer is most likely to pursue. If the seller

20 See p 135, post.
1 See pp 139–141, post.
2 This seems to be assumed in *The Lucy* [1983] 1 Lloyd's Rep 188 at 201–202. Damages *under s 2(1) of the Act* can be awarded even though the contract has been affirmed: *Production Technology Consultants v Bartlett* [1988] 1 EGLR 82.
3 [1957] 1 All ER 325. See p 131, ante.

can discharge the burden of proof imposed on him by s 2(1), the buyer may still succeed in his claim for damages by showing that the statement had contractual force: fault is irrelevant in such an action. If there is no element of fault or contractual intention, the buyer has no *right* to damages, though he has the chance of obtaining a discretionary award of damages in lieu of rescission. But such damages cannot be awarded in addition to rescission so that where the buyer wants to return the car his only hope will be to claim an indemnity, and this hope is (as we shall see) a very faint one. If the right to rescind has been lost, the buyer still has no remedy whatsover for a wholly innocent misrepresentation which does not have contractual force.

The second question relates to the contents of the various rights to damages, ie to the amount recoverable in each type of claim. Here the leading distinction is between claims in tort and claims in contract. The basic difference is this: in tort the plaintiff gets such damages as will put him into the position in which he would have been if the tort *had not been committed*, while in contract he is entitled to be put into the position in which he would have been if the contract *had been performed*. Suppose for example that a person is induced by misrepresentation to buy a car for £500 which would have been worth £750 if the representation had been true but which is actually worth only £400; and suppose further that the car has been delivered and paid for and that it cannot be returned. In tort, it is assumed that the buyer would, if the misrepresentation *had not been made*, not have bought the car at all. He would therefore still have his £500 instead of a car worth £400, and so he gets damages of £100. In contract, the buyer is entitled to be put into the position in which he would have been if the representation *had been true*. In that event he would have had a car worth £750 instead of having one worth £400. His damages are therefore £350. Of course if the buyer would have made a bad bargain even if the representation had been true, he may recover more in tort than in contract. This would be the position in the above case if the car would have been worth only £425 even if the representation was true. Here, applying the above principles, the buyer still gets £100 in tort but only £25 in contract. For the purpose of these distinctions the better view is that a claim under s 2(1) of the Misrepresentation Act would be a claim in tort[4] by virtue of the fiction of fraud. A claim for damages in lieu of rescission under s 2(2) of the Act does not seem to be a claim either in contract or in tort, being independent of fault and contractual intention; and it is not at all clear on what principle such damages will be assessed.

---

4 *F & B Entertainments Ltd v Leisure Enterprises Ltd* (1976) 240 Estates Gazette 455; *André & Cie SA v Ets Michel Blanc & Fils* [1977] 2 Lloyd's Rep 166 at 181; and see p 343, post.

In the above examples the representation is a positive assertion that the subject-matter has a certain quality. They should be contrasted with *Esso Petroleum Co Ltd v Mardon*,[5] where the misrepresentation was that the future annual turnover of the filling station could be estimated at 200,000 gallons. The tenant did not recover the profit which he would have made on such a turnover, even though the oil company was held liable in contract (as well as in tort); for the collateral contract was not that 200,000 gallons would be sold but that the estimate had been prepared with due care. Here it made no practical difference whether the damages were awarded for breach of *this* contract or in tort. They were in fact assessed on what is normally a tort basis, so as to put the tenant into the position in which he would have been if he had not taken the lease.

So far, we have considered only the loss which the buyer suffers because of the lower value of the subject-matter. He may also suffer consequential losses, eg where he loses money in the course of running a business which he has been induced to buy by a misrepresentation as to its profitability.[6] Such losses are only recoverable if they are not 'too remote' and the rules as to remoteness (which are discussed in Chapter 18)[7] are probably more favourable to the plaintiff in tort than in contract. This consideration has to be set against the possibility of recovering more in contract under the principles discussed above; so that the question whether the buyer should press his claim in contract or in tort will often be a finely balanced one.

The various rights to damages must be contrasted with the equitable right to an 'indemnity'. Equity did not award damages for misrepresentation, but it might order the representor to pay a sum of money to the representee, as part of the process of rescission. The object of this process was to restore each party so far as possible to the position he was in before the contract, so that sums expended under the contract had to be repaid. Suppose, for example, that a tenant is by the terms of a lease bound to pay rent to the landlord and rates to the local authority, and that he is also obliged to repair the premises. Any money paid or spent by him in discharge of these obligations will be recoverable if he rescinds for misrepresentation. But this right to an indemnity only exists in respect of sums which the tenant *was bound under the lease* to disburse.[8] He cannot claim an indemnity in respect of his removal expenses, or injury suffered by him or his employees as a result of relying on the landlord's representations as to the physical state of the premises. Such losses result from his acts of moving in and using the premises, and these were not acts which he was under the lease bound

---

[5] [1976] QB 801.
[6] *Doyle v Olby (Ironmongers) Ltd* [1969] 2 QB 158; cf *Archer v Brown* [1985] QB 401.
[7] See pp 333–336, post.
[8] *Whittington v Seale-Hayne* (1900) 16 TLR 181.

to do. He can only recover in respect of them on a claim for damages; and he cannot both rescind *and* claim damages for a misrepresentation which was wholly innocent, and which was not a term of the contract.

vii Compensation orders in criminal cases

Misrepresentation may involve criminal liability: for example, where property, services or a pecuniary advantage is obtained by deception, or where a false trade description is applied to goods.[9] When a person is convicted of such an offence (or indeed of any offence) he may be ordered to pay compensation for any personal injury, loss or damage resulting from the offence.[10] Such an order may be made even though the conditions of civil liability for misrepresentation are not satisfied: for example where a person is convicted of obtaining property by a deception consisting of a misrepresentation of *law*.[11] If the misrepresentation gives rise to both civil and criminal liability, any compensation paid under the order made by the criminal court is taken into account in later civil proceedings, so that the misrepresentor is not made liable twice over.[12]

c Rescission

The word rescission is confusingly used to describe a number of processes, of which three are relevant here. After these have been discussed, we shall consider the circumstances in which the right to rescind may be lost.

i Rescission for misrepresentation

In the first sense, rescission refers to the process of setting a contract aside for misrepresentation. At common law this process was available only in cases of fraud, but equity extended it to all cases of innocent misrepresentation. Misrepresentation (unlike mistake) does not make the contract void. It only gives the representee the option to avoid it. If he exercises the option, the contract comes to an end so that each party is relieved from his obligation to perform. In addition, the representee is entitled to recover anything that he transferred to the other party, on terms of restoring anything that he received under the contract. For example, if a contract of sale is rescinded by a seller for misrepresentation he will get back the goods on terms of paying back the price.

The rule that the contract is voidable and not void has important

---

[9] Theft Act 1968, ss 15, 16; Theft Act 1978, ss 1, 5; Trade Descriptions Act 1968, s 1(a).

[10] Powers of Criminal Courts Act 1973, s 35, as amended by Criminal Justice Act 1988, s 104, cf Financial Services Act 1986, ss 47, 61.

[11] Under the Theft Act 1968, s 15(4).

[12] Powers of Criminal Courts Act 1973, s 38, as substituted by Criminal Justice Act 1988 s 105.

effects on the rights of third parties. If a contract of sale is void because of a mistake as to the identity of the buyer, no property in the goods passes to the buyer, so that the goods can be recovered by the seller from an innocent third party to whom the buyer has resold them.[13] If, on the other hand, the sale is induced by the fraud of the buyer (not leading to a fundamental mistake), a voidable title nevertheless passes to him and can be transferred to an innocent third party who buys the goods without knowledge of the fraud before the seller has rescinded the contract.[14]

For the purpose of the rule just stated, it is, of course, crucial to know exactly when the contract has been rescinded. Rescission may be effected by taking legal proceedings; or extra-judicially, by giving notice to the other party or, where goods have been obtained by fraud, by retaking them. Obviously none of these steps can be taken where the fraudulent party has made off with the goods and cannot be traced. In one such case, it was held that the defrauded seller of a car could rescind the contract by simply notifying the police.[15] The unfortunate result of the decision was that a third party who subsequently in good faith bought the car from the rogue had to give it up to the true owner. In Scotland, it has been held that a notice to the police cannot amount to rescission in such circumstances.[16] This appears to be the preferable view, and its adoption in England has been recommended by the Law Reform Committee.[17]

ii Rescission for breach

The victim of a breach of contract can always claim damages, and in addition he can sometimes 'rescind' the contract. This topic is discussed in Chapter 16; here it suffices to say that, as a general rule, a breach must be *serious* to give rise to a right to rescind for the breach: a *slight* breach gives rise only to a claim for damages. A representation inducing a contract may be incorporated in it as one of its terms: and s 1(a) of the Misrepresentation Act 1967 provides that such incorporation does not affect the right to rescind for misrepresentation. An incorporated misrepresentation may therefore give rise to a right to rescind for misrepresentation even if it only leads to a slight breach, ie to one which is not sufficiently serious to give rise to a right to rescind for breach. However, in such a case, it is probable that the court will exercise its discretion under s 2(2) of the Misrepresentation Act to declare the contract subsisting, in which case the representee will be

[13] *Cundy v Lindsay* (1878) 3 App Cas 459; see p 109, ante.
[14] Eg *Lewis v Averay* [1972] 1 QB 198; see p 111, ante.
[15] *Car and Universal Finance Co Ltd v Caldwell* [1965] 1 QB 525.
[16] *MacLeod v Kerr* 1965 SC 253.
[17] 12th Report (1966) Cmnd 2958 para 16.

limited to his claim for damages *either* for breach of the still subsisting contract, *or* in lieu of rescission under s 2(2). Usually, the former will be the preferable claim.

If the incorporated misrepresentation leads to a breach which is sufficiently serious to give rise to a claim to rescind for breach, the representee has two rights of recission, one for misrepresentation and one for breach. He will almost invariably exercise the latter right, since it has two advantages over the former. First, rescission for breach can be coupled with a claim for damages for the breach,[18] whereas rescission for misrepresentation probably extinguishes any claim for damages for breach, and cannot be claimed together with damages in lieu of rescission. Secondly, a representee who wants, above all, to rescind runs the risk that the court may, at the request of the representor, exercise its discretion under section 2(2) of the Misrepresentation Act 1967 to declare the contract subsisting and to award damages in lieu of rescission. Although the point is not entirely clear, it seems probable that this discretion only applies to rescission for misrepresentation and not to rescission for breach. Hence a person whose main interest is in rescission should, in the case of an incorporated misrepresentation, base his claim on breach.

iii Defensive rescission

Frequently, a party who rescinds will do so because he wants to get back what he gave under the contract. But he may not yet have performed his part and may wish to rely on the misrepresentation simply as a justification for his refusal to perform. This purely defensive use of the misrepresentation is sometimes referred to as rescission; but it is not in all respects governed by the same rules as the process by which a party seeks to get back what he gave under the contract. A party making a claim of the latter kind will only succeed if he at the same time restores what he himself received under the contract. But this requirement of restoration is not always insisted upon where fraud is simply set up as a defence to a claim. Thus an insurance company can rely by way of defence on the fraud of the policyholder, without returning the premiums.[19] Similarly, a person who is induced by fraud to enter into a contract of sale with a buyer with whom he would not have dealt, if he had known the truth, can refuse both to deliver the goods and to pay back the price.[20] The rule does not apply where the representation is negligent or wholly innocent. Its purpose seems to be to deter fraud, particularly where

---

[18] See pp 272, 292, post.
[19] See *Feise v Parkinson* (1812) 4 Taunt 640 at 641; Marine Insurance Act 1906, s 84 (1) and (3) (a).
[20] *Berg v Sadler and Moore* [1937] 2 K B 158.

the fraud is criminal; but it is far from clear why the criminal law is not considered to provide adequate deterrence.

iv Limitations on the right to rescind

The right to rescind is a potential source of hardship to the representor and to third parties. Prejudice to third parties is avoided by the rule that, once an innocent third party has for value acquired an interest in the subject-matter, the contract cannot be rescinded so as to deprive him of that interest.[1] The other limitations on the right to rescind are designed to avoid hardship to the representor; and they can be discussed under three headings: restitution, affirmation and lapse of time.

The requirement of *restitution* means that a person seeking to rescind the contract must be able and willing to restore what he has received under it. This requirement may not, as we have just seen, apply where a victim of fraud simply pleads it as a defence. But if, for example, a buyer wants to rescind in order to get back his money, he must restore the goods; and conversely a seller claiming back his goods must pay back the price. The most difficult cases are those in which restoration is possible in some sense but not in the fullest sense: for example, because the subject-matter has deteriorated or been altered in some way; or because the representee has used it and cannot, strictly speaking, restore the benefit which he has derived from such use.

Deterioration may be due to one of a number of causes. If it is due to the very defect to which the misrepresentation relates, it should obviously not bar rescission: it is precisely on account of such deterioration that the right to rescind is most commonly exercised. Deterioration similarly does not bar the right to rescind where it is due to a wholly extraneous cause, as where goods are damaged by a third party, or where shares decline in value because of a fall in the market.[2] But the position is different where the alteration or deterioration is due to the voluntary act of the representee. Here the general principle is that the change in the subject-matter does bar rescission;[3] but this is subject to a number of qualifications. It does not apply at all where the deterioration occurs simply in the course of a reasonable test carried out to determine the accuracy of the representation. And it is modified where the deterioration or alteration is relatively slight, so that substantial restoration remains possible. In such a case the representee can restore the thing as it is, provided that he also makes an allowance for any benefit which he has obtained as a result of its use. For example, in one case,[4] the purchaser of a phosphate-bearing island

[1] Eg ante, p 110.
[2] *Head v Tattersall* (1871) L R 7 Exch 7; *Armstrong v Jackson* [1917] 2 K B 822.
[3] *Clarke v Dickson* (1858) E B & E 148.
[4] *Erlanger v New Sombrero Phosphate Co* (1878) 3 App Cas 1218.

had worked it, but not worked it out; and it was held that he could rescind on terms of restoring the island and accounting for any profit derived from his operations there. A similar rule applies where the representee has not in any way altered the subject-matter, but has simply used it. Thus, a purchaser of land may go into possession and then discover that there has been a misrepresentation. He will be entitled to rescind on terms of restoring the land and paying a rent for the period of his occupation. The principle of making a money allowance may also apply where a sale is induced by a misrepresentation on the part of the *buyer*, who then incurs expenses (beyond payment of the price) in performing other terms of the contract. A seller claiming rescission in such a case may be obliged, not only to repay the price, but also to make an allowance in respect of those other expenses incurred by the buyer.[5]

The right to rescind is, secondly, barred if the representee *affirms* the contract after he has discovered the truth. Such affirmation may be express, but it can also be inferred from failure to repudiate: for example, from retaining goods, or from staying in possession of land, with knowledge of the truth.[6] Here again, retention for a reasonable period to test the accuracy of the representation will not amount to affirmation of the contract; but further use of the subject-matter after the true facts have been discovered will have this effect. Acts done in ignorance of the true facts will not amount to affirmation and so will not, of themselves, bar the right to rescind *for misrepresentation*, though such acts may sometimes[7] bar the right to rescind for breach.

A third bar to rescission is *lapse of time*. Where the misrepresentation is fraudulent, time for this purpose begins to run from the discovery of the truth, lapse of time being in such cases regarded simply as evidence of affirmation. But where the misrepresentation is innocent, time begins to run from the conclusion of the contract, or perhaps from the time when the truth ought reasonably to have been discovered. In one case,[8] a buyer of a picture innocently said to be 'by J Constable', sought to rescind for misrepresentation five years after he had bought the picture. The claim was held barred by lapse of time, even though the buyer had acted promptly after discovering that the picture was a modern copy, so that he could not be said to have affirmed. In cases of innocent misrepresentation, lapse of time is therefore an independent bar to rescission.

In the circumstances discussed above, the right to rescind is absolutely barred; but it does not follow that rescission will be allowed

[5] *Spence v Crawford* [1939] 3 All E R 271.
[6] Eg *Long v Lloyd* [1958] 2 All E R 402.
[7] See p 290, post.
[8] *Leaf v International Galleries* [1950] 2 K B 86.

merely because none of the bars to rescission has arisen. Under s 2(2) of the Misrepresentation Act 1967, the right to rescind for innocent misrepresentation is subject to the discretion of the court, to declare the contract subsisting and to award damages in lieu of rescission. The sub-section enables the court to refuse to allow rescission in any case in which damages would, in its view, be the more appropriate remedy. However, it may still be in the interest of the party resisting rescission to show that one of the bars to rescission has arisen. For if he can show this rescission *must* be refused: the matter will not be at the discretion of the court.

d Estoppel

Under the doctrine of estoppel, a person who makes precise and unambiguous representation of fact may be prevented from denying that the facts were as he stated them to be, if the person to whom the representation was made was intended to act on it, and did act on it to his detriment. It is generally said that the effect of estoppel is not to create a cause of action, but only to give rise to a defence. Suppose, for example, that A induces B to hire a car by innocently representing that it is in good running order, and that the contract requires B to keep the car in repair. In such a case estoppel would not entitle B to damages if the car was in fact unroadworthy; but it could provide B with a defence if, immediately after the conclusion of the contract, A sued B for failing to remedy the very defects which the car had when it was handed over to him.

Estoppel may, however, help a plaintiff no less than a defendant, as a further example will make clear. Suppose that A is a warehouseman who says to B that there are goods belonging to C in the warehouse and promises to deliver those goods to B, for some consideration moving from B (eg payment of warehouse charges). If there are in fact no goods of C in the warehouse, A may be liable to B on the basis of estoppel. Here estoppel does not create B's cause of action (which is based on A's promise to deliver); but A's representation that C's goods were in the warehouse prevents him from relying on the defence that in fact no such goods were there.[9]

3 NON-DISCLOSURE

a Generally no duty of disclosure

So far in this chapter we have been concerned with active misrepresentations. Of course, such misrepresentations do not have to

---

[9] *Griswold v Haven* 25 N Y 595 (1862); *Coventry v Great Eastern Rly Co* (1883) 11 Q B D 776.

be made in so many words. They may be made by conduct, the stock example being the case where the seller of a house papers over the cracks.[10] A misrepresentation may also be impliedly made where a person states a misleading half-truth. In one case,[11] a solicitor employed by a vendor of land said that he did not know of any restrictive covenants affecting the land. This statement was literally true, but it was held to amount to a misrepresentation, as the solicitor had not given the reason for his ignorance, which was simply that he had failed to read the relevant documents.

Where there is no express or implied misrepresentation, the general rule is that there is no liability for non-disclosure. Thus a seller is not bound to disclose facts known to him but not to the buyer which make the subject-matter less valuable than the buyer had supposed it to be; and conversely a buyer need not disclose facts known to him, but not to the seller, which make the subject-matter more valuable than the seller supposed it to be. The general rule is justified partly by the argument that, in the absence of active misrepresentation, each party takes the risk that the subject-matter may turn out to be worse, or better, than he had supposed; and partly by the difficulty of determining the scope of a general duty of disclosure. It would, for example, be very hard to say just which of the many facts known by a seller about his house must be disclosed to the buyer.

b Exceptions

There are, however, many cases in which some duty of disclosure exists. In these cases the general rule is that a person need only disclose facts which were actually known to him (or his agent) at the time of the conclusion of the contract. Sometimes, however, the duty of disclosure ceases as soon as the parties are bound as a matter of business, even though there is as yet no binding contract. Thus, in contracts of insurance, it ceases when the insurer agrees to accept the risk by initialling a slip, even where there is no legally enforceable contract until the policy is executed.[12] Conversely, a contract may impose a duty of disclosure which continues after its formation and requires one party to inform the other as the occasion arises of certain facts, eg that he has been involved in an accident or convicted of a motoring offence.

The cases in which some duty of disclosure exist are as follows.

i *Change of circumstances*
A person may, in the course of negotiations for the sale of a business,

---

[10] Eg, *Gordon v Selico* (1986) 278 Estates Gazette 53; cf Financial Services Act 1986, s 133.
[11] *Nottingham Patent Brick and Tile Co v Butler* (1886) 16 QBD 778.
[12] *Cory v Patton* (1872) LR 7 QB 304.

make a representation as to its profitability which is perfectly true when made. But if, before any contract is concluded, there is a radical change of circumstances which wholly falsifies that representation, he must disclose this change to the other party.[13] At least this is so if it is still reasonable for the latter to rely on the orginal representation. Where the negotiations have gone on for a very long time, it many no longer be reasonable for him to do this.

The same duty of disclosure has been held to exist where there was a 'change of intention': that is, where during negotiations one party made a statement as to his future commercial policy but changed that policy before the conclusion of the contract.[14] On the other hand, in a more recent case[15] a wife who had been left by her husband received an offer of financial provision from him after saying that she would not remarry. She later decided after all to remarry and then accepted the offer. It was held that she was not bound to disclose her state of mind as her original representation was one of *intention* as opposed to one of *fact*. A better ground for the decision would have been that a statement of intention not to remarry is so intrinsically likely to be changed that it was not reasonable for the husband to have relied on it. As a general principle, there seems to be no good reason for saying that a representation of intention should not be corrected if the representor changes his mind. A representation of present intention is generally regarded as one of fact;[16] and there is no difficulty in cases of this kind in specifying exactly what must be disclosed.

ii Latent defects

A latent defect may not merely affect the value of the subject-matter but also cause further loss or injury to the buyer. In such a case the seller may, if he knows of the defect, be liable in negligence for failing to warn the buyer of its existence: the seller of a car would be liable on this ground if he knew that the car had defects which made it dangerous and if those defects led to and accident in which the buyer was injured.[17]

iii Custom

A duty of disclosure may arise by the custom of a particular trade or market.

iv Contracts uberrimae fidei

A duty of disclosure exists in relation to certain specific contracts on the

---

13 *With v O'Flanagan* [1936] Ch 575; cf Financial Services Act 1986, ss 147, 164.
14 *Traill v Baring* (1864) 4 De G J & Sm 318.
15 *Wales v Wadham* [1977] 2 All E R 125, disapproved (but on another ground only) in *Livesey v Jenkins* [1985] A C 424.
16 See p 123, ante.
17 *Hurley v Dyke* [1979] R T R 265 at 303.

ground that one party to such contracts is in a much better position than the other to know material facts. Such contracts are known as contracts uberrimae fidei. The outstanding illustration of this category is the contract of insurance. Here 'the underwriter knows nothing and the man who asks him to insure knows everything'.[18] Hence the latter is, as a general rule, bound to declare all facts which a reasonably prudent insurer would take into account in deciding whether to accept the risk, or what premium to charge.[19] The insured must, for example, disclose the fact that other underwriters had declined to cover the risk; in the case of life insurance he must disclose any illness, physical or mental, from which he suffers; in the case of an insurance on jewellery, he must disclose previous thefts of jewellery from him. Insurers often stipulate for an even greater degree of protection, by providing that all answers in the proposal form shall form the basis of the contract. The result of such clauses is to enable insurers to avoid liability for misstatements, even though they relate to quite trivial matters, which are not material at all, and even though they were made in the most perfect good faith.[20] Under a contract of insurance, a duty of disclosure may also be imposed on the underwriter: for example, if the insured property had already been destroyed when the policy was taken out, or if the insured had been deceived by his own broker, an underwriter who knows such facts is under a duty to disclosure them to the insured.[1]

Certain agreements between members of a family for settling disputes as to the family property also fall within the class of contracts uberrimae fidei.[2]

v Analogous contracts

In some contracts which are not uberrimae fidei there is a limited duty to disclose: that is, a duty which is not one to disclose all material facts, but a lower duty to disclose *unusual* facts. A creditor to whom a guarantee is given by a surety must, for example, disclose to the surety any *unusual* circumstances, such as terms of the principal contract which the surety would not normally expect it to contain.[3] Thus the duty of disclosure is less exacting under a contract of suretyship than it is under a contract of insurance. The distinction between the two types of contract gives rise to some difficulty, since it is possible to insure

---

18 *Rozanes v Bowen* (1928) 32 Ll L Rep 98 at 102.
19 *Container Transport International Inc v Oceanus Mutual Underwriting Association (Bermuda) Ltd* [1984] 1 Lloyd's Rep 476.
20 The Law Commission has recommended that such clauses should cease to have this effect: Law Com 104 para 7.4.
1 *Banque Financière de la Cité SA v Westgate Insurance Co Ltd* [1988] 2 Lloyd's Rep 513 at 544.
2 *Greenwood v Greenwood* (1863) 2 De G J & Sm 28.
3 *Cooper v National Provincial Bank* [1946] K B 1 at 7.

against a third party's breach of contract. If A makes a contractual promise to B, and C then promises B to make a payment to B, if A fails to perform his promise, the contract between B and C may be one of insurance or suretyship according to the circumstances. So far as B's duty of disclosure is concerned, the vital distinction is this. If C is a person selected by B, the duty of disclosure is the same as in an ordinary contract of insurance, since C will be in a worse position than B to know the facts affecting A's ability to perform. But if C is a person selected by A, C will be in as good a position to know these facts as B, so that B will only be under the more limited duty of disclosure owed to a surety.[4]

A limited duty of disclosure may also arise in contracts for the sale of land. Here it has been said that a seller is bound to disclose unusual defects of title.[5] Certain other cases in which there is a duty of disclosure have been discussed elsewhere in this book, in particular in relation to compromises of invalid claims and to exemption clauses.[6]

vi Relationship of parties

In some cases, a duty of disclosure arises because there is a so-called *fiduciary* relationship between the parties. Such a duty is, for example, owed by an agent to his principal, and by a company promoter to the company. In yet other cases of fiduciary relationships the contract may be set aside, even though full disclosure has been made, unless further conditions to be discussed in chapter 10 are satisfied.[7]

Our concern in this section is with non-disclosure which *induces* a contract; but a duty of disclosure may also arise in the *performance* of a contract: for example, an employee may be bound to disclose the fact that his fellow employees have defrauded the employer.[8] Failure to perform such a duty does not invalidate the contract but amounts to a breach of it. The failure may, however, vitiate a second contract: eg one for the payment of compensation for the 'early retirement' of the employee.[9]

vii Statutory duties of disclosure

Many modern statutes require certain facts to be disclosed in relation to specific contracts. These requirements are designed to protect classes of persons such as investors, or borrowers, or consumers of certain kinds of goods. For example, the Financial Services Act 1986[10]

---

[4] *Trade Indemnity Co Ltd v Workington Harbour Board* [1937] AC 1.

[5] *Rignall Developments Ltd v Halil* [1988] Ch 190.

[6] See pp 35, 72–73, ante.

[7] Post, p 149.

[8] *Sybron Corpn v Rochem Ltd* [1984] Ch 112 at 126–127; for a similar duty in another context, see *The Good Luck* [1988] 1 Lloyd's Rep 514.

[9] *Sybron Corp v Rochem Ltd*, supra.

[10] Ss 146, 163.

imposes extensive duties of disclosure on persons who seek official listings of securities on the stock exchange or who issue a prospectus inviting subscriptions for unlisted securities.

c The effects of non-disclosure

Failure to perform a duty of disclosure can give rise to the same remedies as misrepresentation: that is, to a right to rescind and to a common law right to damages for deceit, and sometimes for negligence.[11] In the case of the statutory duty of disclosure just described, the right to damages appears to be the sole remedy.[12] On the other hand, it has been held that breach of the duty of disclosure which arises in the case of contracts uberrimae fidei gives rise only to a right to rescind and not to one to damages for negligence at common law.[13] Nor does breach of a duty of disclosure normally give rise to liability in damages under s 2(1) of the Misrepresentation Act, since the statutory liability arises where 'a misrepresentation has been made'; and this phrase does not appear to cover simple non-disclosure.[14] The same phrase occurs in s 2(2) of the Act, so that the power of the court to declare a contract subsisting and to award damages in lieu of rescission would not apply merely because a duty of disclosure had been broken. It should, however, be recalled that a misrepresentation may be 'made' by conduct or by stating a half-truth; and it is probable that s 2 of the Act applies to such cases. The section may also apply where a representation is falsified by a change of circumstances. Such a case falls literally within the words 'Where a person enters into a contract after a representation has been made to him . . .' and it is as plausible to say that he is liable because he made the representation, as it is to say that he is liable because he failed to disclose the change of circumstances.

[11] See p 142, ante.
[12] *Re South of England Natural Gas Co* [1911] 1 Ch 573, which seems to be unaffected by the Financial Services Act 1986, ss 150, 166.
[13] *Banque Financière de la Cité SA v Westgate Insurance Co Ltd* [1988] 2 Lloyd's Rep 513.
[14] Ibid at 556.

Chapter 10

Improper pressure

The law in a number of situations gives relief against contracts
obtained by improper pressure. The crucial word here is 'improper'.
Almost every contract is made under some form of economic pressure,
and even where this pressure is considerable—where, in other words,
one party is able to drive a hard bargain—the validity of the contract is
not normally affected. But victims of certain forms of pressure are
protected by the common law of duress and the equitable rules of
undue influence, while further rules for the protection of particular
classes of person have been developed in equity and by legislation.

1 DURESS

The original definition of duress was a very narrow one. It meant
actual or threatened unlawful violence to, or constraint of, the person
of the other contracting party.[1] Later cases reject this narrow view and
recognise that duress may be pleaded in other circumstances: eg where
a person is forced to enter into a contract under a threat to burn his
house down, or one to call his employees out on strike in breach of their
contracts of employment, or one to refuse to perform an earlier
contract (either between the same parties or with a third party).[2]
Whether a threat amounts to duress no longer depends on whether it is
the victim's person, property or financial position that is threatened.
Any threat *can* amount to duress so long as it is 'illegitimate' either
because what is threatened is a legal wrong (as in the above examples)
or because of the nature of the threat itself (as in the case of a
blackmailer's threat to reveal the truth about his victim).[3] Whether it
does amount to duress then depends on its effect on the victim: it must
produce 'coercion of the will which vitiates consent'.[4] In one case,[5] a
contractor had undertaken to erect an exhibition stand and, one week

---

1 See *Latter v Braddell* (1880) 50 LJ QB 166; affd (1881) 50 LJ QB 448.
2 *The Siboen and the Sibotre* [1976] 1 Lloyd's Rep 293; and see the authorities cited in notes
   3 to 5 below.
3 *The Universe Sentinel* [1982] ICR 262 at 289.
4 *Pao On v Lau Yiu Long* [1980] AC 614 at 616.
5 *B & S Contracts and Design Ltd v Victor Green Publications Ltd* [1984] ICR 419; cf *The
   Atlantic Baron* [1979] QB 705 and p 40 ante.

147

before the exhibition was due to open, told his client that the contract would be cancelled unless the client made an extra payment, to meet claims by the contractor's workforce. This threat was held to amount to duress as the consequences of not having the stand available in time would have been disastrous for the client, so that he had no reasonable alternative except to comply with the threat. But a threat to break a contract will not necessarily amount to duress. In another case[6] a person who had made a contract with a company threatened to refuse to perform it unless the directors guaranteed that such performance would not cause him any loss. The directors of the company, thinking that the risk was small and wanting to avoid adverse publicity, gave the guarantee; and the argument that they had done so under duress was rejected as their will had not been coerced. A threat to *enforce* contractual rights will nto amount to duress because there is nothing 'illegitimate' about such a threat. There would, for example, be no duress if a lender threatened to call in a loan repayable on demand even though the lender knew that the borrower would be ruined if the threat were carried out.

The original common law view that duress required unlawful violence to the *person* of the victim was reflected in a line of mid-19th century cases according to which 'duress of goods' did not affect the validity of a contract.[7] It followed that a promise to pay money to prevent the unlawful seizure of goods, or to obtain the release of goods which had been unlawfully detained, could not have been impugned on the ground of duress. But it had also been held in another line of cases that money actually paid in such circumstances could be recovered back by the payor.[8] The two lines of cases are in fact incongruous; and both would now be governed by the broader modern view of duress stated above.

Where a contract is affected by duress the result is to make the contract voidable, not void.[9] Innocent third parties are therefore not prejudiced by the invalidity of the contract.

2   UNDUE INFLUENCE

Equity sometimes gave relief where an agreement had been obtained by some form of pressure, which fell outside the originally narrow common law definition of duress. In one line of cases, for example, contracts obtained by threatening to prosecute the promisor, or his

6 *Pao On v Lau Yiu Long*, supra.
7 Eg *Skeate v Beale* (1840) 11 Ad & El 983.
8 Eg *Astley v Reynolds* (1731) 2 Stra 915.
9 *Pao On v Lau Yiu Long* [1980] AC 614 at 634; *The Universe Sentinel* [1982] ICR 262 at 272, 288.

spouse or close relative, for a criminal offence were set aside on the ground of undue influence.[10]

Equity further gives relief where a transaction is unfair to one of the parties and the relationship between them is such as to give rise to a presumption that one of them exercised undue influence over the other. Such a relationship has been held to exist between parent and child, doctor and patient, solicitor and client, trustee and beneficiary, religious leader and disciple, and in some cases between fiancé and fiancée—but not between husband and wife,[11] nor between banker and customer.[12] The presumption is not however rigidly confined to any particular group of relationships. It applies whenever one party is able to take unfair advantage of the other because of a relationship of trust and confidence existing between them.[13] The mere existence of such a relationship is not, of itself, a ground for relief: the party seeking to set the transaction aside must generally show that it was unfair.[14] It is then up to the party in whom confidence was reposed to rebut the presumption. The most usual (though not the only) way of doing this is by showing that the other party was independently and competently advised before he entered into the transaction.[14a] In some exceptional cases the party seeking to uphold the presumption must himself show that the transaction was fair: this is the position where a solicitor buys from his client or a trustee from his beneficiary.[15]

Relief in cases of undue influence is barred on grounds similar to those discussed in relation to misrepresentation: that is, by inability to make restitution,[16] the intervention of the rights of innocent third parties, by affirmation and by lapse of time.

3 PROTECTION OF PARTICULAR GROUPS OF PERSONS

Even where there was no undue influence (actual or presumed) equity sometimes gave relief because one of the parties to a transaction was thought to require special protection; for example because he was poor or ignorant and unfair advantage had been taken of him. In an

10 Eg *Kaufman v Gerson* [1904] 1 KB 591.
11 *Midland Bank plc v Shephard* [1988] 3 All ER 17.
12 *National Westminister Bank plc v Morgan* [1985] AC 686.
13 *Tate v Williamson* (1866) 2 Ch App 55; *Lloyd's Bank Ltd v Bundy* [1975] QB 326; *Goldsworthy v Brickell* [1987] Ch 378.
14 *National Westminister Bank plc v Morgan* [1985] AC 686 at 706; *Woodstead Finance Ltd v Petrou* [1986] FLR 158; *Midland Bank plc v Shephard*, supra.
14a *Allcard v Skinner* (1887) 36 Ch D 145 at 190.
15 *Wright v Carter* [1903] 1 Ch 27; *Thomson v Eastwood* (1877) 2 App Cas 215.
16 See *O'Sullivan v Management Agency & Music Ltd* [1985] QB 428 (*precise* restitution not necessary).

old case,[17] a poor man was told that he was legally entitled to a share of an estate and was offered 200 guineas in cash if he would relinquish it. He agreed to these terms, even though the share was in fact worth £1,700, and the contract was set aside as it had been 'improvidently obtained'. More recently the same principle was applied where a wife, in the course of divorce proceedings, transferred her share in the matrimonial home to her husband without independent advice and for a grossly inadequate consideration.[18]

One group of persons thought by the courts to need special protection were the so-called 'expectant heirs': that is, persons who raised money by selling reversionary interests in property before they were entitled to possession of it, or even by selling the bare expectancy of inheriting under someone's will or intestacy.[19] Originally such sales could be set aside merely on the ground of undervalue. But this rule was later reversed by legislation[20] and now relief will only be given if the undervalue is so gross as to make the transaction an unconscionable one.

In a number of cases Lord Denning MR has relied on the equitable rules discussed in this chapter, and on a number of other instances,[1] in support of a general principle of 'inequality of bargaining power'. Under this principle, relief would be given against unfair transactions at the suit of a party 'whose bargaining power is grievously impaired by reason of his own needs or desires, or by his own ignorance or infirmity, coupled with undue influence or pressures brought to bear on him by or for the benefit of the other'.[2] The scope of this alleged principle is very wide: it seems to be intended to apply to such diverse transactions as a guarantee of a bank loan obtained from the borrower's father by a bank manager in whom the father placed implicit trust;[3] the renegotiation of a contract;[4] the settlement of a personal injury claim;[5] and the inclusion of an exemption clause in a standard form contract with a consumer.[6] However, the actual decisions in these cases can be explained on other grounds, and were so explained by other members of the courts. Later decisions have rejected the principle for two main reasons. First, its vagueness has drawn the criticism that it would be 'unhelpful because it would render the law uncertain'.[7] Secondly, the need for such a principle has

17 *Evans v Llewellin* (1787) 1 Cox Eq Cas 333.
18 *Creswell v Potter* [1978] 1 WLR 255 n.
19 *Nevill v Snelling* (1880) 15 Ch D 679.
20 Sale of Reversions Act 1867; now Law of Property Act 1925, s 174.
1 Eg the restraint of trade cases, discussed on p 168 post.
2 *Lloyd's Bank Ltd v Bundy* [1975] QB 326 at 339.
3 *Lloyd's Bank Ltd v Bundy* [1975] QB 326 at 339.
4 *D & C Builders Ltd v Rees* [1966] 2 QB 617.
5 *Arrale v Costain Civil Engineering Ltd* [1976] 1 Lloyd's Rep 98.
6 *Levison v Patent Steam Carpet Cleaning Co Ltd* [1978] QB 69 at 78.
7 *Pao On v Lau Yiu Long* [1980] AC 614 at 634.

been greatly reduced by the modern expansion of the concept of duress,[8] and by the fact that Parliament has dealt with a number of specific instances in which inequality of bargaining power might be abused.[9]

One illustration of this legislative approach is to be found in the law relating to 'extortionate credit bargains'.[10] Since the repeal of the usury laws in 1854, there has been no legal restriction of the maximum rate of interest which a moneylender can charge. But under the Consumer Credit Act 1974 an extortionate credit bargain can be 'reopened' by the court. A credit bargain is extortionate if it requires the debtor to make payments which are grossly exorbitant, or if it otherwise grossly contravenes the principles of fair dealing.[11] The power to 'reopen' is a very flexible one. The court can order accounts to be taken, set aside any obligation undertaken by the debtor or by any surety, order the creditor to repay excessive amounts received by him, direct the return to a surety of property given as security, and even alter the terms of the credit agreement or of any security instrument executed in relation to it.[12]

Protection against unfair bargains is provided for consumers under the Fair Trading Act 1973. The Act empowers the Director General of Fair Trading to refer to the Consumer Protection Advisory Committee any 'consumer trade practice'[13] which has or is likely to have the effect of 'subjecting consumers to undue pressure to enter into relevant consumer transactions';[14] or of causing the terms of such transactions to be so adverse to consumers as to be inequitable.[15] Such a reference may lead to legislation against the practice by statutory instrument.[16] This may prohibit the continuance of the practice; and the prohibition can be enforced by criminal penalties and by proceedings before the Restrictive Practices Court.[17] Under these provisions, consumers can be protected against 'high pressure salesmanship', which may be regarded as a kind of 'economic duress'. A similar policy underlies the special statutory rule giving a right to cancel within a cooling-off period to a person who signs a regulated consumer credit agreement in certain circumstances—eg if he (or she) is induced by a representative of the lender to sign the agreement at home.[18]

---

[8] Ante, p 147.
[9] *National Westminster Bank plc v Morgan* [1985] A C 686 at 708.
[10] Consumer Credit Act 1974, ss 137–140.
[11] Ibid s 138(1); see *Coldunell Ltd v Gallon* [1986] Q B 1184.
[12] Consumer Credit Act 1974, s 139(2).
[13] Fair Trading Act 1973, ss 3, 13(1) and 14.
[14] Ibid s 17(2)(c).
[15] Ibid s 17(2)(d).
[16] Fair Trading Act 1973, ss 22, 23; cf p 97, ante.
[17] Ibid ss 35, 37. Civil rights and remedies are not intended to be affected: s 26.
[18] Consumer Credit Act 1974, ss 67–73; cf Insurance Companies Act 1982, s 76; Financial Services Act 1986, s 56.

Chapter 11

Illegality

The general principle that parties can make what contracts they please is subject to the obvious limitation that their contract must not involve the commission of a legal wrong. The law also denies full effect to contracts which, even though they do not involve the commission of a legal wrong, are said to be 'contrary to public policy'. Contracts which involve the commission of a legal wrong, or are contrary to public policy, are said to be illegal, or affected with illegality. In this chapter we shall first consider the various groups of contracts so affected. It will become clear that 'illegality' in the sense here under discussion can vary very much in seriousness from one type of contract to another. It follows that the effects of illegality on contracts are likewise far from uniform; and these effects will be discussed in the concluding section of this chapter.

1 CONTRACTS CONTRARY TO LAW

a Making of the contract forbidden by law

In some cases the very making of a contract is against the law. For example, a contract to 'rig the market' amounts to an indictable conspiracy to defraud and is therefore illegal.[1] A contract to finance another person's litigation in return for a share in the proceeds was also illegal as it amounted to the crime of champerty.[2] Criminal liability in cases of this kind has been abolished, but the rule that the contract is illegal has been expressly preserved.[3] Under this rule, an agreement to remunerate a solicitor by a fee payable only if the litigation ends in the client's favour is illegal.[4] And where the making of a contract is prohibited by a court order, disobedience of the order would be contempt of court and the prohibited contract would be illegal.[5]

Legislation may simply prohibit the making of a contract without rendering it criminal. For example, an Act of 1774 provides that 'no

---

[1] *Scott v Brown* [1892] 2 QB 72.
[2] *Re Thomas* [1894] 1 QB 747.
[3] Criminal Law Act 1967, s 14; *Trendtex Trading Corpn v Crédit Suisse* [1982] AC 679.
[4] *Wallersteiner v Moir (No 2)* [1975] QB 373.
[5] *Clarke v Chadburn* [1985] 1 All ER 211.

insurance shall be made' by a person on the life of another in which he has no insurable interest; and contracts which contravene this prohibition have been held illegal.[6] A modern Act of Parliament would be more likely to provide expressly whether a contract made in disregard of such a statutory prohibition was, or was not, to be illegal. A contract which is not prohibited, but simply declared by statute to be void or voidable or unenforceable, is not illegal.[7]

b Object of the contract contrary to law

A contract may be illegal because of its object. Obviously, a contract for the deliberate *commission of a crime* is illegal; indeed it falls under the previous heading as such a contract would be a criminal conspiracy. A contract may be illegal, even though there is no conspiracy, if one of the parties simply knows that the other intends to use the subject-matter for an illegal purpose: eg where the seller of a car knows that the buyer intends to use it in a smash-and-grab raid. A contract may also have a criminal object where only one party has any criminal intent, or even, under modern criminal statutes, where neither party has such an intent. Here again, there is no criminal conspiracy, but the contract is often to some extent affected by illegality. The difficulties arising from such 'innocent illegality' will be discussed later in this chapter.[8]

Where the object of a contract is the deliberate *commission of a civil wrong*, the contract is often illegal. This would be the position where a contract was made to defraud or defame a third party. But where one of the parties is innocent, the better view is that he can enforce the contract: for example, a printer who innocently prints libellous matter can probably recover his charges.[9] If both parties are innocent, it is clear that the contract is not illegal. It quite commonly happens that A sells goods to B which they both believe to belong to A but which, in fact, belong to C. The contract is not illegal even though A or B (or both of them) may have committed a civil wrong, known as the tort of conversion, against C.

c Method of performance contrary to law

A contract may be capable of being performed in several ways, some of which are perfectly lawful, while another involves the commission of an offence. For example, the law may require a seller of certain goods to be licensed, or to attach statements to them specifying their

[6] Life Assurance Act 1774, s 1; *Harse v Pearl Life Assurance Co Ltd* [1904] 1 K B 558.
[7] Eg Marine Insurance Act 1906, s 4(1); *Re London County Commercial Reinsurance Office* [1922] 2 Ch 67.
[8] See pp 176–179, post.
[9] *Clay v Yates* (1856) 1 H & N 73.

154 *Illegality*

ingredients. In such cases there is nothing illegal in the sale as such: the illegality only arises if the seller does not in fact hold the licence or give the required information. The question whether this makes the contract illegal depends, in these cases, on the court's view of the purpose of the rule of law that is contravened. In one case[10] a shipowner overloaded his ship and so became liable to a fine under the relevant merchant shipping legislation. The owner of some of the goods on the ship argued that the contract of carriage was therefore illegal and that he was not liable to pay the agreed freight. If this argument had been accepted, two consequences would have followed. First, the shipowner would have been subjected to a very severe penalty (in addition to the fine) in the shape of loss of freight; and secondly, the owner of the goods (which in fact arrived safely at the agreed destination) would have obtained a totally undeserved windfall. The court therefore held that the shipowner was entitled to his freight, as the purpose of the legislation was to prohibit overloading and not to invalidate contracts of carriage.

Similar reasoning has been applied where an offence is committed by failing to comply with requirements of form imposed by statute. In one case,[11] a landlord committed an offence by failing to give his tenant a rent-book. It was held that the landlord was nevertheless entitled to sue for the rent, since the purpose of the legislation was simply to punish his failure to give the rent-book and not to invalidate the lease. A fortiori, where the landlord commits an offence by requiring an illegal premium the tenant can enforce the contract, but without having to pay the premium.[12]

A contract may be subject to a licensing or similar requirement under which its performance is legal only if the consent of some public body (such as an export licence or a building permit) has been obtained. Such a contract is not illegal so long as it is expressly or impliedly made subject to such consent.[13] It is only illegal if it is performed without the required consent;[14] or if the parties intend it to be performed even though that consent is not obtained.[15] A licence may also be required for carrying on some specified kind of business, as opposed to the making or performance of a particular contract. If a person carries on such a business without the required licence, the resulting contracts will be illegal if the legislation which imposed the

10 *St John Shipping Corpn v Joseph Rank Ltd* [1957] 1 QB 267.
11 *Shaw v Groom* [1970] 2 QB 504.
12 *Ailion v Spiekermann* [1976] Ch 158—unless the tenant takes the initiative and 'tempts the [landlord] with a cheque book': ibid at 163.
13 Eg *Michael Richards Properties Ltd v Corpn of Wardens St Saviour's Parish* [1975] 3 All ER 416.
14 Eg *J Dennis & Co Ltd v Munn* [1949] 2 KB 327.
15 Eg *Bigos v Bousted* [1951] 1 All ER 92.

requirement also expressly prohibited those contracts.[16] Such a prohibition may also be implied: this was held to be the position at common law where insurers carried on business without the required licence.[17] But in such cases the licencing requirement was imposed on only one party (the insurer) for the protection of the other (the insured); and the preferable solution, now adopted by statute,[18] is that the illegality does not deprive the latter of the right to enforce the contract.

d Promises contingent on the commission of an unlawful act

A contract may be made under which one party promises to pay the other a sum of money on the occurrence of one or more events, including the commission by the other of an unlawful act. In one case,[19] a person who had insured his life for £50,000 committed suicide, and it was held that his estate was not entitled to enforce the policy even though it expressly covered death by suicide. The actual reasoning is obsolete now that suicide is no longer a crime;[20] but the principle remains, that a promise to pay a sum of money to a person on the commission by him of a crime is generally illegal.

Problems of this kind commonly arise where one person promises to indemnify another against liability arising out of the commission of an unlawful act. Such liability may either be criminal or civil, and it may be incurred either deliberately (with guilty intent) or innocently; for the present purpose innocence will be taken to include negligence.

A promise to indemnify a person against *civil* liability innocently incurred is perfectly valid. Such a promise is made expressly whenever an insurance company undertakes to indemnify a person against civil liability (for example, for negligence); and a promise of this kind is enforceable against the insurer even if the negligent conduct also amounts to a crime—as it often does in the case of motor accidents.[1] A promise to indemnify a person against civil liability may also be implied. For example, an agent who in good faith and with his principal's authority sells property which belongs to a third party, may be liable in conversion to the third party; and he is entitled to be indemnified by his principal against such liability.[2] Although there is some doubt on the point, it seems that a promise to indemnify a person against *criminal* liability is also enforceable if the liability is incurred (as

---

[16] Eg *Re Mahmoud and Ispahani* [1921] 2 KB 716; post p 177.

[17] See *Phoenix General Insurance Co of Greece SA v Administratia Asigurarilo de Stat* [1986] 2 Lloyd's Rep 552 (where the statute had not been contravened).

[18] Financial Services Act 1986, s 132.

[19] *Beresford v Royal Insurance Co Ltd* [1938] A C 586.

[20] Suicide Act 1961.

[1] *Tinline v White Cross Insurance* [1921] 3 K B 327.

[2] *Adamson v Jarvis* (1827) 4 Bing 66.

under modern legislation it quite commonly is) without guilty intent. For example a person may drive a car after being told by his insurance agent that he is properly insured. If this is not the case, the driver incurs criminal liability but it has been held that he can nevertheless enforce the agent's implied promise to indemnify him against that liability.[3]

On the other hand, where the wrong is deliberately committed, the general principle is that the promise to indemnify is illegal.[4] This is true whether the promise relates to criminal or to civil liability. If a passenger tells a taxi driver to break the speed limit and promises to pay the fine, the promise is not legally enforceable; and the same is true where a promise is made to indemnify a person against civil liability for deceit,[5] or for publishing a statement which he knows to be defamatory.[6] If a motorist deliberately causes injury to someone, he cannot recover from his insurer the damages which he has to pay the injured party. But the latter has, by statute, a direct right against the motorist's insurance company;[7] and this is not affected by the illegality which prevents the motorist himself from suing the company. If the injured party's right were so affected, the scheme of compulsory third party motor insurance would be seriously weakened.

2 CONTRACTS CONTRARY TO PUBLIC POLICY

Contracts are said to be contrary to public policy when they have a clear tendency to bring about a state of affairs which the law regards as harmful. Obviously, the attitude of the law towards such questions varies from time to time so as to reflect changing social attitudes and economic conditions. The resulting flexibility of the doctrine of public policy is a source of uncertainty, and it could, if carried to extremes, enable courts to invalidate any contracts of which they strongly disapproved. Some judges have stressed this danger and have taken a somewhat restrictive view of the doctrine of public policy. Their attitude was summed up long ago in the statement that public policy is 'a very unruly horse, and when once you get astride it you never know where it will carry you'.[8] Later judges have laid greater stress on the creative role of the courts in this area; and their attitude is, in turn, expressed in the more recent statement that 'With a good man in the saddle the unruly horse can be kept in control.'[9] The present law is

---

3 *Osman v J Ralph Moss Ltd* [1970] 1 Lloyd's Rep 313.
4 *Gray v Barr* [1971] 2 QB 554.
5 *Brown Jenkinson & Co Ltd v Percy Dalton (London) Ltd* [1957] 2 QB 621.
6 *WH Smith & Sons v Clinton* (1908) 99 LT 840.
7 See p 217, post; cf *Gardner v Moore* [1984] AC 548 at 560–561.
8 *Richardson v Mellish* (1824) 2 Bing 229 at 252.
9 *Enderby Town Football Club Ltd v Football Association Ltd* [1971] Ch 591 at 606.

essentially a compromise between these two attitudes.

On the one hand, the courts will not readily invent new 'heads' of public policy, that is, they will not generally apply the doctrine to clauses or contracts to which it has never been applied before. They are more reluctant to extend the doctrine in this way at the present time than they were when it was originally developed; and the reason for this is that the more important fields of public policy are now regarded as primarily a matter for Parliament.[10] It is, for example, unlikely that the courts in Britain would have made a significant contribution to solving the problem of racially discriminatory contracts. They would have regarded the problem as a political one, to be regulated mainly by Parliamentary legislation and not by judicial innovation.

On the other hand, 'where the subject-matter is "lawyer's law"'[11] the courts do still exercise a creative role in the field of public policy in a number of important ways. First, they have relatively little hesitation in extending existing heads of public policy: for example once a contract falls within the general category of being in restraint of trade, the fact that it was made to further a policy of (for example) religious discrimination would quite probably lead to a holding that the restraint was not justified[12] and thus invalid. Secondly, the courts do still occasionally apply the doctrine of public policy to entirely new classes of contracts. For example, in one case[13] the doctrine was applied to a contract by which a trade journal promised not to comment on the affairs of a company, since this could prevent it from exposing even frauds committed by the company; and in another case[14] an agreement purporting to deprive an agricultural tenant of his statutory security of tenure was held to be contrary to public policy. There were no direct precedents for these decisions. Thirdly, the courts sometimes invalidate contracts, or terms of contracts, on grounds that are essentially based on public policy, but they forestall the criticism which an expansion of that doctrine would evoke by simply not mentioning it. Illustrations of this process are provided by the common law limitations on the effectiveness of exemption clauses;[15] and by cases in which it was held that the performance of an existing duty could not constitute consideration.[16]

The following types of contracts are at present regarded by the law as

---

[10] See *Cheall v Association of Professional, Executive, Clerical and Computer Staff* [1983] 2 AC 180 at 191.
[11] *D v National Society for Prevention of Cruelty to Children* [1978] AC 171 at 235.
[12] Cf pp 166–168, post.
[13] *Neville v Dominion of Canada News Co Ltd* [1915] 3 KB 556.
[14] *Johnson v Moreton* [1980] AC 37.
[15] See pp 85–88, ante.
[16] Eg *Morgan v Palmer* (1824) 2 B & C 729 at 736; *Stilk v Myrick* (1809) 2 Camp 317, as reported in 6 Esp 129; see pp 39–40, ante.

contrary to public policy. Contracts in restraint of trade also fall within this group, but give rise to problems of such complexity that it will be convenient to discuss them separately.

a Immoral contracts

A contract is contrary to public policy if its object is to promote 'immorality'. In the present context, immorality seems to refer simply to extramarital sexual intercourse: the cases provide no illustration of any other kind of immorality which invalidates a contract. The principle most obviously makes illegal a promise by a man to pay money to a woman if she will become, or remain, his mistress. The same is true of a contract which indirectly promotes this kind of immorality. For example a contract by which the owner of a brougham let it out to a prostitute, knowing that she intended to use it for the purpose of attracting customers, was held to be illegal.[17] And a contract of employment would be illegal if one of its terms were that the employee should procure prostitutes for the employer's clients.[18]

The original common law view was that all contracts which could be said to promote such immoral purposes were illegal. Recent developments, however, suggest that this approach must now be restricted to contracts of the kind described above, made for purely meretricious purposes, and that it no longer applies to the arrangements of persons who live together in a stable relationship as husband and wife without being married. Such an arrangement may, for example, confer legally enforceable rights in the accommodation which they share,[19] or in a joint bank account.[20] A contract between them to 'pool' their earnings would probably not be contrary to public policy;[1] and the same is true where the father of an illegitimate child promises to pay the mother money for its support.[2] Often the domestic arrangements of such parties will not be contracts for want of contractual intention;[3] but they will no longer be struck down on grounds of public policy.

b Contracts affecting the freedom and stability of marriage

The law of contract makes a number of assumptions about marriage, which are reflected in three sets of rules.

---

[17] *Pearce v Brooks* (1866) LR 1 Exch 213.
[18] See *Coral Leisure Group v Barnett* [1981] ICR 503 at 508.
[19] Eg *Tanner v Tanner* [1975] 3 All ER 776; *Eves v Eves* [1975] 3 All ER 768. See also Domestic Violence and Matrimonial Proceedings Act 1976, s 2(1); *Davis v Johnson* [1979] AC 264.
[20] *Paul v Constance* [1977] 1 All ER 195.
[1] See the American case of *Marvin v Marvin* 557 P 2d 106 (1976).
[2] *Horrocks v Forray* [1976] 1 WLR 230 at 239; cf *Ward v Byham* [1956] 2 All ER 318.
[3] See p 53, ante.

i Restraint of marriage

First, it assumes that everyone should be free to marry, so that a promise not to marry is prima facie invalid. The same is true of a promise by A to pay a sum of money by way of damages to B, in the event of A's marriage, this being in substance a promise not to marry.[4] In such cases the restraint on marriage is total, but if it were limited in such a way as to make it reasonable it might be valid: for example if a person promised not to marry before completing a course of training or study. Moreover, a contract which does not amount to an actual promise not to marry is not invalid merely because it may deter a person from marrying. This would be the position where a contract was made to pay an allowance until marriage, or where some other benefit under a contract was to cease on marriage.

ii Marriage brokage

The law secondly takes the view that the arranging of marriages should not be made into a business; so that a contract to find a spouse for a client in return for a fee is invalid.[5] The law on the point is settled, but the harmful tendencies (if any) of such contracts are scarcely so clear as to justify their invalidation on grounds of public policy. It seems unlikely that 'computer dating' contracts would be held invalid.

iii Protecting existing marriages

The law wants to protect existing marriages; and the law of contract plays some (though probably not a very significant) part in the pursuit of that aim. The overriding principle is that an agreement tending to weaken the marriage bond is invalid. This principle is the basis of three separate rules.

First, an agreement between husband and wife made while they are living together, and providing for the terms of a possible future separation, is invalid; and the same is true where such an agreement is actually made before marriage (as it might be in the case of a 'shotgun' marriage).[6] The reasoning behind the rule is that, if such an agreement were valid, it might give one or other of the parties an incentive to break up the marriage. Obviously, this reasoning does not apply where the marriage has already broken up, so that separation agreements made *after* a separation has occurred are valid.[7] Moreover, an agreement for future separation is valid if made as part·of the reconciliation of parties previously separated.[8] The purpose of this rule

---

[4] *Lowe v Peers* (1768) 4 Burr 2225.
[5] *Hermann v Charlesworth* [1905] 2 K B 123.
[6] *Brodie v Brodie* [1917] P 271.
[7] *Wilson v Wilson* (1848) 1 H L Cas 538.
[8] *Harrison v Harrison* [1910] 1 K B 35.

is to promote reconciliation, which might be less likely if the parties could not provide for future separation.

Secondly, the law at one time invalidated ageements which tended to facilitate divorce, for example by specifying the wife's rights to maintenance. Such agreements were thought to amount, or to lead, to collusion, which was formerly a bar to divorce. Now that collusion has ceased to be a bar to divorce, such agreements are no longer contrary to public policy,[9] and the law provides machinery for submitting them to the court for its approval.[10] An agreement of this kind will only be invalid at common law in the rare case where it amounts to a corrupt bargain, such as a conspiracy to deceive the court.

A third rule relates to promises by married persons to marry. This rule is in a sense obsolete, but the reasoning behind it may still be of some practical importance even to-day. Before 1971, a person who broke a promise to marry was liable in damages for breach of contract. But this action for breach of promise of marriage could not be brought where the promisor was, to the knowledge of the promisee, already married when the promise was made.[11] In that case, the promise was said to have a tendency to break up the existing marriage and to lead to immorality. The idea that the promisor's immunity from liability for breach of promise protected his existing marriage is perhaps open to question; and in any case, the rule did not apply where the marriage had been virtually dissolved by a decree nisi of divorce.[12] The action for breach of promise of marriage was abolished[13] by an Act of 1970; but that Act provides that 'where an agreement to marry is terminated'[14] the parties may have certain rights in each other's property. It is at least arguable that, for this purpose, the 'agreement' must be one which would, before the Act, have been enforceable by an award of damages for breach of promise of marriage; and that, accordingly, the property rights under the Act are not available where one party to the agreement was already married and the other party knew this.

c Contracts excluding the jurisdiction of the courts

The parties to a contract often provide that disputes arising under it shall be settled extra-judicially, by arbitration; and that no action shall be brought on the contract until the decision of the arbitrator has been

---

9 *Sutton v Sutton* [1984] Ch 184 at 194.
10 Matrimonial Causes Act 1973, s 7; Domestic Proceedings and Magistrates' Courts Act 1978, s 6, as substituted by the Matrimonial and Family Proceedings Act 1984, s 10.
11 Eg *Spiers v Hunt* [1908] 1 K B 720.
12 *Fender v St John Mildmay* [1938] A C 1.
13 Law Reform (Miscellaneous Provisions) Act 1970, s 1.
14 Ibid; s 2(1).

obtained.[15] Such arbitration clauses are generally speaking perfectly valid. Indeed, if one of the parties to the contract disregards such a clause and brings an action without going to arbitration, the court may (and in certain cases must[16])stay the action,[17] and so in effect compel a party to resort to arbitration. But the process of arbitration is subject to a considerable degree of judicial control: in particular the court may grant leave to appeal from an arbitrator on a point of law.[18] The original common law position was that any attempt by contract to exclude judicial control of arbitrations was contrary to public policy; for it might lead to the parties being bound by an arbitrator's decision even though it contravened some peremptory rule of law.[19] On the other hand, the impossibility of excluding judicial control was a source of delay in arbitration proceedings; and the Arbitration Act 1979 now makes it possible for the parties to exclude judicial control by means of a written 'exclusion agreement'.[20] In the case of a 'domestic arbitration agreement',[1] however, they can only do so *after* the arbitration has commenced.

The rule that parties cannot effectively exclude the jurisdiction of the courts, has also been applied where a husband in matrimonial proceedings promises to pay his wife an allowance and she, in return, promises not to apply for maintenance. Here the wife's promise is invalid because her right to maintenance is 'a matter of public concern which she cannot barter away'.[2] It follows that she can still apply to the court in spite of her promise not to do so. Alternatively she can, if the agreement is in writing, sue the husband for the promised allowance.[3]

The rule finally applies where the rules of an association purport to give exclusive power to one of the association's committees to construe the rules. Since a question of construction is one of law, the attempt to deprive the courts of their jurisdiction over it is ineffective.[4]

---

15 *Scott v Avery* (1856) 5 H L Cas 811.
16 Arbitration Act 1975, s 1(1) (applicable to certain arbitration agreements with international elements).
17 Arbitration Act 1950, s 4(1). For an exception in the case of certain arbitration agreements in contracts with consumers', see Consumer Arbitration Agreements Act 1988.
18 Arbitration Act 1979, s 1(2); under s 2 the court can also determine preliminary questions of law. For guidelines as to the exercise of the court's discretion to grant leave, see *The Nema* [1982] A C 724.
19 *Czarnikow v Roth, Schmidt & Co* [1922] 2 K B 478.
20 S 3(6).
1 This excludes agreements with certain foreign elements: s 3(7).
2 *Hyman v Hyman* [1929] A C 601 at 629.
3 Matrimonial Causes Act 1973, s 34: not where the agreement is oral, as in *Sutton v Sutton* [1984] Ch 184.
4 *Lee v Showmen's Guild of Great Britain* [1952] 2 Q B 329.

d Contracts which pervert the course of justice

The public has an interest in the enforcement of the criminal law, so that, as a general rule, criminal charges cannot validly be compromised by private agreement between the criminal and the victim. Sometimes, indeed, an agreement to stifle a prosecution may itself amount to the crime of concealing an arrestable offence[5] and be invalid on that ground[6] but even where this is not the case (eg because the offence in question is not an arrestable one) the general principle is that the contract is illegal. For example, agreements to stifle prosecutions for riot, perjury and assaulting a police officer have all been held illegal.[7] On the other hand, it has been held that certain offences of a 'private' nature could be validly compromised. This rule has been applied to such disparate crimes as assaults by a husband and wife on each other and trade-mark offences.[8] In such cases, there was thought to be no strong public interest in prosecuting the offender; and the same may sometimes be true where the victim agrees not to prosecute the criminal, if the latter will make good any loss caused by the offence.

A contract may be illegal under the present heading even though it does not affect criminal proceedings. All that is necessary is that there should be some public interest in the outcome of the proceedings. An agreement to obstruct bankruptcy proceedings is accordingly illegal because of its tendency to prejudice creditors generally.[9] Corrupt agreements relating to matrimonial proceedings are likewise illegal, if they pervert the course of justice.

e Contracts to deceive public authorities

Such contracts often amount to criminal conspiracies but they may be illegal even where this is not the case, eg because one party is innocent. In one case[10] a tenant took a lease of a service flat for £1,200 per annum and signed two documents, under one of which he agreed to pay £450 and under the other £750. The landlord's purpose in splitting the transaction up in this way was to enable him to defraud the rating authorities, but the tenant did not know this. It was held that the

---

[5] Criminal Law Act 1967, s 5(1); and see Police and Criminal Evidence Act 1984, s 24(1) for the definition of 'arrestable offence'.
[6] Ante, p 152.
[7] *Collins v Blantern* (1767) 2 Wils 341; *Keir v Leeman* (1846) 9 Q B 371; *Windhill Local Board v Vint* (1890) 45 Ch D 351.
[8] *McGregor v McGregor* (1888) 21 Q B D 424; *Fisher & Co v Apollinaris Co* (1875) 10 Ch App 297.
[9] *Elliot v Richardson* (1870) L R 5 C P 744.
[10] *Alexander v Rayson* [1936] 1 K B 169; cf *Mitsubishi Corpn v Alafouzos* [1988] 1 Lloyd's Rep 191.

contract was illegal, so that the tenant could not be sued for the rent.[11] A contract of employment would similarly be illegal if its purpose was to defraud the Revenue: eg by providing that the employee should receive 'expenses' in excess of those actually incurred,[12] or that part of his pay should be concealed from the tax authorities.[13]

f Contracts prejudicing the public service

Contracts for the sale of public offices, honours and commissions in the armed forces are illegal as they tend to lead to corruption or inefficiency in the public service.[14] On similar grounds, a contract purporting to bind a Member of Parliament to vote in accordance with the dictates of some person or body outside Parliament is illegal.[15] The making of such a contract is also a breach of Parliamentary privilege.

g Trading with an enemy

It is a statutory offence to trade in time of war with an 'enemy', that is with a person voluntarily resident or carrying on business in enemy occupied territory. A contract which involves trading with an 'enemy' is illegal at common law, though the modern practice is to deal with the matter by war-time legislation.[16]

h Contracts to break the law of a foreign country

A contract is illegal if its purpose is to do an act in a friendly foreign country which is contrary to the law of that country. On this ground, a contract to smuggle whisky into the United States during the prohibition period was held illegal.[17] Similarly, a loan to enable insurgents to launch an armed attack on a friendly foreign country is illegal.[18] Such contracts are contrary to public policy as they are thought to prejudice good foreign relations. But if an English company sold arms to one foreign state, the contract would not be illegal merely because it was known that the arms were to be used in a war with a second foreign country.

---

11 For possible liability in tort if the tenant has defrauded the landlord, see post, p 178.
12 *Miller v Karlinski* (1945) 62 T L R 85; cf *Hyland v J H Barker (North West) Ltd* [1985] I CR 861.
13 Cf *Corby v Morrison* [1980] I C R 564.
14 *Morris v MacCullock* (1763) Amb 432; *Garforth v Fearon* (1787) 1 Hy Bl 328; *Parkinson v College of Ambulance* [1925] 2 K B 1 (cf Honours (Prevention of Abuses) Act 1925).
15 *Amalgamated Society of Railway Servants v Osborne* [1910] A C 87; cf *Lemenda Trading Co Ltd v African Middle East Petroleum Co Ltd* [1988] QB 448.
16 Trading with the Enemy Act 1939.
17 *Foster v Driscoll* [1929] 1 K B 470.
18 *De Wütz v Hendricks* (1824) 2 Bing 314.

i Undue restrictions on personal liberty

In a few very extreme cases, contracts may be illegal on the ground that they unreasonably restrict one party's personal freedom. This was held to be the position where a moneylending contract provided that the borrower should not, without the consent of the lender, change his job or his residence, borrow money elsewhere or dispose of any of his property.[19] Similarly, a contract by which a man assigned the *whole* of his salary, which was his sole means of support, has been held invalid.[20]

3 CONTRACTS IN RESTRAINT OF TRADE

By far the most important group of contracts contrary to public policy are contracts in restraint of trade. The law relating to these contracts provides a particularly good illustration of the flexible nature of the doctrine of public policy. It has undergone many significant changes in the course of history and is even to-day in a considerable state of flux. The overriding principle, however, is clear. Contractual provisions in restraint of trade are prima facie void, but they will be upheld if they are reasonable and not contrary to public interest. They can be divided into the following classes or categories.

a Sale of a business and employment

The first group consists of provisions in contracts for the sale of a business by which the seller undertakes not to compete with the buyer; and of provisions in contracts of employment by which the employee undertakes that he will not, after leaving the employer, compete with him, or take up employment with a competitor. The validity of such restraints depends on three points.

i A 'proprietary interest'

A person who sells a business sells, amongst other things, the goodwill, and the law will protect the buyer's interest in the goodwill by restraining the seller from canvassing the old customers of the business. It will do so even in the absence of a convenant in restraint of trade, for it regards the buyer as having acquired a 'proprietary interest' in the goodwill.[1] This 'proprietary interest' is the buyer's interest in the business which he has bought. It does not extend to his interest in any other business which he already owned or which he

---

[19] *Horwood v Millar's Timber and Trading Co* [1917] 1 K B 305.
[20] *King v Michael Faraday & Partners* [1939] 2 K B 753.
[1] Cf *Trego v Hunt* [1896] A C 7.

hoped thereafter to carry on. If A owns a bookshop in Oxford and buys one from B in Cambridge, A can validly restrain B from setting up another bookshop in Cambridge. But he cannot validly restrain B from setting up a bookshop in Oxford or from selling typewriters in Cambridge. Such restraints would not be related to the relevant proprietary interest, which is one in the goodwill of a bookselling business in Cambridge. Much less could A validly buy off competition by a wholly independent contract not related to the sale of any business at all. If A owned a bookshop in Oxford and B simply threatened to set up a rival bookshop there, A would have no proprietary interest to which a covenant in restraint could be attached. An agreement whereby A promised a sum of money to B, in consideration simply of B's not setting up a bookshop in Oxford, would therefore be invalid. Such an agreement is sometimes called a covenant 'in gross', an expression used to emphasise the point that it is not related to any 'proprietary interest'.

The 'proprietary interest' of an employer is more narrowly defined than that of the buyer of a business. The traditional reason for this distinction is that the courts in restraint of trade cases attach importance to disparity of bargaining power[2] and consider that an employee needs greater protection than the seller of a business. It is also the case that the buyer of a business pays for (amongst other things) freedom from competition, while an employer pays only (or very largely) for the services of the employee. Accordingly, the employer does not have a 'proprietary interest' merely because the business in which the employee works would suffer from competition. He must go further and show one of two things: either that the employee has come into contact with the employer's customers or clients in such a way as to acquire influence over them; or that he has learned the employer's 'trade secrets' (such as secret processes and formulae and 'knowhow')[3] or other confidential information. These interests are again 'proprietary' in the sense that the law protects them, even if there is no stipulation in restraint of trade. The employee can be restrained from soliciting the employer's customers *during employment* and from using or disclosing the employer's trade secrets *at any time*;[4] while the restriction on the use of confidential information is normally limited to the period of employment but may extend beyond it: eg where the employer copies or memorises lists of customers, or where he

---

[2] *A Schroeder Music Publishing Co Ltd v Macaulay* [1974] 1 W L R 1308 at 1315.

[3] *Caribonum Co Ltd v Le Couch* (1913) 109 L T 587; *Commercial Plastics Ltd v Vincent* [1965] 1 Q B 623 at 642.

[4] *Printers and Finishers Ltd v Holloway* [1964] 3 All E R 731; *Wessex Dairies Ltd v Smith* [1935] 2 K B 80.

[5] *Faccenda Chicken Ltd v Fowler* [1986] ICR 297 at 311; cf *A-G v Guardian Newspapers Ltd (No 2)* [1988] 3 All E R 545, 647, 660 (lifelong duty of confidentiality said to exist in *Spycatcher* case).

proposes actually to sell such information as opposed to using it to earn his living.[5] In the absence of any such proprietary interest, a restraint cannot be imposed on an employee merely because he has, in the course of his employment, acquired some general skill,[6] eg because he has been trained by the employer as a skilled electrician or carpenter.

There are borderline cases in which the relationship does not fall into either the employer and employee, or into the vendor and purchaser category: for example, where a restraint is contained in a partnership agreement between solicitors or doctors, or in a contract between a writer or composer and his publisher. In such cases, courts have regard to the relative bargaining power of the parties: thus they would not subject the restraint in the partnership case to the stringent tests that govern the validity of a restraint between employer and employee;[7] while those tests have been applied where a young, and relatively unknown, song-writer promised not to dispose of his work except to a particular publisher, even though there was no employment relationship between the parties.[8]

ii *Reasonableness*

Assuming that there is a 'proprietary interest', the next requirement of validity is that the restraint must be 'reasonable'. This does not mean that the scope of the covenant must be identical with that of the interest. If this were the law, covenants in restraint of trade would be pointless since a 'proprietary interest' is (by definition) protected even in the absence of such a covenant. The 'proprietary interest' of the buyer of a business is merely that the seller should not *solicit* his old customers: not that the seller should not *deal* with them if they come to him of their own accord. It is against such other competition that the buyer can protect himself by a covenant in restraint of trade.[9] The question whether the covenant is reasonable depends primarily on the relation between it and the interest protected; and the covenant will be unreasonable if it goes further than reasonably necessary for the protection of that interest in point of space, time or subject-matter. For example, the buyer of a shop whose customers live within a radius of five miles can validly stipulate that the seller must not set up a similar shop within that radius. But a covenant against competition within a radius of fifty miles would be void, however much the parties both

---

6 *Herbert Morris Ltd v Saxelby* [1916] 1 A C 688.

7 *Bridge v Deacons* [1984] AC 705 at 714; *Kerr v Morris* [1987] Ch 90.

8 See *Schroeder Music Publishing Co Ltd v Macaulay* [1974] 1 WLR 1308.

9 See *John Michael Design plc v Cooke* [1987] ICR 445.

wished to enter into it.[10] Where the nature of the business demands it, a very extensive restraint may be regarded as reasonably necessary. In the leading *Nordenfelt*[11] case, a world-wide restraint was imposed on the Swedish seller of an armaments business to an English company; and the restraint was upheld, since the customers of the business included governments throughout the world. The question whether a covenant is excessive in point of time similarly depends on the length of time for which the business sold would normally be expected to retain its clientèle. So far as subject-matter is concerned, the covenant can only validly restrain the seller from competing with the type of activity carried on by the business sold. Thus it has been held that the seller of an *imitation* jewellery business cannot be restrained from competing with the buyer in the sale of *real* jewellery.[12]

The position is similar in employment contracts. Suppose, for example, that an employer has a 'proprietary interest' in trade secrets. It would be pointless for him to take a covenant against the use of disclosure of these secrets, since he is protected against such conduct even in the absence of the covenant. What he can do is to use the interest as a peg on which to hang a restraint against competition within reasonable limits of space and time. If this were not possible, it would be very hard for the employer to prove that his proprietary interests were being infringed. In particular, it would be hard for him to prove that his trade secrets were being exploited, if the employee could not be restrained from working for a rival concern. On the other hand, where the proprietary interest consists of trade connections, a blanket restraint covering an entire area might be unreasonable, for it would prevent the employee from working in the whole of the area, even though the employer had only had dealings with a relatively small number of persons within it. The law has therefore drawn a distinction, in this group of cases, between *area* covenants and *solicitation* covenants. The latter only restrain the employee from dealing with the employer's customers or clients, and leave the employee free to compete in other respects. The tendency of the courts in recent years has been to strike down area covenants in contracts of employment, but to uphold the less restrictive solicitation covenants. Between employer and employee it may be a further requirement that the covenant must be confined to customers or clients with whom the employee came into contact in the course of his work for the

---

[10] See *Empire Meat Co Ltd v Patrick* [1939] 2 All E R 85; cf *Spencer v Marchington* [1988] IRLR 392.
[11] [1894] A C 535.
[12] *Goldsoll v Goldman* [1915] 1 Ch 292.

employer;[13] but a solicitation covenant between partners has been upheld even where this requirement was not satisfied.[14] All this is not to say that, even in employment contracts, area covenants may not be upheld if the area covered is only a small one. In 1921 the House of Lords still upheld a restraint on a solicitor's managing clerk against practising within seven miles of his principal's office after the end of his employment.[15] But this was before the distinction between area and solicitation covenants had achieved its present prominence; and it is at least arguable that such a restraint would now be regarded as excessive.[16] A restraint in a contract of employment may further be unreasonable for excessive duration. Thus where the employer's clientèle was of a fluctuating nature, a five-year restraint was held to be too long;[17] while, on the other hand, in the case of the solicitor's managing clerk (mentioned above) a life-long restraint was regarded as reasonable. Finally a restraint may be unreasonable because it relates to some form of activity in which the employee was not employed. On this ground, a restraint on a person employed as a tailor against working as a hatter has been held invalid.[18]

In deciding whether a restraint is reasonable, the court also has regard to the adequacy of the consideration given for it and to the relative bargaining strengths of the parties.[19] It follows that where a restraint is imposed on the weaker party the fairness of the bargain is a necessary condition of its reasonableness.[20] In determining the issue of fairness, the court has to take into account not only the extent of the restraint but also the benefits which the contract as a whole confers on the party subject to the restraint.[1] The requirement of fairness must be satisfied in addition to those discussed above; ie the restraint must go no further than necessary for the protection of the interest *and* it must be fair. Where there is no inequality of bargaining power the additional requirement of fairness does not apply.

---

13 *G W Plowman & Son Ltd v Ash* [1964] 2 All E R 10; cf *T Lucas & Co Ltd v Mitchell* [1972] 2 All E R 1035; *Marley Tile Co Ltd v Johnson* [1982] I R L R 75 and see *Mason v Provident Clothing & Supply Co Ltd* [1913] A C 724; *Spencer v Marchington* [1988]IRLR 392.

14 *Bridge v Deacons* [1984] AC 705; cf ante, p 166 (less stringent test of validity of covenants between partners).

15 *Fitch v Dewes* [1921] 2 A C 158.

16 See *Fellowes & Son v Fisher* [1976] Q B 122.

17 *M & S Drapers v Reynolds* [1956] 3 All E R 814.

18 *Attwood v Lamont* [1920] 3 K B 571.

19 *Nordenfelt v Maxim Nordenfelt Guns and Ammunition Co* [1894] A C 535 at 565; *A Schroeder Music Publishing Co Ltd v Macaulay* [1974] 1 W L R 1308 at 1316.

20 Ibid; *Clifford Davis Management Co Ltd v WEA Records Ltd* [1975] 1 W L R 61 at 65.

1 Cf *Alec Lobb (Garages) Ltd v Total Oil (Great Britain) Ltd* [1985] 1 All ER 303; *Bridge v Deacons* [1984] AC 705 at 716.

iii Public interest

A restraint which is reasonable in relation to the interest meriting protection may, nevertheless, be invalid on the ground that it is contrary to the public interest. This requirement is not always clearly separable from that of reasonableness, since both are in the last resort imposed on account of the broad public interest in freedom to trade. But it is possible to imagine a case in which the restraint, though reasonable in the sense that it secures to the buyer no more than the clientèle of the business which he has bought, is one which nevertheless prejudices the public by depriving it of much needed additional services of the kind provided by the business. This might be the position on the sale of a medical practice. A restraint on one of the partners would not be struck down merely on the ground that particular patients wishes to continue to be treated by that partner;[2] but it might be contrary to the public interest if, in the area covered by it, there was a shortage of doctors.

iv Other problems relating to employment

The above discussion of restraints in employment contracts is based on two assumptions. The first is that there is an undertaking not to compete; but it seems that the same rules may apply, even though there is no such undertaking, if the *effect* of the contract is to stifle competition. Thus the doctrine of restraint of trade was applied to a contract under which an employee was, on his retirement, promised a pension on the terms that it would cease to be paid if he competed with the employer.[3] The second assumption is that the undertaking comes into effect *after* the employment has come to an end, so that the rules as to restraint of trade do not normally apply to an undertaking not to compete during employment:[4] indeed, the employee's implied undertaking of faithful service would normally rule out such competition.[5] But there may be exceptional cases in which a restraint operative during employment would be invalid. This would, in particular, be the case where the employment was a long term one, or one giving the employer options to renew, and where such provisions were in fact used to stifle competition.[6]

---

[2] *Kerr v Morris* [1987] Ch 90; cf *Bridge v Deacons* [1984] AC 705 at 720.
[3] *Wyatt v Kreglinger and Fernau* [1933] 1 K B 793; cf *Stenhouse Australia Ltd v Phillips* [1974] A C 391; *Sadler v Imperial Life Assurance Co of Canada* [1988] IRLR 388.
[4] Eg, *Evening Standard v Henderson* [1987] ICR 588.
[5] *Faccenda Chicken Ltd v Fowler* [1986] ICR 277 at 308-309.
[6] Cf *A Schroeder Music Publishing Co Ltd v Macaulay*]1974] 3 All E R 616.

b Restrictive trading and similar agreements

Agreements regulating competition between commercial suppliers of goods or services are subject to the common law of restraint of trade. They differ from the types of restraint so far discussed in that the interest meriting protection does not have to be a 'proprietary' one, that is, one which the law would protect even in the absence of an agreement in restraint of trade. Purely commercial interests, such as 'stability in ... lists of customers'[7] were regarded as sufficient to support the validity of agreements of this kind. Once such an interest was established (and there was rarely any difficulty in doing this) the agreement was subject to the usual requirements of validity: that is, it must be reasonable and not contrary to the public interest. In fact, the courts interpreted these requirements leniently in this class of cases, so that agreements of this kind were only held invalid in the most extreme cases: for example, if the effect of the agreement was to force a party out of business, or if it provided that he could not withdraw from the trade association without the consent of its committee.[8] The common law was reluctant to disturb trading agreements between parties who were supposed to have bargained on equal terms.

But this attitude, though perhaps defensible in disputes between those two parties, might well cause hardship to third parties who suffered from the high prices or scarcities which such agreements could create. Where the validity of the agreement was contested by one of the parties to it, the law could to some extent take account of such hardships, by holding that they made the contract contrary to the public interest. For example, an agreement between employers not to give jobs to each others' former employees might be invalidated on the ground that it unreasonably restricted the employees' opportunities to find work.[9] But this line of attack did nothing to solve the most pressing problem of all, which arose from the fact that agreements of trade associations were rarely broken, since they benefited the parties to them. It was at one time thought that third parties who were prejudiced by such agreements had no cause of action merely on that account. Hence it followed that, though the agreement might not be enforceable, the parties could not be prevented from acting in accordance with it, if they so desired. More recently, the common law began in a few cases to allow third parties to challenge such agreements. In one case,[10] a professional footballer obtained a declaration

---

7 *McEllistrim's Case* [1919] A C 548 at 564.

8 *McEllistrim's Case*, supra.

9 *Kores Manufacturing Co Ltd v Kolok Manufacturing Co Ltd* [1959] Ch 108.

10 *Eastham v Newcastle United Football Club Ltd* [1964] Ch 413; cf *Greig v Insole* [1978] 3 All E R 449.

that the 'retain and transfer' system operated by the Football Association and the Football League was invalid. Similarly, an association which controls entry into a profession may have a rule excluding certain classes of persons from membership. There is some authority for the view that a member of the class can get an injunction to restrain such exclusion if the grounds for it are not relevant to his capacity to work in that profession,[11] for example, if the rule excluded persons on religious or political grounds.

In such cases the courts can intervene in favour of the third party to protect one particular interest traditionally stressed by the common law, namely the 'right to work'. A more general solution to the problem of prejudice to third parties is now provided by legislation. Under the Restrictive Trade Practices Act of 1976[12] certain restrictive trading agreements or arrangements (including in particular price-fixing agreements between suppliers of goods and most services) have to be registered with the Director General of Fair Trading. Once an agreement is registered, its validity may be tested in proceedings brought by the Director before the Restrictive Practices Court. In these proceedings the parties to the agreement must show that it is beneficial in one of a number of specified ways and that it is not, on balance, detrimental to the public at large. If they fail to show this, the agreement is declared void and the parties can be restrained from giving effect to it. If the parties fail to register a registrable agreement, the restriction in it is void and it is unlawful for the parties to give effect to or to enforce the agreement. If they nevertheless do so, they can be restrained from continuing to do so and held liable in damages to any third party who as a result of such conduct suffers loss.

At common law, trade union rules were subject to the restraint of trade doctrine. But this state of the law was reversed by legislation long ago; and the present position is that union rules are not unenforceable by reason only of their being in restraint of trade.[13] They may, however, be invalid on the analogous ground that they provide for unreasonable exclusion or expulsion from a union and so deprive a person of the opportunity of obtaining or retaining certain kinds of employment.[14] A union rule is not, however, contrary to public policy merely because it gives effect to a 'no poaching' agreement between unions;[15] though it might be invalid if, by leading to the expulsion of a member, it put his job in jeopardy.[16]

---

[11] *Nagle v Feilden* [1966] 2 QB 633, a case of sex discrimination which would now be unlawful under the Sex Discrimination Act 1975 and Sex Discrimination Act 1986.

[12] As amended by the Competition Act 1980 and other legislation.

[13] Trade Union and Labour Relations Act 1974, s 2(5).

[14] Employment Act 1980, s 4(1) and (2).

[15] *Cheall v Association of Professional, Executive, Clerical and Computer Staffs* [1983] 2 AC 180.

[16] Ibid p 191.

c Exclusive dealing and service agreements

It commonly happens that a buyer of goods agrees to buy all his
requirements from a particular seller, or that a seller undertakes to sell
his whole output to a particular buyer, or that a person agrees to
employ another as his 'sole agent'. Such agreements only impose a
restraint on one of the parties, and are not within the restrictive trade
practices legislation, as this only applies to agreements imposing
restraints on a number of parties. And at common law, the general
view used to be that exclusive dealing agreements were not invalid for
restraint of trade. But this view was challenged in a line of cases
concerning the so-called 'solus petrol agreements'. Under such an
agreement, a garage proprietor would give a number of undertakings
to an oil company, usually in return for financial help by way of loans
or discounts or both. The purpose of the agreement would of course be
to ensure that the company's brand of petrol, and no other brand, was
to be sold from the garage in question. Hence the agreement would
provide that the proprietor should buy all his petrol from the company;
keep his garage open for the sale of petrol at all reasonable times; and, if
he should sell the garage, that he should obtain similar undertakings
from the buyer. In *Esso Petroleum Ltd v Harper's Garage Ltd*[17] the House
of Lords held that such agreements were within the doctrine of restraint
of trade, and thus required justification. Solus agreements were later
the subject of a report by the Monopolies Commission[18] and the
present practice with respect to them is governed by undertakings
given by the oil companies after that report. But the decision in the *Esso*
case is still important for the guidance which it provides as to the
common law principles governing the validity of exclusive dealing
agreements in general.

The first and most difficult question is which such agreements are
within the common law doctrine of restraint of trade at all. This has
been said to depend on factors such as whether the agreement restrains
or only regulates trade; and whether it is of a kind that has 'passed into
the normal currency of . . . contractual relations'.[19] Under these tests
sole agency and sole distributorship agreements would normally be
held to be outside the doctrine of restraint of trade; but the solus system
was held to be within the doctrine, largely because it was a novel system
which had not yet acquired settled and stereotyped features. However,
even contracts which have acquired such features may be within the
doctrine, especially if they are not freely negotiated but made between
parties of greatly disparate bargaining power. For example, in one case

17 [1968] AC 269.
18 Now the Monopolies and Mergers Commission: see the Fair Trading Act 1973, Pt
   IV; Competition Act 1980, ss 2, 3 and 5.
19 [1968] AC at 332–333.

an unknown song-writer undertook to give his exclusive services to a publisher who made no promise to publish his work. It was held that the contract was subject to the restraint of trade doctrine as it was 'capable of enforcement in an oppressive manner'.[20] It seems probable that in future the courts will hold exclusive dealing and service agreements to be within the restraint of trade doctrine if they contain novel or unusual features; or if there is disparity of bargaining power and the agreement is likely to cause hardship to the weaker party.

If an exclusive dealing agreement is not within the doctrine of restraint of trade, no further question arises as to its validity. If it is within the doctrine, the usual requirements have to be satisfied. First, there must be an interest meriting protection. In the *Esso* case this was described as the oil company's 'network of outlets'[1] and it is clear that (in the terminology used above) a 'commercial' as opposed to a 'proprietary' interest is sufficient. Secondly, the agreement must be reasonable in relation to the interest. In the *Esso* case this was held to depend on the probable effect of breach of the agreement on the oil company's distribution system. A twenty-one-year agreement was held unreasonable, as it attempted to look too far into the uncertain future; but an agreement covering a period of only four and a half years was upheld. Where the restriction is imposed on the weaker party to a relationship of unequal bargaining power, the fairness of the contract is, again, relevant to its reasonableness. This may work in favour of the validity of the restraint: thus in a later case a twenty-one year solus agreement was upheld as the garage proprietor had obtained considerable benefits under it and the oil company had not made any unfair use of its superior bargaining power.[2] In the above case of the songwriter,[3] on the other hand, the restriction extended over five years during which he had to submit all his work to the publishers while they made no promise to publish it and were not bound, if they failed to do so, to pay him more than nominal amounts. The restriction was held invalid as it was neither necessary nor fair. Thirdly, the agreement must not be contrary to the public interest; failure to satisfy this requirement was another ground on which the twenty-one-year agreement was held invalid in the *Esso* case.

d European Community law

Article 85 Treaty of Rome (which has the force of law in the United Kingdom) makes special provision for 'agreements between

---

[20] *A Schroeder Music Publishing Co Ltd v Macaulay* [1974] 1 W L R 1308 at 1314; cf *O'Sullivan v Management Agency & Music Ltd* [1985] QB 428.

[1] [1968] A C at 329.

[2] *Alec Lobb (Garages) Ltd v Total Oil GB Ltd* [1985] 1 All ER 303.

[3] *A Schroeder Music Publishing Co Ltd v Macaulay* [1974] 1 WLR 1308.

undertakings, decisions by associations of undertakings and concerted practices which have as their object or effect the prevention, restriction or distortion of competition within the common market'.[4] Such agreements (etc) are void unless specifically exempted by the Community authorities.[5] An agreement made outside the Community may fall within these provisions if it restricts competition within the Community, eg where 'undertakings' in non-member states agree to fix prices which they charge to customers in member states.[5a] But article 85 does not apply to an agreement which affects trade only within a single member state. It follows that purely domestic agreements which do not affect trade outside the United Kingdom continue to be governed by the rules previously stated in this chapter.[6]

An agreement may be void under the Treaty or specifically exempt under the Treaty, and at the same time fall within the Restrictive Trade Practices Act 1976. The Act deals with this possibility[7] so as to give effect to the general policy that Community principles governing restrictive trade practices should, where they apply, prevail over the domestic rules.

e Restrictions on the use of land

Land is often sold subject to covenants which restrict its use: for example, by prohibiting building, or the carrying on of some particular trade, or of any trade at all. Such restrictive covenants are commonly enforced, and in the *Esso* case it was said that they were not subject to the doctrine of restraint of trade. The reason for this was said to be that the purchaser of the land 'had no previous right to be there at all, let alone to trade there, and when he takes possession of that land, subject to a negative restrictive covenant, he gives up no right or freedom which he previously had'.[8] It follows that even a solus agreement entered into by a purchaser of land as a term of the purchase is perfectly valid, irrespective of its extent. The reasoning is not very satisfactory. It ignores the possibility that a restrictive covenant in a contract of sale may offend the public interest, just as much as one which is contained in a mortgage raised by a person who already owned the garage premises; and there is no doubt that a restriction in such a mortgage is within the doctrine of restraint of trade. Even a restrictive covenant imposed on the sale of land may, by a special statutory provision, be modified or discharged on a number of grounds, one of which is that the continued existence of the covenant 'would impede

---

4 Art 85(1).
5 Arts 85(2) and (3).
5a *Ahlstrom Osakeyhtio v EC Commission* (1988) Times, 29 September.
6 See *Esso Petroleum Co Ltd v Kingswood Motors (Addlestone) Ltd* [1974] QB 142.
7 Ss 5 and 34.
8 [1968] AC 269 at 298.
9 Law of Property Act 1925, s 84 (amended by Law of Property Act 1969, s 28).

some reasonable user of the land for public or private purposes. '9 Since the purchaser will probably have paid less for the hand on account of the restriction, he may be ordered to pay compensation as a condition of being released from the covenant or of having it modified.

f Other agreements

It has been said that the categories of restraint of trade are not closed;[10] for an agreement may restrain trade even though it falls outside the types so far considered. This would, for example, be true of an agreement by one manufacturer not to produce certain goods in competition with another. It is possible that the common law doctrine of restraint of trade might be extended to such agreements. This is not to say that they would be invalid, but merely that they would have to be justified in accordance with the usual requirements of the doctrine. Two further types of agreements are covered by special statutory provisions. Price maintenance agreements were valid at common law, but many such agreements are now void under the Resale Prices Act 1976. Agreements between two persons not to bid against each other at an auction were likewise valid at common law; but it is now provided[11] that, if at least one of the parties to the agreement is a dealer, they may be guilty of an offence. If the agreement not to bid amounts to a crime, it is no doubt illegal and any resulting contract of sale between one of the parties and the owner of the auctioned property can be set aside by the latter.

4 THE EFFECTS OF ILLEGALITY

The most common effect of illegality is to prevent the enforcement of the contract, either wholly or in part. It may also prevent a party who has transferred money or property under the contract from getting it back; and it may invalidate collateral transactions.

a Enforcement of the contract

The law relating to the enforcement of illegal contracts is in a complex and not very satisfactory state. The basic rule is that a guilty party cannot enforce the contract while an innocent party may be able to do so.

i A guilty party cannot enforce the contract

Cases illustrating this rule have already been mentioned: for example, the owner of a brougham who knowingly let it to a prostitute to help her to attract clients could not recover the agreed hire.[12] It makes no

10 [1968] A C at 337.
11 Auctions (Bidding Agreements) Acts 1927–1969.
12 *Pearce v Brooks* (1866) L R 1 Exch 213.

difference that the other party is (as in that case) equally guilty. The defendant to an action on an illegal contract thus gets a windfall, but the rule has been justified on the ground that 'the courts will not lend their aid to such [ie a guilty] a plaintiff.'[13]

The rule, as so far stated, assumes that the illegality arises by reason of the object of the contract. Where it arises by reason of the method of performance, a party is not 'guilty' for the present purpose merely because he breaks the law. We have, for example, seen that a shipowner may be entitled to enforce a contract of carriage by claiming freight in spite of the fact that he had overloaded his ship.[14] He would have been a 'guilty' party only if he had intended all along to perform the contract in an unlawful way, ie if at the time of entering into the contract he had known that he could not perform it lawfully, but only by overloading. If the cargo-owner had 'participated' in the scheme, he, too, would have been a 'guilty' party for the purpose of the present rule. This would have been the position if he had known of the unlawfulness in the method of performance and assented to it in order to benefit from it by saving any extra expense which might be incurred by having his goods lawfully carried.[15]

A party may be 'guilty' for the purpose of the present rule even though he is ignorant of or mistaken about the law, so that he is morally quite innocent. In one case, the owner of a roulette wheel hired it out to enable the hirer to play a form of roulette which was believed by both parties to be lawful, but which was in fact unlawful. It was held that the owner could not sue for the hire as the parties had 'a common design to use the subject-matter for an unlawful purpose'.[16] But this rule is relaxed where a contract can be performed in several ways only one of which is (unknown to the parties) unlawful. If, on discovering that the intended method is unlawful, they actually perform in another, lawful, way, the contract is not affected by illegality;[17] or, to put the point in another way, neither party is treated as a 'guilty' party.

ii   An innocent party may be able to enforce the contract

It will be clear from the foregoing discussion that an innocent party is one who is mistaken about, or ignorant of, the *facts* which constitute the illegality. In *Archbolds (Freightage) Ltd v Spanglett Ltd*[18] a contract was

---

[13] *Holman v Johnson* (1775) 1 Cowp 341 at 343.
[14] *St John Shipping Corp v Joseph Rank Ltd* [1957] 1 QB 267; cf *Coral Leisure Group v Barnett* [1981] ICR 503.
[15] As in *Ashmore, Benson, Pease & Co v A V Dawson Ltd* [1973] 2 All ER 856.
[16] *JM Allan (Merchandising) Ltd v Cloke* [1963] 2 QB 340 at 348; cf *Corby v Morrison* [1980] ICR 564.
[17] *Waugh v Morris* (1873) LR 8 QB 202.
[18] [1961] 1 QB 374.

The effects of illegality 177

made for the carriage of a consignment of whisky; and, in attempting
to perform it, the carrier committed an offence, as the vehicle which he
used was not properly licensed to carry goods belonging to third
parties. But, as the owner of the whisky did not know this, it was held
that he was entitled to damages for breach of the contract of carriage.
In the view of the court, the purpose of the statute which had imposed
the licensing requirement was 'sufficiently served by the penalties
prescribed for the offender; the avoidance of the contract would cause
grave inconvenience and injury to innocent members of the public
without furthering the object of the statute'.[19] Many modern statutes
contain express provisions to this effect: for example, where a motor
vehicle is supplied which does not comply with statutory safety
requirements, the supplier commits an offence, but the validity of the
contract is unaffected.[20]

iii Cases in which the innocent party cannot enforce the contract

There are other cases in which it has been held that even an innocent
party cannot enforce an illegal contract. The leading case arose under
war-time legislation making it an offence to buy or sell (amongst other
things) linseed oil without a licence. A contract for the sale of such oil
was made between a seller who had a licence and a buyer who
fraudulently pretended to the seller that he had one. It was held that the
seller could not get damages for breach of the contract, even though he
did not know of the facts constituting the illegality.[1] Similarly, it has
been held that a builder doing work in the honest, but mistaken, belief
that the requisite licences had been obtained could not recover the
agreed price of the work.[2]

These cases are very hard on the innocent party. They can be
justified (if at all) on the ground that, in this group of contracts, it
would 'further the object of the statute' to deny even an innocent party
a remedy on the contract. In a sense such a denial always has this effect.
It might induce an innocent party to take greater care, before entering
into the contract, to make sure that it was not illegal; and also to back
out of the contract if, before he had performed it, he discovered its
illegality. It may be asked why this reasoning should apply to some
cases of contracts affected by illegality but not to others. One possible
answer is that in the sale and building contracts mentioned above the

---

[19] Ibid at 390.
[20] Road Traffic Act 1972, s 62(1) and (3); cf Fair Trading Act 1973, s 23; Financial
Services Act 1986, ss 5, 56, 57, 131 and 132 (post, p 178); Consumer Protection Act
1987, s 41(3).
[1] *Re Mahmoud and Ispahani* [1921] 2 K B 716; cf *Bedford Insurance Co Ltd v Instituto de
Rességuros do Brasil* [1985] QB 966 at 982.
[2] *J Dennis & Co Ltd v Munn* [1949] 2 K B 327.

plaintiffs claimed to be put into the position in which they would have been if the contract had *been performed*; while in the *Archbolds* case they claimed to be put into the position in which they would have been if the contract had *never been made*. The purpose of the statute is, in general, more likely to be defeated by allowing a claim of the former than of the latter kind.

A second possible answer is that the illegality may arise under legislation passed for the protection of a class; and the purpose of the legislation would scarcely be promoted by denying a remedy on the contract to an innocent member of the class. This situation is illustrated by cases in which insurers committed offences by carrying on business without the requisite licences. The policy of the licensing requirement would not be promoted by denying a right of action on a policy issued in the course of such a business to an innocent insured and, by statute,[3] he is now entitled to enforce the contract, though previously judicial opinion on the point was divided.[4]

iv *Other remedies of the innocent party*

Where the innocent party cannot enforce the illegal contract, the courts have sometimes alleviated the hardship to him by giving him some other remedy.

If he has been induced to enter into the illegal contract by a misrepresentation as to its legality, he may be able to recover damages in tort for the misrepresentation.[5] Such a remedy will again only put the innocent party into the position in which he would have been, if the contract had never been made. It will only give him the amount by which he is worse off as a result of the misrepresentation, and not the amount by which he would have been better off if the contract had been performed. In other words, it will not give him damages for loss of his bargain.[6] Innocence in this context is a relative concept. In a recent case[7] parties to a contract for the sale of a flat for £45,000 agreed to overvalue the fittings so as to save the purchaser some £300 in stamp duty. This made the purchaser a willing party to an attempt to defraud the Revenue;[8] but he nevertheless recovered damages for the vendor's fraud in falsely representing that the flat included a roof garden, the vendor's fraud being regarded as a more serious wrong than the comparatively trivial illegality.

---

3 Financial Services Act 1986, s 132.

4 Contrast *Stewart v Oriental Fire & Marine Insurance Co Ltd* [1985] QB 988 with *Phoenix General Insurance Co of Greece SA v Administratia Asigurarilor de Stat* [1986] 2 Lloyd's Rep 552.

5 *Shelley v Paddock* [1980] QB 348; cf *Burrows v Rhodes* [1899] 1 QB 816.

6 Cf p 134, ante; p 321, post.

7 *Saunders v Edwards* [1987] 2 All ER 651.

8 Ante, p 162.

Alternatively, the innocent party may be able to claim damages for breach of a 'collateral contract' to the effect that the principal contract is lawful. In one case[9] this device was used to allow builders who had, in all innocence, done unlicensed work, to recover the value of the work; and it seems that they recovered exactly the same amount in this action as they would have recovered if they had been able to sue on the illegal contract. The rule is a strange one, for it makes very little sense to say that the public interest precludes enforcement of the contract but does not preclude another remedy which is just as good. In fact, the builders in our case were not careless in failing to see that licences had been obtained (since the owner was an architect on whose word they reasonably relied); and it was too late for them to back out, as they had finished the work. But in these circumstances it would have been better to recognise that there was no public interest against allowing them to sue on the main contract itself. The collateral contract device in the present context is an unnecessary complexity, and it gives the law a strange air of inconsistency.

b Severance

Where only part of a contract is illegal, it may be possible to sever that part and to enforce the rest of the contract. Two situations require discussion.

i Severance of illegal promises

Suppose that A buys a bookshop in Cambridge from B, and B promises not to engage in the bookselling business in Cambridge or in Oxford. Here B's promise is valid so far as it relates to Cambridge but invalid so far as it relates to Oxford; and the question is whether A can sever the valid from the invalid part and prevent B from opening a new bookshop in Cambridge. He can do so if three conditions are satisfied.

First, the illegal promise must not be so seriously illegal as to contaminate the whole contract. Severance would, for example, not be possible where a lawful promise was combined with one deliberately to commit a crime, or to do an immoral act.[10] If a man promised to serve another as a valet and as a pickpocket, he could obviously not be sued for failing to perform even his duties as valet. In practice, the doctrine of severance is most frequently applied to contracts in restraint of trade.

Secondly, the so-called 'blue pencil' test must be satisfied. It must be possible to sever the illegal part by simply deleting words in the contract. The court will not add words, or substitute one word for

[9] *Strongman (1945) Ltd v Sincock* [1955] 2 Q B 525.
[10] See *Bennett v Bennett* [1952] 1 K B 249 at 254.

another, or rearrange words, or in any other way redraft the contract. For example, a contract not to compete within ten miles of a particular place cannot be severed by deleting 'ten' and substituting 'five', even though a five-mile restraint would have been perfectly reasonable. Where the contract is drawn up by laymen, this rule often causes hardship to the party for whose benefit the restraint was intended. On the other hand, it gives little protection to the other party since a draftsman who knows of the 'blue pencil' rule can easily draw up the restraint so as to neutralise its operation.

A promise cannot be severed merely because the 'blue pencil' test is satisfied. The courts have laid down a third requirement: that severance must not change the nature of the contract. Two cases (one on each side of the line) may be cited to illustrate this requirement. In the first,[11] a seller of an imitation jewellery business undertook not to deal in real or imitation jewellery in the United Kingdom and in certain places abroad. It was held that the reference to real jewellery and to the foreign places could be severed, and the rest of the contract enforced. In the second case[12] a general outfitter's business was divided into several departments, and the person employed as head of each department undertook not to compete with the employers, after leaving their service, in the business of *any* of the departments. The effect of the covenant was thus to prevent the head of the tailoring department from competing as a hatter or milliner, and so forth, while the only reasonable restraint would have been one against competing as a tailor. It was held that the contract could not be severed (even though the 'blue pencil' test was satisfied). The convenant was 'one covenant for the protection of the entire business'[13] so that to sever the references to all trades except tailoring would be to alter its entire nature. These two cases show that the courts are more ready to sever covenants between vendor and purchaser than between employer and employee; but it should not be supposed that they will always sever covenants of the former kind, or that they will not, in any circumstances, sever covenants of the latter kind. The requirement that severance must not alter the nature of the contract is easy enough to state, but its operation is very hard to predict. It turns on subtle questions of degree, and even of personal impression.

In the cases so far discussed, the question was whether invalid parts of the promise not to compete could be severed. Even where this cannot be done, the rest of the contract generally remains binding. Thus the fact that a contract contains an invalid promise not to compete will not normally justify breaches of other unrelated terms of the contract, for

---

11 *Goldsoll v Goldman* [1915] 1 Ch 292.
12 *Attwood v Lamont* [1920] 3 K B 571.
13 Ibid at 593.

the contract as a whole will not, merely because of the invalidity of one of its terms, have 'so changed its character as not to be the sort of contract that the parties intended to enter into at all'.[14] The illegality will only invalidate the contract as a whole where one of the main objects of the contract was to secure the restraint. The question in such cases is not whether severance of parts of an illegal covenant will alter the nature of the *covenant*, but whether deletion of the covenant will alter the nature of the *contract* as a whole, by leaving it without subject-matter or by substantially altering its intended subject-matter.[15]

ii Severing illegal parts of the consideration

So far we have considered the question whether the legal part of a promise can be enforced *against* the person making a promise which is partly legal and party illegal. An action may also be brought *by* such a person to enforce the (wholly legal) counter-promise which he has received for it. For example, a builder might have performed his undertaking to do work of which a part was licensed, and the rest unlicensed and therefore illegal. If he sued for the agreed price, the client would argue that part of the consideration for his promise to pay was illegal, while the builder might argue that that part should be severed.

Here again, severance is not allowed if the illegal part of the consideration is immoral, or if the illegality arises from a deliberate violation of the law.[16] In our example, the builder would not be entitled to recover anything if he knew that part of the work was unlicensed; but severance might be possible if he were innocent of the illegality. Whether it actually is possible depends on the importance of the illegal part of the consideration in relation to the contract as a whole. In one case,[17] the perpetrator of a fraud promised to pay the victim £3,000 in return for the latter's promise not to take 'any legal proceedings' in respect of the fraud; and this promise was construed to mean that the victim would not take either civil or criminal proceedings. It was held that the fraudulent party's promise to pay the £3,000 could not be enforced, as a *substantial part* of the consideration for it was the victim's illegal promise to stifle a criminal prosecution. On the other hand if the *main consideration* for a promise is lawful, the promise can be enforced even though there was also some subsidiary illegal consideration. This would normally be the position where an employee agreed to an unreasonably wide stipulation in restraint of trade. He could

---

[14] *Alec Lobb (Garages) Ltd v Total Oil (G B) Ltd* [1985] 1 All E R 303 at 320; cf *Carney v Herbert* [1985] A C 301.
[15] Eg *Amoco Australia Pty Ltd v Rocca Bros Motor Engineering Pty Ltd* [1975] A C 561.
[16] *Bennett v Bennett* [1952] 1 K B 249 at 254.
[17] *Lound v Grimwade* (1888) 39 Ch D 605.

nevertheless sue for his wages since the main consideration for the employer's promise to pay them would be the employee's promise to work, or the performance of it.[18]

The case last put is not strictly one of severance, for the result in such a case is that the employee recovers the *whole* of his wages. This result is probably due to the fact that the illegal part of the consideration (ie the excessive part of the restraint) cannot be precisely valued. Where such valuation is possible, there may be true severance, leading to recovery of so much of the promised payment as is supported by lawful consideration. Thus in one case,[19] a builder innocently did work worth nearly £1,200 when the owner held a licence for work up to only £1,000; and it was held that the builder could recover the latter sum.

c   Recovery of money or property

Where one party to a contract completely fails or refuses to perform it, the other normally has a choice of remedies. He can try to 'enforce' the contract; or to 'undo' it by claiming back any money which he paid or property which he transferred under the contract.[20] In the case of an illegal contract, there is (as we have seen) often no right to enforce the contract; and it is also the general rule that money paid or property transferred under such a contract cannot be claimed back.[1] The rule is supposed to operate as a further deterrent against the making of illegal contracts, by leaving one party entirely at the mercy of the other. On the other hand, it is capable of producing very harsh results, especially where an illegal contract is innocently made; and there are situations in which the purpose of the rule of law which has made the contract illegal is better served by allowing, than by denying, the recovery of money or property. The general rule against non-recovery is therefore subject to the following exceptions.

i   *Statutes for the protection of a class*

The illegality of a contract may arise under a statute passed for the protection of a class of people, such as tenants, or borrowers from moneylenders. Some such statutes expressly provide that a member of the protected class can get back money paid, or property transferred, under the contract; for example, under the Rent Act a tenant can get back money (such as a premium or an excess rent) which he could not legally be required to pay.[2] He can recover an illegal premium even

---

[18] *McFarlane v Daniell* (1938) 38 S R N S W 337, approved in *Carney v Herbert* [1985] A C 301 at 311.

[19] *Frank W Clifford Ltd v Garth* [1956] 2 All E R 323.

[20] See generally ch 18, pp 320–324, post.

[1] Eg *Scott v Brown* [1892] 2 Q B 724.

[2] Rent Act 1977, ss 57, 94, 125; cf Financial Services Act 1986, ss 5, 6, 56, 57, 131 and 132.

though he paid it quite willingly so as to secure preferential treatment for himself.[3] A member of the protected class can get back money or property in these situations at common law, even though there is no express statutory provision to that effect;[4] and he can do so even though the other party has in fact performed his part of the illegal bargain.

ii *Illegal contract made under pressure*

In some cases, recovery of money paid or property transferred has been allowed on the ground that the claimant was 'forced' to enter into the contract by some form of pressure. In one case,[5] an insolvent debtor wanted to make a composition with his creditors, but one creditor would not join in unless the debtor first paid him £50. The debtor was allowed to claim back this £50 on the ground that he had been 'forced' to agree to defraud the other creditors. The result was clearly desirable since the £50 thus became available for distribution among all the creditors.

A person may be 'forced' to enter into an illegal contract not only by the other party but also by extraneous circumstances. This is another reason why a tenant who pays an illegal premium during a housing shortage can get the money back. But the pressure must be of a kind which makes it, in the view of the court, excusable to enter into the illegal transaction. In *Bigos v Bousted*[6] a father made an illegal contract to acquire foreign currency because he wanted to send his daughter abroad as a cure for her recurrent attacks of pleurisy. It was held that he had not been 'forced' to make the illegal contract and that he could not rely on the present exception to the general rule of non-recovery so as to get back securities which he had deposited with the other party to the illegal contract.

iii *Fraud or mistake inducing the illegal contract*

Money paid or property transferred under an illegal contract can be reclaimed by a person who was induced to enter into the contract by the other party's fraudulent representation that the contract was lawful. Under this rule, premiums paid under an illegal insurance have been recovered by an innocent policyholder who was deceived by the insurance company's agent into believing that he had an insurable interest in the subject-matter, when in fact he had none.[7] The rule does

---

[3] *Gray v Southouse* [1949] 2 All ER 1019.
[4] *Kiriri Cotton Co Ltd v Dewani* [1960] AC 192; cf *Nash v Halifax Building Society* [1979] Ch 584.
[5] *Atkinson v Denby* (1862) 7 H & N 934.
[6] [1951] 1 All ER 92.
[7] *Hughes v Liverpool Victoria Legal Friendly Society* [1916] 2 KB 482.

not apply where the misrepresentation was innocent,[8] though there might in such a case, be a right to rescind for misrepresentation;[9] and if this right were exercised it would follow that money paid or property transferred could be claimed back.

In an old case[10] a policy of insurance was taken out on goods in Russia at a time when neither party knew (or could have known) that war had broken out between this country and Russia. This made the policy illegal, but the policy-holder recovered back the premium as he had paid it under a mistake of fact affecting the legality of the contract.

iv Repentance

'Public policy', it has been said, 'is best served by allowing a party to repent before it is too late, and to prevent the completion of the illegal purpose by reclaiming the money paid by him in pursuance of it'.[11] Two points arising out of this statement should be stressed.

First, the claimant must 'repent'—that is, he must voluntarily abandon the illegal purpose. If that purpose is simply frustrated by the other party's failure or refusal to perform, there is no 'repentance' and hence no recovery. This was the position in the case of *Bigos v Bousted*,[12] mentioned above. The party who had agreed to supply the foreign currency simply failed to do so; and the argument that the other party had repented (and that he could recover his securities on this ground) was accordingly rejected.

Secondly, the repentance must come 'before it is too late'. Obviously, it is too late once the illegal purpose has been achieved; and the position is the same if the illegal purpose has been partly performed, at least if the part that has been performed is substantial. On the other hand, the mere fact that acts have been done in preparation for performing the illegal purpose will not prevent recovery. Thus in one case,[13] it was held that property transferred under a scheme to defraud creditors could be reclaimed, as the scheme had not yet been used to defraud any creditor. But in another case[14] money was paid under a scheme to interfere with the course of justice. It was held that the money could not be recovered as some such interference (though less than that bargained for) had actually taken place.

8 *Harse v Pearl Life Assurance Co Ltd* [1904] 1 K B 558; *Edler v Auerbach* [1950] 1 K B 359.
9 P 136, ante.
10 *Oom v Bruce* (1810) 12 East 225.
11 *Harry Parker Ltd v Mason* [1940] 2 K B 590 at 609.
12 [1951] 1 All E R 92.
13 *Taylor v Bowers* (1876) 1 Q B D 291.
14 *Kearly v Thomson* (1890) 24 Q B D 742.

v No reliance on the contract or its illegality

A person may be able to recover money paid or property transferred under an illegal contract if he can establish his right to it without relying on the contract or on its illegality. The law on this subject is complex, technical and not very satisfactory. It approaches the problem by reference to the rules which govern the transfer of proprietary or possessory rights in the subject-matter of illegal contracts; and it largely disregards the more important question whether the purpose of the rule giving rise to the illegality would be promoted or defeated by allowing recovery.

One group of cases concerns the hire or hire-purchase of goods under illegal contracts. Suppose that a television set is hired under such a contract for twelve months. During that period, the owner cannot claim it back. The contract would give the hirer the right to keep possession of the set, and the owner could not rely on the illegality of the contract to negative that right.[15] But after the end of the twelve months, the owner could claim back the set by simply saying that it was his property. His title would exist, quite apart from the contract or its illegality. This is a relatively straightforward case, but some variations of it give rise to more difficulty. Suppose first that, after one month, the hirer sells the set. This will amount to a repudiatory breach of contract,[16] as a result of which the hirer's right to keep possession of the set can be brought to an immediate and premature end by the owner. Hence the owner will be able to claim damages for conversion from the hirer, by simply relying on his ownership of the set; while the hirer will no longer be able to rely on his right to keep possession of the set as that right will have come to an end with the contract. Suppose next that the hirer had simply failed to pay the first month's rent; that a clause in the contract entitled the owner, on such failure, to give notice terminating the contract; and that such notice had been given. Here again, the hirer's right to keep possession of the set would have terminated prematurely, but only as a result of action taken by the owner under a term of the contract. Hence it would seem that the owner was relying on a term of the illegal contract, and in a sense trying to enforce that term, if he claimed the set before the end of the twelve months. In one case of this kind[17] the owner's claim nevertheless succeeded. The reasoning of the case is open to the objection that it deprives the rule that the illegal contract cannot be enforced of much of its practical importance; for the important remedy of claiming the goods back will be equally available against a defaulting hirer whether the contract is

---

[15] Cf *Taylor v Chester* (1869) L R 4 Q B 309 (pledge).
[16] *North Central Wagon and Finance Co v Graham* [1950] 2 K B 7.
[17] *Bowmakers Ltd v Barnet Instruments Ltd* [1945] K B 65 (hire-purchase).

legal or illegal. But the actual result can be justified on the ground that the owner's violation of the law was innocent and that the policy of the relevant legislation (which was to regulate the allocation of scarce resources in time of war) was promoted rather than defeated by allowing the owner to recover his goods.

The position of an owner who has let out goods under a contract of hire or hire-purchase is much more favourable than that of a seller who has sold the goods outright. Here the position is that the entire property in the goods can pass from the seller to the buyer, notwithstanding the illegality of the contract, in accordance with the usual rules which govern the passing of property under a contract of sale.[18] If under these rules the property has passed, the seller cannot get the goods back, since he has no title left on which he can rely. Indeed, if the seller succeeds in physically taking the goods away from the buyer, the latter is legally entitled to claim them back.[19] This is so even though he acquired them under an illegal contract. The buyer is similarly entitled to claim the goods from third parties who have taken them away, or who have disposed of them, in disregard of the buyer's title acquired under the illegal contract.[20] But there are limits to this principle: it has been said not to apply where a plaintiff who has obtained property by means of a criminal fraud claims damages for conversion of 'the very proceeds of the fraudulent conduct'.[1]

A person who has paid money under an illegal contract is again very unlikely to be able to get it back by relying simply on his title. When money is paid over, the payor's entire property in it almost invariably passes to the payee. The only significant exception to this rule occurs where money is deposited with a stakeholder. If money has, for example, been so deposited under an illegal wager, the depositor can claim it back from the stakeholder, so long as the latter has not paid it over to the other party to the wager.[2] Moreover, a person may be able to establish a right to money due under an illegal transaction without relying on the illegality. An agent may make an illegal contract on behalf of his principal with a third party, and receive money from the third party for the account of the principal. In some of the older authorities, it was held that the principal could recover such money from the agent.[3] He could establish his right to it by simply showing that it had been received by his agent on his behalf; and it was not

---

18 *Belvoir Finance Co Ltd v Stapleton* [1971] 1 QB 210.

19 *Singh v Ali* [1960] AC 167.

20 *Belvoir Finance Co Ltd v Stapleton* [1971] 1 QB 210.

1 *Thakewell v Barclays Bank plc* [1986] 1 All ER 676 at 689. For statutory powers to make confiscation orders against convicted offenders, see Criminal Justice Act 1988, Pt VI. There is no such power at common law: *Chief Constable of Leicestershire v M* [1988] 3 All ER 1015 at 1018.

2 Cf *O'Sullivan v Thomas* [1895] 1 QB 698.

3 Eg *Bone v Ekless* (1860) 5 H & N 925.

necessary for him to rely on the illegal contract under which it had been received by the agent.

vi Recovery allowed under certain illegal contracts

The general rule against recovery of money or property is by no means an obviously or universally desirable one; and some of the older authorities, particularly in equity, took the view that recovery should generally be allowed.[4] Traces of this view can still be seen to-day in the rule that money paid in advance by a client under a marriage brokage contract can be claimed back.[5] Obviously, the policy of the rule against these contracts is better served by making the marriage bureau pay back the money even if it has made efforts to promote a match, than by allowing it to keep the money in spite of the fact that it has done nothing. The rule relating to marriage brokage contracts is, at the present time, an isolated one. But it does suggest that, in cases not yet covered by authority, the court should not mechanically apply the general rule of non-recovery. Rather, it should ask itself whether the policy of the rule making the contract illegal is better served by denying or by allowing the recovery of money paid or property transferred under the contract.

d Collateral transactions

The illegality of a principal contract may infect collateral transactions which are in themselves perfectly lawful. Thus a loan of money is illegal if the lender knows that it is going to be used to perform an illegal contract: for example that it is going to be used to pay off another loan which is illegal.[6] On the other hand, some remote connection between the two transactions will not invalidate the collateral transaction. In one case,[7] diamonds were sold under a contract which was illegal as it had been so made as to deceive the revenue authorities of a foreign country.[8] The diamonds were later stolen and the sellers sued their insurers for this loss. The claim succeeded since the sellers could make out their claim under the insurance contract without reference to any illegal conduct on their part, since they had derived no benefit from the illegality,[9] and since the illegality had not in any way contributed to the loss.

---

[4] Eg *Morris v MacCullock* (1763) Amb 432.

[5] *Hermann v Charlesworth* [1905] 2 K B 123.

[6] *Spector v Ageda* [1973] Ch 30; *The American Accord* [1983] 1 A C 168.

[7] *Euro-Diam Ltd v Bathurst* [1988] 1 Lloyd's Rep 228.

[8] Ante; p 162–163.

[9] Contrast *Geismar v Sun Alliance and London Insurance Ltd* [1978] Q B 383 (no action on insurance on goods smuggled into this country).

Chapter 12

Contractual capacity

For various reasons, the law imposes restrictions on the contractual capacities of certain persons or bodies. In this chapter we shall discuss such restrictions as they apply to persons who are below the age of majority, or mentally ill or drunk, and to corporations.

1 MINORS

A minor is a person below the age of majority, which is now fixed at 18.[1] The main purpose of the legal rules regulating the contracts of such persons is to protect them from their inexperience, which may lead them to enter into contracts on unfavourable terms, or into contracts which, though perfectly fair, are simply improvident. On the other hand, the law also wants to prevent undue hardship to adults who deal fairly with minors. One way of achieving both aims would be to require minors' contracts to be made with the authorisation of their guardians. But this expedient was not adopted in English law; instead minors' contracts were divided into a number of classes, ranging from those which are valid to those which do not bind the minor but nevertheless may subject him to certain extra-contractual liability.

In the 19th and early 20th centuries a good deal of litigation arose out of cases in which young men of 'good family' ran up large tradesmen's bills or borrowed substantial sums of money. Such problems no longer commonly occur, especially now that the age of majority has been reduced from 21 to 18. But the question whether minors are bound by contracts can still arise today: for example, out of employment contracts, out of the contracts of young professional athletes or entertainers, and out of hire-purchase agreements made by minors. Claims may also be made *by* the minors either to enforce the liability of the other contracting party or to reclaim money or property with which the minor has parted under the contract. The practical importance of the topic, though reduced by changes in social conditions, remains by no means negligible.

[1] Family Law Reform Act 1969, s 1.

a Contracts which are binding

A minor is bound by contracts for necessaries, and by contracts of employment and analogous contracts.

i *Necessaries*

A minor's liability for necessaries was originally said to exist for his own good: the theory was that he could not get necessaries (except for ready cash) unless the law made him liable.[2] However some of the relevant rules of law make the position of the tradesman so precarious that no reasonable businessman would rely on them in giving credit to a minor; while others fairly obviously exist for the benefit of the tradesman and not for that of the minor.

This is, for example, true of the legal definition of necessaries, which are not confined to necessities. They include all goods and services (such as education[3] or medical or legal advice) which are 'fit to maintain the particular person in the state, station and degree . . . in which he is'.[4] Thus in one old case, even a livery for a minor's servant was held to be a necessary.[5] Obviously, the purpose of this wide definition was to protect persons who gave credit to wealthy minors in respect of goods or services which, in the view of the court, it was reasonable for the minors to have.

Not surprisingly, juries (consisting traditionally of twelve shopkeepers) were inclined to push this broad definition of necessaries beyond its legitimate limits. In one case, 'an Oxford jury held that champagne and wild ducks were necessaries to an . . . undergraduate'.[6] The courts countered this trend by distinguishing between 'luxurious articles of utility' and 'mere luxuries'.[7] The latter could not, as a matter of law, be necessaries; and the courts reserved to themselves the right to determine whether, as a matter of law, the articles were *capable of being* necessaries.[8] It was only if this preliminary question was answered in the affirmative that the case could properly be left to the jury, who then decided whether the goods *actually were* necessaries. This depended partly on the nature of the goods (so that, for instance, a racehorse could never be a necessary); and partly on the minor's actual needs (so that clothes could be necessaries but would not be if the minor already had an adequate supply). So far as the latter requirement was concerned, the law insisted that the goods must actually be necessaries

---

[2] *Ryder v Wombwell* (1868) LR 4 Exch 32 at 38.
[3] *Sherdley v Sherdley* [1988] AC 213 at 225.
[4] *Peters v Fleming* (1840) 6 M & W 42 at 46.
[5] *Hands v Slaney* (1800) 8 Term Rep 578.
[6] HL, 219 Official Report (3rd Series) Col 1225 (1874).
[7] *Chapple v Cooper* (1844) 13 M & W 252 at 258.
[8] *Ryder v Wombwell* (1868) LR 4 Exch 32.

at two points of time: the time at which they were sold and the time when they were delivered to the minor.[9] It was up to the tradesman to prove the difficult negative proposition that the minor was not adequately supplied at both times; and if the minor had an adequate supply, the tradesman's action would fail, even though he did not know this.[10] No doubt these rules were developed to control juries, who were too much inclined to find verdicts against minors; and they have survived, although to-day contract cases are no longer tried by jury.

Even where a minor is liable for necessaries, the rule is that he is only bound to pay a reasonable price.[11] This may be less than he agreed to pay; in theory it may also be more, but for practical purposes this possibility can be ruled out. The fact that the minor is not bound to pay the agreed price has given rise to the view that his liability for necessaries is not contractual at all. It is said to be a liability imposed by law, not because he has agreed, but because he has been supplied.[12] From this it is thought to follow that, if he has not already been supplied, he cannot be liable. On this view, he would not be liable on a so-called 'executory' contract for necessaries ie on one for necessaries to be supplied in the future. In other words, if a minor ordered a suit to be delivered and paid for in a month's time he could cancel the order without being liable for the price or for damages. This view makes little sense if liability for necessaries exists for the minor's own good, and it makes even less sense if such liability exists for the protection of an adult who agrees to supply the minor with his reasonable needs. In one case where the necessaries consisted largely of education (in the art of playing professional billiards), a minor was held liable for repudiating the contract when it remained partly unperformed.[13]

A minor may find that the supplier of necessaries will not give him credit, but that a third person will, either by paying the supplier or by lending money to the minor. A person who pays the supplier can recover the amount so paid (at least if the amount was reasonable) from the minor,[14] who is no worse off than he would be if he had to pay the supplier. A person who lends money to a minor to enable him to pay for necessaries can, however, only recover so much of the loan as was actually used for that purpose.[15] His right is restricted in this way because of the danger that the loan might be misapplied.

9 *Nash v Inman* [1908] 2 K B 1; Sale of Goods Act 1979, s 3.
10 *Barnes v Toye* (1884) 13 Q B D 410.
11 Sale of Goods Act 1979, s 3.
12 *Nash v Inman* [1908] 2 K B 1 at 8.
13 *Roberts v Gray* [1913] 1 K B 520.
14 *Earle v Peale* (1712) 10 Mod Rep 67.
15 *Marlow v Pitfeild* (1719) 1 P Wms 558.

ii *Employment and analogous contracts*

Contracts of employment with children are regulated by various legislative provisions which restrict the age from which children may be employed, and specify conditions and hours of work.[16] Subject to such provisions, the common law rule is that a minor is bound by a contract of employment so long as it is *on the whole* for his benefit. This depends on the terms generally available in the type of employment and locality in question. If the minor is employed on terms which are usual from this point of view, they will normally bind him in spite of the fact that some of them are disadvantageous to him.[17] But they will not bind the minor where they are harsh and oppressive, even though they are no worse than those offered to adults.[18] Contracts of apprenticeship, though formerly regarded as a special category, are now subject to the general rules governing contracts of employment with minors.[19]

These rules also apply to two further groups of contracts. First, they apply to contracts ancillary to contracts of employment, such as contracts to dissolve contracts of employment. Secondly, they apply to contracts which are not strictly contracts of employment but which are analogous to such contracts in enabling the minor to make a living. For example in one case[20] an under-age heavyweight boxer was held to be bound by a term in a contract by which he forfeited his 'purse' if he was disqualified. This term was *on the whole* for his benefit, as it encouraged clean fighting. Similarly, a contract giving a firm of publishers the exclusive right to publish the memoirs of a minor was held binding (in spite of the nature of the work) as it would help him 'to make a start as an author'.[1] On the other hand, it is not true to say that a contract is binding on a minor merely because it is for his benefit and because it helps him to make a living. In particular it is well settled that a minor is not liable on a 'trading contract'. This means primarily a contract by which the minor buys or sells goods as a dealer,[2] but it also extends to certain contracts for the provision of services. An under-age haulage contractor has been held to be a trader. Hence he was not liable on a contract to hire-purchase a lorry;[3] nor would he have been liable for breach of a contract to carry goods in the lorry.

---

[16] Eg Employment of Children Act 1973.

[17] *Clements v London and North Western Rly Co* [1894] 2 QB 482.

[18] *De Francesco v Barnum* (1889) 43 Ch D 165.

[19] See *Gadd v Thompson* [1911] 1 KB 304.

[20] *Doyle v White City Stadium Ltd* [1935] 1 KB 110.

[1] *Chaplin v Leslie Frewin (Publishers) Ltd* [1966] Ch 71 at 95.

[2] *Cowern v Nield* [1912] 2 KB 419.

[3] *Mercantile Union Guarantee Corpn Ltd v Ball* [1937] 2 KB 498.

b Contracts which are binding unless repudiated

In some cases the contract binds both parties, but the minor (though not the other party) can escape liability by repudiating the contract. This rule applies where a minor agrees to buy or sell land,[4] or to take or to grant a lease of land;[5] where a minor enters into a marriage settlement;[6] and where he incurs liability for calls on shares in a company,[7] by either subscribing for the shares or by buying partly paid up shares from a previous holder. It also applies to the relations between a minor and persons with whom he enters into a partnership, in the sense that he is not entitled to any share in the profits of the partnership unless he discharges his obligations under it to the other partners.[8] He is not liable to third parties who deal with the partnership. In all these cases it is said that the minor has acquired an interest in a subject-matter of a permanent nature; and it would be unjust to allow him to retain this, unless he discharged the obligations attached to it. The explanation is not wholly satisfactory, but the law relating to the contracts described above is well settled.

The repudiation may take place either during or after minority. If it takes place during minority it can still be withdrawn either before the minor comes of age or within a reasonable time thereafter.[9] Repudiation after minority is only effective if it takes place within a reasonable time. This is calculated from the date on which the minor attains his majority, and not from the time of the making of the contract or from the time at which the former minor discovered his right to repudiate.[10] The effect of repudiation is to relieve the minor from all future liability under the contract, such as liability for future rent or future calls on shares. On the other hand repudiation is probably not retrospective: it does not free the minor from liabilities which had accrued at the time of repudiation. Nor does repudiation enable the minor to get back money which he has paid under the contract, unless there has been a 'total failure of consideration'. In one case,[11] a minor had applied for shares in a company. The shares were allotted to her and then fell sharply in value. The minor repudiated and thus escaped liability for calls but it was held that she could not get back the money which she had already paid. There had been no 'total failure of consideration' as she had got the very shares for which she had bargained. If there is such failure of consideration, even an adult can recover back money

---

4 *Whittingham v Murdy* (1889) 60 L T 956.
5 *Davies v Benyon-Harris* (1931) 47 T L R 424.
6 *Edwards v Carter* [1893] A C 360.
7 *North Western Rly Co v McMichael* (1850) 5 Exch 114.
8 *Lovell and Christmas v Beauchamp* [1894] A C 607.
9 *North Western Rly Co v McMichael,* supra at 127.
10 *Edwards v Carter* [1893] A C 360.
11 *Steinberg v Scala (Leeds) Ltd* [1923] 2 Ch 452.

paid.[12] A minor's position is however more favourable than an adult's in that the minor can get back money paid even though the total failure was brought about by his own act. This would, for example, be the position if a minor, having paid a deposit under a lease to commence on a future date, repudiated before that date.

A minor may borrow money to enable him to make payments under a contract within the present group and actually use the money for this purpose. He is not bound by the contract of loan, but the lender has rights similar to those of a lender for necessaries.[13]

c Contracts which are not binding on the minor

Here we are concerned with contracts which do not fall within the groups so far discussed. For example, a minor might contract to buy goods which are not necessaries, or to sell goods as a trader, or to go on a luxury world cruise, or he might borrow money or enter into a contract of service which was not beneficial, or into a contract of insurance. Such contracts do not bind the minor; but the fact that he is not bound does not prevent his promise from being good consideration for that of the adult party. That party is therefore bound by the contract,[14] though the remedy of *specific* performance is not available against him.[15] The present group of contracts differs from group **b** above, in that the minor does not have to repudiate to escape liability: if he does nothing, he is not bound. He will, however, become liable on the contract if, after reaching full age, he 'ratifies' it[16] by either declaring himself bound by it or by behaving in such a way as to show that he regards himself as bound.

The minor may perform his part of the contract without being bound to do so: eg by paying for goods which were not 'necessaries'. He is not entitled to the return of the payment merely because the contract did not bind him by reason of his minority.[17] The only circumstances in which he is entitled to get his money back are the same as those in which an adult would be so entitled: eg if he had paid in advance and the goods were never delivered to him, so that there was a 'total failure of consideration';[18] or if the goods were defective and he justifiably rejected them on that ground.[19]

---

12 P 359, post.
13 Ante, p 190, *Nottingham Permanent Benefit Building Society v Thurstan* [1903] A C 6.
14 See *Bruce v Warwick* (1815) 6 Taunt 118; *Wilson v Kearse* (1800) Peake Add Cas 196; *Corpe v Overton* (1833) 10 Bing 252 at 259; *Williams v Moor* (1843) 11 M & W 256; former statutory modifications of the common law rules stated in the text have been removed by the Minors' Contracts Act 1987, ss 1 and 4(2).
15 *Flight v Bolland* (1828) 4 Russ 298.
16 See *Williams v Moor* (1843) 11 M & W 256.
17 *Wilson v Kearse* (1800) Peake Add Cas 196; *Corpe v Overton* (1833) 10 Bing 252 at 259.
18 Post, p 359.
19 Eg post, p 279.

Performance of the contract will also generally involve some dealing with the subject matter: eg goods which are not 'necessaries' may be delivered by an adult seller to the minor. The property in such goods can pass to the minor (in spite of the invalidity of the contract) by such delivery,[20] coupled with the seller's intention to pass the property to the minor. It is true that where a contract is void for mistake as to the identity of the other contracting party, property does not pass;[1] but the case in which the contract does not bind the buyer because of his minority is distinguishable. In the mistake case there is no intention to pass property to the recipient. In the case of the under-age buyer there is such an intention, though it may (if the seller does not know the law) be based on a mistaken view of the binding force of the underlying contract. The view that property passes is also the more desirable one; for to hold the contrary would seriously prejudice innocent third parties who had in turn bought the goods from the minor, and who might have done so long after the minor had come of age.

Property can pass *from*, no less than *to* the minor under a contract which does not bind him: for example, where he delivers goods sold by him as a trader; or where he transfers his copyright in a book or in a musical composition under a contract which does not bind him because it is not, on the whole, beneficial to him.[2]

d Liability in tort

Minors (except for very young children) are subject to the law of tort in the ordinary way: eg they are liable for negligently causing injury or damage, or for converting property that does not belong to them. But a tort is often at the same time a breach of contract: for example where a minor negligently damages a car which he has hired. The law in such cases will not allow the adult to get round the minor's immunity from contractual liability, by suing in tort.[3] But the minor could be held liable in tort if he did something which was wholly outside the acts envisaged by the contract: for example, if he entered the hired car for a stock-car race, or if he sold it.[4]

e Liability in restitution

A minor may be made liable in restitution where he has obtained benefits under a contract but cannot be made to pay for them because

---

[20] *Stocks v Wilson* [1913] 2 K B 235 at 246; the same assumption underlies the Minors' Contracts Act 1987, s 3(1), post, p 195.

[1] *Cundy v Lindsay* (1878) 3 App Cas 459; see p 109, ante.

[2] See *Chaplin v Leslie Frewin (Publishers) Ltd* [1966] Ch 71 (where the contract was held to be binding: ante, p 191).

[3] *Fawcett v Smethurst* (1914) 84 L J K B 473.

[4] Cf *Burnard v Haggis* (1863) 14 C B N S 45; *Ballett v Mingay* [1943] K B 281.

the contract is not binding on him. Section 3(1) of the Minors' Contracts Act 1987 gives the court a wide discretion to impose such liability; but this is expressly said to be without prejudice to any other remedy available to the adult.[5] Other restitutionary remedies therefore still need to be discussed, though generally the adult will make his claim under section 3(1) since the conditions imposed by the subsection are less onerous than those imposed by the earlier rules of equity and common law.

i *Minors' Contracts Act 1987, s 3(1)*

The subsection applies where a contract has been made with a minor and is unenforceable against him because of his minority. In such a case, the court 'may, if it is just and equitable to do so, require [the minor] to transfer to the [other party] any property acquired by the [minor] under the contract, or any property representing it.' The operation of the subsection can be illustrated by supposing that the minor has bought a diamond ring for £500, that the ring has been delivered to him, but that he has not paid the price. The court can then order the minor to return the ring to the seller. Moreover, if the minor were to exchange the ring for a necklace, the court could order the minor to transfer the necklace to the seller as 'property representing' the ring. Similarly, if the minor sold the ring for £400 the court could order the minor to transfer the £400 to the seller;[6] and if the minor used the £400 to buy a bracelet the court could order the minor to transfer the bracelet to the seller. On the other hand, if the minor had spent the £400 on a party to celebrate his coming of age, the court could not make an order under section 3(1) since the minor no longer has either 'the property acquired' or any 'property representing' it; if he had spent £250 out of the £400 on the party, the court could order him to transfer no more than the remaining £150. The fact that the minor may have *other* assets is irrelevant. The court's discretion under section 3(1) exists only to prevent the minor from being enriched by retaining the 'property' obtained under the contract or its identifiable proceeds: to extend the restitutionary remedy beyond this point would come too close to making him liable on a contract that does not bind him. The crucial point is that the minor does not come under a *personal* liability, enforceable against his assets generally. The remedy is *proprietary* in the sense of being enforceable only against a particular asset, ie the property obtained under the contract, or another asset into which it has been transformed. So long as this restriction on the scope of the

5 Section 3(2).
6 'Property' in s 3(1) seems to include money: cf Law Commission Report on Minors' Contracts (Law Com No 134) para 4.21.

remedy is observed, it is immaterial that the *measure* of liability is identical with what was due under the contract. If, in our example of the diamond ring, the minor had happened to resell the ring for exactly the £500 that he had agreed to pay for it, he could be ordered to transfer the whole of that sum, so long as it was still in his hands.

The examples considered in the preceding discussion are relatively straightforward. It is easy to imagine more complex situations in which the minor sells the 'property acquired', pays the money into an active bank account which is already in credit, and (perhaps a month later) draws on the account to make a substitute purchase. In such cases, the process of 'tracing' property into its product can be extremely complex and technical; but the detailed rules governing the process need not be considered here since the discretion conferred on the court by section 3(1) seems to be designed to avoid their complexities. In exercising that discretion, the court can take account of the difficulties of 'tracing' and can refuse to order the minor to 'restore' unless it is clear that the property in respect of which the order is sought does indeed represent the property acquired under the contract.

ii Effects of fraud

A minor might induce an adult to enter into a contract with him by some fraud: for example, he might procure a loan of money, or the delivery of goods on credit, by fraudulently pretending to be of age. At common law, he could not be made liable on the contract merely because he had procured it by fraud;[7] nor could the adult get round the minor's immunity from contractual liability by claiming the amount of the loan, or the value of the goods, as damages in tort for deceit.[8]

These rules unduly favoured fraudulent minors; and equity redressed the balance by ordering a minor who had fraudulently mis-represented his age to restore benefits obtained under the resulting contract. There seems to be no reason now for the adult to resort to this remedy; for it is restricted to cases of fraud while the statutory remedy under section 3(1) of the Minors' Contracts Act 1987 is not so restricted. The statutory remedy is, moreover, clearly available, not only in respect of the very thing obtained under the contract, but also in respect of its proceeds; while it was disputed whether the equitable remedy was available in respect of such proceeds.[9] One clear limitation on the scope of the equitable remedy is illustrated by a case[10] in which a minor had, by fraudulently pretending to be of full age, obtained a loan

---

[7] Eg *Bartlett v Wells* (1862) 1 B & S 836.
[8] *R Leslie Ltd v Sheill* [1914] 3 K B 607.
[9] Ibid at 619, doubting *Stocks v Wilson* [1913] 2 K B 235.
[10] *R Leslie Ltd v Sheill* supra.

of £400. It was held that he could not be made to 'restore' that amount in the absence of evidence that he still had the money or its identifiable proceeds. Once he had dissipated the money, he could not be ordered to pay an equivalent sum out of his other assets. Such authorities on the scope of the equitable remedy are now of interest chiefly as illustrating the sort of circumstances in which the court is, or is not, likely to exercise its discretion to order the minor to make a transfer under section 3(1) of the 1987 Act. The common principle underlying the equitable and the statutory remedy is that both remedies are *proprietary* rather than *personal* (in the sense already explained): they are available in respect of identifiable property only, and not in respect of the minor's assets generally.

iii Liability in quasi-contract

Where one party to a contract has paid a sum of money to the other for some counter-performance, which then is not rendered, he is normally entitled to recover that money in a quasi-contractual action. This is called an action for money had and received to the use of the plaintiff, or an action for money paid on a total failure of consideration.[11] It is a *quasi*-contractual action because the liability to repay is imposed by law irrespective of agreement. Generally, the liability imposed in such an action is a *personal* one in the sense discussed above. It should therefore not be imposed on a minor who has failed to perform a contract which does not bind him. His liability should be restricted to one to restore the actual money or its traceable proceeds: in other words, he should be liable to a *proprietary* remedy only.[12] Unless his liability were restricted in this way, the policy which limits his contractual capacity would be fundamentally disrupted.

The quasi-contractual remedy is available as of right: in this respect, it is preferable (from the adult's point of view) to the remedy under section 3(1) of the Minors' Contracts Act 1987, which is discretionary. On the other hand, the quasi-contractual remedy is subject to two limitations. First, it is (according to one case[13]) available only against a minor who is guilty of fraud. Secondly, it is only available in respect of *money*: there is no quasi-contractual action to recover *goods*. Formerly, these limitations could lead to the regrettable results that a minor could keep something for nothing: for example, where he had simply not paid for goods obtained under a contract which did not bind him, or where he had not delivered goods for which he had been paid. But in such cases he can now be ordered to make restitution under section 3(1)

[11] Pp 359–362, post.
[12] *R Leslie Ltd v Sheill* [1914] 3 K B 607.
[13] *Cowern v Nield* [1912] 2 K B 419.

of the 1987 Act, so that the practical importance of the limitations on the scope of the quasi-contractual remedy has been virtually eliminated.

2 MENTAL PATIENTS

A contract with a mental patient is valid;[14] but to this rule there are two exceptions. First, the contract can be avoided by the patient if the other party knew of his inability to understand the transaction.[15] Secondly, if the patient's disorder is so serious that his property is made subject to the control of the court, any contract amounting to an attempt by him to dispose of the property does not bind him, though it binds the other party.[16] A contract which does not bind the patient becomes binding on him, if he ratifies it after he is cured.[17]

Even where the patient cannot be sued on the contract, he is liable to pay a reasonable price for necessaries supplied to him.[18]

3 DRUNKEN PERSONS

A person cannot avoid liability on a contract merely because, when he made it, his commercial judgment was befuddled by drink; though in equity the remedy of specific performance has occasionally been refused, where one party took advantage of the other's intoxication.[19] The contract is, moreover, voidable by the latter party if he was so drunk that he could not understand the transaction and, if the other party knew this.[20] Such a contract, however, becomes binding if it is ratified when the effects of drink have worn off.[1] A drunken person is, again, liable for necessaries supplied to him while he is suffering from his temporary incapacity to contract.[2]

4 CORPORATIONS

a Charter corporations

Some corporations (such as Universities and Colleges and certain professional associations) are created by Royal Charter. The charter will

14 *Hart v O'Connor* [1985] A C 1000.
15 *Imperial Loan Co v Stone* [1892] 1 Q B 599.
16 *Re Walker* [1905] 1 Ch 160.
17 *Manches v Trimborn* (1946) 115 L J K B 305.
18 Sale of Goods Act 1979, s 3.
19 *Malins v Freeman* (1836) 2 Keen 25 at 34.
20 *Gore v Gibson* (1845) 13 M & W 623.
 1 *Matthews v Baxter* (1873) L R 8 Exch 132.
 2 Sale of Goods Act 1979, s 3.

specify the purposes for which the corporation was created; but such provisions do not restrict the corporation's contractual capacity.[3] Thus a contract may be perfectly valid, although it was not authorised, or was prohibited, by the charter. If the corporation makes such a contract, it runs the risk of having its charter revoked, and its members may take legal proceedings to stop it from entering into contracts which expose it to this risk.[4] But all this does not affect the validity of any such contract which the corporation has actually concluded.

b Statutory corporations

Most corporations are now created by, or under the authority of, statute. Some (such as the nationalised industries) are created by special Acts of Parliament. The great majority of commercial corporations have, since 1862, been created by using the machinery provided for this purpose by the Companies Acts.

i The ultra vires doctrine

The contractual capacity of statutory corporations is limited by the ultra vires doctrine. Under this doctrine, any contract made by the corporation may be invalid if the contract is beyond the powers of the corporation. In order to determine what these are one has to look, in the case of a company incorporated by special Act of Parliament, at the provisions in that Act specifying the corporation's powers; and, in the case of a company incorporated under the Companies Acts, at its memorandum of association. This is a document which must be registered in the Companies Register, where it is open to public inspection. It contains a clause specifying the objects of the company; and any contract for a purpose not stated in the objects clause is ultra vires. For example, in one case[5] a company whose objects clause stated that it had been formed to render services to overseas visitors went into the business of breeding pigs; and it was held that a loan to the company for the purpose of that business was ultra vires.

The reason for the ultra vires doctrine can be seen from this rather extreme example. It is that an investor who puts his money into one kind of business should have some assurance that it will not be used for a wholly different one. He does not, indeed, have a complete assurance, since the company has wide powers to change the objects clause of its memorandum.[6] But such a change can only be made by a special resolution, passed by a three-fourths majority of shareholders;[7]

[3] *Jenkin v Pharmaceutical Society* [1921] 1 Ch 392 at 398.
[4] *Jenkin v Pharmaceutical Society* supra.
[5] *Introductions Ltd v National Provincial Bank Ltd* [1970] Ch 199.
[6] Companies Act 1985, s 4.
[7] Ibid s 378.

so that shareholders are at least entitled to be consulted and to vote before the company enters upon a course of action wholly different from the objects originally stated in its memorandum of association.

In practice, however, the protection which the ultra vires doctrine is supposed to give to investors in the company is very considerably diluted. In the first place, the company can validly make a contract of a kind not actually mentioned in the objects clause if the contract is reasonably incidental to its objects: for example, it can grant short leases of premises not immediately required for the purpose of its business.[8] Secondly, a contract into which the company enters may on its face be quite neutral. This is the position where the company simply borrows money. The contract of loan is not invalid merely because the company uses the money for a purpose which is ultra vires. It would only be invalid if the lender had notice of that purpose when he made the loan.[9] Thirdly, the persons drawing up the memorandum of association often do so in such a way as to give the company a good deal of room for manoeuvre. They tend to include in the objects clause very wide powers, enabling the company to carry on many forms of activity which have little, if any, relation to the business for which the company was originally formed. In one case,[10] the objects clause contained no fewer than thirty objects, enabling the company to carry on almost any kind of business, and concluded with a provision to the effect that no one of these objects should be regarded as subsidiary to any other object. The House of Lords held that effect must be given to this provision, but did so reluctantly since this kind of drafting seriously reduces the protection which the ultra vires doctrine is meant to give to shareholders. To redress the balance, the courts have restricted the scope of such widely drawn objects clauses by distinguishing between *objects* of a company and ancillary *powers*:[11] such powers, though stated in the objects clause, must be exercised only for the purpose of the objects. If they are exercised for other purposes, the resulting transaction is not indeed ultra vires and void. But it is an abuse of the powers of the directors and cannot be enforced by a third party with notice of the facts giving rise to the abuse. For example, where the objects clause empowered a company to give guarantees, it was held that such guarantees could only be given for the legitimate purposes of the company and that a creditor who know that the guarantee had been given for other purposes could not enforce it.[12]

---

8 *Foster v London, Chatham and Dover Rly Co* [1895] 1 QB 711.

9 Cf *Re Jon Beauforte Ltd* [1953] Ch 131; *Rolled Steel Products (Holdings) Ltd v British Steel Corpn* [1986] Ch 246.

10 *Cotman v Brougham* [1918] AC 514; cf *Re Horsley & Weight Ltd* [1982] Ch 442.

11 *Rolled Steel Products (Holdings) Ltd v British Steel Corpn* [1986] Ch 246 at 305.

12 *Rolled Steel* case supra.

ii Qualifications of the doctrine

The ultra vires doctrine used to be a source of hardship to persons who dealt with the company. This hardship arose because an ultra vires contract could not be enforced against the company in any circumstances: not even by a person who had entered into the contract in excusable ignorance of the fact that it was ultra vires. Section 35 of the Companies Act 1985 (re-enacting a change in the law first introduced in 1972[13]) now provides that, where a transaction has been 'decided on by the directors', it shall, in favour of a person dealing with the company in good faith, be deemed to be within the capacity of the company. Such a person is therefore not affected by the ultra vires doctrine: he can enforce the contract against the company even though it was not authorised by the memorandum of association. He must, however, be excusably ignorant of this fact: good faith is negatived if he knew that the transaction was ultra vires or if he could not, in all the circumstances, have been unaware of this fact.[14]

Before the statutory provision just discussed came into force, the law had developed a number of devices by which the lot of the ultra vires contractor was alleviated. These will become much less important now that such a person will generally be able to enforce the contract. But some of them may still occasionally be useful: for example, where the case is not covered by s 35 because the ultra vires contract was not 'decided on by the directors'. A person who cannot, or does not wish to, rely on the subsection has a number of other remedies. If he lends money under an ultra vires loan, and it is used to pay off an intra vires debt, he can recover to the extent to which it has been so used. This does not prejudice the shareholders as the company's total indebtedness is not increased.[15] An ultra vires lender can also recover the money which he has lent, to the extent to which it can still be traced into the company's assets.[16] The weakness of both these remedies is, of course, that they may lead to less than full recovery if only part of the money has been used to pay intra vires debts, or if only part of it is still traceable when the claim is made. Finally, the ultra vires contractor may have a remedy against an officer of the company who has induced him to enter into the contract by representing that it was intra vires. The remedy would be in tort if the officer was guilty of fraud or negligence. If the representation was wholly innocent the officer would still be liable in contract, for breach of a so-called 'implied warranty' that he had authority to make the contract on behalf of the company.[17]

[13] European Communities Act 1972, s 9(1).
[14] *International Sales and Agencies Ltd v Marcus* [1982] 3 All ER 551.
[15] *Blackburn Building Society v Cunliffe, Brooks & Co* (1882) 22 Ch D 61; affd 9 App Cas 857.
[16] *Sinclair v Brougham* [1914] AC 398.
[17] *Firbank's Executors v Humphreys* (1886) 18 QBD 54; see p 262, post.

Suppose that a company had power to borrow up to £10 million and, after this amount had been borrowed, a director negotiated a further loan. He could be held liable for having impliedly represented that the company had not exhausted its borrowing powers. But he would not be liable if his representation related to a matter of law.[18] This rule in practice severely restricted the personal remedy against officers of the company, since a representation as to the meaning of the memorandum of association is one of law.

So far we have considered only the rights of the ultra vires contractor. The further question arises whether the company itself can enforce an ultra vires contract. If the contract is still unperformed on both sides, it probably cannot be enforced by the company, for such enforcement could hardly be ordered without requiring the company to perform its part, and thus sanctioning ultra vires expenditure. If, on the other hand, the contract has been performed by the company, little harm could be done to the shareholders (whom the ultra vires doctrine is meant to protect) by allowing the company to enforce the contract. Probably it can do so,[19] though strictly the purpose of the ultra vires doctrine would be better served by allowing the company to claim back any money paid or property transferred by it under the contract.

---

[18] *Rashdall v Ford* (1866) L R 2 Eq 750.
[19] *Bell Houses Ltd v City Wall Properties Ltd* [1966] 2 Q B 656 at 694.

Chapter 13

The parties to a contract

So far we have assumed that a contract is made simply between two parties, each consisting of one person. Occasionally reference has been made to multilateral contracts between more than two parties: for example, to the situation in which three or more persons agree to compete in a race and to obey certain rules. Here again it is assumed that each party to the contract consists of one person. It is however also possible to have more than one person on each side of the contract. There are four such situations, which will be considered in turn. First, there may be more than one debtor, as where A and B make a promise to X; secondly, there may be more than one creditor, as where A makes a promise to X and Y; thirdly, A may make a contract with X for the benefit of Y; and fourthly, the question may arise whether a contract between A and X can bind Y.

1 PROMISES BY MORE THAN ONE PERSON

Suppose that A and B promise to pay X £10. One possibility is that each has made an entirely *separate* promise, in which case X can claim £10 from each of them ie £20 in all. But another possibility is that A and B have promised together to pay X £10, in which case X cannot get more than £10 in all. The exact legal effect of such a promise depends on whether it is *joint* or *joint and several*. A joint promise is a single promise made by a number of persons; a joint and several promise consists of such a single promise coupled with a seperate promise by each promisor. Promises by a number of persons are deemed to be joint unless they provide the contrary, eg by being framed in the form 'we promise jointly and severally' or 'we, and each of us, promise'.

a Similarities between joint, and joint and several, promises

Whether the promise is joint or joint and several, each promisor is fully liable to the promisee: ie in our example X can recover the full £10 from either A or B (but not from both). But if one debtor pays more than his share, he is entitled to contribution from the other. This is assessed by dividing the debt by the number of debtors who are solvent when the right to contribution arises.[1] Thus if A, B and C promise to

[1] *Hitchman v Stewart* (1855) 3 Drew 271.

204 The parties to a contract

pay £18 to X and A pays the whole sum, he can recover £6 from B and
£6 from C. But, if C is bankrupt at the time of the payment, A can
recover £9 from B. These rules are subject to contrary provision,
express or implied, in the contract. If, for example, A is a principal
debtor while B and C are sureties, obviously A cannot recover contribution from B and C. On the contrary, if B or C or both of them pay
the debt, they are entitled to be wholly indemnified by A.

If the creditor releases one of the co-debtors, the general rule is that
the others are also released;[2] for if they could still be sued they would
then be able to claim contribution from the one who was released and
so deprive the release of its practical force.[3] However, the courts have
drawn a difficult distinction between a release (available to all the
debtors) and a covenant not to sue (available only to the one with whom
it is made). They tend to construe a promise not to sue one debtor as a
covenant not to sue, if it expressly reserves the rights of the creditor
against the other debtors.[4]

If one debtor raises a defence to the claim, this will not avail the
others, if it was personal to him: for example, if one successfully pleads
that he is a minor the others are not released.[5] The position is different
if one debtor's defence goes to the root of the whole claim: for example,
if the defence is that the creditor had not performed his part of the
contract.[6] One special problem is whether a guarantor, who generally
undertakes joint and several liability with the principal debtor, can rely
on a defence available to the latter. The solution to this problem
depends on the policy of the rule giving the debtor his defence. Thus, a
guarantee of an illegal contract cannot be enforced, since to allow enforcement would tend to undermine the rule giving rise to the illegality.[7] On the other hand, a guarantee of an ultra vires contract, which
will in practice often be given by the directors of the company in
question, can be enforced.[8] This rule does not undermine the ultra
vires doctrine since investors in the company (whom that doctrine is
meant to protect) will not be prejudiced if such guarantors are held
liable. Similarly, an adult is liable where he guarantees a debt which
cannot be enforced against the principal debtor by reason of the latter's
minority.[9] The rule that the minor cannot be sued for the debt exists for
his protection alone, and its purpose would not be furthered by
allowing the adult to escape liability on the guarantee.

---

2 *Nicholson v Revill* (1836) 4 Ad & El 675.
3 *Jenkins v Jenkins* [1928] 2 K B 501 at 508.
4 *Price v Barker* (1855) 4 E & B 760.
5 *Lovell and Christmas v Beauchamp* [1894] A C 607.
6 *Pirie v Richardson* [1927] 1 K B 448.
7 *Swan v Bank of Scotland* (1836) 10 Bli N S 627.
8 *Yorkshire Railway Wagon Co v MacLure* (1882) 21 Ch D 309; see pp 199–200, ante.
9 Minors' Contracts Act 1987, s 2; see p 193 ante.

b Differences between joint, and joint and several, promises

At common law, the so-called doctrine of survivorship applied to joint, but not to joint and several, promises. Under this doctrine, if A and B made a joint promise to X and A died, his liability passed to B. If B paid the debt, he could get contribution from A's estate,[10] but X had no right against the estate. The result might be that, if A died and B became bankrupt, X had no substantial rights against anyone. The rule was highly inconvenient in commercial cases and equity in some such cases refused to follow it.[11] It no longer applies to partnership debts;[12] and it is arguable that the topic was one in which there was a conflict between common law and equity, so that the equitable rules now prevail by virtue of the general rule which gives them primacy in cases of such conflict.[13]

There were also procedural distinctions between the two types of promises; but these have lost much of their former importance. At common law, an action on a joint contract had to be brought against all the debtors, whereas one on a joint and several contract could be brought against all the debtors or against any one of them. But the rule in the case of joint debtors is relaxed in some cases: for example, if one of the debtors is abroad, or cannot be traced, or is bankrupt. In all these cases the others can be sued without that one.[14] And in an action against one joint and several debtor the court may order the others to be made parties to the proceedings,[15] so that (for example) contribution between them can be assessed once for all in a single action. Moreover, the rule that all joint debtors had to be sued together, only applied if the one who was sued expressly pleaded the creditor's failure to join the others as parties to the action. There was thus the possibility that judgment might be obtained against only one of the co-debtors; and if that judgment was not satisfied, the creditor would wish to take further proceedings against the others. At common law he could only do so where the debt was joint and several[16] but by statute he can now also do so in the case of joint debts.[17]

---

[10] *Batard v Hawes* (1853) 2 E & B 287.
[11] *Thorpe v Jackson* (1837) 2 Y & C Ex 553.
[12] Partnership Act 1890, s 9.
[13] Judicature Act 1873, s 25 (II); now Supreme Court Act 1981, s 49 (1).
[14] *Wilson Sons & Co Ltd v Balcarres Brook SS Co Ltd* [1893] 1 QB 422; *Robinson v Geisel* [1894] 2 QB 685; Insolvency Act 1986, s 345(4).
[15] RSC Ord 15, r 6 (2) (b).
[16] *Blyth v Fladgate* [1891] 1 Ch 337; contrast *Kendall v Hamilton* (1879) 4 App Cas 504 (joint debt).
[17] Civil Liability (Contribution) Act 1978, s 3.

2 PROMISES TO MORE THAN ONE PERSON

If A promises to pay £10 to X and Y, he may make two separate promises to pay them £10 each, in which case, his total liability is to pay £20. But the promise may be a single promise under which A is not to be liable for more than £10 in all. Here it is necessary to distinguish between cases in which the promise is made to X and Y jointly and those in which it is made to them severally.

a Joint promises

If a promise is made to X and Y jointly they are together entitled to the whole of the promised performance. Suppose that A is tenant of a house owned by X and Y and promises to pay rent of £2,000 per annum to them jointly. As against A neither of the landlords is entitled to any particular share of the £2,000. A is not concerned with any arrangement that X and Y may have made between themselves as to the division of the rent. Moreover, the doctrine of survivorship operates between joint creditors, so that if X dies Y becomes entitled to the whole sum.[18] It also follows from the nature of a promise to two persons jointly that an action on the promise must be brought by both of them together.[19]

b Several promises

If a promise is made to two persons severally, each of them is entitled to his proportionate part of the promised performance. This would, for example, be the position if A issued a policy of insurance in favour of the persons interested in the cargo of a particular ship and if some of the cargo was owned by X and the rest by Y. In the event of a loss, X and Y would each separately be entitled to his due proportion of the policy moneys. It would not be necessary for X and Y to sue A together; and the doctrine of survivorship does not apply to a promise of this kind. If X dies his rights against A pass to X's personal representative and not to his co-creditor.[20] In equity a contract for the repayment of money lent by a number of lenders was presumed to create a several right in each lender.[1] The object of this presumption was to avoid the doctrine of survivorship. It could be rebutted, especially where that doctrine caused no substantive injustice and was administratively convenient: eg where the lenders were trustees and had no beneficial interest in the money.[2]

---

[18] *Anderson v Martindale* (1801) 1 East 497.
[19] *Sorsbie v Park* (1843) 12 M & W 146.
[20] *Withers v Bircham* (1824) 3 B & C 254.
[1] *Steeds v Steeds* (1889) 22 QBD 537.
[2] Ibid at 542.

c Joint and several promises

Section 81 of the Law of Property Act 1925 provides that covenants and contracts under seal made with two or more persons jointly are (unless a contrary intention is expressly stated) to be 'construed as being also made with each of them.' This provision is restricted to promises under seal; it appears to mean that the promise is at the same time both joint and several. The point of s 81 was probably to abolish the doctrine of survivorship except where the creditors clearly intended it to apply; but it seems that promises within the section are also to be treated as several for the purpose of the other rules which apply to several (as opposed to joint) promises.

d Effects of the distinctions

Two of these have already been stated: the doctrine of survivorship and the rule requiring all creditors to sue together only apply to joint promises. The other effects are as follows.

First, payment of the whole debt to, or by the direction of, one joint creditor discharges the debt[3] unless the contract expressly, or by implication, provides that the payment must be made to, or authorised by, all the creditors. Payment of the whole to one of two several creditors does not discharge the debtor's liability to the other, who is separately entitled to his share. Secondly, if a joint creditor releases the debtor, the result is to discharge the whole debt; but a release by a several creditor only discharges his share and not that of any other creditor.[4] Thirdly, the general principle is that a defence available against one creditor is available against the others, if the promise was made to them jointly,[5] but not if it was made to them severally.[6] Finally, a promise to X and Y jointly can be enforced by both of them although the whole consideration was provided by one of them;[7] and the same rule has been said to apply where the promise was 'joint and several' and the promisee who had provided the consideration had died.[8] But it seems unlikely that a promise to X and Y severally can be enforced by X if the whole consideration was provided by Y.

The application of the above rules is complicated by the fact that the same transaction may contain a number of promises, one of which is joint while another is several. For example, where two persons open a joint bank account, the bank's promise to pay the amount standing to

3 *Powell v Brodhurst* [1901] 2 Ch 160 at 164.
4 *Steeds v Steeds* (1889) 22 QBD 537.
5 *P Samuel & Co v Dumas* [1924] AC 431 at 445.
6 *Hagedorn v Bazett* (1813) 2 M & S 100.
7 Cf. *Coulls v Bagot's Executor and Trustee Co Ltd* [1967] ALR 385.
8 *McEvoy v Belfast Banking Co* [1935] AC 24 at 43.

the credit of the account may be made to them jointly (so as to be enforceable only by both of them together).[9] But a further promise to honour only instructions given by both account holders has been held to be a separate promise made to each of them, so that the bank was liable to one of them where, without his knowledge or authority, it allowed the other to draw on the account.[10]

3 PROMISES IN FAVOUR OF A THIRD PARTY

This situation differs from the one which has just been discussed in that A makes no promise directly to Y. The only contract is between A and X, and Y is merely an intended, or third party, beneficiary. Suppose that X takes out an insurance policy with the A company in favour of Y. Here Y is not a party to the contract between A and X but a third party beneficiary. An arrangement involving A, X and Y may, moreover, be so constituted that Y is not a beneficiary at all.[11] Suppose that A sells goods to X who directs A to deliver them at Y's warehouse. Here the intention is in all probability not to confer any benefit on Y but simply to tell A how to perform his promise to X. There is a further possibility: Y may not be a mere beneficiary of a contract between A and X, but an immediate party to a *separate* contract between himself and A. An arrangement involving three parties may in law be analysed as consisting of two contracts: a main contract between A and X and a collateral contract between A and Y. Such an analysis has, for example, been adopted where a car belonging to Y was damaged in a road accident and repaired by A (a garage) on the instructions of X (an insurance company). It was held that the main contract to repair the car was between A and X, but that there was also a collateral contract between A and Y under which A was liable in damages for undue delay in carrying out the repairs.[12]

Assuming, however, that the arrangement in question is a contract for the benefit of a third party, the question then arises as to the legal effects of such a contract. In discussing this question, we shall consider in turn the relations between the promisor and the third party, those between the promisor and the promisee, and those between the promisee and the third party.

a Privity of contract

The general rule of English law is that rights arising under a contract can be enforced or relied upon only by the parties to the contract.[13]

---

9 *Brewer v Westminster Bank Ltd* [1952] 2 TLR 568.
10 *Catlin v Cyprus Finance Corpn (London) Ltd* [1983] QB 759.
11 Cf *Thavorn v Bank of Credit and Commerce International S A* [1985] 1 Lloyd's Rep 259.
12 *Charnock v Liverpool Corpn* [1968] 3 All ER 473; cf ante, p 31.
13 *Tweddle v Atkinson* (1861) 1 B & S 393; *Dunlop Pneumatic Tyre Co Ltd v Selfridge & Co Ltd* [1915] AC 847.

There are two main reasons for this so-called doctrine of privity of contract. One is that the third party is usually a gratuitous beneficiary. As such, he could not enforce the promise even if it had been made to him, since he provided no consideration for it;[14] and it is hard to see why he should be better off when the promise is not made to him at all. The second is that the courts have been anxious to preserve the power of the contracting parties to put an end to their contract or to alter it; and if a third party acquired rights under the contract that power would be lost or at any rate very severely restricted.

The most common application of the doctrine of privity is to cases in which A promises X to pay a sum of money to Y. This is the position where X insures his life with A in favour of Y, and the general rule is that Y is not entitled to enforce the policy.[15] Another example is provided by the leading case of *Beswick v Beswick,*[16] where X transferred his business to his nephew A, who promised X that after X's death he would pay £5 per week to X's widow (Y). It was assumed by the House of Lords that the widow could not in her own right enforce the nephew's promise, as it had not been made to her but to her husband.

b Other effects of the contract

Although, under the doctrine of privity, a contract under which A makes a promise to X for the benefit of Y cannot be enforced by Y, it remains binding between A and X. The fact that the promise was made for the benefit of a third party does, however, give rise to a number of special problems.

i *Promisee's remedies*

X may be entitled to an order of specific performance, and if such an order is made A will be compelled to perform in favour of Y. This is what happened in *Beswick v Beswick*. On X's death, his widow Y became his administratrix and so for legal purposes represented him. In her capacity as representative of X she obtained an order directing the nephew (A) to make the promised payments to her in her personal capacity. The result was that a promise in favour of a third party was enforced exactly in accordance with its terms. But this result can only be reached if A's promise is of such a kind that it is specifically enforceable: this requirement would, for example, exclude the remedy where A had promised X to render personal services to Y.[17] Moreover, enforcement of the promise in favour of Y *requires the co-operation of X*. If

---

[14] Ante, pp 31.
[15] *Re Sinclair's Life Policy* [1938] Ch 799. For another, more doubtful, application, see p 86, ante.
[16] [1968] AC 58.
[17] See p 354, post.

X refuses to sue A, Y cannot force him to do so; nor can Y force X to sue for specific performance if X chooses to pursue some other remedy.

The most obvious other remedy is for X to claim damages from A. Such a claim will clearly succeed where A's failure to pay Y had caused loss to X. This would be the position where X was indebted to Y and looked to the payment by A to Y as a means of discharging that debt. X could also show that he had suffered loss if as a result of A's breach he had to spend money in making some other provision for Y: for example, if he had to take out another policy of insurance in favour of Y because his policy with A had been wrongfully repudiated by A. Where X has suffered loss, he is entitled to damages in respect of that loss even though he made the contract both for his own benefit and for that of Y.[18] For example, where a man had booked a package holiday for himself, his wife and his children, but the accommodation provided fell seriously short of that promised, he recovered damages from the tour operator for his mental distress. In assessing those damages, account was taken of the fact that his own distress was increased by witnessing that of his wife and children.[19] But as a general rule X cannot recover substantial damages from A in respect of loss suffered by Y.[20] Thus in *Beswick v Beswick* it was said that the damages recoverable by X's estate would have been only nominal since A's breach had caused no loss to the estate, but only to Y.[1] The rule is subject to a number of exceptions, one of which may provide an alternative explanation for the package holiday case just mentioned. It has been suggested that the booking of family holidays and the ordering of meals in restaurants may call for special treatment,[2] so that the person who makes the booking or orders the meal can recover damages in respect of loss suffered by other members of the party.

As an alternative to damages, X might claim the return of any payment he had made under the contract: for example, in the insurance cases he might sue A for the return of his premiums; or he might claim that A should pay X the policy moneys, ie the sums which under the contract A had promised to pay to Y. But a claim for the return of premiums will often be less advantageous than one for the policy moneys; and if the contract says that these are to be paid to Y it is very doubtful whether they can be successfully claimed by X.[3]

---

[18] See *Radford v De Froberville* [1978] 1 All ER 33.

[19] *Jackson v Horizon Holidays Ltd* [1975] 3 All ER 92, as explained in *Woodar Investment Development Ltd v Wimpey Construction (UK) Ltd* [1980] 1 W L R 277 at 283, 293, 297.

[20] *Woodar Investment* case, supra; cf p 317, post.

[1] [1968] A C especially at 102.

[2] *Woodar Investment* case, supra, at 283; other exceptions arise where X contracts as agent or trustee for a third party.

[3] See *Cleaver v Mutual Reserve Fund Life Association* [1892] 1 Q B 147, criticised in *Coulls v Bagot's Executor and Trustee Co Ltd* [1967] A L R 385 at 410.

An action by X for damages, for return of the money paid by him, or for the sum agreed to be paid under the contract, will not be of any help to Y: the success of such an action would simply lead to a judgment for a sum of money in favour of X. But in the exceptional cases in which X can recover damages in respect of loss suffered by Y, the court could, perhaps, direct X to hold or use the proceeds of the judgment for the benefit of Y. There is some support for this view where A is bound to make a payment to X to enable X to pay off a debt or obligation to Y;[4] and it is possible that a similar order could be made in a case involving a contract for the benefit of a third party.[5]

ii *Position between promisee and third party*

Where A has actually performed in favour of Y, for example by making the promised payment to him, X might claim that Y should hand that payment over to X. It is unlikely that X himself will make such a claim, since this would defeat his intention to benefit Y. But if X has gone bankrupt or died the claim may be put forward for the benefit of his creditors or of the persons entitled under his will. As a general rule claims of this kind will fail, so that Y can keep the money for his own benefit. X (or someone standing legally in his shoes) can only claim the money from Y if Y received it as X's nominee. In such a case Y would not be a true third party beneficiary, but merely a person to whom A was authorised to make a payment (or to render some other performance) due under the contract to X.[6]

X may also claim the money before it has actually been paid over to Y. Often A is quite willing to pay either X or Y, so long as the payment is made in such a way as to discharge him from his liability under the contract. Since our basic assumption is that Y has no enforceable rights under the contract, there is nothing to stop A and X from agreeing to vary the contract, so as to make the money payable to X. Such a variation, however, requires the consent of *both* parties to the contract: A is not bound to pay X merely because X asks him to do so. He would only be bound to do this if the contract on its true construction obliged him to pay Y, or such other person (including X), as X might direct. In cases of doubt, the answer to this question of construction would probably depend on whether it mattered to A whether the payment was received by Y or by someone else. If A is an insurance company, the destination of the payment will usually not matter in the least to the company, whose only concern will be to ensure that its obligation to pay is effectively discharged. On the other hand, if A is Y's close

---

[4] *Allen v Waters* [1935] 1 K B 200; *Cunningham v Harrison*]1973] Q B 942 at 952; but see *Donnelly v Joyce* [1974] Q B 454 at 462-463.

[5] *Jackson v Horizon Holidays Ltd*]1975] 1 W L R 1468 at 1473.

[6] As in *Coulls v Bagot's Executor and Trustee Co Ltd* [1967] A L R 385.

relation, A may have an interest in seeing that the payment is made to
Y, since, if it were diverted to X, A might feel obliged to make some
other provision for Y's support.[7]

c Scope of the doctrine of privity

The doctrine of privity prevents a person from enforcing rights (or
relying on defences) which *arise under* a contract to which he is not a
party. It does not mean that he may not indirectly benefit from the
contract: for example, payment by A of part of Y's debt to X, which X
accepts in full settlement, may discharge that debt.[8] The contract
between A and X may also be one of the circumstances giving Y a right
to sue A in tort. Two such situations call for discussion.

i Liability in negligence

A contract between A and X may give rise to a relationship between A
and Y in which A owes a duty of care to Y: eg if it results in Y's goods
being carried in A's ship. If, in the course of performing that contract,
A negligently damages those goods, he will be liable in tort to Y.[9] On
the same principle, professional advisers, such as surveyors and
solicitors, have been held liable in tort to persons other than the clients
who had engaged them.[10] Perhaps the most controversial extension of
such liability was made in *Junior Books Ltd v Veitchi Co Ltd*,[11] where X
had contracted to build a factory for Y and had then entered into a subcontract with A for the flooring. There was no contract between A and
Y; but it was held that defects in A's work, causing the floor to crack,
would, if due to A's negligence, make him liable in tort to Y.[11a]

Such tort liability is, however, in many ways less extensive than
liability for breach of contract. First, A's liability in tort depends on
fault, while contract liability is often strict.[12] Secondly, A can only be
liable in tort to Y if his negligence in *performing* his contract with X
causes loss to Y: if in the *Junior Books* case A had simply refused to
perform that contract, he would not have been liable in tort to Y[13] even
though his refusal had led to delay in the completion of the factory and
so caused loss of profits to Y. The third, and most important, point is
that A's contract with X does not give rise to a duty of care to Y *merely*
because the breach of the contract causes loss to Y. There must, in

---

7   Cf *Re Stapleton-Bretherton, Weld-Blundell v Stapleton-Bretherton* [1941] Ch 482.

8   *Hirachand Punamchand v Temple* [1911] 2 K B 330.

9   *The Antonis P Lemos* [1985] A C 711.

10 Eg *Ross v Caunters* [1980] Ch 297; *Al Kandari v J R Brown & Co* [1988] 1 All E R 833;
    Yianni v Edwin Evans & Sons [1982] Q B 438.

11 [1983] 1 A C 520.

11a Where there *is* a contract between A and Y, it may define A's duty to Y exhaustively,
    so as to exclude liability in tort, as in *Greater Nottingham Co-operative Society Ltd v Cemen-
    tation Piling and Foundations Ltd* [1988] 2 All E R 971.

12 Post, p 266.

13 Cf *The Zephyr* [1985] 2 Lloyd's Rep 529 at 538.

addition, be a relationship of 'proximity' between A and Y. In the *Junior Books* case there were many special or a unique[13a] factors giving rise to such a relationship: in particular, A was nominated as the flooring sub-contractor by Y, A knew of Y's special requirements, and Y had relied on A's special skills.

These special factors have been emphasised in later cases so as to restrict the scope of the decision in the *Junior Books* case. It has, moreover, been held that Y can only rely on that case as giving him a right of action in tort if he has suffered some physical harm as a result of A's carelessness. In the *Junior Books* case, this requirement was satisfied: the defects in the floor had caused it to crack. But the position is different where A's breach of his contract with X causes no physical harm at all, but only financial loss, to Y.[14] In one case, Y engaged X to sell his car, and X in turn employed A in the matter. A negligently paid the proceeds over to an imposter, so that they were lost to Y. There was no contract between Y and A; and it was held that Y had no claim against A in tort, for to allow such a claim would 'come perilously close to abolishing the doctrine of privity altogether.'[15]

Even where A's breach of his contract with X does result in physical harm, three further requirements normally restrict A's tort liability. First, Y can only sue A in tort for causing damage to property if, when the harm was done, Y was the owner or possessor of the thing in question: it is not enough for him to have agreed to buy the thing from X and to have suffered loss in the sense of having to pay the price in spite of the harm done by A (eg in breach of a contract between A and X to carry the thing to Y).[16] Secondly, the harm must normally be, not to the very thing supplied by A under his contract with X, but to *other* property belonging to Y. Thus where A sold goods to X who resold them to Y, it was held that A was not liable in tort to Y merely because the goods had disintegrated on account of a defect in them amounting to a breach of A's contract with X.[17] Thirdly, even where other property belonging to Y is destroyed or damaged as a result of a defect in A's performance of his contract with X, the damages which Y can recover from A are normally restricted to the value of that property and the profits which could have been derived *from it*: the claim does not extend to further profits which Y could have earned by making use of *the goods supplied by A* under his contract with X if they had not been

---

[13a] *D & F Estates Ltd v Church Comrs for England* [1988] 2 All E R 992 at 1003.

[14] *Tate & Lyle Industries Ltd v Greater London Council* [1983] 2 A C 509 at 530–31; *London Congregational Union Inc v Harriss and Harriss* [1988] 1 All E R 15 at 25; *Simaan General Contracting Co v Pilkington Glass Ltd (No 2)* [1988] 1 All E R 791; cf *Pacific Associates Inc v Baxter* (1988) Times, 28 December.

[15] *Balsamo v Medici* [1984] 1 W L R 951 at 959–960.

[16] *The Aliakmon* [1986] A C 785.

[17] *Aswan Engineering Co v Lupdine Ltd* [1987] 1 W L R 1.

defective.[18] Damages of the latter kind are normally available only in a contractual action, in which the aim of the award is to put the plaintiff into the position in which he would have been if the contract had been performed. In a tort action, that object is merely to put him into the position in which he was before the tort had been committed. The tort damages awarded in the *Junior Books* case did, indeed, relate to defects in the very thing supplied and include items normally recoverable only in a contractual action (such as the cost of making good the very thing supplied, ie the defective floor). But this aspect of the case is best explained by reference to the special or unique circumstances (mentioned above) which gave rise to the duty; and the general rule is that such damages are not available where a stranger to a contract sues one of the contracting parties in tort. The rule is illustrated by a later case in which defective plastering had been done, under a contract between A and X, in a flat which was later let to Y. The House of Lords held that Y could not, in a tort action against A, recover the cost of making good the defects in the plaster.[18a]

ii Intimidation

The tort of intimidation is committed where A, by threats of unlawful conduct directed at X, induces X to act to the detriment of Y. For this purpose, a breach of contract is an unlawful act,[19] so that A would be liable for intimidation to Y if, by threatening to break his contract with X, he induced X to stop doing business with Y. In such a case, Y is not enforcing the contract between A and X:[20] his claim is for damages for the loss which A has inflicted on him by means of his unlawful threat against X.

d Exceptions to the doctrine of privity

Although the doctrine of privity can to some extent be explained on both theoretical and practical grounds,[1] it is also open to criticism. It can cause inconvenience where it prevents enforcement of the contract by the person (Y) who has the greatest interest in enforcing it: this would often be the result of a strict application of the doctrine to commercial transactions involving (as they commonly do) more than two parties. Worse still, it can cause injustice, for it may enable the promisor (A) to break his contract with relative impunity, since there may be no very effective remedy against him: this might be the position if the contract was not specifically enforceable and if the court refused to award X more than nominal damages on the ground that the breach

---

18   *Muirhead v Industrial Tank Specialities Ltd* [1986] QB 507.
18a   *D & F Estates Ltd v Church Comrs for England* [1988] 2 All ER 992.
19   *Rookes v Barnard* [1964] AC 1129.
20   Ibid at 1168, 1208.
1   See p 205, ante.

had caused him no loss.[2] These defects have led the House of Lords to indicate that it might be willing to reconsider the doctrine of privity if legislation for this purpose is not brought forward.[3] In the meantime, the law has mitigated the defects just mentioned by developing a number of exceptions to the doctrine. The most important of these are as follows:

i *Agency, assignment and land law*

Under the law of agency, an agreement between A and X can give rise to a contract between A and Y if X, in making the agreement, acted on behalf of and with the authority of either A or Y. This exception is discussed in chapter 15. Another exception arises where a contractual right between A and X is transferred to Y, who thus becomes entitled to enforce it against A. This process is called assignment and is discussed in chapter 14. Further exceptions to the doctrine of privity exist in the land law. For a detailed account of these exceptions, reference should be made to specialised works on that subject, but one example may be given here. Suppose that A sells a house to X and covenants not to build on an adjoining field which A retains. X then sells the house to Y with the benefit of the covenant. The result is that, if the proper conditions are satisfied, Y will be able to enforce A's promise not to build on the field. All these exceptions are well established and there is relatively little doubt as to their scope.

ii *Trusts of promises*

This is a more controversial exception. When A made a promise to X for the benefit of Y, X was sometimes regarded as trustee for Y of the benefit of A's promise. In that event, Y could sue A on the promise; though he had to join X to the action (as co-plaintiff if X was willing to join or as co-defendant if he was not) so that A was not exposed to the risk of being sued twice on the same promise. This trust device was for example applied where a broker (Y) negotiated a charterparty in which the shipowners (A) promised the charterer (X) to pay a commission to Y. It was held that X was trustee for Y of A's promise, which could therefore be enforced by Y against A.[4] Such a trust may be created even though the contract does not contain the word 'trust' or 'trustee'. The crucial factor, in determining whether there is a trust, is the intention of the parties to the contract and primarily that of the promisee (X).[5]

[2] See p 210, ante.
[3] *Beswick v Beswick* [1968] AC 58 at 72; *Woodar Investment Development Ltd v Wimpey Construction (UK) Ltd* [1980] 1 WLR 277 at 281; *Swain v Law Society* [1983] 1 AC 598 at 611.
[4] *Affréteurs Réunis SA v Leopold Walford (London) Ltd* [1919] AC 801.
[5] *Swain v Law Society* [1983] 1 AC 598 at 620.

The first requirement of such a trust is that X must intend to take the promise for the benefit of Y. This point may seem to be so obvious that it scarcely needs to be stated; but sometimes third parties do try to enforce promises which were not intended for their benefit at all. In one case,[6] a landowner (X) granted a lease of sporting rights to A who promised to keep down rabbits. X then let the land to Y on the terms that X was not to be liable to Y for damage done by rabbits. It was held that X was not trustee of A's promise, since he had taken it for his own benefit and not for the benefit of Y. Conversely, the fact that X did *not* intend the promise to be for his own benefit may support the conclusion that there was a trust in favour of Y.[7]

Secondly, the intention of X to benefit Y must be final and irrevocable. Thus where X took out a life insurance policy for the benefit of his godson Y it was held that there was no trust in favour of Y since the policy contained an option entitling X to surrender it for his own benefit.[8] On the other hand, a trust is not negatived merely because the contract names several beneficiaries between whom X can choose. In one case[9] A promised X to pay an annuity after his death to X's widow or (if X so directed) to his children. It was held (in the absence of a direction to pay the children) that there was a trust in favour of the widow.

Thirdly, a trust will not be created merely because an intention to benefit the third party is shown and no power to revoke that benefit is reserved. There must be an 'intention to create a trust' and this is a most elusive requirement. It appears, in principle, to involve an intention on the part of X, both to confer a benefit on Y, and also to assume fiduciary responsibilities towards him. But the decided cases do not make it at all clear when this requirement is satisfied. One pair of cases will suffice to illustrate the point. In the nineteenth-century case of *Re Flavell*,[9] A and X were carrying on business in partnership. On X's retirement, A promised X to provide after X's death for his widow, Y. It was held that there was a trust of the promise in favour of Y. But more recently in *Re Schebsman*[10] a similar promise, made by A to his retiring employee X for the benefit of the latter's widow Y, was held not to create a trust in her favour (though this decision did not prejudice her as A was in fact ready to make the promised payment to her). Such cases suggest that the courts have become less willing than they once were to apply the trust device to escape from the doctrine of privity. The reason for this change of attitude is that the implication of a trust in favour of Y would make it impossible for A and X to vary or abrogate the contract by mutual consent; and the courts are reluctant to deprive them of this right, unless the intention to create a trust is clearly shown to exist. The courts will most readily infer such an

---

6 *West v Houghton* (1879) 4 C P D 197.

7 *Lyus v Prowsa Developments Ltd* [1982] 2 All ER 953.

8 *Re Sinclair's Life Policy* [1938] Ch 799.

9 *Re Flavell* (1883) 25 Ch D 89.

10 [1944] Ch 83.

intention where X is under some legal obligation to provide for Y: for example where Y is X's employee, the contract of employment requires X to insure Y against accidents and X effects such insurance with company A for Y's benefit.

iii Insurance

The doctrine of privity can be particularly inconvenient in relation to contracts of insurance. In this area many exceptions to the doctrine have therefore been created by legislation. It is, for example, common for the owner of a car to take out a policy of insurance covering, not only himself, but any person driving the car with his consent. By statute, such a person is entitled to the benefit of the policy.[11] Moreover, a motor insurance policy must (and other policies in practice may) cover the policyholder against certain liabilities to third parties. Here the insurance company (A) does not actually promise the policyholder (X) to pay the accident victim (Y). A's promise is rather to pay X any amount which X has to pay Y. Obviously, Y has a substantial interest in the performance of A's promise; and by statute he may in certain circumstances enforce X's right against A.[12] Where Y is the victim of a motor accident, he has further rights under an agreement originally made between the Motor Insurers' Bureau and the Minister of Transport.[13] Under this agreement, the Bureau undertakes to pay the victim any amount which he cannot recover from the driver or insurer, 'in respect of any liability which is required to be covered by a policy of insurance' under the statutory scheme of compulsory third party motor insurance. This agreement may not technically be enforceable by the accident victim.[14] But it can be enforced by the appropriate Minister;[15] and the Bureau has never relied on the doctrine of privity to escape liability under the agreement.

Under the Solicitors Act 1974 a scheme has been set up for the compulsory insurance of solicitors against liability for professional negligence. This takes the form of a contract by which insurers promise the Law Society to provide indemnity insurance for solicitors. The scheme gives rise to rights and duties between the insurers and solicitors, by way of exception to the doctrine of privity.[16]

A further exception to the doctrine exists in relation to life insurance. It is common for a person to insure his or her life for the benefit of his or her spouse or children; and by statute such a policy creates 'a trust in favour of the objects therein named.'[17]

[11] Road Traffic Act 1972, s 148 (4).
[12] Third Parties (Rights against Insurers) Act 1930, s 1; Road Traffic Act 1972, ss 149, 150.
[13] [1964] 2 QB 745 at 770; *White v London Transport Executive* [1971] 2 QB 721.
[14] See *Gardner v Moore* [1984] AC 548 at 556.
[15] See *Gurtner v Circuit* [1968] 2 QB 587.
[16] *Swain v Law Society* [1983] 1 AC 598.
[17] Married Women's Property Act 1882, s 11.

A final group of cases which fall under this heading are those in which several persons have an interest in certain property, and that property is insured by one of them. Under various statutes, the benefit of that insurance may be available to the other persons who have interests in the property. For example, if premises are let to a tenant and insured by him against fire, the landlord can claim under the policy; and vice versa.[18] Again, where a house which has been sold is damaged between contract and conveyance, any insurance money received by the seller must be paid over to the buyer on completion of the purchase, thus indirectly giving the buyer the benefit of the seller's insurance.[19]

iv *Law of Property Act 1925, s 56(1)*

This subsection provides that '*A person may take* an immediate or other interest in land or other property, or *the benefit of any* condition, right of entry, covenant or *agreement over or respecting land or other property* , *although he may not be named as a party to the conveyance or other instrument.*' The italicised words might appear at first sight to suggest that the subsection had abolished the doctrine of privity in all cases of written agreements affecting 'property'. Moreover, the Act provides that, unless the context indicates the contrary, 'property' includes 'any thing in action'.[20] Now a promise by A to X is a 'thing in action' and, accordingly, it was at one time argued that a written promise by A to X to pay money to Y could be enforced by Y against A, by virtue of section 56 (1).[1] But this view was rejected by the House of Lords in *Beswick v Beswick.*[2] It was there held that s 56(1) gave the widow no right in her personal capacity to sue on the promise to pay her an annuity, which had been made to her husband by his nephew. This interpretation was justified primarily by reference to the history of the subsection, which had (with modifications) replaced an earlier enactment.[3] This, in turn, had been passed to change an old rule of common law under which a person could not take certain benefits under a deed inter partes unless he was *named as a party* to the deed. A deed 'inter partes' was one expressed to be 'between A of the first part, B of the second part . . . ' etc. In the case of such a deed, it was often necessary for a person seeking to enforce it to be both *named* (and not merely described, eg as the owner of certain land) and to be named *as a party* (ie he had to be

---

18 Fires Prevention (Metropolis) Act 1774, s 83; *Portavan Cinema Co Ltd v Price and Century Insurance Co* [1939] 4 All E R 601; cf *Mark Rowlands Ltd v Berni Inns Ltd* [1986] Q B 211.
19 Law of Property Act 1925, s 47.
20 Ibid s 205 (1); cf p 223, post.
1 Eg in the Court of Appeal in *Beswick v Beswick* [1966] Ch 538.
2 [1968] A C 58; see p 210, ante.
3 Real Property Act 1845, s 5.

named as 'X of the nth part.') The main purpose of s 56(1) and its predecessor was simply to reverse this old rule: and this point is reflected in the wording of the subsection. It says that a person may take the benefit of an agreement over or respecting property, although he may not '*be named as a party*': not although he may not *be a party*. The general view is that the subsection only applies in favour of persons to whom the instrument purports to make a grant, or with whom it purports to make a covenant:[4] such persons can take the benefit of the instrument even though it does not actually name them. A covenant in favour of 'the owner of Blackacre' would thus fall within its provisions, at least if the owner was an ascertainable person at the time when the covenant was made.[5] But the great majority of promises in favour of third parties are not covered by the subsection.

4 PROMISES PURPORTING TO BIND A THIRD PARTY

a The general rule

As a general rule, a contract between A and X does not bind Y. Where the contract purports to impose some positive obligation on Y, the rule may seem to be too obvious to need stating. Clearly Y cannot be liable to pay A £10 merely because A and X have made a contract to this effect. This follows from the nature of contractual obligations, which are essentially based on consent. But the rule also applies where the contract between A and X simply purports to deprive Y of some right or otherwise to impair Y's freedom of action. For example, a contract between A and X may contain an exemption clause purporting to protect A against liability to Y; and, as we saw in chapter 7,[6] the general rule is that Y is not bound by such a clause if he is not a party to the contract.

The general rule that a person is not bound by a contract to which he is not a party is regarded as an aspect of the doctrine of privity. It is subject to a number of exceptions; and there is also an important group of cases which falls outside the scope of the rule.

b Exceptions to the general rule

Most of the exceptions to the doctrine of privity only entitle a third party to the benefit of a contract and do not subject him to any obligations under it. No one has, for example, suggested that a third party can be bound by a contract under the trust exception. But under some

---

[4] *White v Bijou Mansions* [1937] Ch 610; affd [1938] Ch 351.
[5] *Re Ecclesiastical Comrs Conveyance* [1936] Ch 430.
[6] See p 87, ante.

of the other exceptions, a person can be bound (no less than entitled) under a contract to which he is not directly a party. The most important of these is agency (to be discussed in chapter 15): it is perfectly possible for Y to become liable to A under a contract made between A and X, if X in making the contract acted as A's or Y's agent. The point has already been made in relation to exemption clauses, which may also restrict the rights of a third party on a number of other grounds, discussed in chapter 7.[7] Some of the exceptions to the doctrine of privity which are recognised by the land law are also relevant in the present context. For example, if Y buys land from X, he may be bound by a restrictive covenant affecting the land even though that covenant was made between X and A, an adjoining occupier.

c Scope of the general rule

The general rule states that Y is not bound by a contract between A and X, so that its terms cannot be enforced against him. But the existence of the contract may restrict Y's freedom of action in a number of other ways. The most important of these are as follows:

i *Contract creating proprietary interests or possessory rights*

This class of cases is best discussed by reference to two illustrations, which are not intended to be exhaustive. Suppose first that X agrees to sell a Rembrandt to A and then agrees to sell the same painting to Y. Since the contract between X and A is specifically enforceable,[8] its effect in equity is to confer on A a proprietary interest in the painting; and this would prevail against Y unless he bought without notice of the earlier contract.[9] Similar reasoning applies where possession of the subject-matter is transferred under the contract. Suppose that X hires his car out to A and then sells it to Y. Although Y is not bound to perform any obligations which X may have undertaken in his contract with A, he is nevertheless bound to respect A's right to retain possession of the car in accordance with the terms of A's contract with X.

ii *Interference with contractual rights*

In the cases put above, A had, under his contract with X, acquired a proprietary interest in, or possession of, the subject-matter of the contract. Greater difficulty arises where A has no such proprietary or

---

[7] See p 88, ante.

[8] Post, p 352.

[9] Cf *Swiss Bank Corpn v Lloyd's Bank Ltd* [1982] A C 584 at 598, 613 (where the actual decision was that there was *no* specifically enforceable agreement); *The Stena Nautica (No 2)* [1982] 2 Lloyd's Rep 336 (where specific enforcement was again refused).

possessory interest, but does have some commercial interest in the disposition of the subject-matter. This possibility can be discussed by considering some further illustrations.

First, A may enter into a contract with X which imposes restrictions on subsequent dealings with the subject-matter. In one case,[10] X bought a new car and covenanted with A (the British Motor Trade Association) not to resell the car for one year, without first offering it to A at a price not above the list price. The purpose of the covenant was to stop profiteering at a time when cars were in very short supply. Within the year, Y, with knowledge of the covenant, bought the car from X and he was held liable to A. The liability was not for breach of contract, but in tort for knowingly interfering with A's contractual rights against X, ie with A's right to have the car offered to him. Put generally, the point is that contracts do not only create rights and duties between the contracting parties. They also impose an obligation on third parties not to interfere with the performance of contractual duties of which they are aware. But this principle will not apply to all cases in which a contract between A and X imposes restrictions on subsequent dealings with the subject-matter and Y then, with knowledge of the restrictions, acts inconsistently with them. Suppose that a manufacturer (A) sells goods to a wholesaler (X) who enters into a price maintenance agreement with A. By this agreement, X undertakes (i) not to resell the goods above or (more commonly) below a specified price and (ii) to extract a similar undertaking from any retailer (Y) to whom he may resell the goods. If X resells to Y and extracts the undertaking, he *performs* his contract with A, so that Y can no longer be guilty of wrongful interference with it. Nor can A at common law sue Y on the contract between X and Y, since A is not a party to it.[11] But by statute A can enforce the price maintenance agreement against Y provided that Y has actual notice of it.[12] Of course it is assumed that the agreement is itself valid. Most *minimum* resale price maintenance agreements are now void so that they cannot be enforced against any one.[13]

A second type of contract which may affect a third party is one which requires the *use* of a particular thing for its performance. The most common commercial illustration is the time or voyage charter-party. Under such a contract the charterer does not get possession of the ship. The contract amounts simply to an undertaking by the shipowner to provide a service: namely to carry cargo in the particular ship which has been chartered. Now a ship may first be chartered by X to A and

[10] *British Motor Trade Association v Salvadori* [1949] Ch 556.
[11] *Dunlop Pneumatic Tyre Co Ltd v Selfridge & Co Ltd* [1915] AC 847.
[12] Resale Prices Act 1976, s 26.
[13] Ibid ss 9, 14.

then (while the charterparty is still in force) she may be sold by X to Y. The question then arises whether A can enforce his rights under the charterparty in any way against Y. One case supports the view that the charterparty between A and X gave A an equitable interest in the ship which he could enforce by restraining a purchaser with notice of the charterparty from using the ship inconsistently with it.[14] But this view was criticised, particularly because an equitable interest can be enforced against a purchaser with only 'constructive notice' of it: that is, against somebody who did not actually know of the contract between A and X, but who could have discovered it by making reasonable enquiries. This doctrine of constructive notice works well enough in relation to contracts for the acquisition of interests in land which are only concluded and performed after careful investigations. But its introduction into the field of commercial contracts, which are much more quickly made and performed, is generally regarded as undesirable. Hence, in a latter case of the same kind, the argument that the charterer had an equitable interest in the ship was rejected.[15] But the case leaves open the possibility that Y may be liable in tort to A for wrongfully interfering with the contract between A and X.[16] The advantage of this approach is that Y is only liable in tort if at the time of his contract with X he had *actual knowledge* of the earlier contract between A and X. He is not liable if at that time he had only constructive notice of the earlier contract; nor even if he acquired actual knowledge of it between making his own contract with X and calling for its performance.[17] Hence the doctrine of constructive notice is kept out of this branch of the law; while justice is done by preventing Y from using the ship inconsistently with a charterparty of which he knew at the time of his purchase, and the existence of which presumably affected the price he paid.

---

14 *Lord Strathcona SS Co v Dominion Coal* [1926] AC 108; it is now clear that such an interest only arises where the contract is specifically enforceable: see p 220, ante.

15 *Port Line Ltd v Ben Line Steamers Ltd* [1958] 2 QB 146.

16 As in *British Motor Trade Association v Salvadori* [1949] Ch 556, see p 221, ante.

17 See *Swiss Bank Corpn v Lloyd's Bank Ltd* [1979] Ch 548 at 568–569, 569–573; varied [1982] AC 584 at 598; affd [1982] AC 584 at 610.

Chapter 14

Transfer of contractual rights

A contract can be regarded in two ways: as the source of an obligation and as an asset. Suppose that A buys goods from X for £100 payable in a month's time. From one point of view, the effect of the contract is to oblige A to do something, ie to pay X £100. From another point of view, A's promise to pay is an asset and can be dealt with as such by X. For example, X may go to his banker Y and ask Y to advance money at once, on the strength of A's promise to pay the £100. If Y agrees to do this, he may ask X to transfer to him the rights which X has against A under the original contract of sale. This process of transferring contractual rights is called 'assignment'. It is effected by a transaction between only two parties. In the above example, these are X, who will be called the creditor or assignor, and Y, who will be called the assignee. The important point is that the debtor (A) is not a party to the transaction: in other words, an assignment does not require the consent of the debtor. The effect of an assignment is to transfer the assignor's rights to the assignee, who thus becomes entitled to sue the debtor on the contract.

The development of the law on this topic has been profoundly influenced by the different approaches to it adopted at common law and in equity. Even today, the subject cannot be understood without some knowledge of the position before the merger of common law and equity in 1875, when the Judicature Act 1873 came into force.

1 LAW AND EQUITY

Before 1875 common law and equity had different substantive rules on the subject of assignment. The two systems were also administered in separate courts, and this gave rise to procedural difficulties in enforcing an assignee's rights.

a Substantive differences

We must begin by distinguishing between *choses in possession* and *choses in action*. The former are things that can be physically seized; the latter are rights that can only be asserted by bringing legal proceedings. A contractual right, eg to the payment of £100, is a chose in action. The person to whom the money is owed cannot simply seize it; he must bring an action for the amount. At common law, choses in action could not be assigned. It was thought (or said) that such assignment might lead to officious intermeddling in litigation;[1] and such intermeddling formerly constituted a wrong, known as 'maintenance', or as 'champerty' if the intermeddler was to share in the proceeds of the litigation.[2] Equity, however, did not regard the assignee as an officious intermeddler,[3] but rather as a person who had acquired an interest in property. It therefore enforced assignments of choses in action. Hence the basic rule was that choses in action were not assignable at common law, but were assignable in equity.

There were, however, exceptions to the common law rule; and these still exist in the present law. The most important relates to negotiable instruments. The nature of such instruments will be more fully explained later in this chapter;[4] the only point to be made here is that they were regarded as transferable at common law. The common law, moreover, recognises at least three methods by which someone other than the original creditor can become entitled to sue the original debtor. The first of these is *novation*. This is a contract between debtor, creditor and a third party, by which it is agreed that the debt will henceforth be owed, not to the creditor, but to the third party. Assuming that the third party has provided consideration for the debtor's new promise to pay him, he can enforce that promise. The second common law method has no accepted technical name but may be called *acknowledgment*. The creditor asks his debtor to pay a third party and the debtor agrees to do so and notifies the third party. The result is that the third party can sue the debtor; and it seems that he can do so even though he has not provided any consideration for the debtor's promise.[5] Thirdly, the creditor can give the third party a *power of attorney*, making him his agent to sue the debtor on the creditor's behalf and freeing him from an agent's usual liability to account to his principal (the creditor) for the proceeds of the action. None of these common law methods, however, quite do the work of assignment. The first two require the consent of the debtor; and the third has two disadvantages: as a general rule, it is revocable by the creditor, and it is often revoked by his death.[6]

b Procedural difficulties

To understand these difficulties it is first necessary to draw yet a further distinction, namely that between legal and equitable choses in action.

---

[1] *Fitzroy v Cave* [1905] 2 K B 364 at 372.
[2] P 152, ante; see now Criminal Law Act 1967 ss 13, 14.
[3] *Wright v Wright* (1750) 1 Ves Sen 409 at 411.
[4] See p 235, post.
[5] *Shamia v Joory* [1958] 1 Q B 448.
[6] See pp 263–264, post.

A legal chose in action was one which could be sued for in a common law court, such as a debt due under a contract. An equitable chose in action was a right which could only be sued for in the Court of Chancery, such as the right to receive the income of a trust fund. Where the assignment was of an equitable chose, there was no procedural difficulty in enforcing it. The assignee could simply sue the trustee in the Court of Chancery for the income which had been assigned; and if the trustee were later sued in the same Court by the assignor, he could make good his defence by relying on the assignment and on his payment to the assignee. Where, on the other hand, the assignment was of a legal chose, the position was more complicated. Equity could not simply allow the assignee to sue the debtor for the debt in the Court of Chancery. For one thing, that court did not enforce ordinary legal debts. For another, such a course could cause hardship to the debtor. If he were later sued again in a common law court by the assignor for the same debt, he would have to go to the trouble of taking separate proceedings in Chancery to restrain the common law action. To avoid these difficulties, equity allowed the assignee to use the name of the assignor for the purpose of suing the debtor in a common law court; and if the assignor refused to allow his name to be used for this purpose the Court of Chancery could compel him to do so. In this way effect was given to the assignment without exposing the debtor to the risk of a second action by the assignor, whose right against the debtor would have been consumed by the original action, brought in his name.

2 EFFECTS OF THE JUDICATURE ACT 1873

This Act affected the law as to assignment in two ways.

a Removal of procedural difficulties

The procedural difficulties mentioned above disappeared when a new High Court (created by the Act) took over the functions of the old courts of common law and equity, and administered both systems concurrently. The assignee of a chose in action could now sue for it in the High Court. He could do so whether the chose was a legal or an equitable one, since all Divisions of the High Court could now recognise both legal and equitable claims. Nor need the debtor fear a subsequent action in a different court, since there was now only a single system of courts. Hence the requirement that the assignee of a legal chose must sue in the name of the assignor became obsolete;[7] though, as we shall see, it is still sometimes desirable to have the assignor as well as the

[7] *Weddell v JA Pearce & Major* [1988] Ch 26 at 40.

assignee before the court in any action brought by either of them against the debtor.

b Statutory assignment

The state of affairs outlined above was recognised by a provision in the Judicature Act 1873 which is now reproduced in s 136(1) of the Law of Property Act 1925. This provides that an assignment of a 'debt or other legal thing in action' transfers to the assignee the legal right to the debt or thing in action; and that the assignee can sue for the debt in his own name. The assignment, however, only has these effects if three conditions laid down in the statute are satisfied: the assignment must be 'absolute', it must be 'by writing under the hand of the assignor', and written notice of the assignment must have been given to the debtor. If these requirements are *not* satisfied the assignment may still be valid under the old rules of equity. It is therefore still necessary to distinguish between statutory assignments and equitable assignments. An equitable assignment may be an assignment of a legal or of an equitable chose: it is simply one which fails to comply with the statutory requirements. The most important effect of the distinction is this: if the assignment is statutory, the assignee can sue the debtor *alone*, but if it is equitable he may have to *join the assignor* to the action. He will have to do so, first, in those cases in which, under the old rules of equity, he had to sue in the name of the assignor: that is, if the chose is legal but not if it is equitable. Secondly, he will have to join the assignor whenever the latter retains an interest in the subject-matter of the action. The first of these rules is simply an historical survival. But the second reflects an important principle: that both assignor and assignee must be brought before the court when the absence of one of them might prejudice the debtor. This principle has been carried into effect by judicial interpretation of the requirement stated in s 136(1) that the assignment must be 'absolute'.

i 'Absolute assignment'

The courts have tended to classify assignments as absolute or non-absolute with an eye on the consequences. When it was desirable to have the assignor before the court, they have said that the assignment was not absolute—with the result that the assignment was only equitable so that the assignor had to be joined to the action. A convenient starting point for the discussion is the distinction, drawn in s 136(1), between absolute assignments and assignments 'by way of charge'. The distinction may be illustrated by the following example. A is X's tenant at a rent of £100 per month. X borrows £500 from Y and, as security for the loan, he assigns to Y his right to the monthly rent due from A. Of course X and Y do not intend that A is to go on paying Y after Y's loan to X (together with interest) has been repaid; and they may provide for this in one of two ways. First, they may say that A is to pay Y *'until Y's loan to X has been repaid'*. In that case, neither A nor the court could (in the absence of X) tell how much (if anything) ought to be paid by A to Y. For X might have used money from another source to pay off the loan to Y and the question whether he has done so cannot be satisfactorily determined either by A or by the court in the absence of X. As it is thus desirable to have X before the court, the assignment will be classified as not absolute (but by way of charge), with the result that X must be joined to the action.[8] Secondly, X and Y may say that, when Y's loan to X has been repaid, the right to receive the rent from A is *to be reassigned* to X. Here A and the court have (even in the absence of X) no difficulty in knowing whether A is bound to pay X or Y. For the crucial point is not whether X has paid off the loan made by Y, but simply whether Y has reassigned to X the right to receive the rent from A. The reassignment will only bind A when he receives notice of it: until then he can safely pay Y, and the court can safely give judgment in favour of Y, even in the absence of X. As X is not a necessary party to the action, the assignment is absolute so that Y can sue A without joining X as a party to the action.[9] Of course, if the debt had been repaid, Y's failure to reassign might be a breach of contract between him and X; but such a breach would not affect the question whether A was bound to pay X or Y.

The reason why an assignment by way of charge is not absolute is that it will *automatically* come to an end on the occurrence of a condition subsequent, viz, the discharge of the assignor's debt to the assignee. The same reasoning can apply to other conditions: eg if X assigns rent due from A to his son Y 'so long as Y continues his studies at Oxford.' Here A will want to have the question whether Y is still continuing those studies settled in such a way that neither X nor Y can subsequently dispute it. Hence it is desirable to have both X and Y before the court; and the assignment will be classified as not absolute in order to produce this result. Similar reasoning would apply where the condition was precedent:[10] eg where the assignment was expressed to take effect only 'when Y begins his studies at Oxford.'[11]

It is also settled that an assignment of part of a debt is not absolute.[12] When X assigns to Y £50 out of the £100 which A owes to X, A does not have any difficulty in determining how much he is bound to pay respec-

8 Cf *Durham Bros v Robertson* [1898] 1 QB 765.

9 Cf *Tancred v Delagoa Bay Rly* (1889) 23 QBD 239.

10 See ante, p 24 for the distinction between conditions precedent and subsequent.

11 Cf *The Halcyon The Great* [1984] 1 Lloyd's Rep 283.

12 *Williams v Atlantic Assurance Co Ltd* [1933] 1 KB 81 at 100.

tively to X and Y. But if Y could sue A without joining X, A might be prejudiced in another way; for he might want to deny that he was liable to pay at all. Suppose that Y made a claim and A wanted to raise the defence that the contract had been procured by fraud, or that he was exonerated by X's breach. Even if he could establish such a defence in the absence of X, he would then have to establish it all over again if he were later sued for the other £50 by X. Obviously, this hardship would be even more severe if X by a series of assignments had split the debt into (say) ten or more parts. To avoid this hardship *all* the interested parties must join in the action. It follows that even the original creditor cannot sue for his part without joining the assignee or assignees.[13]

ii *'Debt or other legal thing in action'*

A 'debt' within s 136(1) is a fixed sum due under contract or otherwise. The phrase 'other legal thing in action' is not confined to legal (as opposed to equitable) choses in action. It means any right which, though formerly not assignable at common law, was assignable in equity by the ordinary process of equitable assignment.[14] But where some special statutory provision governs the transfer of rights, that provision, and that provision only, has to be complied with. Thus 136(1) does not apply to transfers of bills of lading, policies of life and marine insurance, and shares in companies, all such transfers being regulated by special statutory provisions.[15]

iii *Assignor disputing validity of the assignment*

The assignor may want to dispute the validity of the assignment: for example, on the ground that it was procured by fraud, or made in pursuance of a contract which was broken by the assignee or which was ineffective. Here the only substantial dispute will be between assignor and assignee, the debtor being only concerned to pay whichever of them turns out to be entitled to the debt. In such a case s 136(1) provides for a form of proceedings in which the debtor drops out of the dispute and the issue is left to be contested by the real protagonists in the case ie the assignor and the assignee.

3 ASSIGNMENT DISTINGUISHED FROM AUTHORITY TO PAY

The essential feature of an assignment is that it is a transfer of a debt to the assignee. So long as the assignor's intention to make such a transfer

---

13 *Walter and Sullivan Ltd v J Murphy & Son Ltd* [1955] 2 QB 584.
14 *Torkington v Magee* [1902] 2 KB 427 at 430 (revsd on another ground [1903] 1 KB 644).
15 Bills of Lading Act 1855, s 1; Policies of Assurance Act 1867; Marine Insurance Act 1906, s 50; Companies Act 1985, s 182(1).

is clear, no particular words need be used to constitute an assignment. Generally an assignment will take the form of a communication between assignor and assignee; but this is not necessary. A direction to the debtor may amount to an assignment, so long as the debtor is thereby 'given to understand that the debt has been made over by the creditor to some third person.'[16] Where the assignment takes this form, it must, however, also be communicated to the assignee.[17] The exact reason for this requirement is obscure, though it can perhaps be justified as preserving the essential nature of an assignment as a transaction between assignor and assignee.

Although an assignment may take the shape of a direction to the debtor, it is not every such direction that amounts to an assignment. The direction may amount only to an authority to the debtor to pay the third party. This means that the debtor will be discharged if he pays the third party, but the third party will not acquire any rights against the debtor. The point may be illustrated by reference to the common case of a person who draws a cheque on his bank in favour of a third party. This is regarded as a direction to the bank to pay the third party, so that the bank is justified in debiting the customer's account if it pays the third party; and if it refuses to pay him it may be liable to the customer for breach of contract. But the cheque is not an assignment of part of the customer's bank balance, so that the payee does not acquire any right which he can enforce directly against the bank.[18]

4 FORMALITIES

A statutory assignment must be 'by writing under the hand of the assignee'.[19] An assignment which is not statutory may, however, still be effective as an equitable assignment.

Equity laid down no formal requirements for assignments, and the general rule is that no writing or other form is necessary for the validity of an equitable assignment. Such an assignment can therefore be made orally. This general rule is however subject to a number of exceptions. By statute a 'disposition of an equitable interest' has to be in writing,[20] and this requirement will generally apply to assignments of equitable choses. Other statutes provide for the registration of certain assignments:[1] the purpose of these provisions is to safeguard a person's creditors against the risk that he may secretly assign away all (or a class) of

---

16 *William Brandt's Sons & Co v Dunlop Rubber Co* [1905] A C 454 at 462.
17 *Re Hamilton* (1921) 124 L T 737.
18 Cf Bills of Exchange Act 1882, s 53(1).
19 Law of Property Act 1925, s 136(1).
20 Law of Property Act 1925, s 53(1).
 1 Companies Act 1985, ss 395, 396; Insolvency Act 1986, s 344.

the debts owed to him. Finally, a contract may provide that the rights arising under it are only to be assigned by a written document; and it seems that such a provision must be complied with before an effective assignment can be made.

5 NOTICE TO THE DEBTOR

An equitable assignment is perfectly valid between assignor and assignee even though no notice of it has been given to the debtor.[2] Nevertheless there are three reasons why notice to the debtor should, if possible, be given.

First, the notice may turn the assignment into a statutory assignment and so enable the assignee to sue the debtor without joining the assignor as a party to the action. To have this effect, the notice must be in writing. It may be given by either the assignor or the assignee.[3]

Secondly, the notice perfects the assignee's title as against the debtor.[4] Once the debtor has received notice of the assignment, he is bound to pay the assignee. If he disregards the notice and pays the assignor, he runs the risk of having to make a further payment to the assignee.[5] For this purpose, the notice does not have to be in any particular form: it may thus be given orally.

Thirdly, notice is important to determine questions of priorities between competing assignees. Suppose that a debt of £100 is assigned to Y as security for a loan of £75 and then to Z as security for a further loan of £75. The rule is that Y and Z rank in the order in which they give notice to the debtor.[6] If the right which is assigned is equitable, the notice must be in writing;[7] but where the chose is legal even an oral notice will secure priority.

6 CONSIDERATION

An assignment is primarily a transfer of property, and as such it may be valid without consideration. Just as X can make a gift of a car to Y, so X can make a gift to Y of the £100 which A owes to X. Nevertheless, there is much dispute on the question exactly when a gratuitous assignment of a chose in action is binding. There are two reasons why this

2 *Holt v Heatherfield Trust Ltd* [1942] 2 K B 1.
3 *Holt v Heatherfield Trust Ltd* [1942] 2 K B 1.
4 *Warner Bros Records Inc v Rollgreen Ltd* [1976] Q B 430.
5 *Brice v Bannister* (1878) 3 Q B D 569.
6 *Dearle v Hall* (1828) 3 Russ 1.
7 Law of Property Act 1925, s 137(3).

question gives rise to so much difficulty. The first is that it is often hard to tell the difference between an actual assignment of a chose in action and a promise to make such an assignment. A mere promise to give is, of course, only binding if the requisites of a valid contract are fulfilled. Secondly, an attempt to make a gift may fail because the steps required by law to make it effective have not been taken. Here the rule is that equity will not perfect an imperfect gift: it will not, in other words, compel the donor to do what is necessary to make the gift effective.[8] Such compulsion would only be exercised if the attempt to make a gift could be construed as a promise to make a gift, *and* if that promise was binding as a contract. Here again, consideration would be necessary. Indeed the rule of equity was stricter than that of the common law. Equity would not aid a 'volunteer',[9] so that the mere presence of nominal consideration, or of a seal, was not enough to induce equity to perfect an imperfect gift.

There were, therefore, under the old law, and still are in the present law, cases in which an assignment must be supported by consideration. Even where this is the position, the point that there was no consideration is, however, not one which can be taken by *the debtor*.[10] He has to pay the debt in any event and is only concerned to ensure that he pays it to a person who can give a good discharge. The cases with which we are concerned are those in which *the assignor* wishes to dispute the assignment on the ground that it is gratuitous: in other words, where it is claimed that the debt should not be paid to the assignee, but to the assignor (or, more probably, to those who legally represent the assignor on his death or bankruptcy). The cases may be divided into three categories: those in which an attempt is made to assign rights which are not yet in existence, those in which the purported assignment amounts to an incomplete gift, and those in which it amounts to a completed gift.

a Attempts to assign future rights

An assignment is the present transfer of a contractual right, and there can be no such transfer of a right which does not yet exist. An attempt to assign such a right can only operate as a promise to assign and will therefore have to be supported by consideration.[11] This would, for example, be the position where a person purported to assign the benefit of a contract which had not yet actually been concluded and which he merely expected to make. On the other hand there may be a present right under an existing contract to a future payment and such a right

---

[8] *Milroy v Lord* (1862) 4 De G F & J 264.
[9] See p 2a, ante.
[10] *Walker v Bradford Old Bank* (1884) 12 Q B D 511.
[11] *Glegg v Bromley* [1912] 3 K B 474.

can no doubt be assigned.[12] For example, a landlord can assign rent which will become due on a future day under an existing lease. Such an assignment will be effective without consideration provided that it amounts to a completed gift, in accordance with the rules and distinctions to be discussed below.

b Incomplete gifts

The notion of an incomplete gift can most readily be understood by reverting to the simple case of the gift of a chattel, such as a picture. Here the law provides two ways in which the gift may effectively be made: by delivery or by deed of gift.[13] If the donor fails to make the gift in one of these two ways, the gift is incomplete. This would, for example, be the position if the donor simply wrote to the donee, saying 'I hereby give you the picture hanging over my mantelpiece.' Similar reasoning may apply to the gift of incorporeal property. In the leading case of *Milroy v Lord*[14] the owner of shares in a company wanted to make a gift of them and for that purpose executed a deed of gift. But the only way in which the legal title to the shares could be transferred was by the execution of an 'instrument of transfer' followed by registration in the books of the company. Since these steps had not been taken, the gift was incomplete; and this will always be the case when *something more must be done by the donor to transfer the subject-matter* of the gift to the donee.

Now any attempt to apply this reasoning to the assignment of an ordinary contractual right comes up against this difficulty. At common law there could be no assignment, and hence no transfer at all, of a chose in action. In equity, there were no rules specifying *how* an assignment must be executed, except for the statutory requirement that a disposition of an equitable interest must be in writing.[15] At first sight, one might therefore suppose that *any* assignment (or in the case of an equitable interest any written assignment) was sufficient to transfer the property to the assignee and that consideration was *never* necessary. On the other hand where the assignment was of a legal chose it could be said that the assignor always had to do 'something more' to transfer the property, namely to allow his name to be used in an action against the debtor in a common law court. This argument at first sight leads to the view that consideration should *always* be necessary for the validity of an assignment of a legal chose. In fact, the courts did not accept either of these arguments. They sometimes upheld and sometimes struck down gratuitous assignments of choses in action. The test of validity was not

---

12 Eg *Hughes v Pump House Hotel Co Ltd* [1902] 2 K B 190.
13 *Cochrane v Moore* (1890) 25 Q B D 57.
14 (1862) 4 De G F & J 264.
15 Law of Property Act 1925, s 53(1), reproducing Statute of Frauds 1677, s 9.

whether the assignee could sue without the co-operation of the assignor. The test was whether he had made a completed gift.

c Completed gifts

The question whether an assignment is a completed gift is one to which no simple answer can be given. The answer depends on whether the assignment is statutory or equitable; and, if equitable, on the reason why it falls into this category.

i Statutory assignment

A statutory assignment is a completed gift, so that consideration is not necessary for its validity.[16] As the statute provides that such an assignment transfers the legal right to the chose in action to the assignee, there is obviously nothing more that the assignor has to do to transfer the property.

ii Equitable assignments

An assignment may be equitable (as opposed to statutory) for a number of reasons.

First, written notice of the assignment may not have been given to the debtor. In this case the assignment may be valid without consideration.[17] The reason is that notice may be given by the assignee, so that there is nothing more that the assignor *must* do to transfer the property.

Secondly, the assignment itself may not be in writing. Here one possible view is that the assignor has not done all that is required of him to transfer the property since he has not executed a statutory assignment (or a document which the assignee can turn into such an assignment by giving notice). Hence, it is said, the gift is incomplete.[18] The other view is that, although the statute specifies a way in which a transfer of a chose in action *may* be made, it does not in terms say that such a transfer *must* be made in that way. Hence an oral assignment may still be a completed gift in equity, if the intention to make such a gift is clear.[19] The latter seems to be the preferable view, since there is nothing in the statute to restrict the effects of assignments in equity; and equity laid down no requirements as to the manner of making assignments. It will be recalled that a gift of a chattel may be made in two ways, and it would not be surprising or odd if a gift of a chose in action could also be made in two ways, by statutory and by equitable assignment.

[16] *Harding v Harding* (1886) 17 Q B D 442.
[17] *Holt v Heatherfield Trust Ltd* [1942] 2 K B 1.
[18] *Olsson v Dyson* (1969) 120 C L R 365.
[19] *German v Yates* (1915) 32 T L R 52.

Thirdly, the assignment may not be absolute. Where it is not absolute because it is of part of a debt, there seems to be no reason in principle why the assignment should not be a completed gift. This could, for example, be the position where X assigned to Y half the rent due to him from A. Where the assignment is by way of charge, on the other hand, it would not be intended as a gift at all, but as security for a loan by the assignee to the assignor. This would usually provide consideration for the assignment: the consideration would consist either in the making of the loan or, if it had already been made, in the assignee's forbearance to enforce the loan.[20] An assignment might also fail to be absolute because it is made subject to some other condition. Here the position would seem to be that the assignment can be a complete gift if the condition can be performed without the co-operation of the assignor; but, if the condition requires some further act of the assignor, the gift would be imperfect until that act had been done. For example, an assignment to pay for work *already* done (and so constituting past consideration) would not be a completed gift if it were made 'subject to inspection and approval' of the work by the assignor.[1]

7 THE ASSIGNEE'S TITLE

The basic principle is that the position of the assignee, as against the debtor, should be no better than that of assignor. The object of the principle is to safeguard the debtor from the prejudice which he would suffer if he had to pay more to the assignee than he would have had to pay to the assignor. Hence the rule is that an assignee takes 'subject to . . . equities'.[2] The phrase is a little misleading, in that the debtor can rely against the assignee on legal no less than on equitable defences. The rule and its limits can be illustrated by the following examples.

Suppose that A agrees to buy a car from X for £2,000 and X assigns to Y the benefit of A's promise to pay the £2,000. In an action by Y, A can rely on such defences as the following: that he was induced to buy the car by the fraud of X;[3] or that X had failed to deliver the car;[4] or that (before notice of the assignment was received) A and X had rescinded the contract by mutual consent. A more difficult situation arises if the car which is delivered to A lacks qualities which X said it had, with the result that A suffers loss. The untruth of X's statement

20 See p 34, ante.
 1 Cf *Re McArdle* [1951] Ch 669.
 2 *Mangles v Dixon* (1852) 3 H L Cas 702 at 732.
 3 Cf *Pickersgill Sons Ltd v London and Provincial Marine and General Insurance Co Ltd* [1912] 3 K B 614 (non-disclosure).
 4 Cf *Tooth v Hallet* (1869) 4 Ch App 242.

about the car may amount to a breach of contract or only to a misrepresentation. In the former case, there is no doubt that A can reduce his liability to Y by the amount of the loss.[5] In the latter case, A is entitled to rescind the contract and, if he does so, he can avoid liability to Y. But he may have lost the right to rescind, and in a case where this was the position it was held that A could not rely against Y on the loss which he had suffered as a result of the fraud of X.[6] This seems to be a regrettable result as it cuts across the policy that the right assigned should not be worth more in the hands of the assignee than it would have been worth in the hands of the assignor; and the preferable view is that A should be able to rely *by way of defence* on loss suffered through the fraud of X, even in an action brought by Y. Of course, if, in the above cases, A suffers loss in excess of £2,000 he cannot *claim* the excess from Y since Y himself is not guilty of breach of contract or of fraud. The loss can only be relied on to reduce or extinguish Y's claim. Any excess must be claimed from X.

So far it has been assumed the only transaction between A and X is the contract, the benefit of which has been assigned to Y. But A may wish to set up against Y a debt which has become due to him from X under a second, independent transaction. For example, X may lend £100 to A and assign the debt to Y. Later, A may sell goods to X for £125; and when A is sued by Y for the £100 he may rely on the fact that £125 has become due to him from X (and has not been paid) under the sale. In substance A is here relying on the sale as a kind of payment of the original loan; so that the rules (already discussed)[7] as to payment by the debtor to the assignor after notice of the assignment apply to determine the effect of the later transaction. In other words, A's defence will succeed if he entered into the sale before he had notice that the original debt of £100 had been assigned, but not if he entered into the sale after he had such notice.[8] In the latter case A suffers no hardship. He cannot expect to pay off the £100 which X had lent him by delivering goods to X under a contract of sale made after having had notice that the £100 was no longer owed to X but was owed to Y.

8 NEGOTIABILITY DISTINGUISHED FROM ASSIGNMENT

Certain documents are, by the custom of merchants, negotiable instruments. The most important such document is the bill of exchange. This

---

[5] Cf *Government of Newfoundland v Newfoundland Rly* (1888) 13 App Cas 199.
[6] *Stoddart v Union Trust Ltd* [1912] 1 K B 181.
[7] See p 230, ante.
[8] Cf *Stevens v Venables* (1862) 30 Beav 625.

takes the form of a written order by X (the drawer) on A (the drawee), requiring A to pay a sum of money either to X or to a named third person (the payee) or to bearer. When A accepts the order he becomes liable as acceptor on the bill. A common type of bill of exchange is a cheque, which is a bill of exchange drawn on a banker payable on demand.[9] The rules which regulate the transfer of a negotiable instrument differ in a number of ways from those which govern the ordinary assignment of a chose in action.

First, a negotiable instrument is transferable by delivery. If it is payable to bearer, delivery is all that is necessary. If it is payable to a named person, the transfer requires both indorsement (ie the payee's signature) and delivery. The transfer does not need to be in writing, nor is it necessary to give written notice to the debtor.

Secondly, the transferee of a negotiable instrument does not take 'subject to equities' if he is a 'holder in due course'. Such a holder is a person who has in good faith given value for the instrument, provided that the instrument is valid and regular on its face, not overdue and not to the holder's knowledge dishonoured. There is a presumption that a holder is a holder in due course. This presumption does not apply where the instrument is affected by fraud, duress or illegality, but even then the holder can sue on the instrument if he proves that he gave value for it in good faith.[10] The reason for all these rules is that, in commercial practice, a bill of exchange is treated almost as cash, so that it would be most undesirable to allow the validity of such an instrument to be disputed on some ground that was not apparent on its face.

Thirdly, consideration is not necessary for the validity of *the transfer* of a negotiable instrument[11] so that the transferor cannot deny the validity of the transfer on the ground it was gratuitous. Consideration is, however, necessary for the validity of *the original contract* contained in the instrument, though even this requirement is modified in two ways in relation to bills of exchange. Past consideration, in the shape of an antecedent debt or liability, is sufficient; and a holder of the bill can enforce it if consideration has at *any* time been given for the bill, even though the holder himself provided no consideration.[12]

9 LIMITS ON ASSIGNABILITY

The law in general treats contractual rights as assignable; but it only treats them in this way so long as this does not prejudice the debtor or offend some public interest.

9 Bills of Exchange Act 1882, s 73.
10 Bills of Exchange Act 1882, ss 29, 30.
11 *Easton v Pratchett* (1835) 1 Cr M & R 798 at 808.
12 Bills of Exchange Act 1882, s 27(1) & (2).

a Prejudice to the debtor

The cases in which assignment may cause prejudice to the debtor can be grouped under two heads.

i Personal contracts

In general it is thought to make no difference to a contracting party in whose favour he performs. This is most obviously true in the case of a money debt. If A owes £100 to X he normally suffers no prejudice if instead of having to pay X he has to pay an assignee, Y. This is assumed to be true even where X is an indulgent and Y an exacting creditor. If A wants to protect himself against having to pay anyone except X, he can do so by expressly providing in the original contract that its benefit is not to be assignable.[13]

There is, however, a group of contracts which are said to be 'personal'. These are contracts in which it would be unreasonable to expect one party (A) to perform in favour of anyone except the other (X). Where this is the case, the benefit of A's obligations cannot be assigned. The leading illustration of this principle is provided by contracts of employment. Here it is well settled that an employer cannot assign the benefit of his employee's obligation to serve. The purpose of the rule is said to be to preserve the employee's right freely to choose whom he will serve;[14] and the rule continues to apply even though, in these days of take-overs and mergers, the right of choice is sometimes illusory. Another illustration of the principle is that a person who has taken out a policy of motor insurance cannot assign the benefit of the policy. The contract is 'personal' in the sense that the insurance company will probably have relied on the policy-holder's driving record in issuing the policy.[15] Even a commercial contract for the sale of goods may be a 'personal' contract. In one case[16] A, a wholesaler, agreed to deliver goods on credit to X who was experienced in the business of reselling the goods by retail. It was held that the contract could not be assigned to Y, who had no experience in that line of business, since to allow this would impose on A quite different commercial risks from those which he had undertaken.

Difficult problems sometimes arise where A makes a long-term contract to supply X with raw materials for the purpose of X's business, and that business is later taken over by Y (a much larger concern) to whom X purports to assign the benefit of the contract with A. In a sense the contract is 'personal' since A may have relied on his estimate of X's requirements in entering into the contract, or in fixing his price.

---

[13] *Helstan Securities Ltd v Hertfordshire County Council* [1978] 3 All ER 262.
[14] *Nokes v Doncaster Amalgamated Collieries Ltd* [1940] AC 1014 at 1026.
[15] *Peters v General Accident and Life Assurance Corpn Ltd* [1937] 4 All ER 628.
[16] *Cooper v Micklefield Coal and Lime Co Ltd* (1912) 107 LT 457.

Nevertheless, if the contract on its true construction limits A's liability to the quantity of goods which X could reasonably have required, it will normally be regarded as assignable.[17] But it will not be so regarded if it contains other provisions intended to confer a benefit on A which he will lose as a result of a purported assignment. Thus in one case[18] A undertook to supply X with all the eggs which X should need in his bakery for one year, and X agreed not to buy eggs elsewhere during the year. X sold his business to Y, to whom he purported to assign the benefit of the contract with A. It was held that A was not bound to supply eggs to Y since X's promise not to buy eggs elsewhere could not be enforced against Y, and it would be unjust to subject A to all the burdens of the contract while depriving him of one of its important benefits.

ii *Danger of maintenance or champerty*

Equity rejected the common law's view that assignments in general were invalid on the ground that they *might* lead to maintenance or champerty.[19] In equity, an assignment was, however, regarded as invalid if it was *in fact likely* to lead to undesirable interference by one person in litigation which was properly the concern of another. The principle has survived the abolition of maintenance and champerty as legal wrongs. It is most clearly illustrated by the rule that rights of action in tort cannot, in general, be assigned.[20] Thus if A defames X or negligently injures him, X cannot assign to Y his right to claim damages from A. To allow such assignments would, it is thought, lead to undesirable speculation in claims of this kind. Where there is no such danger the assignment may be allowed. This accounts for a well established exception to the general rule: an insurance company which has compensated the victim of a tort can take an assignment of the victim's rights against the tortfeasor.[1] Indeed, to the extent to which it has compensated the victim, it can assert his rights against the tortfeasor even without assignment.[2]

Rights to damages which cannot be assigned are sometimes called 'mere' rights of action; but the phrase is not particularly helpful in distinguishing between those contractual rights which can and those which cannot be assigned. The distinction certainly does not depend on the existence of a dispute as to liability: it is clear that a debt can be

---

17 *Tolhurst v Associated Portland Cement Co* [1903] A C 414.

18 *Kemp v Baerselman* [1906] 2 K B 604.

19 See p 224, ante.

20 *Defries v Milne* [1913] 1 Ch 98.

 1 *King v Victoria Insurance Co* [1896] A C 250.

 2 *Hobbs v Marlowe* [1978] A C 16 at 37.

assigned even though the debtor denies liability to pay it.[3] Nor does it turn on the nature of the right or claim assigned. There can be an assignment not only of a right to a fixed sum of money but also of a right to some other performance. The first possibility is illustrated by the case where a seller of goods assigns his right to the price, and the second by the case where the buyer assigns his right to receive the goods. Even where a contract has already been broken, the right to claim damages for the breach can then be assigned, so long as the assignment is not in fact likely to lead to undesirable interference in litigation which is properly the exclusive concern of the assignor.[4] Thus in one case[5] a seller of land assigned to the buyer his right to damages against a tenant of the land for breaches of covenant in the lease. The assignment was held valid: it did not lead to maintenance or champerty as the outcome of the litigation was no longer primarily the concern of the seller, but rather that of the buyer (ie the assignee) since the sale had given him a proprietary interest in the land. Similar reasoning may apply where the assignee has 'a genuine commercial interest'[6] in the outcome of the litigation. Thus in another case[7] a bank had financed a contract for the sale of cement by one of its customers and later took an assignment from that customer of his claim for damages for wrongful failure to pay for the cement. It was held that such an assignment *could* have been valid by reason of the bank's commercial interest in the transaction; and it probably *would* have been upheld if it had been taken with a view to the enforcement of the claim by the bank itself.[8] But in fact it had been taken for the express purpose of enabling the bank to sell the claim to a third party with a view to dividing the profit to be made from it (which amounted to nearly seven million dollars) between the third party and the bank. In view of these facts the assignment was held to be champertous and therefore invalid.

b Public policy

The assignment of certain rights is invalid on grounds of public policy. For example, a wife cannot assign a right to the payments which her husband may be ordered to make to her in matrimonial proceedings: if she could do this she might anticipate the allowance and be left without means of support.[9] It has also been held that a 'public officer' cannot

---

[3] *County Hotel and Wine Co v London and North Western Rly Co* [1918] 2 K B 251 at 258.
[4] *Weddell v J A Pearce & Major* [1988] Ch 26 at 43.
[5] *Ellis v Torrington* [1920] 1 K B 399.
[6] *Trendtex Trading Corpn v Crédit Suisse* [1982] A C 679 at 703.
[7] *Trendtex Trading Corpn v Crédit Suisse,* supra.
[8] *Brownton Ltd v Edward Moore Inbucon Ltd* [1985] 3 All E R 499.
[9] *Watkins v Watkins* [1896] P 222.

assign his salary.[10] This rule is said to be necessary to enable such a person to maintain the dignity of his office, but this argument now looks decidedly old fashioned. Another possible justification for the rule is that it prevents corruption, but the rule does not seem to be a very powerful instrument for this purpose, especially as it does not apply to officers paid out of local funds.[11] The assignability of many other payments out of public funds is expressly forbidden by various statutory provisions.[12]

10 INVOLUNTARY ASSIGNMENT

So far, we have considered the assignment of rights, by act of the parties or of one of them. Assignment may also come about by operation of law on the death or bankruptcy of one of the contracting parties.

a Death

When a contracting party dies, his rights pass to his personal representatives who can claim any performance due to the deceased under the contract, or damages for its breach. Where the contract has not been fully performed by the deceased, the personal representatives may be entitled to complete performance so as to earn the sum to be paid to the deceased: for example, the personal representatives of a deceased seller may deliver the goods and claim the price. But they will not be entitled to complete the performance of an obligation of the deceased which was 'personal,' ie such that the other contracting party would be entitled to refuse to accept performance from anyone except the deceased.

b Bankruptcy

On the bankruptcy of a contracting party, contractual rights to which he was entitled at the time of the bankruptcy are 'deemed to have been assigned' to his trustee in bankruptcy.[13] The trustee can claim performance of the contract, or damages for its breach; or he may be entitled to complete performance of the bankrupt's obligations so as to earn the agreed sum. Once again, the trustee cannot take this last course if the contract is 'personal' in the sense discussed above. But, since the bankrupt is still physically available to perform the contract,

---

[10] *Liverpool Corpn v Wright* (1859) 28 LJ Ch 868.
[11] *Re Mirams* [1891] 1 QB 594.
[12] Eg Child Benefit Act 1975, s 12; Social Security Act 1975, s 87.
[13] Insolvency Act 1986, s 311(4).

the trustee may employ him to do so; and, if the other party in this way gets what he bargained for, he will have to pay the agreed sum to the trustee.[14] The rule that choses in action pass to the trustee in bankruptcy is, however, subject to a number of limitations.

First, certain rights do not pass on the ground that they are 'personal'. This word is here used in a sense quite different from that discussed above: namely, to refer to the personal affairs of the bankrupt. For example, the bankrupt's right to damages for breach of a contract to render him medical services does not pass to his trustee.[15] The underlying theory is that the bankrupt's creditors are entitled to his property, but not to any sums due to him as compensation for injury to his person. It seems that this rule has survived the statutory definitions of the bankrupt's 'property' (which vests in his trustee) so as to include 'things in action.'[16]

Secondly, special provisions apply to the bankrupt's right to payments in the nature of income (eg under a contract of employment). These may not vest in the trustee because they will often not arise until after the commencement of the bankruptcy.[17] But the trustee can apply to the court for an order directing such income to be paid to him; and in deciding how much of the income is to be paid to the trustee the court will take into account 'what appears . . . to be necessary for meeting the reasonable domestic needs of the bankrupt and his family.'[18] The rule is designed to encourage the bankrupt to work so as to maintain himself and his family.

11 ASSIGNMENT DISTINGUISHED FROM TRANSFER OF LIABILITIES

Assignment is the transfer of a *right* without the consent of the debtor. The law does not recognise any converse process by which a liability can be transferred without the consent of the creditor. Suppose that X has lent £100 to A. He cannot be deprived of his right to sue A merely because B has contracted with A to pay the debt. Moreover, as a general rule the assignee of a contractual right does not become liable to perform any obligations which the assignor may have owed to the debtor under the contract. Suppose, for example, that a builder assigns to his bank monies due or to become due to him under a building contract. The bank does not, by virtue of the assignment, become liable to the builder's client for any breach of contract by the builder; though

---

[14] *Ex p Shine* [1892] 1 QB 522.
[15] *Drake v Beckham* (1849) 2 HL Cas 579 at 627.
[16] Insolvency Act 1986, ss 306, 403.
[17] Ibid s 283(1)(a).
[18] Ibid s 310(2).

the client may be able to rely on such a breach by way of defence to the bank's claim.[19]

There are, however, cases in which one person becomes liable to perform an obligation originally undertaken by another, or discharges such an obligation by actually performing it. These are discussed below; it will be seen that in none of them is there any true transfer of liability.

a Novation

We have seen that novation can be used so as to substitute one creditor for another and so in a sense to do the work of assignment.[20] Similarly, A, B and X can enter into a contract whereby A's obligation to X is discharged and B agrees to perform what A had undertaken. Strictly this is not a transfer of A's liability. What happens is that A's obligation ceases to exist and a new one is undertaken by B. This new obligation would not, for example, necessarily be affected by any defence which A had against X.

b Benefit and burden

Occasionally an assignee of a contractual right is subject to liabilities under the contract under the so-called principle of benefit and burden. For example, in one case[1] a mining company acquired land on a Pacific island under contracts obliging it to return the land after it was worked out to its former owners and to replant it. The company transferred its rights under these contracts to commissioners subject to the covenants contained in them; and the commissioners promised the company to keep it indemnified against claims by the landowners under these covenants. Soon afterwards the company was wound up; and many years later the commissioners were held liable to the landowners for breach of the covenant to replant. An intention that they should be so liable was inferred from the circumstances in which they came to the transaction: in particular from the facts that they had expressly promised the company to discharge the burdens of the contracts when they took the benefits, and that the company was about to go into liquidation. The exceptional nature of these circumstances suggests that the scope of the principle of benefit and burden is likely to be a narrow one. Certainly it will not apply to the ordinary case where only a contractual right is assigned. Even where it does apply, the liability is not strictly *transferred*: the assignor is not released by it from his original liability under the contract.

---

19 See *Young v Kitchin* (1878) 3 Ex D 127.
20 See p 224, ante.
1 *Tito v Waddell (No 2)* [1977] Ch 106 at 289–303.

c Operation of law

Sometimes contractual liabilities are, in a sense, transferred by operation of law. For example, the personal representatives of a deceased contracting party are bound to apply his assets in discharging his contractual liabilities. Similarly, the trustee of a bankrupt contractor is bound to distribute his assets among his creditors. In these cases the personal representative or trustee in bankruptcy is not, of course, *personally* liable on the contracts, so that strictly speaking there is no transfer of liabilities. In addition, a trustee in bankruptcy can disclaim an onerous or unprofitable contract,[2] though if he does so the bankrupt's estate will be liable in damages for breach of the contract.

By statute, the indorsement of a bill of lading (which is a document evidencing a contract for the carriage of goods by sea) may transfer not only the rights but also the liabilities of the original shipper.[3] Thus the indorsee may become liable to pay freight under a contract which has been transferred to him. But even here there is no true transfer of liability, for the original shipper is not relieved of his liability under the contract.[4]

d Vicarious performance

A's obligation to X may be discharged if B performs it. This is most obviously true where X actually agrees to accept performance from B in discharge of A's obligation. Suppose that A owes £100 to X and B offers to pay this sum (or a smaller sum) to X in satisfaction of A's debt. If X accepts the payment on these terms, A's debt is discharged.[5]

More difficulty arises where X is unwilling to accept performance from B but wishes to insist on personal performance from A. The general rule is that he is not entitled to do so. In one case,[6] for example, A let out railway wagons to X and agreed to keep them in repair for 7 years. During that period A transferred the benefit of the contract to B, to whom he also delegated the task of performing the obligation to repair. It was held that X could not object to B's performance of this obligation so long as B did the work efficiently. The creditor(X) is only entitled to object to vicarious performance in two types of cases.

First, and most obviously, X can object to performance by B if the contract expressly or by implication provides that a particular obligation will be performed by A and by no one else. For example, in one

---

[2] Insolvency Act 1986, s 315; cf ibid, s 178.
[3] Bills of Lading Act 1855, s 1.
[4] Ibid s 2.
[5] *Hirachand Punamchand v Temple* [1911] 2 K B 330.
[6] *British Waggon Co v Lea & Co* (1880) 5 Q B D 149.

case[7] a dry-cleaning contract contained the words 'whilst every care is exercised in cleaning . . . garments . . .', it was held that the cleaner (A) was not entitled to delegate performance of the cleaning operation to a subcontractor (B), since A could not take care of the garment while it was being cleaned by B.

Secondly, the creditor can object to vicarious performance of an obligation which is 'personal' in the sense that it is unreasonable to require him to accept performance from anyone except the other contracting party.[8] For example, an employee is not entitled to perform his duties as such by a substitute. Similarly, it has been held that the duties of a warehouseman under a contract to store goods and those of an estate agent instructed to find a purchaser for a house cannot be delegated to a third party.[9] The same may even be true of a contract for the sale of goods: for example where the buyer has entered into the contract in special reliance on the seller's reputation as a manufacturer or supplier of goods of a particular quality.[10]

Vicarious performance is sometimes called 'assignment of liabilities'. But this is a misleading description since, in none of the cases discussed under this heading, is any liability *transferred*. In one case[11] A contracted to repair X's car. He delegated performance of the work to a subcontractor, B, who did the work defectively, so that X was injured. As X had consented to the employment of a subcontractor, he clearly could not have refused to accept vicarious performance. But this did not relieve A from liability under the contract,[12] so that A was held liable to X for B's defective workmanship. Nor, on the other hand, would B have been liable under the contract to X if he had simply refused to do the work. B's only liability to X would have been in tort if he had been negligent in doing the work.

7 *Davies v Collins* [1945] 1 All ER 247.
8 *Robson v Drummond* (1831) 2 B & Ad 303.
9 *Edwards v Newland* [1950] 2 KB 534; *John McCann & Co v Pow* [1974] 1 WLR 1643.
10 *Johnson v Raylton, Dixon & Co* (1881) 7 QBD 438.
11 *Stewart v Reavell's Garage* [1952] 2 QB 544.
12 Where there is *no* contract between A and X, the employment by A of a competent sub-contractor (B) is likely to relieve A from liability in tort for negligence: *D & F Estates Ltd v Church Comrs for England* [1988] 2 All ER 992.

Chapter 15

Agency

1 INTRODUCTION

Agency is both a general principle of the law of contract and at the same time a special contract. The *general principle* is that, where an agent is authorised by a principal to enter into a contract on the principal's behalf with a third party, and does so, then a contract is created between principal and third party. For the purpose of this principle, it is first necessary to show that the relationship of principal and agent has arisen; and this generally depends on an agreement between the principal and the agent. Often, that agreement will amount to a *special contract* giving rise to rights and duties on either side. Our sole concern in this book, however, will be with agency as a general contract principle.

There is an important difference between the legal and the commercial concept of agency. In a commercial sense, it is, for example, common to refer to a car dealer as 'agent' for a particular manufacturer. But when such a dealer sells a car to a customer, he does not normally make a contract of sale between the customer and the manufacturer. What he does is to buy the car from the manufacturer and to resell it to the customer. Hence, if the car is defective, the customer's only remedy under the contract of sale is against the dealer; though he may have a remedy against the manufacturer in contract under the latter's 'guarantee', or in tort[1] if the defect results in personal injury or in loss of, or damage to, the customer's other property. It is also possible for the dealer to act partly on his own and partly on someone else's behalf. This is commonly the position where a car is supplied on hire-purchase, the bulk of the purchase price being provided by a finance company, which may buy the car from the dealer and then let it out on hire-purchase to the customer. Here the dealer is considered to act on his own behalf (and not as the customer's agent) when he sells the car to the finance company[2]; but he may be the agent of the finance company to accept the customer's offer to enter into a hire-purchase

---

[1] For negligence at common law, and irrespective of negligence under the Consumer Protection Act 1987, Pt I.
[2] *Mercantile Credit Co Ltd v Hamblin* [1965] 2 QB 242 at 269; cf Consumer Credit Act 1974 s 56(3)(a).

agreement, and for various other purposes.[3] Similarly an estate agent instructed to negotiate the sale of a house by private treaty may act on his client's behalf for certain purposes: eg for the purpose of making representations about the property.[4] But for other purposes he is not an agent in the legal sense. For example, he has normally no power to make a contract of sale between his client and a prospective purchaser; nor does he normally act on the client's behalf when receiving a precontract deposit from such a purchaser. The agent holds such a deposit on trust for the purchaser;[5] and if the purchaser asks for its return (as he is entitled to do at any time before a binding contract has been concluded) the liability to repay it falls on the agent and not on his client.[6] All this is only 'normally' true; it is possible, if unusual, for the client expressly to authorise the agent to make a contract on his behalf,[7] or to receive a deposit.[8]

A person who makes a contract between two others is sometimes the agent of both of them. An auctioneer is the agent of the seller for the purpose of making a contract of sale between him and the highest bidder. But he is also the agent of the highest bidder for the purpose of signing any memorandum required to make the sale enforceable.[9]

2 CREATION OF AGENCY

In the normal case, agency arises by agreement:[10] that is the principal actually authorises the agent to act on his behalf and the agent agrees to do so. But sometimes agency arises by operation of law, even though the principal has not actually authorised the agent to act on his behalf; and it may arise ex post facto by ratification.

a Actual authority

Actual authority may be express or implied.

i *Express authority*

An agent's authority is express to the extent to which it is conferred in so many words. An express appointment need not take any particular form. It may be oral even though the contract which the agent is

---

3 *Northgran Finance Ltd v Ashley* [1963] 1 QB 476; Consumer Credit Act 1974, ss 57(3), 69(6) and 102.
4 *Sorrell v Finch* [1977] AC 728 at 753.
5 Estate Agents Act 1979, s 13(1)(a).
6 *Sorrell v Finch,* supra; for interest on the deposit, see the Estate Agents Act 1979, s 15.
7 Cf eg *Spiro v Lintern* [1973] 1 WLR 1002 at 1006.
8 Eg *Ryan v Pilkington* [1959] 1 All ER 689, as explained in *Sorrell v Finch,* supra, at 750.
9 *Wilson & Sons v Pike* [1949] 1 KB 176; *Leeman v Stocks* [1951] Ch 941.
10 *Garnac Grain Co Inc v Faure and Fairclough Ltd* [1968] AC 1130 at 1137.

authorised to make has to be in, or evidenced in, writing.[11] But authority to execute a deed under seal must itself be under seal: such authority is known as a power of attorney.

ii Implied authority

The terms of an express appointment may not exhaustively specify all that the agent is in fact authorised to do. He may have implied authority to do acts which are reasonably incidental to the execution of his express authority. The scope of this incidental authority depends on the circumstances of each case. It is thus a question of fact whether an agent who is employed to sell property has authority to sign a memorandum to make the sale enforceable; or to give an undertaking as to the quality of the subject-matter. Generally an agent who is authorised to sell has no implied authority to receive payment.[12]

Where an agent is authorised to make a contract in a particular market he further has implied authority to act in accordance with any relevant custom of the market. This is so whether or not the principal knows of the custom. But the agent only has such customary authority if the custom is 'reasonable'. This means that the custom must not be actually inconsistent with the express instructions given to the agent or with the relationship of principal and agent. Where an agent is employed to buy for the principal, a custom of the market entitling him to buy on his own account and then to resell to the principal is unreasonable.[13] It converts the agent into a seller, thus giving him an incentive to secure the highest possible price, while his duty as agent is to buy for the principal as cheaply as he can.

In the cases so far considered, implied authority supplements an authority which has been expressly conferred. It is also possible for the very existence of the authority to be implied: for example, a wife has implied authority to pledge her husband's credit for household necessaries.[14] The implication is based on the existence of a domestic establishment which is managed by the wife, and not on the legal relationship of husband and wife. Hence the wife has no such implied authority if there is no domestic establishment (eg because the parties live in an hotel);[15] but if there is such an establishment the implied authority may exist even though the parties are not married.[16] A child, as such, has generally no authority to pledge the credit of either

---

11 *Heard v Pilley* (1869) 4 Ch App 548.
12 *Butwick v Grant* [1924] 2 K B 483.
13 *Robinson v Mollett* (1875) L R 7 H L 802.
14 *Jewsbury v Newbold* (1857) 26 L J Ex 247.
15 *Debenham v Mellon* (1880) 6 App Cas 24.
16 *Blades v Free* (1829) 9 B & C 167; *Hamilton v Forrester* (1825) 3 S 572.

parent;[17] though a child could no doubt have implied authority as manager of the household.

The implied authority here discussed is *actual* authority. It can therefore be negatived by express contrary instructions from the principal. But the mere fact that the principal has given such instructions may not exonerate him from liability on contracts made by the agent: he may still be liable under the rules discussed below.

b   Authority by operation of law

A principal may be liable on contracts which he has not actually authorised, and even on those which he has expressly forbidden, in the following cases.

i   *Apparent authority*

An agent (A) who in fact has no authority to contract on behalf of the principal (P) may nevertheless *appear* to the third party (X) to have such authority. P may then be bound by the contract if the appearance of authority resulted from his words or conduct. In one case[18] P owned a jeweller's shop and regularly paid X for goods ordered by his manager A for resale in the shop. A then left P's employment, ordered more jewellery from X, and made off with it. It was held that P was liable to X on the ground that A still appeared to X to have authority to bind P. In such a case, A is said to have *general* apparent authority, extending to all transactions which the manager of a shop normally has authority to conclude.[19] Even where A has no such authority by virtue of the position into which P has placed him, he may have *specific* apparent authority by virtue of an express representation by P that A had authority to enter into a particular contract on his behalf.[20] Once an appearance of authority has been created in either of these two ways, the onus is on P to give notice to X that A no longer has authority to contract on P's behalf.

This doctrine of apparent authority is of great practical importance. It applies if the following conditions are satisfied. First, the representation must be made *by the principal*: P is not liable merely because A has represented that he has an authority that he actually lacks.[1] Secondly, the representation must be made *to the third party* with whom the agent has purported to contract: that party cannot rely on a representation made to someone else. Both these rules may be illustrated by supposing

---

17 *Mortimore v Wright* (1840) 6 M & W 482.
18 *Summers v Solomon* (1857) 7 E & B 879; cf *United Bank of Kuwait v Hammoud* [1988] 3 All E R 418.
19 *The Ocean Frost* [1986] A C 717 at 777.
20 Ibid (where a claim on this basis failed).
1 *A-G for Ceylon v Silva* [1953] A C 461; *The Ocean Frost* [1986] A C 717 at 778.

that, in the case of the jeweller, A had ordered jewellery on credit from a new supplier, Y, alleging that he had P's authority to do so. Here P would not be liable to Y, since Y could not rely either on the representation made *by* A or on that made *to* X. Thirdly, the representation must be *one of fact and not one of law*. For this purpose the construction of a document is a question of law. Hence the doctrine of apparent authority does not apply where P shows X the document by which A is appointed and X believes that it bears one meaning when, on its true construction, it bears another. Fourthly, the third party must have *relied on the representation*; and this requirement can only be satisfied if the representation was actually known to him.[2] Fifthly, the third party cannot invoke the doctrine of apparent authority if he *knew that the representation was false*; or if he had a reasonable opportunity of discovering the truth but failed to take it. This would be the position if he was shown a document setting out the limits of the agent's authority but did not read it.[3]

Under the fourth of the above rules *actual knowledge of the representation* is necessary to establish a case of apparent authority; but under the fifth rule apparent authority is negatived where the third party *ought to have known the truth*. This distinction is particularly important in relation to contracts made with companies, which necessarily contract through agents. The authority of such agents may be set out in the company's memorandum and articles of association, which are registered and open to public inspection. For some purposes, third parties are deemed to have 'constructive notice' of these documents: that is, they are deemed to know what is in them even though they have not in fact read them.[4] But a third party cannot rely on something of which he does not actually know, so that the doctrine of constructive notice cannot be used against the company *to establish* a case of apparent authority. Such a case may, however, arise quite apart from the provisions of the registered documents: for example, where persons who have power to appoint a manager for the company represent that they have appointed A, when they have not effectively done so.[5] The more difficult question is whether the doctrine of constructive notice can be used in favour of the company, that is to *negative* a case of apparent authority. Here a number of distinctions have to be drawn. The law starts with the principle that the third party is deemed to know of any limitation set out in the registered documents, so that he cannot rely on an appearance of authority which is inconsistent with the terms of those documents. This would be the position where a managing director

[2] *The Ocean Frost* [1986] AC 717 at 778.
[3] *Jacobs v Morris* [1902] 1 Ch 816.
[4] *Mahony v East Holyford Mining Co Ltd* (1875) LR 7 HL 869.
[5] See *Freeman and Lockyer v Buckhurst Park Properties (Mangal) Ltd* [1964] 2 QB 480.

purported to enter into a contract which could, under the articles, only be made by the full board acting on the company's behalf. But this rule could cause hardship to the third party, and it has accordingly been modified in a number of ways. In the first place, the third party is not concerned with the 'internal management' of the company.[6] Thus if the articles empower the board to appoint a managing director, and the agent acts as such without having been duly appointed, the third party is entitled to rely on the appearance of authority thus created;[7] always assuming that the other requirements of apparent authority are satisfied. Secondly, if the transaction has been 'decided on by the directors' a third party who enters into it in good faith is by statute protected from the operation of the doctrine of constructive notice.[8] He is not bound to enquire whether the registered documents in any way limited the power of the directors to enter into the transaction.

A principal may sometimes be liable for his agent's forgery on the basis of apparent authority. This was held to be the position where a solicitor's clerk obtained money from a client on the security of forged title deeds; for the solicitor had impliedly represented that the clerk had authority to conclude mortgage transactions on his behalf.[9] But the third party cannot rely on the doctrine of apparent authority where the agent forges the principal's signature: in such a case the third party's belief is not that the agent had authority to sign *on the principal's behalf*, but that the signature actually was that of the principal.[10]

Even where the requirements of apparent authority are not satisfied, a person may sometimes be liable on an analogous ground. For example, where a person 'stands by' knowing that his signature has been or will be forged, he may be 'estopped' from denying that the signature was genuine.[11] The same principle was applied where a wife purported to enter into a contract to sell her husband's house although she had no authority, actual or apparent, to do so. At this stage the husband would not have been bound by the contract. But later he met the buyer, led him to believe that there was a binding contract, and allowed him to have work done on the house. It was held that the husband was estopped from denying his wife's authority to enter into the contract, as he had induced the buyer to believe that she had such authority, and to act to his prejudice in reliance on that belief.[12]

6 *Royal British Bank v Turquand* (1856) 6 E & B 327.
7 *Freeman & Lockyer v Buckhurst Park Properties (Mangal) Ltd* [1964] 2 QB 480 at 506.
8 Companies Act 1985, s 35.
9 *Uxbridge Permanent Benefit Building Society v Pickard* [1939] 2 KB 248.
10 Eg *Ruben v Great Fingall Consolidated* [1906] AC 439.
11 *Greenwood v Martin's Bank Ltd* [1933] AC 51. For estoppel, see p 141, ante.
12 *Spiro v Lintern* [1973] 3 All ER 319 at 323; *Worboys v Carter* (1987) 283 Estates Gazette 307.

ii *Usual authority*

This expression sometimes refers to certain cases of either implied or apparent authority. But it will be used here in a third sense, which may be illustrated by reference to the case of *Watteau v Fenwick*. P employed A as manager of his public house and expressly told A not to buy any goods (except bottled ales and mineral waters) from third parties. A nevertheless bought cigars (for the purposes of the business) from X, but he did so in his own name, without referring to P. Obviously A had no actual authority to buy the cigars, as he had been expressly told not to make such contracts. Nor was the case one of apparent authority, as X did not believe that A was P's agent but thought that A was buying on his own account. P was nevertheless held liable for the price of the cigars, on the ground that the contract was within the class of acts 'usually confided to an agent of that character'.[13] The decision has aroused much controversy but it seems on the whole to promote justice. Where the contract is made in the course of the principal's business, he will generally benefit from it; and it seems reasonable that he should equally be liable in the exceptional cases where the contract is to his disadvantage, whether as a result of the agent's dishonesty or for some other reason.

iii *Authority of necessity*

In some circumstances a person who acts for another in an emergency is said to have authority of necessity, and so to become the latter's agent. Three illustrations of the principle may be given.

First, the master of a ship may find it necessary to raise money quickly, for example to make repairs without which the ship cannot pursue her voyage. If he cannot get instructions from the shipowner in time, he has authority to borrow on the shipowner's credit, to borrow on the security of the ship or cargo, and even to sell part of the cargo.[14]

Secondly, a power of sale is conferred by statute on a bailee of uncollected goods if he has given notice to the bailor of his intention to sell, or if he has failed to trace the bailor after having taken reasonable steps to do so.[15]

Thirdly, agency of necessity may arise where one person intervenes to save another's life or property, and in certain analogous cases. The outstanding illustration of this rule is to be found in the law of maritime salvage, under which a person who goes to the aid of a ship in distress at sea[16] and saves life or property is entitled to some payment for his

13 [1893] 1 QB 346 at 348–349.
14 See *Notara v Henderson* (1872) LR 7 QB 225.
15 Torts (Interference with Goods) Act 1977, ss 12 and 13 and Sch 1.
16 See *The Goring* [1988] 1 All ER 641.

efforts; and if he takes the salvaged goods to a place of safety he has authority of necessity to warehouse them there, so as to prevent them from deteriorating.[17] Occasionally, the courts have been prepared to apply this principle outside the area of maritime salvage. For example, in *Great Northern Rly Co v Swaffield*[18] a railway company spent money on feeding and stabling a horse which the owner had failed to collect; and it was held that the owner was liable to reimburse the company. The decision is based on obvious humanitarian grounds; but the general rule is that a person who, without authority, preserves another's property is not entitled to any recompense: it is thought that the owner should not be subjected to obligations without his consent.[19] A distinction must, however, be drawn between the mere preservation of property and its improvement. Where the owner claims the return of property which has actually been improved, he often has to make some allowance for an increase in value which is due to the improver's efforts.[20]

As the above cases show, authority of necessity produces three quite different consequences. First, it may enable the 'agent' to make a contract between the 'principal' and a third party. This is its effect where a shipmaster borrows on the owner's credit. Secondly, it may enable the 'agent' to dispose of the principal's property either wholly or by way of security: this is illustrated by the shipmaster's power to create a security over the ship or to sell the cargo, and by the bailee's power to sell uncollected goods. Thirdly, it may entitle the agent to recompense or reimbursement, as in the salvage and analogous cases. Strictly, our concern in this chapter should only be with the first of these consequences. This alone involves an application of the general contract principle that an agent can make a contract between his principal and a third party, and it has been suggested that the phrase 'agency of necessity' should be used to refer only to cases of this kind.[1] But such a narrow use of the phrase obscures the fact that often the same circumstances which produce one of the consequences just described will also lead to another. Thus in the *Swaffield* case the actual question was whether the railway company was entitled to be reimbursed; but if the company had made a contract with a livery stable on the owner's behalf, that contract might well have bound the owner on the ground that the company had authority of necessity.

---

17 *The Winson* [1982] A C 939.
18 (1874) L R 9 Exch 132.
19 *Falcke v Scottish Imperial Assurance Co* (1886) 34 Ch D 234 at 248.
20 See *Munro v Wilmott* [1949] 1 K B 295, the facts of which would not be covered by ss 12 and 13 and Sch 1 of Torts (Interference with Goods) Act 1977; cf (in cases of mistake) ibid s 6 and *Greenwood v Bennett* [1973] Q B 195.
1 *The Winson* [1982] A C 939 at 958.

iv Other cases of agency by operation of law

In a number of other cases an agent is attributed to a person by operation of law. Thus when a company is first formed its original directors
are, by statute, declared to be its agents.[2] Sometimes the court can
appoint an agent for a person: for example it does so when it appoints
someone to manage the affairs of a mental patient.[3]

c Ratification

Where an agent makes a contract without being authorised to do so,
the principal may become a party to that contract by subsequent
ratification. This may be express, where the principal says in so many
words that he adopts the agent's act. It may also be inferred from conduct: for example where the agent without authority buys goods which
the principal then uses or resells. Ratification will only be inferred,
however, if the principal has a free choice in the matter. Suppose that
an agent without authority enters into a contract for the repair of the
principal's property. Ratification cannot be inferred merely from the
fact that the principal takes back his own property on which the work
has been done.[4]

i Conditions to be satisfied

Ratification can only take effect if the following conditions are
satisfied.

First, the agent must purport to act for the principal. This does not
mean that he must intend to act for the principal, who may be able to
ratify even though the agent intended to act for his own benefit and in
fraud of the principal.[5] What the rule does mean is that the agent must
make it appear to the third party that he was acting for a principal. The
principal does not have to be named, so that an unauthorised contract
made by an agent simply 'on behalf of my principal' can be ratified.
But ratification is not possible where an agent makes an unauthorised
contract *in his own name*, so that the third party thinks that he is dealing
with the agent and with no one else.[6] If this were not the law, anyone
who might benefit from a contract between two other persons could
acquire rights under it by ratification, even though he had not previously authorised the contract. Such a possibility would virtually
nullify the doctrine of privity of contract.

Secondly, the principal must have been in existence when the

[2] Companies Act 1985, s 282.
[3] *Plumpton v Burkinshaw* [1908] 2 K B 572.
[4] *The Liddesdale* [1900] A C 190.
[5] *Re Tiedemann and Ledermann Frères* [1899] 2 Q B 66.
[6] *Keighley Maxsted & Co v Durant* [1901] A C 240.

unauthorised contract was made. This rule looks logical, but it leads to the awkward result that a company cannot ratify contracts made by its promoters on its behalf before its incorporation.[7] As a practical matter it is often necessary to make such contracts; and various attempts have been made to circumvent the rule. None of these wholly solves the problem of creating mutually binding obligations between the company and the third party. Under the most recent legislation the contract takes effect (subject to any agreement to the contrary) as a contract between the agent and the third party;[8] but this is still unsatisfactory as the company itself does not acquire any direct rights or liabilities under the contract.

Thirdly, the principal must have had the capacity to enter into the unauthorised contract when it was made. A company therefore cannot ratify a contract which was ultra vires when it was made.[9] This is so even though the company later altered its memorandum of association so that at the time of ratification the contract was intra vires. This rule has lost most of its importance now that a person who enters into an ultra vires contract with a company can often enforce it even without ratification.[10] But the rule could still have some practical effect where the ultra vires contractor acquired no rights under the original contract,[11] or where it was the company which tried to rely on the ratification. Even in such cases, however, the company may still be able to make the transaction effective by 'adopting' it. But this does not have the same legal effect as ratification of the original contract. It can only operate prospectively, by creating an entirely new contract, whereas ratification has (as we shall see) retrospective effect. Thus if the third party withdraws from the transaction before it is 'adopted', the company cannot hold him to it.

Fourthly, there is a group of rules which limits the time for ratification. The general rule is that ratification must come within a reasonable time.[12] Ratification is also too late if it comes after the time fixed for performance,[13] or at a time when the principal himself could not have made the contract. On the latter ground an unauthorised insurance of property cannot generally be ratified after the property

---

[7] *Kelner v Baxter* (1866) LR 2 CP 174.
[8] Companies Act 1985, s 36(4); only applicable where the company is incorporated in the United Kingdom: see *Rover International v Cannon Films Sales Ltd (No 2)* [1987] 3 All E R 986; revsd in part (1988) Financial Times, 10 June.
[9] *Ashbury Rly Carriage and Iron Co v Riche* (1875) LR 7 H L 653. The company may be liable irrespective of ratification under Companies Act 1985, s 35: see p 201, ante.
[10] See p 201, ante.
[11] See p 201, ante.
[12] *Re Portuguese Consolidated Copper Mines* (1890) 45 Ch D 16.
[13] *Dibbins v Dibbins* [1896] 2 Ch 348.

has been destroyed;[14] but exceptionally a contract of marine insurance can be ratified even after a loss has occurred.[15]

Fifthly, a nullity (such as a contract prohibited by statute)[16] cannot be ratified. This principle is sometimes used to explain the rule that a principal cannot ratify his agent's act in forging his signature.[17] Another reason for this rule is that the agent does not pretend that he is signing *on behalf* of the principal, but that the signature *actually is* that of the principal. Hence he does not purport to act on behalf of the principal within the first of our ratification rules. A principal may, however, be liable on a forged signature on the ground of estoppel.[18]

ii Relation back

Ratification gives the unauthorised act the same effect as it would have had, if it had been originally authorised. In the leading case,[19] A without authority purported to buy a house from X on P's behalf. X repudiated the transaction and P then ratified. It was held that the ratification related back to the time of the unauthorised transaction between A and X, so that X was liable to P. This doctrine of 'relation back' has been criticised on the ground that it gives P the option of holding X to the contract while X has no corresponding option to hold P. But if P does not ratify, X has (as we shall see) a remedy against A;[20] and, as soon as X discovers A's lack of authority, he can force the issue by calling on P to ratify promptly. Any undue delay by P at this stage would make the ratification too late under the time rules discussed above.[1] Further, if A and X are conscious of a doubt as to A's authority, they can contract expressly 'subject to ratification'; and if they do so, the doctrine of 'relation back' does not apply.[2] Nor does it apply if A and X by mutual consent agree to cancel the contract before P ratifies.[3] In view of all these limitations on its scope, the doctrine of 'relation back' does not seem to be unjust in its practical operation.

3 EFFECTS OF AGENCY

The most important effects of agency are first that the agent can make a contract between principal and third party; and secondly that the agent

---

14 *Grover & Grover Ltd v Mathews* [1910] 2 K B 401.
15 Marine Insurance Act 1906, s 86.
16 *Bedford Insurance Co Ltd v Instituto de Resseguros do Brasil* [1985] Q B 966 at 986.
17 *Brook v Hook* (1871) L R 6 Ex 89.
18 See p 250, ante.
19 *Bolton Partners v Lambert* (1889) 41 Ch D 295.
20 See pp 261–263, post.
1 Ante, p 254 at n 12.
2 *Watson v Davies* [1931] 1 Ch 455.
3 *Walter v James* (1871) L R 6 Ex 124.

himself is not a party to this contract. Both these principles are, however, subject to exceptions and the detailed rules governing the relations between principal and third party, and those between agent and third party, will be discussed below. As a special contract, agency also gives rise to reciprocal rights and duties between principal and agent: these, as already stated, are outside the scope of this book.

a Relations between principal and third party

It will be convenient under this heading to consider first the rights and secondly the liabilities of the principal. Before these can be discussed a distinction must be drawn between disclosed and undisclosed principals. A *disclosed* principal is one of whose existence the third party was aware at the time of contracting. He is called a named principal if the third party also knew his name, and an unnamed principal if the third party knew of his existence but did not know his name. A principal is *undisclosed* if at the time of contracting the third party was unaware of his existence. In this situation the agent, though carrying out the principal's instructions, does not reveal this fact to the third party, who thinks that he is dealing with the agent and with no one else.

i Rights of principal

As a general rule, the principal is entitled to enforce the contract against the third party.[4] Where the principal is disclosed, this rule causes no injustice to the third party, since he knows at the time of contracting that he is undertaking a liability towards someone other than the agent. But where the principal is undisclosed, his intervention might well prejudice the third party who at the time of contracting thought that he was dealing with the agent and with no one else. One rule which reduces the possibility of such prejudice is that the third party can set up against the undisclosed principal any defence that he could have raised against the agent.[5] But even this rule does not deal adequately with two situations in which personal considerations enter into the contract. First, the third party may have wanted to deal with the agent *and with no one else*, for example because the contract was 'personal'—ie of a kind that could not be assigned or vicariously performed.[6] If this is the position, the third party is not bound to accept and pay for performance from the undisclosed principal. Secondly, the third party, though perfectly willing to deal with persons other than the agent, *may not have wanted to deal with the undisclosed principal*. In one case[7] the managers of a theatre had refused to sell a first night ticket to a

---

4 *Langton v Waite* (1868) LR 6 Eq 165.
5 *Browning v Provincial Insurance Co of Canada* (1873) LR 5 PC 263 at 272.
6 *Collins v Associated Greyhound Racecourses Ltd* [1930] 1 Ch 1.
7 *Said v Butt* [1920] 3 KB 497; see also *Nash v Dix* (1898) 78 LT 445; *Dyster v Randall* [1926] Ch 932.

dramatic critic who had been hostile to them in the past. The critic then sent a friend to buy the ticket, ostensibly for the latter's own use; and it was held that the critic had acquired no rights under the contract which had thus been made. Although the authorities on the point are not easy to reconcile, the position seems to be that the undisclosed principal cannot intervene *if he knew* that the third party did not want to deal with him. If the principal *did not know* this, he could probably intervene unless it could be inferred from the 'personal' nature of the contract, or from its express or implied terms, that its benefit was not to be assigned.

A third party from whom money is due under the contract may pay this money to the agent; and the agent may abscond or become insolvent before he has paid the money over to the principal. The question then arises whether the third party is discharged by the payment, or whether he must make a second payment to the principal. If at the time of the payment the principal was still undisclosed, the third party is discharged, for he has paid the only creditor of whose existence he knew.[8] But if at that time the principal was disclosed, the third party is not discharged:[9] he knows that his creditor is the principal and if he pays someone else he does so at his own risk. Payment to an agent for a disclosed principal will only discharge the third party if the agent has authority (whether actual, apparent or usual) to receive payment.

It is also possible that the agent had, before the contract was made, incurred some debt to the third party; and the third party may try to set this debt off against the principal's claim. Suppose that A owes X £20 and then on P's behalf sells and delivers goods to X for a price of £100. The extent of X's liability to P depends on whether P was at the time of contracting a disclosed or an undisclosed principal. If P was a disclosed principal, X must pay P the full £100.[10] But if P was an undisclosed principal, X need only pay P £80; for in this case X believed that he was dealing with A alone, and he could therefore reasonably expect that the price of the goods would be reduced by the amount that A owed him.[11] If X simply did not know whether A was acting for a principal or on his own behalf, this reasoning does not apply; and in such a case he is once again liable to pay the full £100 to P.[12]

ii Liabilities of principal

The general rule is that the principal is liable to the third party under the contract. This is so whether the principal was disclosed or

[8] *Curlewis v Birkbeck* (1863) 3 F & F 894.
[9] *Linck, Moeller & Co v Jameson & Co* (1885) 2 T L R 206.
[10] Cf *Mildred v Maspons* (1883) 8 App Cas 874.
[11] Cf *George v Clagett* (1797) 7 Term Rep 359.
[12] *Cooke v Eshelby* (1887) 12 App Cas 271.

undisclosed. The rules which limit the undisclosed principal's rights under the contract exist only to protect the third party and therefore do not limit the liability of the principal. A third party who discovers the existence of an undisclosed principal thus gets a benefit for which he did not bargain, in that he can sue two persons (the principal and the agent) on the contract.[13] But the principal can hardly complain about this as he initiated the transaction.

Some difficulty arises where the principal gives his agent the money to pay the third party, and the agent fails to pay it over and absconds or becomes insolvent. The general rule is that the principal must then make a second payment to the third party.[14] This rule clearly applies where the principal is disclosed; and the better view is that it also applies where the principal is undisclosed.[15] Of course it may be hard on the principal to have to pay twice; but generally a debtor must see that his creditor is paid, and he bears any risk inherent in the method that he has chosen for transmitting the payment. The principal is only discharged by a payment to the agent if the third party has expressly requested (or has otherwise induced) him to pay in this way.[16]

b Relations between agent and third party

As a general rule an agent is not a party to the contract that he makes between his principal and the third party. But there are many exceptions so that the agent is often liable to, and sometimes acquires rights against, the third party.

i Agent may be a party to the contract

The first group of cases in which the agent is a party to the contract are those in which he intends to undertake personal responsibility. Where the contract is in writing, the question whether the agent had this intention is one of construction; and the answer to it depends on the way in which the agent is described in the body of the document and on the way in which he signs it. Obviously he is not a party if he is described, and signs, as agent. But where the document is not clear a distinction has to be drawn between 'words of representation', which negative the intention to assume personal liability, and words which merely describe the professional or commercial capacity of the agent. Words which are merely descriptive are perfectly consistent with an intention to assume personal liability. Such an intention was, for example, held

---

[13] This does not mean that he will be *paid* twice over: see pp 260–261, post.

[14] *Irvine v Watson* (1880) 5 Q B D 414.

[15] *Heald v Kenworthy* (1855) 10 Exch 739; contra, *Armstrong v Stokes* (1872) L R 7 Q B 598.

[16] *Smyth v Anderson* (1849) 7 C B 21; cf *Wyatt v Hertford* (1802) 3 East 147.

to exist under a contract containing the words 'We, as solicitors, undertake . . .'.[17] Even the words 'as agents' may be descriptive when they are used in their commercial and not in their strictly legal sense.[18] Normally a person who signs an order on company notepaper with the addition 'Director' would not be personally liable; but in one case[19] a director who in this way signed an order for repairs to *his own* boat was held personally liable on the contract. The words 'on behalf of' or 'per procurationem' will generally be regarded as words of representation; but they may simply mean that the person on whose behalf the agent has signed *is*, and not that the agent is *not*, to be a party to the contract.[20] Where the agent is, under the above rules, personally liable he can normally also enforce the contract; but if the parties so intend it is possible for him to be liable without at the same time being entitled.

Secondly, the agent is a party to the contract (so that he can both sue and be sued on it) where the principal is undisclosed.[1] The rule does not apply where the principal is only unnamed.[2] In such a case the rights and liabilities of the agent depend on the principles stated in the preceding paragraph; though it may be relatively easier to infer that he intended to undertake personal responsibility where the principal is unnamed than where he is named.[3]

Thirdly, the agent may be a party to the contract where he purports to act for a principal but in fact acts on his own behalf. It has accordingly been held that the agent can enforce the contract where he intends to act for himself but purports to act for an unnamed principal, eg by buying 'on behalf of my principal'.[4] But the position is different where he names the principal: ie where he buys 'on behalf of my principal P'. Here the third party may have relied on P's commercial reputation in entering into the contract, so that he could be prejudiced by having to perform in favour of the agent.[5] Where the principal is unnamed, the possibility of such prejudice to the third party is remote; though it might arise in a situation (similar to that discussed above) in which the third party was willing to contract with *anyone except* the agent.[6]

---

17 *Burrell v Jones* (1819) 3 B & Ald 47.
18 *Parker v Winlow* (1857) 7 E & B 942; cf pp 245–246, ante.
19 *The Swan* [1968] 1 Lloyd's Rep 5.
20 *The Sun Happiness* [1984] 1 Lloyd's Rep 381.
1 *Sims v Bond* (1833) 5 B & Ad 389 at 393.
2 See *Universal Steam Navigation Co v James McKelvie & Co* [1923] AC 492.
3 See *N & J Vlassopulos Ltd v Ney Shipping Ltd* [1977] 1 Lloyd's Rep 478.
4 *Schmaltz v Avery* (1851) 16 QB 655; criticised in the Scottish case of *Hill Steam Shipping Co v Hugo Stinnes Ltd* 1941 SC 324.
5 *Bickerton v Burrell* (1816) 5 M & S 383; *Fellowes v Gwydyr* (1829) 1 Russ & M 83.
6 Ante pp 256–257; cf *The Remco* [1984] 2 Lloyd's Rep 205.

Fourthly, the agent may be a party to the contract if he intends and purports to contract for a non-existent principal. This is the position where an agent purports to make a contract on behalf of a company which does not yet exist: by statute the contract has effect as a contract entered into by the agent, who is liable on it accordingly.[7] The statutory rule can be excluded by contrary agreement, but the agent will not escape liability merely by contracting 'as agent'.[8] He must establish that there was an agreement exonerating him from liability. This is a question of fact in each case.[9]

So far it has been assumed that the agent purports to act on behalf of the unformed company, as where he signs the contract 'A, on behalf of P plc.' But it is also possible for him simply to sign the contract in the company's name, as where he signs 'P plc, A (director).' In the latter case he does not say that he is contracting on behalf of the company, but that the signature *is* that of the company. At common law there was no contract if the company did not in fact exist when the document was signed.[10] But by statute the agent may be treated as a party to the contract, in the absence of contrary agreement.[11]

Finally, an agent may acquire rights or be subject to liabilities under the contract by virtue of a relevant custom or usage, or by special statutory provision.[12]

ii Position where agent is a party to the contract

Where the agent is a party to the contract, the principal may, and often will, also be a party; but this does not mean that the third party is either liable or entitled twice over.

So far as the third party's *liabilities* are concerned, the first rule is that if he performs in favour of the principal, he is under no further liability to the agent. If, on the other hand the third party performs in favour of the agent he is only discharged if the principal was undisclosed, or if the agent was authorised to receive performance: the rules on this topic have been dicussed above.[13] Under these rules a third party who pays the agent may have to make a second payment to the principal. If principal and agent both claim performance, then the principal generally has the prior claim, to which that of the agent must yield.[14]

---

[7] Companies Act 1985, s 36(4).
[8] *Phonogram Ltd v Lane* [1982] QB 938 at 944.
[9] Cf the common law position as stated in *Black v Smallwood* [1966] ALR 744.
[10] *Newborne v Sensolid (GB) Ltd* [1954] 1 QB 45.
[11] Companies Act 1985, s 36(4).
[12] Eg Insolvency Act 1986, s 44(1).
[13] See p 257, ante.
[14] *Atkinson v Cotesworth* (1825) 3 B & C 647.

So far as the third party's rights are concerned, the first question is whether the agent's undertaking was not merely one of personal, but one of *exclusive*, liability. If it was of the latter kind, the third party cannot claim performance from the principal at all.[15] But more commonly both principal and agent will be liable on the contract: this is, for example, the position where the agent contracts for an undisclosed principal. There are three possibilities in cases of this kind. First, the third party may have actually received performance from either the principal or the agent; and in that case he cannot sue the other. Secondly, the third party may have 'elected' to hold either the principal or the agent liable; and the effect of this is again that the third party cannot then sue the other.[16] What amounts to 'election' is a question of fact. If the third party took legal proceedings against the agent, this would be strong (though not conclusive) evidence of election to hold the agent liable.[17] The reason for this doctrine of 'election' appears to be that the third party's conduct in (for example) claiming performance from the agent might lead the principal to believe that no claim would be made against him, and accordingly to settle his own accounts with the agent.[18] If there has been no such action in reliance, it is hard to see in what way a principal (or agent) is prejudiced by the third party's unsuccessful attempt to obtain payment from the agent (or principal). In practice the courts can, when there is no such prejudice, refuse to apply the doctrine by finding as a fact that the conduct of the third party does not amount to election.[19] Thirdly, the third party may have actually obtained judgment against principal or agent; and if their liability was joint it used to be the law that the third party could not then sue the other even though the judgment was not satisfied.[20] Now the mere fact that the third party has obtained a judgment against principal or agent is no longer a bar to proceedings against the other;[1] though it might, presumably, still amount to an 'election'.

iii Agent acting without authority

An agent who purports to enter into a contract on behalf of a principal is taken to represent that he had authority to make the contract. If he had no such authority and knew this, he is liable in tort to the third party for fraud; and he might be liable in negligence if he ought to have

---

[15] Eg *Thomson v Davenport* (1829) 9 B & C 78.
[16] *Debenhams Ltd v Perkins* (1925) 133 L T 252 at 254.
[17] See *Scarf v Jardine* (1882) 7 App Cas 345.
[18] Eg *Davison v Donaldson* (1882) 9 Q B D 623.
[19] Eg *Clarkson Booker v Andjel* [1964] 2 Q B 775.
[20] See p 205, ante.
[1] Civil Liability (Contribution) Act 1978, s 3.

known of his want of authority. But the law goes further and holds the agent liable even though he in good faith and without negligence believed that he had authority when he had none. He is said to have impliedly warranted that he had the authority which he purported to have; and liability for breach of the implied warranty is quite independent of fault in the sense of fraud or negligence.[2] Thus an agent would be liable if his authority had come to an end as a result of the principal's death or insanity, even though he did not know and could not reasonably have known of these events.[3] This rule can cause hardship to the agent, who may have acted in the most perfect good faith. The hardship is alleviated by a special statutory provision under which the agent is not liable to the third party if he acts under a power of attorney in ignorance of the fact that it has been revoked.[4]

The agent's liability for breach of implied warranty of authority is further limited by a number of rules of common law. He is, in the first place, not liable if the representation was one of law; and for this purpose a representation as to the construction of the document from which the agent's authority is derived is treated as one of law.[5] Secondly, the agent is not liable if the third party knew (or must be taken to have known) that the agent had no authority.[6] Thirdly, the agent is not liable if, though he had no actual authority, the principal is nevertheless liable to the third party under the rules relating to apparent or usual authority;[7] or if the principal ratifies. In such cases the third party can sue the principal, so that the agent's want of authority does not cause the third party any loss. Finally, it has been held that the doctrine of breach of implied warranty of authority does not apply to agents of the Crown.[8] This limitation on the scope of the doctrine has been criticised on the ground that it puts such agents in an unduly favourable position. On the other hand, it would be most unreasonable to make civil servants personally liable for the very large sums often involved in government contracts.

The effect of these statutory and common law rules is certainly to mitigate the harshness of the doctrine of implied warranty of authority; but it would be more satisfactory to confine the doctrine to cases in which the agent knew, or was negligent in not knowing, of his want of authority. The general principle of strict liability can, in spite of the various limitation on the doctrine, still lead to harsh results.[9]

---

[2] *Collen v Wright* (1857) 8 E & B 647.
[3] *Yonge v Toynbee* [1910] 1 K B 215.
[4] Powers of Attorney Act 1971, s 5(1).
[5] *Rashdall v Ford* (1886) L R 2 Eq 750.
[6] *Halbot v Lens* [1901] 1 Ch 344.
[7] *Rainbow v Howkins* [1904] 2 K B 322; but see *Yonge v Toynbee* [1910] 1 K B 215.
[8] *Dunn v Macdonald* [1897] 1 Q B 555.
[9] Eg *V/O Rasnoimport v Guthrie & Co Ltd* [1966] 1 Lloyd's Rep 1.

4 TERMINATION OF AGENCY

Agency is often a contract, and any event which terminates that contract will bring the relation of principal and agent to an end. To take the most obvious cases: the parties may terminate the relation by mutual consent; or the contract may provide that it is to expire at the end of a fixed time.

A common way of terminating agency is by notice, which may be given by either party to the other. Where a contract of agency prescribes a period of notice, the giving of such a notice will terminate the agency; where no period of notice is specified, a reasonable period of notice will have the same effect.[10] A notice which specifies too short a period is a breach of contract, giving rise to liability in damages, but it is nevertheless *effective*: that is, it terminates the relation of principal and agent.[11]

At common law, agency may come to an end by operation of law on the death or total disability of either party; on the bankruptcy of the principal; and on that of the agent if it makes him unfit to perform his duties.

The events listed above terminate the relationship of principal and agent and the agent's actual authority (whether express or implied) to contract on behalf of the principal. They do not necessarily put an end to authority which exists independently of the principal's consent. For example, a principal who terminates the agent's actual authority by notice to the agent may still be liable on the basis of apparent authority on contracts made by the agent after receipt of the notice. To avoid such liability, the principal must further give notice *to the third party* that he has terminated the agent's authority. There is considerable confusion in the authorities on the exact effects at common law of the principal's death or incapacity; but the better view seems to be that these events, too, only terminate actual authority and do not affect apparent authority unless the third party has notice of them.[12] Where the agent's authority is conferred by a power of attorney, a third party who deals with the agent without notice of revocation can, by statute, treat the transaction as valid as if the power had still been in·existence.[13]

In some cases agency is 'irrevocable' in the sense that an attempt by the principal to revoke it is not merely wrongful, *but ineffective*; and in the sense that it survives such events as the principal's death, legal disability or bankruptcy. At common law this is the position where the

---

[10] *Martin-Baker Aircraft Co Ltd v Canadian Flight Equipment Ltd* [1955] 2 Q B 556.

[11] *Denmark Productions Ltd v Boscobel Productions Ltd* [1969] 1 Q B 699.

[12] *Drew v Nunn* (1879) 4 Q B D 661; contrast *Yonge v Toynbee* [1910] 1 K B 215; *Blades v Free* (1829) 9 B & C 167.

[13] Power of Attorney Act 1971, s 5(2).

agent's authority is 'coupled with an interest'.[14] Obviously it is not sufficient for this purpose to show that the agent has an interest in earning his commission; for, if it were, all commercial agencies would be irrevocable. The rule refers to cases in which the agency is created to protect some *previously existing* interest of the agent. It could, for example, apply where P owed money to A and then authorised A to sell some of P's property and to repay himself out of the proceeds. The authority would not be irrevocable if P's indebtedness to A first arose *after* the authority had been conferred.[15] There are, finally, statutory restrictions on the revocability of certain powers of attorney. Such a power is irrevocable if it expressly so provides and if it is given to secure a proprietary interest or the performance of an obligation.[16] And a power of attorney which is expressed to continue in spite of the principal's supervening incapacity[17] is not revoked by such incapacity, but only in that event suspended till registered with the court.[18] Such an 'enduring power' can then only be revoked with the consent of the court;[19] and the agent and the third party are protected if in good faith they act in ignorance of the incapacity, and in certain other cases.[20]

---

[14] *Carmichael's Case* [1896] 2 Ch 643.

[15] *Smart v Sandars* (1848) 5 C B 895.

[16] Powers of Attorney Act 1971, s 4.

[17] Enduring Powers of Attorney Act 1985, s 2.

[18] Ibid, s 1(1)(a) and (b),6.

[19] Ibid, ss 7(1)(a),8(3).

[20] Ibid, ss 1(1)(c),9.

Chapter 16

Performance and breach

Every contract imposes certain obligations on at least one of the parties. If the contract is unilateral, it imposes an obligation on only one of the parties. In the more common case of a bilateral contract, obligations are imposed on both parties, and each of the parties may be subject to more than one obligation. Under an ordinary contract for the sale of goods, for example, the seller will be obliged to deliver the goods, and he may be obliged to ensure that they are of a certain quality, or fit for a particular purpose. The buyer, on the other hand, will be obliged to accept the goods and to pay for them.

A party who fails to perform his obligations under the contract will generally be in breach, so that performance and breach can be regarded as two sides of the same coin. But failure to perform is not invariably a breach. It may be excused either under the doctrine of frustration (which is discussed in chapter 17) or for reasons stated later in the present chapter. Our concern here will be with four topics: the nature of the duty to perform; the rules governing the method of performance; the effects of failure to perform (not amounting to frustration); and repudiation before performance has actually become due.

1 THE DUTY TO PERFORM

a Terms of the contract

It goes almost without saying that the extent of the duty to perform depends primarily on the terms of the contract. Performance must be exactly in accordance with these terms. It will not suffice for the party who is under the duty to do something else that is as good, or almost as good, or even better. If some latitude is required, the contract must expressly provide for it: for example, by saying that a seller is to deliver 'about' a certain quantity of goods, or that a ship is 'expected to arrive' at 'about' a stated time. Such stipulations are very common in commercial contracts. Unless they are included, failure to perform exactly in accordance with the contract is prima facie a breach.

So far it has been assumed that the terms of the contract clearly specify the duties of the party alleged to be in breach. But there may be, and often is, dispute as to the exact meaning of terms in the contract which impose these obligations; and sometimes a more fundamental question arises, namely whether the defendant is under any duty at all, or under any duty of the kind which he is alleged to have broken. There may be no such duty: in one case[1] a carrier agreed with the Admiralty that, for eleven years, he would convey from Dover to Calais such mail as he should be asked to carry. It was held that the Admiralty was under no duty to give him any mail to carry but only under one to pay him at the contract rate for such mail as he actually carried. Similarly, a contract by which A binds himself to supply B with such quantities of (for example) steel as B may order, or as B may require in a particular business, does not bind B to give any orders, or to carry on his business in such a way that any relevant requirements will arise. On the other hand, obligations which are not expressly stated can sometimes be implied. A contract of employment, for example, may simply say that the employer is to pay wages without making it clear whether he must actually provide work. In the past, the general rule was that the employer was only bound to pay,[2] since the employee would not normally be prejudiced if he did not work but still received his wages. But there were exceptions: for example, if an actor was engaged to perform in a play, he had to be given an opportunity of appearing.[3] More recently, it has been suggested that the old general rule is out of keeping with the fact that the law now recognises a 'right to work'; and that consequently (at least in the case of a skilled worker) the employer impliedly undertakes actually to provide work. Thus an employer may be liable in damages for breach of contract if he sends a worker home, even on full pay.[4]

b Standard of duty

Once it has been determined *what* each contracting party must do, the next question is this: is a party liable for *any* failure in performance, or only for a failure which can, in some sense, be said to be due to his fault?

Contractual liability is in many cases strict: that is, it arises quite independently of fault. The point is most clearly illustrated by the case of a man who cannot pay the agreed price for goods that he has bought, simply because his bank has failed: there is no doubt that he is in breach of contract.[5] Similarly, a seller of goods may be unable to deliver because he is let down by his suppliers or because he is unable to find

---

1 *Churchward v R* (1865) LR 1 QB 173.

2 *Turner v Sawdon* [1901] 2 KB 653.

3 *Herbert Clayton and Jack Waller Ltd v Oliver* [1930] AC 209.

4 *Langston v Amalgamated Union of Engineering Workers* [1974] 1 All ER 980. See further *Langston v Amalgamated Union of Engineering Workers (No 2)* [1974] ICR 510 (no *specific* enforcement cf p 354, post).

5 Cf *Universal Corpn v Five Ways Properties Ltd* [1979] 1 All ER 552.

shipping space to get the goods to their agreed destination:[6] again he is in breach even though his inability to deliver was not due to any failure on his part to take reasonable steps to secure performance. The same principle can apply to defects of quality. In one case[7] a buyer of milk became ill because the milk was infected with typhoid germs; and it was held that the seller was in breach of contract even though he had taken all reasonable precautions to ensure that the milk was pure. Perhaps the most striking case of all was one in which a bottle of lemonade was supplied by manufacturers to a shopkeeper who sold it to a customer. The lemonade contained carbolic acid and it was held that the shopkeeper (though in no moral sense at 'fault') was liable to the customer for breach of contract.[8] The principle of strict liability seems also to apply where goods are supplied under a contract other than one of sale: eg under a contract of hire.[9]

There are, however, a number of situations in which fault is relevant to the issue of contractual liability. First, a supervening event may discharge a contract under the doctrine of frustration, to be discussed in chapter 17; but a party cannot rely on such an event as a ground of discharge if he has himself voluntarily brought it about, or (generally) if its occurrence is due to his negligence.[10] Secondly, there are some contracts which do not impose a strict duty to produce a specified result, but only a duty to use reasonable care and skill, or best endeavours, to bring it about. This standard of liability commonly applies where a person contracts to supply a service in the course of a profession or business.[11] Thus a doctor who contracts to provide medical treatment is not normally understood to guarantee its success:[12] he is only bound to show reasonable care and skill.[13] The same is true of contracts calling for the exercise of some other professional skills, for example as a solicitor.[14] Architects occupy an intermediate position: they are only liable for negligence in respect of errors of supervision,[15] but may be strictly liable for defects of design.[16]

---

[6] *Lewis Emanuel & Son Ltd v Sammut* [1959] 2 Lloyd's Rep 629; *Intertradex SA v Lesieur-Tourteaux SARL* [1978] 2 Lloyd's Rep 509.

[7] *Frost v Aylesbury Dairy Co Ltd* [1905] 1 KB 608.

[8] *Daniels v White & Son* [1938] 4 All ER 258.

[9] See Supply of Goods and Services Act 1982, ss 4, 9; cf Supply of Goods (Implied Terms) Act 1973, ss 9-11 as substituted by Consumer Credit Act 1974, Sch 4, para 35.

[10] Post, pp 309–310.

[11] Supply of Goods and Services Act 1982, s 13.

[12] See *Eyre v Measday* [1986] 1 All ER 488; *Thake v Maurice* [1986] QB 644.

[13] Eg *Gold v Haringey Health Authority* [1987] 2 All ER 888.

[14] *Clark v Kirby-Smith* [1964] Ch 506.

[15] *Bagot v Stevens, Scanlan & Co Ltd* [1966] 1 QB 197.

[16] *Independent Broadcasting Authority v EMI Electronics* (1980) 14 BLR 1. Cases of strict liability at common law are preserved by Supply of Goods and Services Act 1982, s 16 (2) (a).

The principle of strict liability was also applied where a firm had contracted to repair a car and in the course of so doing fitted connecting rods supplied by a reputable manufacturer. The rods suffered from latent defects and gave way, causing extensive damage; and the repairers were held liable even though they had taken all reasonable care.[17] The distinction between this case and those of the professional services is that the car-repairing contract contains both a supply and a service element.[18] Liability for defects in the components *supplied* is strict, by analogy to sale. Liability for short-comings in the *service* element probably depends on fault, ie on failure to use reasonable care and skill.

Fault is finally relevant in the case of those conditional contracts, in which one party impliedly undertakes to bring about the occurrence of the condition.[19] For example, a contract may be made to sell goods for overseas delivery and it may be known to both parties that the goods cannot be exported without licence. In such a case, the seller is not normally bound to do more than to make reasonable efforts to get the licence.[20] If such efforts are made and fail, the seller will not be in breach merely because he cannot lawfully deliver the goods in accordance with the contract.

The standard of duty normally imposed by law can be varied by the terms of the contract. Thus it is possible (if unlikely) for a medical practitioner to guarantee the success of his treatment; while conversely the parties can (subject to statutory restrictions)[1] reduce a duty which is prima facie strict to one of reasonable diligence.

c Excuses for non-performance

Not every failure to perform a contractual promise is a breach. The failure may be excused by some rule of law, or by the terms of the contract.

One situation in which an excuse can be said to be provided by law is that in which the duty to perform has not yet arisen. If, for example, goods are sold for cash on delivery and the seller has failed to deliver, then obviously the buyer need not pay. But even after the duty to perform has come into existence, excuses for non-performance may be provided by supervening events outside the control of the parties. Such an event may so seriously affect performance as to frustrate the contract. In that case (as we shall see in chapter 17) it will discharge *both* parties from all their obligations under the contract. But a

---

[17] *GH Myers & Co v Brent Cross Service Co* [1934] 1 KB 46.
[18] See *Young & Marten Ltd v McManus Childs Ltd* [1969] 1 AC 454.
[19] Ante, p 24.
[20] *Re Anglo-Russian Merchant Traders* [1917] 2 KB 679.
[1] See pp 88–97, ante.

supervening event may also have less drastic effects. For example, an employee who does not go to work because he is temporarily ill is not in breach. The illness operates as an excuse for non-performance. But it does not frustrate the contract unless it is so serious as to make effective resumption of work impossible.[2] Except in such a case, the employee is bound to go back to work when his illness is over. In the meantime the employer is prima facie bound to go on paying wages,[3] unless his obligation to do so is excluded by the express or implied terms of the contract.[4]

Excuses provided by the contract take two common forms. First, the contract may contain a clause entitling a party to cancel or to terminate. Hire-purchase agreements, for example, often expressly (or as a matter of law[5]) confer on the hirer the right to terminate by notice. If the hirer exercises that right his failure thereafter to pay instalments is obviously not a breach—though he will be in breach if he simply fails to pay without going through the motions of terminating in accordance with his right to do so. Secondly, a contract which would normally impose a strict duty may provide that, if one party cannot perform for some reason beyond his control, he is to be excused. For example, a charterparty prima facie imposes a strict duty on the charterer to provide the agreed cargo, but it may contain an 'exception' for failure to perform this duty in circumstances not due to the fault of the charterer. If such circumstances arise, the charterer's failure to perform will be excused and will not constitute a breach.[6]

A party relying on an excuse for non-performance must show that it existed at the time of his refusal or failure to perform.[7] If he can show this, he is not in breach even though at that time he did not state the excuse (or even know of it) but gave some other, insufficient ground.[8] For example, if a seller tenders goods which suffer from a defect justifying their rejection the buyer is entitled to reject them; and it makes no difference that at the time of rejection he did not specify the defect, or alleged the existence of another defect which he could not substantiate.[9] In support of the rule, it can be said that it prevents the party in breach (the seller in our example) from benefiting from concealment of defects. On the other hand, the seller may be as ignorant of the defects as the buyer, and in such a case the rule can cause him considerable surprise and hardship. It therefore does not

---

[2] Eg, *Marshall v Harland and Wolff Ltd* [1972] 2 All ER 715 post, p 300.
[3] *Marrison v Bell* [1939] 2 KB 187.
[4] *Mears v Safecar Security Ltd* [1983] QB 54.
[5] Consumer Credit Act 1974, s 99.
[6] *The Angelia* [1973] 2 All ER 144.
[7] See *British and Beningtons Ltd v North Western Cachar Tea Co Ltd* [1923] AC 48.
[8] Eg *Ridgway v Hungerford Market Co* (1835) 3 Ad & El 171.
[9] Eg *Arcos Ltd v EA Ronaasen & Son* [1933] AC 470.

apply where failure to specify the defect deprives him of the chance of putting matters right:[10] eg by making a second tender of conforming goods within the period fixed for delivery; or where his conduct is in some other way affected by the buyer's failure to specify the true ground of rejection: eg where he spends time or money in investigating or trying to put right a different objection which the buyer raises at the time of rejection, but later fails to substantiate.[11] The buyer will also be unable to rely on a defect which would have justified rejection if at the time of rejection his right to reject had already been barred on one of the grounds to be discussed later in this chapter: eg by acceptance.[12]

2 METHOD OF PERFORMANCE

Performance is generally due without demand[13] but this rule is subject to a number of qualifications. It obviously does not apply where the contract provides for performance 'on demand'.[14] A demand is also necessary where, without it, a party cannot reasonably be expected to know that performance is required: for example, where a landlord who has covenanted to keep premises in repair has no means of knowing that they are in need of repair until a notice to this effect has been given to him by his tenant.[15]

Often performance by one party (such as payment or delivery) cannot be completed unless the other party co-operates by accepting it. In such cases, the obligation of the former party is to tender performance. A tender of money requires actual production of the money: a statement that the debtor is ready and willing to pay is only an offer to tender. A tender of less than the amount due is bad;[16] and the same is true where a debtor tenders more than is due and asks for change.[17]

A payment by cheque is normally regarded as a conditional payment which becomes absolute when the cheque is honoured.[18] On the other hand, where goods or services are paid for by credit card or charge card, such payment is regarded as absolute. It follows that, if the card

---

10 *Andrē et Cie v Cook Industries Inc* [1987] 2 Lloyd's Rep 463.
11 Cf *The Lena* [1981] 1 Lloyd's Rep 68 at 79; *The Eurometal* [1981] 1 Lloyd's Rep 337 at 341.
12 *Panchaud Frères SA v Etablissements General Grain Co Ltd* [1970] 1 Lloyd's Rep 53, as explained in *B B Exploration (Libya) Ltd v Hunt* [1979] 1 W L R 783 at 810-811, affd Post p 287.
13 *Walton v Mascall* (1844) 13 M & W 452.
14 See *Bank of Boroda v Panessar* [1987] Ch 335.
15 *Calabar Properties Ltd v Stitcher* [1984] 1 W L R 287 at 298.
16 *Dixon v Clark* (1848) 5 C B 365.
17 *Betterbee v Davis* (1811) 3 Camp 70.
18 *Re Romer and Haslam* [1893] 2 Q B 286.

issuing company should fail to pay the supplier, the latter's sole remedy is against the company.[19] He is not entitled to claim the price from the customer, since it would be unjust to make the customer liable for immediate full payment in cash when he had contracted on credit terms. The customer's only liability is to the company, in accordance with the agreement under which it issued the card to him.

Performance must of course be in accordance with the terms of the contract which may specify not only the nature but also the manner of the performance required: for example it may state how, where and when goods are to be delivered and paid for. A tender of performance which does not comply with these requirements is defective; but if it is rejected on that ground and a second 'good' tender is made within the contract period, the good tender must normally be accepted.[20]

A troublesome type of provision is one which allows for alternative methods of performance without making it clear which party has the right to choose between them. The law in some cases resolves the uncertainty by more or less arbitrary rules: for example if a loan is repayable in 'one or two years' the option is the borrower's;[1] if a lease is for seven, fourteen or twenty-one years, the option is the tenant's.[2] In other cases there is no general rule. For example a contract may provide for delivery of goods 'in April' without stating whether it is the buyer or the seller who is entitled to specify the exact delivery date. The question in such cases is one of construction, depending on the nature and terms of the contract as a whole.

3 RESCISSION FOR FAILURE IN PERFORMANCE

Failure to perform a contract will generally be a breach. As such it will give rise to the usual remedies for enforcing the contract, either specifically or by an award of damages. These remedies are discussed in chapter 18. But a person who does not get what he bargained for may also seek to 'terminate' or 'rescind' the contract, and he may be entitled to do this even though the other party's failure to perform was not a breach.[3] 'Rescission' here does not mean that the contract is wholly brought to an end, much less that it is retrospectively annulled, as in cases of misrepresentation.[4] In particular, where the failure in

[19] *Re Charge Card Services Ltd* [1988] 3 All E R 702.
[20] *Tetley v Shand* (1871) 25 L T 658.
[1] *Reed v Kilburn Co-operative Society* (1875) L R 10 Q B 264.
[2] Ibid at 265.
[3] Eg because he had an excuse for non-performance: see p 268, ante.
[4] Ante, p 136; for criticism of the terminology, see *Photo Production Ltd v Securicor Transport Ltd* [1980] A C 827 at 844-851; for its continued use, see eg *Bunge Corpn v Tradax SA* [1981] 2 All ER 513 at 548, 549; *Berger & Co Inc v Gill & Duffus SA* [1984] A C 382 at 390, 391.

performance amounts to a breach, rescission for that breach does not deprive the injured party of his right to damages for the breach. To say that a party can rescind for breach (or other failure in performance) refers to three different, though related, processes. The first is a simple refusal to perform, as where a buyer of defective goods refuses to pay for them. The second is a refusal to accept further performance, as where a buyer of goods by instalments refuses to accept further deliveries on the ground that those already made are not in accordance with the contract. The third is a claim by the injured party to be returned, so far as possible, to the pre-contract position: for example, where a buyer rejects defective goods and asks for his money back.

Such claims to rescind the contract will sometimes be more advantageous to the injured party than claims for enforcement. For one thing, refusal to perform, or to accept performance, is a kind of self-help, free from the delays and risks of legal proceedings. For another, it will often be more reasonable to allow a buyer to whom defective goods are tendered to reject them, rather than to require him to accept and pay, and then to seek his remedy in damages.

On the other hand, rescission is also used for the more questionable purpose of enabling a party to get out of a bad bargain. Suppose that A has sold goods to B at a price of £100, to be delivered and paid for in six months. When the goods are delivered they are found to be defective in some way which reduces their value by 10 per cent; but by this time the market value of such goods has declined to £40. If B were entitled to rescind, he could save himself £60 by buying equivalent goods elsewhere; while if his only claim were one for damages it would yield no more than £4. Conversely, the value of the goods at the time fixed for delivery may have risen to £200 and A may seek to rescind on the ground that B has failed strictly to perform the terms as to payment. This failure may not cause A any appreciable loss at all, but if it entitles him to rescind he will be able to avoid his liability to deliver the goods for the original price. This desire to get out of a bad bargain seems to be a very common motive for rescission; certainly it appears again and again in the reported cases on this topic. Rescission can also lead to another kind of hardship where a party has only performed in part but cannot complete. He may by such part performance have conferred benefits on the other party which the latter cannot restore. This would be the position where A contracts to paint B's house for a lump sum payable on completion, but only manages to do three-quarters of the work. To allow B to refuse to make *any* payment can clearly cause hardship to A.

There may thus be strong practical reasons both for and against allowing rescission; and the courts have had much difficulty in balancing the competing interests of the parties. This difficulty accounts for the very complex state of the rules which determine the availability of rescission and the grounds on which the right to rescind may be barred. After considering these, we shall discuss the rule that rescission is not automatic but a matter for the choice of the injured party.

a The order of performance

The right to rescind, in the sense of simply refusing to perform, depends in the first place on the provisions of the contract with regard to the order in which the acts of performance on both sides are to be done. The possible situations are best discussed by taking some simple examples. First, A agrees to work for B at a monthly salary. Here A's performance is said to be a *condition precedent* to B's duty to pay. This means that B only becomes liable to pay the agreed salary at the end of the month; and B will not be bound to make the payment if, before then, A has repudiated the contract by refusing to do the work.[5] Secondly, A agrees to sell goods to B for cash on delivery (and in the absence of a contrary provision it will be assumed that a sale is on these terms).[6] Here delivery and payment are said to be *concurrent conditions*: that is, neither party need perform until the other is ready and willing to do so; and if, before such an exchange of the goods for the price has taken place, one party repudiates the contract, the other will be entitled to rescind so as to be permanently relieved of his obligations under it. Thirdly, performance by one party may be due in spite of a breach by the other. For example, a landlord is not entitled to refuse to perform his covenant to repair simply because the tenant is in arrears with his rent.[7] The obligations of the parties in these cases are sometimes said to arise out of *independent covenants*.

The rule that A's failure to perform a condition precedent or concurrent condition justifies B's refusal to perform is subject to a qualification. It does not apply if, before performance from A became due, B without justification indicated that he would refuse to accept such performance and if A accepted that repudiation.[8] Such acceptance puts an end to A's own duty to perform and entitles him to claim damages for wrongful repudiation from B.[9]

b Failure in performance must generally be serious

Performance may be in the agreed order, but be deficient in quantity or quality, or be made or tendered after the agreed time. The general principle in such cases is that the right to rescind depends on the

---

[5] *Miles v Wakefield Metropolitan District Council* [1987] A C 539.
[6] Sale of Goods Act 1979, s 28.
[7] *Taylor v Webb* [1937] 2 K B 283.
[8] Post, p 294.
[9] *British and Beningtons Ltd v North Western Cachar Tea Co Ltd* [1923] A C 48, H L; *Berger & Co Inc v Gill & Duffus SA* [1984] A C 382; contrast *The Simona* [1988] 2 All E R 742 and *Segap Garages Ltd v Gulf Oil (Great Britain) Ltd* (1988) Times, 24 October where the repudiation was *not* accepted.

seriousness of the failure in performance. The question is said to be whether the failure deprives the injured party of 'substantially the whole benefit',[10] which it was intended that he should obtain; or whether it 'goes to the root' of the contract. If it does, the injured party can rescind. If its effect is less serious, the injured party will, as a general rule, have to accept and pay for the defective performance. His only remedy (assuming that the failure is a breach) will be in damages.[11] This requirement that the failure must be serious is subject to many important exceptions which will be discussed later in this chapter. Our present concern is with the requirement itself, which is often expressed in vague, general phrases, such as those quoted above. But behind this façade of vague language the courts have applied a number of essentially practical tests.

i Adequacy of damages

The first of these tests is this: will the injured party be adequately protected by an action for damages, or does he *need* the more drastic remedy of rescission? This point is well illustrated by a line of cases concerning breaches by sellers of contracts for the sale of land. If the breach simply is that the seller cannot convey the whole area of land comprised in the contract, then compensation in money will often be an adequate remedy, at least where the reduction in area does not seriously interfere with the use to which the purchaser intended to put the land.[12] This situation should be contrasted with a case in which premises in Covent Garden were sold under a contract which provided that 'no offensive trade' was to be carried on. Investigation of the title revealed that the premises were subject to a covenant against carrying on many quite inoffensive trades, including the sale of fruit. It was held that the purchaser could rescind (and so get back his deposit) as damages for the particular breach were so hard to assess as to be an inadequate remedy.[13] The same test was applied where the English distributor for a French tile manufacturer was persistently (but only slightly) late in making payments under the contract. It was held that the French manufacturer could not rescind since he suffered no loss except a small amount of interest on the sums paid late; and this could easily be made good by an award of damages.[14]

---

10 *Photo Production Ltd v Securicor Transport Ltd* [1980] A C 827 at 849.
11 See eg *Wade v Waldron* 1910 SC 571.
12 Eg *Aspinalls to Powell and Scholefield* (1889) 60 L T 595.
13 *Flight v Booth* (1834) 1 Bing N C 370; cf *Walker v Boyle* [1982] 1 W L R 495.
14 *Decro-Wall International SA v Practitioners in Marketing Ltd* [1971] 2 All ER 216.

ii Reasonableness of accepting further performance

A second test, which is particularly important where a contract calls for continued performance over a period of time, is whether it is reasonable to require the injured party to continue to accept performance of the contract in the light of the failure that has occurred. In deciding this question, the courts have regard to a number of factors. One is the ratio of the failure to the performance that was bargained for. Thus in one case[15] 100 tons of rag flock were sold for delivery by instalments and it was held that defects in only $1\frac{1}{2}$ tons did not justify the buyers' refusal to accept further deliveries. In another case[16] a tenor had been engaged for the 1875 season at Covent Garden, which was to last for three and a half months; and it was held that his failure (on account of illness) to attend rehearsals on four out of the six days before the season opened did not justify his dismissal. Another important factor is the state of uncertainty as to the future which has been created by the failure in performance. The case of the tenor may, from this point of view, be contrasted with one in which a soprano had been engaged to take the leading female part in a new opera. She was ill on the opening night and this fact was held to justify her dismissal, as the illness 'was a serious one of uncertain duration'.[17] The same test is often applied to determine whether failure to remedy the unseaworthiness of a chartered ship justifies rescission of the charterparty.[18]

No exhaustive list can be given of the factors which influence decisions in cases of this kind. In an American case,[19] rescission of a contract to supply milk to State schools and hospitals for a year was held to be justified on the ground that on three occasions in the first two weeks live maggots or dirt had been found in the milk. All that one can say about such a case is that the court found the breach so shocking as to conclude that the State could not reasonably be expected to take further supplies from this source.

iii Ulterior motives

A third test which the courts sometimes apply is this: was the injured party really rescinding because of the prejudice caused to him by the failure in performance, or was he using the failure as an excuse for getting out of a bad bargain? If the latter was his real motive the courts are reluctant to hold that the failure was sufficiently serious; for

[15] *Maple Flock Co Ltd v Universal Furniture and Products (Wembley) Ltd* [1934] 1 KB 148.
[16] *Bettini v Gye* (1876) 1 QBD 183.
[17] *Poussard v Spiers and Pond* (1876) 1 QBD 410 at 415.
[18] *Hong Kong Fir Shipping Co Ltd v Kawasaki Kisen Kaisha Ltd* [1962] 2 QB 26; *The Hermosa* [1982] 1 Lloyd's Rep 570.
[19] *Hershey Farms v State* 110 NYS 2d 324 (1952).

'contracts are made to be performed and not to be avoided according to the whims of market fluctuation'.[20] In one case[1] a contract was made for the carriage of coal which arrived damaged and was also worth less at the destination than the freight. It was held that the owner of the coal could not refuse to pay freight: refusal here was not motivated by the fact that the coal was damaged but by the fall in the market at the destination. In another case[2] a ship which had been chartered for twenty-four months was unseaworthy and needed extensive repairs. When these were completed, the charterparty had seventeen months to run. Meanwhile there had been a 'catastrophic fall' in freight rates.[3] There was no evidence that the unseaworthiness and consequent delays had caused the charterer any loss; on the contrary, they benefited him as he did not, under the terms of the contract, have to pay the (very high) rate of agreed hire while the ship was undergoing repairs. In these circumstances the court refused to allow the charterer to rescind. The decision may well have been influenced by the fact that, under a long-term charterparty, the commercial risk of a fall in freight rates is on the charterer; and this risk should not be thrown back on the shipowner in consequence of breaches which caused the charterer no (or no serious) loss. This flexible and realistic approach to the problem of rescission should be contrasted with that which is adopted in cases falling within the exceptions to the requirement of serious failure, to be discussed in the following paragraphs.

c Exceptions to the requirement of serious failure

It is often hard to predict whether a failure in performance will be regarded as sufficiently serious to justify rescission. To promote greater certainty, the law therefore allows rescission in a number of cases irrespective of the seriousness of the failure. These exceptions to the requirement of serious failure can, however, lead to injustice. For example, they may allow a party to rescind even though this will lead to his being unjustly enriched,[4] and even though his motive for rescinding is simply to get out of a bad bargain.[5] The risk of such injustice has in turn led to judicial and legislative restrictions on the scope of the exceptions.[6]

---

20 *The Hansa Nord* [1976] QB 44 at 71.
1 *Dakin v Oxley* (1864) 15 CBNS 646.
2 *Hong Kong Fir Shipping Co Ltd v Kawasaki Kisen Kaisha Ltd* [1962] 2 QB 26.
3 Ibid at 39.
4 See pp 278, 289–290, post.
5 See p 280, post.
6 See pp 281–282, 291.

i Express provisions

A contract may contain an express provision giving one party the right
to cancel in specified circumstances. For example, a charterparty may
provide that the charterer can cancel if the ship is not at the port of
loading by the end of a specified time, or that the shipowner can
withdraw the ship if the hire is not punctually paid; a hire-purchase
agreement may provide that the owner can terminate if the hirer does
not keep up his payments; or a lease may provide that the landlord can
forfeit if the tenant commits any breach of covenant. The law starts
with the principle that, in the interests of commercial certainty, such
provisions can be literally enforced, so that rescission will be allowed
for even a quite trivial breach.[7] But the resulting hardship to the party
in breach is mitigated in two ways. First, the rescinding party must act
exactly in accordance with the term giving him the right to cancel: he
cannot, for example, cancel *before* the specified event has occurred,
merely because such occurrence has become virtually certain.[8]
Secondly, the law sometimes grants the party in breach relief against
the express term: for example, by allowing a defaulting tenant or hire-
purchaser extra time in which to perform his obligations.[9] Such 'relief
against forfeiture' is, however, only available where rescission would
deprive the party in breach of 'proprietary or possessory rights'[10]
acquired by him under the contract: eg where it would deprive a tenant
or hire-purchaser of the premises or goods which were the subject
matter of the contract. It is (at least between parties bargaining on
equal terms) not available merely because rescission would deprive the
party in breach of valuable *contractual* rights, such as a charter's rights
to services to be performed by the shipowner under a long-term
charterparty.[11]

ii Entire and severable obligations

In some cases, a party is entitled to refuse to perform if the other has not
fully completed performance of his part. He can do this if the other
party's obligation is *entire* , but not if it is *severable*. The distinction is
most easily illustrated by reference to contracts for the carriage of
goods by sea. If the contract provides that the freight is to be paid at the
agreed destination, the carrier cannot recover anything for carrying

---

[7] *The Laconia* [1977] A C 850; *The Chikuma* [1981] 1 All ER 652; *The Scaptrade* [1983]
2 AC 694; such clauses do not seem to be within s 3(2)(b) of the Unfair Contract
Terms Act 1977 (see p 92, ante).
[8] *The Afovos* [1983] 1 W L R 195, H L; cf *The Mihalis Angelos* [1971] 1 Q B 164.
[9] Eg Law of Property Act 1925, s 146; Consumer Credit Act 1974, s 88.
[10] *The Scaptrade* [1983] 2 A C 694 at 702.
[11] See the authorities cited in n 7, supra; cf *Sport International Bussum B V v Inter-Footwear
Ltd* [1984] 1 W L R 776; contrast *B I C C Ltd v Burndy Corpn* [1985] Ch 232.

the goods part of the way: the obligation to get the goods to the destination is entire.[12] On the other hand if the contract provides for freight at so much *per ton* the obligation is severable with regard to the quantity carried, so that the carrier can recover a proportionate part of the freight if he carries less than the agreed amount to the agreed destination.[13] And if the carrier carries the cargo to the agreed destination but it arrives damaged, he is entitled to full freight unless the damage is so serious as to make the goods quite useless to the cargo-owner.[14] Of course, in all these cases the carrier is liable in damages if his failure in performance amounts to a breach. A contract for the sale of goods imposes an entire obligation with regard to quantity. Hence if the seller delivers too little, or too much, the buyer is (unless the discrepancy is minimal or the contract provides for a margin) entitled to refuse to accept and pay.[15] But such a contract does not impose an entire obligation with regard to quality: the right to reject for defects of quality depends on different distinctions to be discussed below.[16] A contract of employment which provides for payment at the end of a fixed period or periods imposes an entire obligation to serve for the stipulated period: thus if the contract provides for payment monthly in arrear and the employee leaves in breach of contract (or is justifiably dismissed) before the end of the month, he is not entitled to his agreed pay for that month; nor, at common law, to any part of it.[17] But if, in the course of the month, he has committed some minor breach of contract, eg by doing bad work, he will be entitled to his pay, less damages for the breach.[18] A similar distinction exists in the case of building contracts. In *Sumpter v Hedges*[19] a builder contracted with a landowner to build two houses on the latter's land for a lump sum of £560; but he was unable to complete the work as he ran out of money. It was held that the builder could not recover the agreed sum as the obligation to complete was entire; nor, for reasons to be discussed later, could he recover the reasonable value of his work. In practice the resulting hardship to the builder is mitigated by stipulations for progress payments; and in *Sumpter v Hedges* itself substantial payments on account had in fact been made to the builder. Moreover, if the houses had been completed late, or defectively, the landowner could

---

[12] *St Enoch Shipping Co v Phosphate Mining Co* [1916] 2 K B 624.

[13] *Ritchie v Atkinson* (1808) 10 East 295.

[14] *Dakin v Oxley* (1864) 15 C B N S 646 at 667.

[15] Sale of Goods Act 1979, s 30 (1).

[16] See pp 279-283, post.

[17] *Boston Deep Sea Fishing & Ice Co v Ansell* (1888) 39 Ch D 339; and cf ante p 273. For possible rights under the Apportionment Act 1870, see p 291, post.

[18] *Miles v Wakefield Metropolitan District Council* [1987] A C 539 at 570; for restrictions on the right to deduct damages from wages, see Wages Act 1986, Pt I.

[19] [1898] 1 Q B 673.

not have refused to pay merely on account of these breaches: his right
to rescind in such a case would have depended on the seriousness of the
breach.[20]

iii Conditions, warranties and intermediate terms

The availability of rescission may turn on the question whether the
term which is not performed is a condition or a warranty or an
intermediate term. A warranty (in modern legal usage) is a term which
affects some relatively minor or subsidiary aspect of the subject-matter
of the contract. Breach of it gives rise to a right to claim damages but
not, in general, to a right to rescind the contract. A condition, on the
other hand, is a term which affects an important aspect of the subject-
matter. Breach of it entitles the victim not only to claim damages but
also to rescind the contract. An intermediate term is one which falls
between the categories of conditions and warranties. Breach of such a
term justifies rescission only where it leads, or amounts, to a serious
failure in performance; where the breach does not have this effect, the
injured party's only remedy is in damages.

The distinction between conditions and warranties is in some cases
based on the intention of the parties, as expressed in the contract. Thus
a provision giving the buyer the right to reject goods if they did not
possess a specified quality would be classified as a condition, as this
would give effect to the intention of the parties.[1] But the mere use of the
word 'condition' will not be conclusive, for the word may have been
used in a non-technical sense to mean simply a term of the contract (as
in the phrase 'our conditions of contract'). In one case[2] a four-year distributorship agreement made it a 'condition' that the distributor would
visit six named customers once a week. It was held that the contract
could not be rescinded merely because this term had been broken. The
parties could not have intended rescission to be available if only one out
of a possible 1,400 or so visits was not paid; indeed they had elsewhere
in the contract laid down a procedure for 'determination' for 'material
breach'.

Often, however, the contract gave no clue as to the intention of the
parties in this respect; and in such cases the distinction between
conditions and warranties was originally based on the seriousness of
the failure to perform. Where the term broken was so important that it
was unreasonable to require the injured party to accept and pay, it
was classified as a condition. Where it was less important, so that
damages were an adequate remedy, it was classified as a warranty.

[20] *Hoenig v Isaacs* [1952] 2 All ER 176.
[1] Eg *Bannerman v White* (1861) 10 CBNS 844; cf *Bergerco USA v Vegoil Ltd* [1984]
1 Lloyd's Rep 440.
[2] *Schuler A G v Wickman Machine Tool Sales Ltd* [1974] AC 235.

Unfortunately, however, the distinction between conditions and warranties came to be overlaid with technicalities, so that to some extent its original purpose was obscured. This development took place because the courts came to classify terms as conditions or warranties by reference to authority, rather than by reference to their importance in individual contracts. Certain commonly found terms thus became conditions as a matter of law, and had to be so treated irrespective of the effects of failure to perform them in a particular case.[3] It was, for example, held to be a condition in a contract for the sale of goods that the goods must correspond with the contractual 'description'; and this rule has received statutory recognition in the Sale of Goods Act.[4] The buyer can therefore reject goods which do not answer the contractual description, even though their failure to do so does not prejudice him seriously, or at all. In one case[5] timber staves were bought for the purpose of making cement barrels and were described in the contract as being $\frac{1}{2}$" thick. It was held that the buyer was justified in rejecting them on the ground that they were $\frac{9}{16}$" thick, even though they were perfectly suitable for making cement barrels, and even though the buyer's motive for rejection was in all probability the fall in the market price of timber. The same principle applies to the common case of goods being sold on the terms that they are to be shipped (or have been shipped) in a specified period, eg as a 'September shipment'. Such words are part of the description of the goods[6] so that the buyer can reject if the goods were shipped on 1 October even though this does not prejudice him in the least and even though his motive for rejecting is that the market has fallen. This type of reasoning, whereby any breach of a term justifies rescission, once that term has been classified as a condition, is particularly common in relation to contracts for the supply of goods, in which many terms are classified as conditions by statute. But it is by no means confined to such contracts. It is for example settled that in a charterparty a statement that the ship is at the time of the contract in a particular port, or one that she will sail on a named day, is a condition.[7] Breach of such a term will therefore automatically and as a matter of law justify rescission.

Judicial or statutory classification of particular terms as warranties is less common. Of the many terms implied by the Sale of Goods Act into contracts for the sale of goods, only one is classified as a warranty: namely the implied term that the goods are free from charges in favour

---

3 *Bunge Corpn v Tradax SA* [1981] 1 W L R 711 at 724; cf ibid 715-716, 718.
4 Originally enacted in 1893; see now Sale of Goods Act 1979, s 13.
5 *Acros Ltd v E A Ronaasen & Son* [1933] A C 470.
6 *Bowes v Shand* (1877) 2 App Cas 455.
7 *Behn v Burness* (1863) 3 B & S 751; *Glaholm v Hays* (1841) 2 Man & G 257.

of third parties.[8] In such cases damages (enabling the buyer to pay off the charge) will generally be an adequate remedy.

Where a term has been classified by law as a condition its breach gives rise to an automatic right to rescind even though there is no evidence that the parties so intended, even though the breach did not prejudice the injured party seriously or at all, and even though his motive in rescinding was simply to escape from a bad bargain. This position has been described as 'excessively technical';[9] and the courts have mitigated its rigours by sometimes placing terms not previously classified as conditions or warranties into the category of intermediate terms.[10] The point may be illustrated by reference to a charterparty under which the shipowner fails to provide a seaworthy ship. Such a failure amounts to a breach of an intermediate term, so that the charterer is not entitled to rescind merely because the ship is unseaworthy;[11] but he may be entitled to do so on one of the other grounds discussed in this chapter: eg if the unseaworthiness leads to a delay which causes him serious prejudice, or which brings a cancelling clause into play. Certain terms in contracts for the sale of goods have similarly been classified as intermediate. In one case,[12] citrus pulp pellets were sold under a contract which provided that they were to be 'shipped in good condition'. Some of the goods were not so shipped, and the buyer purported to reject the whole consignment; later he re-acquired it through an intermediary for little more than a third of the original contract price and used it (as he had intended all along) to manufacture cattle food. The court was clearly unwilling to allow the buyer in this way to escape from a bad bargain. It held that the broken term was not a condition but an intermediate term and that the effect of the breach was not sufficiently serious to justify rescission. Such decisions raise the difficult problem of determining when previously unclassified terms will be classified as intermediate terms and when as conditions.

On the one hand, classification of terms as intermediate can be said to promote justice, by preventing a party from rescinding for ulterior motives where the breach has not caused him any serious loss. Accordingly, a number of cases support the view that previously

---

[8] Sale of Goods Act 1979, s 12 (2).
[9] *Reardon Smith Line Ltd v Hansen Tangen* [1976] 1 W L R 989 at 998. For proposals for reform, see Law Commission Report on Sale and Supply of Goods (Law Com No 120) para 4.21.
[10] As in *Federal Commerce and Navigation Ltd v Molena Alpha Inc* [1979] A C 757.
[11] *Hong Kong Fir Shipping Co Ltd v Kawasaki Kisen Kaisha Ltd* [1962] 2 Q B 26.
[12] *The Hansa Nord* [1976] Q B 44.

unclassified terms should be classified as intermediate,[13] unless a contrary intention clearly appears from the terms of the contract.[14]

On the other hand, classification of terms as conditions can be said to promote certainty; for it will enable an injured party in a future case to know, as soon as the term has been broken, that he is entitled to rescind: he will not need to go into the difficult question whether the breach has serious effects. In *Bunge Corpn v Tradax Export SA*[15] a contract for the sale of goods provided that the goods were to be delivered on board a ship to be provided by the buyers in June. The contract required the buyers to give at least 15 days' notice of the ship's readiness to load; and the House of Lords held that this provision was a condition. It followed that the sellers could rescind simply on the ground that the buyers' notice had reached them five days too late. At the same time, the House of Lords recognised that 'the courts should not be too ready to interpret contractual clauses as conditions'.[16] The effect of the decision is therefore not to reject the approach that the court should 'lean in favour'[17] of classifying terms as intermediate but to qualify it in relation to stipulations which specify a fixed time for performance in commercial contracts. Such stipulations are likely to be classified as conditions because their punctual performance is often vital[18] in dealings with commodities which fluctuate rapidly in value; and because breach of such stipulations is easy to establish, so that their classification as conditions promotes certainty by making it clear to the injured party that he can safely rescind if the other party has not performed by the specified day.

There are, finally, two situations in which rescission may be available as a remedy for breach of warranty. The first arises where a statement of fact which induced the making of the contract is later incorporated in it as a warranty. Such incorporation does not affect the right to rescind *for misrepresentation*;[19] but if the matter misrepresented does not seriously prejudice the injured party the court will probably exercise its discretion to declare the contract subsisting,[20] so that the only remedy will be in damages. The second arises where, though the broken term is a warranty, its breach in fact causes very serious prejudice to the injured party: eg if a breach of warranty in a contract to

13 Eg *Federal Commerce and Navigation Ltd v Molena Alpha Inc* [1979] AC 757; *Bremer Handelsgesellschaft m b H v Vanden Avenne-Izegem PVBA* [1978] 2 Lloyd's Rep 109 at 113; *Tradax International SA v Goldschmidt SA* [1977] 2 Lloyd's Rep 604.
14 Eg *Tradax Export SA v European Grain and Shipping Ltd* [1983] 2 Lloyd's Rep 100.
15 [1981] 2 All ER 513; *Toepfer v Lenersan-Poortman NV* [1980] 1 Lloyd's Rep 143.
16 [1981] 2 All ER 513 at 541-542.
17 *Tradax International SA v Goldschmidt SA* [1977] 2 Lloyd's Rep 604 at 612.
18 See *The Post Chaser* [1981] 2 Lloyd's Rep 695 at 700.
19 Misrepresentation Act 1967, s 1 (a); p 137, ante.
20 Ibid s 2 (2); pp 132-133, ante.

supply a wedding dress made the dress useless on the day of the wedding. There is some support for the view that in such cases rescission would be justified even though the term broken was only a warranty.[1] If this is right, a warranty differs from an intermediate term only in that it *generally* does not give rise to a right to rescind: not in that it can *never* do so.

iv Breach of fundamental term

In chapter 7 we saw that a breach of a fundamental term justified rescission; and normally such a breach will amount to a serious failure in performance. But this is not invariably true, since the concept of fundamental term has, like that of condition, become technical. Sometimes, a term is fundamental merely because it has been so classified by authority; and any breach of it then justifies rescission. This is, for example, true where a carrier of goods by sea deviates:[2] it makes no difference that the deviation is 'for practical purposes irrelevant'.[3] Hence, paradoxically, the right to rescind for breach of a fundamental term sometimes constitutes an exception to the requirement of serious failure in performance.

v Manner of breach

A breach which is in itself trivial will not justify rescission *merely* because it was deliberate. A shipowner would not, for example, be entitled to rescind a charterparty merely because the charterer had deliberately delayed loading for a single day.[4] But where the breach is deliberate it may justify rescission (even though its effects are not such as to satisfy the normal requirement of serious failure in performance) on the ground that its deliberate nature was evidence of the guilty party's 'intention no longer to be bound by the contract'.[5] Thus the effects of unseaworthiness may not in themselves be so serious as to justify rescission of a charterparty; but if the shipowner, before delivery of the ship, refused to remedy the unseaworthiness, the charterer would (so long as the defect is not trivial) be entitled to rescind on that ground.[6] However, the mere fact that the breach was deliberate does not necessarily show that the guilty party intended no

---

[1] *Astley Industrial Trust Ltd v Grimley* [1963] 1 W L R 584 at 599; *The Hansa Nord* [1976] Q B 44 at 83.

[2] See p 79, ante.

[3] *Suisse Atlantique Société D'Armament Maritime SA v N V Rotterdamsche Kolen Centrale* [1967] 1 A C 361 at 423.

[4] *Suisse Atlantique* case [1967] 1 A C 361 at 435.

[5] *Freeth v Burr* (1874) L R 9 C P 208 at 213 (sale); *Laws v London Chronicle Ltd* [1959] 2 All E R 285 (employment).

[6] *Hong Kong Fir Shipping Co Ltd v Kawasaki Kisen Kaisha Ltd* [1962] 2 Q B 26 at 56–64.

longer to be bound by the contract. Thus in one case[7] a buyer of land refused to perform, believing in good faith and in reliance on legal advice that his refusal was justified. The advice turned out to be wrong; but it was held that the buyer had not repudiated since he had throughout declared himself ready to perform if his belief, that he was not bound to do so, should turn out to be mistaken.

It does not follow from the above cases that a deliberate breach will *only* justify rescission where it is evidence of the guilty party's intention no longer to be bound by the contract; for the breach may be sufficiently serious irrespective of such an intention. This was the position where a shipowner wrongfully refused to perform a charterparty except in such a way as would make further performance useless to the charterer. It was held that the charterer was entitled to rescind even though the shipowner in fact intended to keep the contract in being (this being in his interest as freight rates had fallen).[8]

vi *Unilateral contracts and options*

So far we have been concerned with cases in which the failure of one party to perform a promise justifies the refusal of the other to perform his counterpromise. This analysis, however, does not fit the case of a unilateral contract in which only one party makes a promise. Where A promises to pay B £100 if B walks from London to York, B makes no promise and is not bound to do anything. But A can refuse to pay if B gives up the walk before he reaches York. B's completing the walk is here a condition of A's liability; and B must strictly comply with that condition. If he abandons the walk so much as one mile short of York, A can refuse to pay. This rule is particularly important in relation to options which also only bind one of the parties (though their exercise will generally lead to a contract binding both). It goes without saying that an option to purchase can only be exercised within the stipulated time; and the other conditions of its exercise must also be strictly performed.[9] In one case[10] a tenant was given an option to renew his lease provided that *all* the covenants of the lease had been duly performed. He purported to exercise the option but it was held that the landlord was not bound to renew as the tenant was in breach of some of the covenants of the original lease. The landlord would only have been bound to renew if the tenant had cured those breaches by the time he came to exercise the option.[11]

---

7   *Woodar Investment Development Ltd v Wimpey Construction UK Ltd* [1980] 1 All ER 571; cf *Mersey Steel and Iron Co v Naylor Benzon & Co* (1884) 9 App Cas 434.
8   *Federal Commerce and Navigation Co Ltd v Molena Alpha Inc* [1979] AC 757.
9   *Hare v Nicoll* [1966] 2 QB 130.
10   *West Country Cleaners (Falmouth) Ltd v Saly* [1966] 3 All ER 210.
11   *Bass Holdings Ltd v Morton Music Ltd* [1987] 2 All ER 1001.

d Stipulations as to time

Stipulations as to the time of performance are divided by law into two kinds. Some such stipulations are treated as being 'of the essence of the contract'. Failure to perform a stipulation of this kind gives rise automatically to a right to rescind. Others are regarded as less important. Failure to perform these does not automatically give rise to a right to rescind, though it may do so under one of the headings already discussed: eg because the delay amounts to a serious failure in performance. The distinction may be illustrated by reference to contracts for the sale of goods, in which prima facie a stipulation as to the time of making delivery is of the essence of the contract;[12] but one as to the time of taking delivery,[13] or of payment, is not.[14] In other words, a buyer can rescind if delivery is not made within the agreed time; but a seller cannot rescind merely because the buyer delays in taking delivery or in paying for the goods. These are only prima facie rules. They can be excluded by express provisions that time is (or is not) to be of the essence, and also by other circumstances. For example, a stipulation as to the time of payment will be of the essence if the goods are perishable, and one as to the time of taking delivery will be of the essence where the contract requires the buyer to provide a ship on which the goods can be loaded within a specified time.[15]

For historical reasons, contracts for the *sale of land* call for separate treatment. At common law, time was of the essence of such contracts. Hence if the buyer was not ready to pay, or the seller to convey, on the day named in the contract, then the other party could rescind. Equity did not follow this rigid rule. It generally regarded time as a matter of subsidiary importance in such contracts, and it therefore enforced them, even after the time fixed for performance,[16] so long as the delay did not amount to a serious breach. By statute, the equitable rule now prevails,[17] so that rescission is no longer available to one party merely because the other party has failed to perform at the agreed time. Thus a party who refuses to perform on account of the delay can be sued for specific performance or damages.[18] But the delay remains a breach, so that, if no attempt is made to rescind, and the contract is actually performed late, the victim of the delay will be entitled to damages.[19] A

---

[12] *Hartley v Hymans* [1920] 3 K B 475 at 484.

[13] *Woolfe v Horne* (1877) 2 Q B D 355.

[14] Sale of Goods Act 1979, s 10 (1).

[15] *The Osterbek* [1973] 2 Lloyd's Rep 86; *Bunge Corpn v Tradax SA* [1981] 2 All ER 513.

[16] *Parkin v Thorold* (1852) 16 Beav 59.

[17] Law of Property Act 1925, s 41 (re-enacting the Judicature Act 1873, s 25 (1)); *United Scientific Holdings Ltd v Burnley Borough Council* [1978] A C 904 at 940.

[18] *Stickney v Keeble* [1915] A C 386 at 404.

[19] *Raineri v Miles* [1981] A C 1050.

party who wishes to avoid the risk of being held to the contract in spite of the other's delay can expressly provide that time is to be 'of the essence'. Even if time is not originally of the essence, the injured party is not bound to wait indefinitely for performance. He can (after the contract date for performance has gone by) give notice to the other party calling upon him to perform by the end of a specified period. A contract for the sale of land generally stipulates how much notice must be given for this purpose; failing that, the period of notice must be reasonable.[20] If *either* party then fails to perform by the end of that period, the other can rescind.[1]

Even in equity time is of the essence of a contract for the sale of land if delay in performance is in fact likely to have a serious effect. This is, for example, the position where the subject-matter of the contract is a short leasehold, since such a property tends to depreciate rapidly.[2] Similarly time is of the essence in so-called 'commercial' contracts for the sale of land, such as contracts for the sale of business premises as a going concern, or of land intended for rapid commercial development.[3] Now that land and houses fluctuate violently in value, the distinction between these 'commercial' and other contracts begins to look artificial. But it does still exist so that time would not be regarded as being of the essence of a contract for the sale of ordinary domestic premises as a private residence. Time may, finally, in a sense be of the essence where the contract is conditional and specifies a time by which the condition is to be satisfied: eg where the contract is subject to planning permission being obtained in six months. Here the stipulation as to time is not one as to the performance of the contract. It affects the more fundamental question whether a binding contract of sale is to come into existence at all; and this question must be resolved within the stipulated time.[4]

e Limits on rescission

The right to rescind a contract for failure in performance may be lost, or the exercise of the right may be limited, on one of the following grounds:

i Waiver

The injured party may know that a breach has occurred which would normally give him the right to rescind. But if he nevertheless indicates

---

20 *Stickney v Keeble,* supra; cf *British and Commonwealth Group plc v Quadrex Holdings* Inc (1988) Times, 8 December.
1 *Finkielkraut v Monohan* [1949] 2 All ER 234; *Quadrangle Development and Construction Co Ltd v Jenner* [1974] 1 All ER 729.
2 *Hudson v Temple* (1860) 29 Beav 536.
3 *Lock v Bell* [1931] 1 Ch 35; *Bernard v Williams* (1928) 44 TLR 437.
4 *Aberfoyle Plantations v Cheng* [1960] AC 115.

that he will perform the contract, or that he will accept late or defective performance, then he will be taken to have 'waived' his right to rescind for the breach in question, in the sense of having elected to affirm the contract.[5] This type of waiver must be distinguished from that discussed in chapter 3, by which a party purports wholly to relinquish contractual rights.[6] Our present concern is with cases in which the injured party only waives his right to rescind, while retaining his right to damages. Such waiver does not give rise to problems of consideration; for even defective performance, coupled with damages, *may* be more beneficial than rescission. The element of reliance, which serves as a substitute for consideration in the type of waiver discussed in chapter 3,[7] is therefore not necessary for the waiver of the right to rescind with which we are here concerned.[8] All that is necessary for the purpose of this kind of waiver is that the injured party should have known that he had the right to rescind[9] and that he should by some 'unequivocal act or statement'[10] have indicated that he would not exercise that right.

ii Part performance of the contract

Rescission often causes hardship to the party in breach, and this hardship tends to become more severe the further performance or purported performance of the contract has gone. Suppose that a seller has delivered goods at a distant place, or that a shipowner has sent his ship half-way round the world to begin performance of a charterparty, or that a builder has nearly completed a house which he had contracted to build. Such persons would clearly suffer hardship if at this stage the buyer or charterer or landowner could still rescind; and as a general guide it can be said that the courts become less ready to allow rescission, the further performance has gone. This does not mean that the right to rescind is lost merely because the contract has been partly performed, as a backward glance at *Sumpter v Hedges* [11] will show; but there can be no doubt about the general policy. A particularly clear illustration of it is to be found in the rule that a buyer of goods cannot reject them for breach of condition after he has 'accepted' them.[12]

---

5 *Bentsen v Taylor* [1893] 2 QB 274; Sale of Goods Act 1979, s 11(2).
6 See pp 40–43, ante; and cf p 59 ante.
7 Ante, p 42.
8 See *The Athos* [1981] 2 Lloyd's Rep 74 at 87-88; approved on this point [1983] 1 Lloyd's Rep 127; *Peyman v Lanjani* [1985] Ch 457 at 493, 500-501.
9 *Peyman v Lanjani* [1985] Ch 457.
10 *The Mihalios Xilas* [1979] 2 All ER 1044 at 1049.
11 [1898] 1 QB 673; p 278 ante; cf also such cases as *Hershey Farms v State* 110 N Y S 2d 324 (1952), p 275, ante; *Thorpe v Fasey* [1949] Ch 649 appears to take a contrary view but to be explicable on the ground that there was no sufficiently serious breach.
12 Sale of Goods Act 1979, s 11(4).

Acceptance is here a technical concept. A buyer is deemed to have accepted the goods in three situations: when he intimates to the seller that he accepts the goods; when the goods have been delivered to him and, after reasonable opportunity of examining them, he does an act inconsistent with the ownership of the seller, such as reselling the goods and delivering them to a sub-buyer; and when he retains them for more than a reasonable time without intimating to the seller that he rejects them.[13] A buyer may 'accept' goods even though he does not yet know of the breach of condition. In this respect the requirements of acceptance differ strikingly from those of waiver.

'Acceptance' only bars the right to rescind *for breach of condition*. There are two cases in which a buyer who has 'accepted' may still be able to rescind.

First, the seller may have made a misrepresentation inducing the contract. In that case, the buyer may be able to rescind the contract even though the misrepresentation has become a term of the contract,[14] and the right to rescind *for misrepresentation* is probably not lost merely because the buyer has 'accepted' the goods. It may be lost on analogous grounds discussed in chapter 9, such as affirmation and lapse of time.[15] But these could be more favourable to the buyer than the rules as to acceptance: in particular, affirmation presupposes knowledge of the truth. On the other hand, the right to rescind for misrepresentation is subject to the discretion of the court[16] while the right to rescind for breach can be exercised as of right.

Secondly, the seller may have committed a breach which is more serious than a breach of condition and it seems that the right to rescind for such a breach will not be barred merely by 'acceptance'. Suppose that peas are sold by sample, that the seller delivers peas in bags, and that the peas are not in accordance with the sample. If the buyer keeps the peas for more than a reasonable time without opening the bags he will be deemed to have 'accepted' them and so to have lost his right to rescind for breach of condition. But if the bags contain beans, the buyer will not lose his right to rescind by 'acceptance', for in this case the seller's breach goes beyond a mere breach of condition: it amounts to a total failure to perform.[17] The right to rescind for such a failure will only be lost if the buyer, after discovering the truth, indicates that he will keep the beans. In such a case he can be said to have 'waived' the right to rescind, or possibly to have made a new contract to buy beans.

---

13 Sale of Goods Act 1979, s 35.
14 Misrepresentation Act 1967, s 1 (a).
15 See p 140, ante.
16 Misrepresentation Act 1967, s 2(2).
17 See *Chanter v Hopkins* (1838) 4 M & W 399 at 404; and p 79, ante.

iii Terms of the contract

Commercial sellers of goods often try to protect themselves against
rescission by clauses which provide that certain breaches by the seller
shall give rise only to a claim for damages and not to a right to reject or
rescind. Similarly, contracts for the sale of land often provide that
errors and misdescriptions shall not annul the sale but shall give rise to
a claim for compensation only. Such non-rejection or non-cancellation
clauses are prima facie effective. They are, however, regarded as
exemption clauses; and accordingly they are subject to the rules,
discussed in chapter 7, which limit the effectiveness of such clauses. In
particular, they are strictly construed against the parties seeking to rely
on them; they are presumed, as a matter of construction, not to apply
to breaches of a particularly serious kind;[18] and they may be ineffective, or subject to the requirement of reasonableness, under the Unfair
Contract Terms Act 1977 or the Misrepresentation Act 1967.[19]

iv New contract

Where performance by one party (A) is incomplete or defective, the
other (B) may be entitled to rescind *the contract* . But B may nevertheless
be under some liability to A in respect of the performance actually
rendered.

This is most obviously so where A's failure to complete performance
is due to B's wrongful refusal to accept it. In one case[20] A agreed to
write a serial for B's magazine; and, when A had done a substantial
part of the work, B discontinued the publication. A was not entitled to
the *agreed remuneration* but recovered a reasonable recompense for the
work he had done.

A similar liability also arises where A fails to complete performance
in accordance with the contract but B nevertheless voluntarily accepts
A's partial or defective performance. The point may be illustrated by
further reference to *Sumpter v Hedges* [1] where the builder was not entitled
to the *agreed price* as the unperformed obligation to complete the two
houses was an entire one. His claim for the reasonable value of his work
also failed as the landowner had not accepted it *voluntarily*: the partly
completed houses were on his land and so he really had no choice in the
matter. On the other hand the landowner had also used building
materials left lying loose on the site by the builder. It was held that he
had voluntarily accepted these materials and that he was liable for their
reasonable value. A similar distinction exists where a carrier by sea

18 *J Aron & Co (Inc) v Comptoir Wegimont* [1921] 3 K B 435.
19 See pp 88–96, ante; *Walker v Boyle* [1982] 1 All ER 634.
20 *Planché v Colburn* (1831) 8 Bing 14.
 1 [1898] 1 Q B 673; see p 278, ante.

fails to carry goods to the agreed destination but delivers them at an intermediate port. A new contract may be inferred if the carrier so delivers the goods at the request of their owner,[2] but no such inference will be drawn merely because the owner of the goods takes possession of them at the intermediate port where they have been unloaded without his consent.[3] Similarly, where an employee refuses to perform the work that he was employed to do, he is not entitled to his wages;[4] but he may be entitled to a reasonable sum if the employer voluntarily accepts work falling short of that required under the contract.[5] The object of the rule that the acceptance must be voluntary is to protect the injured party against having to pay for a performance different from that for which he bargained. This may be particularly necessary where damages would not adequately compensate him for the loss which he has suffered. On the other hand the rule may lead to unjust enrichment where the value of the performance received by the victim exceeds the loss caused by the breach. Under the rule in *Sumpter v Hedges* the landowner could get a nearly completed building for nothing. There appears to be an element of penalty in this rule; and it would be better if the party in breach could recover the value to the victim of the performance actually rendered and retained, less any loss suffered by the victim in consequence of the failure to complete performance.[6]

v Both parties in breach

This possibility is illustrated by a group of arbitration cases in which the claimant is guilty of such serious delays as to make a satisfactory trial impossible. It thereupon becomes the duty of the other party to apply to the arbitrator for directions to put an end to the delay. If he fails to do so, neither party can rescind as 'both [are] in breach of their contractual obligations to each other'.[7] It is possible (if unlikely) for the arbitration agreement to be brought to an end by other means: eg where the delay is coupled with other circumstances, and together they support the inference that the parties have abandoned the agreement by mutual consent.[8]

---

[2] *Christy v Row* (1808) 1 Taunt 300.
[3] Cf *Hopper v Burness* (1876) 1 CPD 137.
[4] See *Miles v Wakefield Metropolitan District Council* [1987] AC 539.
[5] A point left open in *Miles v Wakefield Metropolitan District Council*, supra.
[6] See Law Commission Paper 121; not to be implemented: see Law Commission, 19th Annual Report, para 2.11.
[7] *Bremer Vulkan Schiffbau und Maschinenfabrik v South India Shipping Corpn Ltd* [1981] AC 909; *The Hannah Blumenthal* [1983] 1 AC 854. For criticism, see *The Antclizo* [1988] 2 All ER 513.
[8] See ante, p 7.

vi *Apportionment Act 1870*

This Act provides that certain 'periodical payments in the nature of income' shall, unless the contract otherwise provides, 'be considered as accruing from day to day and shall be apportionable in respect of time accordingly'.[9] The Act applies to such payments as rents, annuities, dividends, salaries and pensions.[10] If, for example, a person who was entitled to a monthly salary died in the third week of the month, he would be entitled to a proportionate part of his month's pay. The terms of the Act are wide enough to lead to the same result even where the employee leaves in breach of contract or is lawfully dismissed during the month; but judicial opinion is divided on the question whether a party in breach can take advantage of the provisions of the Act.[11]

f The option to rescind

At this stage we shall assume that there has been a failure in performance which justifies rescission. Three further points now require discussion.

i *No automatic rescission*

A breach of contract gives the injured party an option to rescind. It does not automatically discharge the contract;[12] for if it did a party could rely on his own breach of the contract to excuse himself from further performance of it. For this reason, the rule applies even if the contract provides that the contract is to become 'void' in the event of breach.[13] From this point of view, the effects of breach differ from those of frustration, which (as we shall see in chapter 17) does automatically discharge both parties. But although in cases of breach discharge depends on the election of the injured party, his freedom of choice is to some extent curtailed by law. Suppose, for example, that an employee is wrongfully dismissed in breach of contract. The dismissal does not automatically terminate the contract,[14] but the damages which the

---

[9] Ss 2, 7.
[10] S 5.
[11] *Clapham v Draper* (1885) Cab & El 484; *Moriarty v Regent's Garage Co* [1921] 1 K B 423; on appeal [1921] 2 K B 766.
[12] *Heyman v Darwins Ltd* [1942] A C 356 at 361; *Photo Production Ltd v Securicor Transport Ltd* [1980] A C 827; *Rigby v Ferodo Ltd* [1987] ICR 457.
[13] See *Davenport v R* (1877) 3 App Cas 115; *New Zealand Shipping Co Ltd v Société des Ateliers et Chantiers de France* [1919] A C 1. Contrast *Cheall v Association of Professional Executive Clerical and Computer Staff* [1983] 1 All E R 1130 (breach of agreement with third party); *Thompson v ASDA-MFI Group plc* [1988] 2 All E R 722 (no breach).
[14] *Gunton v Richmond-upon-Thames London Borough Council* [1981] Ch 448; *Dietman v London Borough of Brent* [1987] I C R 737; for the converse situation (repudiatory breach by employee) cf *Evening Standard Co Ltd v Henderson* [1987] I C R 588; *Miles v Wakefield Metropolitan District Council* [1987] A C 539.

employee can recover will be reduced to the extent that he failed to mitigate his loss. If he mitigates by obtaining other employment, he will have put it out of his power to perform the original contract and so be taken to have exercised his option to rescind that contract.[15] The mitigation rules do not compel the injured party to exercise that option, but they provide him with strong incentive to do so.[16] They may, conversely, provide him with an incentive to accept a performance which he was entitled to reject: for example where a seller on a rising market offers delivery after the agreed time, and it would be reasonable for the buyer to accept such delivery. Although the buyer is not *bound* to accept such delivery, his unreasonable refusal to do so will be taken into account in reducing his damages.[17]

ii *Effects of rescission*

Rescission is sometimes said to terminate or discharge the contract; but this is true only in a qualified sense. The exact effects of rescission are best considered by looking in turn at the position of the injured party and at that of the party failing to perform.

The injured party is released from future obligations under the contract: for example, a buyer who exercises his right to rescind an instalment contract need not accept and pay for future deliveries. But he is not released from obligations already accrued at the time of rescission: he must, for example, pay for instalments already delivered before that time, except to the extent that they are themselves defective and are lawfully rejected. If they are thus rejected, the buyer is entitled to get back the money paid for them: to this extent rescission operates retrospectively.

The party who has failed to perform is also released from future (but not from accrued) obligations *to perform*. If, for example, a party to whom instalment payments are due under a contract lawfully rescinds for the other party's breach, the latter cannot be sued for instalments which would have become due *after* the date of rescission.[18] But he is not released from his liability to pay instalments which had become due *before* that date.[19] Nor is he released from liability in *damages* if his failure to perform amounted to a repudiatory breach, giving the other party the right to rescind. Thus if a hire-purchase agreement is

---

15 As in *Dietman's* case, supra.
16 *Gunton's* case, supra, at 468.
17 *The Solholt* [1983] 1 Lloyd's Rep 605 cf p 338, post.
18 Cf *Financings Ltd v Baldock* [1963] 2 Q B 104 at 110 (hire-purchase); *U C B Leasing Ltd v Holtom* [1987] R T R 362.
19 *Hyundai Shipbuilding & Heavy Industries Co Ltd v Pournaras* [1978] 2 Lloyd's Rep 502; *Hyundai Heavy Industries Co Ltd v Papadopoulos* [1980] 2 All E R 29; *Moschi v Lep Air Services* [1973] A C 331 at 354-355; for an exception see p 348, post.

wrongfully repudiated by the hirer, the owner can rescind and recover not only any payments due at the time of rescission, but also damages for wrongful repudiation.[20] These can include loss suffered after rescission: eg because the owner can only let the subject-matter out to another customer on terms which are less profitable to him than those of the original contract with the defaulting party.[1] Damages can similarly be recovered where a contract for the sale of goods or of land is rescinded by one party on account of the other's breach[2]. There is no inconsistency between rescinding for breach and claiming damages: in this respect rescission for breach differs from rescission for misrepresentation.[3] The reason for the difference seems to be that misrepresentation affects the formation of the contract, so that a party who rescinds on this ground in effect says that there was never a properly formed contract. A party who rescinds for breach makes no similar allegation: his complaint is simply that the contract has not been properly performed.

Finally, an injured party who first rescinds cannot then affirm and claim performance. This follows from the rule that rescission releases the other party from his obligation to perform. The result may also be justified on the ground that that party may have acted in reliance on the belief that, after rescission, he would no longer be called on to perform.

iii Effects of affirmation

If the injured party affirms (or simply fails to rescind) the obligations of both parties remain in force.[3a] For example, an employee may commit a breach justifying his dismissal; but if he is not dismissed and continues to perform duties under the contract, the employer will be liable to pay such part of the employee's salary or wages as has become due, less any damages caused by the breach.[4]

The fact that the *obligations* of the parties remain in force does not

---

[20] There is no such liability where the injured party rescinds under an express term for a breach not amounting to a repudiation: *Financings Ltd v Baldock*, supra; the contrary decision reluctantly reached in *Lombard North Central plc v Butterworth* [1987] Q B 527 can perhaps be explained on the ground that the term broken was a condition.

[1] *Yeoman Credit v Waragowski* [1961] 3 All ER 145; *Photo Production Ltd v Securicor Transport Ltd* [1980] A C 827 at 849.

[2] *Millar's Machinery Co Ltd v David Way & Son* (1935) 40 Com Cas 204; *Buckland v Farmer and Moody* [1978] 3 All ER 929; *Johnson v Agnew* [1980] A C 367; *Berger & Co Inc v Gill & Duffus SA* [1984] A C 382; *The Blankenstein* [1985] 1 All E R 475, C A.

[3] See pp 136–137, ante.

[3a] *Segap Garages Ltd v Gulf Oil (Great Britain) Ltd* (1988) Times, 24 October.

[4] See *Sim v Rotherham Metropolitan Borough Council* [1987] Ch 216; and cf *Miles v Wakefield Metropolitan District Council* [1987] A C 539 on the question how much has become due (ante, p 290).

lead to any conclusions about the remedies for their enforcement. A party who elects to keep the contract alive may in fact be prevented (by the other's wrongful repudiation) from performing his own obligations: for example a wrongfully dismissed employee may be prevented from doing the work that he was engaged to do. In such a case, his only remedy will be by way of damages: he will not be entitled to the agreed wages.[5] Even where the wrongful repudiation does *not* prevent the injured party from performing, affirmation of the contract will not necessarily enable him to secure remedies for the *specific* enforcement of the other's obligations. The circumstances in which such remedies are available will be discussed in chapter 18.[6]

We have seen that an injured party cannot rescind and then affirm; but the converse is not true. If he first affirms, the guilty party is clearly not released; nor will the injured party's efforts to secure performance of themselves amount to an 'unequivocal act or statement' that he will in no circumstances rescind, so as to give rise to a waiver.[7] Hence if those efforts prove fruitless the injured party can still rescind. This is so even if the injured party has actually gone to court and obtained an order of specific performance, with which the guilty party has failed to comply. It is then open to the injured party to apply to the court to dissolve the order, to put an end to the contract, and to claim damages for its breach.[8]

4 ANTICIPATORY BREACH

One of the parties to a contract may, before the time fixed for performance, *renounce* the contract by indicating that he will refuse to perform it, or *disable himself* from performing it by some act or omission making such performance impossible. He is then said to commit an 'anticipatory' (as opposed to an actual) breach. The other party can either 'accept' the breach or keep the contract alive by continuing to press for performance.[9]

a Accepting the breach

The injured party can 'accept' the breach either by bringing an action on the contract, or by giving notice to the other party and acting accordingly. The legal effects of accepting the breach are as follows.

[5] See post, p 350.
[6] See pp 351–358, post.
[7] See p 287, ante.
[8] *Johnson v Agnew* [1980] AC 367 at 394.
[9] *Micheal v Hart & Co* [1902] 1 KB 482.

i Rescission

Acceptance of an anticipatory breach amounts to a rescission of the contract. For the purpose of this rule it is assumed that the breach is one that would, if it were actual, justify rescission: ie that it would be of the degree of seriousness discussed earlier in this chapter,[10] or that it would fall within an exception to that requirement, eg because it would amount to a breach of condition.[11] However, where the right to rescind arises *only* under an express provision for cancellation,[12] it cannot be exercised on account of a merely anticipatory breach. Suppose that a charterparty gives a charterer the right to cancel if the ship is not at the port of loading by 1 June. He is not entitled to cancel on 25 May even though on that day the ship is so far from the port of loading that she cannot possibly reach it in less than ten days.[13]

In cases of anticipatory breach, the injured party may rescind before the time fixed for performance; and a question therefore arises as to the time at which the breach must be of such a nature as to justify rescission. Is the relevant time that of rescission or that fixed for performance? This depends on the type of anticipatory breach in question. In the case of a *refusal to perform* that refusal must be 'clear' and 'absolute'[14] and the refusal can be inferred from conduct where the party in breach has 'acted in such a way as to lead a reasonable man to conclude that [he] did not intend to fulfil [his] part of the contract'.[15] Whether a reasonable man would draw this conclusion is to be judged by reference to *the time of rescission*.[16] But the position is different where the ground of rescission is the other party's *prospective inability* (as opposed to his refusal) to perform. The injured party may at the time of rescission reasonably believe that the other party will be unable to perform in accordance with the contract, and that the resulting actual breach will be sufficiently serious to justify rescission. Nevertheless if it turns out that the other party can perform, or that his breach is not of the required degree of seriousness, rescission will not be justified.[17] This rule is likely to be inconvenient in practice since normally the injured party, when faced with an anticipatory breach, will want to know at once whether he remains bound by the contract, or whether he

---

[10] See pp 273–276, ante.

[11] See p 279, ante; that a breach of condition suffices for this purpose is assumed in *Universal Cargo Carriers Corpn v Citati* [1957] 2 QB 401.

[12] See p 277, ante.

[13] *The Mihalis Angelos* [1971] 1 QB 164; a dictum in *The Afovos* [1983] 1 All ER 449 at 455, limiting the doctrine of anticipatory breach to 'fundamental' breaches occurs in the context of such express provisions and should be restricted to this situation.

[14] *The Hermosa* [1982] 1 Lloyd's Rep 570 at 572.

[15] Ibid at 580.

[16] Ibid at 573; *The Sanko Iris* [1987] 1 Lloyd's Rep 487.

[17] *Universal Cargo Carriers Corpn v Citati* [1957] 2 QB 401 at 449-450.

is free to make alternative arrangements. The rule does not apply where there has been an *actual* breach and the only doubt relates to the prospective effects of that breach. In such a case, the injured party is entitled to rescind if, when he did so, he reasonably believed that the effects of the breach would be of the required degree of seriousness.[18]

Where the injured party justifiably rescinds, both parties are released from their duty to perform future obligations, but the guilty party is liable in damages. To make good his claim for damages, the injured party need not perform, or even show that he could have performed, his own future obligations;[19] for after rescission his failure or inability to perform them can no longer amount to a breach. *Other* future events may, however, affect the damages to which he is entitled, and even reduce them to a nominal amount: this possibility is explained in chapter 18.[20]

ii Damages

The most striking feature of the doctrine of anticipatory breach is that a victim can sue for damages *at once*.[1] He does not have to wait until the time fixed for performance arrives. Suppose that A on 1 January agrees to employ B with effect from 1 October and that on 1 February A repudiates the contract. B can immediately bring proceedings against A, and, if the case comes to trial quickly, he may even get his damages before 1 October. This result is open to the objection that A's obligation is accelerated: he may have to pay damages before he was due to perform. But the doctrine of anticipatory breach is nevertheless generally regarded as a convenient one. Its merit is that it tends to reduce loss by making it possible for the parties to have their dispute determined with a minimum of delay.

Once the victim has accepted the breach, his right to damages is not defeated by actual or possible supervening events. In the case put, A could not avoid liability by at this stage indicating that he was, after all, ready to employ B;[2] or by arguing that he or B might die before 1 October, and that the contract would then be frustrated.[3] Subsequent events may affect the amount recoverable,[4] but not the right to damages itself.

[18] *Hong Kong Fir Shipping Co Ltd v Kawasaki Kisen Kaisha Ltd* [1962] 2 QB 26 at 57.
[19] *British and Beningtons Ltd v North Western Cachar Tea Co Ltd* [1923] AC 48.
[20] Post, p 333.
[1] *Hochster v De la Tour* (1853) 2 E & B 678.
[2] Cf *Danube etc Rly v Xenos* (1863) 13 CBNS 825.
[3] Cf *Synge v Synge* [1894] 1 QB 466.
[4] Cf supra at n. 20.

b Keeping the contract alive

The victim of an anticipatory breach may elect to keep the contract alive, in the hope of securing its actual performance: this is likely to be more beneficial in practice than even a successful lawsuit. By taking this course, the victim also keeps open the possibility of·being able to claim specific performance or the agreed sum.[5] His damages may also be assessed on a different, and to him more favourable, basis.[6] On the other hand he will not receive anything until (at the earliest) the time fixed for performance; and he runs the risk of losing his rights under the contract as a result of events occurring after the anticipatory breach: for example, on account of some supervening event which frustrates the contract,[7] or which entitles the other party to cancel the contract under one of its express terms.[8]

[5] See pp 349–358, post.
[6] See pp 332–333, post.
[7] *Avery v Bowden* (1855) 5 E & B 714; (1856) 6 E & B 953.
[8] *The Simona* [1988] 2 All ER 742.

Chapter 17

Frustration

We saw in chapter 16 that a contracting party may be in breach even though his failure to perform is not due to any want of care or diligence on his part. For example, a seller who undertakes to ship goods from a certain port within a stated time may be liable in damages if he fails to do so, even though his failure is simply due to the fact that no ship which could carry the goods left that port within the time.[1] On the other hand, the seller would not be liable if, before the relevant time, the port were destroyed by an earthquake. In that case the contract is said to have been frustrated by supervening impossibility. The distinction between the two cases is an obvious, almost intuitive, one, which it is not altogether easy to put into words. In our first case the seller undertakes that there will be a ship, perhaps realising that there is an element of risk about such an undertaking. But in the second he does not undertake that there will be a port: this is simply assumed by both parties. When a fundamental assumption of this kind is falsified by subsequent events the doctrine of frustration comes into play.

The effect of the doctrine is to discharge the contract by operation of law. If follows that *both* parties are discharged, even though only one party's obligation has become impossible to perform. In our last example, both seller and buyer are discharged, even though it remains physically possible for the buyer to pay the price. The law regards the contract as a kind of common venture, having as its object the *exchange* of the goods for the price; and if that 'common object' cannot be fulfilled, then both parties are at once discharged from all their obligations under the contract. This automatic and total discharge of the contract is a somewhat drastic solution to a difficult problem. It can occasionally lead to hardship and inconvenience almost as great as the opposite view (formerly held, but now abandoned, by the law) that a contract is not discharged by supervening impossibility of performance. Accordingly, the doctrine of frustration has been kept within narrow limits by two trends, one judicial and the other commercial. The judges have insisted that the supervening event must destroy a *fundamental* assumption on which the contract was based; and they have also limited the scope of the doctrine in a number of other ways. Businessmen have, for their part, taken steps to 'draft out' frustration. In other words they have, where possible, said in the contract what was

[1] See pp 266–267, ante.

298

to happen if supervening events interfered with performance. Where they have done so, these provisions will generally apply and will exclude the doctrine of frustration. In the rest of this chapter, we shall consider first the normal operation of the doctrine of frustration, secondly some limitations on its scope, and thirdly the exact legal consequences of frustration.

1 OPERATION OF THE DOCTRINE

A contract may be frustrated if it becomes impossible to perform; or if the purpose of the contract is frustrated; or if performance becomes illegal.

a Impossibility.

Supervening events may make performance impossible in the following situations:

i *Destruction of the subject-matter.*

The most obvious cause of impossibility is the destruction of the subject-matter of the contract. In *Taylor v Caldwell*[2] the Surrey Gardens and Music Hall were hired out by the defendants to the plaintiff 'for the purpose of giving four grand concerts' on four named days in June, July and August 1861. Before the first of those days the Music Hall was accidentally burnt down. The plaintiffs claimed damages in respect of their wasted advertising expenses, but the claim failed as the destruction of the Music Hall had frustrated the contract. The case shows that the destruction need not be total for the Surrey Gardens (with their many attractions) appear to have survived undamaged. In other words, 'destruction' in the present context does not mean complete physical destruction, but destruction of the commercial characteristics of the subject-matter.

Even the destruction of the subject-matter will not always frustrate a contract; for it may be governed by rules of law which place the 'risk of loss' on one party or the other. The point may be illustrated by supposing that A has agreed to instal machinery in B's factory. If, before the work is completed, the *factory* is destroyed the contract is frustrated.[3] But if only the *machinery* is destroyed, A must do the work again at no extra cost;[4] for the risk of loss, so far as the work is concerned, is (unless the contract otherwise provides) on the builder until completion.

---

[2] (1863) 3 B & S 826.
[3] *Appleby v Myers* (1867) L R 2 C P 651.
[4] Ibid at 660.

ii Death or incapacity

A contract is frustrated by the death of a party who had undertaken a 'personal' obligation. A contract of employment, for example, can be frustrated by the death of either party; and the same would be true if either party were permanently incapacitated from performance.

iii Unavailability

A contract may also be frustrated where the subject-matter, though not destroyed, ceases to be available for the purpose of performing the contract. A contract for the sale of goods may thus be frustrated if the goods are requisitioned;[5] and a charterparty may be frustrated if the ship is requisitioned or detained, or if cargo is unavailable by reason of a strike. In such cases, considerable difficulties can arise if the unavailability is only temporary: the test in such cases is whether performance would, as a result of the delay, become 'as a matter of business a totally different thing'[6] from that originally undertaken. This would most obviously be the position (so that the contract would be frustrated) where the contract contained a seasonal element: for example, where a ship which had been chartered to carry spring vegetables was requisitioned and not released till the autumn.[7] Charterparties were similarly held to have been frustrated where the ships were detained for long periods in the course of the Gulf War between Iran and Iraq.[8] But a case in which a chartered ship was requisitioned during the First World War fell on the other side of the line, so that the contract was not frustrated: the charterparty was a long-term one and it seemed likely, when the ship was requisitioned, that she would be released in time to render substantial services under the charterparty.[9]

Similar principles apply where a party who is under an obligation of 'personal' performance is temporarily unavailable, eg as a result of illness or conscription. Thus a contract to give a musical performance on a particular day may be frustrated by the performer's illness on that day;[10] and a long-term contract of employment may be frustrated by the employee's illness if it is so serious as to make it unlikely that performance can be resumed.[11] This is so even though the contract is terminable on relatively short notice, since many such contracts are

---

5 *Re Shipton, Anderson & Co* [1915] 3 K B 676.
6 *Bank Line Ltd v Arthur Capel & Co* [1919] A C 435 at 460.
7 Cf *Jackson v Union Marine Insurance Co Ltd* (1874) L R 10 C P 125 at 140.
8 Eg *The Evia (No 2)* [1983] 1 A C 736; *The Wenjiang* [1983]1 Lloyd's Rep 400.
9 *Tamplin SS Co Ltd v Anglo-Mexican Petroleum Co* [1916] 2 A C 397.
10 *Robinson v Davison* (1871) L R 6 Exch 269.
11 See *Condor v The Barron Knights Ltd* [1966] 1 W L R 87; *Marshall v Harland & Wolff Ltd* [1972] 2 All ER 715; *Hart v A R Marshall & Sons (Bulwell) Ltd* [1978] 2 All ER 413.

intended to last, and in fact do last, for many years.[12] A less serious illness may give the employee an excuse for non-performance[13] and may entitle the employer to terminate;[14] but it will not discharge both parties automatically under the doctrine of frustration.

iv Failure of a particular source.

A contract may be frustrated if its subject-matter is to be taken from a source which fails. Thus where a farmer contracted to sell potatoes out of a crop to be grown on his land, it was held that the contract was frustrated when the crop was attacked by disease and failed.[15] But a contract is not frustrated merely because a source contemplated by only *one* of the parties (but not by the other) has failed. In one case a seller of timber expected to get supplies from abroad but the buyer did not know this. It was held that the contract was not frustrated when the seller was cut off by war from his foreign source of supply.[16] Where *both* parties contemplate the source that fails, the contract may be frustrated even though the contract does not actually refer to that source; but there would be no frustration if it would have been commercially reasonable to provide against such failure: eg by contracting 'subject to availability' or 'subject to shipment'.

v Method of performance impossible

Where a contract provides that it is to be performed in a particular way, impossibility in the method of performance may frustrate it. This was for example held to be the position where goods were to be carried in a named ship in January, and the ship was stranded and so unable to carry the goods in that month.[17] Here the stipulation as to the method of performance was considered to mean that the contract was to be performed *only* in the specified manner. Where this is not the case, the contract will not be frustrated *merely* because performance by the agreed method becomes impossible. For example a contract of carriage would not be frustrated merely because part of the agreed route was blocked, so long as there was still some other (and commercially reasonable) way of reaching the agreed destination. The contract would only be frustrated if performance by the available method differed *fundamentally* from that originally agreed or from that which both parties expected to be used. The judicial approach to questions of

---

12 *Notcutt v Universal Equipment Co (London) Ltd* [1986] 3 All E R 582.
13 See p 269, ante.
14 *Poussard v Spiers and Pond* (1876) 1 Q B D 410; ante, p 275.
15 *Howell v Coupland* (1876) 1 Q B D 258.
16 *Blackburn Bobbin Co Ltd v T W Allen & Sons Ltd* [1918] 2 K B 467.
17 *Nickoll and Knight v Ashton, Edridge & Co* [1901] 2 K B 126.

this kind is illustrated by a group of cases which arose out of the closing
of the Suez Canal in 1956 and again in 1967. In some of these cases
goods were sold at inclusive prices covering the cost of the goods and
their carriage from Red Sea ports to European ports. The sellers had,
no doubt, fixed the price on the assumption that they would be able to
ship the goods via Suez. Shipment via the Cape of Good Hope was
twice as expensive and would reduce the seller's expected profit.
Nevertheless it was held that these contracts were not frustrated by the
closing of the Canal.[18] Similar decisions were reached in cases
involving contracts of a carriage which had been made on the
assumption that the ship would use the Canal.[19] If the contract was one
to carry the goods to an agreed destination for a fixed charge, it would
be the carrier who would suffer hardship in consequence of having to
use a longer and more expensive route. If, on the other hand, the
contract provided for payment at so much per day, the owner of the
goods would suffer hardship in having to pay an unexpectedly large
amount for getting the goods to the agreed destination. Yet in neither
of these situations would the contract normally be frustrated. It would
require very strong facts (such as, perhaps, a contract to carry
perishable goods from Port Sudan to Alexandria and the subsequent
closure of the Canal) to bring about such a result.

vi Alternatives

Alternatives may relate either to *what* is to be done under the contract
or to *how* it is to be done. The first possibility is illustrated by a charterparty giving the shipowner the option to nominate one of two ships.
Such a contract is frustrated if, after he has made the nomination, the
nominated ship is destroyed.[20] The second possibility is illustrated by a
contract of sale requiring the seller to ship the goods from one of a range
of ports. Supervening impossibility of shipment from one or more of
those ports does not frustrate the contract so long as shipment from one
of them remains possible.[1]

vii Impossibility contrasted with impracticability.

Attempts are sometimes made to argue that a contract is frustrated
because supervening events have very greatly increased the expense of
performance to one party. In such cases performance, though not
impossible, is said to be 'impracticable'.[2] But in English law such

18 *Tsakiroglou & Co Ltd v Noblee Thorl GmbH* [1962] A C 93.
19 *The Eugenia* [1964] 2 QB 226; *Palmco Shipping Inc v Continental Ore Corpn* [1970] 2 Lloyd's Rep 21.
20 See *The Didymi and Leon* [1984] 1 Lloyd's Rep 583; *The Badagry* [1985] 1 Lloyd's Rep 395.
1 Eg *The Furness Bridge* [1977] 2 Lloyd's Rep 367.
2 See the American Restatement, *Contracts* 2d § 261.

impracticability is not a ground of frustration. This appears from the Suez cases, in one of which it was said that 'an increase of expense is not a ground of frustration'.[3] In another case[4] a builder agreed to build council houses for a local authority for a fixed price; but (as a result of delays due to labour shortages) found that he could only complete the work at a substantial loss. His argument that the contract was frustrated was again rejected by the House of Lords. A severe increase in cost may excuse a party under an express contractual provision for supervening events;[5] but it will not discharge the contract under the common law doctrine of frustration.

Problems of this kind are particularly acute when long-term contracts are made for the supply of some commodity and the costs to the supplier increase, sometimes to many times the contract price. Paradoxically, the supplier's position is relatively favourable where the contract does not specify any time limit; for in such a case he is normally entitled to terminate the contract by reasonable notice: this was held to be the position where a contract had been made to supply water to a hospital 'at all times hereafter' for a fixed charge, and in the course of some 56 years the cost to the supplier had risen to over 18 times the contract price.[6] But no such avenue of escape is open to the supplier where the contract is expressed to last for a fixed period, such as 10 years, nor can the supplier in such a case rely on an increase in cost as a ground of frustration.[7] In practice he is likely to protect himself by express provisions for 'flexible pricing.'

Although an increase in cost to one party will not frustrate a contract, other events falling short of impossibility may have this effect. The point is illustrated by a case in which, after a contract for the sale of sugar had been made between a Cuban and a Chilean state trading organisation, there was a total breakdown of diplomatic and commercial relations between the two countries in consequence of the overthrow of the Marxist government in Chile. The contract was held to be frustrated, not because of any hardship to either party, but because in the changed conditions there was no longer any realistic possibility of securing its performance.[8]

---

[3] *Tsakiroglou & Co Ltd v Noblee Thorl GmbH* [1962] AC 93 at 115.

[4] *Davies Contractors Ltd v Fareham UDC* [1956] AC 696.

[5] Eg *Tradax Export SA v André & Cie SA* [1976] 1 Lloyd's Rep 416 at 423.

[6] *Staffordshire Area Health Authority v South Staffordshire Waterworks Co* [1978] 3 All ER 769; for special circumstances excluding the right to terminate such a contract by notice, see *Watford Borough Council v Watford Rural District Council* (1987) Times, 18 December.

[7] *Kirklees Metropolitan Borough Council v Yorkshire Woollen District Transport Co* (1978) 77 LGR 448.

[8] *The Playa Larga* [1983] 2 Lloyd's Rep 171.

b Frustration of purpose.

In cases to be discussed under this heading, performance is, again, not impossible; but one party argues that the contract ought to be discharged because the other's performance is no longer of any use to him. The argument was accepted in a series of cases which arose when the coronation of King Edward VII had to be postponed because of the sudden illness of the King. Before this happened, many people had bought seats on stands or hired rooms which overlooked the routes of the coronation processions; and it remained physically possible for them to sit on the stands or to use the rooms. But the contracts were nevertheless held to be frustrated, except where they expressly provided for the event.[9] They were not regarded simply as contracts to provide seats or rooms at high prices, but as contracts to provide facilities for watching the processions.

The application of the doctrine of frustration to these 'coronation seat' cases may seem sensible enough; but the courts were not prepared to extend the doctrine beyond this point. Many other contracts were made in the expectation that the coronation, and related festivities, would take place as planned. But by no means all such contracts were frustrated. For example in one case[10] a contract was made for the hire of a pleasure boat to watch the naval review which was to be held at Spithead at the time of the coronation, and for a day's cruise round the fleet. The review was cancelled but the fleet remained at Spithead; and it was held that the contract was not frustrated. No doubt the hirer could have made a profit by taking trippers out to watch the review; and very probably he could not charge enough to cover his outlay for the lesser attraction of a cruise round the fleet. But the terms of the contract made it impossible to say that it was a contract to provide facilities for watching the review. It was a contract for the hire of a boat, though for one party it turned out to be a much worse bargain than he had hoped. As a general rule, a contract is not frustrated merely because supervening events prevent a party from putting the subject-matter to its intended use. For example, a contract to buy property for redevelopment is not frustrated merely because between contract and completion the property is listed as being of special architectural or historic interest, so that redevelopment becomes impossible or more difficult, and the value of the property is very considerably reduced.[11] Nor is a contract for the sale of goods frustrated merely because the buyer's purpose to export them from, or to import them into, a particular county is defeated by export or import restrictions.[12] The

[9] Post, p 307.
[10] *Herne Bay Steam Boat Co v Hutton* [1903] 2 K B 683.
[11] *Amalgamated Investment and Property Co Ltd v John Walker & Sons Ltd* [1976] 3 All E R 509.
[12] Eg *Congimex Companhia Geral de Comercio Importadora e Exportadora SARL v Tradax Export SA* [1983] 1 Lloyd's Rep 250.

doctrine of frustration will not enable a party to escape from a contract merely because it has turned out for him to be a bad bargain. There must, as in the coronation cases, be a 'cessation . . . of [a] . . . state of things going to the root of the contract and essential to its performance'.[13]

c Supervening illegality

A contract is discharged if its performance becomes illegal. Thus a contract would be frustrated if it provided for the export of goods to (or the import of goods from) a place which, in the course of a war, became enemy territory;[14] or if its performance was prohibited by legislation.[15] Such discharge is not based on the injustice of holding the parties to the contract in the changed circumstances, but rather on public policy: if the parties were not discharged they might be tempted to perform the contract and so to break the law. It should follow that supervening illegality in respect of even a subsidiary obligation should operate as an excuse for the non-performance of that obligation,[16] though it would not frustrate the whole contract. It would only have this effect if it defeated the main purpose of the contract.[17] The test to be applied here is the same as that already discussed in relation to partial destruction of the subject-matter.[18]

d Time of frustration

As a general rule, the effect of supervening events on a contract must be assessed by reference to the time when they occur, so that the rights of the parties are not left indefinitely in suspense.[19] Thus a contract of carriage can be frustrated if, as a result of war, it becomes highly probable that the only possible route will be blocked; and it makes no difference that the route is then, quite unexpectedly, reopened within the time fixed for performance.[20] But this rule cannot apply without qualification where the alleged ground of frustration is a delay which may turn out to be either slight or serious. In such cases the contract is not frustrated as soon as the delay begins, but only when it has gone on for so long that a reasonable businessman would conclude that it was likely to interfere fundamentally with performance.[1]

---

13 *Krell v Henry* [1903] 2 K B 740 at 748.
14 *Fibrosa Spolka Akcyjna v Fairbairn, Lawson Combe, Barbour Ltd* [1943] A C 32; cf *Re Badische Co* [1921] 2 Ch 331.
15 Eg *Denny Mott & Dickson Ltd v James B Fraser & Co Ltd* [1944] A C 265.
16 See p 306, post.
17 As in *Denny, Mott & Dickson Ltd v James B Fraser & Co Ltd* [1944] A C 265.
18 Ante, p 299.
19 *Bank Line Ltd v Arthur Capel & Co* [1919] A C 435 at 454.
20 *Embiricos v Sydney Reid & Co* [1914] 3 K B 45.
1 *The Nema* [1982] A C 724; *The Wenjiang (No 2)* [1983] 1 Lloyd's Rep 400 at 403.

e Leases

The doctrine of frustration can apply to leases,[2] but such transactions will only rarely be frustrated. One reason for this is that leases are often long-term transactions; and a temporary interruption of the tenant's use of the premises will hardly ever be long enough to bring about frustration.[3] If the lease is of a house which is later destroyed, the lease will usually contain express provisions[4] for that event (such as covenants to insure and rebuild), and these will exclude frustration. Indeed, in the present period of rising prices it will generally be in the interests of the tenant to argue against frustration; for if the lease is frustrated he will have to surrender a valuable site to the landlord many years before the agreed time. Such considerations account for the narrow scope of the doctrine of frustration in relation to leases. Thus it has been held that leases were not frustrated by the destruction[5] or requisitioning[6] of the premises, or by legislation which prevented the tenant from using the premises as he had intended.[7] In the most recent case, a 10-year lease of a warehouse was held not to be frustrated when the only access road was closed by a local authority for 20 months some four years before the end of the tenancy.[8] But a lease could be frustrated if it was a short lease for a particular purpose: eg if a person took a lease of a furnished house for six months and the house was then burnt down.

Even where the whole lease is not frustrated, supervening events may give a party an excuse for non-performance of a particular term in the lease. Thus if either party undertakes to do building work which becomes illegal, failure to do the work at the agreed time will be excused[9] even though the lease remains in being.

f Sale of land

A contract for the sale of land can be frustrated;[10] but a contract for the sale of a house is not frustrated merely because, before completion of the contract by conveyance, the house is destroyed.[11] The purchaser

---

[2] *National Carriers Ltd v Panalpina (Northern) Ltd* [1981] A C 675.

[3] See p 300, ante.

[4] See pp 307–308, post, for the effect of such provisions.

[5] *Denman v Brise* [1949] 1 K B 22.

[6] *Matthey v Curling* [1922] 2 A C 180.

[7] *London and Northern Estates Co v Schlesinger* [1916] 1 K B 20; *Cricklewood Property and Investment Trust Ltd v Leighton's Investment Trust Ltd* [1945] A C 221.

[8] *National Carriers Ltd v Panalpina (Northern) Ltd* [1981] A C 675.

[9] *Sturcke v S W Edwards Ltd* (1971) 23 P & C R 185 at 190, criticising *Eyre v Johnson* [1946] K B 481, *contra*.

[10] This is assumed in *Amalgamated Investment and Property Co Ltd v John Walker & Sons Ltd* [1976] 3 All ER 509.

[11] *Paine v Meller* (1801) 6 Ves 349.

commonly protects himself against loss by insuring the house as soon as the contract of sale becomes legally binding.

2 LIMITATIONS ON THE DOCTRINE

Even where the supervening events are such that they are capable of frustrating the contract, they will not necessarily have this effect. The operation of the doctrine of frustration may be excluded by the following factors.

a Contractual provisions

The common law relating to frustration leads to 'all or nothing' solutions. If the doctrine applies, the contract is completely at an end; if it does not apply the contract remains in full force. Businessmen tend to prefer, and to provide for, intermediate solutions. In some of the coronation seat cases, for example, the contracts provided that, if the procession were postponed, the tickets should be valid for the day on which the procession eventually did take place; or that the ticket-holders should get their money back less a small sum to cover the other party's expenses.[12] When the coronation was postponed, these provisions took effect to the exclusion of the doctrine of frustration.

Where a contract contains a provision of this kind, it is, however, a question of construction whether the provision does indeed cover the events which have occurred. In one case[13] a contract to build a reservoir in six years provided that the builder should have an extension of time for delays 'however occasioned'. This provision was interpreted as giving him a period of grace only in the event of non-frustrating delays. It did not cover the delays which had actually occurred when government intervention in the First World War brought the work to a halt, and forced the builder to sell his construction plant. Hence the builder's plea of frustration succeeded. Moreover, the mere fact that the contract makes *some* provision for a supervening event will not exclude frustration if the provision is not *complete*. A charterparty may, for example, provide that the *shipowner* is not to be liable for delays due to certain events beyond his control. Such a clause will not prevent the *charterer* from relying on the delay (if long enough) as a ground of frustration. The reason is that the provision deals only with *one* possible consequence of the delay, namely its effect on the liability of the shipowner for breach. It says

---

[12] *Victoria Seats Agency v Paget* (1902) 19 T L R 16; *Clark v Lindsay* (1903) 19 T L R 202.
[13] *Metropolitan Water Board v Dick, Kerr & Co* [1918] A C 119.

nothing about the liabilities of the charterer, which can therefore still be discharged by frustration.[14]

Frustration may be excluded, not only by an express term, but also by an implication which arises from the nature of the transaction. It has, for example, been held that a contract for the management of the ship was not discharged merely by the loss of the ship, since the parties must have intended the managers, after the loss, to attend to such matters as the settlement of claims arising out of it and the repatriation of the crew.[15]

A contractual provision for the event will not exclude frustration in certain cases of supervening illegality. For example if one of the contracting parties becomes an alien enemy the contract would not be saved by even the clearest express provision for that event. The parties cannot 'contract out' of the particularly strong public policy against aiding the enemy economy in time of war.[16] On the other hand, clauses dealing with export or import prohibition are commonly upheld:[17] they assume that the prohibition will be observed and do not subvert its purpose.

There is, finally, the converse possibility that a contract may expressly provide for discharge on the occurrence of specified events (such as strikes or other obstacles to performance), whether or not these events bring about a change of circumstances which would be sufficiently fundamental to frustrate the contract. If the specified event occurs, the contract is discharged under the express term and not under the doctrine of frustration.

b Foreseen and foreseeable events

In many frustration cases, the courts have stressed the unexpected nature of the supervening event.[18] These statements suggest that there can be no frustration if, at the time of contracting, the parties actually foresaw that the event would, or was likely to, occur. This view is based on the assumption that, in these circumstances, the parties freely took the risk that the event might occur. Such a risk would no doubt be reflected in the contract price; and if the parties did not want to take that risk, they could easily provide against it. Of course, for the purpose of this argument, it is necessary to define exactly what it is that the parties foresaw. The fact that they foresaw *a* delay does not prevent

---

[14] See *Jackson v Union Marine Insurance Co Ltd* (1874) L R 10 C P 125; cf *The Adelfa* [1988] 2 Lloyd's Rep 466 at 471.

[15] *The Maira (No 2)* [1985] 1 Lloyd's Rep 300, C A; affd on other grounds [1986] 2 Lloyd's Rep 12, H L.

[16] *Ertel Bieber & Co v Rio Tinto Co Ltd* [1918] A C 260.

[17] Eg *Johnson Matthey Bankers Ltd v State Trading Corpn of India Ltd* [1984] 1 Lloyd's Rep 427.

[18] Eg *Krell v Henry* [1903] 2 K B 740 at 752.

frustration if *the* delay which occurred was of a wholly different order of magnitude and was not foreseen. Nor is the doctrine of frustration excluded merely because the parties (or one of them) could, as a remote contingency, have foreseen that the event would occur. No doubt it was, in this sense, 'reasonably foreseeable' that Edward VII (who was then 60 years old) might fall ill at the time fixed for his coronation, but this did not prevent the doctrine of frustration from applying in the coronation cases. Some judicial statements go even further and assert that a contract can be frustrated even by an event which was precisely foreseen.[19] But it is hard to see why, in such cases, the courts should reallocate contractual risks which have been consciously undertaken; and the preferable view seems to be that, if parties contract with reference to a risk of which they were aware, they should not normally be able to rely on the doctrine of frustration. They should only be able to do so if the contract indicates that they had *not* intended to provide for the risk: eg by stipulating that, if the event were to occur, they would 'leave the lawyers to sort it out.'[20] If the lawyers' efforts to do so ended in deadlock, the contract could be frustrated.[1]

Special considerations apply where a contract is frustrated because its performance would, after the outbreak of war, involve trading with the enemy. Here the contract is discharged as a matter of public policy even if the event was clearly foreseen. Thus a contract for the export of goods from this country to Germany made in August 1939 would have been frustrated by the outbreak of war on September 3, however much that event was anticipated by both parties.

c Self-induced frustration

A party cannot rely on 'self-induced' frustration,[2] that is on an obstacle to performance brought about by his own voluntary conduct. This is most obviously true where that conduct is in itself a breach of the contract. Thus a charterer who in breach of contract orders the ship into a war zone, with the result that she is detained there, cannot rely on the detention as a ground of frustration.[3] The position is the same where the breach of *both* parties gives rise to a delay that would (if there had been no breach) have frustrated the contract.[4] A party likewise

---

[19] *W J Tatem Ltd v Gamboa* [1939] 1 K B 132 at 138; *The Eugenia* [1964] 2 Q B 226 at 239; *Nile Co for the Export of Agricultural Crops v H & J M Bennett (Commodities) Ltd* [1986] 1 Lloyd's Rep 555 at 582.

[20] *The Eugenia;* supra, at 234.

[1] Cf *Autry v Republic Productions Inc* 180 P 2d 888 (1947).

[2] *Bank Line Ltd v Arthur Capel & Co* [1919] A C 435 at 452; *Maritime National Fish Ltd v Ocean Trawlers Ltd* [1935] A C 524.

[3] *The Eugenia* [1964] 2 Q B 226.

[4] *The Hannah Blumenthal* [1983] 1 AC 854.

cannot rely as a ground of discharge on an event which was due to his deliberate act, even though that act is not itself a breach.[5] For example, a singer who had contracted to give a concert on a specified day could not rely on inability to perform as a result of his imprisonment after conviction for unlawfully dealing in drugs. Even negligence in bringing about the event would generally exclude frustration: for example, the defendants in *Taylor v Caldwell*[6] would not have been able to rely on the doctrine if the fire had been due to their negligence. In principle the position should be the same where a singer was unable to perform because she had carelessly caught cold; but as the effect of such conduct on a person's health is hard to foresee it may be that the plea of frustration would be available in such a case.[7]

The purpose of the rule that a party cannot rely on self-induced frustration is to deprive that party of the benefit of the doctrine of discharge: the rule must not be allowed to prejudice the *other* party. It follows that the party whose conduct has brought about the event cannot rely on it as a ground of discharge; but the other party may be able to do so. For example, an employee who is prevented from working by a sentence of imprisonment cannot rely on this fact as frustrating the contract;[8] but his employer could so rely on it, with the result that he would not be liable for unfair dismissal.[9]

The question whether frustration is indeed due to the voluntary act of a party can give rise to difficult questions in the following type of case. Suppose A has planted a crop of potatoes in a field which is normally expected to yield 200 tons. He agrees to sell 100 tons of this expected crop to X and 100 tons of it to Y; but, as a result of events beyond his control, the total yield is only 100 tons. If A delivers that amount to X, Y will argue that frustration of his contract was brought about by A's voluntary act; and if A delivers the 100 tons to Y, X will have a similar argument. Yet it seems inconsistent with the principle of frustration to hold A liable for failing to deliver the 100 tons which were not produced. So long as A acts reasonably in allocating the actual yield, it seems that he will be under no liability.[10] He might act reasonably in delivering 50 tons to each buyer, or in delivering the whole 100 tons to the first of the two buyers to have contracted with him.[11]

5 *Denmark Productions Ltd v Boscobel Productions Ltd* [1969] 1 Q B 699.
6 (1863) 3 B & S 826, p 289, ante.
7 See *Joseph Constantine SS Line v Imperial Smelting Corpn Ltd* [1942] A C 154 at 166-167.
8 Cf *Sumnal v Statt* (1984) 49 P & C R 367 (imprisonment of tenant no excuse for failing to perform covenant to reside in farmhouse).
9 *F C Shepherd & Co Ltd v Jerrom* [1987] Q B 301.
10 See *Bremer Handelsgesellschaft m b H v Continental Grain Co* [1983] 1 Lloyd's Rep 269.
11 See *Bremer Handelsgesellschaft m b H v C Mackprang Jr* [1979] 1 Lloyd's Rep 221 at 224; *Intertradex S A v Lesieur Tourteaux SARL* [1978] 2 Lloyd's Rep 509.

3 LEGAL CONSEQUENCES OF FRUSTRATION

a In general

The main legal effect of frustration is to bring the contract automatically to an end. No steps to 'rescind' it need be taken by either party; and the obligations of both are immediately terminated. Hence the odd result sometimes comes about, that a party actually makes a profit out of the frustrating event. Suppose that a ship is chartered for 12 months and then requisitioned. Normally one would expect the charterer to claim frustration, as he does not get the services of the ship. But if the compensation for requisition is more than the agreed hire, the shipowner may claim frustration so as to get the larger sum; and in a number of cases such claims have in fact been allowed.[12] It might be better if the doctrine were restricted so as to discharge only the party prejudiced by the event. This is, indeed, the position in cases of 'self-induced' frustration, where the party bringing about the event cannot rely on it as a ground of discharge, while the other party can do so.[13]

b The Law Reform (Frustrated Contracts) Act 1943

At common law, frustration does not retrospectively annul the contract: it only brings the contract to an end as from the occurrence of the frustrating event. This rule gives rise to difficult problems of adjustment where one party has, or should have, performed some or all of his obligations before the time of frustration. Considerable powers to make such adjustments are given to the courts by the Law Reform (Frustrated Contracts) Act 1943.

i *Prepayment of money*

Suppose that under a contract of sale payment is due on August 10 and delivery on October 10. The contract is frustrated on September 10, when payment has not yet been made. As frustration does not operate retrospectively one might suppose that the buyer would remain liable to pay, while the seller's obligation to deliver was discharged. But this result would often be very unjust. Section 1(2) of the 1943 Act therefore provides that money due but not paid before frustration ceases to be payable; and that, if the money has actually been paid, it must be paid back. Thus frustration is given some retrospective effect. But this may in turn lead to injustice where the person to whom the prepayment was due has incurred expenses, eg in manufacturing the goods, or in packing them up for despatch. The subsection therefore goes on to

---

[12] Eg *Bank Line Ltd v Arthur Capel & Co* [1918] AC 435.
[13] *FC Shepherd & Co Ltd v Jerrom* [1987] QB 301; ante, p 310.

provide that a person to whom a prepayment was made (or due) may
be allowed, at the court's discretion, to keep (or recover) a reasonable
sum not exceeding the amount of the prepayment to cover his
expenses. What is a reasonable sum depends on all the circumstances.
The crucial question will be whether the expenses have not only been
incurred but wasted. For example, where manufacturing expenses
have been incurred, the test will be whether the thing which has been
made can be readily sold to another customer. The court cannot under
the subsection allow more than the amount actually expended or more
than the amount which has been (or should have been) prepaid. Thus if
£100 was prepaid and £75 expended the court cannot allow more than
£75; and if £100 was prepaid and £150 expended the court cannot allow
more than £100.

ii Other benefits

Payments of money made before the time of frustration present
relatively little difficulty, since money can always be paid back. But
greater difficulty arises where, before frustration, one party has
conferred on the other some benefit in kind. Suppose that A, a builder
agrees to install a central heating system in B's house under a contract
providing for payment on completion; and that, when the work is
nearly finished, the house is accidentally burnt down. In such a case the
builder cannot recover *the agreed sum* . But he may have a remedy under
section 1(3) of the 1943 Act. This provides that if one party (B) has
'obtained a valuable benefit . . . before the time of discharge' as a
result of anything done by the other party (A) in or for the purpose of
the performance of the contract, then A can recover from B such sum as
the court thinks just, not exceeding the value of the benefit. Under this
subsection, the court must first identify and value the benefit obtained
by B: it does so by reference to what has been received by B, not to the
cost incurred by A. Secondly, the court must determine what is the
'just' sum to be awarded to A: here the cost of performance to A can be
taken into account; and where the cost incurred by A was less than the
value of the benefit received by B that cost formed the basis of the
award.[14] A further problem is that in our example the benefit received
by B was destroyed by the frustrating event. Although the contrary has
been suggested,[15] it is submitted that this fact is not relevant to the
question whether B has obtained a valuable benefit; for in order to
determine this question the Act requires the court to look at the
position as it was *before* the frustrating event. Thus the fact that the
house was burnt down does not affect the court's *power* to award

[14] *B P Exploration Co (Libya) Ltd v Hunt* (No 2) [1982] 1 All ER 925; affd [1983] 2 A C 352.
[15] *B P Exploration Co (Libya) Ltd v Hunt* (No 2) [1979] 1 W L R 783 at 801.

something under section 1(3); though it is a factor which may be taken into account when the court assesses the 'just' sum actually to be awarded.[16]

iii Severability

Suppose that A agrees to install a central heating system in B's house on the terms that £300 is to be paid when the pipes are laid, a further £300 when the radiators are installed and a final £400 when the boiler has been installed *and* the system is in operation. After the boiler has been installed but *before* it is connected, the house is accidentally burnt down. If nothing has been paid, A is entitled to the first two instalments (ie £600) in full. He can, in addition, recover such sum as the court thinks just in respect of the 'valuable benefit' conferred on B by work done during the third stage of the contract; for the 1943 Act provides[17] that the provisions of s 1 (discussed above) shall apply to each severable part of a contract as if it were a separate contract.

iv Exceptions

The Act can be excluded by contrary agreement:[18] for example by a provision that money paid under a contract is not to be refundable in any event.

The Act does not apply to contracts for the carriage of goods by sea, to contracts of insurance, and to contracts for the sale of specific goods where the cause of frustration is the perishing of the goods.[19] In these cases the effects of frustration were, before the Act, governed by well settled rules. For example, if freight was paid in advance no part of it could be reclaimed even though the contract was frustrated before the goods reached the agreed destination;[20] if freight was payable at the destination nothing could be recovered for any 'valuable benefit' conferred by carrying the goods (before frustration) to an intermediate port;[1] if goods were insured for three months against fire no part of the premium could be reclaimed merely because after one month the goods were destroyed by water;[2] and the effect of the destruction of specific goods was governed by special rules in the Sale of Goods Act 1979.[3] It was thought more important to preserve the certainty of these

---

[16] Law Reform (Frustrated Contracts) Act 1943, s 1(3) (b).
[17] S 2(4).
[18] S 2(3) (a). See *B P Exploration Co (Libya) Ltd v Hunt* (No 2) [1983] 2 A C 352 (where the contract was held not to have excluded the Act).
[19] s 2(5).
[20] *Byrne v Schiller* (1871) L R 6 Exch 319.
[1] See pp 277–278, ante.
[2] Cf *Tyrie v Fletcher* (1777) 2 Cowp 666 at 668.
[3] S 7 (originally enacted in 1893).

rules than to extend the powers of adjustment created by the 1943 Act to cases of this kind. The argument is not wholly convincing, and the wording of the Act at this point gives rise to some strange distinctions. For example, a person who has agreed to buy *specific* goods and has paid for them in advance may, because the Act is excluded, get the *whole* price back if the goods are destroyed.[4] But if the goods are *not* specific he may (under the Act) get back his price *less* an allowance for the seller's expenses; and this is also the position if the cause of frustration is not the destruction of specific goods but their requisition. It is hard to see any justification for these distinctions.

---

[4] Under the common law rule laid down in the *Fibrosa* case [1943] AC 32.

Chapter 18

Remedies for breach of contract

1 CLASSIFICATION

Remedies for breach of contract can be divided into judicial and non-judicial remedies. Judicial remedies are those that must be sought by taking proceedings in a court of law or before an arbitrator; non-judicial remedies are those that are sought in some other way. In some areas of the law, an important non-judicial remedy is self-help: for example the owner of goods which are wrongfully detained by another person may be entitled simply to seize those goods. In this sense, self-help is not generally available as a remedy for breach of contract. Suppose that A agrees to sell a car to B for £5,000. If B does not pay, A cannot simply seize £5,000 belonging to B; nor can B, if A refuses to deliver, seize the car, at least so long as A remains owner of it. Of course the purely defensive 'remedy' of refusing to perform on account of the other party's breach is a kind of self-help. This has been discussed in chapter 16. Our present concern is with judicial remedies.

Judicial remedies can further be subdivided into criminal and civil remedies. Occasionally, the same conduct may amount to a breach of contract and to a criminal offence: for example, where a landlord cuts off his tenant's gas supply[1] or where a supplier of goods applies a false trade description to them.[2] In the criminal proceedings, the offender may be ordered to pay compensation for any personal injury, loss or damage resulting from the offence.[3] This power will often be exercisable in a contractual context—eg where a person has been induced to buy goods because a false trade description has been applied to them.[4] But a compensation order may be made even though the false statement never became part of the contract, so that there was no breach. In general, a breach of contract does not involve any criminal liability. It is purely and simply a civil wrong, and our concern will be with civil remedies for breach.

---

[1] Protection from Eviction Act 1977, s 1; *McCall v Abelesz* [1976] QB 585.

[2] Trade Descriptions Act 1968, s 1(1)(a).

[3] Powers of Criminal Courts Act 1973, s 35 as amended by Criminal Justice Act 1988, s 104.

[4] Trade Descriptions Act 1968, s 1(1)(a). The offence is committed when the false description is *applied*, even though no sale results.

Civil remedies may further be subdivided according to the nature of the relief claimed. The injured party may claim specific relief, damages or restitution.

A claim for specific relief is one for the actual performance of the defaulting party's undertaking. It is usually associated with the so-called equitable remedies of specific performance and injunction but a common law action to recover the agreed sum due under a contract (eg an action for the price, or for wages) is also a claim for specific relief.

Alternatively, the injured party may claim compensation for the fact that he has not received the agreed performance. Such compensaion takes the form of damages in money. It is placed at the beginning of our account of remedies since it is the remedy which is most frequently discussed in the reported cases on the subject.

A claim for restitution arises when the plaintiff has, in performing his part of the contract, conferred a benefit on the defendant and seeks to get back that benefit or its value. For example, a buyer who has paid in advance but has not received delivery may claim the return of his money. Where precise restitution is physically impossible, the plaintiff will claim the reasonable value of the benefit: for example he may claim the value of services rendered in partial performance of a contract which cannot be fully performed because it has been frustrated. As the last example shows, claims for restitution are by no means limited to cases of *breach* of contract; but, as they are sometimes available on breach, it is convenient to discuss them in this chapter.

2 DAMAGES

Damages are always available, and can be claimed as of right, whenever a contract has been broken. In this respect they differ from claims for specific relief or restitution, which may be subject to the discretion of the court and to other restrictions to be discussed later in this chapter. Even if the injured party has not proved any loss, he is entitled to nominal damages. Claims for nominal damages may be brought simply to establish the existence of a legal right. An action for a declaration is now a more appropriate remedy for this purpose, and actions for nominal damages have become something of a rarity in contract cases. They will not be further considered here. Our concern will be with the principles governing awards of substantial damages.

a The compensatory principle

The first of these principles is that the purpose of damages is to compensate the plaintiff. This principle has a number of important consequences.

i Loss to plaintiff the criterion

As a general rule, damages are based on loss to the plaintiff[5] and not on gain to the defendant. For example, where a shipowner in breach of contract withdraws his ship from a charterparty, the charterer's damages are based on his loss and not on any profit made by the shipowner from other employment of the ship.[6] Gain to the defendant is, however, exceptionally taken into account in a number of situations. If the defendant in breach of contract abuses a 'fiduciary' position (eg if an agent makes a profit by using confidential information acquired in his capacity as agent) he must account for any profit so made.[7] On the conclusion of a contract for the sale of land, the vendor is regarded as trustee of the land for the purchaser and if in breach of the contract the vendor resells the land to a third party at a profit, the purchaser is in equity entitled to that profit.[8] Liability in these cases is not based on breach of contract as such, but on equitable principles. At common law a defendant who in breach of contract uses the plaintiff's property must pay a reasonable rental value even though the plaintiff would not himself have used the property or let it out to anyone else.[9] This liability appears, however, to be based, not on gain to the defendant, but on the fact that the plaintiff has lost the chance of letting the property out to someone else. Similarly, where a developer built houses in breach of restrictive covenant, the injured party recovered damages even though the breach did not reduce the value of his land. The damages were based on the amount which the landowner might have charged the developer for permission to build.[10]

ii Meaning of 'loss'

If the plaintiff is to get substantial damages, he must show that he has suffered loss. 'Loss' here means any harm to the person or property of the plaintiff, and any amount by which the plaintiff's wealth is diminished in consequence of the breach. Suppose that a seller has contracted to deliver a car on October 1, and in breach of contract he delivers it a month later. The buyer has suffered loss in not having the car for a month and this would be so even if the car would not have been of any use to him during that month, eg because he was ill or abroad for the whole period in question. Such factors could affect the *amount* of loss suffered, but the plaintiff is not generally deprived of his right to

[5] Or, in certain exceptional cases, to a third party: see p 210, ante.
[6] *The Siboen and the Sibotre* [1976] 1 Lloyd's Rep 293, 337.
[7] *Regal (Hastings) Ltd v Gulliver* [1942] 378; 1 All E R cf *A-G v Guardian Newspapers Ltd (No 2)* [1988]. 3 All E R 545 at 644, 664 (the *Spycatcher* case); partners are under a similar liability: Partnership Act 1890, ss 29, 30.
[8] See *Lake v Bayliss* [1974] 2 All E R 1114.
[9] *Penarth Dock Engineering Co Ltd v Pounds* [1963] 1 Lloyd's Rep 359.
[10] *Wrotham Park Estate Co v Parkside Homes Ltd* [1974] 2 All E R 321.

damages merely because it is shown that he would (or would not) have used the subject-matter of the contract in a particular way. Exceptionally, the fact that the plaintiff had resold the subject-matter may be relevant for the purpose of showing that he suffered no loss: this point is further discussed below.[11]

In determining whether the plaintiff has suffered loss, regard must be had to his overall position in consequence of the breach. Suppose that a seller who has not been paid fails to deliver on a falling market. No doubt the buyer is deprived of the goods which were due to him; but at the same time he is released from his obligation to pay the price, and he can buy substitute goods more cheaply in the market. Hence he has not suffered any overall loss. Similarly, the buyer will suffer no loss if he accepts goods which are not in accordance with the contract but which are not in fact any less valuable than the goods which the seller ought to have delivered.

Even where the plaintiff has suffered loss, the overall position must similarly be considered in determining the extent of the loss. Benefits which the plaintiff obtains in consequence of the breach are therefore set off against the prejudice that he suffers; and it is the difference between these two amounts which constitutes his loss. Thus an employee who is wrongfully dismissed must set off against his lost wages any amounts earned in substitute employment. The court will not generally award damages which will actually put the plaintiff into a better position than that in which he would have been, if the breach had not occurred.[12] But an exception may be made to this principle where its strict application would create a practical dilemma for the injured party. The exception is illustrated by a case[13] in which A rebuilt his factory after it had been burnt down as a result of B's breach of contract. It was held that A could recover the whole cost of rebuilding without making any allowance for the fact that he now had a new factory, worth more than the old one which had been destroyed. To take this benefit into account would, in effect, have forced A to spend money on improvements which he might not have wanted, or which he could not have afforded; for he had no reasonable alternative but to rebuild and had done so in order to mitigate his loss.[14]

iii No punitive damages

The purpose of damages for breach of contract is to compensate the plaintiff and not to punish the defendant. In tort actions, the courts

[11] See p 327, post.
[12] *Philips v Ward* [1956] 1 All E R 874; *Perry v Sidney Phillips & Son* [1982] 3 All E R 705.
[13] *Harbutt's Plasticine Ltd v Wayne Tank and Pump Co Ltd* [1970] 1 Q B 447, overruled, but not on this point, in *Photo Production Ltd v Securicor Transport Ltd* [1980] A C 827.
[14] Post, p 337.

occasionally mark their disapproval of the defendant's conduct by awarding damages in excess of the plaintiff's loss. They may, for example, do so where a person publishes a book, with a view to profit, knowing that it contains defamatory matter.[15] Such punitive (or exemplary) damages cannot be awarded in a purely contractual action.[16] However, the same conduct may amount both·to a breach of contract and to a tort: for example, where a landlord unlawfully evicts his tenant. In such a case the tenant can recover punitive damages if he frames his claim in tort.[17]

iv *Injury to feelings*

Punitive damages must be distinguished from damages for injured feelings. The latter are awarded not to punish the defendant, but to compensate a plaintiff for an injury which he has actually suffered, even though it may not be an economic one. Although such damages are often awarded in tort actions, their availability for breach of contract is limited: a person cannot recover damages merely because the breach of a contract made in the course of his business causes him distress;[18] nor can a wrongfully dismissed employee recover extra damages because the manner of his dismissal was 'harsh and humiliating'.[19] But damages for injured feelings or distress can be recovered in a contractual action where it is the very object of the contract to promote the enjoyment or comfort of the injured party. Such damages have, for example, been awarded against package tour operators for failing to provide holiday accommodation of the standard required by the contract;[20] against an airline for failing to get guests to wedding celebrations in accordance with its contract;[1] against a photographer for breaking his contract to take wedding photographs;[2] (in California) against embalmers whose efforts failed to achieve the degree of preservation required by the contract;[3] against a surveyor who negligently failed to draw his client's attention to defects in a house which the client later bought as his home;[4] against a landlord for breach of his covenant to repair a flat, leaving it so damp as to be uninhabitable;[5] and against

---

[15] *Cassell & Co Ltd v Broome* [1972] A C 1027.
[16] *Perera v Vandiyar* [1953] 1 W L R 672.
[17] *Drane v Evangelou* [1978] 2 All E R 437.
[18] *Hayes v Dodds* [1988] N L J R259.
[19] *Addis v Gramophone Co Ltd* [1909] A C 488 at 493; *Shove v Downs Surgical plc* [1984] 1 All E R 7; *Bliss v South East Thames Regional Health Authority* [1987] I C R 700.
[20] *Jarvis v Swans Tours Ltd* [1973] Q B 233.
[1] *Chande v East African Airways Corpn* [1964] E A 78.
[2] *Diesen v Samson* 1971 S L T 49.
[3] *Chelini v Nieri* 196 P 2d 915 (1948).
[4] *Perry v Sidney Phillips & Son* [1982] 3 All E R 705.
[5] *Calabar Properties Ltd v Stitcher* [1984] 1 WLR 287.

the seller of a defective car for the vexation caused to the buyer when the car broke down and would not restart.[6]

Damages for injured feelings must further be distinguished from damages for 'anxiety'. There is good sense in the rule that damages of the latter kind cannot generally be recovered in a contractual action.[7] Some uncertainty always exists about the performance of a contract. Hence 'anxiety' is a risk to which anyone who enters into a contract voluntarily exposes himself, and in respect of which he should not get compensation. Such damages were, for example, refused where an architect was sued for breach of a contract to supervise the conversion of a house into flats which were intended to be let (and not to be used for the client's personal occupation).[8] The same reasoning does not, however, apply where the very object of a contract is to remove a previously existing source of anxiety. Damages for failing to achieve that object have accordingly been recovered from a solicitor who failed to take necessary steps in non-molestation proceedings, so that the molestation of his client continued.[9]

b Kinds of loss recoverable

The statement that the plaintiff is to be compensated for his loss is not, in itself, particularly helpful. For a breach of contract may cause different kinds of loss and we have to ask for which of these compensation will be given.

i Expectations

The first, and most important, principle is that the law protects the expectations created by a contract. Damages are therefore awarded to put the plaintiff into the position in which he would have been if the contract had actually been performed;[10] or in other words the plaintiff is entitled to damages for loss of his bargain. This may involve compensation for two quite separate expectations. Suppose that A agrees to sell a piece of machinery to B but fails to deliver it. Here B is deprived first of the actual thing contracted for, ie the machinery; and secondly of the chance of making a profitable use of it until he can get a substitute. He may get damages (in accordance with the principles to be discussed below) in respect of both of these items of loss. This protection of expectations created by the contract is the feature which

---

[6] *Bernstein v Pamson Motors (Goldens Green) Ltd* [1987] 2 All E R 220; cf *U C B Leasing Ltd v Holtom* [1987] R T R 362.
[7] *Cook v* [1967] 1 All E R 299.
[8] *Hutchinson v Harris* (1978) 10 B L R 19.
[9] *Heywood v Wellers* [1976] Q B 446.
[10] *Robinson v Harman* (1848) 1 Exch 850 at 855.

distinguishes contractual actions from actions in tort;[11] and it is particularly important where the plaintiff has made a good bargain. Suppose that A agrees to sell goods to B for £100. At the time fixed for delivery they are worth £150. If A fails to deliver, B's damages will be based on the value of the goods that he ought to have received: ie the damages will be £150 if B has already paid for the goods and £50 if he has not. The same principle applies where A warrants that the goods are of 'grade 1' quality and he delivers goods of 'grade 2' quality. If B 'accepts' the goods, his damages will be based on the difference between what he has actually received (grade 2 goods) and what he ought to have received (grade 1 goods). As we saw in chapter 9, the position is different where A does not *warrant* but only *represents* that the goods have a certain quality. Here B may be entitled to damages in tort for misrepresentation and in such an action expectations created by the representation are not protected. All that B will get is the difference between what he received and the price which he paid.[12]

ii Reliance

The plaintiff may incur expenses or other losses in reliance on the contract. For example, a buyer may be required by the contract to collect the goods, and if he takes steps to do so but the seller fails to provide the goods, then the buyer will have wasted the costs of collection. Expenses may also be wasted if the plaintiff incurs them for the purpose of making use of the subject-matter, even though he is not required by the contract to incur them. For example a buyer's costs of installing machinery may turn out to be useless because it is not up to the standard laid down in the contract. Subject to restrictions which will be mentioned below, the plaintiff is entitled to be compensated for such reliance loss. He may even be able to recover in respect of expenses incurred *before* the contract. In one case[13] a television company incurred preliminary expenses of £2,750 for the purpose of making a film. They then engaged an actor for the leading part, and he later repudiated the contract. He was held liable for the £2,750 as reliance loss. The company had relied on their contract with him, not in incurring the expediture, but in allowing it to be wasted: that is, in forbearing to look for someone else to play the part.

<hr>

11 See ante, p 5; in the *Junior Books* case [1983] 1 A C 520 damages in tort were awarded for loss of expectations created by a contract to which the claimant was not a party, but the case is unlikely to be followed on this point: see ante, p 214.
12 See p 134, ante.
13 *Anglia Television Ltd v Reed* [1972] 1 Q B 60.

iii Restitution

The nature of a claim for restitution has already been explained.[14] Such a claim may arise where the injured party has, in performing his part of the contract, conferred a benefit on the other party. It is, for example, available where the defaulting party has wholly failed to perform his part of the contract. Thus if a seller has been paid in advance and then refuses to deliver the goods, he is liable to *restore* the price to the buyer. The effect of such a claim is to put both parties into the position in which they would have been if the contract had never been made. In this respect it differs from a claim for loss of expectations, which is meant to put the plaintiff into the position in which he would have been if the contract had been performed. It also differs from a claim for reliance loss: this may put the injured party into the position in which he would have been if the contract had never been made, but it will often leave the guilty party in a worse position. Reliance loss may be recoverable even though the guilty party has not received any benefit. As a general rule,[15] restitution is available only in respect of such benefits. A claim for restitution may not strictly be one for 'damages', being based on gain to the defendant, rather than on loss to the plaintiff. But it is mentioned here so that its relation to claims for damages for expectation and reliance loss can be discussed.

iv Relation between expectation, reliance and restitution claims

This is a complex subject, but three leading principles are clear.

First, the plaintiff can often choose whether to base his claim on expectation, reliance or restitution. It is important to stress that the defendant has no similar choice: he cannot insist that the plaintiff should only get reliance loss or restitution. If the defendant could do this, it would be too easy for him to get out of a bad bargain: for example, a seller who had sold goods for less than they were worth could simply pay back the price. Obviously in such a case the buyer would not want his money back, but damages for loss of his bargain.

Secondly, the plaintiff's choice is in some respects limited. Sometimes he cannot claim for loss of expectation. Where the value of his expectation is so speculative that it cannot be satisfactorily proved, he will only be able to claim reliance loss and restitution.[16] In many cases the plaintiff cannot get restitution. For example, a claim to get back money paid under a contract will only succeed if the breach is sufficiently serious to amount, or to give rise, to a 'total failure of

---

[14] See p 316, ante.
[15] For an exception see p 364, post.
[16] *McRae v Commonwealth Disposals Commission* (1950) 84 C L R 377 at 411.

consideration' in the sense discussed later in this chapter.[17] Where this requirement is satisfied, restitution can be claimed even though it will leave the plaintiff better off than he would have been if the contract had been performed. This will be the position whenever the plaintiff has made a bad bargain. Suppose he has paid £100 in advance for goods which are worth only £75. If the seller fails to deliver, the buyer will get back the whole of his £100. The law will not limit the seller's liability to £75 for, if it did this, the end result would be that the seller would keep £25 for doing absolutely nothing. On the other hand, the court will *not* allow the plaintiff his *whole reliance* loss if this would clearly leave him better off than he would have been if the contract had been performed.[18] Suppose A contracts to sell aero engines to B for £100 m, and that he has incurred development expenses of £150 m when B repudiates the contract. Here A cannot get more than £100 m even if he claims reliance loss. Any further loss to A is the result, not of B's breach, but of the fact that A has made a bad bargain; and there is no compelling reason in this example for shifting that loss to B, since B will not (as in our previous example) be enriched if a ceiling of £100 m is placed on his liability. It does not follow that a claim for reliance loss can never yield more than one for loss of expectation: it may do so where the plaintiff cannot prove the value of his expectation; or where the value of the expectation is speculative. In the case of the television film mentioned above, the company's profits might or might not have exceeded the £2,750 recovered as reliance loss. The company did not have to prove what these profits would be. Its claim for reliance loss would only have been reduced to the level of its expectations if the actor could have proved that the profits would *certainly* have been less than the amount of the reliance expenditure.[19]

Thirdly, although the plaintiff *may* often be able to choose between expectation, reliance and restitution, it does not follow that he *must* choose: in other words, the various claims can sometimes be combined. In one case[20] machinery was delivered and paid for, and installed by the buyer. It was then found not to be in accordance with the contract and the buyer recovered the price he had paid (restitution), his installation expenses (reliance) and the net profits which he had lost because his productive capacity was reduced in consequence of the breach (expectation). Of course the buyer could not have got the restitution and reliance items plus his *gross* profits, for this would give him these profits plus the costs of earning them, and so in effect give

---

[17] See pp 359–361, post.
[18] *C and P Haulage v Middleton* [1983] 3 All E R 94.
[19] *C C C Films (London) Ltd v Impact Quadrant Films Ltd* [1985] Q B 16.
[20] *Millar's Machinery Co Ltd v David Way & Son* (1935) 40 Com Cas 204.

him damages twice over the same loss.[1] But, so long as this danger of duplicating damages is avoided, there is no reason why claims of the kind here described should not be combined. A further example may help to make this clear. Suppose A agrees to sell to B a shipload of oil to be collected from A's installations in the Persian Gulf; B intends (as A well knows) to carry the oil to his refinery at Southampton. B pays for the oil and sends a tanker out to collect it, but A refuses to deliver. Here B should be able to recover the price (restitution), the expense wasted in sending out the tanker (reliance) and the difference, if any, between the Persian Gulf price of the oil and the contract price. What he cannot do is to claim both the cost of sending out the tanker and the difference between the contract price and the *Southampton* price, for the cost of sending out the tanker is part of the expense of getting the oil to Southampton and of thereby raising its value to the price at that place.

v Consequential and incidental loss

The expression 'consequential loss' is used in the law of contract in several senses. First it is used simply to refer to loss of profits, that is to an element of expectation loss. Secondly, it is used to refer to reliance loss, such as expense wasted by a buyer in attempting to collect goods which the seller wrongfully refuses to deliver. But our present concern is with a third meaning of the expression. The breach may not merely deprive the plaintiff of what he bargained for; further harm may result from the defect in the defendant's performance. Suppose that the seller of a cow in breach of contract delivers an animal that is diseased. The buyer has bargained for a healthy cow, and he can get the difference in value between this and the diseased animal as damages for loss of his bargain. But he may also have put the diseased cow with his other cattle which in consequence were infected and died. He can recover the value of those cattle as a consequential loss in the present sense.[2] Yet it is hardly realistic to say that the buyer expected not to lose the other cattle or that he put the cow which he had bought with the others in reliance on her not being diseased. In fact the possibility of injury to the other cattle would probably not have crossed his mind at all. There is no doubt such consequential loss may be recoverable, but it does not fit easily into the categories of expectation and reliance.

The same is true of a further type of loss. Suppose a seller fails to deliver and the buyer makes a substitute purchase. Even if the price of the substitute is the same as that of the goods originally bought, the buyer will have suffered some loss: namely, the administrative

---

[1] *Cullinane v British Rema Manufacturing Co* [1954] 1 Q B 292; *T C Industrial Plant Pty Ltd v Robert's Queensland Pty Ltd* [1964] A L R 1083.
[2] *Smith v Green* (1875) 1 C P D 92.

expenses of making the second contract. There is no doubt that he can recover such loss[3] which (following an American usage) may be called incidental loss.[4]

c Valuing the loss

For the purpose of an award of damages, plaintiff's loss has to be translated into money terms. This process of valuation or assessment gives rise to many problems.

i The bases of assessment

The first of these is to determine the basis on which the assessment is to be made. Where the claim is for reliance loss, the basis is the cost to the plaintiff of his action or forbearance in reliance on the contract. Where the claim is for restitution, the basis is the benefit obtained by the defendant. But where the claim is for expectation loss, or for consequential loss (in the third of the above senses) there are at least two possible bases of assessment. These will be called 'difference in value' and 'cost of cure'.

In some cases both of these bases of assessment will lead to the same result. Where a seller of goods fails to deliver, the buyer is entitled to damages based on the cost of substitute goods; and this can be described either as the difference in value between what he has got (nothing) and what he should have got (the goods), or as the cost of 'curing' the seller's breach. But there are other cases in which the choice between the two bases can be of crucial importance. In an American case[5] a company took a mining lease of agricultural land and covenanted that it would, at the end of its mining operations, restore the land to its former state. The cost of the work would have been $29,000, but the effect of doing it would have been to increase the value of the land by only $300. The company refused to do the work, and it was held that the damages were $300 (difference in value) and not $29,000 (cost of cure). In England a similar rule is laid down by statute for assessing damages for breach of a tenant's covenant to repair.[6] The common law position is more complex. Difference in value is clearly the basis where the plaintiff does not cure the defect but disposes of the subject-matter.[7] On the other hand, there is support for the view that

---

[3] *Robert Stewart & Sons Ltd v Carapanayoti & Co Ltd* [1962] 1 All E R 418.
[4] Uniform Commercial Code, s 2-715 (1).
[5] *Peevyhouse v Garland Coal Mining Co* 382 P 2d 109 (1962).
[6] Landlord and Tenant Act 1927, s 18 (1).
[7] *Perry v Sidney Phillips & Son* [1982] 3 All E R 705; *Calabar Properties Ltd v Stitcher* [1984] 1 W L R 287 at 299.

the plaintiff is entitled to the higher cost of cure if he can establish that he has actually incurred that cost or that he will definitely do so.[8] If, however, the plaintiff insisted on cure when its cost was not merely greater than, but wholly out of proportion to, the resulting benefit to him, he would have failed to perform his duty to mitigate.[9] In such a case he should recover only on a difference in value basis.[10] The choice between the two bases of assessment is not governed by any fixed or general rule: there are only prima facie rules, and even these are not rigidly applied. Two illustrations may be given.

First a seller in breach of contract delivers defective goods. The Sale of Goods Act 1979 here states that prima facie the damages are based on the difference between the actual value of the goods and the value which they would have had, if they had been in accordance with the contract.[11] The rule is probably based on the assumption that the defect is one that cannot be cured: for example, that the goods are of a different commercial grade from that contracted for. The rule is only a prima facie one: if the defect is one that can be cured (for example, if a car has defective brakes) the court would probably award the cost of cure.[12]

Secondly, a builder in breach of contract fails to complete the work which he has contracted to do, or to execute it in accordance with the specifications. Here the law starts with the assumption that the damages will be based on cost of cure.[13] This is reasonable since normally the owner will in fact need to cure the defects: a house without a roof, or a central heating system which does not work, is of no use to him. But the breach, while not making the building appreciably less useful to the owner, may yet be very expensive to cure. This was the position in an American case[14] in which the builder, as a result of a muddle in his office, used the 'wrong' brand of pipe. This was no worse than that required by the contract; and it was, by the time the breach was discovered, firmly embedded in the concrete. It was held that the owner's damages should be assessed on a difference in value basis, since 'cure' would require the substantial destruction of the completed building, to no good purpose. Since there was in fact no difference in value, the damages would be nominal.

---

[8] *Tito v Waddell (No 2)* [1977] Ch 106 at 333; *Radford v De Froberville* [1978] 1 All E R 33; *Dean v Ainley* [1987] 3 All E R 748; cf *County Personnel (Employment Agency) Ltd v Alan R Pulver* [1987] 1 All E R 289 (cost of extricating plaintiff from transaction in which he had been negligently advised).

[9] See p 338, post.

[10] Cf (in tort) *Darbishire v Warran* [1963] 3 All E R 310, [1963] 1 W L R 1067; *C R Taylor (Wholesale) Ltd v Hepworths Ltd* [1977] 2 All E R 784.

[11] S 53 (3). If the price has not been paid, the buyer can simply reduce it by the above amount: s 53 (1) (a).

[12] Cf *Charterhouse Credit Co Ltd v Tolly* [1963] 2 Q B 683 at 711–712 (hire-purchase).

[13] *Hoenig v Isaacs* [1952] 2 All E R 176; and cf the cases cited in n 8 supra.

[14] *Jacob and Youngs v Kent* 129 N E 889 (1921).

ii Relevance of market values

Where damages are based on difference in value, or on the cost of a substitute, the question arises whether they are to be based on the *actual* difference or cost, or on market values. The question is most easily discussed by taking the common cases of failure by a seller to deliver goods, or by a buyer to accept and pay for them. There is said to be a 'market' for goods if there is a place in which they can be bought and sold at a price fixed by supply and demand.[15]

Where a seller wrongfully fails to deliver, the buyer is entitled to the value of the goods, less the price if he has not yet paid it. If there is no market the court has to assess that value as best it can. Relevant factors include the cost of a reasonably close substitute, and the price at which the buyer may have resold the goods to a sub-buyer at or about the time of the seller's breach. If there is a market, the value of the goods is prima facie assessed by reference to it so that the buyer (assuming that he has not yet paid) will be entitled to the amount (if any) by which the market price exceeds the contract price.[16] The reason for the rule is that 'the buyer is entitled to the expense of putting himself in the position of having those goods, and this he can do by going into the market and purchasing them at the market price'.[17] This principle applies where goods are bought for resale, no less than where they are bought for use. Suppose that A sells 100 tons of wheat to B for £x per ton and B then sells 100 tons of wheat to C for £x + 3 per ton, intending to deliver to C the wheat that is due from A. Later A fails to deliver the wheat; and at this time the market value of the wheat is £x + 5 per ton. B's damages will prima facie be £5 per ton and not £3 per ton.[18] The theory is that, as B saw the market rise, he might have bought another 100 tons of wheat (say at £x + 1) to supply to C, and still have had the benefit of his contract with A. Similar reasoning applies in the converse situation. If the sale to C was at £x + 5 and the market price at the date of breach was £x + 3, B's damages will prima facie be £3 per ton, for he could have bought at £x + 3 to supply C.[19] But such reasoning only applies where B is not bound to deliver to C the very same wheat that be bought from A. Suppose that A sells to B the cargo of wheat *of a named ship* at £x per ton and B resells *that cargo* for £x + 5 per ton. Here B's loss will be £5 per ton even if the market price of similar wheat at the date of A's default was £x + 3 per ton. The point is that B could not pass on to C *other* wheat bought in the market at £x + 3 per ton since C was only

15 *Dunkirk Colliery Co v Lever* (1878) 9 Ch D 20.
16 Sale of Goods Act 1979, s 51(3).
17 *Williams Bros v E T Agius Ltd* [1914] A C 510 at 531.
18 *Williams Bros v E T Agius Ltd,* supra.
19 *Williams v Reynolds* (1865) 6 B & S 495.

bound to accept, and to pay £x + 5 per ton for, the particular cargo in question.[20]

Similar principles apply where a buyer wrongfully fails to accept and pay for the goods. Here the assumption is that, on the buyer's default, the seller will sell the goods to someone else, and his damages will be based on the proceeds of the substitute sale. If there is no market, the damages will be based on the actual proceeds so long as the substitute sale was, in all the circumstances, one which it was reasonable to make. If there is a market, the damages are prima facie assessed by reference to it so that the seller will be entitled to the amount (if any) by which the contract price exceeds the market price.[1] The fact that the seller has actually resold above or below the market price is irrelevant, unless the sale is of particular goods, as opposed to a sale of a quantity of some generic marketable commodity.

The rules stated above are concerned only with valuing one of the plaintiff's expectations, namely his expectation of getting the performance promised to him. They do not necessarily lay down the limits of his recovery, for the plaintiff may also have another expectation, that of getting a profit out of the subject-matter. This is obvious enough where the seller is in breach and the buyer loses profits which he expected to make out of the use of the goods. He may lose such profits during the time it takes him to get a substitute; if so, he can recover damages even though the actual cost or market price of the substitute does not exceed the contract price. A somewhat similar possibility exists where the buyer is in breach. Suppose that a car dealer (A) agrees to sell a new car to a customer (B) for £5,000 and that B wrongfully refuses to accept and pay. A thereupon sells the car to C for £5,000 and claims damages from B for the loss of his profit on the contract with him. A's case is that he would, if B had not defaulted, have made two sales and two profits and that he has lost one of these. Such a claim will succeed if A can show that he would, but for B's breach, have performed not only his contract with B, but also that with C: eg if A could have got twenty cars from the manufacturers and have found only ten customers, including B and C. The result of B's default in such a case is that A loses one sale.[2] But A would not be entitled to damages for loss of his profit on the contract with B in the converse case in which he can only get ten cars but can find twenty customers.[2a] Here A will still make the maximum number of ten sales in spite of B's default. The only loss he suffers is a small amount of incidental loss, that is, the extra expense of negotiating the

---

20   *Williams Bros v E T Agius Ltd,* supra, at 523; it is assumed that the resale is not too remote a consequence: see pp 333–336, post, and Re *R & H Hall Ltd and W H Pim Jr & Co's Arbitration* (1928) 139 L T 50.

1   Sale of Goods Act 1979, s 50(3).

2   *W L Thompson Ltd v Robinson (Gunmakers) Ltd* [1955] Ch 177.

2a   *Charter v Sullivan* [1957] 2 Q B 117.

sale with C. The position is the same if the sale is of a unique object (such as a second-hand car): here there can obviously be only one sale and one profit, and this is not lost if C buys for the same price that B had agreed to pay.[3]

iii Speculative damages

A breach of contract may deprive the plaintiff of the chance of gaining some benefit; and in principle damages can be recovered for the loss of such a chance. In one case[4] a girl recovered damages for loss of the chance of taking part in the final stages of a beauty contest; and in another[5] a waiter recovered damages for loss of the chance of earning tips. Damages are also very commonly awarded for 'loss of profits' even though there was only a chance, and not any certainty, that such profits would be made. In all these cases the value of the chance is to some extent a matter of speculation. The court not only has to value the expected benefit but also to take in account the likelihood of its being actually received by the plaintiff. Suppose that a tennis player is, in breach of contract, excluded from a tournament in which the winner is to get a prize of £50,000. The damages for loss of the chance of winning will be less than £50,000. The amount will depend on the stage at which the player was excluded and on his chance of winning; obviously the top seed excluded from the final will get more than an unseeded player excluded from the first round. The fact that the chance cannot be valued precisely is, in these cases, no ground for saying that it has no value at all. But where the chance is very highly speculative the court may feel that it cannot sensibly value it. In such a case the court will refuse to award damages for loss of the chance (which is a form of expectation) and instead confine the plaintiff to a claim for reliance loss.[6]

iv Taxation

The plaintiff in a contractual action may claim damages for loss of some benefit which would, if he had received it, have been taxable in his hands. This is most obviously true where an employee claims damages for wrongful dismissal. Such damages are (subject to the rules as to mitigation, to be discussed below) based on the amounts which the employee would have earned under the contract. To award the plaintiff those amounts in full might result in his actually making a profit out of the breach; for if he had earned his salary or wages he might have had to pay income tax, while the damages may be tax

---

[3] *Lazenby Garages Ltd v Wright* [1976] 2 All ER 770 (BMW car).
[4] *Chaplin v Hicks* [1911] 2 KB 786.
[5] *Manubens v Leon* [1919] 1 KB 208.
[6] *McRae v Commonwealth Disposals Commission* (1950) 84 CLR 377 at 411.

free. In such circumstances, the plaintiff will therefore recover the amount that he would have earned under the broken contract less any tax that he would have had to pay on those earnings.[7] The exact amount of tax to be deducted will depend on the personal circumstances of the plaintiff in each case.

Two conditions must be satisfied before the plaintiff's tax liability is taken into account in assessing damages. First, the benefit which the plaintiff has lost must be one which would, if he had received it, have been taxable in his hands. Loss of income would, but the mere failure to get a capital asset would not, be such a benefit.[8] Thus the incidence of taxation would be irrelevant where a seller wrongfully failed to deliver goods and the buyer made a claim for damages based on the extra cost of obtaining substitute goods. Secondly, the damages themselves must not be taxable, for if the plaintiff has to pay tax on the damages he will obviously not make any profit out of the breach by being awarded his gross loss. In the case of wrongful dismissal, damages are taxable to the extent to which they exceed £30,000.[9] Hence the plaintiff's damages must be reduced by reference to his tax liability where his lost income is less than £30,000; where it is more, the court will first assess his net loss and then award such sum as will, after tax on the sum so assessed be equal to that loss.[10]

v Alternatives

Suppose that A agrees to sell to B for £50 'a ton of coal or a ton of coke'. At the time fixed for delivery a ton of coal is worth £55, and a ton of coke £51. If A refuses to deliver, B's damages will depend on who had the right to choose between the two performances. The general rule is that damages will be assessed on the assumption that each party will exercise the choice most advantageous to himself:[11] hence the damages will be £1 if A had the right to choose but £5 if the contract gave that right to B. But this rule will not be rigidly applied so as to produce absurd or inconvenient results. If, in our example A had the right to choose and had in fact chosen coal before refusing to

---

[7] *Beach v Reed Corrugated Cases Ltd* [1956] 2 All E R 652; cf in tort *British Transport Commission v Gourley* [1956] A C 185.

[8] Cf *Spencer v Macmillan's Trustees* 1958 S C 300.

[9] Income and Corporation Taxes Act 1988, ss 148, 188(4), as amended by Finance Act 1988, s 74.

[10] *Parsons v BNM Laboratories Ltd* [1964] 1 Q B 95; *Shove v Downs Surgical plc* [1984] 1 All E R 7.

[11] *Kaye Steam Navigation Co Ltd v W & R Barnett Ltd* (1932) 48 T L R 440; *The Rijn* [1981] 2 Lloyd's Rep 267; cf *Paula Lee Ltd v Robert Zehil & Co Ltd* [1983] 2 All E R 390.

deliver, the damages would be assessed on that basis.[12] Again, suppose A sells goods to B on the terms that they are to be delivered on any day in a given month to be chosen by A. If by the end of the month A has not delivered, damages will be assessed by reference to the market price on the last day of the month—not by reference to the market price on the particular day of the month on which that price was lowest.[13] The latter basis would lead to too much uncertainty, whatever its theoretical merits might be.

vi *Time for assessment*

As costs and prices fluctuate, the exact amount of damages will depend on the point of time by reference to which the assessment is made. The law starts with the principle of assessment by reference to the time of breach. This principle is, for example, stated in the Sale of Goods Act 1979. Where a buyer fails to accept and pay (or where a seller fails to deliver), damages are prima facie based on the market price at the time when the goods ought to have been accepted (or delivered), or, if no time was fixed, at the time of the refusal to accept (or deliver).[14] This rule should not, however, be interpreted too literally. The injured party may be given a reasonable time to consider the position, and damages may then be assessed by reference to the end of that reasonable time and not by reference to the very day of breach.[15] Even with this qualification, the principle of assessment by reference to the time of breach is not an inflexible one; and it will not be applied in the following situations.

First, the breach may not be known to the injured party as soon as it is committed. In that case damages will normally be assessed by reference to the time at which the breach was, or reasonably should have been, discovered. This rule is often applied where a builder does defective work and the defects do not become apparent for some time after the work was done. In one such case[16] the cost of making good the defects was £16,800 when the defective work was done, but £21,300 when the breach was discovered; and it was held that the builder was liable for the latter sum.

Secondly, the injured party may know of the breach but be unable

[12] *Toprak Mahsulleri Ofisi v Finagrain Cie Commerciale Agricole et Financière SA* [1979] 2 Lloyd's Rep 98; *Shipping Corpn of India Ltd v Naviera Letasa SA* [1976] 1 Lloyd's Rep 132 at 137-138.
[13] Cf *Harlow and Jones Ltd v Panex (International) Ltd* [1967] 2 Lloyd's Rep 509; *Phoebus D Kyprianou Co v Wm H Pim Jr & Co Ltd* [1977] 2 Lloyd's Rep 570 (both cases of buyer's breach).
[14] Ss 50(3), 51(3).
[15] *C Sharpe & Co Ltd v Nosawa* [1917] 2 K B 814; cf *Bremer Handelsgesellschaft m b H v Vanden Avenne-Izegem* [1978] 2 Lloyd's Rep 109 at 117.
[16] *East Ham Borough Council v Bernard Sunley Ltd* [1966] A C 406.

332 Remedies for breach of contract

at once to act on that knowledge. Suppose that a seller has despatched goods to the buyer, and that, while they are en route, the buyer wrongfully refuses to pay. The seller may be unable to resell the goods while they are in transit, and, if so, the damages may therefore be assessed by reference to the market value of the goods as soon as the transit is over, or as soon thereafter as it is reasonable for the seller to resell.

Thirdly, it may in all the circumstances be quite unreasonable to expect the injured party to act on his knowledge of the breach by making a substitute contract. He cannot be expected to do so where he continues, after breach, to negotiate in the hope of securing eventual performance, or where he is actually suing for specific performance of the contract. In such cases damages are assessed by reference to the time when it becomes clear that performance will not be obtained: ie when the negotiations break down,[17] when the court refuses to order specific performance,[18] or when it becomes clear that the defendant will not comply with an order for specific performance and the plaintiff elects instead to seek damages.[19]

vii Anticipatory breach

The victim of an anticipatory breach can either continue to press for performance or 'accept' the breach.[20]

If he takes the former course, the time for assessment is governed by the same rules that apply in cases of actual breach. It follows that damages will (subject to the exceptions just discussed) be assessed by reference to the time when the contract ought to have been performed, and not by reference to the time of repudiation.[1]

The prima facie rule of assessment by reference to the time of breach also applies where the victim 'accepts' the breach;[2] but here it is subject to the important qualification that, on 'accepting' the breach, the injured party must mitigate his loss in accordance with the principles to be discussed later in this chapter.[3] This means that he will be expected to make a substitute contract on, or within a reasonable time of, his acceptance of the breach.[4] Thus the damages

---

17 *Radford v De Froberville* [1978] 1 All E R 33; *Toprak Mahsulleri Ofisi v Finagrain Cie Commerciale Agricole et Financière SA* [1979] 2 Lloyd's Rep 98; *The Aktion* [1987] 1 Lloyd's Rep 283 at 314.

18 *Wroth v Tyler* [1974] Ch 30 as explained in *Radford v De Froberville*, supra; *Domb v Isoz* [1980] Ch 548 at 559; *Meng Leong Development Pte Ltd v Jip Hong Trading Co Pte Ltd* [1985]A C 511.

19 *Johnson v Agnew* [1980] A C 367 at 401.

20 Ante, p 294.

1 *Tai Hing Cotton Mill Ltd v Kamsing Knitting Factory* [1979] A C 91.

2 *Roper v Johnson* (1873) L R 8 C P 167.

3 See pp 337–340, post.

4 *Roth v Taysen, Townsend & Co* (1895) 1 Com Cas 240.

will be assessed by reference to any relevant market when that substitute contract should have been made—not when the original contract should have been performed. However, the burden of proving that such a substitute contract could have been made lies on the party in breach;[5] and, if he cannot show this, the damages will be assessed by reference to the market when he should have performed. The further question arises whether, in applying the principle of looking to that time, the court can take into account future events (other than market movements) between the anticipatory breach and the time fixed for performance. Where the victim has 'accepted' the anticipatory breach, the court clearly cannot take into account the probability that the victim himself might subsequently have committed a breach justifying the guilty party's repudiation; for the victim's 'acceptance' of the anticipatory breach relieves him from his obligation to perform in the future, so that his failure to do so can no longer be a breach.[6] But the contract may give the guilty party a right to cancel on the occurrence of an *event* (such as the late arrival of a chartered ship) even though that event did not amount to a *breach* by the victim. If the guilty party can show that such an event would *certainly* have occurred, and that he would have exercised his right to cancel on account of it, then the contract will be of no value to the injured party, whose damages will therefore be nominal.[7]

d Methods of limiting damages

A breach of contract may be a starting point of a series of events which cause loss to the plaintiff; but the law will not hold the defendant liable for all such loss. Sometimes it will regard the loss as too remote, or as not having a sufficiently strong causal connection with the breach. Sometimes it will take the view that the plaintiff should have mitigated the loss, or that he suffered it (wholly or in part) as the result of his own default. And sometimes it will limit the defendant's liability by more or less arbitrary rules of law.

i Remoteness

The principle that damages will not be awarded for losses which are 'too remote' is illustrated by the leading case of *Hadley v Baxendale*.[8] A shaft in the plaintiffs' mill at Gloucester broke and had to be sent to the makers at Greenwich to serve as a pattern for a new one. The

---

[5] *Roper v Johnson*, supra.
[6] *Berger & Co Inc v Gill & Duffus SA* [1984] A C 382 at 391; ante, p 273; contrast *The Simona* [1988] 2 All E R 742 (breach *not* accepted).
[7] *The Mihalis Angelos* [1971] 1 Q B 164 at 210; cf p 296, ante.
[8] (1854) 9 Exch 341.

defendants undertook to carry the shaft to Greenwich, but in breach of contract delayed its delivery for a few days, during which the mill was kept idle. The plaintiffs claimed damages for the resulting loss of profits but the court regarded this loss as too remote a consequence of the breach. The underlying idea is that it is undesirable to make a defendant pay for such remote loss, for to hold him liable might either deter him from entering into contracts at all, or lead to an undue raising of charges to meet such liability. The defendant will only be liable if one of two rules laid down in *Hadley v Baxendale* is satisfied.

First, the loss must arise 'naturally, ie, according to the usual course of things, from such breach of contract itself.'[9] This test was not satisfied in *Hadley v Baxendale* because 'in the great multitude of cases'[10] a carrier's delay in delivering a broken mill shaft would not keep the mill idle: the millers might have had, or been able to get, a spare shaft. The case should from this point of view be contrasted with the later *Victoria Laundry*[11] case, in which a large boiler was sold to a laundry. In breach of contract the sellers delivered the boiler twenty-two weeks late, so that the buyers could not use it (as they had intended to do) to expand their business. It was held that the sellers were liable for the general loss of profits suffered by the buyers. Having regard to the subject-matter, the likelihood of such loss was obviously very much greater in the *Victoria Laundry* case than in *Hadley v Baxendale*.

Secondly, the defendant may be liable if the loss was such 'as may reasonably be supposed to have been in the minds of both parties at the time they made the contract as the probable result of the breach.'[12] This depends in the first place on what the defendant knew of the plaintiff's circumstances; and in *Hadley v Baxendale* the defendants did not know enough to make them liable under this rule. It seems that they knew that the plaintiffs' mill was stopped, but not that it would remain idle until the new shaft arrived from Greenwich.[13] In the *Victoria Laundry* case the defendants knew that the plaintiffs were in the laundry business; but not that the plaintiffs wanted the boiler for the purpose of some exceptionally lucrative government contracts. Hence the defendants were not liable for the actual loss suffered because the plaintiffs could not perform *those contracts*, but only for loss of ordinary profits.

Under the second rule in *Hadley v Baxendale* the defendant is not liable if he is ignorant of the special circumstances; but it does not

---

[9] Ibid at 354.
[10] Ibid at 356.
[11] [1949] 2 K B 528.
[12] *Hadley v Baxendale* (1854) 9 Exch 341 at 354.
[13] See the report in 18 Jur 358.

follow that he will be liable *merely* because he knows of them. To impose this degree of liability there must be 'some knowledge *and acceptance* by one party of the purpose and intention of the other in entering into the contract.'[14] No doubt the plaintiffs' purpose in making the contract of carriage in *Hadley v Baxendale* was to get their mill started again; but, even if the defendants had known all the facts, they could scarcely be said to have accepted this purpose as the basis of the contract. Such acceptance could, however, be inferred where A contracts to carry B's goods to a particular market in which B wishes to make contracts of sale. In *The Heron II*[15] the defendants agreed to carry a cargo of sugar belonging to the plaintiffs from Constanza to Basrah 'with all convenient speed'. The plaintiffs intended to sell the sugar on the sugar market in Basrah; and, although the defendants did not know this, they did know that there was a sugar market there, and they must have known that it was not unlikely that the plaintiffs would want to sell the sugar in that market.[16] In breach of contract the defendants called at various ports out of the direct route, taking on and discharging cargo, so that they took twenty-nine instead of twenty days to reach Basrah. During the extra nine days, the price of sugar at Basrah fell so that the plaintiffs obtained some £4,000 less for the sugar than they would have done if the ship had gone straight to Basrah. The House of Lords held that the defendants were liable for this loss, since, in the light of their knowledge of the circumstances, it was one which they should reasonably have had in their contemplation. And in the circumstances it seems correct to say that they not only knew of the plaintiffs' purpose but 'accepted' it in the sense above discussed: that is, that they contracted to get the cargo to the particular market without undue delay. On the other hand, they could not have contemplated the terms of individual transactions: accordingly, if the delay had prevented the plaintiffs from performing an exceptionally profitable contract sale for more than the market price, the defendants would not have been liable for this loss.[17]

Before *The Heron II* it had become common to say that a loss was not too remote if it could reasonably have been foreseen; and the references in that case to the contemplation of the parties suggest that the House of Lords was applying a foreseeability test of some kind. Nevertheless the case marks a change of emphasis. Reasonable foreseeability is also established as a test of remoteness in the law of torts; and in that branch of the law a reasonable person is credited with the capacity to foresee some consequences which are by no means

14 *Weld-Blundell v Stephens* [1920] AC 956 at 980.
15 [1969] 1 AC 350.
16 Ibid at 382.
17 Cf *The Rio Claro* [1987] 2 Lloyd's Rep 173.

obvious or even very probable. In the law of contract a much higher degree of foreseeability is required. There must, as it was put in *The Heron II*, be a 'serious possibility' or a 'real danger'[18] that the loss will occur; and references to 'foreseeability' as a test of remoteness in contract must be understood in this sense.

The effect of *The Heron II* is that damages will in general be more severely limited in contract than in tort; but it does not follow that this will invariably be the case. The point was further considered in *H Parsons (Livestock) Ltd v Uttley Ingham & Co Ltd*[19] where the defendants committed a breach of contract in failing to see that a pig-food hopper supplied by them to the plaintiffs was properly ventilated. In consequence the food became mouldy and many of the pigs died from a rare intestinal disease. The defendants were held liable for the resulting loss, that is, for the value of the pigs that died and for the profit that would have been made by selling those pigs. The ground for the decision seems to be that the contract test of remoteness was satisfied as there was a 'serious possibility' that the pigs would become ill.[20] The court, moreover, recognised that the tests of remoteness differed in contract and tort in certain cases. The distinction can be justified on the ground that a contracting party can often draw unusual risks to the other party's attention before the contract is made (and so make him liable for them); while the victim of a tort has no such opportunity as he usually has no previous relations with the wrongdoer.[1] But this justification would lose its force where a contracting party in fact had no such opportunity to protect himself; nor would it make sense to maintain different tests where the same facts gave rise to a cause of action both in contract and in tort.[2] In either of these situations the plaintiff could probably rely on the more favourable tort test. In other cases the more restrictive test stated in *The Heron II* will continue to apply to damages for breach of contract.[3]

ii Causation

A plaintiff can only recover damages if there is some causal connection between the breach and his loss. Suppose that a ship founders in a storm and it is later discovered that she was technically unseaworthy because she was not carrying a proper medicine chest.[4] The unsea-

---

[18] Ibid at 414, 415, 425.
[19] [1978] QB 791.
[20] Ibid at 812.
[1] *The Heron II* [1969] 1 AC 350 at 386.
[2] Cf *Archer v Brown* [1985] QB 401 at 418.
[3] *The Pegase* [1981] 1 Lloyd's Rep 175 at 181.
[4] For this example of 'unseaworthiness', see *Hong Kong Fir Shipping Co v Kawasaki Kisen Kaisha Ltd* [1962] 2 QB 26 at 62.

worthiness would be a breach of any contract for the carriage of goods on board which the shipowner may have made. But the owner of goods on the ship would not be entitled to damages merely on that account because such a breach would not normally have caused the ship to sink.

On the other hand, the plaintiff may recover full damages even though the breach is not the sole cause of the loss. If the breach 'is one of two causes, both co-operating and both of equal efficacy, it is sufficient to carry a judgment in damages'.[5] In the leading *Monarch SS Co Ltd*[6] case a contract was made in April 1939 to carry goods from Manchuria to Sweden. The ship was delayed by unseaworthiness and so failed to get to Sweden before the outbreak of war in September 1939. Instead she was ordered to a Scottish port where the goods had to be transferred to neutral vessels. The carriers were held liable for the cost of transhipment even though the loss was caused by a combination of unseaworthiness and the acts of the British authorities. Neither factor was the sole cause of the loss, and both could be said to have operated with 'equal efficacy'. Similarly, a ship hardly ever sinks *merely* because she is unseaworthy; and the shipowner will often be liable if the loss is caused by a combination of unseaworthiness and ordinary sea perils. On the other hand, it was said in the *Monarch Steamship* case that the shipowner would not be liable if the ship had been delayed by un-seaworthiness and then been struck by a typhoon, for in that case the unseaworthiness would have had no 'real' but only a 'fortuitous' connection with the loss.[7]

iii Mitigation

The victim of a breach of contract is said to be under a 'duty to mitigate' his loss. The word 'duty' is here used in an unusual sense. It merely means that the victim is not entitled to recover damages for a loss that he should have avoided: not that he is liable for failing to avoid it. This 'duty' has two aspects.

First, the injured party must take all reasonable steps to minimise his loss. One application of this principle has already been considered. When a buyer fails to accept and pay for goods, or a seller to deliver them, the other party is expected to go into the market and to make a substitute contract at the relevant time, which is prima facie the time of breach. If he fails to do so and the market then moves against him, he cannot recover the extra loss which he suffers, as this

---

[5] *Heskell v Continental Express Ltd* [1950] 1 All E R 1033 at 1048; cf *The Silver Sky* [1981] 2 Lloyd's Rep 95.
[6] [1949] A C 196.
[7] [1949] A C 149 at 215, approving a statement in the lower (Scottish) court: 1947 S C 179 at 193.

is due to his failure to mitigate.[8] Another application of the principle
is that an employee who is wrongfully dismissed must make reasonable efforts to find another comparable job. The crucial point is that
the injured party must, and need only,[9] act reasonably. Thus an
employee who is wrongfully dismissed is not bound to take another
job if this will involve an appreciable reduction in status;[10] nor is he
bound to accept an offer of re-employment from an employer who has
wrongfully dismissed him in circumstances of personal humiliation.[11]
But sometimes a party may be required to accept an offer of performance from the party in breach even on terms other than those
originally agreed. In one case[12] a person who had agreed to sell crêpe
de chine on credit refused to deliver except for cash, and the buyer
immediately bought against him in the market, which had risen. It
was held that the buyer should have mitigated by accepting the
seller's offer of cash deliveries. Where a seller cannot deliver on time,
the buyer may similarly be required to mitigate by accepting an offer
of late delivery.[13] In such cases the injured party remains entitled to
damages for any loss suffered by him as a result of the difference
between the newly offered performance and that originally bargained
for; and if the defaulting party's offer purports to take away that
right, it need not be accepted.[14]

The 'duty' to mitigate requires the injured party to make a *substitute*
contract to replace that which has been broken. So far we have
assumed that the new contract is indeed a true substitute for the
broken one. But suppose that A reserves one of the hundred rooms in
B's hotel and then in breach of contract cancels the reservation. C
now wishes to book a room in the hotel. If the other ninety-nine
rooms in the hotel are taken, B is bound to mitigate by letting A's
room to C; but if less than ninety-nine rooms are taken, B is fully
entitled to put C into one of the empty rooms and to claim damages
from A.

The second aspect of the 'duty' to mitigate is that the injured party
must not take unreasonable steps actually to increase the loss.[15] In the
case just put, it would probably not be reasonable for B to spend
money in getting the room ready for A's occupation *after* A had
cancelled his reservation. But there are other cases in which it would
be reasonable for the injured party to incur expenses after the

---

[8] See pp 327–329, ante, cf *The Elena d'Amico* [1980] 1 Lloyd's Rep 75 at 79.
[9] See *London and South of England Building Society v Stone* [1983] 3 All E R 105.
[10] *Yetton v Eastwoods Froy Ltd* [1966] 3 All E R 353.
[11] *Payzu Ltd v Saunders* [1919] 2 K B 581 at 589.
[12] *Payzu Ltd v Saunders,* supra.
[13] *The Solholt* [1983] 1 Lloyd's Rep 605.
[14] *Strutt v Whitnell* [1975] 2 All E R 510.
[15] *The Borag* [1981] 1 All E R 856.

breach–particularly if he was bound by commercial or moral obligations to third parties to do so. The point is strikingly illustrated by a
case[16] in which an English firm had printed banknotes for the Bank of
Portugal, and in breach of contract allowed them to get into the hands
of a rogue who put them into circulation. The Bank then cancelled
the notes and bought them up in exchange for good notes, even
though it was not legally bound to do so. It was held that the printers
were liable for the face value of the notes, and not merely for
the cost of reprinting, as the Bank had acted reasonably, having
regard to its commercial obligations.

So far we have considered the *duty* to mitigate. The law also
recognises a distinct, though related, idea: that the loss is *in fact*
mitigated if the plaintiff has benefited from or as a result of the
breach. This can happen in various ways. First, the plaintiff may
benefit by being relieved of his own obligations under the contract. If
a seller fails to deliver, the buyer need not pay, and the amount which
he saves is taken into account in assessing his loss. Secondly, the
plaintiff may benefit from performing his 'duty' to mitigate: for,
example, a wrongfully dismissed employee may get a substitute job
and so receive wages. As such benefits are taken into account even if
they are not obtained, it is obvious that they must equally be taken
into account if they are obtained. Thirdly, the plaintiff may benefit as
a result of something which he actually did in consequence of the
breach even though he was not required to do so in performing his
'duty' to mitigate. A skilled worker may be wrongfully dismissed
and, if he cannot find comparable employment, he may take a job as
an unskilled labourer. His actual earnings as a labourer will be taken
into account in assessing damages.[17]

This example should be contrasted with a case[18] in which a contract
of employment restricted the employee's right to invest in competing
companies. On wrongful dismissal, the employee was freed from this
restriction, and made such an investment. It was held that his profit
on the investment was 'not a direct result of his dismissal' but a 'collateral benefit',[19] and that it should not be taken into account. The
distinction between the two types of benefit has in some cases given
rise to difficult questions of causation.[20] One rule which is clearly
established, however, is that the plaintiff need not bring into account

---

16 *Banco de Portugal v Waterlow & Sons Ltd* [1932] AC 452.
17 Cf *Edwards v Society of Graphical and Allied Technicians* [1971] Ch 354. For mitigation in
   cases of *unfair* dismissal (which does not usually involve any *breach* of contract) see
   Employment Protection (Consolidation) Act 1978, s 74(4).
18 *Laverack v Woods of Colchester* [1967] 1 QB 278.
19 Ibid at 290.
20 Eg *British Westinghouse Co v Underground Electric Rlys Co of London* [1912] AC 673.

any benefits which he has received under a policy of insurance taken out by him against the loss caused by the breach.[1]

iv Default of the victim

Where the victim of a breach of contract fails to mitigate, the loss is partly due to his default in the sense that he *failed to avoid* the consequences of an event brought about by the other party's breach. There is, however, another group of cases in which the event causing loss is *partly brought about* by conduct of the plaintiff. Goods on board a ship may be damaged partly because the carrier failed to stow them properly and partly because the shipper did not provide adequate packing; or the hirer of a car may be injured partly because the brakes were defective and partly because he drove too fast. In the law of tort such conduct on the part of the victim is known as contributory negligence. At common law its effect was to bar the plaintiff's claim completely if he had the 'last opportunity' of avoiding the accident; but where the defendant had the last opportunity the plaintiff recovered in full. This unsatisfactory 'all or nothing' solution has been altered by the Law Reform (Contributory Negligence) Act 1945. The Act provides that where the plaintiff suffers loss partly as a result of his own 'fault' and partly as a result of the 'fault' of the defendant, he can nevertheless recover damages; but the court can reduce his damages in proportion to the effect which his fault had in causing the loss. 'Fault' is defined in section 4 of the Act to mean 'negligence . . . or other act or omission which gives rise to liability in tort or would, apart from this Act, give rise to the defence of contributory negligence'. The question arises whether the contributory negligence rules can be applied to contractual actions.

For the purpose of answering this question, the cases must be divided into three categories. First the defendant's conduct constitutes both a breach of contract and a tort: this would be the position where a carrier for reward failed to observe the duty of care which he owed to a passenger both under the contract and under the general law. If the passenger was injured partly as a result of this breach of duty and partly as a result of his own carelessness, there is no doubt that the contributory negligence rules would apply.[2] The rules would similarly apply where the defendant was in breach of a duty of care arising from a contract to render professional services;[3] for such a

---

[1] *Bradburn v Great Western Rly Co* (1874) LR 10 Exch 1; *The Yasin* [1979] 2 Lloyd's Rep 45; contrast *Mark Rowlands Ltd v Berni Inns Ltd* [1986] QB 211, where the rule was excluded by the terms of the contract.

[2] Cf *Sayers v Harlow UDC* [1958] 2 All ER 342; *Sole v WJ Hallt Ltd* [1973] QB 574.

[3] *De Meza v Apple* [1974] 1 Lloyd's Rep 508 (auditor); affd [1975] 1 Lloyd's Rep 498 where the applicability of the 1945 Act was left open; *Forsikringsaktieselskapet Vesta v Butcher* [1988] 1 Lloyd's Rep 19; affd without reference to this point, 26 January 1989.

breach is now recognised as giving rise to liability in both contract and tort.[4] Secondly, the defendant is in breach of contract without being in any way careless.[5] In such a case the Law Reform (Contributory Negligence) Act could not apply because the definition of 'fault' in the Act connotes some degree of carelessness; and the question whether the defendant was liable in full or not at all would depend on the principles of causation discussed earlier in this chapter. Thus in one case[6] a dealer supplied a defective trailer coupling to a customer who went on using it, after it was obviously broken, until there was an accident. It was held that the dealer was not liable as the accident had been caused by the customer's use of the coupling when he knew that it was broken, and not by the fact that it was defective when sold. Thirdly, the defendant is liable for breach of a contractual duty of care, but that carelessness does not make him liable in tort. In one case, the Act was said to apply to such a situation,[7] but the case concerned a careless professional adviser and would probably now be regarded as falling into our first category. More recently, it has been suggested that 'negligence' in the Act refers *only* to tortious negligence:[8] if this view prevails, the Act will not apply to the third category of cases.

In the situations so far discussed, the loss is caused partly by the breach of contract and partly by the plaintiff's own careless conduct; but that conduct does not amount to a legal wrong against the defendant. Where the plaintiff's conduct does amount to such a wrong and each party suffers loss, those losses may be apportioned (quite apart from the Act) on the ground that they resulted from two independent actionable wrongs. Each party can then recover to the extent that his loss was caused by the other's wrongful act.[9] Thus if responsibility for the event were equally divided between the parties, each would be liable for half the loss suffered by the other.

v Special rules

In two cases damages are limited by special rules.

The first relates to failure to pay a fixed sum of money when due. The obvious remedy for such failure is an action for that sum, and in

---

[4] *Esso Petroleum Co Ltd v Mardon* [1976] QB 801 at 819; *Midland Bank Trust Co Ltd v Hett Stubbs and Kemp* [1979] Ch 384; except where the contract exhaustively defines the defendant's duty: cf ante p 212 n 11a.

[5] See p 266, ante.

[6] *Lexmead (Basingstoke) Ltd v Lewis* [1982] AC 225; cf *The Good Luck* [1988] 1 Lloyd's Rep 514 at 555.

[7] *De Meza v Apple* [1974] 1 Lloyd's Rep 508 (affd [1975] 1 Lloyd's Rep 498, where the point was left open), cited without disapproval in *Forsikringsaktieselskapet Vesta v Butcher* [1988] 1 Lloyd's Rep 19, at 23–24; and see ante p 340 n 3.

[8] Ibid at 35.

[9] *Tenant Radiant Heat Ltd v Warrington Development Corpn* (1987) Times, 19 December.

addition interest can be recovered if the contract provides for it in the
event of late payment. Even in the absence of such a provision, the
court has a discretionary power to award interest so long as the action
is begun before the principal sum due has been paid.[10] If the payment
is simply made late, the person to whom it was due cannot *then* claim
interest unless the contract so provides. The rule can work hardship in
times of inflation but it survives in spite of repeated criticism.[11] It
used, moreover, to be thought that no further damages (other than
interest) could be recovered for failure to pay money when due.[12] But
this rule, too, was hard to justify;[13] and it no longer prevents a
plaintiff from recovering *special* damages in respect of a particular loss
which is not too remote.[14] Thus in one case[15] the defendant was late in
making a substantial payment, knowing that the plaintiff needed it to
complete the purchase of a new home. As a result of the delay, the
plaintiff incurred various extra charges in connection with his
purchase; and it was held that he could recover these as damages for
late payment. Damages can similarly be recovered where a bank
wrongfully refuses to honour a customer's cheque;[16] and where a
person fails to perform an undertaking to subscribe for debentures in
a company,[17] or to provide a letter of credit under a contract for the
sale of goods.[18]

Secondly, it was settled by the House of Lords in *Bain v Fothergill*[19]
that a person who has contracted to sell land and then finds that he
cannot show good title is not liable to the purchaser for loss of his
bargain. He is only liable for the purchaser's cost of investigating the
title. In times of rapidly fluctuating house prices, the rule is likely to
cause hardship to purchasers, and its abolition has been recommended by the Law Commission.[20] Meanwhile, the rule does not
apply where the vendor could make his title good (eg by paying off a
charge on the land, or by taking steps to put an end to a tenancy) but
refuses to do so.[1] Moreover, if the vendor represents that his title is

10 Supreme Court Act 1981, s 35A, as amended by Administration of Justice Act 1982,
s 15 and Sch I.
11 *London, Chatham & Dover Rly Co v South Eastern Rly Co* [1893] A C 429 at 437; *La Pintada*
[1985] A C 104.
12 *Fletcher v Tayleur* (1855) 17 C B 21 at 29.
13 *Wallis v Smith* (1882) 21 Ch D 243 at 257 ('not quite consistent with reason').
14 *The Lips* [1987] 3 All E R 110 at 116; *International Minerals and Chemical Corpn v Karl O
Helm A G* [1986] 1 Lloyd's Rep 81.
15 *Wadsworth v Lydall* [1981] 2 All E R 401, approved in *La Pintada* [1985] A C 104 at 127.
16 *Prehn v Royal Bank of Liverpool* (1870) L R 5 Exch 92.
17 *Wallis Chlorine Syndicate Ltd v American Alkali Co Ltd* (1901) 17 T L R 656.
18 *Trans Trust S P R L v Danubian Trading Co Ltd* [1952] 2 Q B 297.
19 (1874) L R 7 H L 158.
20 Law Com No 166, para 4.2.
1 *Day v Singleton* [1899] 2 Ch 320; *Re Daniel* [1917] 2 Ch 405; *Malhotra v Choudhury* [1980]
Ch 52; *Sharneyford Supplies Ltd v Edge* [1987] Ch 305.

good when it is actually defective, he will be liable in deceit if at the time of contracting he knew of the defect;[2] and under s 2(1) of the Misrepresentation Act 1967 if he cannot prove that he on reasonable grounds believed his representation to be true.[3] Since this liability arises in tort, it would seem that the purchaser would not recover damages for loss of his bargain;[4] but his claim for reliance loss would not be limited (as it is when the rule in *Bain v Fothergill* applies) to the cost of investigating the vendor's title.

e Penalties and liquidated damages

Under the rules so far discussed, the amount which will be recoverable on breach of contract is often hard to predict. The parties may try to remove this uncertainty by providing that a fixed sum is to be paid[5] on breach. If the sum is a reasonable estimate of the probable loss the provision will be valid; a provision of this kind is known as a *liquidated damages* clause. Sometimes, however, the purpose of the provision is not to make a genuine pre-estimate of loss but to bring pressure to bear on one of the parties to perform his part of the contract. Such a provision is known as a *penalty* clause and is invalid.

i Rules for distinguishing between them

The category into which a particular clause falls depends on the construction of the clause as a whole. Thus the mere fact that the parties have called it a 'liquidated damages' or 'penalty' clause is not decisive either way. In the leading case of *Dunlop Ltd v New Garage Ltd*[6] four rules of construction were formulated for distinguishing between the two types of provisions.

The first, and most important, rule is that a clause is penal 'if the sum stipulated for is extravagant and unconscionable in amount in comparison with the greatest loss that could conceivably be proved to have followed from the breach'. An illustration given in one of the cases, though far-fetched, catches the spirit of the rule: it would be a penalty if a builder promised to pay £1 million on failure to do building work worth £50.[7]

---

2 *Bain v Fothergill*, supra, at 207.
3 See pp 129, 134, ante.
4 *Sharneyford Supplies Ltd v Edge* [1987] Ch 305 at 323, disapproving a contrary dictum in *Watts v Spence* [1976] Ch 165 at 175 and describing damages for misrepresentation as damages 'in tort'.
5 Or that a 'payment in kind' is to be made: see *Jobson v Johnson* (1988) Independent, 22 June.
6 [1915] AC 79 at 87-88 (the order in which the rules are stated in the text differs, for purposes of exposition, from that in the *Law Reports*).
7 *Clydebank Engineering Co v Don Jose Ramos Yzquierdo y Castaneda* [1905] AC 6 at 10.

The second rule, which is really a corollary of the first, is that a provision will be regarded as a valid liquidated damages clause if 'the consequences of breach are such as to make precise pre-estimation an impossibility'; and if, in addition, the actual amount bears a reasonable relation to the probable consequences of breach. In *Dunlop Ltd v New Garage Ltd*, a contract for the sale of tyres imposed numerous restrictions on resales and provided that the buyer should pay the seller £5 for every tyre sold or offered in breach of these restrictions. This provision was held valid since such breaches had a general tendency to disrupt the seller's business organisation, though the exact loss flowing from each breach was almost impossible to quantify.

The third rule lays down a presumption that a clause is penal if it makes the same sum payable on one or more of several breaches which must cause different amounts of loss. For example in one case[8] a lease provided that the tenant should pay £3 'for every ton of *hay or straw* which shall be sold off the premises during the last twelve months of the tenancy.' This was held to be a penalty because hay was worth more than straw. Similarly, a provision in a hire-purchase agreement would be a penalty if it provided that three-quarters of the hire-purchase price should be paid on the hirer's default as compensation for depreciation; for the depreciation would obviously be greater if the hirer defaulted in the twelfth month than it would be if he defaulted in the first.[9] The rule can, however, give rise to some very odd results.[10] If it applies, the clause is invalid even though the actual breach is quite a serious one, and one for which the stipulated sum would be a reasonable pre-estimate. A draftsman who knows of the rule can generally avoid it by proportioning the sum payable to the seriousness of the breach, or to its probable effects. In the hire-purchase cases, for example, the amount payable as compensation for depreciation can be increased in proportion to the time for which the hirer has had the goods (making allowance for payments which he has made under the agreement).[11] Similarly, where the breach consists of delay, the contract may provide that a fixed sum is to be paid for each week (or other period) of delay.[12]

The fourth rule deals with the situation in which the breach consists only in not paying a fixed sum of money and the contract provides in that event for the payment of a greater sum. Such a provision is

---

[8] *Willson v Love* [1896] 1 QB 626.

[9] *Landom Trust Ltd v Hurrell* [1955] 1 All ER 839.

[10] The court may be able to avoid these by refusing to construe the clause literally as in *Webster v Bosanquet* [1912] AC 398 (provisions for payment of £500 if defendant sold 'the whole or any part' of his tea crop to anyone except plaintiff *held* valid as 'any part' meant any substantial part).

[11] Eg *Phonographic Equipment* (1958) *Ltd v Muslu* [1961] 3 All ER 626.

[12] *Clydebank Engineering case*, supra.

invariably penal. Thus if £50 is owed under a contract which provides that on default in punctual payment the debtor should be liable to pay £1,000, the stipulation would be a penalty. This is obviously a sensible result, but it could equally well be explained on the ground that the sum of £1,000 was 'extravagant and unconscionable'. The fourth rule can, however, apply even where this is not the case, eg where £55 is due on failure punctually to pay £50. The view that such a provision was penal was originally based on the old rule that damages (other than interest) could not be awarded for failure to pay money when due. Special damages can now be recovered for such a breach if the plaintiff can show that the delay has caused a particular loss which is not too remote;[13] and it may be that the present rule too, will no longer apply where it was likely, at the time of contracting, that late payment would cause such loss. The courts have recognised that, unless the rule is so limited, it can invalidate perfectly reasonable bargains, and they have therefore interpreted it restrictively. It does not, for instance, apply to a provision merely because it accelerates the liability of a debtor (by providing that on his failure punctually to pay one instalment the others shall at once become due);[14] and this is so even though in a commercial sense early payment in fact costs more. And, although the rule invalidates increases for late payment, the parties can achieve much the same result by agreeing to a discount for early payment: such an agreement is perfectly valid.

ii *Effects of the distinction*

A provision for liquidated damages is, as a general rule, fully effective. Thus on the one hand the injured party can recover the stipulated amount even though it exceeds his actual loss. On the other hand, the injured party cannot recover more than the stipulated amount even though his actual loss is greater.[15] In the latter situation, the liquidated damages clause operates to limit liability, but its legal nature is nevertheless distinct from that of a limitation of liability clause. Under a limitation clause the injured party recovers this loss up to the stipulated amount. Under a liquidated damages clause, on the other hand, the injured party simply recovers the stipulated amount and the amount of his loss (if any) is quite irrelevant.[16]

By contrast, a penalty clause is disregarded for all purposes. The injured party will therefore recover his loss in accordance with

[13] See p 342, ante.
[14] *Protector Loan Co v Grice* (1880) 5 QBD 592; *The Angelic Star* [1988] 1 Lloyd's Rep 122.
[15] *Cellulose Acetate Silk Co Ltd v Widnes Foundry (1925) Ltd* [1933] AC 20.
[16] For this reason, such clauses are probably not affected by the Unfair Contract Terms Act 1977; cf p 89, ante.

the normal rules. Usually the sum thus assessed will be less than the penalty; but the rule applies equally if the loss is greater than the penalty.[17] There are two reasons why this apparently paradoxical situation may arise. First, the question whether a stipulation is a penalty has to be determined by reference to the time of *contracting* and it is possible for a sum which was 'extravagant and unconscionable' at that time to fall short of a loss which may arise at the time of *breach*. Secondly, a clause may be penal under the third or fourth of the rules of construction discussed above even though it is not 'extravagant and unconscionable' at all; and in such a case it is easily possible for the stipulated amount to fall short of the loss which is actually suffered and recoverable under the normal rules.

iii Scope of the distinction

The distinction between penalties and liquidated damages only applies to sums payable *on breach*. In one case[18] a professional footballer suffered an injury which was thought to have put him permanently out of the game; and he was paid £500 under a policy of insurance on the terms that the money was to be repaid if he again played professional football. This was not a penalty since the player had made no promise not to play again and therefore committed no breach by so doing. More difficulty arises when the same sum is payable on several events of which some are breaches while others are not. For example a hire-purchase agreement may require the hirer to bring his payments up to a fixed minimum if the agreement is terminated; and the agreement may be terminated *either* by the owner on account of the hirer's breach *or* by a notice given by the hirer. Here the distinction between penalties and liquidated damages applies if the agreement is terminated for breach, but not if it is lawfully terminated by notice.[19] The paradoxical result is that the hirer who terminates his contract lawfully may be worse off than one who breaks it; for in the former case he is liable for the whole of the stipulated sum, while in the latter he may be able to avoid such liability if he can show that the stipulation is a penalty. If the agreement is one under which the amount of credit does not exceed £15,000, the hirer has a special statutory right to terminate on payment of half the hire-purchase price, and if he exercises this right the court may, instead of the statutory minimum payment, award such sum as will

---

[17] *Wall v Rederiaktiebolaget Luggude* [1915] 3 K B 66.
[18] *Alder v Moore* [1961] 2 Q B 57; cf *Export Credits Guarantee Department v Universal Oil Products Co* [1983] 2 All E R 205 (distinction inapplicable to sums payable under one contract on breach of another contract with a third party).
[19] *Campbell Discount Co Ltd v Bridge* [1961] 1 Q B 445. On appeal, the House of Lords was evenly divided on the point: [1962] A C 600.

adequately compensate the owner for his loss.[20] But this special provision does not alter the general (and unsatisfactory) rule that the distinction between penalties and liquidated damages only applies where there has been a breach.

f Advance payments

One of the parties to a contract may make, or agree to make, an advance payment to the other. If the payee then fails to perform, he must pay the money back. But if the payor defaults after making the payment the rights of the parties with respect to it depend on the distinction between a deposit and a part payment.

A deposit is a sum paid 'as a guarantee that the contract shall be performed'.[1] The payee is generally entitled to keep it[2] (unless the contract otherwise provides); though there is some support for the view that he must pay back if it amounts to a penalty,[3] as opposed to a provision for liquidated damages.[4] In the case of a contract for the sale of land, moreover, the court has a discretion to order the repayment of a deposit.[5] It has been said that the discretion will be exercised 'where justice requires it';[6] but it does not seem that the court will order the return of the normal 10 per cent deposit to a purchaser who simply defaults.[7]

A part payment is simply a payment on account of the price. Whether such a payment must be returned depends on the nature of the contract under which it was made. If repayment would restore both parties to their precontract position, the money must be paid back. This is the position where a part payment is made by a buyer under a contract of sale:[8] the buyer will get his money back and the seller will keep (or get back) the subject-matter of the sale. On the other hand, where the part payment is in respect of work done by the payee under the contract, then he cannot be restored to his precontract position; and so he is entitled to keep the part payment.[9]

---

[20] Consumer Credit Act 1974, s 100 (1) and (3).
[1] *Howe v Smith* (1884) 27 Ch D 89 at 95.
[2] *Howe v Smith,* supra.
[3] *Public Works Comr v Hills* [1906] A C 368.
[4] *Pye v British Automobile Commercial Syndicate Ltd* [1906] 1 K B 425.
[5] Law of Property Act 1925, s 49 (2).
[6] *Schindler v Pigault* (1975) 30 P & C R 328 at 336; *Universal Corpn v Five Ways Properties Ltd* [1979] 1 All E R 552 at 555.
[7] *James Macara Ltd v Barclay* [1944] 2 All E R 31 at 32 (affd [1945] K B 148); *Michael Richard Properties Ltd v St Saviour's Parish, Southwark Corpn of Wardens* [1975] 3 All E R 416.
[8] *Dies v British International Mining Corpn* [1939] 1 K B 724.
[9] *Hyundai Shipbuilding and Heavy Industries Co Ltd v Pournaras* [1978] 2 Lloyd's Rep 502; *Hyundai Heavy Industries Ltd v Papadopoulos* [1980] 2 All E R 29; cf *The Scaptrade* [1983] 2 A C 694 at 703.

Again these rules can be excluded by express contrary provisions. These give rise to particular difficulty where a contract of sale provides for payment by instalments and allows the vendor to rescind the contract and to forfeit instalments already paid if the purchaser defaults. If the purchaser has made substantial payments, the operation of such forfeiture clauses can be extremely harsh. The courts will often help him to avoid the forfeiture by giving him extra time to pay.[10] But if, at the end of that time, he still cannot pay, the general view is that the vendor can enforce the forfeiture so long as he was not guilty of unconscionable conduct in procuring the contract.[11] Some judges have, however, expressed the view that the vendor cannot take this step if it would be unconscionable for him to keep the part payment;[12] and where the forfeited amount is excessive in relation to the vendor's actual loss this would certainly be the fairer view.

Where a deposit or part payment has been promised but not paid when due, the person to whom it was promised may rescind the contract on account of the non-payment, and the question then arises whether he can nevertheless sue for the promised payment. This depends on whether the payment, if it had been made, would have been one that he was entitled to keep under the rules just stated. Thus he can generally sue for the promised payment if it was a deposit,[13] for rescission does not restrospectively affect accrued rights. But he could not sue for the payment if, exceptionally, the deposit was one that he was liable to restore. This would be the position where the deposit was penal, or such that the court would order its return in the exercise of its discretion to do so under a contract for the sale of land.[14] Similarly, the prospective payee could not sue for a part payment due under such a contract; for it would be absurd to allow him to recover the payment in one action when he would have to return it in another.[15] But where the contract is one under which a part payment, if made, could be retained, then a promise to pay it remains enforceable after rescission of the contract.[16]

---

[10] *Starside Properties Ltd v Mustapha* [1974] 2 All E R 567.

[11] *Mussen v Van Diemen's Land Co* [1938] Ch 253; *Galbraith v Mitchenall Estates Ltd* [1965] 2 Q B 473.

[12] *Stockloser v Johnson* [1954] 1 Q B 476 at 485, 491; cf Law Commission Working Paper No 61 Pt V.

[13] *Dewar v Mintoft* [1912] 2 K B 373; *Millichamp v Jones* [1983] 1 All E R 267; *The Blankenstein* [1985] 1 All E R 475 at 488 (disapproving *Lowe v Hope* [1970] Ch 94).

[14] See p 347, ante.

[15] *McDonald v Dennys Lascelles Ltd* (1933) 48 C L R 457; *Johnson v Agnew* [1980] A C 367 at 396; cf p 347 ante at note 8.

[16] *Hyundai Shipbuilding and Heavy Industries Co Ltd v Pournaras* [1978] 2 Lloyd's Rep 502; *Hyundai Heavy Industries Ltd v Papadopoulos* [1980] 2 All E R 29.

3 ACTION FOR AN AGREED SUM

One of the parties to a contract generally undertakes to pay a sum of money: for example a buyer promises to pay an agreed price, or an employer promises to pay agreed wages. An action for such an agreed sum is one for specific relief,[17] and also differs from an action for damages in its practical effect, for it may lead to a different measure of recovery. Of course this is not always the case. If a seller of goods has delivered and the buyer has not paid, it makes no difference whether the seller claims the price or his loss, for his loss is in fact the amount of the price. But in more complex situations it might, on a claim for damages, be argued that the whole of the seller's loss was not recoverable because (for example) part of it was too remote; or a dispute might arise as to the basis on which the loss should be quantified. On a claim for an agreed sum, such arguments or issues are irrelevant, though an issue of mitigation may (as we shall see) sometimes arise. It is therefore important to know exactly when an action for an agreed sum can be brought. This depends on three factors.

First and most obviously it depends on the terms of the contract. Suppose an employee is under his contract entitled to wages monthly in arrear. If he is wrongfully dismissed on the second day of the month, he is only entitled to damages, and not to his agreed wages. On the other hand, goods may be sold on the terms that they are to be paid for on 1 November and to be delivered a month later. If the buyer fails to pay on 1 November, the seller can sue for the price.[18] In the examples so far given, there is no suggestion that the person to whom payment was promised was himself in default. If he was, his claim for the agreed sum would (even if it were otherwise available) fail if his breach was such as to justify rescission, in the sense discussed in chapter 16.

The right to bring an action for the price may, secondly, be restricted by rules of law. The contract may define the point at which the *duty* to pay the agreed sum arises; but it does not follow that the *action* for the price is always available at that point. Suppose that goods are sold on the terms that they are to remain the seller's property till paid for, and that they are to be paid for by cash on delivery. If the buyer wrongfully rejects the seller's tender of delivery he can be sued for damages but not for the price. Under the Sale of Goods Act 1979 the *duty* to pay arises on tender of delivery; but the *action* for the price is (where no day is fixed for payment) only available where the property in the goods has passed to the buyer.[19]

---

[17] See p 316, ante.

[18] Sale of Goods Act 1979, s 49 (2).

[19] S 49(1); *Stein Forbes & Co v County Tailoring Co* (1916) 86 L J K B 448; but see *Workman, Clark & Co v Lloyd Brazileno* [1908] 1 K B 968.

The purpose of making the seller claim damages (and not the price) is to encourage him to mitigate by making efforts to resell the goods elsewhere.

The right to sue for the agreed sum depends, thirdly, on the conduct of the injured party in relation to the other party's breach. As we saw in chapter 16, the injured party may elect to terminate the contract or to keep it alive. If he elects to terminate, he loses any right which might otherwise have accrued to him in the future to claim the agreed sum.[20] If the injured party elects to keep the contract alive, there are some cases in which he is clearly entitled to sue for the agreed sum. This is the position where he has already done all that is required of him to make the action available: for example, if a seller of goods at the time of the repudiation has already transferred the property in them to the buyer.[1] On the other hand, the injured party will not be entitled to sue for the agreed sum if he has not yet done all that is required of him to make the action available, and if he cannot do the required acts without the co-operation of the other party. An employee who is wrongfully dismissed cannot sue *for his wages* merely because he has throughout the period of employment declared his readiness to go back to work.[2] These are clear cases, but the position is much more controversial where, at the time of breach, the injured party has not yet done what is required to make the action available, and can do it without the co-operation of the party in breach. In *White & Carter (Councils) Ltd v McGregor*[3] A agreed to advertise B's garage business for three years. B purported to cancel the contract on the day on which it was made, but A nevertheless displayed the advertisements and his claim for the agreed price was upheld by a majority of the House of Lords. The decision has been criticised on the ground that A should have mitigated by reletting the advertising space. If he had done this, B would not have been forced to pay for something which he did not want; and A (it is said) would have been no worse off, for he could have recovered by way of damages any amount by which the proceeds of reletting fell short of the sum to be paid by B. The argument is sound in principle, but on the facts of the case it was probably not substantiated. It presupposes that the demand for advertising space exceeded the supply, so that A could have relet the space intended for B; but it was up to B to show this and the decision can be explained on the ground that B had failed to prove that A could or should have mitigated.[4] The argument also assumes that A

---

[20] See p 292, ante.

[1] See preceding paragraph.

[2] *Denmark Productions Ltd v Boscobel Productions Ltd* [1969] 1 QB 699; *Roberts v Elwells Engineers Ltd* [1972] 2 QB 586.

[3] [1962] AC 413.

[4] Cf pp 333, ante.

had no other legitimate interest in going ahead with performance. Such an interest might have arisen by reason of commitments to third parties. This was, for example, the position where a charterparty was wrongfully repudiated by the charterer. The shipowner was held entitled to insist on continued performance, and so to sue for the agreed hire; and one reason for the decision was that he had assigned the hire to his bank, to whom he was therefore obliged to keep the contract in being.[5] On the other hand, where there is no such legitimate interest in insisting on continued performance, the mitigation rules can apply even to an action for the agreed sum. This view is supported by another charterparty case[6] in which the charterer undertook to make certain repairs to the ship before redelivery and to pay the agreed hire till then. He failed to do the repairs; but it was held that the owner was not entitled to refuse to accept redelivery, and to sue for the agreed hire. As the cost of the repairs far exceeded the value which the ship would have had after they were done,[7] the owner had no legitimate interest in insisting on their execution and the payment of hire. He should therefore have mitigated by accepting redelivery of the unrepaired ship; and his only remedy was in damages.

4 SPECIFIC ENFORCEMENT

A contract may be specifically enforced by a court order telling the defendant actually to perform his undertaking. Such an order may be positive or negative according to the nature of the undertaking. The court may (positively) order the defendant to do something, for example to convey a house, or to deliver a picture. Such an order is known as one of specific performance. Alternatively, the court may (negatively) order the defendant to forbear from doing something which he has promised not to do, for example it may restrain him from competing with the plaintiff. Such an order is known as an injunction.

Disobedience of an order of specific performance or of an injunction is contempt of court, and can be punished in the last resort by imprisonment of the defendant. Because it may have this drastic effect, the courts have traditionally been somewhat reluctant to order specific performance. But such an order can also be enforced in

5 *The Odenfeld* [1978] 2 Lloyd's Rep 357.
6 *Attica Sea Carriers Corpn v Ferrostaal Poseidon Bulk Reederei GmbH* [1976] 1 Lloyd's Rep 250; cf *The Alaskan Trader* [1983] 2 Lloyd's Rep 645.
7 Cf p 326, ante.

various other ways, without putting the defendant under any personal constraint:[8] for example, by ordering the delivery or conveyance of something to the plaintiff. The principal argument for restricting the availability of specific performance has thus lost a good deal of its force; so that there is a corresponding trend towards some expansion in the scope of the remedy. Moreover, that argument never applied to an award of a sum of money in an action for an agreed sum: this could always be enforced by levying execution on the defendant's property. For this reason actions for an agreed sum are not subject to the restrictions on specific performance discussed below.

a Specific performance

The common law did not specifically enforce obligations except those to pay money. With this exception, there was, and is, no *right* to specific performance: the remedy is equitable and (like most such remedies) discretionary. Its scope is limited in a number of ways, of which the following are the most important.

i *Damages must be 'inadequate'*

Specific performance will not be ordered where the plaintiff can be adequately protected by an award of damages. This will generally be the case where he has bought shares or generic goods which are available in the market.[9] On the seller's default, the buyer can go into the market, get a substitute, and recover any extra cost by way of damages. Specific performance will, on the other hand, be ordered where no satisfactory substitute can be obtained: for example where the sale is of land or of a house, or of 'unique' goods such as an heirloom or a great work of art.[10] At one time the courts took a narrow view of this category, in keeping with the restrictive view of specific performance noted above.[11] More recently the tendency has been to ask not whether damages are 'adequate' but whether specific performance is the more appropriate remedy.[12] The category of 'unique' goods has been extended to include goods needed by the buyer in his business and not elsewhere available: for example, during the petrol shortage of 1973 an oil company was ordered not to

---

[8] *Miliangos v George Frank (Textiles) Ltd* [1976] A C 443 at 494, 497; *The Messiniaki Tolmi* [1983] 2 A C 787.

[9] *Re Schwabacher* (1907) 98 L T 127 at 128.

[10] Eg *Pusey v Pusey* (1684) 1 Vern 273.

[11] Eg *Cohen v Roche* [1927] 1 K B 169 (Heppelwhite chairs).

[12] *Beswick v Beswick* [1968] A C 58; *Evans Marshall & Co Ltd v Bertola SA* [1973] 1 W L R 349 at 379

break its contract to supply petrol to a garage.[13] Specific performance can also be ordered of contracts to supply 'commercially unique' goods, such as ships[14] or machinery; but if such goods are readily available from another source, the contract will not be specifically enforced.[15] Damages may also be regarded as the less appropriate remedy for other reasons: for example, because of the difficulty of assessing them. Thus a contract to execute a mortgage as security for a loan,[16] and a contract that a debt is to be repaid out of specific property,[17] can be specifically enforced since the exact value of having such security rights is uncertain.

ii *Discretion of the court*

Even where specific performance is the more appropriate remedy, it will not necessarily be ordered. The remedy is a discretionary one, though the discretion is 'to be governed as far as possible by fixed rules and principles'.[18] In particular, there are three grounds on which the remedy may be refused.

The first is undue hardship to the defendant. On this ground specific performance may be refused where the cost of performance to the defendant is wholly out of proportion to the benefit which performance will confer on the plaintiff;[19] or where, as a result of severe financial misfortune and incapacitating illness, specific performance would cause exceptional personal distress to the defendant.[20] But specific performance would not be refused merely because the vendor of a house was caught on a rising market and so had difficulty in buying alternative accommodation with the proceeds of sale.[1]

Secondly, specific performance may be refused because the contract itself was grossly unfair. For this purpose it is not enough to show simply that the price was too low; but the remedy will be refused if, in addition, the claimant took unfair advantage of his superior knowledge or if he exploited his superior bargaining strength by

---

13 *Sky Petroleum Ltd v VIP Petroleum Ltd* [1974] 1 All ER 954; cf *Howard E Perry v British Railways Board* [1980] 1 WLR 1375 at 1383.
14 *Behnke v Bede Shipping Co Ltd* [1927] 1 KB 649; *The Oro Chief* [1983] 2 Lloyd's Rep 509 at 520–521.
15 *Société des Industries Metallurgiques SA v Bronx Engineering Co Ltd* [1975] 1 Lloyd's Rep 465; *The Stena Nautica (No 2)* [1982] 2 Lloyd's Rep 336.
16 *Ashton v Corrigan* (1871) LR 13 Eq 76.
17 See *Swiss Bank Corpn v Lloyd's Bank Ltd* [1982] AC 584 (where the contract was held to contain no such term).
18 *Lamare v Dixon* (1873) LR 6 HL 414 at 423.
19 *Tito v Waddell (No 2)* [1977] Ch 106 at 326; cf *Redland Bricks Ltd v Morris* [1970] AC 652.
20 *Patel v Ali* [1984] Ch 283.
1 *Mountford v Scott* [1975] Ch 258.

rushing the other party into the transaction. Thus where an antique dealer bought valuable china jars from a widow for a fifth of their real value it was said that he could not specifically enforce the contract.[2]

Thirdly, specific performance may be refused if the court in some other way disapproves of the plaintiff's conduct: for example, if he refuses to perform a term to which he had clearly agreed, but which could not be enforced against him because it was not evidenced in writing.[3] Unfair conduct of the plaintiff may suffice even if it does not amount to a breach of any promise. Thus specific enforcement of a solus agreement[4] against a garage was refused where the oil company, by giving discounts to other garages, had made it impossible for the defendant to trade except at a loss.[5]

iii *Personal Service*

The court will not specifically enforce a contract of personal service.[6] One reason for this rule was that to order the employee to work would unduly interfere with his personal liberty; and it is now provided by statute that no court shall compel an employee to do any work by ordering specific performance of a contract of employment or by restraining the breach of such a contract by injunction.[7] Conversely it was thought that to order specific enforcement against the employer would be a futile attempt to enforce the continuance of a 'personal' relationship against the wish of one of the parties. The principle is maintained in the law relating to unfair dismissal (which may not be a breach of contract at all). The employer may be ordered to reinstate or re-engage the employee;[8] but if he refuses to do so, the employee's only remedy, in the last resort, is an award of compensation. As a practical matter, an employer may actually be forced to reinstate an employee whom he would rather dismiss; or to dismiss one whom he is quite willing to keep. The courts have recognised these changes in the nature of the employment relationship. In one case[9] an employer was forced by union pressure to dismiss an employee in breach of contract. The court restrained the dismissal and thus in effect reinstated the employee. Reinstatement can also be ordered where

---

[2] *Falcke v Gray* (1859) 4 Drew 651.

[3] See *Martin v Pycroft* (1852) 2 De G M & G 785.

[4] See p 172, ante.

[5] *Shell U K Ltd v Lostock Garage Ltd* [1976] 1 W L R 1187.

[6] *Johnson v Shrewsbury and Birmingham Rly* (1853) 3 De G M & G 914.

[7] Trade Union and Labour Relations Act 1974, s 16.

[8] Employment Protection (Consolidation) Act 1978 ss 69-71. 'Re-engagement' means giving the employee a new job; 'reinstatement' means giving him his old job back.

[9] *Hill v C A Parsons Ltd* [1972] Ch 305; cf *Irani v Southampton and South West Hampshire Health Authority* [1985] I C R 590; *Powell v Brent London Borough Council* [1988] I C R 176.

the relation between the parties is not a purely contractual one: for example where a public employee is dismissed in violation of statutory conditions governing his employment.[10]

iv *Other contracts*

There are certain other contracts which will not be specifically enforced. Specific performance will not be ordered of a promise without consideration, even though it is binding at law because it is under seal.[11] The reason for the rule is that equity will not aid a 'volunteer' (ie a person who has given no consideration).[12] A contract will not be specifically enforced against a party who has the right to terminate it, for he could, by exercising that right, make the order of court nugatory.[13] A contract which is sufficiently certain to be legally binding may yet be too vague to be specifically enforceable. As disobedience of an order of specific performance may lead to imprisonment, the defendant must be told by the order exactly what he is to do. Thus a contract to publish an article cannot be specifically enforced if the text has not been agreed.[14]

v *Difficulty of supervision*

Specific performance is sometimes refused on the ground that the defendant has undertaken continuous duties, the performance of which the court cannot, or is unwilling, to supervise. On this ground, specific performance has been refused of a landlord's undertaking to have a porter 'constantly in attendance';[15] of a contract to deliver goods by instalments;[16] of an obligation to operate signals;[17] and of a contract to build.[18] But the courts no longer regard such 'difficulty' of supervision as decisive. Where the duties are not to be performed by the defendant personally, he can be ordered to enter into a contract to procure their performance: such an order has been made against a lessor of luxury flats who had covenanted to employ a resident porter to perform certain specified tasks.[19] And contracts to build can be specifically enforced if the work to be done is sufficiently defined, the defendant is in possession of the land, and damages would not

---

[10] *Malloch v Aberdeen Corpn* [1971] 2 All ER 1278.
[11] See *Cannon v Hartley* [1949] Ch 213.
[12] *Jefferys v Jefferys* (1841) Cr & Ph 138.
[13] *Sheffield Gas Co v Harrison* (1853) 17 Beav 294; *Gregory v Wilson* (1852) 9 Hare 683.
[14] *Joseph v National Magazine Co Ltd* [1959] Ch 14.
[15] *Ryan v Mutual Tontine Association* [1893] 1 Ch 116.
[16] *Dominion Coal Co v Dominion Iron and Steel Co* [1909] AC 293.
[17] *Powell Duffryn Steam Coal Co v Taff Vale Rly* (1874) 9 Ch App 331.
[18] *Flint v Brandon* (1803) 8 Ves 159.
[19] *Posner v Scott-Lewis* [1987] Ch 25.

adequately compensate the plaintiff.[20] The defendant will in most cases obey the court's order simply because it has been made; and where his performance is alleged to be defective it can be 'supervised' by an expert appointed by the court instead of by the court itself.

vi Impossibility

The court will not order specific enforcement where performance of the contract is impossible. If, for example, a husband sold land belonging to his wife, he could not be ordered to convey it.[1] Nor will the court specifically enforce an agreement to assign a lease if (under the terms of the lease) the assignment requires the consent of the landlord, and he refuses to give his consent.[2]

vii Mutuality of remedy

Under the so-called doctrine of mutuality of remedy, specific performance will not be ordered if the court cannot at the same time ensure that the unperformed obligations of the plaintiff will also be specifically performed.[3] Suppose that A promises to convey a house to B in return for B's promise to work for A for 10 years. Here B cannot get specific performance against A because his own promise to work cannot be specifically enforced against him. The reason why the court will not force A to convey the land is that it cannot ensure that he will receive the services from B. If the court did order A to convey and B then refused to do the work, A could only claim damages; and if B were insolvent this remedy would be worth very little. Obviously this reasoning would not apply if B claimed specific performance *after* he had done the work; and in such a case B's claim would succeed.[4] As our example shows, the question whether the requirement of mutuality is satisfied has to be determined by reference to the state of affairs at the time of the hearing[5]—not (as was formerly thought) to that at the time of contracting.

b Injunction

Where a contract contains a negative promise (such as a promise not to build, or not to compete), the breach of that promise may be

---

20 Eg *Wolverhampton Corpn v Emmons* [1901] 1 K B 515; *Jeune v Queens Cross Properties Ltd* [1974] Ch 97; cf *Calabar Properties Ltd v Stitcher* [1984] 1 W L R 287; Landlord and Tenant Act 1985, s 17.

1 See *Castle v Wilkinson* (1870) 5 Ch App 534. Cf *Watts v Spence* [1976] Ch 165. If the husband has an interest in the land, he can be ordered to convey that interest, but not his wife's.

2 *Warmington v Miller* [1973] Q B 877.

3 *Price v Strange* [1978] Ch 337 at 367-368.

4 *Price v Strange*, supra; cf *Sutton v Sutton* [1984] Ch 184.

5 *Price v Strange*, supra.

restrained by injunction. Such an order is known as a prohibitory injunction where it directs the defendant not to break the promise in the future; and as a mandatory injunction where it directs the defendant to undo a breach committed in the past: eg to pull down a house built in breach of a restrictive covenant.[6]

An injunction will not be granted if its practical effect would be to compel the performance of a contract which is not specifically enforceable. For example an injunction will not be granted to restrain an employee from breaking his obligation to work[7] or (normally[8])to restrain an employer from dismissing the employee.[9] This would be so even if the contract contained a provision which was negative in form, such as a promise 'not to dismiss' for a given period.

A contract which is not specifically enforceable may, however, contain a narrower negative promise. In the leading case of *Lumley v Wagner*[10] the defendant agreed to sing at the plaintiff's theatre twice a week for three months, and she also promised not to use her talents at any other theatre during that period. It was held that she could be restrained by injunction from breaking this negative promise. In such cases the effect of the injunction may be to put some pressure on the defendant to perform the positive obligation. But that is no objection to the granting of the injunction unless the pressure is so severe as to be, for practical purposes, irresistible. In one case[11] a film actress was restrained from breaking a promise not to act for third parties: it was said that she could still earn her living by doing other work. In a more recent case,[12] however, a pop group promised not to make recordings for anyone except the plaintiff, whom they had appointed as their manager for five years. An injunction to restrain the group from breaking this promise was refused as it would 'as a practical matter' force them to continue to employ the plaintiff. Where an employee promises not to work *in any capacity* except for the employer, an injunction will similarly be refused[13] (unless the employer continued to pay the employee while the injunction was in force[14]); for if it were granted the only 'choice' left to the employee would be one between remaining idle and performing his positive obligation to serve.

The fear of putting too much pressure on an employee is further reflected in the rule that an injunction will only be issued against him

---

[6] As in *Wakeham v Wood* (1982) 43 P & C R 40.

[7] *Whitwood Chemical Co v Hardman* [1891] 2 Ch 416.

[8] For an exception see p 354, ante.

[9] *Chappell v Times Newspapers Ltd* [1975] 2 All E R 233.

[10] (1852) 1 De G M & G 604.

[11] *Warner Bros Pictures Inc v Nelson* [1937] 1 K B 209.

[12] *Page One Records Ltd v Britton* [1968] 1 W L R 157.

[13] *Ehrman v Bartholomew* [1898] 1 Ch 671.

[14] *Evening Standard Co Ltd v Henderson* [1987] I C R 588.

where the contract contains an *express* negative promise. But where no question of employment is involved, the courts will sometimes *imply* a negative promise in a contract which is not specifically enforceable. If, for example, A makes a promise (positive in form) to buy *all* his requirements of coal from B for a certain period, a negative promise (not to buy elsewhere) can readily be implied, and be enforced by injunction.[15] This may, indeed, put pressure on him to buy from B. But, in cases of sale, direct specific performance is refused not because it is *undesirable* in itself (as a form of undue personal constraint) but simply because it is thought to be *unnecessary* (damages being regarded as an appropriate remedy). Hence the objection to indirect specific performance through an injunction is much less strong in the sale than in the employment cases.

c Damages and specific performance or injunction

Originally, courts of equity did not award damages. It followed that if the court in its discretion refused to order specific performance or to issue an injunction, in spite of the fact that the plaintiff had a legally enforceable claim, he would have to take separate proceedings in a common law court for damages. This position was changed by an Act of 1858[16] which gave the court of Chancery power to award damages in addition to or 'in substitution for . . . specific performance' or injunction. This power is now vested in the High Court;[17] but there will normally be little point in invoking it since that court has power to grant all remedies to which a party is entitled:[18] eg to award damages as well as, or instead of, specific relief. There are, however, still situations in which it may be to the plaintiff's advantage to invoke the power created by the 1858 Act. In particular, damages may be awarded under the Act where there is no cause of action at law: eg for breach of an oral contract for the sale of land, so long as the equitable rules as to part performance are satisfied;[19] or where specific performance is sought before actual breach of a contract to be performed in the future.[20]

There was also formerly some support for the view that, while at common law damages were to be assessed by reference to the time of breach,[1] under the Act they were to be assessed by reference to the

---

[15] Cf *Metropolitan Electric Supply Co v Ginder* [1901] 2 Ch 799.

[16] Chancery Amendment Act 1858, s 2.

[17] Supreme Court Act 1981, s 50.

[18] Supreme Court Act 1981, s 49.

[19] *Price v Strange* [1978] Ch 337 at 358; for the requirement of written evidence and the doctrine of part performance, see pp 58, 60, ante.

[20] For specific performance in such a case, see *Hasham v Zenab* [1960] AC 316.

[1] See p 331, ante.

time of judgment.[2] This was thought to follow from the fact that under the Act damages were awarded '*in substitution* . . . *for* specific *performance*'; for if the value of the subject-matter had risen between the time of breach and the time of judgment damages assessed by reference to the time of breach would, it was said, be no true substitute for performance. But the common law also pursues the general objective of putting the plaintiff into the position in which he would have been '*if* the contract had been *performed*'.[3] This seems to mean much the same as the words quoted from the 1858 Act; and we have also seen that the common law does not invariably assess damages by reference to the time of breach.[4] The House of Lords has therefore held that damages are to be assessed in the same way under the Act as at common law.[5] In particular, if the plaintiff ought to have made a substitute contract, damages will be assessed by reference to the time when that contract should have been made. The plaintiff cannot, on a rising market, inflate his damages by asking for them to be assessed under the Act at the later time of judgment; for to allow him to do so would conflict with the requirement that he must take all reasonable steps to mitigate his loss.[6]

5 RESTITUTIONARY REMEDIES

The general nature of a claim for restitution on breach of contract has already been outlined: it is a claim for the return of the injured party's performance, or for its reasonable value. Assuming that the injured party is entitled to restitution, the exact nature of his remedy depends on the kind of benefit which he has conferred on the party in breach. If the injured party has made a payment of money, he can get it back; if he has rendered some other performance, he is entitled to recompense for its reasonable value.

a Recovery of money

A person who has paid money under a contract can recover it back in the following circumstances.

i *Total failure of consideration*

First, he can do so if there has been a 'total failure of consideration'. The word 'consideration' is (rather confusingly) here used in a sense

---

[2] *Wroth v Tyler* [1974] Ch 30.
[3] *Robinson v Harman* (1848) 1 Exch 850 at 855; see p 320, ante.
[4] See pp 331–332, ante.
[5] *Johnson v Agnew* [1980] A C 367 at 400.
[6] See p 337, ante.

different from that which it bears in relation to the formation of contracts. There it can, and often does, refer to a promise to perform. Here it generally refers to the *performance* of the promise.[7] There is a 'total failure of consideration' if the plaintiff has not received any part of the performance for which he bargained. This would be the position if a buyer of goods paid in advance and the seller failed to deliver. In such a case the buyer can, at his option, claim damages or the return of his money. He will take the former course if the market has risen and the latter if it has fallen. As a general rule, money can only be reclaimed if the failure of consideration is *total* and not if it is only *partial*. The failure would, for example, be partial where A paid B in advance for a month's work and B left in breach of contract after ten days. In such a case it would be unfair to allow A to get back all his money when he had had the benefit of B's work for the ten days; and it might not be satisfactory to allow him to get back a proportionate part, since the hardest part of B's work might have come at the beginning. Where there is no such difficulty in making an apportionment, the person making the advance payment may sometimes be able to get back part of it. Suppose that A pays B £100 in advance for five tons of coal and B delivers only three tons. Here A can keep the three tons and get back £40.[8]

There may, moreover, be a total failure of consideration even though the plaintiff has received *some* benefit under the contract, if that was not *the* benefit for which he bargained. Suppose, for example, that A sells a car to B, and that at the time of the sale he and B in good faith believe that the car belongs to A. But in fact it belongs to X, who, some months later, traces it and claims it from B. Here B has had the use of the car during the intervening period; but it has been held that this is not *the* benefit for which he bargained, namely, a car to which he would have title as owner. Hence there is a total failure of consideration, and B can get back the *whole* of the price from A.[9] According to one view,[10] this result is unjust since B gets the use of the car for nothing; and on this view B should only get back the price less some allowance for the use of the car. On the other hand, it is not easy to see why B should, in effect, pay A for having had the use of a car which belonged to X, particularly as X might be able to sue B in tort for the value of the use of the car. In such a case, the present rule, allowing B to get back the whole price, seems to be at least as fair as any of the alternatives which have been suggested. The position

---

7 *Fibrosa case* [1943] A C 32 at 48.

8 Cf *Ebrahim Dawood Ltd v Heath Ltd* [1961] 2 Lloyd's Rep 512.

9 *Rowland v Divall* [1923] 2 K B 500; cf *Rover International Ltd v Cannon Film Sales Ltd (No 2)* (1988) Financial Times, 10 June.

10 Law Reform Committee, 12th Report (Cmnd 2958) para 36; but Law Commission Paper No 160, para 6.5 regards the subject as too difficult for legislative reform.

would be different if all claims of X in relation to the car had been settled by A (or, where the car had passed through a number of hands, by some earlier person in the chain of sellers and buyers). In one case,[11] A in good faith acquired a car, not knowing that it was subject to a hire-purchase agreement under which X (a finance company) was its owner. He sold it to B, who kept it for nearly a year before it was claimed by X. At this stage, B claimed the price back from A, and the claim succeeded in full, even though, after it was made, the original hire-purchaser had paid off X, so that B could have safely kept the car. Had he done so, he would have suffered no loss; and the actual outcome of the case was that he had nearly a year's use of the car for nothing. Since there was no longer any risk of his being sued by X, this result seems to be unnecessary for B's protection. Where B does have to return the car to X, his claim against A is not limited to one for the return of the price. He can, in addition, recover any other loss (such as money spent on repairing the car) by way of damages.[12]

ii *Rescission of the contract*

Even where the plaintiff has received some part of the benefit for which he bargained, he may be entitled to rescind the contract, either for misrepresentation or for breach.[13] One consequence of such rescission is that the plaintiff can refuse to accept, or that he can return, the defendant's performance. In this way he may be able to bring about a total failure of consideration and so to get his money back: for example, a buyer to whom short delivery has been made can reject it and recover the whole of the price. The claimant's use of the subject-matter may bar his right to rescind;[14] but where it does not have this effect, the question whether it prevents the failure of consideration from being total depends on the tests already stated. Suppose that the hire-purchaser of a car keeps it for some months and then lawfully rejects it because it is defective. Here the failure of consideration will not be total since, for the period in question, the hirer had what he bargained for: namely the use of the car and the valid option to purchase it. Hence his remedy is in damages;[15] these are indeed sometimes based on the instalments paid, but any benefit obtained by the hirer from the use of the car is also taken into account.[16] On the other hand, he could get his money back in full if he had never had a

---

[11] *Butterworth v Kingsway Motors* [1954] 2 All ER 694.

[12] *Mason v Burningham* [1949] 2 KB 545.

[13] See pp 136 et seq, and 271 et seq, ante.

[14] See pp 139–141, 287–288, ante.

[15] *Yeoman Credit Ltd v Apps* [1962] 2 QB 508.

[16] Eg *Charterhouse Credit Co Ltd v Tolly* [1963] 2 QB 683; strictly, the damages should be based on the *value* of the subject-matter and not on the *price* paid.

valid option to purchase at all: eg because the other party to the contract did not own the car.[17]

iii Frustration

The rights of a party to recover back money paid under a frustrated contract have been discussed in chapter 17. The only point that needs to be stressed here is that under the Law Reform (Frustrated Contracts) Act 1943[18] a payment can be reclaimed even though the failure of consideration was not total. This does not lead to injustice to a payee who has performed in part; for under the Act the court can make adjustments in his favour in respect of expenses incurred, and valuable benefits conferred, by the payee under the contract.

iv Invalid contracts

Money can sometimes be recovered back on the ground that the contract under which it was paid was invalid. This is the position where the contract was wholly void for mistake.[19] The special rules which govern the recovery of money under contracts made with persons under an incapacity, and under illegal contracts, are discussed in chapters 12 and 11.

b Recompense

A person who has conferred a benefit on the other contracting party by rendering a service, or by transferring property, will normally claim the sum of money which the other party has agreed to pay for that performance. As a general rule, the court will simply enforce the agreement to pay and will do so literally, according to the terms of the agreement. It will not award a party more than the agreed sum merely because his performance was unexpectedly onerous;[20] nor will it award less merely because the agreed sum was excessive. Nor will the court award anything at all if the event on which payment was to be made has not occurred: as we saw in chapter 16, a party who fails to complete performance of an entire obligation cannot usually recover anything.[1] The reason for all these rules is that, generally speaking, the court must enforce the contract which the parties have made and not make a different contract for them. But in some cases this reasoning does not apply, while in others there are good reasons for departing from it. In such situations a party who cannot sue for

---

[17] Cf *Warman v Southern Counties Car Finance Ltd* [1949] 2 K B 576.
[18] See pp 311–312, ante.
[19] Eg *Branwhite v Worcester Works Finance Ltd* [1969] 1 A C 552.
[20] *Gilbert & Partners v Knight* [1968] 2 All E R 248.
[1] See pp 277–279, ante.

an agreed sum may nevertheless be able to sue for a reasonable remuneration.

First, he may be able to do this where, though the parties have clearly entered into a contract, no sum is ever agreed. Thus if a contract for the sale of goods does not fix the price, the seller is entitled to a reasonable price;[2] and if a contract for services does not fix the remuneration, a reasonable sum must be paid.[3] The same result may be reached where the failure to fix a price has the effect that no contract is ever concluded: if the parties nevertheless believe that there is a contract, or that one will come into existence, a reasonable sum must be paid for goods or services supplied in that belief.[4]

Secondly, the contract under which the parties have fixed the sum to be paid may be void. In one case[5] a managing director's appointment was void because neither he nor those who appointed him had the necessary qualification shares in the company; and it was held that he was entitled to a reasonable remuneration for his work.

Thirdly, a reasonable remuneration may be payable under a contract which has been frustrated. Where a valuable benefit (other than money) is conferred on one of the parties *before* frustration, the other can ask for a reasonable sum under the Law Reform (Frustrated Contracts) Act 1943.[6] Sometimes, however, the parties may continue to act under a contract, believing that it remains in force, when, as a matter of law, it has been frustrated. It seems that a party who in this belief confers a benefit on the other *after* frustration can recover a reasonable sum.[7]

Fourthly, it may sometimes be proper for the court to disregard a valid express contract and to award a reasonable sum. Thus where necessaries have been sold and delivered to a minor, he is only liable for a reasonable price and not for any higher price that he may have agreed to pay.[8]

Finally, the court may sometimes award a reasonable sum even though the event on which payment was to be made has not occurred. If one party is prevented by the other's breach from completing performance of an entire obligation, he can claim a reasonable sum

---

[2] Sale of Goods Act 1979, s 8 (2).
[3] Supply of Goods and Services Act 1982, s 15.
[4] *Peter Lind & Co v Mersey Docks* [1972] 2 Lloyds's Rep 234; *British Steel Corpn v Cleveland Bridge and Engineering Co Ltd* [1984] 1 All ER 504.
[5] *Craven-Ellis v Canons Ltd* [1936] 2 KB 403; cf *Rover International Ltd v Cannon Film Sales Ltd (No 2)* (1988) Financial Times, 10 June.
[6] See p 312, ante.
[7] *The Massalia* [1961] 2 QB 278; overruled on the issue of frustration, but not on the present point, in *The Eugenia* [1964] 2 QB 226.
[8] Sale of Goods Act 1979, s 3; see p 190, ante.

for the performance which he has actually rendered. This would be the position where a house-owner in breach of contract refused to allow a builder to complete the agreed work. Where performance is prevented by the other party's breach, restitution is available in spite of the fact that no actual benefit has been received by the defendant.[9] Even if the failure to complete was due to the claimant's own breach, he can nevertheless recover a reasonable sum, or a pro rata payment, if the other party 'voluntarily' accepted the partial performance.[10] Such acceptance is sometimes treated as evidence of a 'new contract' without any express term as to remuneration.

9 Eg *Planché v Colburn* (1831) 8 Bing 14.
10 See p 289, ante; dicta in *Miles v Wakefield Metropolitan District Council* [1987] AC 539 at 553, 561 seem to suggest that acceptance, whether voluntary or not, suffices.

Index

Acceptance
bilateral contract, 16–17
communication of, 11–12
conduct, by, 10
contract comes into existence on, 10
counter-offer, 10–11
express, 10
none identifiable, 21
offer,
  knowledge, requirement of, 16
  method prescribed by, 15
  must correspond with, 10
postal,
  accident in post, risk put on offeror,
    13
  convenience, 14
  general rule, 12–13
  limitations,
    address, 13
    postal strike, 13
    second class mail, use of, 13
    stamp, 13
    telex, use of, 13
  offeror's power to withdraw offer,
    curtailment of, 13
  revocation, 14
  time of posting, contract made at, 14
  Uniform Law, effect of, 14–15
  when operative, 12–13
promise contained in, 10
rescission, effect on, 288
silence as, 15–16
Acceptor
meaning, 7
Administrative action
exemption clause, control of, 96–97
Advertisement
invitation to treat, as, 8
offer, as, 8
reward, of, as offer, 8
Affirmation
rescission, effects on, 293–294
Agency
creation of,
  actual authority,
    express, 246–247

Agency – *continued*
creation of – *continued*
  actual authority – *continued*
    implied, 247–248
  generally, 246
  operation of law,
    authority by,
      apparent, 248–250
      generally, 248
      necessity, 251–252
      usual, 251
    other cases, 253
  ratification,
    conditions to be satisfied, 253–
      255
    generally, 253
    relation back, 255
effects of,
  generally, 255–256
  third party,
    agent, relations with,
      agent acting without authority,
        261–263
      agent is party, 260–261
      agent may be party, 258–260
      generally, 258
    principal, relations with,
      generally, 256
      rights of principal, 256–258
general principle, 245–246
legal distinguished from commercial
  concept of, 245–246
termination of, 263–264
third party, promise in favour of, 215
Agreement
acceptance. *See* ACCEPTANCE
bargaining power, regard to, 3
condition precedent, subject to, 24
condition subsequent, subject to, 24
conditional, 24
consideration. *See* CONSIDERATION
contents of contract, does not determine, 2–3
contract, meaning, 1
contract results from, 2
counter-offer, 10–11

Agreement — *continued*
　description of contract as, qualification
　　of, 2–3
　discretionary, 53
　domestic, 53–54
　gentlemen's, 6
　hire-purchase. *See* HIRE-PURCHASE
　　AGREEMENT
　incomplete,
　　formal agreement not executed,
　　　23–24
　　long-term contract, 22–23
　　market values, reference to, 23
　　subject to contract, 23
　master, 85
　mistake in recording,
　　document, rectification of, 118–119
　　restrictions, 120–121
　　types, 119–120
　objective test, 2
　offer. *See* OFFER
　process by which parties reach, analysis
　　of, 7
　scope of contract, does not determine,
　　2–3
　social, 53–54
　vague,
　　commercial contract, 21–22
　　contractual intention, 52–53
　　generally, 21
　　hire-purchase, 22
　　sale of goods, 22–23
　　valuation, 23
Ambiguity
　representation must be unambiguous,
　　125
Analogous contract
　disclosure, duty of, 144–145
Anticipatory breach. *See* BREACH OF
　CONTRACT
Assignment
　absolute, 226–228
　assignee's title, 234–235
　authority to pay, distinguished from,
　　228–229
　consideration,
　　completed gifts,
　　　equitable assignment, 233–234
　　　generally, 233
　　　statutory assignment, 233
　　future rights, attempts to assign,
　　　231–232
　　generally, 230–231
　　incomplete gifts, 232–233
　debtor, notice to, 230

Assignment — *continued*
　equitable, 233–234
　formalities, 229–230
　generally, 223
　involuntary,
　　bankruptcy, 240–241
　　death, 240
　　generally, 240
　Judicature Act 1873, effects of,
　　procedural difficulties, removal of,
　　　225–226
　　statutory assignment,
　　　absolute, 226–228
　　　assignor disputing validity, 228
　　　debt, 228
　　　generally, 226
　　　other legal thing in action, 228
　law and equity,
　　generally, 223
　　procedural difficulties, 224–225
　　substantive differences, 223–224
　limits on assignability,
　　debtor, prejudice to,
　　　champerty, danger of, 238–239
　　　maintenance, danger of, 238–239
　　　personal contract, 237–238
　　generally, 236
　　public policy, 239–240
　meaning, 223
　negotiability distinguished from, 235–
　　236
　statutory, 226–228, 233
　third party, promise in favour of, 215
　transfer of liabilities, distinguished
　　from,
　　benefit and burden, 242
　　generally, 241–242
　　novation, 242
　　operation of law, 243
　　vicarious performance, 243–244
Association
　arbitrary exclusion from, 4
Auction sale
　fall of hammer, effect of, 9
　offer, when made, 9
　without reserve, 9
Authority. *See* AGENCY

Bankruptcy
　involuntary assignment, 240–241
Bargaining
　power,
　　agreement qualified with regard to,
　　　3
　　inequality of, 150–151

Bargaining — *continued*
supervised, exemption clause and, 96
unfair bargain, protection against, 151
Belief
statement of, 123
Beneficiary
undue influence over, 149
Benefit
consideration, doctrine of, 27–28
Benefit and burden
assignment, 242
Bilateral contract
acceptance, 10, 16–17
Bill of exchange
antecedent debt or liability is good consideration for, 30
Breach of contract
anticipatory,
accepting breach,
damages, 296, 332–333
generally, 294
rescission, 295–296
generally, 294
keeping contract alive, 297
damages for, 130–132
negligence, liability for, 76–77
rescission for. *See* RESCISSION
seriousness,
generally, 77–78
legal effects of rule, 81–84
scope of rule, 78–81
Business
liability, 88–89
meaning, 89n

Car-park
automatic, notice displayed at entrance, as offer, 8
Carelessness
non est factum, restrictions on doctrine, 118
Carriage
contract may relate to, 1
offer, when and by whom made, 9–10
Causation
damages limited by, 336–337
Champerty
danger of, 238–239
meaning, 224
Child
undue influence over, 149
Choses in action
choses in possession distinguished from, 223–224

Choses in action — *continued*
meaning, 223
Choses in possession
choses in action distinguished from, 223–224
meaning, 223
Circumstances
change in, duty of disclosure, 142–143
Claim
doubtful, 35
invalid, 35
liquidated, 44
Client
undue influence over, 149
Collateral contract
parol evidence rule, 70–71
Collateral transactions
illegality, effects of, 187
Collective agreement
binding in honour only, 52
Commercial contract
vague terms, 21–22
Common calling
person engaged in, 4
Common carrier
freedom of contract, exception to general rule of, 4
Common law
assignment. *See* ASSIGNMENT
duress, 148
equity distinguished from, 6
exemption clause, effectiveness of, 85–88
mistake. *See* MISTAKE
negligence at, damages for, 128–129
Communication
acceptance, of, 11–12
long-distance, instantaneous methods of, 13
Compensation
damages. *See* DAMAGES
order, criminal case, 136
Condition
occurrence of, termination of offer, 20
precedent, agreement subject to, 24
rescission, availability of, 279–283
subsequent, condition subject to, 24
Conduct
acceptance by, 10
silence as acceptance, 16
Consent
mistake. *See* MISTAKE
Consideration
adequacy, irrelevance of, 28–29

Consideration − *continued*
  assignment,
    completed gifts,
      equitable assignment, 233−234
      generally, 233
      statutory assignment, 233
    future rights, attempts to assign,
      231−232
    generally, 230−231
    incomplete gifts, 232−233
  benefit, notion of, 27−28
  bilateral contract, 25
  compromise, 34−35
  debt, part payment of, 44−47
  detriment, notion of, 27−28
  estoppel,
    convention, by, 43
    promissory, 41−43
    proprietary, 47−49
  existing duties as,
    generally, 35−36
    one party's obligation,
      variations increasing, 39−40
      variations reducing, 40−41
    original parties,
      modification of contract between,
        38−39
      rescission of contract between,
        38−39
    public duty, 36
    third party, duty imposed by con-
      tract with, 37−38
  forbearance,
    compromise and, 34−35
    doubtful claim, 35
    generally, 34
    invalid claim, 35
    no promise to forbear, case involv-
      ing, 34−35
  illegal part of, severance of, 181−182
  irrevocable offer, 49−50
  meaning, 25−26
  nominal, 28−29
  past, insufficiency of, 30
  promise,
    gratuitous, 26−27
    mutual, 31−33
    onerous, 26−27
  promisee, must move from, 31
  reciprocity as basic notion of, 25
  sale of goods, contract for, 25
  total failure, 359−361
Consistency
  course of dealing, 75

Consumer
  dealing as, meaning, 89
Consumer credit agreement
  formal requirements, 56
Contents of contract
  agreement does not determine, 2−3
  express terms, ascertainment of, 62−63
  generally, 62
  implied terms,
    custom, by, 65−66
    fact, in, 2−3, 63−64
    law, in, 2−3, 64−65
    usage, by, 65−66
  parol evidence rule. See PAROL EVI-
    DENCE RULE
Contract
  agreement. See AGREEMENT
  analogous, 144−145
  bilateral. See BILATERAL CONTRACT
  breach. See BREACH OF CONTRACT
  capacity to contract. See CONTRACTUAL
    CAPACITY
  collateral. See COLLATERAL CONTRACT
  contents. See CONTENTS OF CONTRACT
  contract to make, 22
  enforcement. See ENFORCEMENT OF
    CONTRACT
  failure to perform. See BREACH OF CON-
    TRACT
  formal requirements. See FORMAL
    REQUIREMENTS OF CONTRACT
  freedom of, 3−4
  frustration. See FRUSTRATION
  general theory, 1−2
  illegality. See ILLEGALITY
  improper pressure, obtained by. See
    IMPROPER PRESSURE
  intention. See CONTRACTUAL INTEN-
    TION
  invalid, 362
  meaning, 1
  misrepresentation. See MISREPRESENTA-
    TION
  mistake. See MISTAKE
  parties to. See PARTIES TO CONTRACT
  performance. See PERFORMANCE
  remedies for breach. See REMEDIES
  rights, transfer of. See ASSIGNMENT
  terms. See TERMS OF CONTRACT
  third party, with. See THIRD PARTY
  uberrimae fidei, 143−144
  unilateral. See UNILATERAL CONTRACT
Contracts
  general theory, 1−2
  plural term, use of, 1

Contractual capacity
  corporation,
    charter, 198–199
    statutory,
      generally, 199
      ultra vires doctrine,
        generally, 199–200
        qualifications of, 201–202
  drunken person, 198
  generally, 188
  mental patient, 198
  minor,
    binding contract,
      analogous contract, 191
      employment, 191
      necessaries, for, 189–190
      unless repudiated, 192–193
    contract not binding on, 193–194
    inexperience, protection from, 188
    liability,
      quasi-contract, in, 197–198
      restitution, in,
        fraud, effects of, 196–197
        generally, 194–195
        Minors' Contracts Act 1987,
          s 3(1), 195–196
      quasi-contract, liability in, 197–198
      tort, in, 194
    meaning, 188
Contractual intention
  agreement,
    discretionary, 53
    domestic, 53–54
    social, 53–54
    vague, 52–53
  express provisions, 51–52
  generally, 51
  other illustrations, 54–55
Contractual rights
  interference with, 220–222
  transfer of. *See* ASSIGNMENT
Convenience
  postal acceptance, of, 14
Convention
  estoppel by, 43
Corporation
  charter, 198–199
  contractual capacity, 198–202
  statutory,
    generally, 199
    ultra vires doctrine,
      generally, 199–200
      qualifications of, 201–202

Counter-offer
  battle of forms, importance in, 10–11
  meaning, 10
  rules relating to, 10–11
Counter-promise
  promise is no consideration for, 32
Court
  jurisdiction of, contract excluding, 160–161
  specific performance, discretion as to, 353–354
Criminal case
  compensation order in, 136
Custom
  disclosure, duty of, 143
  parol evidence rule, 68–69
  terms implied by, 65–66
Customer
  offer coming from, 8

Damages
  adequacy of, 274
  advance payments, 347–348
  anticipatory breach, 296, 332–333
  breach of contract, for, 130–132
  compensatory principle,
    generally, 316
    injury to feelings, 319–320
    loss,
      meaning, 317–318
      plaintiff, to, 317
    no punitive damages, 318–319
  criminal case, compensation order in, 136
  fraud, for, 127–128
  generally, 316
  inadequate, 352–353
  injunction, and, 358–359
  kinds of loss recoverable,
    claims for expectation, reliance and restitution, relation between, 322–324
    consequential, 324–325
    expectations, 320–321
    incidental, 324–325
    reliance, 321
    restitution, 322
  limitation of,
    causation, 336–337
    default of victim, 340–341
    generally, 333
    mitigation, 337–340
    remoteness, 333–336
    special rules, 341–343

Damages — *continued*

liquidated, penalties distinguished from, 343–347

Misrepresentation Act 1967, s 2(1), under, 129–130

negligence at common law, for, 128–129

penalties, liquidated damages distinguished from, 343–347

punitive, 318–319

relationship between various rights to, 133–136

rescission, in lieu of, 132–133, 274

specific performance, and, 358–359

speculative, 329

valuation of loss,

alternatives, 330–331

anticipatory breach, 332–334

assessment,

bases of, 325–326

time for, 331–332

generally, 325

market values, relevance of, 328–329

speculative damages, 329

taxation, 329–330

Death

frustration by, 300

involuntary assignment, 240

termination of offer, 20–21

Debt

authority to pay distinguished from assignment, 228–229

meaning, 228

part payment, 44–47

written acknowledgement by debtor, 30

Debtor

assignment. *See* ASSIGNMENT

prejudice to, 237–238

Defence

equitable, oral evidence may be relied on for, 67

Detriment

consideration, doctrine of, 27–28

Disciple

undue influence over, 149

Disclosure

generally no duty of, 141–142

statutory duties of, 145–146

See also NON-DISCLOSURE

Discretionary agreement

contractual intention, 53

Doctor

patient, undue influence over, 149

Document

complete contractual, distinguished from informal memorandum, 69–70

mistake,

rectification, 118–119

signed under, 116–118

parol evidence rule, 68, 69–70

written, meaning of terms, 68

Domestic agreement

contractual intention, 53–54

Drunken person

contractual capacity, 198

Duress

contract obtained by, 147–148

meaning, 147

Employers' association

collective agreement, 52

Employment

contract may relate to, 1

minor, contractual capacity of, 191

personal service, 354–355

Enemy

trading with, 163, 305

Enforcement of contract

expectation interest, protection of, 5–6

failure to use required form, effect of, 59, 60

illegality,

generally, 175

guilty party cannot enforce, 175–176

innocent party,

ability to enforce, 176–177

cases in which unable to enforce, 177–178

other remedies, 178–179

reasons for, 4–6

reliance interest, protection of, 5

restitution interest, protection of, 5

specific,

generally, 351–352

injunction,

damages and, 358–359

generally, 356–358

specific performance. *See* SPECIFIC PERFORMANCE

Equity

assignment. *See* ASSIGNMENT

common law distinguished from, 6

mistake, relief for, 102–103

undue influence, contract obtained by, 148–149

volunteer, refusal to aid, 29

Estoppel
convention, by, 43
misrepresentation, effect of, 141
promissory, 41–43
proprietary, 47–49
European Economic Community
restraint of trade, 173–174
Evidence
writing, contract evidenced in, 58
See also PAROL EVIDENCE RULE
Exclusive dealing agreement
restraint of trade, 172–173
Exemption clause
administrative action, 96–97
common law, effectiveness at, 85–88
incorporation,
course of dealing, 74–75
generally, 73
notice, 73–74
signature, 73
other legislative techniques, 96–97
scope,
construction, generally, 75–76
negligence, liability for, 76–77
seriousness of breach,
generally, 77–78
legal effects of rule, 81–84
scope of rule, 78–81
supervised bargaining, 96
See also UNFAIR CONTRACT TERMS ACT
1977
Expectant heir
special protection, 150
Expectation interest
protection of, 5–6
Expectations
loss of, damages, 320–321
Express terms
ascertainment of, 62–63
Extortionate credit bargain
protection relating to, 151

Fact
implied terms, 2–3, 63–64
representation of, 122
Failure to perform contract. *See* BREACH
OF CONTRACT
Forbearance
generally, 34
no promise to forbear, case where, 34–35
promise, need to establish causal connection with, 34–35
Foreign country
law, contract to break, 163

Formal requirements of contract
assignment, 229–230
failure to use required form, effect of,
admissibility in evidence, on, 61
binding nature of contract, on, 59
enforcement, on, 59, 60
validity of contract, on, 59
form generally not required, 57
nature of, 56
purpose of, 56
types,
memorandum in writing, 58
note in writing, 58
seal, contract made under, 57
writing, contract must be in, 57
written particulars, 58
written contract,
rescission, 61
variation, 61
Forms
battle of, 10–11
purchase, 11
sales, 11
Fraud
damages for, 127–128
exemption clause, 85–86
illegal contract, inducing, 183–184
minor, contractual capacity of, 196–197
mutual promise procured by, 33
Freedom of contract
common calling, person engaged in, 4
principle of, 3–4
Frustration
generally, 298–299
legal consequences of,
generally, 311
Law Reform (Frustrated Contracts)
Act 1943,
exceptions, 313–314
generally, 311
money, prepayment of, 311–312
other benefits, 312–313
severability, 313
limitations on doctrine,
contractual provisions, 307–308
foreseeable events, 308–309
foreseen events, 308–309
generally, 307
self-induced frustration, 309–310
money, recovery of, 362
operation of doctrine,
generally, 299
impossibility,
alternatives, 302

Frustration — *continued*
  operation of doctrine — *continued*
    impossibility — *continued*
      death, 300
      failure of particular source, 301
      impracticability, contrasted with, 302−303
      incapacity, 300
      method of performance impossible, 301−302
      subject-matter, destruction of, 299
      unavailability, 300−301
    lease, 306
    purpose, 304−305
    sale of land, 306−307
    supervening illegality, 305
    time of frustration, 305
  self-induced, 309−310
Future
  rights, attempts to assign, 231−232
  statement as to, 123−124

Gazumping
  enforcement of contract, failure of, 6
Gift
  completed, 233−234
  incomplete, 232−233
  promise to accept, 32
Goods
  price-cutting, supply may not be refused on grounds of, 4
  sale of,
    consideration, 25
    contract may relate to, 1
    vague agreement, 22−23

Hire
  contract may relate to, 1
Hire-purchase agreement
  exemption clause, 75−76
  formal requirements, 56
  vague, 22
Honour clause
  effect of, 51−52

Illegality
  effects of,
    collateral transactions, 187
    enforcement,
      generally, 175
      guilty party, by, 175−176
      innocent party,
        cases in which unable to enforce, 177−178

Illegality — *continued*
  effects of — *continued*
    enforcement — *continued*
      innocent party — *continued*
        other remedies, 178−179
        when able to enforce, 176−177
    generally, 175
    money, recovery of,
      class, statutes for protection of, 182−183
      fraud, 183−184
      generally, 182
      mistake, 183−184
      no reliance on contract, 185−187
      pressure, illegal contract made under, 183
      repentance, 184
      whether allowable, 187
    property, recovery of,
      class, statutes for protection of, 182−183
      fraud, 183−184
      generally, 182
      mistake, 183−184
      no reliance on contract, 185−187
      pressure, illegal contract made under, 183
      repentance, 184
      when allowable, 187
    severance,
      consideration, illegal part of, 181−182
      generally, 179
      illegal promise, of, 179−181
  frustration, 305
  general principle, 152
  law, contract contrary to,
    making of, 152−153
    object, 153
    performance, 153−155
    unlawful act, promise contingent on commission of, 155−156
  public policy, contrary to,
    enemy, trading with, 163
    foreign country, contract to break law of, 163
    generally, 156−158
    immoral contract, 158
    jurisdiction of court, contract excluding, 160−161
    justice, contract which perverts course of, 162
    marriage, contract affecting freedom and stability of,
      brokage, 159

Illegality — *continued*
public policy, contrary to — *continued*
marriage, contract affecting freedom and stability of — *continued*
existing marriage, protection of,
159—160
generally, 158
restraint of marriage, 159
personal liberty, undue restrictions
on, 164
public authorities, contract to
deceive, 162—163
public service, contract prejudicing,
163
supervening, 305
trade, contract in restraint of,
business, sale of,
generally, 164
proprietary interest, 164—165
public interest, 169
reasonableness, 166—167
employment,
generally, 164
other problems relating to, 169
proprietary interest, 165—166
public interest, 169
reasonableness, 167—168
European Community law, 173—174
exclusive dealing agreement, 172—
173
generally, 164
land, restrictions on use of, 174—175
other agreements, 175
restrictive trading, 170—171
service agreement, 172—173
trade union rules, 171
Immoral contract
public policy, contrary to, 158
Implied terms
custom, by, 65—66
fact, in, 2—3, 63—64
law, in, 2—3, 64—65
parol evidence rule, 67
usage, by, 65—66
Impossibility
specific enforcement and, 356
See also FRUSTRATION
Impracticability
impossibility contrasted with, 302—303
Improper pressure
duress, 147—148
generally, 147
illegal contract made under, 183

Improper pressure — *continued*
particular groups of persons, protection of, 149—151
undue influence, 148—149
Incapacity
frustration by, 300
termination of offer, 20—21
Incomplete agreement. *See* AGREEMENT
Injunction
damages and, 358—359
specific enforcement, 356—358
Injured feelings
damages for, 319—320
Innkeeper
freedom of contract, exception to general rule of, 4
Insurance
third party, promise in favour of, 217—
218
Intention. *See* CONTRACTUAL INTENTION
Intimidation
third party, promise in favour of, 214
Invalid contract
money, recovery of, 362
Invitation to treat
examples, 8
making of, 8
offer, 8—9

Justice
course of, contract which perverts, 162

Land
agreement subject to contract, 23
law, promise in favour of third party,
215
restrictive covenants, 174—175
sale of,
contract may relate to, 1
frustration, 306—307
time of performance, 285—286
Lapse
termination of offer by, 19—20
Latent defects
disclosure, duty of, 143
Law
assignment. *See* ASSIGNMENT
contract contrary to,
making of, 152—153
object, 153
performance, 153—155
unlawful act, promise contingent on
commission of, 155—156
foreign country, of, contract to break,
163

Law — *continued*
implied terms, 2–3, 64–65
statement of, 124
Lease
contract may relate to, 1
frustration of, 306
Letter
postal acceptance. *See* ACCEPTANCE
Liability
business, 88–89
exclusion of, 89
exemption clause, 76–77
minor, of,
restitution, in,
fraud, effects of, 196–197
generally, 194–195
Minors' Contracts Act 1987, s 3(1), 195–196
quasi-contract, liability in, 197–198
tort, in, 194
misrepresentation, for. *See* MISREPRE-SENTATION
negligence, for, 76–77
negligence, in, 212–214
restriction of, 89
transfer of, distinguished from assignment,
benefit and burden, 242
generally, 241–242
novation, 242
operation of law, 243
vicarious performance, 243–244
Liquidated damages
penalties distinguished from, 343–347
See also DAMAGES
Loss
meaning, 317–318
See also DAMAGES
Lost property
advertisement of reward, as offer, 8

Maintenance
danger of, 238–239
meaning, 224
Market values
damages, relevance on, 327–329
Marriage
brokage, 159
existing, protection of, 159–160
freedom of, contract affecting, 158–160
restraint of, 159
stability of, contract affecting, 158–160

Memorandum
informal, distinguished from complete contractual document, 69–70
writing, in, 58
Mental patient
contractual capacity, 198
Minor
contractual capacity. *See* CONTRAC-TUAL CAPACITY
Misrepresentation
complexity of law, 122
effects of,
damages,
breach of contract, 130–132
criminal case, compensation order in, 136
fraud, 127–128
generally, 127
Misrepresentation Act 1967, s 2(1), 129–130
negligence at common law, 128–129
relationship between various rights to, 133–136
rescission, in lieu of, 132–133
estoppel, 141
generally, 127
mistake, 127
rescission,
breach, for, 137–138
defensive, 138–139
generally, 136
misrepresentation, for, 136–137
right to rescind, limitations on, 139–141
exemption clause, 85–86
general requirements,
fact, representation of,
belief, 123
future, statement as to, 123–124
generally, 122
law, statement of, 124
opinion, 123
liability, other conditions,
generally, 125
material, representation must be, 125
representation, reliance on, 125–127
unambiguous, representation must be, 125
meaning, 122
mistake, relationship with, 127
rescission for, 136–137, 288
See also NON-DISCLOSURE

Mistake
  agreement, in recording,
    rectification of document, 118−119
    restrictions, 120−121
    types, 119−120
  common law,
    contract exceptionally void at, 113−114
    contract valid at, 113
    contract void at, 103−104
    fundamental mistake at, 99−102
  documents,
    rectification of, 118−119
    signed under, 116−118
  effects of,
    common law,
      contract exceptionally void at, 113−114
      contract valid at, 113
      contract void at, 103−104
    one party, risk of mistake taken by, 104−105
    rescission on terms, 106−107, 115−116
    specific performance, bar to, 105−106, 114−115
  equity gives relief, 102−103
  generally, 98−99
  illegal contract, inducing, 183−184
  misrepresentation, relationship with, 127
  negativing consent,
    effects,
      common law,
        contract exceptionally void at, 113−114
        contract generally valid at, 113
        rescission on terms, 115−116
        specific performance, bar to, 114−115
      generally, 107−108
    types,
      contract, 112
      generally, 108
      person, 108−111
      subject-matter, 108
      terms, 111−112
  non est factum, doctrine of,
    generally, 116−117
    restrictions,
      carelessness, 118
      generally, 117
      nature of mistake, 117−118
      persons who can rely on doctrine, 117

Mistake − *continued*
  nullifying consent,
    effects,
      common law, contract void at, 103−104
      one party, risk taken by, 104−105
      rescission on terms, 106−107
      specific performance, bar to, 105−106
    generally, 99
    types,
      common law, fundamental mistake at, 99−102
      equity, relief given by, 102−103
      generally, 99
  rescission on terms, 106−107, 115−116
  specific performance, bar to, 105−106, 114−115
  types of,
    agreement, mistake in recording, 119−120
    common law, fundamental mistake at, 99−102
    contract, inducing, 112
    equity gives relief, 102−103
    generally, 108
    person, 108−111
    subject-matter, 108
    terms, 111−112
Mitigation
  damages limited by, 337−340
Money
  advance payments, 347−348
  agreed sum, action for, 349−351
  damages. *See* DAMAGES
  prepayment of, effect of frustration on, 311−312
  recompense, 362−364
  recovery of,
    class, statutes for protection of, 182−183
    consideration, total failure of, 359−361
    fraud, 183−184
    frustration, 362
    generally, 182
    invalid contract, 362
    mistake, 183−184
    no reliance on contract, 185−187
    pressure, illegal contract made under, 183
    repentance, 184
    rescission, 361−362
    when allowable, 187

Mortgage
contract may relate to, 1
Mutual promise
consideration, as, 31–33

Necessaries
minor's liability for, 189–190
Necessity
authority of, 251–252
Negligence
common law, at, damages for, 128–129
liability for, 76–77
liability in, 212–214
Negotiability
assignment distinguished from, 235–236
New contract
rescission, limits on, 289–290
Newspaper
advertisement, as invitation to treat, 8
Non est factum, doctrine of
generally, 116–117
restrictions on,
carelessness, 118
generally, 117
mistake, nature of, 117–118
persons who can rely, 117
Non-disclosure
effects of, 146
exceptions,
analogous contract, 144–145
change of circumstances, 142–143
contract uberrimae fidei, 143–144
custom, 143
generally, 142
latent defects, 143
parties, relationship of, 145
statutory duties of disclosure, 145–146
no duty of disclosure, 141–142
Non-performance
excuses for, 268–270
See also BREACH OF CONTRACT
Note
writing, in, 58
Notice
exemption clause contained in, 73–74
Novation
assignment, 242

Offer
auction sale, 9
carriage of passengers, 9–10
counter-offer, 10–11

Offer — *continued*
customer, coming from, 8
essential feature, 8
examples, 8
irrevocable, 49–50
meaning, 7
none identifiable, 21
objective test, 7
rejection, 19
tender, 8–9
termination of,
death, 20–21
generally, 18
incapacity, 20–21
lapse, 19–20
occurrence of condition, 20–21
rejection, 19
withdrawal, 18–19
to whom made, 7
withdrawal, 18–19

Offeree
meaning, 7
Offeror
meaning, 7
withdrawal of offer, curtailment of power, 13
Opinion
statement of, 123
Option
rescission, availability of, 284

Parent
child, undue influence over, 149
Parol evidence rule
exceptions,
collateral contract, 70–71
contents of contract, rule only relates to, 66–67
custom, 68–69
documents, 69–70
equitable defence, oral evidence relied on for, 67
implied terms, 67
oral warranty, evidence of, 67
rectification, 69
subsequent variation or rescission of contract, 67–68
written document, 68
generally, 66
Parties to contract
exemption clause, effectiveness of, 86–88
generally, 203

Parties to contract — *continued*
  original, contract between,
    modification, 38−39
    rescission, 38−39
  promise by. *See* PROMISE
  relationship of,
    duty of disclosure, 145
    interference with, 4
Passenger
  carriage of, when and by whom offer
    made, 9−10
Patient
  undue influence over, 149
Penalties
  liquidated damages distinguished from,
    343−347
Performance
  duty to perform,
    non-performance, excuses for, 268−
      270
    standard of, 266−268
    terms of contract, 265−266
  frustration. *See* FRUSTRATION
  generally, 265
  impossibility. *See* FRUSTRATION
  method of,
    contrary to law, 153−155
    generally, 270−271
    impossibility, 301−302
  order of, 273
  part, 287−288
  rescission. *See* RECISSION
  vicarious, 243−244
Person
  mistake as to, 108−111
  undue influence, special protection
    relating to, 149−151
Personal contract
  debtor, prejudice to, 237−238
Personal liberty
  undue restrictions on, 164
Personal service
  contract of, specific enforcement of,
    354−355
Petrol
  indication of price, as invitation to
    treat, 8
Possessory rights
  contract creating, 220
Postal acceptance. *See* ACCEPTANCE
Pressure. *See* IMPROPER PRESSURE
Principal. *See* AGENCY
Privity, doctrine of
  exceptions,
    agency, 215

Privity, doctrine of — *continued*
  exceptions — *continued*
    assignment, 215
    generally, 214−215
    insurance, 217−218
    land law, 215
    Law of Property Act 1925, s 56(1),
      218−219
    trust of promises, 215−217
  general rule, 208−209
  scope,
    generally, 212
    intimidation, 214
    negligence, liability in, 212−214
Profession
  exclusion from, 4
Promise
  acceptance, contained in, 10
  forbearance, need to establish causal
    connection with, 34−35
  gratuitous, 26−27
  illegal, severance of, 179−181
  more than one person,
    by,
      generally, 203
      joint, and joint and several,
        differences between, 205
        similarities between, 203−204
    to,
      distinctions, effects of, 207−208
      generally, 206
      joint, 206
      joint and several, 207
      several, 206
  mutual, as consideration, 31−33
  obligation arises out of, 3
  onerous, 26−27
  past, 30
  third party,
    in favour of,
      generally, 208
      other effects of contract,
        generally, 209
        promise and third party, posi-
          tion between, 211−212
        promisee's remedies, 209−211
    privity of contract,
      agency, 215
      assignment, 215
      doctrine, 208−209
      exceptions in doctrine, 214−219
      insurance, 217−218
      intimidation, 214
      land law, 215

Promise — *continued*
  third party — *continued*
    in favour of — *continued*
      privity of contract — *continued*
        Law of Property Act 1925, s 56(1), 218–219
        negligence, liability in, 212–214
        scope of doctrine, 212–214
        trust of promises, 215–217
      purporting to bind,
        exceptions to general rule, 219–220
        general rule, 219
        scope of general rule,
          contractual rights, interference with, 220–222
          generally, 220
          possessory rights, contract creating, 220
          proprietary interests, contract creating, 220
  trust of, 215–217
  unlawful act, contingent on commission of, 155–156
Promisee
  consideration must move from, 31
  third party, promise in favour of, position relating to, 211–212
  remedies, 209–211
Property
  recovery of,
    class, statutes for protection of, 182–183
    fraud, 183–184
    generally, 182
    mistake, 183–184
    no reliance on contract, 185–187
    pressure, illegal contract made under, 183
    repentance, 184
    when allowable, 187
Proprietary interests
  contract creating, 220
Public authority
  contract to deceive, 162–163
Public duty
  consideration, as, 36
Public interest
  freedom of contract, exceptions to general rule, 4
Public policy
  assignment, limits on, 239–240
  contract contrary to,
    enemy, trading with, 163

Public policy — *continued*
  contract contrary to — *continued*
    foreign country, contract to break law of, 163
    generally, 156–158
    immoral contract, 158
    jurisdiction of court, contract excluding, 160–161
    justice, contract which perverts, 162
    marriage, contract affecting freedom and stability of,
      brokage, 159
      existing marriage, protection of, 159–160
      generally, 158
      restraint of marriage, 159
    personal liberty, undue restrictions on, 164
    public authorities, contract to deceive, 162–163
    public service, contract prejudicing, 163
  repentance, 184
Public service
  contract prejudicing, 163

Quasi-contract
  minor, liability of, 197–198

Race discrimination
  freedom of contract, 4
Ratification
  agency, creation of,
    conditions to be satisfied, 253–255
    generally, 253
    relation back, 255
Reasonableness
  further performance, of accepting, 275
  requirement of,
    cases to which applicable, 91–93
    generally, 91
    rules relating to, 93–94
Receipt
  contractual document distinguished from, 73
Reciprocity
  consideration, basic notion of, 25
Recovery
  money, of. *See* MONEY
  property, of. *See* PROPERTY
Rectification
  document, of, 118–119
  parol evidence rule, 69
Reliance
  loss of, damages, 321

Reliance interest
protection of, 5
Religious leader
disciple, undue influence over, 149
Remedies
agreed sum, action for, 349–351
classification,
judicial,
civil, 315–316
criminal, 315
non-judicial, 315
damages. *See* DAMAGES
enforcement. *See* ENFORCEMENT OF
CONTRACT
illegal contract, relating to. *See*
ILLEGALITY
mutuality, 356
rescission. *See* RESCISSION
restitutionary,
generally, 359
recompense, 362–364
recovery of money,
consideration, total failure of,
359–361
frustration, 362
invalid contract, 362
rescission of contract, 361–362
specific enforcement. *See* ENFORCE-
MENT OF CONTRACT
Remoteness
damages limited by, 333–336
Repentance
illegality, effects of, 184
Representation. *See* MISREPRESENTATION
Rescission
anticipatory breach, 295–296
breach of contract, for,
failure must be serious,
damages, adequacy of, 274
exceptions to requirement,
conditions, 279–283
entire obligations, 277–279
express provisions, 277
fundamental term, breach of,
283
generally, 276
intermediate terms, 279–283
manner of breach, 283–284
options, 284
severable obligations, 277–279
unilateral contract, 284
warranties, 279–283
further performance, reasonableness of accepting, 275
ulterior motives, 275–276

Rescission – *continued*
breach of contract, for – *continued*
generally, 137–138, 271–273
limits on,
Apportionment Act 1870, 291
both parties in breach, 290
generally, 286
new contract, 289–290
part performance, 287–288
terms of contract, 289
waiver, 286–287
option to rescind,
affirmation, effects of, 293–294
effects of rescission, 292–293
generally, 291
no automatic rescission, 291–292
order of performance, 273
time, stipulations as to, 285–286
damages in lieu of, 132–133, 274
defensive, 138–139
misrepresentation, for, 136–137, 288
mistake, effect of, 106–107, 115–116
money, recovery of, 361–362
original parties, contract between, 38–
39
parol evidence rule, 67–68
right to rescind, limitations on, 139–
141
written contract, of, 61
Restitution
interest, protection of, 5
loss of, damages, 322
minor, liability of,
fraud, effects of, 196–197
generally, 194–195
Minors' Contracts Act 1987, s 3(1),
195–196
quasi-contract, 197–198
remedies. *See* REMEDIES
Reward
advertisement of, as offer, 8
Rights. *See* CONTRACTUAL RIGHTS

Sale
goods, of. *See* GOODS
land, of. *See* LAND
Seal
contract required to be made under, 57
Service agreement
restraint of trade, 172–173
Severance
consideration, illegal part of, 181–182
frustration, effect of, 313
generally, 179
illegal promise, of, 179–181

Sex discrimination
 freedom of contract, 4
Shares
 sale of, contract may relate to, 1
Shop
 special offer, as invitation to treat, 8
Signature
 exemption clause, 73
Silence
 acceptance, as, 15–16
Social agreement
 contractual intention, 53–54
Solicitor
 client, undue influence over, 149
Specific performance
 court, discretion of, 353–354
 damages, and, 358–359
 damages must be inadequate, 352–353
 generally, 352
 impossibility, 356
 mistake, refusal on ground of, 105–106, 114–115
 mutuality of remedy, 356
 other contracts, 355
 personal service, 354–355
 supervision, difficulty of, 355–356
Standard terms
 preparation of, 72
 See also EXEMPTION CLAUSE
Subject-matter
 destruction of, 299
 mistake as to, 108

Taxation
 damages, 329–330
Telephone
 acceptance by, 13
Telex
 acceptance by, 13, 15
Tender
 indefinite amount, for, 8–9
 invitation to treat, 8–9
 offer, 8–9
Termination of offer. *See* OFFER
Terms of contract
 duty to perform, 265–266
 express, ascertainment of, 62–63
 implied. *See* IMPLIED TERMS
 ineffective, 90–91
 intermediate, 279–283
 mistake as to, 111–112
 partly effective, 94–95
 rescission on, 106–107, 115–116
 standard, 72
 See also EXEMPTION CLAUSE

Third party
 agency,
  agent, relations with, 258–263
  principal, relations with, 256–258
 contract with, duty imposed by, 37–38
 exemption clause, effectiveness of, 86–88
 part payment accepted by creditor from, 45
 promise. *See* PROMISE
Time
 damages, assessment of, 331–332
 frustration, of, 305
 performance, of, 285–286
Title
 assignee, of, 234–235
Tort
 intimidation, 214
 minor, liability of, 194
Trade
 contract in restraint of,
  business, sale of,
   proprietary interest, 164–165
   public interest, 169
   reasonableness, 166–167
  employment,
   generally, 164
   other problems relating to, 169
   proprietary interest, 165–166
   public interest, 169
   reasonableness, 167–168
  European Community law, 173–174
  exclusive dealing agreement, 172–173
  generally, 164
  land, restrictions on use of, 174–175
  other agreements, 175
  restrictive trading agreement, 170–171
  service agreement, 172–173
 enemy, with, 163, 305
Trade association
 collective agreement, 52
Trade union
 restraint of trade doctrine, rules subject to, 171
Tradesmen's circular
 advertisement in, as invitation to treat, 8
Transfer of contractual rights. *See* ASSIGNMENT
Trust
 promises, of, 215–217
Trustee
 beneficiary, undue influence over, 149

Uberrimae fidei
disclosure, duty of, 143–144
Unavailability
frustration by, 301
Undue influence
contract obtained by, 148–149
Unfair Contract Terms Act 1977
business liability, 88–89
cases not covered by, 95–96
consumer, dealing as, meaning, 89
evasion, restrictions on, 95
generally, 88
ineffective terms, 90–91
liability,
exclusion of, 89
restriction of, 89
partly effective terms, 94–95
reasonableness, requirement of,
cases to which applicable, 91–93
generally, 91
rules relating to, 93–94
terminology, 88–90
**Uniform Law on Formation of Con-
tracts for International Sale of
Goods**
postal acceptance, 14–15
Unilateral contract
acceptance, 10, 17–18
rescission, availability of, 284
Unlawful act. *See* ILLEGALITY

Usage
terms implied by, 65–66

Vague agreement. *See* AGREEMENT
Valuation
vague agreement, 23
Variation
increasing one party's obligations, 39–
40
parol evidence rule, 67–68
reducing one party's obligation, 40–41
written contract, of, 61
Volunteer
equity refuses to aid, 29
meaning, 29
Voucher
contractual document distinguished
from, 73

Waiver
rescission, limits on, 286–287
Warranty
oral, 67
rescission, availability of, 279–283
Writing
contract required to be in, 57
memorandum in, 58
note in, 58
Written particulars
formal requirements, 58